C0-AZV-848

# Stata Reference Manual
## Release 7
### Volume 3 Q-St

Stata Press
College Station, Texas

Control charts may be used to define the goal of a repetitive process; to control that process; and to determine if the goal has been achieved. Walter A. Shewhart of Bell Telephone Laboratories devised the first control chart in 1924. In 1931, Shewhart published *Economic Control of Quality of Manufactured Product*. According to Burr (1976, 29), "Few fields of knowledge have ever been so completely explored and charted in the first exposition." Shewhart (1931, 6) states: ". . . a phenomenon will be said to be controlled when, through the use of past experience, we can predict, at least within limits, how the phenomenon may be expected to vary in the future. Here it is understood that prediction within limits means that we can state, at least approximately, the probability that the observed phenomenon will fall within given limits."

For more information on quality control charts, see Burr (1976), Duncan (1986), Harris (1999), or Ryan (1989).

## cchart

▷ Example

cchart graphs a c chart, the number of nonconformities in a unit, where *defect_var* records the number of defects in each inspection unit and *unit_var* records the unit number. The unit numbers need not be in order. For instance,

```
. describe
Contains data
  obs:           25                      Defects in 25 samples
  vars:           2
  size:         300 (99.9% of memory free)

              storage  display    value
variable name  type    format     label     variable label

sample         float   %9.0g                Subassembly number
defects        float   %9.0g                Number of defects

Sorted by:
     Note:  dataset has changed since last saved
. list in 1/5
        sample    defects
  1.        1         77
  2.        2         64
  3.        3         75
  4.        4         93
  5.        5         45
```

*(Graph on next page)*

. cchart defects sample, ylabel xlabel title(c Chart for Radio Subassemblies)

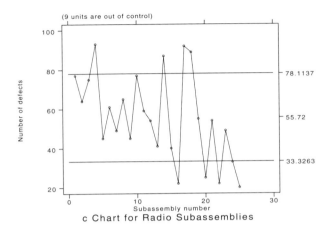

c Chart for Radio Subassemblies

The expected number of defects is 55.72, with lower- and upper-control limits of 33.3263 and 78.1137, respectively. Nine units are out of control.                                                                 ◁

## pchart

▷ Example

pchart graphs a p chart, the fraction of nonconforming items in a subgroup, where *reject_var* records the number rejected in each inspection unit, *unit_var* records the inspection unit number, and *ssize_var* records the number inspected in each unit.

For instance, if you have data on the number of railway frames rejected from a random sample from each day's output:

```
. describe
Contains data from pchart.dta
  obs:           5                     Number rejected by day
  vars:          3                     20 Jul 2000 11:19
  size:         80 (99.9% of memory free)
```

| variable name | storage type | display format | value label | variable label |
|---|---|---|---|---|
| day | float | %9.0g | | Day |
| rejects | float | %9.0g | | Number rejected |
| ssize | float | %9.0g | | Sample size |

```
Sorted by:
. list in 1/5
        day      rejects       ssize
  1.     26          19          50
  2.      8          13          50
  3.     17          11          50
  4.     16           3          50
  5.     25          18          50
```

```
. pchart rejects day ssize, ylabel xlabel
```

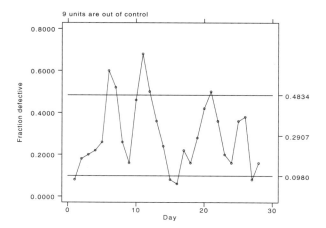

Obviously, this is a manufacturing process with a considerable rejection rate. The average rejection rate is .2907 (29 percent) and the lower- and upper-control limits are .0980 and .4834, respectively. Nine units are out of control.

In our example, the sample sizes are fixed at 50, so the `ssize` variable contains 50 for each observation. It is not necessary that sample sizes be fixed, however. Pretend our data were slightly different:

```
. list in 1/5

         day     rejects       ssize
1.        26          19          72
2.         8          13          72
3.        17          11          72
4.        16           3          70
5.        25          18          70
. pchart rejects day ssize, ylabel xlabel
```

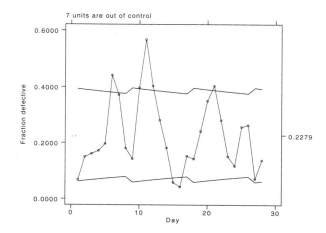

In this case, the control limits are, like the sample size, no longer constant. The `stabilize` option will stabilize the control chart:

    . pchart rejects day ssize, ylabel xlabel stabilize

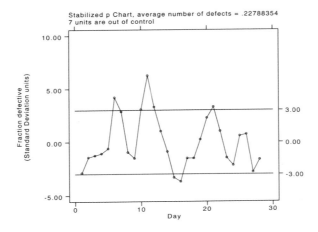

⊲

## rchart

▷ Example

`rchart` displays an R chart showing the range for repeated measurements at various times. Variables within observations record measurements. Observations represent different samples.

For instance, say we take five samples of five observations each. In our first sample, our measurements are 10, 11, 10, 11, and 12. The data are

    . list

         m1    m2    m3    m4    m5
    1.   10    11    10    11    12
    2.   12    10     9    10     9
    3.   10    11    10    12    10
    4.    9     9     9    10    11
    5.   12    12    12    12    13

*(Graph on next page)*

```
. rchart m1-m5, connect(l)
```

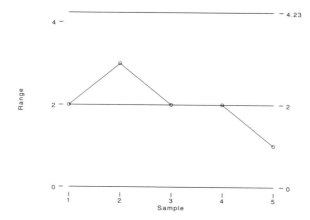

The expected range in each sample is 2 with lower- and upper-control limits of 0 and 4.23, respectively. If we knew that the process standard deviation is 0.3:

```
. rchart m1-m5, connect(l) std(.3)
```

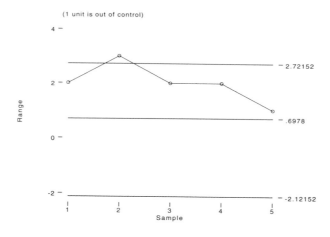

*(Continued on next page)*

# xchart

▷ Example

xchart graphs an $\overline{X}$ chart for repeated measurements at various times. Variables within observations record measurements. Observations represent different samples. Using the same data as in the previous example:

. xchart m1-m5, connect(l)

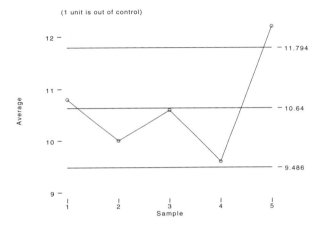

The average measurement in the sample is 10.64 and the lower- and upper-control limits are 9.486 and 11.794, respectively. If we knew from prior information that the mean of the process is 11:

. xchart m1-m5, connect(l) mean(11)

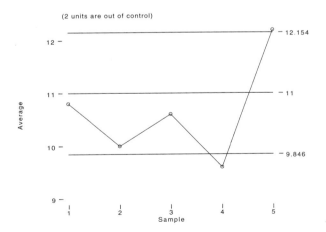

If we also knew that the standard deviation of the process is 0.3:

```
. xchart m1-m5, connect(l) mean(11) std(.3)
```

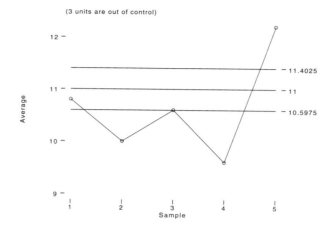

Finally, **xchart** allows you to specify your own control limits if you wish:

```
. xchart m1-m5, connect(l) mean(11) lower(10) upper(12)
```

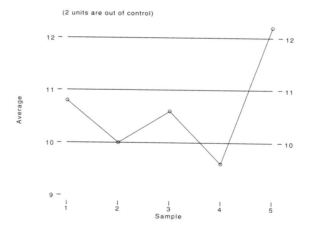

*(Continued on next page)*

## shewhart

▷ Example

shewhart displays a vertically aligned $\overline{X}$ and R chart in the same image. To produce the best-looking combined image possible, you will want to use the xchart and rchart commands separately and then combine the graphs. shewhart, however, is more convenient.

Using the same data as previously, but realizing that the standard deviation should have been 0.4:

. shewhart m1-m5, connect(l) mean(11) std(.4)

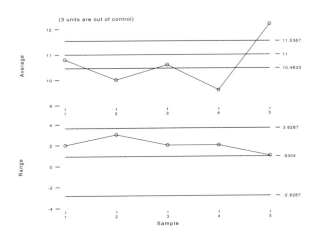

◁

## Methods and Formulas

cchart, pchart, rchart, xchart, and shewhart are implemented as ado-files.

For the c chart, the number of defects per unit $C$ is taken to be a value of a random variable having a Poisson distribution. If $k$ is the number of units available for estimating $\lambda$, the parameter of the Poisson distribution, and if $C_i$ is the number of defects in the $i$th unit, then $\lambda$ is estimated by $\overline{C} = \sum_i C_i/k$. Then,

$$\text{central line} = \overline{C}$$
$$\text{UCL} = \overline{C} + 3\sqrt{\overline{C}}$$
$$\text{LCL} = \overline{C} - 3\sqrt{\overline{C}}$$

Control limits for the p chart are based on the sampling theory for proportions, using the normal approximation to the binomial. If $k$ samples are taken, the estimator of $p$ is given by $\overline{p} = \sum_i x_i / \sum_i n_i$, where $x_i$ is the number of defects in the $i$th sample of size $n_i$. The central line and the control limits are given by

$$\text{central line} = \overline{p}$$
$$\text{UCL} = \overline{p} + 3\sqrt{\overline{p}(1-\overline{p})/n_i}$$
$$\text{LCL} = \overline{p} - 3\sqrt{\overline{p}(1-\overline{p})/n_i}$$

Control limits for the R chart are based on the distribution of the range of samples of size $n$ from a normal population. If the standard deviation of the process $\sigma$ is known,

$$\text{central line} = d_2\sigma$$

$$\text{UCL} = D_2\sigma$$

$$\text{LCL} = D_1\sigma$$

where $d_2$, $D_1$, and $D_2$ are functions of the number of observations in the sample and are obtained from the table published in Beyer (1976).

When $\sigma$ is unknown,

$$\text{central line} = \overline{R}$$

$$\text{UCL} = (D_2/d_2)\overline{R}$$

$$\text{LCL} = (D_1/d_2)\overline{R}$$

where $\overline{R} = \sum_i R_i/k$ is the range of the $k$ sample ranges $R_i$.

Control limits for the $\overline{X}$ chart are given by

$$\text{central line} = \overline{x}$$

$$\text{UCL} = \overline{x} + (3/\sqrt{n})\sigma$$

$$\text{LCL} = \overline{x} - (3/\sqrt{n})\sigma$$

if $\sigma$ is known. If $\sigma$ is unknown

$$\text{central line} = \overline{x}$$

$$\text{UCL} = \overline{x} + A_2\overline{R}$$

$$\text{LCL} = \overline{x} - A_2\overline{R}$$

where $\overline{R}$ is the average range as defined above and $A_2$ is a function (*op. cit.*) of the number of observations in the sample.

## References

Beyer, W. H., ed. 1976. Factors for computing control limits. In *Handbook of Tables for Probability and Statistics*. 2d ed. 451–465. Cleveland, OH: The Chemical Rubber Company.

Burr, I. W. 1976. *Statistical Quality Control Methods*. New York: Marcel Dekker.

Duncan, A. J. 1986. *Quality Control and Industrial Statistics*. 5th ed. Homewood, IL: Irwin.

Harris, R. L. 1999. *Information Graphics: A Comprehensive Illustrated Reference*. New York: Oxford University Press.

Ryan, T. P. 1989. *Statistical Methods for Quality Improvement*. New York: John Wiley & Sons.

Saw, S. L. C. and T. W. Soon. 1994. sqc1: Estimating process capability indices with Stata. *Stata Technical Bulletin* 17: 18–19. Reprinted in *Stata Technical Bulletin Reprints*, vol. 3, pp. 174–175.

Shewhart, W. A. 1931. *Economic Control of Quality of Manufactured Product*. New York: D. Van Nostrand Company.

## Also See

**Related:**    [R] **serrbar**

**Background:**    *Stata Graphics Manual*

# Title

qreg — Quantile (including median) regression

# Syntax

qreg *depvar* [*indepvars*] [*weight*] [if *exp*] [in *range*] [, level(#) quantile(#)
    nolog iterate(#) wlsiter(#) trace ]

iqreg *depvar* [*indepvars*] [if *exp*] [in *range*] [, level(#) quantiles(# #)
    reps(#) nolog ]

sqreg *depvar* [*indepvars*] [if *exp*] [in *range*] [, level(#) quantiles(# [# [# ...]])
    reps(#) nolog ]

bsqreg *depvar* [*indepvars*] [if *exp*] [in *range*] [, level(#) quantile(#) reps(#) ]

_qreg [*depvar* [*indepvars*] [*weight*] [if *exp*] [in *range*]] [, level(#) quantile(#)
    iterate(#) trace accuracy(#) ]

by ... : may be used with qreg, iqreg, sqreg, and bsqreg; see [R] **by**.

qreg and _qreg allow aweights and fweights; see [U] **14.1.6 weight**.

qreg, iqreg, sqreg, and bsqreg share the features of all estimation commands; see [U] **23 Estimation and post-estimation commands**.

qreg may be used with sw to perform stepwise estimation; see [R] **sw**.

# Syntax for predict

*For* qreg, iqreg, *and* bsqreg

    predict [*type*] *newvarname* [if *exp*] [in *range*] [, { xb | stdp | residuals } ]

*For* sqreg

    predict [*type*] *newvarname* [if *exp*] [in *range*] [, equation(*eqno* [,*eqno*])
    { xb | stdp | stddp | residuals } ]

These statistics are available both in and out of sample; type predict ... if e(sample) ... if wanted only for the estimation sample.

# Description

qreg estimates quantile (including median) regression models, also known as least-absolute value models (LAV or MAD) and minimum L1-norm models.

iqreg estimates interquantile range regressions, regressions of the difference in quantiles. The estimated variance–covariance matrix of the estimators (VCE) is obtained via bootstrapping. iqreg has a limit of 336 *indepvars*.

sqreg estimates simultaneous-quantile regression. It produces the same coefficients as qreg for each quantile. Reported standard errors will be similar, the difference being that sqreg obtains an estimate of the VCE via bootstrapping and the VCE includes between-quantiles blocks. Thus, one can test and construct confidence intervals comparing coefficients describing different quantiles. sqreg has a limit of 336/$q$ *indepvars* where $q$ is the number of quantiles specified.

bsqreg is the same as sqreg with one quantile. sqreg is faster than bsqreg. However, bsqreg is not limited to 336 coefficients.

_qreg is the internal estimation command for quantile regression. _qreg is not intended to be used directly; interested users should see *Methods and Formulas* below.

## Options

level(#) specifies the confidence level, in percent, for confidence intervals. The default is level(95) or as set by set level; see [U] **23.5 Specifying the width of confidence intervals**.

quantile(#) (for qreg, bsqreg, and _qreg) specifies the quantile to be estimated and should be a number between 0 and 1, exclusive. For qreg and bsqreg numbers larger than 1 are interpreted as a percent. The default value of 0.5 corresponds to the median.

quantiles(# #) (for iqreg) specifies the quantiles to be compared. The first number must be less than the second and both should be between 0 and 1, exclusive. Numbers larger than 1 are interpreted as a percent. Not specifying this option is equivalent to specifying quantiles(.25 .75), meaning the interquartile range.

quantiles(# [# [# ...]]) (for sqreg) specifies the quantiles to be estimated and should contain numbers between 0 and 1, exclusive. Numbers larger than 1 are interpreted as a percent. The default value of 0.5 corresponds to the median.

nolog suppresses the iteration log for the qreg command and the displaying of periods after each replication for the iqreg and sqreg commands.

iterate(#) specifies the maximum number of iterations that will be allowed to find a solution. The default value is 16,000 and the range is 1 to 16,000.

wlsiter(#) specifies the number of weighted least squares iterations that will be attempted before the linear programming iterations are started. The default value is 1. If there are convergence problems—something we have never observed—increasing this number should help.

trace specifies that the coefficients are to be printed on each iteration.

reps(#) specifies the number of bootstrap replications to be used to obtain an estimate of the variance–covariance matrix of the estimators (standard errors). reps(20) is the default.

This default is arguably too small. reps(100) would perform 100 bootstrap replications. reps(1000) would perform 1,000.

accuracy(#) should not be specified; it specifies the relative accuracy required for the linear programming algorithm. If the potential for improving the sum of weighted deviations by deleting an observation from the basis is less than this on a percentage basis, the algorithm will be said to have converged. The default value is $10^{-10}$.

▷ Example

Returning to real data, the equation for the 25th percentile of `price` based on `weight`, `length`, and `foreign` in our automobile data is

```
. qreg price weight length foreign, quant(.25)
Iteration  1:  WLS sum of weighted deviations =  84014.501

Iteration  1: sum of abs. weighted deviations =  84083.651
Iteration  2: sum of abs. weighted deviations =  70700.381
  (output omitted )
Iteration  6: sum of abs. weighted deviations =  69603.554
```

| .25 Quantile regression | | Number of obs = | 74 |
|---|---|---|---|
| Raw sum of deviations 83825.5 (about 4187) | | | |
| Min sum of deviations 69603.55 | | Pseudo R2   = | 0.1697 |

| price | Coef. | Std. Err. | t | P>\|t\| | [95% Conf. Interval] | |
|---|---|---|---|---|---|---|
| weight | 1.831789 | .6680931 | 2.74 | 0.008 | .4993193 | 3.164259 |
| length | 2.845558 | 24.78057 | 0.11 | 0.909 | -46.57774 | 52.26885 |
| foreign | 2209.925 | 434.631 | 5.08 | 0.000 | 1343.081 | 3076.77 |
| _cons | -1879.775 | 2808.067 | -0.67 | 0.505 | -7480.287 | 3720.738 |

Note that, in comparison with our previous median regression, the coefficient on `length` now has a positive sign and the coefficients on `foreign` and `weight` are reduced. The actual lower quantile is $4,187, substantially less than the median $4,934. It appears that the factors are weaker in this part of the distribution.

We can also estimate the upper quartile as a function of the same three variables:

```
. qreg price weight length foreign, quant(.75)
Iteration  1:  WLS sum of weighted deviations =  102589.61

Iteration  1: sum of abs. weighted deviations =  104678.5
Iteration  2: sum of abs. weighted deviations =  101523.41
  (output omitted )
Iteration  7: sum of abs. weighted deviations =  98395.936
```

| .75 Quantile regression | | Number of obs = | 74 |
|---|---|---|---|
| Raw sum of deviations 159721.5 (about 6342) | | | |
| Min sum of deviations 98395.94 | | Pseudo R2   = | 0.3840 |

| price | Coef. | Std. Err. | t | P>\|t\| | [95% Conf. Interval] | |
|---|---|---|---|---|---|---|
| weight | 9.22291 | 2.653578 | 3.48 | 0.001 | 3.930515 | 14.51531 |
| length | -220.7833 | 80.13906 | -2.76 | 0.007 | -380.6156 | -60.95098 |
| foreign | 3595.133 | 1727.704 | 2.08 | 0.041 | 149.336 | 7040.93 |
| _cons | 20242.9 | 8534.528 | 2.37 | 0.020 | 3221.325 | 37264.48 |

This tells a very different story: `weight` is much more important and `length` is now significant—with a negative coefficient! The prices of high-priced cars seem to be determined by other factors than the prices of low-priced cars.

◁

❑ Technical Note

One explanation for having substantially different regression functions for different quantiles is that the data are heteroskedastic, as we will demonstrate below. The following statements create a sharply heteroskedastic set of data:

```
. drop _all

. set obs 10000
obs was 0, now 10000

. gen x = .1 + .9 * uniform()

. gen y = x * uniform()^2
```

Let us now estimate the regressions for the 5th and 95th quantiles:

```
. qreg y x, quant(.05)
Iteration  1:  WLS sum of weighted deviations =  1201.2755

Iteration  1: sum of abs. weighted deviations =  1201.5026
Iteration  2: sum of abs. weighted deviations =  1102.7415
 (output omitted )
Iteration 11: sum of abs. weighted deviations =  481.45251

.05 Quantile regression                         Number of obs =     10000
  Raw sum of deviations 481.4977 (about .00358914)
  Min sum of deviations 481.4525                Pseudo R2     =    0.0001
```

| y | Coef. | Std. Err. | t | P>\|t\| | [95% Conf. Interval] |
|---|-------|-----------|---|---------|----------------------|
| x | .0028206 | .0012194 | 2.31 | 0.021 | .0004303 | .0052109 |
| _cons | -.0004743 | .0017975 | -0.26 | 0.792 | -.0039978 | .0030493 |

```
. qreg y x, quant(.95)
Iteration  1:  WLS sum of weighted deviations =   1609.799

Iteration  1: sum of abs. weighted deviations =  1610.2774
Iteration  2: sum of abs. weighted deviations =  1489.5823
 (output omitted )
Iteration 11: sum of abs. weighted deviations =  898.04445

.95 Quantile regression                         Number of obs =     10000
  Raw sum of deviations 1043.312 (about 1.3505412)
  Min sum of deviations 898.0445                Pseudo R2     =    0.1392
```

| y | Coef. | Std. Err. | t | P>\|t\| | [95% Conf. Interval] |
|---|-------|-----------|---|---------|----------------------|
| x | .8879752 | .023791 | 37.32 | 0.000 | .8413401 | .9346103 |
| _cons | .0174503 | .035114 | 0.50 | 0.619 | -.0513803 | .0862808 |

The coefficient on x, in particular, differs markedly between the two estimates. For the mathematically inclined, it is not too difficult to show that the theoretical lines are $y = .0025\,x$ for the 5th percentile and $y = .9025\,x$ for the 95th, numbers in close agreement with our numerical results.

❏

## Estimated standard errors

qreg estimates the variance–covariance matrix of the coefficients using a method of Koenker and Bassett (1982) and Rogers (1993). This is described in *Methods and Formulas* below. Rogers (1992) reports that, while this method seems adequate for homoskedastic errors, it appears to understate the standard errors for heteroskedastic errors. The irony is that exploring heteroskedastic errors is one of the major benefits of quantile regression. Gould (1992, 1997) introduced generalized versions of qreg that obtain estimates of the standard errors using bootstrap resampling (see Efron and Tibshirani 1993 or Wu 1986 for an introduction to bootstrapped standard errors). The iqreg, sqreg, and bsqreg commands provide a bootstrapped estimate of the entire variance–covariance matrix of the estimators.

▷ Example

The first example of qreg on real data above was a median regression of price on weight, length, and foreign using the automobile data. Here is the result of repeating the estimation using bootstrapped standard errors:

```
. bsqreg price weight length foreign
(estimating base model)
(bootstrapping ...................)
Median regression, bootstrap(20) SEs          Number of obs =        74
  Raw sum of deviations    142205 (about 4934)
  Min sum of deviations 108822.6              Pseudo R2     =    0.2347
```

| price | Coef. | Std. Err. | t | P>\|t\| | [95% Conf. Interval] | |
|---|---|---|---|---|---|---|
| weight | 3.933588 | 3.12446 | 1.26 | 0.212 | -2.297951 | 10.16513 |
| length | -41.25191 | 83.71266 | -0.49 | 0.624 | -208.2116 | 125.7077 |
| foreign | 3377.771 | 1040.209 | 3.25 | 0.002 | 1303.14 | 5452.402 |
| _cons | 344.6494 | 7053.301 | 0.05 | 0.961 | -13722.72 | 14412.01 |

The coefficient estimates are the same—indeed, they are obtained using the same technique. Only the standard errors differ. Therefore, the $t$ statistics, significance levels, and confidence intervals also differ.

Since bsqreg (as well as sqreg and iqreg) obtains standard errors by randomly resampling the data, the standard errors it produces will not be the same from run to run unless you first set the random number seed to the same number; see [R] generate.

By default, bsqreg, sqreg, and iqreg use 20 replications. You can control the number of replications by specifying the reps() option:

```
. bsqreg price weight length foreign, reps(1000)
(estimating base model)
(bootstrapping .................(output omitted)...)
Median regression, bootstrap(1000) SEs        Number of obs =        74
  Raw sum of deviations    142205 (about 4934)
  Min sum of deviations 108822.6              Pseudo R2     =    0.2347
```

| price | Coef. | Std. Err. | t | P>\|t\| | [95% Conf. Interval] | |
|---|---|---|---|---|---|---|
| weight | 3.933588 | 2.670425 | 1.47 | 0.145 | -1.392407 | 9.259583 |
| length | -41.25191 | 69.64623 | -0.59 | 0.556 | -180.1569 | 97.65311 |
| foreign | 3377.771 | 1095.176 | 3.08 | 0.003 | 1193.511 | 5562.031 |
| _cons | 344.6494 | 5944.856 | 0.06 | 0.954 | -11511.99 | 12201.29 |

A comparison of the standard errors is informative:

| variable | qreg | bsqreg reps(20) | bsqreg reps(1000) |
|---|---|---|---|
| weight | .8602 | 2.930 | 2.646 |
| length | 28.87 | 82.27 | 69.87 |
| foreign | 577.3 | 912.4 | 1081. |
| _cons | 3260. | 7455. | 6039. |

The results shown above are typical for models with heteroskedastic errors. (Note that our dependent variable is price; had our model been in terms of ln(price), the standard errors estimated by qreg and bsqreg would have been nearly identical.) Also note that, even in the case of heteroskedastic errors, 20 replications is generally sufficient for hypothesis tests against 0.

◁

## Interquantile and simultaneous-quantile regression

Consider a quantile-regression model where the $q$th quantile is given by

$$Q_q(y) = a_q + b_{q,1}x_1 + b_{q,2}x_2$$

For instance, the 75th and 25th quantiles are given by

$$Q_{.75}(y) = a_{.75} + b_{.75,1}x_1 + b_{.75,2}x_2$$
$$Q_{.25}(y) = a_{.25} + b_{.25,1}x_1 + b_{.25,2}x_2$$

The difference in the quantiles is then

$$Q_{.75}(y) - Q_{.25}(y) = (a_{.75} - a_{.25}) + (b_{.75,1} - b_{.25,1})x_1 + (b_{.75,2} - b_{.25,2})x_2$$

qreg estimates models such as $Q_{.75}(y)$ and $Q_{.25}(y)$. iqreg estimates interquantile models such as $Q_{.75}(y) - Q_{.25}(y)$. The relationships of the coefficients estimated by qreg and iqreg are exactly as shown: iqreg reports coefficients that are the difference in coefficients of two qreg models and, of course, iqreg reports the appropriate standard errors which it obtains by bootstrapping.

sqreg is like qreg in that it estimates the equations for the quantiles

$$Q_{.75}(y) = a_{.75} + b_{.75,1}x_1 + b_{.75,2}x_2$$
$$Q_{.25}(y) = a_{.25} + b_{.25,1}x_1 + b_{.25,2}x_2$$

The coefficients it obtains are the same as would be obtained by estimating each equation separately using qreg. sqreg differs from qreg in that it estimates the equations simultaneously and obtains an estimate of the entire variance–covariance matrix of the estimators by bootstrapping. Thus, one can perform hypothesis tests concerning coefficients both within and across equations.

For example, to obtain estimates of the above model, you could type

```
. qreg y x1 x2, q(.25)
. qreg y x1 x2, q(.75)
```

Doing this, you would obtain estimates of the parameters but you could not test whether $b_{.25,1} = b_{.75,1}$ or, equivalently $b_{.75,1} - b_{.25,1} = 0$. If your interest really is in the difference of coefficients, you could type

```
. iqreg y x1 x2, q(.25 .75)
```

The "coefficients" reported would be the difference in quantile coefficients. Alternatively, you could estimate both quantiles simultaneously and then test the equality of the coefficients:

```
. sqreg y x1 x2, q(.25 .75)
. test [q25]x1 = [q75]x2
```

Whether you use iqreg or sqreg makes no difference in terms of this test. sqreg, however, because it estimates the quantiles simultaneously, allows testing other hypotheses. iqreg, by focusing on quantile differences, presents results in a way that is easier to read.

Finally, sqreg can estimate quantiles singly,

```
. sqreg y x1 x2, q(.5)
```

and can thereby be used as a substitute for the slower bsqreg. (Gould (1997) presents timings demonstrating that sqreg is faster than bsqreg.) sqreg can also estimate more than two quantiles simultaneously:

```
. sqreg y x1 x2, q(.25 .5 .75)
```

▷ Example

In demonstrating qreg, we performed quantile regressions using the automobile data. We discovered that the regression of price on weight, length, and foreign produced vastly different coefficients for the .25, .5, and .75 quantile regressions. Here are the coefficients we obtained:

| Variable | 25th percentile | 50th percentile | 75th percentile |
|---|---|---|---|
| weight | 1.83 | 3.93 | 9.22 |
| length | 2.85 | -41.25 | -220.8 |
| foreign | 2209.9 | 3377.8 | 3595.1 |
| _cons | -1879.8 | 344.6 | 20242.9 |

All we can say, having estimated these equations separately, is that price seems to depend differently on the weight, length, and foreign variables depending on which portion of the price distribution we examine. We cannot be more precise because the estimates have been made separately. With sqreg, however, we can estimate all the effects simultaneously:

```
. sqreg price weight length foreign, q(.25 .5 .75) reps(100)
(estimating base model)
(bootstrapping ............... (output omitted) .....)
Simultaneous quantile regression          Number of obs =        74
   bootstrap(100) SEs                      .25 Pseudo R2 =    0.1697
                                           .50 Pseudo R2 =    0.2347
                                           .75 Pseudo R2 =    0.3840
```

| price | Coef. | Bootstrap Std. Err. | t | P>\|t\| | [95% Conf. Interval] | |
|---|---|---|---|---|---|---|
| **q25** | | | | | | |
| weight | 1.831789 | 1.574777 | 1.16 | 0.249 | -1.309005 | 4.972583 |
| length | 2.845558 | 38.63523 | 0.07 | 0.941 | -74.20998 | 79.9011 |
| foreign | 2209.925 | 1008.521 | 2.19 | 0.032 | 198.494 | 4221.357 |
| _cons | -1879.775 | 3665.184 | -0.51 | 0.610 | -9189.753 | 5430.204 |
| **q50** | | | | | | |
| weight | 3.933588 | 2.529541 | 1.56 | 0.124 | -1.111423 | 8.978599 |
| length | -41.25191 | 68.62258 | -0.60 | 0.550 | -178.1153 | 95.6115 |
| foreign | 3377.771 | 1017.422 | 3.32 | 0.001 | 1348.586 | 5406.956 |
| _cons | 344.6494 | 6199.257 | 0.06 | 0.956 | -12019.38 | 12708.68 |
| **q75** | | | | | | |
| weight | 9.22291 | 2.483676 | 3.71 | 0.000 | 4.269374 | 14.17645 |
| length | -220.7833 | 86.17422 | -2.56 | 0.013 | -392.6524 | -48.91422 |
| foreign | 3595.133 | 1147.216 | 3.13 | 0.003 | 1307.083 | 5883.184 |
| _cons | 20242.9 | 9414.242 | 2.15 | 0.035 | 1466.79 | 39019.02 |

The coefficient estimates above are the same as those previously estimated although the standard error estimates are a little different. sqreg obtains estimates of variance by bootstrapping. Rogers (1992) provides evidence that, in the case of quantile regression, the bootstrap standard errors are better than those calculated analytically by Stata.

The important thing here, however, is that the full covariance matrix of the estimators has been estimated and stored and thus it is now possible to perform hypothesis tests. Are the effects of weight the same at the 25th and 75th percentiles?

```
. test [q25]weight = [q75]weight
 ( 1)   [q25]weight - [q75]weight = 0.0

       F(  1,     70) =     8.97
            Prob > F =    0.0038
```

It appears that they are not. We can obtain a confidence interval for the difference using lincom:

```
. lincom [q75]weight-[q25]weight
 ( 1)  - [q25]weight + [q75]weight = 0.0
```

| price | Coef. | Std. Err. | t | P>|t| | [95% Conf. Interval] | |
|---|---|---|---|---|---|---|
| (1) | 7.391121 | 2.467548 | 3.00 | 0.004 | 2.469752 | 12.31249 |

Indeed, we could test whether the weight and length set of coefficients are equal at the three quantiles estimated:

```
. quietly test [q25]weight = [q50]weight
. quietly test [q25]weight = [q75]weight, accum
. quietly test [q25]length = [q50]length, accum
. test [q25]length = [q75]length, accum
 ( 1)   [q25]weight - [q50]weight = 0.0
 ( 2)   [q25]weight - [q75]weight = 0.0
 ( 3)   [q25]length - [q50]length = 0.0
 ( 4)   [q25]length - [q75]length = 0.0

       F(  4,     70) =     2.43
            Prob > F =    0.0553
```

iqreg focuses on one quantile comparison but presents results that are more easily interpreted:

```
. iqreg price weight length foreign, q(.25 .75) reps(100) nolog
```

| .75-.25 Interquartile regression | | | Number of obs = | 74 |
|---|---|---|---|---|
| bootstrap(100) SEs | | | .75 Pseudo R2 = | 0.3840 |
| | | | .25 Pseudo R2 = | 0.1697 |

| price | Coef. | Bootstrap Std. Err. | t | P>|t| | [95% Conf. Interval] | |
|---|---|---|---|---|---|---|
| weight | 7.391121 | 2.467548 | 3.00 | 0.004 | 2.469752 | 12.31249 |
| length | -223.6288 | 83.09868 | -2.69 | 0.009 | -389.3639 | -57.89376 |
| foreign | 1385.208 | 1193.557 | 1.16 | 0.250 | -995.2671 | 3765.683 |
| _cons | 22122.68 | 9009.159 | 2.46 | 0.017 | 4154.478 | 40090.88 |

Looking only at the .25 and .75 quantiles (the interquartile range), the iqreg command output is easily interpreted. Increases in weight corresponds significantly to increases in price dispersion. Increases in length corresponds to decreases in price dispersion. The foreign variable does not significantly change price dispersion.

Do not make too much of these results; the purpose of this example is simply to illustrate the `sqreg` and `iqreg` commands and to do so in a context that suggests why analyzing dispersion might be of interest.

Note that `lincom` after `sqreg` produced the same $t$ statistic for the interquartile range of `weight` as did the `iqreg` command above. In general they will not agree exactly due to the randomness of bootstrapping unless the random number seed is set to the same value before estimation (as was done in this case).

◁

Gould (1997) presents simulation results showing that the coverage—the actual percentage of confidence intervals containing the true value—for `iqreg` is appropriate.

## Saved Results

`qreg` saves in `e()`:

Scalars

| | | | |
|---|---|---|---|
| `e(N)` | number of observations | `e(sum_adev)` | sum of absolute deviations |
| `e(df_m)` | model degrees of freedom | `e(sum_rdev)` | sum of raw deviations |
| `e(df_r)` | residual degrees of freedom | `e(f_r)` | residual density estimate |
| `e(q)` | quantile requested | `e(convcode)` | 0 if converged; otherwise, |
| `e(q_v)` | value of the quantile | | return code for why nonconvergence |

Macros

| | | | |
|---|---|---|---|
| `e(cmd)` | qreg | `e(predict)` | program used to implement |
| `e(depvar)` | name of dependent variable | | `predict` |

Matrices

| | | | |
|---|---|---|---|
| `e(b)` | coefficient vector | `e(V)` | variance–covariance matrix of the estimators |

Functions

| | |
|---|---|
| `e(sample)` | marks estimation sample |

`iqreg` saves in `e()`:

Scalars

| | | | |
|---|---|---|---|
| `e(N)` | number of observations | `e(sumrdv0)` | lower quantile sum of raw deviations |
| `e(df_r)` | residual degrees of freedom | `e(sumrdv1)` | upper quantile sum of raw deviations |
| `e(reps)` | number of replications | `e(sumadv0)` | lower quantile sum of absolute deviations |
| `e(q0)` | lower quantile requested | `e(sumadv1)` | upper quantile sum of absolute deviations |
| `e(q1)` | upper quantile requested | `e(convcode)` | 0 if converged; otherwise, return code for why nonconvergence |

Macros

| | | | |
|---|---|---|---|
| `e(cmd)` | iqreg | `e(vcetype)` | covariance estimation method |
| `e(depvar)` | name of dependent variable | `e(predict)` | program used to implement `predict` |

Matrices

| | | | |
|---|---|---|---|
| `e(b)` | coefficient vector | `e(V)` | variance–covariance matrix of the estimators |

Functions

| | |
|---|---|
| `e(sample)` | marks estimation sample |

`sqreg` saves in `e()`:

Scalars

| | | | |
|---|---|---|---|
| `e(N)` | number of observations | `e(reps)` | number of replications |
| `e(n_q)` | number of quantiles requested | `e(sumrdv#)` | sum of raw deviations for q# |
| `e(q#)` | the quantiles requested | `e(sumadv#)` | sum of absolute deviations for q# |
| `e(df_r)` | residual degrees of freedom | `e(convcode)` | 0 if converged; otherwise, return code for why nonconvergence |

Macros

| | | | |
|---|---|---|---|
| `e(cmd)` | `sqreg` | `e(vcetype)` | covariance estimation method |
| `e(depvar)` | name of dependent variable | `e(predict)` | program used to implement `predict` |

Matrices

| | | | |
|---|---|---|---|
| `e(b)` | coefficient vector | `e(V)` | variance–covariance matrix of the estimators |

Functions

| | |
|---|---|
| `e(sample)` | marks estimation sample |

`bsqreg` saves in `e()`:

Scalars

| | | | |
|---|---|---|---|
| `e(N)` | number of observations | `e(q_v)` | value of the quantile |
| `e(df_r)` | residual degrees of freedom | `e(sum_adev)` | sum of absolute deviations |
| `e(reps)` | number of replications | `e(sum_rdev)` | sum of raw deviations |
| `e(q)` | quantile requested | `e(convcode)` | 0 if converged; otherwise, return code for why nonconvergence |

Macros

| | | | |
|---|---|---|---|
| `e(cmd)` | `bsqreg` | `e(predict)` | program used to implement `predict` |
| `e(depvar)` | name of dependent variable | | |

Matrices

| | | | |
|---|---|---|---|
| `e(b)` | coefficient vector | `e(V)` | variance–covariance matrix of the estimators |

Functions

| | |
|---|---|
| `e(sample)` | marks estimation sample |

`_qreg` saves in `r()`:

Scalars

| | | | |
|---|---|---|---|
| `r(N)` | number of observations | `r(ic)` | number of iterations |
| `r(df_m)` | model degrees of freedom | `r(f_r)` | residual density estimate |
| `r(sum_w)` | sum of the weights | `r(q)` | quantile requested |
| `r(sum_adev)` | sum of absolute deviations | `r(q_v)` | value of the quantile |
| `r(sum_rdev)` | sum of raw deviations | `r(convcode)` | 1 if converged; 0 otherwise |

# Methods and Formulas

`qreg`, `iqreg`, `sqreg`, and `bsqreg` are implemented as ado-files.

According to Stuart and Ord (1991, 1084), the method of minimum absolute deviations was first proposed by Boscovich in 1757 and was later developed by Laplace; Stigler (1986, 39–55) and Hald (1998, 97–103, 112–116) provide historical details. According to Bloomfield and Steiger (1980), Harris (1950) subsequently observed that the problem of minimum absolute deviations could be turned into the linear programming problem that was first implemented by Wagner (1959). Interest has grown in this method due to interest in robust methods. Statistical and computational properties of minimum absolute deviation estimators are surveyed by Narula and Wellington (1982).

Define $q$ as the quantile to be estimated; the median is $q = .5$. For each observation $i$, let $r_i$ be the residual

$$r_i = y_i - \sum_j \beta_j x_{ij}$$

Define the multiplier $h_i$

$$h_i = \begin{cases} 2q & \text{if } r_i > 0 \\ 2(1-q) & \text{otherwise} \end{cases}$$

Then the quantity being minimized with respect to $\beta_j$ is $\sum_i |r_i|h_i$. Thus, quantiles other than the median are estimated by weighting the residuals. For example, if we want to estimate the 75th percentile, we weight the negative residuals by 0.50 and the positive residuals by 1.50. It can be shown that the criterion is minimized when 75 percent of the residuals are negative.

This is set up as a linear programming problem and solved via linear programming techniques as suggested by Armstrong, Frome, and Kung (1979), and used by courtesy of Marcel Dekker Inc. The definition of convergence is exact in the sense that no amount of added iterations could improve the solution. Each step is described by a set of observations through which the regression plane passes, called the *basis*. A step is taken by replacing a point in the basis if the sum of weighted absolute deviations can be improved. If this occurs, a line is printed in the iteration log. The linear programming method is started by doing a weighted least squares (WLS) regression to identify a good set of observations to use as a starting basis.

The variances are estimated using a method suggested by Koenker and Bassett (1982). This method can be put into a form recommended by Huber (1967) for M-estimates where

$$\text{cov}(\beta) = \mathbf{R}_2^{-1} \mathbf{R}_1 \mathbf{R}_2^{-1}$$

and $\mathbf{R}_1 = \mathbf{X}'\mathbf{W}\mathbf{W}'\mathbf{X}$ (in the Huber formulation) and $\mathbf{W}$ is a diagonal matrix with elements

$$W_{ii} = \begin{cases} q/f_{\text{residuals}}(0) & \text{if } r > 0 \\ (1-q)/f_{\text{residuals}}(0) & \text{if } r < 0 \\ 0 & \text{otherwise} \end{cases}$$

and $\mathbf{R}_2$ is the design matrix $\mathbf{X}'\mathbf{X}$. This is derived from formula 3.11 in Koenker and Bassett, although their notation is much different. $f_{\text{residuals}}()$ refers to the density of the true residuals. There are many things that Koenker and Bassett leave unspecified, including how one should obtain a density estimate for the errors in real data. It is at this point we offer our contribution (Rogers 1993).

We first sort the residuals and locate the observation in the residuals corresponding to the quantile in question, taking into account weights if they are applied. We then calculate $w_n$, the square root of the sum of the weights. Unweighted data are equivalent to weighted data where each observation has weight 1, resulting in $w_n = \sqrt{n}$. For analytically weighted data, the weights are rescaled so that the sum of the weights is the number of observations, resulting in $\sqrt{n}$ again. For frequency-weighted data, $w_n$ literally is the square root of the sum of the weights.

We locate the closest observation in each direction such that the sum of weights for all closer observations is $w_n$. If we run off the end of the dataset, we stop. We calculate $w_s$, the sum of weights for all observations in this middle space. Typically, $w_s$ is slightly greater than $w_n$.

The residuals obtained after quantile regression have the property that if there are $k$ parameters, then exactly $k$ of the residuals must be zero. Thus, we calculate an adjusted weight $w_a = w_s - k$. The density estimate is the distance spanned by these observations divided by $w_a$. Because the distance spanned by this mechanism converges toward zero, this estimate of density converges in probability to the true density.

The pseudo $R^2$ is calculated as

$$1 - \frac{\text{sum of weighted deviations about estimated quantile}}{\text{sum of weighted deviations about raw quantile}}$$

This is based on the likelihood for a double exponential distribution $e^{h_i |r_i|}$.

# References

Armstrong, R. D., E. L. Frome, and D. S. Kung. 1979. Algorithm 79-01: A revised simplex algorithm for the absolute deviation curve fitting problem. In *Communications in Statistics, Simulation and Computation* B8(2), 175–190. New York: Marcel Dekker.

Bloomfield, P. and W. Steiger. 1980. Least absolute deviations curve-fitting. *SIAM Journal on Scientific and Statistical Computing* 1: 290–301.

Efron, B. and R. Tibshirani. 1993. *An Introduction to the Bootstrap.* New York: Chapman & Hall.

Gould, W. W. 1992. sg11.1: Quantile regression with bootstrapped standard errors. *Stata Technical Bulletin* 9: 19–21. Reprinted in *Stata Technical Bulletin Reprints*, vol. 2, pp. 137–139.

——. 1997. sg70: Interquantile and simultaneous-quantile regression. *Stata Technical Bulletin* 38: 14–22. Reprinted in *Stata Technical Bulletin Reprints*, vol. 7, pp. 167–176.

Gould, W. W. and W. H. Rogers. 1994. Quantile regression as an alternative to robust regression. *1994 Proceedings of the Statistical Computing Section.* Alexandria, VA: American Statistical Association.

Hald, A. 1998. *A History of Mathematical Statistics from 1750 to 1930.* New York: John Wiley & Sons.

Harris, T. 1950. Regression using minimum absolute deviations. *The American Statistician* 4: 14–15.

Huber, P. J. 1967. The behavior of maximum likelihood estimates under non-standard conditions. *Proceedings of the Fifth Berkeley Symposium on Mathematical Statistics and Probability* 1: 221–233.

——. 1981. *Robust Statistics.* New York: John Wiley & Sons.

Koenker, R. and G. Bassett, Jr. 1982. Robust tests for heteroscedasticity based on regression quantiles. *Econometrica* 50: 43–61.

Narula, S. C. and J. F. Wellington. 1982. The minimum sum of absolute errors regression: A state of the art survey. *International Statistical Review* 50: 317–326.

Rogers, W. H. 1992. sg11: Quantile regression standard errors. *Stata Technical Bulletin* 9: 16–19. Reprinted in *Stata Technical Bulletin Reprints*, vol. 2, pp. 133–137.

——. 1993. sg11.2: Calculation of quantile regression standard errors. *Stata Technical Bulletin* 13: 18–19. Reprinted in *Stata Technical Bulletin Reprints*, vol. 3, pp. 77–78.

Rousseeuw, P. J. and A. M. Leroy. 1987. *Robust Regression and Outlier Detection.* New York: John Wiley & Sons.

Stigler, S. M. 1986. *The History of Statistics.* Cambridge, MA: Belknap Press of Harvard University Press.

Stuart, A. and J. K. Ord. 1991. *Kendall's Advanced Theory of Statistics, Vol. 2.* 5th ed. New York: Oxford University Press.

Wagner, H. M. 1959. Linear programming techniques for regression analysis. *Journal of the American Statistical Association* 54: 206–212.

Wu, C. F. J. 1986. Jackknife, bootstrap and other resampling methods in regression analysis. *Annals of Statistics* 14: 1261–1350 (including comments and reply).

## Also See

| | |
|---|---|
| **Complementary:** | [R] **adjust**, [R] **lincom**, [R] **linktest**, [R] **mfx**, [R] **predict**, [R] **sw**, [R] **test**, [R] **testnl**, [R] **vce**, [R] **xi** |
| **Related:** | [R] **bstrap**, [R] **regress**, [R] **rreg** |
| **Background:** | [U] **16.5 Accessing coefficients and standard errors**, [U] **23 Estimation and post-estimation commands** |

# Title

quadchk — Check sensitivity of quadrature approximation

# Syntax

quadchk $\left[ \#_1 \left[ \#_2 \right] \right]$ $\left[ , \underline{noo}utput \right]$

# Description

quadchk checks the quadrature approximation used in the random-effects estimators of the following commands:

    xtclog
    xtintreg
    xtlogit
    xtpois with the normal option
    xtprobit
    xttobit

quadchk re-estimates the model, starting from the converged answer, for different numbers of quadrature points and then compares the different solutions.

# Options

$\#_1$ and $\#_2$ specify the number of quadrature points to use in the comparison runs of the previous model. The default is to use $n_q - 4$ and $n_q + 4$ points, where $n_q$ is the number of quadrature points used in the estimation of the original model.

nooutput suppresses the iteration log and output of the re-estimated models.

# Remarks

Some random-effects estimators in Stata use Gauss–Hermite quadrature to compute the log likelihood and its derivatives. The quadchk command provides a means to look at the numerical soundness of the quadrature approximation.

Using the converged coefficients of the original model as starting values, the model is re-estimated using two different numbers of quadrature points. The log likelihood and coefficient estimates for the original model and the two re-estimated models are then compared. If the quadrature approach is not valid, then the number of quadrature points will affect the stability of the estimation results. This instability will result in the re-estimated models' log likelihoods and coefficient estimates differing, sometimes dramatically, from the original model's results.

As a rule of thumb, if the coefficients do not change by more than a relative difference of $10^{-4}$ (0.01%), then the choice of quadrature points does not significantly affect the outcome and the results may be confidently interpreted. However, if the results do change appreciably—greater than a relative difference of $10^{-2}$ (1%)—then one must question whether the model can be reliably estimated using the quadrature approach.

Two aspects of random-effects models have the potential to make the quadrature approximation inaccurate: large group sizes and large correlations within groups. These factors can also work in tandem, decreasing or increasing the reliability of the quadrature. For example, if the within-group correlation $\rho$ is small, say $\rho < 0.25$, then Gauss–Hermite quadrature may be reliable for group sizes as big as 50–100. However, when $\rho$ is large, say greater than 0.4, simulations have shown that the quadrature can break down for group sizes as small as 20.

It is easy to see why the quadrature breaks down when group sizes are large or when $\rho$ is big. The likelihood for a group is an integral of a normal density (the distribution of the random effects) times a product of cumulative normals. There are $T_i$ cumulative normals in the product, where $T_i$ is the number of observations in the $i$th group. The Gauss–Hermite quadrature procedure is based on the assumption that the product of normals can be approximated by a polynomial. When $T_i$ is large or $\rho$ is big, this assumption is no longer valid.

Note that when this assumption breaks down badly, increasing the number of quadrature points will not solve the problem. Increasing the number of quadrature points is equivalent to increasing the degree of the polynomial approximation. However, the points are positioned according to a set formula. When the number of points is increased, the range spanned by the points is also increased, and, on average, the points are only slightly closer together. If the true function is, for instance, very concentrated around zero, increasing the number of points is of little consequence because the additional points will mostly pick up the shape of the function far from zero.

When quadchk shows that the coefficient estimates change appreciably with different numbers of quadrature points, this indicates that the polynomial approximation is poor, and increasing the number of quadrature points will not help. You can convince yourself of this by continuing to increase the number of quadrature points. As you do this, the coefficient estimates will continue to change. In cases such as this, all coefficient estimates should be viewed with suspicion; one cannot claim that the results produced with larger numbers of quadrature points are more accurate than those produced with fewer points.

Simulations have shown that estimates of coefficients of independent variables that are constant within groups are especially prone to numerical instability. Hence, if your model involves independent variables of this sort, then it is especially important to run quadchk.

If the quadchk command indicates that the estimation results are sensitive to the number of quadrature points, one may want to consider an alternative such as a fixed-effects, pooled, or population-averaged model. Alternatively, if a different random-effects model is available that is not estimated via quadrature (e.g., xtpois, re), then that model may be a better choice.

▷ Example

In this example, we synthesize data according to the model

$$y = 0.05\,\mathtt{x1} + 0.08\,\mathtt{x2} + 0.08\,\mathtt{x3} + 0.1\,\mathtt{x4} + 0.1\,\mathtt{x5} + 0.1\,\mathtt{x6} + 0.1$$

$$\mathtt{z} = \begin{cases} 1 & \text{if } y \geq 0 \\ 0 & \text{if } y < 0 \end{cases}$$

where the intrapanel correlation is 0.5 and the x1 variable is constant within panel. We first fit a random-effects probit model, and then we check the stability of the quadrature calculation:

```
. xtprobit z x1-x6, i(id)

Fitting comparison model:

Iteration 0:   log likelihood = -4152.5328
Iteration 1:   log likelihood = -4138.4434
```

```
Iteration 2:    log likelihood = -4138.4431
Fitting full model:
rho =  0.0      log likelihood = -4138.4431
rho =  0.1      log likelihood =  -3603.06
rho =  0.2      log likelihood = -3448.0667
rho =  0.3      log likelihood =  -3382.909
rho =  0.4      log likelihood = -3356.2536
rho =  0.5      log likelihood = -3354.0627
rho =  0.6      log likelihood = -3376.4348
Iteration 0:    log likelihood = -3354.0627
Iteration 1:    log likelihood = -3352.1745
Iteration 2:    log likelihood = -3349.6987
Iteration 3:    log likelihood = -3349.6926
```

```
Random-effects probit                      Number of obs      =      6000
Group variable (i) : id                    Number of groups   =       300

Random effects u_i ~ Gaussian              Obs per group: min =        20
                                                          avg =      20.0
                                                          max =        20

                                           Wald chi2(6)       =     36.15
Log likelihood  = -3349.6926               Prob > chi2        =    0.0000
```

| z | Coef. | Std. Err. | z | P>\|z\| | [95% Conf. Interval] | |
|---|---|---|---|---|---|---|
| x1 | .1156763 | .0554911 | 2.08 | 0.037 | .0069157 | .2244369 |
| x2 | .1005555 | .066227 | 1.52 | 0.129 | -.0292469 | .230358 |
| x3 | .1542187 | .0660852 | 2.33 | 0.020 | .0246942 | .2837432 |
| x4 | .1257616 | .0375776 | 3.35 | 0.001 | .0521109 | .1994123 |
| x5 | .1366003 | .0654695 | 2.09 | 0.037 | .0082824 | .2649182 |
| x6 | .0870325 | .0453489 | 1.92 | 0.055 | -.0018496 | .1759147 |
| _cons | .1098393 | .0500502 | 2.19 | 0.028 | .0117426 | .2079359 |
| /lnsig2u | -.0791821 | .0971059 | -0.82 | 0.415 | -.2695062 | .1111419 |
| sigma_u | .9611824 | .0466682 | | | .8739317 | 1.057144 |
| rho | .4802148 | .0242385 | | | .4330283 | .5277569 |

```
Likelihood ratio test of rho=0:      chi2(1) =   1577.50     Prob > chi2 = 0.0000
. quadchk
Refitting model quad() =  8
  (output omitted )

Refitting model quad() = 16
  (output omitted )
```

|  | Quadrature check | | |  |
|---|---|---|---|---|
|  | Fitted quadrature 12 points | Comparison quadrature 8 points | Comparison quadrature 16 points |  |
| Log likelihood | -3349.6926 | -3354.6372 | -3348.3881 | |
|  | | -4.9446636 | 1.3045064 | Difference |
|  | | .00147615 | -.00038944 | Relative difference |
| z: x1 | .11567632 | .16153997 | .07007833 | |
|  | | .04586365 | -.04559799 | Difference |
|  | | .3964826 | -.39418607 | Relative difference |
| z: x2 | .10055552 | .10317831 | .09937417 | |
|  | | .00262279 | -.00118135 | Difference |
|  | | .02608296 | -.01174825 | Relative difference |

| z: | | | | |
|---|---|---|---|---|
| x3 | .1542187 | .15465369 | .15150516 | |
| | | .00043499 | -.00271354 | Difference |
| | | .00282062 | -.0175954 | Relative difference |

| z: | | | | |
|---|---|---|---|---|
| x4 | .12576159 | .12880254 | .1243974 | |
| | | .00304096 | -.00136418 | Difference |
| | | .02418032 | -.01084739 | Relative difference |

| z: | | | | |
|---|---|---|---|---|
| x5 | .13660028 | .13475211 | .13707075 | |
| | | -.00184817 | .00047047 | Difference |
| | | -.01352977 | .00344411 | Relative difference |

| z: | | | | |
|---|---|---|---|---|
| x6 | .08703252 | .08568342 | .08738135 | |
| | | -.0013491 | .00034883 | Difference |
| | | -.0155011 | .00400808 | Relative difference |

| z: | | | | |
|---|---|---|---|---|
| _cons | .10983928 | .11031299 | .09654975 | |
| | | .00047371 | -.01328953 | Difference |
| | | .00431278 | -.12099065 | Relative difference |

| lnsig2u: | | | | |
|---|---|---|---|---|
| _cons | -.07918213 | -.18133823 | -.05815644 | |
| | | -.1021561 | .02102569 | Difference |
| | | 1.2901408 | -.26553574 | Relative difference |

We see that the x1 variable (the one that was constant within panel) changed with a relative difference of nearly 40%! Hence, we conclude that we cannot trust the quadrature approximation for this model, and all results are considered suspect.

◁

## ▷ Example

In this example, we synthesize data exactly the same way as in the previous example, but we make the intrapanel correlation equal to 0.1 instead of 0.5. We again fit a random-effects probit model and check the quadrature:

```
. xtprobit z x1-x6, i(id) nolog
```

| | | | | |
|---|---|---|---|---|
| Random-effects probit | | Number of obs | = | 6000 |
| Group variable (i) : id | | Number of groups | = | 300 |
| Random effects u_i ~ Gaussian | | Obs per group: min = | | 20 |
| | | avg = | | 20.0 |
| | | max = | | 20 |
| | | Wald chi2(6) | = | 39.43 |
| Log likelihood  = -4065.3144 | | Prob > chi2 | = | 0.0000 |

| z | Coef. | Std. Err. | z | P>\|z\| | [95% Conf. Interval] |
|---|---|---|---|---|---|
| x1 | .0246934 | .0251121 | 0.98 | 0.325 | -.0245255    .0739123 |
| x2 | .1300122 | .0587907 | 2.21 | 0.027 | .0147847    .2452398 |
| x3 | .1190411 | .0579539 | 2.05 | 0.040 | .0054535    .2326287 |
| x4 | .1391966 | .0331817 | 4.19 | 0.000 | .0741617    .2042316 |
| x5 | .0773645 | .0578455 | 1.34 | 0.181 | -.0360106    .1907395 |
| x6 | .0862025 | .0401185 | 2.15 | 0.032 | .0075716    .1648334 |
| _cons | .0922659 | .0244394 | 3.78 | 0.000 | .0443656    .1401661 |
| /lnsig2u | -2.34394 | .1575243 | -14.88 | 0.000 | -2.652682    -2.035198 |
| sigma_u | .3097561 | .0243971 | | | .2654468    .3614618 |
| rho | .0875487 | .0125837 | | | .0658239    .1155566 |

Likelihood ratio test of rho=0:     chi2(1) =     110.19      Prob > chi2 = 0.0000

```
. quadchk, nooutput
```

```
Refitting model quad() =  8
Refitting model quad() = 16
```

Quadrature check

| | Fitted quadrature 12 points | Comparison quadrature 8 points | Comparison quadrature 16 points | |
|---|---|---|---|---|
| Log likelihood | -4065.3144 | -4065.3173 | -4065.3144 | |
| | | -.00286401 | -4.767e-06 | Difference |
| | | 7.045e-07 | 1.172e-09 | Relative difference |
| z: x1 | .02469338 | .02468991 | .02469426 | |
| | | -3.463e-06 | 8.851e-07 | Difference |
| | | -.00014023 | .00003584 | Relative difference |
| z: x2 | .13001225 | .13001198 | .13001229 | |
| | | -2.663e-07 | 4.027e-08 | Difference |
| | | -2.048e-06 | 3.097e-07 | Relative difference |
| z: x3 | .11904112 | .11901865 | .1190409 | |
| | | -.00002247 | -2.199e-07 | Difference |
| | | -.00018879 | -1.847e-06 | Relative difference |
| z: x4 | .13919664 | .13918545 | .13919696 | |
| | | -.00001119 | 3.232e-07 | Difference |
| | | -.00008037 | 2.322e-06 | Relative difference |
| z: x5 | .07736447 | .0773757 | .07736399 | |
| | | .00001123 | -4.849e-07 | Difference |
| | | .00014516 | -6.268e-06 | Relative difference |
| z: x6 | .0862025 | .08618573 | .08620282 | |
| | | -.00001677 | 3.264e-07 | Difference |
| | | -.00019454 | 3.786e-06 | Relative difference |
| z: _cons | .09226589 | .09224255 | .09226531 | |
| | | -.00002334 | -5.753e-07 | Difference |
| | | -.00025297 | -6.236e-06 | Relative difference |
| lnsig2u: _cons | -2.3439398 | -2.3442475 | -2.3439384 | |
| | | -.00030763 | 1.450e-06 | Difference |
| | | .00013124 | -6.187e-07 | Relative difference |

Here we see that the quadrature approximation is stable, even for the coefficient of x1. With this result, you can confidently interpret the results.

Again, note that the only difference between this example and the previous one is the value of $\rho$. The quadrature approximation works wonderfully for small to moderate values of $\rho$, but it breaks down for large values of $\rho$. Indeed, for large values of $\rho$, one should do more than question the validity of the quadrature approximation; one should question the validity of the random-effects model itself.

◁

## Methods and Formulas

quadchk is implemented as an ado-file.

## Also See

Complementary:        [R] **xtclog**, [R] **xtintreg**, [R] **xtlogit**, [R] **xtpois**,
                      [R] **xtprobit**, [R] **xttobit**

# Title

| |
|---|
| **query** — Display system parameters |

# Syntax

query

# Description

query displays the settings of various Stata parameters.

# Remarks

query provides more system information than you will want to know. It is not important that you understand every line of output query produces if all you need is one piece of information. Here is what happens when you type query:

```
. query
                                                            ── Status
        type │ float              linesize │ 79
     virtual │ off                pagesize │ 28
        more │ on                       dp │ period
        rmsg │ off                   trace │ off
     matsize │ 40                    level │ 95
     adosize │ 128                 logtype │ smcl
    graphics │ on                  linegap │ 1
                                                            ── Files
         log │ (closed)
      cmdlog │ (closed)
```

The output is broken into two divisions: status and files. We generated the above output using Stata for Windows.

Information on each of the entries can be found in

|  | Status: | | | |
|---|---|---|---|---|
| | type | [R] **generate** | linesize | [R] **log** |
| | virtual | [R] **memory** | pagesize | [R] **more** |
| | more | [R] **more** | dp | [R] **format** |
| | rmsg | [P] **rmsg** | trace | [P] **program** |
| | matsize | [R] **matsize** | level | [R] **level** |
| | adosize | [P] **sysdir** | logtype | [R] **log** |
| | graphics | *Stata Graphics Manual* | linegap | [R] **view** |
| Files: | | | | |
| | log | [R] **log** | | |
| | cmdlog | [R] **log** | | |

In general, the parameters displayed by query can be changed by set; see [R] **set**.

34

## Also See

Complementary:    [R] **set**

Related:    [R] **format**, [R] **generate**, [R] **level**, [R] **log**, [R] **matsize**,
[R] **memory**, [R] **more**, [R] **view**,
[P] **program**, [P] **rmsg**, [P] **sysdir**

# Title

| |
|---|
| **range** — Numerical ranges, derivatives, and integrals |

# Syntax

range *varname* #$_{\text{first}}$ #$_{\text{last}}$ $\left[\text{#}_{\text{obs}}\right]$

dydx *yvar xvar* $\left[\text{if } exp\right]$ $\left[\text{in } range\right]$ , <u>g</u>enerate(*newvar*) $\left[\text{ replace }\right]$

integ *yvar xvar* $\left[\text{if } exp\right]$ $\left[\text{in } range\right]$ $\left[\text{, <u>g</u>enerate(*newvar*) replace <u>t</u>rapezoid}\right.$

$\quad$ <u>i</u>nitial(#) $\left.\right]$

by ... : may be used with dydx and integ; see [R] **by**.

# Description

range generates a numerical range, which is useful for evaluating and graphing functions. dydx and integ calculate derivatives and integrals of numeric "functions".

# Options

<u>g</u>enerate(*newvar*) specifies the name of the new variable to be created. It must be specified with dydx.

replace specifies that if an existing variable is specified for generate(), it should be overwritten.

trapezoid requests that the trapezoidal rule $\big($the sum of $(x_i - x_{i-1})(y_i + y_{i-1})/2\big)$ be used to compute integrals; the default is cubic splines. Cubic splines will give superior results for most smooth functions; for irregular functions, trapezoid may give better results.

initial(#) specifies the initial condition for calculating definite integrals; see *Methods and Formulas* below. If not specified, the initial condition is taken as 0.

# Remarks

range, dydx, and integ allow you to extend Stata's graphics capabilities beyond the realm of data analysis and into mathematics. (See Gould 1993 for another command that draws functions.)

range constructs the variable *varname* taking on values #$_{\text{first}}$ to #$_{\text{last}}$, inclusive, over #$_{\text{obs}}$. If #$_{\text{obs}}$ is not specified, the number of observations in the current dataset is used.

range may be used to produce increasing sequences such as

. range x 0 12.56 100

or it may be used to produce decreasing sequences:

. range z 100 1

▷ Example

To graph $y = e^{-x/6}\sin(x)$ over the interval $[0, 12.56]$, we can type

```
. range x 0 12.56 100
obs was 0, now 100
. gen y = exp(-x/6)*sin(x)
```

Here is a graph of the data:

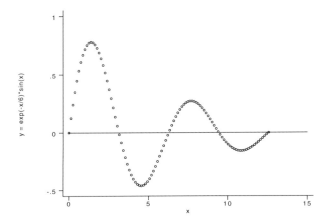

We estimate the derivative using dydx, and compute the relative difference between this estimate and the true derivative.

```
. dydx y x, gen(dy)
. gen dytrue = exp(-x/6)*(cos(x) - sin(x)/6)
. gen error = abs(dy - dytrue)/dytrue
```

The error is greatest at the endpoints as one would expect. The error is approximately 0.5% at each endpoint, but the error quickly falls to less than 0.01%.

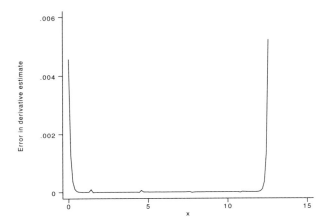

We now estimate the integral using `integ`:

```
. integ y x, gen(iy)
number of points = 100
integral        = .85316396
. gen iytrue = (36/37)*(1 - exp(-x/6)*(cos(x) + sin(x)/6))
. display iytrue[_N]
.85315901
. display abs(r(integral) - iytrue[_N])/iytrue[_N]
5.799e-06
. gen diff = iy - iytrue
```

The relative difference between the estimate $\big($stored in `r(integral)`$\big)$ and the true value of the integral is about $6 \times 10^{-6}$. A graph of the absolute difference (`diff`) is shown below. Note that here error is cumulative. Again, most of the error is due to a relatively poorer fit near the endpoints.

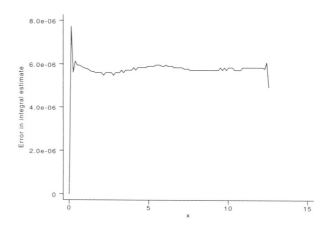

◁

> ## Example

Stata is not limited solely to graphing functions—it can draw parameterized curves as well. For instance, consider the curve given by the polar coordinate relation $r = 2\sin(2\theta)$. The conversion of polar coordinates to parameterized form is $(y, x) = (r\sin\theta, r\cos\theta)$, so

```
. range theta 0 2*_pi 400
(obs was 100, now 400)
. gen r = 2*sin(2*theta)
. gen y = r*sin(theta)
. gen x = r*cos(theta)
. graph y x, c(l) s(i) noaxis yline(0) xline(0)
```

*(Graph on next page)*

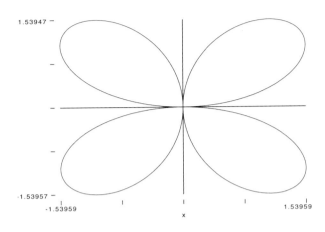

## Saved Results

integ saves in r():

Scalars
r(N_points)   number of unique $x$ points          r(integral)   estimate of the integral

## Methods and Formulas

range, dydx, and integ are implemented as ado-files.

Consider a set of data points $(x_1, y_1), \ldots, (x_n, y_n)$ generated by a function $y = f(x)$. dydx and integ first fit these points with a cubic spline. The cubic spline is then analytically differentiated (integrated) to give an approximation for the derivative (integral) of $f$.

The cubic spline (see, for example, Press et al. (1992)) consists of $n - 1$ cubic polynomials $P_i(x)$, with the $i$th one defined on the interval $[x_i, x_{i+1}]$:

$$P_i(x) = y_i a_i(x) + y_{i+1} b_i(x) + y_i'' c_i(x) + y_{i+1}'' d_i(x)$$

where

$$a_i(x) = \frac{x_{i+1} - x}{x_{i+1} - x_i} \qquad\qquad b_i(x) = \frac{x - x_i}{x_{i+1} - x_i}$$

$$c_i(x) = \frac{1}{6}(x_{i+1} - x_i)^2 a_i(x)[\{a_i(x)\}^2 - 1] \qquad d_i(x) = \frac{1}{6}(x_{i+1} - x_i)^2 b_i(x)[\{b_i(x)\}^2 - 1]$$

and $y_i''$ and $y_{i+1}''$ are constants whose values will be determined as described below. The notation for these constants is justified by the fact that $P_i''(x_i) = y_i''$ and $P_i''(x_{i+1}) = y_{i+1}''$.

Since $a_i(x_i) = 1$, $a_i(x_{i+1}) = 0$, $b_i(x_i) = 0$, and $b_i(x_{i+1}) = 1$. Therefore, $P_i(x_i) = y_i$ and $P_i(x_{i+1}) = y_{i+1}$. Thus, the $P_i$ jointly define a function that is continuous at the interval boundaries. It is also desirable that the first derivative be continuous at the interval boundaries; that is,

$$P_i'(x_{i+1}) = P_{i+1}'(x_{i+1})$$

The above $n-2$ equations (one equation for each point except the two endpoints) and the values of the first derivative at the endpoints, $P_1'(x_1)$ and $P_{n-1}'(x_n)$, determine the $n$ constants $y_i''$.

The value of the first derivative at an endpoint is set to the value of the derivative obtained by fitting a quadratic to the endpoint and the two adjacent points; namely, we use

$$P_1'(x_1) = \frac{y_1 - y_2}{x_1 - x_2} + \frac{y_1 - y_3}{x_1 - x_3} - \frac{y_2 - y_3}{x_2 - x_3}$$

and a similar formula for the upper endpoint.

dydx approximates $f'(x_i)$ using $P_i'(x_i)$.

integ approximates $F(x_i) = F(x_1) + \int_{x_1}^{x_i} f(x)\,dx$ using

$$I_0 + \sum_{k=1}^{i-1} \int_{x_k}^{x_{k+1}} P_k(x)\,dx$$

where $I_0$ (an estimate of $F(x_1)$) is the value specified by the initial(#) option. If the trapezoid option is specified, integ approximates the integral using the trapezoidal rule:

$$I_0 + \sum_{k=1}^{i-1} \frac{1}{2}(x_{k+1} - x_k)(y_{k+1} + y_k)$$

If there are ties among the $x_i$, the mean of $y_i$ is computed at each set of ties, and the cubic spline is fit to these values.

## Acknowledgment

The present versions of dydx and integ were inspired by the dydx2 command written by Patrick Royston of the MRC Clinical Trials Unit, London.

## References

Gould, W. W. 1993. ssi5.1: Graphing functions. *Stata Technical Bulletin* 16: 23–26. Reprinted in *Stata Technical Bulletin Reprints*, vol. 3, pp. 188–193.

——. 1997. crc46: Better numerical derivatives and integrals. *Stata Technical Bulletin* 35: 3–5. Reprinted in *Stata Technical Bulletin Reprints*, vol. 6, pp. 8–12.

Press, W. H., S. A. Teukolsky, W. T. Vetterling, and B. P. Flannery. 1992. *Numerical Recipes in C, The Art of Scientific Computing*. 2d ed. Cambridge: Cambridge University Press.

## Also See

**Complementary:**      [R] **egen**, [R] **obs**

# Title

> **recast** — Change storage type of variable

# Syntax

> recast *type varlist* $\left[\, ,\ \texttt{force}\,\right]$
>
> where *type* is byte, int, long, float, double, or str#.

# Description

> recast changes the storage type of the variables identified in *varlist* to *type*.

# Options

> force makes recast unsafe by causing the variables to be given the new storage type even if that will cause a loss of precision, introduction of missing values, or, in the case of string variables, the truncation of strings.
>
> force should be used with caution. force is for those instances where you have a variable saved as a double but would now be satisfied to have the variable stored as a float even though that would lead to a slight rounding of its values.

# Remarks

> See [U] **15 Data** for a description of storage types. Also see [R] **compress** and [R] **destring** for alternatives to recast.

▷ Example

> recast refuses to change a variable's type if that change is inappropriate for the values actually stored, so it is always safe to try:

```
. describe headroom

              storage  display    value
variable name   type   format     label      variable label

headroom        float  %6.1f                  Headroom (in.)
. recast int headroom
headroom:  37 values would be changed; not changed
```

Our attempt to change headroom from a float to an int was ignored—if the change had been made, 37 values would have changed. Here is an example where the type can be changed:

```
. describe mpg

              storage  display    value
variable name   type   format     label      variable label

mpg             int    %8.0g                  Mileage (mpg)
```

41

```
. recast byte mpg
. describe mpg
```

| variable name | storage type | display format | value label | variable label |
|---|---|---|---|---|
| mpg | byte | %8.0g | | Mileage (mpg) |

recast works with string variables as well as numeric variables, and it provides all the same protections:

```
. describe make
```

| variable name | storage type | display format | value label | variable label |
|---|---|---|---|---|
| make | str18 | %-18s | | Make and Model |

```
. recast str16 make
make:  2 values would be changed; not changed
```

recast can be used both to promote and to demote variables:

```
. recast str20 make
. describe make
```

| variable name | storage type | display format | value label | variable label |
|---|---|---|---|---|
| make | str20 | %-20s | | Make and Model |

◁

## Methods and Formulas

recast is implemented as an ado-file.

## Also See

| | |
|---|---|
| **Related:** | [R] **compress**, [R] **destring** |
| **Background:** | [U] **15.2.2 Numeric storage types**, |
| | [U] **15.4.4 String storage types** |

# Title

> **recode** — Recode categorical variable

# Syntax

> recode *varname* *rule* [*rule* ...] [*=el] [if *exp*] [in *range*]

where

> *rule* is of the form      *element* [*element*...] = *el*
>
> *element* is of the form    { *el* | *el/el* }
>
> and *el* is              { # | min | max }

# Description

recode changes the contents of *varname* according to the *rules*. If if *exp* or in *range* is specified, values of *varname* outside the range are left unmodified. min and max provide a convenient way to refer to the observed minimum and maximum values of *varname*. Combined with if *exp* and in *range*, min and max are determined over the restricted sample.

# Remarks

Despite the complexity of the syntax diagram, recode is easy to use:

| | |
|---|---|
| recode x 1=2 | is the same as replace x=2 if x==1 |
| recode x 1=2 3=4 | changes 1 to 2 and 3 to 4 in x |
| recode x 1=2 2=1 | interchanges 1 and 2 in x |
| recode x 1=2 2=1 *=3 | same as above and changes all other values to 3 |
| recode x 1/5=2 | changes 1 through 5 in x to 2 |
| recode x 1 3 4 5 = 6 | changes 1, 3, 4, and 5 to 6 |
| recode x 1 3/5 = 6 | changes 1 and 3 through 5 to 6 |
| recode x 1 3/5=6 2 8=3 | also changes 2 and 8 to 3 |
| recode x 1 3/5=6 2 8=3 *=1 | and all remaining to 1 |
| recode x min/5=min | recodes minimum through 5 to minimum |
| recode x .=9 | changes missing to 9 |
| recode x 9=. | changes 9 to missing |

# Methods and Formulas

recode is implemented as an ado-file.

# Also See

**Complementary:**      [R] **generate**

**Related:**            [R] **mvencode**

# Title

> **reg3** — Three-stage estimation for systems of simultaneous equations

# Syntax

*Basic syntax*

> reg3 $(depvar_1\ varlist_1)\ (depvar_2\ varlist_2)\ \dots (depvar_N\ varlist_N)$
>
> $\big[weight\big]\ \big[\texttt{if}\ exp\big]\ \big[\texttt{in}\ range\big]$

*Full syntax*

> reg3 $\big(\big[eqname_1\colon\big]depvar_{1a}\ \big[depvar_{1b}\dots=\big]varlist_1\ \big[,\ \underline{\text{noc}}\text{onstant}\ \big]\big)$
>
> $\big(\big[eqname_2\colon\big]depvar_{2a}\ \big[depvar_{2b}\dots=\big]varlist_2\ \big[,\ \underline{\text{noc}}\text{onstant}\ \big]\big)$
>
> $\dots$
>
> $\big(\big[eqname_N\colon\big]depvar_{Na}\ \big[depvar_{Nb}\dots=\big]varlist_N\ \big[,\ \underline{\text{noc}}\text{onstant}\ \big]\big)$
>
> $\big[weight\big]\ \big[\texttt{if}\ exp\big]\ \big[\texttt{in}\ range\big]\ \big[,\ \underline{\text{ex}}\text{og}(varlist)\ \underline{\text{en}}\text{dog}(varlist)\ \underline{\text{inst}}(varlist)$
>
> $\underline{\text{a}}\text{llexog}\ \underline{\text{ireg3}}\ \underline{\text{c}}\text{onstraints}(numlist)\ \big\{\ \underline{\text{ols}}\ \big|\ \underline{\text{sure}}\ \big|\ \underline{\text{m}}\text{vreg}\ \big|\ \text{2sls}\ \big|\ \text{3sls}\ \big\}$
>
> dfk dfk2 $\underline{\text{small}}$ $\underline{\text{noc}}$onstant $\underline{\text{corr}}(correlation)$ $\underline{\text{first}}$ $\underline{\text{level}}(\#)$ $\underline{\text{noh}}$eader
>
> $\underline{\text{not}}$able $\underline{\text{nof}}$ooter $maximize\_options$ $\big]$

by ... : may be used with reg3; see [R] **by**.

aweights and fweights are allowed; see [U] **14.1.6 weight**.

*depvar* and *varlist* may contain time-series operators; see [U] **14.4.3 Time-series varlists**.

reg3 shares the features of all estimation commands; see [U] **23 Estimation and post-estimation commands**.

Explicit equation naming (*eqname*:) cannot be combined with multiple dependent variables in an equation specification.

# Syntax for predict

> predict $\big[type\big]$ *newvarname* $\big[\texttt{if}\ exp\big]$ $\big[\texttt{in}\ range\big]$ $\big[,\ \underline{\text{equation}}(eqno\ \big[,eqno\big])\ \text{xb}$
>
> stdp $\underline{\text{res}}$iduals $\underline{\text{difference}}$ stddp $\big]$

These statistics are available both in and out of sample; type predict ... if e(sample) ... if wanted only for the estimation sample.

# Description

   reg3 estimates a system of structural equations, where some equations contain endogenous variables among the explanatory variables. Estimation is via three-stage least squares (3SLS); see Zellner and Theil (1962). Typically, the endogenous explanatory variables are dependent variables from other equations in the system. reg3 supports iterated GLS estimation and linear constraints.

   reg3 can also estimate systems of equations by seemingly unrelated regression (SURE), multivariate regression (MVREG), and equation-by-equation ordinary least squares (OLS) or two-stage least squares (2SLS).

44

## Nomenclature

Under 3SLS or 2SLS estimation, a *structural equation* is defined as one of the equations specified in the system. *Dependent variable* will have its usual interpretation as the left-hand-side variable in an equation with an associated disturbance term. All dependent variables are explicitly taken to be *endogenous* to the system and as such are treated as correlated with the disturbances in the system's equations. Unless specified in an `endog()` option, all other variables in the system are treated as *exogenous* to the system and uncorrelated with the disturbances. The exogenous variables are taken to be *instruments* for the endogenous variables.

## Options

`noconstant` omits the constant term (intercept). When specified on an equation, `noconstant` omits the constant term for that equation. When specified with the overall options, `noconstant` omits the constant from the instrument list (i.e., the intercept is omitted from the first-stage regressions). The latter usage is rare.

`exog`(*varlist*) specifies additional exogenous variables that are not included in any of the system equations. This can occur when the system contains identities that are not estimated. If implicitly exogenous variables from the equations are listed here, `reg3` will just ignore the additional information. Specified variables will be added to the exogenous variables in the system and used in the "first-stage" as instruments for the endogenous variables. By specifying dependent variables from the structural equations, `exog()` can be used to override their endogeneity.

`endog`(*varlist*) identifies variables in the system that are not dependent variables, but are endogenous to the system. These variables must appear in the variable list of at least one equation in the system. Again, the need for this identification often occurs when the system contains identities. For example, a variable that is the sum of an exogenous variable and a dependent variable may appear as an explanatory variable in some equations.

`inst`(*varlist*) specifies a full list of all exogenous variables and may not be used with the `endog()` or `exog()` options. It must contain a full list of variables to be used as instruments for the endogenous regressors. Like `exog()`, the list may contain variables not specified in the system of equations. This option can be used to achieve the same results as the `endog()` and `exog()` options and the choice is a matter of convenience. Any variable not specified in the *varlist* of the `inst()` option is assumed to be endogenous to the system. As with `exog()`, including the dependent variables from the structural equations will override their endogeneity.

`allexog` indicates that all right-hand-side variables are to be treated as exogenous—even if they appear as the dependent variable of another equation in the system. This option can be used to enforce a seemingly unrelated regression or multivariate regression estimation even when some dependent variables appear as regressors.

`ireg3` causes `reg3` to iterate over the estimated disturbance covariance matrix and parameter estimates until the parameter estimates converge. Although usually successful, there is no guarantee that the iteration will converge to a stable point. Under seemingly unrelated regression, this iteration converges to the maximum likelihood estimates.

`constraints`(*numlist*) specifies by number the linear constraint(s) (see [R] **constraint**) to be applied to the system. In addition to providing constraints for three-stage least squares, the `constraint` option can be combined with `exog()`, `sure`, `mvreg` or explicitly independent equations to produce constrained seemingly unrelated regression or constrained multivariate regression. See [U] **14.1.8 numlist** for shorthand ways of specifying several constraints in *numlist*.

ols causes `reg3` to perform equation-by-equation OLS on the system—even if dependent variables appear as regressors and/or the regressors differ for each equation; see [R] **mvreg**. `ols` implies `allexog`, `dfk`, `small`, and `corr(independent)`; `nodfk` and `nosmall` may be specified to override `dfk` and `small`.

Note that the covariance of the coefficients between equations is not estimated under this option and that cross-equation tests should not be performed after estimation with `ols`. For cross-equation testing, use `sureg` or `3sls` (the default).

sure causes `reg3` to perform a seemingly unrelated regression estimation of the system—even if dependent variables from some equations appear as regressors in other equations; see [R] **sureg**. `sure` is a synonym for `allexog`.

mvreg is identical to `sure` except that the disturbance covariance matrix is estimated with an OLS degrees of freedom adjustment—the `dfk` option. If the regressors are identical for all equations, the parameter point estimates will be the standard multivariate regression results. If any of the regressors differ, the point estimates are those for seemingly unrelated regression with an OLS degrees-of-freedom adjustment in computing the covariance matrix. `nodfk` and `nosmall` may be specified to override `dfk` and `small`.

2sls causes `reg3` to perform equation-by-equation two-stage least squares on the full system of equations. This option implies `dfk`, `small`, and `corr(independent)`.

Note that cross-equation testing should not be performed after estimation with this option. With `2sls` no covariance is estimated between the parameters of the equations. For cross-equation testing use full `3sls`.

3sls specifies the full three-stage least squares estimation of the system and is the default for `reg3`.

dfk specifies the use of an alternate divisor in computing the covariance matrix for the equation residuals. As an asymptotically justified estimator, `reg3` by default uses the number of sample observations $n$ as a divisor. When the `dfk` option is set, a small-sample adjustment is made and the divisor is taken to be $\sqrt{(n - k_i)(n - k_j)}$, where $k_i$ and $k_j$ are the numbers of parameters in equations $i$ and $j$ respectively.

dfk2 specifies the use of an alternate divisor in computing the covariance matrix for the equation errors. When the `dfk2` option is set, the divisor is taken to be the mean of the residual degrees of freedom from the individual equations.

small specifies that small sample statistics are to be computed. It shifts the test statistics from $\chi^2$ and $Z$ statistics to $F$ statistics and $t$ statistics. This option is primarily intended to support multivariate regression. While the standard errors from each equation are computed using the degrees of freedom for the equation, the degrees of freedom for the $t$ statistics are all taken to be those for the first equation. This poses no problem under multivariate regression because the regressors are the same across equations.

corr(*correlation*) specifies the assumed form of the correlation structure of the equation disturbances and is rarely requested explicitly. For the family of models estimated by `reg3` the only two allowable correlation structures are <u>independent</u> and <u>unstructured</u>. The default is `unstructured`.

This option is used almost exclusively to estimate a system of equations by two-stage least squares or to perform OLS regression with `reg3` on multiple equations. In these cases, the correlation is set to `independent`, forcing `reg3` to treat the covariance matrix of equation disturbances as diagonal in estimating model parameters. Thus, a set of two-stage coefficient estimates can be obtained if the system contains endogenous right-hand-side variables; or OLS regression can be imposed, even if the regressors differ across equations. Without imposing independent disturbances, `reg3` would estimate the former by three-stage least squares and the latter by seemingly unrelated regression.

Note that any tests performed after estimation with the independent option will treat coefficients in different equations as having no covariance; cross-equation tests should not be used after specifying `corr(independent)`.

`first` requests that the first-stage regression results be displayed during estimation.

`level(#)` specifies the confidence level, in percent, for confidence intervals. The default is `level(95)` or as set by `set level`; see [U] **23.5 Specifying the width of confidence intervals**.

`noheader` suppresses display of the header reporting the estimation method and the table of equation summary statistics.

`notable` suppresses display of the coefficient table.

`nofooter` suppresses display of the footer reporting the list of endogenous variables in the model.

*maximize_options* control the iteration process when `ireg3` is specified; see [R] **maximize**. You should never have to specify them.

## Options for predict

`equation(`*eqno*`[,`*eqno*`])` specifies to which equation you are referring.

> `equation()` is filled in with one *eqno* for options `xb`, `stdp`, and `residuals`. `equation(#1)` would mean the calculation is to be made for the first equation, `equation(#2)` would mean the second, and so on. Alternatively, you could refer to the equations by their names. `equation(income)` would refer to the equation named income and `equation(hours)` to the equation named hours.

> If you do not specify `equation()`, results are as if you specified `equation(#1)`.

> `difference` and `stddp` refer to between-equation concepts. To use these options, you must specify two equations; e.g., `equation(#1,#2)` or `equation(income,hours)`. When two equations must be specified, `equation()` is not optional.

`xb`, the default, calculates the fitted values—the prediction of $x_j b$ for the specified equation.

`stdp` calculates the standard error of the prediction for the specified equation. It can be thought of as the standard error of the predicted expected value or mean for the observation's covariate pattern. This is also referred to as the standard error of the fitted value.

`residuals` calculates the residuals.

`difference` calculates the difference between the linear predictions of two equations in the system. With `equation(#1,#2)`, `difference` computes the prediction of `equation(#1)` minus the prediction of `equation(#2)`.

`stddp` is allowed only after you have previously estimated a multiple-equation model. The standard error of the difference in linear predictions $(x_{1j} b - x_{2j} b)$ between equations 1 and 2 is calculated.

For more information on using `predict` after multiple-equation estimation commands, see [R] **predict**.

## Remarks

    `reg3` estimates systems of structural equations where some equations contain endogenous variables among the explanatory variables. Generally, these endogenous variables are the dependent variables of other equations in the system, though not always. The disturbance is correlated with the endogenous variables—violating the assumptions of ordinary least squares. Further, since some of the explanatory variables are the dependent variables of other equations in the system, the error terms among the equations are expected to be correlated. `reg3` uses an instrumental variable approach to produce consistent estimates and generalized least squares (GLS) to account for the correlation structure in the disturbances across the equations. Good general references on three-stage include Kmenta (1997) and Greene (2000, 692–693).

Three-stage least squares can be thought of as producing estimates from a three-step process.

**Stage 1.** Develop instrumented values for all endogenous variables. These instrumented values can simply be considered as the predicted values resulting from a regression of each endogenous variable on all exogenous variables in the system. This stage is identical to the first step in two-stage least squares and is critical for the consistency of the parameter estimates.

**Stage 2.** Obtain a consistent estimate for the covariance matrix of the equation disturbances. These estimates are based on the residuals from a two-stage least squares estimation of each structural equation.

**Stage 3.** Perform a GLS-type estimation using the covariance matrix estimated in the second stage and with the instrumented values in place of the right-hand-side endogenous variables.

❑ Technical Note

The estimation and use of the covariance matrix of disturbances in three-stage is almost identical to the seemingly unrelated regression (SURE) method—**sureg**. As with SURE, the use of this covariance matrix improves the efficiency of the three-stage estimator. Even without the use of the covariance matrix the estimates would be consistent. (They would be two-stage least squares estimates.) This improvement in efficiency comes with a caveat. All the parameter estimates now depend on the consistency of the covariance matrix estimates. If a single equation in the system is misspecified, the disturbance covariance estimates will be inconsistent and the resulting coefficients will be biased and inconsistent. Alternately, if each equation is estimated separately by two-stage least squares ([R] **regress**) only the coefficients in the misspecified equation are affected.

❑

❑ Technical Note

Under certain conditions when all equations are just identified, the three-stage least squares estimates "fold-up" to the two-stage least squares estimates available from **ivreg**. This behavior is directly analogous to SURE producing the same results as equation-by-equation ordinary least squares when all the equations in the system have the same independent variables. Conceptually, the covariance of the errors in these cases adds no additional information to the system. While we can estimate the covariance matrix of the equation errors, this information simply "folds-up" in the final estimates of the coefficients. However, as with **sureg**, estimating an exactly identified system with **reg3** can have advantages over equation-by-equation two-stage. After estimation with **reg3**, tests involving coefficients in separate equations can be easily performed using **test** or **testnl**.

❑

▷ Example

A very simple macro-economic model could be postulated that relates consumption (**consump**) to private and government wages paid (**wagepriv** and **wagegovt**). Simultaneously, private wages could be postulated to depend on consumption, total government expenditures (**govt**), and the lagged stock of capital in the economy (**capital1**). While this is not a very plausible model, it does meet the criterion of being simple. This model could be written

$$\text{consump} = \beta_0 + \beta_1 \, \text{wagepriv} + \beta_2 \, \text{wagegovt} + \epsilon_1$$

$$\text{wagepriv} = \beta_3 + \beta_4 \, \text{consump} + \beta_5 \, \text{govt} + \beta_6 \, \text{capital1} + \epsilon_2$$

Assuming this is the full system, consump and wagepriv will be endogenous variables, with wagegovt, govt, and capital1 exogenous. Data for the US economy on these variables are taken from Klein (1950). This model can be estimated with reg3 by typing

```
. reg3 (consump wagepriv wagegovt) (wagepriv consump govt capital1)
Three-stage least squares regression
```

| Equation | Obs | Parms | RMSE | "R-sq" | chi2 | P |
|---|---|---|---|---|---|---|
| consump | 22 | 2 | 1.776297 | 0.9388 | 208.017 | 0.0000 |
| wagepriv | 22 | 3 | 2.372443 | 0.8542 | 80.03506 | 0.0000 |

| | Coef. | Std. Err. | z | P>\|z\| | [95% Conf. Interval] | |
|---|---|---|---|---|---|---|
| consump | | | | | | |
| wagepriv | .8012754 | .1279329 | 6.26 | 0.000 | .5505314 | 1.052019 |
| wagegovt | 1.029531 | .3048424 | 3.38 | 0.001 | .432051 | 1.627011 |
| _cons | 19.3559 | 3.583772 | 5.40 | 0.000 | 12.33184 | 26.37996 |
| | | | | | | |
| wagepriv | | | | | | |
| consump | .4026076 | .2567312 | 1.57 | 0.117 | -.1005764 | .9057916 |
| govt | 1.177792 | .5421253 | 2.17 | 0.030 | .1152461 | 2.240338 |
| capital1 | -.0281145 | .0572111 | -0.49 | 0.623 | -.1402462 | .0840173 |
| _cons | 14.63026 | 10.26693 | 1.42 | 0.154 | -5.492552 | 34.75306 |

```
Endogenous variables:   consump wagepriv
Exogenous variables:    wagegovt govt capital1
```

Without showing the two-stage least square results, it should be noted that the consumption function in this system falls under the conditions noted earlier. That is, the two-stage and three-stage least squares coefficients for the equation are identical.

◁

▷ Example

Some of the most common simultaneous systems encountered are supply and demand models. A very simple system could be specified as

$$\text{qDemand} = \beta_0 + \beta_1 \, \text{price} + \beta_2 \, \text{pcompete} + \beta_3 \, \text{income} + \epsilon_1$$

$$\text{qSupply} = \beta_4 + \beta_5 \, \text{price} + \beta_6 \, \text{praw} + \epsilon_2$$

$$\text{Equilibrium condition}: \quad \text{quantity} = \text{qDemand} = \text{qSupply}$$

where

        quantity is the quantity of a product produced and sold

        price is the price of the product

        pcompete is the price of a competing product

        income is the average income level of consumers

        praw is the price of raw materials used to produce the product

In this system, price is assumed to be determined simultaneously with demand. The important statistical implications are that price is not a predetermined variable and that it is correlated with the disturbances of both equations. The system is somewhat unusual: quantity is associated with two disturbances. This really poses no problem because the disturbances are specified on the behavioral demand and supply equations—two separate entities. Often one of the two equations is rewritten to place price on the left-hand side making this endogeneity explicit in the specification.

To provide a concrete illustration of the effects of simultaneous equations, we can simulate data for the above system using known coefficients and disturbance properties. Specifically, we will simulate the data as follows:

$$\text{qDemand} = 40 - 1.0\,\text{price} + 0.25\,\text{pcompete} + 0.5\,\text{income} + \epsilon_1$$

$$\text{qSupply} = 0.5\,\text{price} - 0.75\,\text{praw} + \epsilon_2$$

where

$$\epsilon_1 \sim N(0, 2.4)$$

$$\epsilon_2 \sim N(0, 3.8)$$

For comparison, we can estimate the supply and demand equations separately by OLS. The estimates for the demand equation are

```
. regress quantity price pcompete income
```

| Source | SS | df | MS |  | Number of obs = | 49 |
|---|---|---|---|---|---|---|
|  |  |  |  |  | F( 3, 45) = | 1.00 |
| Model | 23.1579302 | 3 | 7.71931008 |  | Prob > F    = | 0.4004 |
| Residual | 346.459313 | 45 | 7.69909584 |  | R-squared   = | 0.0627 |
|  |  |  |  |  | Adj R-squared = | 0.0002 |
| Total | 369.617243 | 48 | 7.70035923 |  | Root MSE    = | 2.7747 |

| quantity | Coef. | Std. Err. | t | P>\|t\| | [95% Conf. Interval] | |
|---|---|---|---|---|---|---|
| price | .1186265 | .1716014 | 0.69 | 0.493 | -.2269965 | .4642495 |
| pcompete | .0946416 | .1200815 | 0.79 | 0.435 | -.1472149 | .3364981 |
| income | .0785339 | .1159867 | 0.68 | 0.502 | -.1550754 | .3121432 |
| _cons | 7.563261 | 5.019479 | 1.51 | 0.139 | -2.54649 | 17.67301 |

The OLS estimates for the supply equation are

```
. regress quantity price praw
```

| Source | SS | df | MS |  | Number of obs = | 49 |
|---|---|---|---|---|---|---|
|  |  |  |  |  | F( 2, 46) = | 35.71 |
| Model | 224.819549 | 2 | 112.409774 |  | Prob > F    = | 0.0000 |
| Residual | 144.797694 | 46 | 3.14777596 |  | R-squared   = | 0.6082 |
|  |  |  |  |  | Adj R-squared = | 0.5912 |
| Total | 369.617243 | 48 | 7.70035923 |  | Root MSE    = | 1.7742 |

| quantity | Coef. | Std. Err. | t | P>\|t\| | [95% Conf. Interval] | |
|---|---|---|---|---|---|---|
| price | .724675 | .1095657 | 6.61 | 0.000 | .5041307 | .9452192 |
| praw | -.8674796 | .1066114 | -8.14 | 0.000 | -1.082077 | -.652882 |
| _cons | -6.97291 | 3.323105 | -2.10 | 0.041 | -13.66197 | -.2838471 |

Examining the coefficients from these regressions, we note that they are not very close to the known parameters used to generate the simulated data. In particular, the positive coefficient on `price` in the demand equation stands out. We constructed our simulated data to be consistent with economic theory—people demand less of a product if its price rises and more of a product if their personal income rises. Although the `price` coefficient is statistically insignificant, the positive value contrasts starkly with what is predicted from economic price theory and the $-1.0$ value that we used in the simulation. Likewise, we are disappointed with the insignificance and level of the coefficient on average `income`. The supply equation has correct signs on the two main parameters, but their levels are quite different from the known values. In fact, the coefficient on `price` (.724675) is different from the simulated parameter (0.5) at the 5% level of significance.

All these problems are to be expected. We explicitly constructed a simultaneous system of equations that violated one of the assumptions of least squares. Specifically, the disturbances were correlated with one of the regressors—`price`.

Two-stage least squares can be used to address the correlation between regressors and disturbances. Using instruments for the endogenous variable, `price`, two-stage will produce consistent estimates of the parameters in the system. Let's use `ivreg` to see how our simulated system behaves when estimated using two-stage least squares.

```
. ivreg quantity (price = praw) pcompete income
```

Instrumental variables (2SLS) regression

| Source | SS | df | MS |  |  |
|---|---|---|---|---|---|
| Model | -313.325605 | 3 | -104.441868 |  |  |
| Residual | 682.942847 | 45 | 15.1765077 |  |  |
| Total | 369.617243 | 48 | 7.70035923 |  |  |

Number of obs = 49
F( 3, 45) = 2.68
Prob > F = 0.0579
R-squared = .
Adj R-squared = .
Root MSE = 3.8957

| quantity | Coef. | Std. Err. | t | P>\|t\| | [95% Conf. Interval] | |
|---|---|---|---|---|---|---|
| price | -1.015817 | .3904865 | -2.60 | 0.013 | -1.802297 | -.229337 |
| pcompete | .3319504 | .1804334 | 1.84 | 0.072 | -.031461 | .6953619 |
| income | .5090607 | .2002977 | 2.54 | 0.015 | .1056405 | .9124809 |
| _cons | 39.89988 | 11.24242 | 3.55 | 0.001 | 17.25648 | 62.54329 |

Instrumented: price
Instruments: pcompete income praw

```
. ivreg quantity (price = pcompete income) praw
```

Instrumental variables (2SLS) regression

| Source | SS | df | MS |  |  |
|---|---|---|---|---|---|
| Model | 219.125463 | 2 | 109.562732 |  |  |
| Residual | 150.491779 | 46 | 3.27156042 |  |  |
| Total | 369.617243 | 48 | 7.70035923 |  |  |

Number of obs = 49
F( 2, 46) = 18.42
Prob > F = 0.0000
R-squared = 0.5928
Adj R-squared = 0.5751
Root MSE = 1.8087

| quantity | Coef. | Std. Err. | t | P>\|t\| | [95% Conf. Interval] | |
|---|---|---|---|---|---|---|
| price | .5773133 | .1806137 | 3.20 | 0.003 | .2137567 | .9408698 |
| praw | -.7835496 | .1354534 | -5.78 | 0.000 | -1.056203 | -.5108961 |
| _cons | -2.550694 | 5.442299 | -0.47 | 0.642 | -13.50547 | 8.404086 |

Instrumented: price
Instruments: praw pcompete income

We are now much happier with the estimation results. All the coefficients from both equations are quite close to the true parameter values for the system. In particular, the coefficients are all well within 95% confidence intervals for the parameters. We do note that the missing $R$-squared in the demand equation seems unusual; there will be more discussion of that later.

Finally, this system could be estimated using three-stage least squares. To demonstrate how large systems might be handled and to avoid multi-line commands, we will use global macros (see [P] **macro**) to hold the specifications for our equations.

```
. global demand "(qDemand: quantity price pcompete income)"
. global supply "(qSupply: quantity price praw)"
. reg3 $demand $supply, endog(price)
```

Note that we must specify `price` as endogenous since it does not appear as a dependent variable in either equation. Without this option, `reg3` would assume that there are no endogenous variables in the system and produce seemingly unrelated regression (`sureg`) estimates. The `reg3` output from our series of commands is

```
Three-stage least squares regression
```

| Equation | Obs | Parms | RMSE | "R-sq" | chi2 | P |
|----------|-----|-------|------|--------|------|---|
| qDemand | 49 | 3 | 3.739686 | -0.8540 | 8.681517 | 0.0338 |
| qSupply | 49 | 2 | 1.752501 | 0.5928 | 39.24858 | 0.0000 |

| | Coef. | Std. Err. | z | P>\|z\| | [95% Conf. Interval] | |
|---|-------|-----------|---|---------|----------------------|---|
| qDemand | | | | | | |
| price | -1.014345 | .3742036 | -2.71 | 0.007 | -1.74777 | -.2809194 |
| pcompete | .2647206 | .1464194 | 1.81 | 0.071 | -.0222561 | .5516973 |
| income | .5299146 | .1898161 | 2.79 | 0.005 | .1578819 | .9019472 |
| _cons | 40.08749 | 10.77072 | 3.72 | 0.000 | 18.97726 | 61.19772 |
| | | | | | | |
| qSupply | | | | | | |
| price | .5773133 | .1749974 | 3.30 | 0.001 | .2343247 | .9203019 |
| praw | -.7835496 | .1312414 | -5.97 | 0.000 | -1.040778 | -.5263213 |
| _cons | -2.550694 | 5.273067 | -0.48 | 0.629 | -12.88571 | 7.784327 |

```
Endogenous variables:   quantity price
Exogenous variables:    pcompete income praw
```

As noted earlier, the use of three-stage least squares over two-stage least squares is essentially an efficiency issue. The coefficients of the demand equation from three-stage are very close to the coefficients from two-stage and those of the supply equation are identical. The latter case was mentioned earlier for systems with some exactly identified equations. However, even for the demand equation, we do not expect the coefficients to change systematically. What we do expect from three-stage are more precise estimates of the parameters given the validity of our specification and `reg3`'s use of the covariances among the disturbances. This increased precision is exactly what is observed in the three-stage results. The standard errors of the three-stage estimates are 3 to 20% smaller than those for the two-stage estimates.

Let's summarize the results. With OLS, we got obviously biased estimates of the parameters. No amount of data would have improved the OLS estimates—they are inconsistent in the face of the violated OLS assumptions. With two-stage least squares we obtained consistent estimates of the parameters and these would have improved with more data. With three-stage least squares, we obtained consistent estimates of the parameters that are more efficient than those obtained by two-stage. ◁

❏ Technical Note

We noted earlier that the $R$-squared was missing from the two-stage estimates of the demand equation. Now, we see that the $R$-squared is negative for the three-stage estimates of the same equation. How can we have a negative $R$-squared?

In most estimators, other than least squares, the $R$-squared is no more than a summary measure of the overall in-sample predictive power of the estimator. The computational formula for $R$-squared is $R$-squared $= 1 - RSS/TSS$, where $RSS$ is the residual sum of squares (sum of squared residuals) and $TSS$ is the total sum of squared deviations about the mean of the dependent variable. In a standard linear model with a constant, the model from which the $TSS$ is computed is nested within the full model from which $RSS$ is computed—they both have a constant term based on the same data. Thus, it must be that $TSS \geq RSS$ and $R$-squared is constrained between 0 and 1.

For two- and three-stage least squares some of the regressors enter the model as instruments when the parameters are estimated. However, since our goal is to estimate the structural model, the actual values, not the instruments for the endogenous right-hand-side variables, are used to determine $R$-squared. The model residuals are computed over a different set of regressors from those used to estimate the model. The two- and/or three-stage estimates are no longer nested within a constant-only model of the dependent variable and the residual sum of squares is no longer constrained to be smaller than the total sum of squares.

A negative $R$-squared in three-stage least squares should be taken for exactly what it is—an indication that the structural model predicts the dependent variable worse than a constant-only model. Is this a problem? It depends on your application. Note that three-stage least squares applied to our contrived supply-and-demand example produced very good estimates of the known true parameters. Still, the demand equation produced an $R$-squared of $-0.854$. How do we feel about our parameter estimates? This should be determined by the estimates themselves, their associated standard errors, and the overall model significance. On this basis, negative $R$-squared and all, we feel pretty good about all the parameter estimates for both the supply and demand equations. Would we want to make predictions about equilibrium quantity using the demand equation alone? Probably not. Would we want to make these quantity predictions using the supply equation? Possibly, based on in-sample predictions, they seem better than those from the demand equations. However, both the supply and demand estimates are based on limited information. If we are interested in predicting quantity, a reduced form equation containing all our independent variables would usually be preferred.

❏

❏ Technical Note

As a matter of syntax, we could have specified the supply-and-demand model on a single line without using global macros.

*(Continued on next page)*

```
. reg3 (quantity price pcompete income) (quantity price praw), endog(price)
```

Three-stage least squares regression

| Equation | Obs | Parms | RMSE | "R-sq" | chi2 | P |
|---|---|---|---|---|---|---|
| quantity | 49 | 3 | 3.739686 | -0.8540 | 8.681517 | 0.0338 |
| 2quantity | 49 | 2 | 1.752501 | 0.5928 | 39.24858 | 0.0000 |

| | Coef. | Std. Err. | z | P>\|z\| | [95% Conf. Interval] | |
|---|---|---|---|---|---|---|
| **quantity** | | | | | | |
| price | -1.014345 | .3742036 | -2.71 | 0.007 | -1.74777 | -.2809194 |
| pcompete | .2647206 | .1464194 | 1.81 | 0.071 | -.0222561 | .5516973 |
| income | .5299146 | .1898161 | 2.79 | 0.005 | .1578819 | .9019472 |
| _cons | 40.08749 | 10.77072 | 3.72 | 0.000 | 18.97726 | 61.19772 |
| **2quantity** | | | | | | |
| price | .5773133 | .1749974 | 3.30 | 0.001 | .2343247 | .9203019 |
| praw | -.7835496 | .1312414 | -5.97 | 0.000 | -1.040778 | -.5263213 |
| _cons | -2.550694 | 5.273067 | -0.48 | 0.629 | -12.88571 | 7.784327 |

Endogenous variables:   quantity price
Exogenous variables:    pcompete income praw

However, in this case, reg3 has been forced to create a unique equation name for the supply equation—2quantity. Both the supply and demand equations could not be designated as quantity, so a number was prefixed to the name for the supply equation.

We could have specified

```
. reg3 (qDemand: quantity price pcompete income) (qSupply: quantity price praw)
>   , endog(price)
```

and obtained exactly the same results and equation labeling as when we used global macros to hold the equation specifications.

In the absence of explicit equation names, reg3 always assumes that the dependent variable should be used to name equations. When each equation has a different dependent variable, this rule causes no problems and produces easily interpreted result tables. If the same dependent variable appears in more than one equation, however, reg3 will create a unique equation name based on the dependent variable name. Since equation names must be used for cross-equation tests, you have more control in this situation if explicit names are placed on the equations.

❑

▷ Example

Klein's (1950) model of the US economy is often used to demonstrate system estimators. It contains several common features which will serve to demonstrate the full syntax of reg3. The Klein model is defined by the following seven relationships.

$$c = \beta_0 + \beta_1 p + \beta_2 p1 + \beta_3 w + \epsilon_1 \tag{1}$$

$$i = \beta_4 + \beta_5 p + \beta_6 p1 + \beta_7 k1 + \epsilon_2 \tag{2}$$

$$wp = \beta_8 + \beta_9 y + \beta_{10} y1 + \beta_{11} yr + \epsilon_3 \tag{3}$$

$$y = c + i + g \tag{4}$$

$$p = x - t - wp \tag{5}$$

$$k = k1 + i \tag{6}$$

$$w = wg + wp \tag{7}$$

The variables in the model are listed below. Two sets of variable names are shown. The concise first name uses traditional economics mnemonics while the second name provides more guidance for everyone else. The concise names serve to keep the specification of the model small (and quite understandable to economists).

| Short Name | Long Name | Variable Definition | Type |
|---|---|---|---|
| c | consump | Consumption | endogenous |
| p | profits | Private industry profits | endogenous |
| p1 | profits1 | Last year's private industry profits | exogenous |
| wp | wagepriv | Private wage bill | endogenous |
| wg | wagegovt | Government wage bill | exogenous |
| w | wagetot | Total wage bill | endogenous |
| i | invest | Investment | endogenous |
| k1 | capital1 | Last year's level of capital stock | exogenous |
| y | totinc | Total income/demand | endogenous |
| y1 | totinc1 | Last year's total income | exogenous |
| g | govt | Government spending | exogenous |
| t | taxnetx | Indirect bus. taxes + net exports | exogenous |
| yr | year | Year - 1931 | exogenous |

Equations 1–3 are behavioral and contain explicit disturbances ($\epsilon_1$, $\epsilon_2$, and $\epsilon_3$). The remaining equations are identities which specify additional variables in the system and their "accounting" relationships with the variables in the behavioral equations. Some variables are explicitly endogenous by appearing as dependent variables in Equations 1–3. Others are implicitly endogenous as linear combinations which contain other endogenous variables (e.g., w, and p). Still other variables are implicitly exogenous by appearing in the identities but not the behavioral equations (e.g., wg and g).

Using the concise names, Klein's model may be estimated with the command

(*Continued on next page*)

```
. reg3 (c p p1 w) (i p p1 k1) (wp y y1 yr), endog(w p y) exog(t wg g)
Three-stage least squares regression
```

| Equation | Obs | Parms | RMSE | "R-sq" | chi2 | P |
|---|---|---|---|---|---|---|
| c | 21 | 3 | .9443305 | 0.9801 | 864.5909 | 0.0000 |
| i | 21 | 3 | 1.446736 | 0.8258 | 162.9808 | 0.0000 |
| wp | 21 | 3 | .7211282 | 0.9863 | 1594.751 | 0.0000 |

| | Coef. | Std. Err. | z | P>\|z\| | [95% Conf. Interval] | |
|---|---|---|---|---|---|---|
| **c** | | | | | | |
| p | .1248904 | .1081291 | 1.16 | 0.248 | −.0870387 | .3368194 |
| p1 | .1631439 | .1004382 | 1.62 | 0.104 | −.0337113 | .3599992 |
| w | .790081 | .0379379 | 20.83 | 0.000 | .715724 | .8644379 |
| _cons | 16.44079 | 1.304549 | 12.60 | 0.000 | 13.88392 | 18.99766 |
| **i** | | | | | | |
| p | −.0130791 | .1618962 | −0.08 | 0.936 | −.3303898 | .3042316 |
| p1 | .7557238 | .1529331 | 4.94 | 0.000 | .4559805 | 1.055467 |
| k1 | −.1948482 | .0325307 | −5.99 | 0.000 | −.2586072 | −.1310893 |
| _cons | 28.17785 | 6.793768 | 4.15 | 0.000 | 14.86231 | 41.49339 |
| **wp** | | | | | | |
| y | .4004919 | .0318134 | 12.59 | 0.000 | .3381388 | .462845 |
| y1 | .181291 | .0341588 | 5.31 | 0.000 | .1143411 | .2482409 |
| yr | .149674 | .0279352 | 5.36 | 0.000 | .094922 | .2044261 |
| _cons | 1.797216 | 1.115854 | 1.61 | 0.107 | −.3898181 | 3.984251 |

```
Endogenous variables:  c i wp w p y
Exogenous variables:   p1 k1 y1 yr t wg g
```

We used the `exog()` option to identify `t`, `wg`, and `g` as exogenous variables in the system. These variables must be identified because they are part of the system but do not appear directly in any of the behavioral equations. Without this option, `reg3` would not know they were part of the system. The `endog()` option specifying `w`, `p`, and `y` is also required. Without this information, `reg3` would be unaware that these variables are linear combinations which include endogenous variables.

❑ Technical Note

Rather than listing additional endogenous and exogenous variables, we could specify the full list of exogenous variables in an `inst()` option.

```
. reg3 (c p p1 w) (i p p1 k1) (wp y y1 yr), inst(g t wg yr p1 k1 y1)
```

or, equivalently,

```
. global conseqn "(c p p1 w)"
. global inveqn  "(i p p1 k1)"
. global wageqn  "(wp y y1 yr)"
. global inlist  "g t wg yr p1 k1 y1"
. reg3 $conseqn $inveqn $wageqn, inst($inlist)
```

Macros and explicit equations can also be mixed in the specification

. reg3 $conseqn (i p p1 k1) $wageqn, endog(w p y) exog(t wg g)

or

. reg3 (c p p1 w) $inveqn (wp y y1 yr), endog(w p y) exog(t wg g)

Placing the equation-binding parentheses in the global macros was also arbitrary. We could have used

. global consump "c p p1 w"
. global invest "i p p1 k1"
. global wagepriv "wp y y1 yr"

. reg3 ($consump) ($invest) ($wagepriv), endog(w p y) exog(t wg g)

reg3 is tolerant of all combinations, and these commands will produce identical output.

❏

Switching to the full variable names, we can estimate Klein's model with the commands below. We will use global macros to store the lists of endogenous and exogenous variables. Again, this is not necessary: these lists could have been typed directly on the command line. However, assigning the lists to local macros makes additional processing easier if alternate models are to be estimated. We will also use the ireg3 option to produce the iterated estimates.

(*Continued on next page*)

```
. global conseqn "(consump profits profits1 wagetot)"
. global inveqn  "(invest profits profits1 capital1)"
. global wageqn  "(wagepriv totinc totinc1 year)"
. global enlist "wagetot profits totinc"
. global exlist "taxnetx wagegovt govt"
. reg3 $conseqn $inveqn $wageqn, endog($enlist) exog($exlist) ireg3
Iteration 1:   tolerance =  .37125491
Iteration 2:   tolerance =  .18947121
Iteration 3:   tolerance =  .10764015
 (output omitted )
Iteration 24:  tolerance =  7.049e-07
Three-stage least squares regression, iterated
```

| Equation | Obs | Parms | RMSE | "R-sq" | chi2 | P |
|---|---|---|---|---|---|---|
| consump | 21 | 3 | .9565088 | 0.9796 | 970.3072 | 0.0000 |
| invest | 21 | 3 | 2.134327 | 0.6209 | 56.77951 | 0.0000 |
| wagepriv | 21 | 3 | .7782334 | 0.9840 | 1312.188 | 0.0000 |

| | Coef. | Std. Err. | z | P>\|z\| | [95% Conf. Interval] | |
|---|---|---|---|---|---|---|
| **consump** | | | | | | |
| profits | .1645096 | .0961979 | 1.71 | 0.087 | -.0240348 | .3530539 |
| profits1 | .1765639 | .0901001 | 1.96 | 0.050 | -.0000291 | .3531569 |
| wagetot | .7658011 | .0347599 | 22.03 | 0.000 | .6976729 | .8339294 |
| _cons | 16.55899 | 1.224401 | 13.52 | 0.000 | 14.15921 | 18.95877 |
| **invest** | | | | | | |
| profits | -.3565316 | .2601568 | -1.37 | 0.171 | -.8664296 | .1533664 |
| profits1 | 1.011299 | .2487745 | 4.07 | 0.000 | .5237098 | 1.498888 |
| capital1 | -.2602 | .0508694 | -5.12 | 0.000 | -.3599022 | -.1604978 |
| _cons | 42.89629 | 10.59386 | 4.05 | 0.000 | 22.13271 | 63.65987 |
| **wagepriv** | | | | | | |
| totinc | .3747792 | .0311027 | 12.05 | 0.000 | .3138191 | .4357394 |
| totinc1 | .1936506 | .0324018 | 5.98 | 0.000 | .1301443 | .257157 |
| year | .1679262 | .0289291 | 5.80 | 0.000 | .1112263 | .2246261 |
| _cons | 2.624766 | 1.195559 | 2.20 | 0.028 | .2815124 | 4.968019 |

```
Endogenous variables:  consump invest wagepriv wagetot profits totinc
Exogenous variables:   profits1 capital1 totinc1 year taxnetx wagegovt govt
```

◁

## ▷ Example

As a simple example of constraints, Equation 1 above may be rewritten with both wages explicitly appearing (rather than as a variable containing the sum). Using the longer variable names, we have

$$\text{consump} = \beta_0 + \beta_1 \text{profits} + \beta_2 \text{profits1} + \beta_3 \text{wagepriv} + \beta_{12} \text{wagegovt} + \epsilon_1$$

To retain the effect of the identity in Equation 7, we need $\beta_3 = \beta_{12}$ as a constraint on the system. We obtain this result by defining the constraint in the usual way and then specifying its use in reg3. Since reg3 is a system estimator, we will need to use the full equation syntax of constraint. Note the assumption that the following commands are entered after the model above has been estimated. We are simply changing the definition of the consumption equation (consump) and adding a constraint on two of its parameters. The remainder of the model definition is carried forward.

```
. global conseqn "(consump profits profits1 wagepriv wagegovt)"

. constraint define 1 [consump]wagepriv = [consump]wagegovt

. reg3 $conseqn $inveqn $wageqn, endog($enlist) exog($exlist) constr(1) ireg3
note:  additional endogenous variables not in the system have no effect
       and are ignored:  wagetot
Iteration 1:    tolerance =   .3712547
Iteration 2:    tolerance =  .18947105
Iteration 3:    tolerance =  .10764002
 (output omitted)
Iteration 24:   tolerance =  7.049e-07

Three-stage least squares regression, iterated

Constraints:
 ( 1)  [consump]wagepriv - [consump]wagegovt = 0.0
```

| Equation | Obs | Parms | RMSE | "R-sq" | chi2 | P |
|----------|-----|-------|------|--------|------|---|
| consump | 21 | 3 | .9565086 | 0.9796 | 970.3076 | 0.0000 |
| invest | 21 | 3 | 2.134326 | 0.6209 | 56.77954 | 0.0000 |
| wagepriv | 21 | 3 | .7782334 | 0.9840 | 1312.188 | 0.0000 |

| | Coef. | Std. Err. | z | P>\|z\| | [95% Conf. Interval] | |
|---|-------|-----------|---|--------|---------------------|---|
| **consump** | | | | | | |
| profits | .1645097 | .0961978 | 1.71 | 0.087 | -.0240346 | .353054 |
| profits1 | .1765639 | .0901001 | 1.96 | 0.050 | -.0000291 | .3531568 |
| wagepriv | .7658012 | .0347599 | 22.03 | 0.000 | .6976729 | .8339294 |
| wagegovt | .7658012 | .0347599 | 22.03 | 0.000 | .6976729 | .8339294 |
| _cons | 16.55899 | 1.224401 | 13.52 | 0.000 | 14.1592 | 18.95877 |
| **invest** | | | | | | |
| profits | -.3565311 | .2601567 | -1.37 | 0.171 | -.8664288 | .1533666 |
| profits1 | 1.011298 | .2487744 | 4.07 | 0.000 | .5237096 | 1.498887 |
| capital1 | -.2601999 | .0508694 | -5.12 | 0.000 | -.359902 | -.1604977 |
| _cons | 42.89626 | 10.59386 | 4.05 | 0.000 | 22.13269 | 63.65984 |
| **wagepriv** | | | | | | |
| totinc | .3747792 | .0311027 | 12.05 | 0.000 | .313819 | .4357394 |
| totinc1 | .1936506 | .0324018 | 5.98 | 0.000 | .1301443 | .257157 |
| year | .1679262 | .0289291 | 5.80 | 0.000 | .1112263 | .2246261 |
| _cons | 2.624766 | 1.195559 | 2.20 | 0.028 | .281512 | 4.968019 |

```
Endogenous variables:  consump invest wagepriv wagetot profits totinc
Exogenous variables:   profits1 wagegovt capital1 totinc1 year taxnetx govt
```

As expected, none of the parameter or standard error estimates have changed from the previous estimates (before the seventh significant digit). We have simply decomposed the total wage variable into its two parts and constrained the coefficients on these parts. The warning about additional endogenous variables was just reg3's way of letting us know that we had specified some information that was irrelevant to the estimation of the system. We had left the variable wagetot in our endog macro. It does not mean anything to the system to specify wagetot as endogenous since it is no longer in the system. That's fine with reg3 and fine for our current purposes.

We can also impose constraints across the equations. For example, the admittedly meaningless constraint of requiring profits to have the same effect in both the consumption and investment equations could be imposed. Retaining the constraint on the wage coefficients, we would estimate this constrained system.

```
. constraint define 2 [consump]profits = [invest]profits
. reg3 $conseqn $inveqn $wageqn, endog($enlist) exog($exlist) constr(1 2) ireg3
note:  additional endogenous variables not in the system have no effect
       and are ignored:  wagetot
Iteration 1:   tolerance =  .14279266
Iteration 2:   tolerance =  .0325390
Iteration 3:   tolerance =  .00307811
Iteration 4:   tolerance =  .00016903
Iteration 5:   tolerance =  .00003409
Iteration 6:   tolerance =  7.763e-06
Iteration 7:   tolerance =  9.240e-07

Three-stage least squares regression, iterated

Constraints:
 ( 1)  [consump]wagepriv - [consump]wagegovt = 0.0
 ( 2)  [consump]profits - [invest]profits = 0.0
```

| Equation | Obs | Parms | RMSE | "R-sq" | chi2 | P |
|----------|-----|-------|------|--------|------|---|
| consump  | 21  | 3     | .9504669 | 0.9798 | 1019.537 | 0.0000 |
| invest   | 21  | 3     | 1.247066 | 0.8706 | 144.5728 | 0.0000 |
| wagepriv | 21  | 3     | .7225276 | 0.9862 | 1537.453 | 0.0000 |

|          | Coef. | Std. Err. | z | P>\|z\| | [95% Conf. Interval] | |
|----------|-------|-----------|---|--------|-----------|------------|
| **consump** | | | | | | |
| profits  | .1075413 | .0957767 | 1.12 | 0.262 | -.0801777 | .2952602 |
| profits1 | .1712756 | .0912613 | 1.88 | 0.061 | -.0075932 | .3501444 |
| wagepriv | .798484 | .0340876 | 23.42 | 0.000 | .7316734 | .8652946 |
| wagegovt | .798484 | .0340876 | 23.42 | 0.000 | .7316734 | .8652946 |
| _cons    | 16.2521 | 1.212157 | 13.41 | 0.000 | 13.87631 | 18.62788 |
| **invest** | | | | | | |
| profits  | .1075413 | .0957767 | 1.12 | 0.262 | -.0801777 | .2952602 |
| profits1 | .6443378 | .1058682 | 6.09 | 0.000 | .43684 | .8518356 |
| capital1 | -.1766669 | .0261889 | -6.75 | 0.000 | -.2279962 | -.1253375 |
| _cons    | 24.31931 | 5.284325 | 4.60 | 0.000 | 13.96222 | 34.6764 |
| **wagepriv** | | | | | | |
| totinc   | .4014106 | .0300552 | 13.36 | 0.000 | .3425035 | .4603177 |
| totinc1  | .1775359 | .0321583 | 5.52 | 0.000 | .1145068 | .240565 |
| year     | .1549211 | .0282291 | 5.49 | 0.000 | .099593 | .2102492 |
| _cons    | 1.959788 | 1.14467 | 1.71 | 0.087 | -.2837242 | 4.203299 |

```
Endogenous variables:  consump invest wagepriv wagetot profits totinc
Exogenous variables:   profits1 wagegovt capital1 totinc1 year taxnetx govt
```

◁

## ❑ Technical Note

Identification in a system of simultaneous equations involves the notion that there is sufficient information to estimate the parameters of the model given the specified functional form. Under-identification usually manifests itself as a singular matrix in the three-stage least squares computations. The most commonly violated order condition for two- or three-stage least squares involves the number of endogenous and exogenous variables. There must be at least as many noncollinear exogenous variables in the remaining system as there are endogenous right-hand-side variables in an equation. This condition must hold for each structural equation in the system.

Put as a set of rules:

1. Count the number of right-hand-side endogenous variables in an equation and call this $m_i$.

2. Count the number of exogenous variables in the same equation and call this $k_i$.

3. Count the total number of exogenous variables in all the structural equations plus any additional variables specified in an `exog()` or `inst()` option and call this $K$.

4. If $m_i > (K - k_i)$ for any structural equation ($i$), then the system is underidentified and cannot be estimated by three-stage least squares.

We are also possibly in trouble if any of the exogenous variables is linearly dependent. We must have $m_i$ linearly independent variables among the exogenous variables represented by $(K - k_i)$.

The complete conditions for identification involve rank-order conditions on several matrices. For a full treatment, see Theil (1971) or Greene (2000, 692).

❏

# Saved Results

`reg3` saves in `e()`:

Scalars

| | | | | |
|---|---|---|---|---|
| `e(N)` | number of observations | | `e(F_#)` | $F$ statistic for eqn. # (`small` only) |
| `e(k_eq)` | number of equations | | `e(rmse_#)` | root mean square error for eqn. # |
| `e(mss_#)` | model sum of squares for equation # | | `e(ll)` | log likelihood |
| `e(df_m#)` | model degrees of freedom for equation # | | `e(chi2_#)` | $\chi^2$ for equation # |
| `e(rss_#)` | residual sum of squares for equation # | | `e(p_#)` | significance for equation # |
| `e(df_r)` | residual degrees of freedom (`small` only) | | `e(ic)` | number of iterations |
| `e(r2_#)` | $R$-squared for equation # | | `e(cons_#)` | 1 when equation # has a constant; 0 otherwise |

Macros

| | | | | |
|---|---|---|---|---|
| `e(cmd)` | `reg3` | | `e(wtype)` | weight type |
| `e(depvar)` | name(s) of dependent variable(s) | | `e(wexp)` | weight expression |
| `e(exog)` | names of exogenous variables | | `e(method)` | requested estimation method |
| `e(endog)` | names of endogenous variables | | `e(small)` | `small` |
| `e(eqnames)` | names of equations | | `e(predict)` | program used to implement `predict` |
| `e(corr)` | correlation structure | | | |

Matrices

| | | | | |
|---|---|---|---|---|
| `e(b)` | coefficient vector | | `e(V)` | variance–covariance matrix of the estimators |
| `e(Sigma)` | $\widehat{\Sigma}$ matrix | | | |

Functions

| | |
|---|---|
| `e(sample)` | marks estimation sample |

# Methods and Formulas

`reg3` is implemented as an ado-file.

The most concise way to represent a system of equations for three-stage least squares requires that we think of the individual equations and their associated data as being stacked. `reg3` does not expect the data in this format, but it is a convenient shorthand. The system could then be formulated as

$$
\begin{bmatrix} \mathbf{y}_1 \\ \mathbf{y}_2 \\ \vdots \\ \mathbf{y}_M \end{bmatrix} = \begin{bmatrix} \mathbf{Z}_1 & 0 & \cdots & 0 \\ 0 & \mathbf{Z}_2 & \cdots & 0 \\ \vdots & \vdots & \ddots & \vdots \\ 0 & 0 & \cdots & \mathbf{Z}_M \end{bmatrix} \begin{bmatrix} \beta_1 \\ \beta_2 \\ \vdots \\ \beta_M \end{bmatrix} + \begin{bmatrix} \epsilon_1 \\ \epsilon_2 \\ \vdots \\ \epsilon_M \end{bmatrix}
$$

In full matrix notation this is just

$$
\mathbf{y} = \mathbf{Z}\,\mathbf{B} + \epsilon
$$

The $\mathbf{Z}$ elements in these matrices represent both the endogenous and exogenous right-hand-side variables in the equations.

We also assume that there will be correlation between the disturbances of the equations so that we may write

$$
E(\epsilon\epsilon') = \mathbf{\Sigma}
$$

where the disturbances are further assumed to have an expected value of 0; $E(\epsilon) = 0$.

The "first-stage" of three-stage least squares regression requires developing instrumented values for the endogenous variables in the system. These can be derived as the predictions from a linear regression of each endogenous regressor on all exogenous variables in the system; or, more succinctly, as the projection of each regressor through the projection matrix of all exogenous variables onto the regressors. Designating the set of all exogenous variables as $\mathbf{X}$ we have

$$
\widehat{\mathbf{z}}_i = \mathbf{X}(\mathbf{X}'\mathbf{X})^{-1}\mathbf{X}'\mathbf{z}_i \quad \text{for each } i
$$

Taken collectively, these $\widehat{\mathbf{Z}}$ contain the instrumented values for all the regressors. They take on the actual values for the exogenous variables and first-stage predictions for the endogenous variables. Given these instrumented variables, we can form a generalized least squares (GLS) or Aitken (1935) estimator for the parameters of the system

$$
\widehat{\mathbf{B}} = \left\{ \widehat{\mathbf{Z}}'(\mathbf{\Sigma}^{-1} \otimes \mathbf{I})\widehat{\mathbf{Z}} \right\}^{-1} \widehat{\mathbf{Z}}'(\mathbf{\Sigma}^{-1} \otimes \mathbf{I})\mathbf{y}
$$

All that remains is to obtain a consistent estimator for $\mathbf{\Sigma}$. This estimate can be formed from the residuals of two-stage least squares estimates of each equation in the system. Alternately, and identically, the residuals can be computed from the estimates formed by taking $\mathbf{\Sigma}$ to be an identity matrix. This maintains the full system of coefficients and allows constraints to be applied when the residuals are computed.

Taking $\mathbf{E}$ to be the matrix of residuals from these estimates, we can produce a consistent estimate of $\mathbf{\Sigma}$ as

$$
\widehat{\mathbf{\Sigma}} = \frac{\mathbf{E}'\mathbf{E}}{n}
$$

where $n$ is the number of observations in the sample. An alternate divisor for this estimate can be obtained with the dfk option as outlined under options.

Placing our estimate of $\widehat{\mathbf{\Sigma}}$ into the GLS estimating equation, we obtain

$$\widehat{\mathbf{B}} = \left\{ \widehat{\mathbf{Z}}'(\widehat{\mathbf{\Sigma}}^{-1} \otimes \mathbf{I})\widehat{\mathbf{Z}} \right\}^{-1} \widehat{\mathbf{Z}}'(\widehat{\mathbf{\Sigma}}^{-1} \otimes \mathbf{I})\mathbf{y}$$

as the three-stage least squares estimates of the system parameters.

The asymptotic variance–covariance matrix of the estimator is just the standard formulation for a GLS estimator

$$\mathbf{V}_{\widehat{\mathbf{B}}} = \left\{ \widehat{\mathbf{Z}}'(\widehat{\mathbf{\Sigma}}^{-1} \otimes \mathbf{I})\widehat{\mathbf{Z}} \right\}^{-1}$$

Iterated three-stage least squares estimates can be obtained by computing the residuals from the three-stage parameter estimates, using these to formulate a new $\widehat{\mathbf{\Sigma}}$, and recomputing the parameter estimates. This process is repeated until the estimates $\widehat{\mathbf{B}}$ converge—if they converge. Convergence is not guaranteed. When estimating a system by SURE, these iterated estimates will be the maximum likelihood estimates for the system. The iterated solution can also be used to produce estimates that are invariant to choice of system and restriction parameterization for many linear systems under full three-stage least squares.

The exposition above follows the parallel developments in Greene (2000) and Kmenta (1997).

The computational formulas for the statistics produced by predict can be found in [R] **predict** and [R] **regress**.

## References

Aitken, A. C. 1935. On least squares and linear combination of observations. *Proceedings, Royal Society of Edinburgh* 55: 42–48.

Greene, W. H. 2000. *Econometric Analysis*. 4th ed. Upper Saddle River, NJ: Prentice–Hall.

Klein, L. 1950. *Economic fluctuations in the United States 1921–1941*. New York: John Wiley & Sons.

Kmenta, J. 1997. *Elements of Econometrics*. 2d ed. Ann Arbor: University of Michigan Press.

Theil, H. 1971. *Principles of Econometrics*. New York: John Wiley & Sons.

Weesie, J. 1999. sg121: Seemingly unrelated estimation and the cluster-adjusted sandwich estimator. *Stata Technical Bulletin* 52: 34–47. Reprinted in *Stata Technical Bulletin Reprints*, vol. 9, pp. 231–248.

Zellner, A. and H. Theil. 1962. Three stage least squares: simultaneous estimate of simultaneous equations. *Econometrica* 29: 63–68.

## Also See

| | |
|---|---|
| **Complementary:** | [R] **adjust**, [R] **constraint**, [R] **lincom**, [R] **mfx**, [R] **predict**, [R] **test**, [R] **testnl**, [R] **xi** |
| **Related:** | [R] **biprobit**, [R] **cnsreg**, [R] **ivreg**, [R] **mvreg**, [R] **regress**, [R] **sureg** |
| **Background:** | [U] **16.5 Accessing coefficients and standard errors**, [U] **23 Estimation and post-estimation commands**, [R] **maximize** |

# Title

> **regress** — Linear regression

# Syntax

<u>regress</u> *depvar* [*varlist*] [*weight*] [<u>if</u> *exp*] [<u>in</u> *range*] [, <u>l</u>evel(#)

    <u>b</u>eta <u>hascons</u> <u>no</u>constant <u>tsscons</u> <u>r</u>obust <u>cl</u>uster(*varname*)

    hc2 hc3 <u>noh</u>eader <u>ef</u>orm(*string*) <u>depname</u>(*varname*) <u>mse</u>1 plus ]

by ... : may be used with regress; see [R] **by**.

aweights, fweights, iweights, and pweights are allowed; see [U] **14.1.6 weight**.

*depvar* and the *varlist* following *depvar* may contain time-series operators; see [U] **14.4.3 Time-series varlists**.

regress shares the features of all estimation commands; see [U] **23 Estimation and post-estimation commands**.

regress may be used with sw to perform stepwise estimation; see [R] **sw**.

# Syntax for predict

<u>predict</u> [*type*] *newvarname* [<u>if</u> *exp*] [<u>in</u> *range*] [, *statistic* ]

where *statistic* is

| | |
|---|---|
| xb | $\mathbf{x}_j\mathbf{b}$, fitted values (the default) |
| <u>pr</u>(*a*,*b*) | $\Pr(y_j \mid a < y_j < b)$ |
| e(*a*,*b*) | $E(y_j \mid a < y_j < b)$ |
| <u>ystar</u>(*a*,*b*) | $E(y_j^*)$, $y_j^* = \max\{a, \min(y_j, b)\}$ |
| <u>c</u>ooksd | Cook's distance |
| <u>l</u>everage \| <u>hat</u> | leverage (diagonal elements of hat matrix) |
| <u>res</u>iduals | residuals |
| <u>rsta</u>ndard | standardized residuals |
| <u>rstu</u>dent | studentized (jackknifed) residuals |
| stdp | standard error of the prediction |
| stdf | standard error of the forecast |
| stdr | standard error of the residual |
| * <u>cov</u>ratio | COVRATIO |
| * <u>dfb</u>eta(*varname*) | DFBETA for *varname* |
| * <u>dfits</u> | DFITS |
| * <u>w</u>elsch | Welsch distance |

where *a* and *b* may be numbers or variables; *a* equal to '.' means $-\infty$; *b* equal to '.' means $+\infty$.

Unstarred statistics are available both in and out of sample; type predict ... if e(sample) ... if wanted only for the estimation sample. Starred statistics are calculated only for the estimation sample even when if e(sample) is not specified.

64

## Description

regress estimates a model of *depvar* on *varlist* using linear regression.

Here is a short list of other regression commands that may be of interest. See [R] **estimation commands** for a complete list.

| | | |
|---|---|---|
| anova | [R] **anova** | an easier way to estimate regressions with many dummy variables |
| cnreg | [R] **tobit** | censored-normal regression |
| heckman | [R] **heckman** | Heckman selection model |
| intreg | [R] **tobit** | interval regression |
| ivreg | [R] **ivreg** | instrumental variables (2SLS) regression |
| newey | [R] **newey** | regression with Newey–West standard errors |
| prais | [R] **prais** | Prais–Winsten regression and Cochrane–Orcutt regression |
| qreg | [R] **qreg** | quantile (including median) regression |
| reg3 | [R] **reg3** | three-stage least squares regression |
| rreg | [R] **rreg** | a type of robust regression |
| sureg | [R] **sureg** | seemingly unrelated regression |
| svyintreg | [R] **svy estimators** | interval regression with survey data |
| svyivreg | [R] **svy estimators** | instrumental variables regression with survey data |
| svyreg | [R] **svy estimators** | linear regression with survey data |
| tobit | [R] **tobit** | tobit regression |
| treatreg | [R] **treatreg** | treatment effects model |
| truncreg | [R] **truncreg** | truncated regression |
| xtabond | [R] **xtabond** | Arellano–Bond linear, dynamic panel-data estimator |
| xtintreg | [R] **xtintreg** | panel data interval regression models |
| xtreg | [R] **xtreg** | fixed- and random-effects linear models |
| xtregar | [R] **xtregar** | fixed- and random-effects linear models with an AR(1) disturbance |
| xttobit | [R] **xtintreg** | panel data tobit models |

## Options

level(*#*) specifies the confidence level, in percent, for confidence intervals. The default is level(95) or as set by set level; see [U] **23.5 Specifying the width of confidence intervals**.

beta asks that normalized beta coefficients be reported instead of confidence intervals.

hascons indicates that a user-defined constant or its equivalent is specified among the independent variables in *varlist*. Some caution is recommended when specifying this option as resulting estimates may not be as accurate as they otherwise would be. Use of this option requires "sweeping" the constant last, so the moment matrix must be accumulated in absolute rather than deviation form. This option may be safely specified when the means of the dependent and independent variables are all "reasonable" and there are not large amounts of collinearity between the independent variables. The best procedure is to view hascons as a reporting option—estimate with and without hascons and verify that the coefficients and standard errors of the variables not affected by the identity of the constant are unchanged. If you do not understand this warning, it is best to avoid this option.

noconstant suppresses the constant term (intercept) in the regression.

tsscons forces the total sum of squares to be computed as though the model has a constant; i.e., as deviations from the mean of the dependent variable. This is a rarely used option that has an effect only when specified with noconstant. It affects only the total sum of squares and all results derived from the total sum of squares.

robust specifies that the Huber/White/sandwich estimator of variance is to be used in place of the traditional calculation. This alternative variance estimator produces consistent standard errors even if the data are weighted or the residuals are not identically distributed. robust combined with cluster() further allows residuals which are not independent within cluster (although they must be independent between clusters). See [U] **23.11 Obtaining robust variance estimates**.

If you specify pweights, robust is implied; see [U] **23.13 Weighted estimation**.

cluster(*varname*) specifies that the observations are independent across groups (clusters) but not necessarily independent within groups. *varname* specifies to which group each observation belongs; e.g., cluster(personid) in data with repeated observations on individuals. cluster() affects the estimated standard errors and variance–covariance matrix of the estimators (VCE), but not the estimated coefficients; see [U] **23.11 Obtaining robust variance estimates**. cluster() can be used with pweights to produce estimates for unstratified cluster-sampled data, see [U] **23.13 Weighted estimation**, but also see [R] **svy estimators** for a command designed especially for survey data.

cluster() implies robust; specifying robust cluster() is equivalent to typing cluster() by itself.

hc2 and hc3 specify an alternate bias correction for the robust variance calculation. hc2 and hc3 may not be specified with cluster(). In the unclustered case, robust uses $\widehat{\sigma}_j^2 = \{n/(n-k)\}u_j^2$ as an estimate of the variance of the $j$th observation, where $u_j$ is the calculated residual and $n/(n-k)$ is included to improve the overall estimate's small-sample properties.

hc2 instead uses $u_j^2/(1-h_{jj})$ as the observation's variance estimate, where $h_{jj}$ is the diagonal element of the hat (projection) matrix. This is unbiased if the model really is homoskedastic. hc2 tends to produce slightly more conservative confidence intervals.

hc3 uses $u_j^2/(1-h_{jj})^2$ as suggested by Davidson and MacKinnon (1993), who report that this tends to produce better results when the model really is heteroskedastic. hc3 produces confidence intervals that tend to be even more conservative.

See Davidson and MacKinnon (1993, 554–556) for more discussion on these two bias corrections. The names hc2 and hc3 are based on their notation, page 554; robust without hc2 or hc3 corresponds to HC1 in their notation.

hc2 and hc3 imply robust; typing robust hc2 (or robust hc3) is equivalent to typing hc2 (or hc3) by itself.

noheader suppresses the display of the ANOVA table and summary statistics at the top of the output; only the coefficient table is displayed. This option is often used in programs and ado-files.

eform(*string*) is used only in programs and ado-files that employ regress to estimate models other than linear regression. eform() specifies the coefficient table is to be displayed in "exponentiated form" as defined in [R] **maximize** and that *string* is to be used to label the exponentiated coefficients in the table.

depname(*varname*) is used only in programs and ado-files that employ regress to estimate models other than linear regression. depname() may be specified only at estimation time. *varname* is recorded as the identity of the dependent variable even though the estimates are calculated using *depvar*. This affects the labeling of the output—not the results calculated—but could affect subsequent calculations made by predict, where the residual would be calculated as deviations from *varname* rather than *depvar*. `depname()` is most typically used when *depvar* is a temporary variable (see [P] **macro**) used as a proxy for *varname*.

`mse1` is used only in programs and ado-files that employ `regress` to estimate models other than linear regression. `mse1` sets the mean square error to 1, forcing the variance–covariance matrix of the estimators to be $(\mathbf{X'DX})^{-1}$ (see *Methods and Formulas* below) and affecting calculated standard errors. Degrees of freedom for $t$ statistics are calculated as $n$ rather than $n - k$.

`plus` specifies that a '+' sign be inserted in the last line of dashes of the regression output. You may want to specify this if you are creating a `smcl` log.

## Options for predict

`xb`, the default, calculates the linear prediction.

`pr(a,b)` calculates $\Pr(a < \mathbf{x}_j\mathbf{b} + u_j < b)$, the probability that $y_j|\mathbf{x}_j$ would be observed in the interval $(a, b)$.

> $a$ and $b$ may be specified as numbers or variable names; *lb* and *ub* are variable names;
> `pr(20,30)` calculates $\Pr(20 < \mathbf{x}_j\mathbf{b} + u_j < 30)$;
> `pr(lb,ub)` calculates $\Pr(lb < \mathbf{x}_j\mathbf{b} + u_j < ub)$;
> and `pr(20,ub)` calculates $\Pr(20 < \mathbf{x}_j\mathbf{b} + u_j < ub)$.
>
> $a = .$ means $-\infty$; `pr(.,30)` calculates $\Pr(\mathbf{x}_j\mathbf{b} + u_j < 30)$;
> `pr(lb,30)` calculates $\Pr(\mathbf{x}_j\mathbf{b} + u_j < 30)$ in observations for which $lb = .$
> (and calculates $\Pr(lb < \mathbf{x}_j\mathbf{b} + u_j < 30)$ elsewhere).
>
> $b = .$ means $+\infty$; `pr(20,.)` calculates $\Pr(\mathbf{x}_j\mathbf{b} + u_j > 20)$;
> `pr(20,ub)` calculates $\Pr(\mathbf{x}_j\mathbf{b} + u_j > 20)$ in observations for which $ub = .$
> (and calculates $\Pr(20 < \mathbf{x}_j\mathbf{b} + u_j < ub)$ elsewhere).

`e(a,b)` calculates $E(\mathbf{x}_j\mathbf{b} + u_j \mid a < \mathbf{x}_j\mathbf{b} + u_j < b)$, the expected value of $y_j|\mathbf{x}_j$ conditional on $y_j|\mathbf{x}_j$ being in the interval $(a, b)$, which is to say, $y_j|\mathbf{x}_j$ is censored.
$a$ and $b$ are specified as they are for `pr()`.

`ystar(a,b)` calculates $E(y_j^*)$ where $y_j^* = a$ if $\mathbf{x}_j\mathbf{b} + u_j \le a$, $y_j^* = b$ if $\mathbf{x}_j\mathbf{b} + u_j \ge b$, and $y_j^* = \mathbf{x}_j\mathbf{b} + u_j$ otherwise, which is to say, $y_j^*$ is truncated. $a$ and $b$ are specified as they are for `pr()`.

`cooksd` calculates the Cook's $D$ influence statistic (Cook 1977).

`leverage` or `hat` calculates the diagonal elements of the projection hat matrix.

`residuals` calculates the residuals.

`rstandard` calculates the standardized residuals.

`rstudent` calculates the studentized (jackknifed) residuals.

`stdp` calculates the standard error of the prediction. It can be thought of as the standard error of the predicted expected value or mean for the observation's covariate pattern. This is also referred to as the standard error of the fitted value.

`stdf` calculates the standard error of the forecast. This is the standard error of the point prediction for a single observation. It is commonly referred to as the standard error of the future or forecast value. By construction, the standard errors produced by `stdf` are always larger than those by `stdp`; see *Methods and Formulas*.

`stdr` calculates the standard error of the residuals.

covratio calculates COVRATIO (Belsley, Kuh, and Welsch 1980), a measure of the influence of the $j$th observation based on considering the effect on the variance–covariance matrix of the estimates. The calculation is automatically restricted to the estimation subsample.

dfbeta(*varname*) calculates the DFBETA for *varname*, the difference between the regression coefficient when the $j$th observation is included and excluded, said difference being scaled by the estimated standard error of the coefficient. *varname* must have been included among the regressors in the previously estimated model. The calculation is automatically restricted to the estimation subsample.

dfits calculates DFITS (Welsch and Kuh 1977) and attempts to summarize the information in the leverage versus residual-squared plot into a single statistic. The calculation is automatically restricted to the estimation subsample.

welsch calculates Welsch distance (Welsch 1982) and is a variation on dfits. The calculation is automatically restricted to the estimation subsample.

# Remarks

Remarks are presented under the headings

> *Ordinary least squares*
> *Treatment of the constant*
> *Robust standard errors*
> *Weighted regression*
> *Instrumental variables and two-stage least squares regression*
> *Prediction standard errors*
> *Influence statistics*
> *Prediction with weighted data*

For a discussion and examples of influence statistics and diagnostic statistics from predict— including leverage, residuals, standardized residuals, studentized residuals, DFITS, Cook's $D$, Welsch distance, and COVRATIO; see [R] **regression diagnostics**. The use of other predict options is covered in predict.

regress performs linear regression, including ordinary least squares and weighted least squares. For a general discussion of linear regression, see Draper and Smith (1998), Johnston and DiNardo (1997), or Kmenta (1997).

See Wooldridge (2000) for an excellent treatment of estimation, inference, interpretation, and specification testing in linear regression models. This presentation stands out due to its clarification of the statistical issues, as opposed to the algebraic issues.

See Hamilton (1992) for an integration of graphical and regression methods for performing data analysis illustrated throughout with Stata output. Chatterjee, Hadi, and Price (2000) explain regression analysis using examples containing typical problems that one encounters when performing exploratory data analysis. We also recommend Weisberg (1985), who emphasizes the importance of the assumptions of linear regression and problems resulting from these assumptions; Rawlings (1988), who presents a broad development from regression to analysis of variance; and Ramsey and Schafer (1996), who give a friendly introduction with a wide range of real scientific examples. For a discussion of model selection techniques and exploratory data analysis, see Mosteller and Tukey (1977). Finally, if you are interested in the history of regression, see Plackett (1972). Least squares, which dates back to the 1790s, was discovered independently by Legendre and Gauss.

# Ordinary least squares

▷ Example

Suppose we have data on the mileage rating and weight of 74 automobiles. The variables in our data are mpg, weight, and foreign. The last variable assumes the value 1 for foreign and 0 for domestic automobiles. We wish to estimate the model

$$\text{mpg} = \beta_0 + \beta_1\text{weight} + \beta_2\text{weight}^2 + \beta_3\text{foreign} + \epsilon$$

We do this by creating a new variable called weightsq and then typing regress mpg weight weightsq foreign:

```
. generate weightsq=weight^2
. regress mpg weight weightsq foreign
```

| Source | SS | df | MS | |
|---|---|---|---|---|
| Model | 1689.15372 | 3 | 563.05124 | |
| Residual | 754.30574 | 70 | 10.7757963 | |
| Total | 2443.45946 | 73 | 33.4720474 | |

```
Number of obs =      74
F(  3,    70) =   52.25
Prob > F      =  0.0000
R-squared     =  0.6913
Adj R-squared =  0.6781
Root MSE      =  3.2827
```

| mpg | Coef. | Std. Err. | t | P>\|t\| | [95% Conf. Interval] | |
|---|---|---|---|---|---|---|
| weight | -.0165729 | .0039692 | -4.18 | 0.000 | -.0244892 | -.0086567 |
| weightsq | 1.59e-06 | 6.25e-07 | 2.55 | 0.013 | 3.45e-07 | 2.84e-06 |
| foreign | -2.2035 | 1.059246 | -2.08 | 0.041 | -4.3161 | -.0909002 |
| _cons | 56.53884 | 6.197383 | 9.12 | 0.000 | 44.17855 | 68.89913 |

◁

❑ Technical Note

regress produces a variety of summary statistics along with the table of regression coefficients. If it is not obvious to you how to read the output—and there is no reason it ought to be—then you should read this technical note.

At the upper left, regress reports an analysis-of-variance (ANOVA) table. The column headings SS, df, and MS stand for 'Sum of Squares', 'degrees of freedom', and 'Mean Square', respectively. In the previous example, the total sum of squares is 2,443.5: 1,689.2 accounted for by the model and 754.3 left unexplained. Since the regression included a constant, the total sum reflects the sum after removal of means, as does the sum of squares due to the model.

The table also reveals that there are 73 total degrees of freedom (counted as 74 observations less 1 for the mean removal), of which 3 are consumed by the model, leaving 70 for the residual.

The mean square error is defined as the residual sum of squares divided by the corresponding degrees of freedom.

To the right of the ANOVA table are presented other summary statistics. The $F$ statistic associated with the ANOVA table is 52.25. The statistic has 3 numerator and 70 denominator degrees of freedom. The $F$ statistic tests the hypothesis that all coefficients *excluding the constant* are zero. The chance of observing an $F$ statistic that large or larger is reported as 0.0000, which is Stata's way of indicating a number smaller than 0.00005. The $R$-squared ($R^2$) for the regression is 0.6913, and the $R$-squared adjusted for degrees of freedom ($R_a^2$) is 0.6781. The root mean square error, labeled Root MSE, is 3.2827. Note that the root mean square error is the square root of the mean square error reported for the residual in the ANOVA table.

Finally, Stata produces a table of the estimated coefficients. The first line of the table indicates that the left-hand-side variable is `mpg`. Thereafter follow the four estimated coefficients. Our estimated model is

$$56.54 - 0.0166\,\texttt{weight} + 1.59 \cdot 10^{-6}\,\texttt{weightsq} - 2.20\,\texttt{foreign}$$

Reported to the right of the coefficients in the output are the standard errors. For instance, the standard error for the coefficient on `weight` is 0.0039692. The corresponding $t$ statistic is $-4.175$, which has a two-sided significance level of 0.000. This number indicates that the significance is less than 0.0005. The 95% confidence interval for the coefficient is $[-.024, -.009]$.

❑

## ▷ Example

`regress` shares the features of all estimation commands. Among other things, this means that after running a regression, you can use `test` to test hypotheses about the coefficients, `vce` to examine the covariance matrix of the estimators, and `predict` to obtain predicted values, residuals, and influence statistics. See [U] **23 Estimation and post-estimation commands**.

It also means that no matter how many commands have intervened between now and the last regression, typing `regress` without arguments redisplays the previous results. When replaying results, you may specify options that affect the way they are displayed.

Let's imagine that we meant to specify the `beta` option to obtain beta coefficients (regression coefficients normalized by the ratio of the standard deviation of the regressor to the standard deviation of the dependent variable). Even though we forgot, we can specify the option now:

```
. regress, beta
```

| Source | SS | df | MS | | | |
|---|---|---|---|---|---|---|
| Model | 1689.15372 | 3 | 563.05124 | | | |
| Residual | 754.30574 | 70 | 10.7757963 | | | |
| Total | 2443.45946 | 73 | 33.4720474 | | | |

| | Number of obs = | 74 |
|---|---|---|
| | F( 3, 70) = | 52.25 |
| | Prob > F = | 0.0000 |
| | R-squared = | 0.6913 |
| | Adj R-squared = | 0.6781 |
| | Root MSE = | 3.2827 |

| mpg | Coef. | Std. Err. | t | P>\|t\| | Beta |
|---|---|---|---|---|---|
| weight | -.0165729 | .0039692 | -4.18 | 0.000 | -2.226321 |
| weightsq | 1.59e-06 | 6.25e-07 | 2.55 | 0.013 | 1.32654 |
| foreign | -2.2035 | 1.059246 | -2.08 | 0.041 | -.17527 |
| _cons | 56.53884 | 6.197383 | 9.12 | 0.000 | . |

◁

## Treatment of the constant

`regress` allows you to treat a regression's constant or intercept in a variety of ways. `regress` ordinarily includes a constant. The `noconstant` option allows you to suppress it.

## ▷ Example

We wish to estimate a regression of the `weight` of an automobile against its `length`, and we wish to impose the constraint that the weight is zero when the length is zero.

If we simply regress weight length, we are estimating the equation

$$\text{weight} = \beta_0 + \beta_1 \text{length} + \epsilon$$

In this case, a length of zero corresponds to a weight of $\beta_0$. We want to force $\beta_0$ to be zero or estimate an equation that does not include an intercept:

$$\text{weight} = \beta_1 \text{length} + \epsilon$$

We do this by specifying the noconstant option:

```
. regress weight length, noconstant
```

| Source | SS | df | MS | | |
|---|---|---|---|---|---|
| Model | 703869302 | 1 | 703869302 | Number of obs = | 74 |
| Residual | 14892897.8 | 73 | 204012.299 | F( 1, 73) = | 3450.13 |
| | | | | Prob > F = | 0.0000 |
| | | | | R-squared = | 0.9793 |
| | | | | Adj R-squared = | 0.9790 |
| Total | 718762200 | 74 | 9713002.70 | Root MSE = | 451.68 |

| weight | Coef. | Std. Err. | t | P>|t| | [95% Conf. Interval] | |
|---|---|---|---|---|---|---|
| length | 16.29829 | .2774752 | 58.74 | 0.000 | 15.74528 | 16.8513 |

In our data, length is measured in inches and weight in pounds. We discover that each inch of length adds 16 pounds to the weight.

◁

## ❑ Technical Note

You may wish to run a regression in which you specify the constant term yourself—you do not want Stata to add one automatically. Most commonly, this occurs when you wish to include a set of mutually exclusive indicator variables. hascons is a variation of the noconstant option—it tells Stata not to add a constant to the regression because we have already done so, either directly or indirectly. (Please see the warning about using hascons in *Options* above.)

For instance, let's now re-estimate our model of weight as a function of length and include separate constants for foreign and domestic cars. Our dataset already has an indicator variable called foreign marking foreign-made automobiles, so we create a corresponding domestic variable and estimate the regression:

```
. generate domestic=~foreign
. regress weight length domestic foreign, hascons
```

| Source | SS | df | MS | | |
|---|---|---|---|---|---|
| Model | 39647744.7 | 2 | 19823872.3 | Number of obs = | 74 |
| Residual | 4446433.70 | 71 | 62625.8268 | F( 2, 71) = | 316.54 |
| | | | | Prob > F = | 0.0000 |
| | | | | R-squared = | 0.8992 |
| | | | | Adj R-squared = | 0.8963 |
| Total | 44094178.4 | 73 | 604029.841 | Root MSE = | 250.25 |

| weight | Coef. | Std. Err. | t | P>|t| | [95% Conf. Interval] | |
|---|---|---|---|---|---|---|
| length | 31.44455 | 1.601234 | 19.64 | 0.000 | 28.25178 | 34.63732 |
| domestic | -2850.25 | 315.9691 | -9.02 | 0.000 | -3480.274 | -2220.225 |
| foreign | -2983.927 | 275.1041 | -10.85 | 0.000 | -3532.469 | -2435.385 |

❑

## ❏ Technical Note

You are probably wondering how the `hascons` and the `noconstant` options differ. After all, in both cases `regress` suppressed the constant term. There is a subtle distinction. We can most easily reveal it by re-estimating the last regression, specifying `noconstant` rather than `hascons`:

```
. regress weight length domestic foreign, noconstant
```

| Source | SS | df | MS |
|---|---|---|---|
| Model | 714315766 | 3 | 238105255 |
| Residual | 4446433.70 | 71 | 62625.8268 |
| Total | 718762200 | 74 | 9713002.70 |

```
Number of obs =      74
F(  3,     71) = 3802.03
Prob > F      =  0.0000
R-squared     =  0.9938
Adj R-squared =  0.9936
Root MSE      =  250.25
```

| weight | Coef. | Std. Err. | t | P>\|t\| | [95% Conf. Interval] | |
|---|---|---|---|---|---|---|
| length | 31.44455 | 1.601234 | 19.64 | 0.000 | 28.25178 | 34.63732 |
| domestic | -2850.25 | 315.9691 | -9.02 | 0.000 | -3480.274 | -2220.225 |
| foreign | -2983.927 | 275.1041 | -10.85 | 0.000 | -3532.469 | -2435.385 |

If you compare this output with that produced by the previous `regress` command, you will find that they are almost, but not quite, identical. The parameter estimates and their associated statistics—the second half of the output—are identical. The overall summary statistics and the ANOVA table—the first half of the output—are different.

In the first case, the $R^2$ is shown as 0.8992; in this case, it is shown as 0.9938. In the first case, the $F$ statistic is 316.54; now it is 3802.03. If you look more closely, you will notice that the numerator degrees of freedom are different as well. In the first case, the numerator degrees of freedom are 2; now they are 3. Which is correct?

Both are. When you specify the `hascons` option, the ANOVA table and its associated statistics are adjusted for the explanatory power of the constant. The regression in effect has a constant; it is just written in such a way that a separate constant is unnecessary. When you specify the `noconstant` option, no such adjustment is made.

❏

## ❏ Technical Note

Since `regress` adjusts the ANOVA table for the effectively included constant when you specify the `hascons` option, you may wonder what happens when you make a mistake. What happens when you specify a model that does not, in effect, have a constant and include the `hascons` option?

`regress` watches for that case and, if it occurs, adds a constant to your regression automatically. Let's estimate a model of `weight` on `length` and specify the `hascons` option to see what happens:

```
. regress weight length, hascons
(note: hascons false)
```

| Source | SS | df | MS |
|---|---|---|---|
| Model | 39461306.8 | 1 | 39461306.8 |
| Residual | 4632871.55 | 72 | 64345.4382 |
| Total | 44094178.4 | 73 | 604029.841 |

```
Number of obs =      74
F(  1,     72) = 613.27
Prob > F      =  0.0000
R-squared     =  0.8949
Adj R-squared =  0.8935
Root MSE      =  253.66
```

| weight | Coef. | Std. Err. | t | P>|t| | [95% Conf. Interval] | |
|---|---|---|---|---|---|---|
| length | 33.01988 | 1.333364 | 24.76 | 0.000 | 30.36187 | 35.67789 |
| _cons | -3186.047 | 252.3113 | -12.63 | 0.000 | -3689.02 | -2683.073 |

Even though we specified hascons, regress included a constant anyway. It also added a note to our output: "Note: hascons false". When you specify hascons you are telling Stata that you think you have included a constant or a set of variables that effectively add up to a constant. Stata verifies that what you think is indeed correct.

❏

## ❏ Technical Note

Even if you are specifying what amounts to a constant, you do not have to specify the hascons option. regress is always on the lookout for collinear variables and drops them as necessary. For instance:

```
. regress weight length domestic foreign
```

| Source | SS | df | MS | | Number of obs = | 74 |
|---|---|---|---|---|---|---|
| | | | | | F( 2, 71) = | 316.54 |
| Model | 39647744.7 | 2 | 19823872.3 | | Prob > F = | 0.0000 |
| Residual | 4446433.70 | 71 | 62625.8268 | | R-squared = | 0.8992 |
| | | | | | Adj R-squared = | 0.8963 |
| Total | 44094178.4 | 73 | 604029.841 | | Root MSE = | 250.25 |

| weight | Coef. | Std. Err. | t | P>|t| | [95% Conf. Interval] | |
|---|---|---|---|---|---|---|
| length | 31.44455 | 1.601234 | 19.64 | 0.000 | 28.25178 | 34.63732 |
| domestic | (dropped) | | | | | |
| foreign | -133.6775 | 77.47615 | -1.73 | 0.089 | -288.1605 | 20.80555 |
| _cons | -2850.25 | 315.9691 | -9.02 | 0.000 | -3480.274 | -2220.225 |

❏

## Robust standard errors

regress with the robust option substitutes a robust variance matrix calculation for the conventional calculation and, if you also specify cluster(), allows relaxing the assumption of independence within groups. How this works is explained in [U] **23.11 Obtaining robust variance estimates**. Below we show you how well this works.

## ▷ Example

Specifying the robust option (without cluster()) is equivalent to requesting White-corrected standard errors in the presence of heteroskedasticity. Let us use the automobile data and, in the process of looking at the energy efficiency of cars, analyze a variable with considerable heteroskedasticity.

We will examine the amount of energy—measured in gallons of petrol—that the cars in the data need to move 1,000 pounds of their weight 100 miles. We are going to examine the relative efficiency of foreign and domestic cars.

```
. gen gpmw = ((1/mpg)/weight)*100*1000
```

```
. summarize gpmw
```

| Variable | Obs | Mean | Std. Dev. | Min | Max |
|---|---|---|---|---|---|
| gpmw | 74 | 1.682184 | .2426311 | 1.09553 | 2.30521 |

In these data, the engines consume between 1.10 and 2.31 gallons of gas to move 1,000 pounds of the car's weight 100 miles. Were we to run a regression with conventional standard errors of gpmw on foreign, we would obtain

```
. regress gpmw foreign
```

| Source | SS | df | MS |
|---|---|---|---|
| Model | .936705572 | 1 | .936705572 |
| Residual | 3.36079459 | 72 | .046677703 |
| Total | 4.29750017 | 73 | .058869865 |

```
Number of obs =      74
F(  1,     72) =   20.07
Prob > F       =  0.0000
R-squared      =  0.2180
Adj R-squared  =  0.2071
Root MSE       =  .21605
```

| gpmw | Coef. | Std. Err. | t | P>\|t\| | [95% Conf. Interval] | |
|---|---|---|---|---|---|---|
| foreign | .2461526 | .0549487 | 4.48 | 0.000 | .1366143 | .3556909 |
| _cons | 1.609004 | .0299608 | 53.70 | 0.000 | 1.549278 | 1.66873 |

regress with the robust option, on the other hand, reports

```
. regress gpmw foreign, robust
```

```
Regression with robust standard errors
```

```
Number of obs =      74
F(  1,     72) =   13.13
Prob > F       =  0.0005
R-squared      =  0.2180
Root MSE       =  .21605
```

| gpmw | Coef. | Robust Std. Err. | t | P>\|t\| | [95% Conf. Interval] | |
|---|---|---|---|---|---|---|
| foreign | .2461526 | .0679238 | 3.62 | 0.001 | .1107489 | .3815563 |
| _cons | 1.609004 | .0234535 | 68.60 | 0.000 | 1.56225 | 1.655758 |

The point estimates are the same (foreign cars need one-quarter gallon more gas) but the standard errors differ by roughly 20 percent. Conventional regression reports the 95% confidence interval as $[.14, .36]$ whereas the robust standard errors make the interval $[.11, .38]$.

Which is right? gpmw, for your information, is a variable with considerable heteroskedasticity:

```
. tabulate foreign, summarize(gpmw)
```

| Car type | Summary of gpmw Mean | Std. Dev. | Freq. |
|---|---|---|---|
| Domestic | 1.6090039 | .16845182 | 52 |
| Foreign | 1.8551565 | .30186861 | 22 |
| Total | 1.6821844 | .24263113 | 74 |

In [U] **23.11 Obtaining robust variance estimates**, we show another example using linear regression where it makes little difference whether we specify robust. The linear-regression assumptions were true and we obtained nearly linear-regression results. The advantage of the robust estimate is that in neither case did we have to check assumptions.

◁

❏ Technical Note

When you specify `robust`, `regress` purposefully suppresses displaying the ANOVA table as it is no longer appropriate in a statistical sense even though, mechanically, the numbers would be unchanged. That is, sums of squares remain unchanged, but the meaning you might be tempted to give those sums is no longer relevant. The $F$ statistic, for instance, is no longer based on sums of squares; it becomes a Wald test based on the robustly estimated variance matrix. Nevertheless, `regress` continues to report the $R^2$ and the root MSE even though both numbers are based on sums of squares and are, strictly speaking, irrelevant. In this, the root MSE is more in violation of the spirit of the robust estimator than is $R^2$. As a goodness-of-fit statistic, $R^2$ is still fine; just do not use it in formulas to obtain $F$ statistics because those formulas no longer apply. The Root MSE is valid as long as you take its name literally—it is the square root of the mean square error. Root MSE is no longer a prediction of $\sigma$ because there is no single $\sigma$; the variance of the residual varies observation by observation.

❏

▷ Example

Options `hc2` and `hc3` modify the robust variance calculation. In the context of linear regression without clustering, the idea behind the robust calculation is to somehow measure $\sigma_j^2$, the variance of the residual associated with the $j$th observation, and then to use that estimate to improve the estimated variance of $\widehat{\beta}$. Since residuals have (theoretically and practically) mean 0, one estimate of $\sigma_j^2$ is the observation's squared residual itself—$u_j^2$. A finite-sample correction could improve that by multiplying $u_j^2$ by $n/(n-k)$ and, as a matter of fact, `robust` uses $\{n/(n-k)\}u_j^2$ as its estimate of the residual's variance.

The `hc2` and `hc3` alternatives focus on the finite-sample adjustment $n/(n-k)$. For instance, if the residuals are homoskedastic, it can be shown that the expected value of $u_j^2$ is $\sigma^2(1-h_{jj})$ where $h_{jj}$ is the diagonal element of the projection (hat) matrix. $h_{jj}$ has average value $k/n$, so $1-h_{jj}$ has average value $1-k/n=(n-k)/n$. Thus, the default robust estimator $\widehat{\sigma}_j=\{n/(n-k)\}u_j^2$ amounts to dividing $u_j^2$ by the average of the expectation.

`hc2` divides $u_j^2$ by $1-h_{jj}$ itself and so should yield better estimates if the residuals really are homoskedastic.

`hc3` divides $u_j^2$ by $(1-h_{jj})^2$ and has no such clean interpretation. Davidson and MacKinnon (1993) show that $u_j^2/(1-h_{jj})^2$ approximates a more complicated estimator that they obtain by jackknifing (MacKinnon and White 1985).

Here are the results of re-estimating our efficiency model using `hc2` and `hc3`:

```
. regress gpmw foreign, hc2
Regression with robust standard errors            Number of obs =      74
                                                  F(  1,   72) =   12.93
                                                  Prob > F      =  0.0006
                                                  R-squared     =  0.2180
                                                  Root MSE      =  .21605
```

| gpmw | Coef. | Robust HC2 Std. Err. | t | P>|t| | [95% Conf. Interval] | |
|---|---|---|---|---|---|---|
| foreign | .2461526 | .0684669 | 3.60 | 0.001 | .1096662 | .3826389 |
| _cons | 1.609004 | .0233601 | 68.88 | 0.000 | 1.562437 | 1.655571 |

```
. regress gpmw foreign, hc3
Regression with robust standard errors                Number of obs =      74
                                                      F( 1,     72) =   12.38
                                                      Prob > F      =  0.0008
                                                      R-squared     =  0.2180
                                                      Root MSE      =  .21605
```

| gpmw | Coef. | Robust HC3 Std. Err. | t | P>\|t\| | [95% Conf. Interval] | |
|---|---|---|---|---|---|---|
| foreign | .2461526 | .069969 | 3.52 | 0.001 | .1066719 | .3856332 |
| _cons | 1.609004 | .023588 | 68.21 | 0.000 | 1.561982 | 1.656026 |

◁

## ▷ Example

With `cluster()`, `robust` is able to relax the assumption of independence. Below we have 34,139 observations on 4,782 women aged 16 to 46. Data were collected on these women between 1970 and 1988. We are going to estimate a classic earnings model and we begin by ignoring the fact that each woman appears an average of 7.14 times in the data:

```
. regress ln_wage age age2 grade
```

| Source | SS | df | MS | | |
|---|---|---|---|---|---|
| Model | 1545.54213 | 3 | 515.180711 | | |
| Residual | 4971.00723 | 28504 | .17439683 | | |
| Total | 6516.54937 | 28507 | .228594709 | | |

```
                      Number of obs =   28508
                      F( 3, 28504) = 2954.07
                      Prob > F      =  0.0000
                      R-squared     =  0.2372
                      Adj R-squared =  0.2371
                      Root MSE      =  .41761
```

| ln_wage | Coef. | Std. Err. | t | P>\|t\| | [95% Conf. Interval] | |
|---|---|---|---|---|---|---|
| age | .0559055 | .00331 | 16.89 | 0.000 | .0494177 | .0623933 |
| age2 | -.00069 | .0000548 | -12.59 | 0.000 | -.0007975 | -.0005826 |
| grade | .0812137 | .0010887 | 74.60 | 0.000 | .0790799 | .0833476 |
| _cons | -.3535855 | .048165 | -7.34 | 0.000 | -.4479911 | -.2591799 |

We can be reasonably certain that the standard errors reported above are meaningless. Without a doubt, a woman with higher-than-average wages in one year typically has higher-than-average wages in other years. One way to deal with this would be to estimate a random-effects model—and we are going to do that—but first, let's estimate the model using `regress`, with the `robust` option, and specifying `cluster(id)`, meaning that only observations with differing person ids are truly independent:

```
. reg ln_wage age age2 grade, robust cluster(id)
Regression with robust standard errors                Number of obs =   28508
                                                      F( 3,  4707) =  932.70
                                                      Prob > F      =  0.0000
                                                      R-squared     =  0.2372
Number of clusters (idcode) = 4708                    Root MSE      =  .41761
```

| ln_wage | Coef. | Robust Std. Err. | t | P>\|t\| | [95% Conf. Interval] | |
|---|---|---|---|---|---|---|
| age | .0559055 | .004344 | 12.87 | 0.000 | .0473892 | .0644218 |
| age2 | -.00069 | .0000737 | -9.36 | 0.000 | -.0008345 | -.0005455 |
| grade | .0812137 | .0021609 | 37.58 | 0.000 | .0769774 | .08545 |
| _cons | -.3535855 | .0634761 | -5.57 | 0.000 | -.4780284 | -.2291426 |

For the purposes of comparison, we focus on the grade coefficient which, in economics jargon, can be interpreted as the rate of return to schooling. The 95% confidence interval we previously estimated—an interval we do not believe—is [.079, .083]. The robust interval is twice as wide, being [.077, .085].

As we said, one "correct" way to estimate this model is by random-effects regression. Here is the random-effects result:

```
. xtreg ln_wage age age2 grade, re
Random-effects GLS regression              Number of obs       =     28508
Group variable (i) : idcode                Number of groups    =      4708

R-sq:  within  = 0.1087                     Obs per group: min =         1
       between = 0.3240                                     avg =       6.1
       overall = 0.2360                                     max =        15

Random effects u_i ~ Gaussian               Wald chi2(3)       =   5159.11
corr(u_i, X)       = 0 (assumed)            Prob > chi2        =    0.0000

    ln_wage |     Coef.   Std. Err.      z     P>|z|     [95% Conf. Interval]
------------+----------------------------------------------------------------
        age |    .053857    .0026955    19.98   0.000     .0485739    .0591401
       age2 |  -.0006114    .0000447   -13.69   0.000    -.0006989   -.0005238
      grade |   .0796087    .0019842    40.12   0.000     .0757196    .0834978
      _cons |  -.3701401    .0451443    -8.20   0.000    -.4586214   -.2816589
------------+----------------------------------------------------------------
    sigma_u |  .30512356
    sigma_e |  .30246103
        rho |  .50438207   (fraction of variance due to u_i)
```

Robust regression estimated the 95% interval [.077, .085] and xtreg estimates a similar [.076, .083]. Which is better? The random-effects regression estimator assumes a lot. If we check some of those assumptions by performing a Hausman test, we obtain

```
. xthausman
Hausman specification test
                    ——— Coefficients ———
                      Fixed      Random
    ln_wage |        Effects     Effects       Difference
------------+----------------------------------------------
        age |       .0539076     .053857        .0000506
       age2 |      -.0005973    -.0006114        .000014
      grade |       .0363027     .0796087       -.043306

    Test:  Ho:  difference in coefficients not systematic
                chi2(  3) = (b-B)´[S^(-1)](b-B), S = (S_fe - S_re)
                          =     62.31
                Prob>chi2 =    0.0000
```

The Hausman test casts grave suspicions on the random-effects model we just estimated and so we should be very careful in interpreting those results.

Meanwhile, our robust regression results still stand as long as we are careful about the interpretation. The correct interpretation is that, were the data collection repeated (on women sampled the same way as in the original sample), and were we to re-estimate the model, 95% of the time we would expect the estimated coefficient on grade to be in the range [.077, .085].

Even with robust regression, you must be careful about going beyond that statement. In this case, the Hausman test is probably picking up something that differs within and between person and so would cast doubt on our robust regression model in terms of interpreting [.077, .085] to contain the rate of return to additional schooling, economy-wide, for all women, without exception.    ◁

## Weighted regression

regress can perform weighted as well as unweighted regression. You indicate the weight by specifying the [*weight*] qualifier. By default, regress assumes analytic weights; see the technical note below.

▷ Example

Suppose you have Census data recording the death rate (drate) and median age (medage) for each state. The data also record the region of the country in which each state is located and the overall population of the state:

```
. describe
Contains data from census.dta
  obs:            50                          1980 Census data by state
  vars:            5                          6 Jul 2000 17:06
  size:         1,550 (99.9% of memory free)

              storage  display     value
variable name   type   format      label       variable label

state          str14   %-14s                   State
drate          float   %9.0g                   Death Rate
pop            long    %12.0gc                 Population
medage         float   %9.2f                   Median age
region         byte    %-8.0g      cenreg      Census region

Sorted by:
     Note:  dataset has changed since last saved
```

We can use the xi command to automatically create and include dummy variables for region. Since the variables in the regression reflect means rather than individual observations, the appropriate method of estimation is analytically weighted least squares (Johnston and DiNardo 1997), where the weight is total population:

```
. xi: regress drate medage I.region [w=pop]
I.region           _Iregion_1-4         (naturally coded; _Iregion_1 omitted)
(sum of wgt is    2.2591e+08)
```

| Source | SS | df | MS | | |
|---|---|---|---|---|---|
| Model | 4096.6093 | 4 | 1024.15232 | | |
| Residual | 1238.40987 | 45 | 27.5202192 | | |
| | | | | | |
| Total | 5335.01916 | 49 | 108.877942 | | |

Number of obs = 50
F( 4, 45) = 37.21
Prob > F = 0.0000
R-squared = 0.7679
Adj R-squared = 0.7472
Root MSE = 5.246

| drate | Coef. | Std. Err. | t | P>\|t\| | [95% Conf. Interval] |
|---|---|---|---|---|---|
| medage | 4.283183 | .5393329 | 7.94 | 0.000 | 3.196911   5.369455 |
| _Iregion_2 | .3138738 | 2.456431 | 0.13 | 0.899 | -4.633632   5.26138 |
| _Iregion_3 | -1.438452 | 2.320244 | -0.62 | 0.538 | -6.111663   3.234758 |
| _Iregion_4 | -10.90629 | 2.681349 | -4.07 | 0.000 | -16.30681   -5.505777 |
| _cons | -39.14727 | 17.23613 | -2.27 | 0.028 | -73.86262   -4.431915 |

To weight the regression by population, we added the qualifier [w=pop] to the end of the regress command. Our qualifier was vague (we did not say [aweight=pop]), but unless told otherwise, Stata assumes analytic weights in the case of regress. Stata informed us that the sum of the weight is $2.2591 \cdot 10^8$; there were approximately 226 million people residing in the U.S. according to our 1980 data.

xi provides one way to include dummy variables and can be used with any estimation command. In the special case of linear regression, another alternative would be to use anova with the regress option. This would probably be better, but only because anova has special logic to estimate models with many dummy variables, which uses less memory and computer time.

◁

❑ **Technical Note**

Once you estimate a weighted regression, you may obtain the appropriately weighted variance–covariance matrix of the estimators using vce and perform appropriately weighted hypothesis tests using test.

In the weighted regression in the previous example, we see that _Iregion_4 is statistically significant but that _Iregion_2 and _Iregion_3 are not. We use test to test the joint significance of the region variables:

```
. test _Iregion_2 _Iregion_3 _Iregion_4
 ( 1)   _Iregion_2 = 0.0
 ( 2)   _Iregion_3 = 0.0
 ( 3)   _Iregion_4 = 0.0
       F(  3,    45) =     9.84
            Prob > F =    0.0000
```

The results indicate that the region variables are jointly significant.

❑

❑ **Technical Note**

You may also specify fweight frequency weights with regress. Frequency weights are appropriate when the data do not reflect cell means but instead represent replicated observations. Whether you specify aweights or fweights will not change the parameter estimates, but will change the corresponding significance levels.

For instance, if we specified [fweight=pop] in the weighted regression example above—which would be statistically incorrect—Stata would treat the data as if the data represented 226 million independent observations on death rates and median age. The data most certainly do not represent such—they represent 50 observations on state averages.

With aweights, Stata treats the number of observations on the process as the number of observations in the data. When you specify fweights, Stata treats the number of observations as if it were equal to the sum of the weights; see *Methods and Formulas* below.

❑

❑ **Technical Note**

A popular request on the help line is to describe the effect of specifying [aweight=*exp*] with regress in terms of transformation of the dependent and independent variables. The mechanical answer is that typing

```
. regress y x1 x2 [aweight=n]
```

is equivalent to estimating the model:

$$y_j\sqrt{n_j} = \beta_0\sqrt{n_j} + \beta_1 x_{1j}\sqrt{n_j} + \beta_2 x_{2j}\sqrt{n_j} + u_j\sqrt{n_j}$$

This regression will reproduce the coefficients and covariance matrix produced by the `aweighted` regression. The mean square errors (estimate of the variance of the residuals) will, however, be different. The transformed regression reports $s_t^2$, an estimate of $\mathrm{Var}(u_j\sqrt{n_j})$. The `aweighted` regression reports $s_a^2$, an estimate of $\mathrm{Var}(u_j\sqrt{n_j}\sqrt{N/\sum_k n_k})$, where $N$ is the number of observations. Thus,

$$s_a^2 = \frac{N}{\sum_k n_k}s_t^2 = \frac{s_t^2}{\bar{n}} \tag{1}$$

The logic for this adjustment is as follows: Consider the model

$$y = \beta_0 + \beta_1 x_1 + \beta_2 x_2 + u$$

Assume that, were this model estimated on individuals, $\mathrm{Var}(u) = \sigma_u^2$, a constant. Assume that individual data are not available; what is available are averages $(\bar{y}_j, \bar{x}_{1j}, \bar{x}_{2j})$ for $j = 1, \ldots, N$, and each average is calculated over $n_j$ observations. Then it is still true that

$$\bar{y}_j = \beta_0 + \beta_1 \bar{x}_{1j} + \beta_2 \bar{x}_{2j} + \bar{u}_j$$

where $\bar{u}_j$ is the average of $n_j$ mean 0 variance $\sigma_u^2$ deviates and so itself has variance $\sigma_{\bar{u}}^2 = \sigma_u^2/n_j$. Thus, multiplying through by $\sqrt{n_j}$ produces

$$\bar{y}_j\sqrt{n_j} = \beta_0\sqrt{n_j} + \beta_1\bar{x}_{1j}\sqrt{n_j} + \beta_2\bar{x}_{2j}\sqrt{n_j} + \bar{u}_j\sqrt{n_j}$$

and $\mathrm{Var}(\bar{u}_j\sqrt{n_j}) = \sigma_u^2$. The mean square error $s_t^2$ reported by estimating this transformed regression is an estimate of $\sigma_u^2$. Alternatively, the coefficients and covariance matrix could be obtained by `aweighted regress`. The only difference would be in the reported mean square error, which from equation (1), is $\sigma_u^2/\bar{n}$. On average, each observation in the data reflects the averages calculated over $\bar{n} = \sum_k n_k/N$ individuals, and thus this reported mean square error is the average variance of an observation in the dataset. One can retrieve the estimate of $\sigma_u^2$ by multiplying the reported mean square error by $\bar{n}$.

More generally, `aweight`s are used to solve general heteroskedasticity problems. In these cases, one has the model

$$y_j = \beta_0 + \beta_1 x_{1j} + \beta_2 x_{2j} + u_j$$

and the variance of $u_j$ is thought to be proportional to $a_j$. If the variance is proportional to $a_j$, it is also proportional to $\alpha a_j$, where $\alpha$ is any positive constant. Not quite arbitrarily, but with no loss of generality, let us choose $\alpha = \sum_k(1/a_k)/N$, the average value of the inverse of $a_j$. We can then write $\mathrm{Var}(u_j) = k\alpha a_j\sigma^2$, where $k$ is the constant of proportionality that is no longer a function of the scale of the weights.

Dividing this regression through by the $\sqrt{a_j}$,

$$y_j/\sqrt{a_j} = \beta_0/\sqrt{a_j} + \beta_1 x_{1j}/\sqrt{a_j} + \beta_2 x_{2j}/\sqrt{a_j} + u_j/\sqrt{a_j}$$

produces a model with $\mathrm{Var}(u_j/\sqrt{a_j}) = k\alpha\sigma^2$, which is the constant part of $\mathrm{Var}(u_j)$. Notice in particular that this variance is a function of $\alpha$, the average of the reciprocal weights; if the weights are scaled arbitrarily, then so is this variance.

We can also estimate this model by typing

```
. regress y x1 x2 [aweight=1/a]
```

This will produce the same estimates of the coefficients and covariance matrix; the reported mean square error is, from equation (1), $\{N/\sum_k(1/a_k)\}k\alpha\sigma^2 = k\sigma^2$. Note that this variance is independent of the scale of $a_j$.

❏

## Instrumental variables and two-stage least squares regression

An alternate syntax for **regress** can be used to produce instrumental variable (two-stage least squares) estimates.

$$\left[\text{by } varlist:\right] \underline{\text{regr}}\text{ess } depvar \left[varlist_1 \left[(varlist_2)\right]\right] \left[weight\right] \left[\text{if } exp\right] \left[\text{in } range\right]$$

$$\left[, \text{ } regress \text{ } options \text{ }\right]$$

This syntax is mainly used by programmers developing estimators using the instrumental variables estimates as intermediate results. **ivreg** is normally used to directly estimate these models; see [R] **ivreg**.

With this syntax, **regress** estimates a structural equation of *depvar* on *varlist*$_1$ using instrumental variables regression; (*varlist*$_2$) indicates the list of instrumental variables. With the exception of **hc2** and **hc3**, all standard **regress** options are allowed.

## Prediction standard errors

▷ Example

Using the example from [R] **predict**, you have data on automobiles, including the mileage rating (**mpg**), the car's weight (**weight**), and whether the car is foreign (**foreign**). You wish to estimate the following model:

$$\text{mpg} = \beta_1\text{weight} + \beta_2\text{weight}^2 + \beta_3\text{foreign} + \beta_4$$

We first create the **weight**$^2$ variable and then type the **regress** command:

```
. use auto
(1978 Automobile Data)
. generate weight2 = weight^2
. regress mpg weight weight2 foreign
```

| Source | SS | df | MS | | |
|---|---|---|---|---|---|
| Model | 1689.15372 | 3 | 563.05124 | Number of obs = | 74 |
| Residual | 754.30574 | 70 | 10.7757963 | F( 3, 70) = | 52.25 |
| | | | | Prob > F = | 0.0000 |
| | | | | R-squared = | 0.6913 |
| | | | | Adj R-squared = | 0.6781 |
| Total | 2443.45946 | 73 | 33.4720474 | Root MSE = | 3.2827 |

| mpg | Coef. | Std. Err. | t | P>\|t\| | [95% Conf. Interval] | |
|---|---|---|---|---|---|---|
| weight | -.0165729 | .0039692 | -4.18 | 0.000 | -.0244892 | -.0086567 |
| weight2 | 1.59e-06 | 6.25e-07 | 2.55 | 0.013 | 3.45e-07 | 2.84e-06 |
| foreign | -2.2035 | 1.059246 | -2.08 | 0.041 | -4.3161 | -.0909002 |
| _cons | 56.53884 | 6.197383 | 9.12 | 0.000 | 44.17855 | 68.89913 |

That done, we can now obtain the predicted values from the regression. We will store them in a new variable called **pmpg** by typing **predict pmpg**. Since **predict** produces no output, we will follow that by summarizing our predicted and observed values.

```
. predict pmpg
(option xb assumed; fitted values)
```

```
. summarize pmpg mpg
    Variable │      Obs        Mean    Std. Dev.         Min         Max
─────────────┼───────────────────────────────────────────────────────────
        pmpg │       74     21.2973    4.810311    13.59953    31.86288
         mpg │       74     21.2973    5.785503          12          41
```

◁

## ▷ Example

As shown using this same example in [R] **predict**, we can just as easily obtain predicted values from the model using a wholly different dataset from the one on which the model was estimated. The only requirement is that the data have the necessary variables, which in this case are `weight`, `weight2`, and `foreign`.

Using the data on two new cars (the Pontiac Sunbird and the Volvo 260) from the `newautos.dta` dataset, we can obtain out-of-sample predictions (or forecasts) by typing

```
. generate weight2=weight^2
. predict mpg
(option xb assumed; fitted values)
. list
                  make    weight    foreign    weight2        mpg
1. Pont. Sunbird           2690    Domestic    7236100    23.47137
2.        Volvo 260        3170    Foreign     1.00e+07    17.78846
```

The Pontiac Sunbird has a predicted mileage rating of 23.5 mpg whereas the Volvo 260 has a predicted rating of 17.8 mpg. By way of comparison, the actual mileage ratings are 24 for the Pontiac and 17 for the Volvo.

◁

`predict` can calculate the standard error of the forecast (`stdf` option), the standard error of the prediction (`stdp` option), and the standard error of the residual (`stdr` option). It is easy to confuse `stdf` and `stdp` because both are often called the prediction error. Consider the prediction $\widehat{y} = \mathbf{x}_j\mathbf{b}$, where $\mathbf{b}$ is the estimated coefficient (column) vector and $\mathbf{x}$ is a (row) vector of independent variables for which we want the prediction. First, $\widehat{y}$ has a variance due to the variance of the estimated coefficient vector $\mathbf{b}$,

$$\mathrm{Var}(\widehat{y}_j) = \mathrm{Var}(\mathbf{x}_j\mathbf{b}) = s^2 h_j$$

where $h_j = \mathbf{x}_j(\mathbf{X}'\mathbf{X})^{-1}\mathbf{x}_j'$ and $s^2$ is the mean square error of the regression. Do not panic if you do not understand all of this algebra—just remember that $\mathrm{Var}(\widehat{y}_j) = s^2 h_j$, whatever are $s^2$ and $h_j$. `stdp` calculates this quantity. This is the error in our prediction due to our uncertainty about $\mathbf{b}$.

If we are about to hand this number out as our forecast, however, there is another error. According to our model, the true value of $y$ is given by

$$y = \mathbf{x}\mathbf{b} + \epsilon = \widehat{y} + \epsilon$$

and thus, the $\mathrm{Var}(y) = \mathrm{Var}(\widehat{y}) + \mathrm{Var}(\epsilon) = s^2 h + s^2$, which is the square of `stdf`. `stdf`, then, is the sum of the error in our prediction plus the residual error.

`stdr` has to do with an analysis-of-variance decomposition of $s^2$, the estimated variance of $y$. The standard error of the prediction is $s^2 h$ and therefore $s^2 h + s^2(1 - h) = s^2$ decomposes $s^2$ into the prediction and residual variances.

▷ Example

Returning to our model of mpg on weight, weight$^2$, and foreign, we previously predicted the mileage rating for the Pontiac Sunbird and Volvo 260 as 23.5 and 17.8 mpg respectively. We now want to put a standard error around our forecast. Remember, the data for these two cars were in newautos.dta:

```
. use newautos, clear
(New Automobile Models)

. gen weight2=weight*weight

. predict mpg
(option xb assumed; fitted values)

. predict se_mpg, stdf

. list

              make    weight   foreign    weight2        mpg      se_mpg
  1. Pont. Sunbird      2690   Domestic   7236100   23.47137    3.341823
  2.     Volvo 260      3170    Foreign   1.00e+07   17.78846    3.438714
```

Thus, an approximate 95% confidence interval for the mileage rating of the Volvo 260 is $17.8 \pm 2 \cdot 3.44 =$ $[10.92, 24.68]$.

◁

## Influence statistics

We will briefly introduce the Cook's $D$ and leverage (hat) statistics. A broader range of influence statistics are discussed in more detail in [R] **regression diagnostics**.

▷ Example

Continuing with our regression model of mpg on weight, weight$^2$, and foreign, we obtain and examine Cook's distance measure of influence:

```
. predict distance, cooksd

. summarize distance, detail

                          Cook's D

        Percentiles       Smallest
  1%      8.95e-06        8.95e-06
  5%       .0000226        .0000209
 10%       .0000806        .0000226      Obs                    74
 25%        .000337        .0000226      Sum of Wgt.            74

 50%       .0023156                      Mean             .0152965
                          Largest        Std. Dev.        .0354097
 75%       .0181588        .0821998
 90%        .038079        .0822987      Variance         .0012538
 95%       .0821998        .0846101      Skewness         4.944938
 99%       .2607084        .2607084      Kurtosis         32.77605
```

We discover that we have one highly influential observation. We can uncover its identity by listing it:

```
. list make mpg if distance>.2

          make       mpg
 71. VW Diesel        41
```

The VW Diesel is the only diesel car in our data.

◁

## ▷ Example

The diagonal elements of the projection matrix, obtained by the **hat** option, are a measure of distance in explanatory variable space.

```
. predict xdist, hat
. summarize xdist, detail
```

```
                              Leverage

            Percentiles     Smallest
    1%        .0251334       .0251334
    5%        .0255623       .0251334
   10%        .0259213       .0253883      Obs                   74
   25%        .0278442       .0255623      Sum of Wgt.           74

   50%         .04103                      Mean            .0540541
                             Largest       Std. Dev.       .0459218
   75%        .0631279       .1593606
   90%        .0854584       .1593606      Variance        .0021088
   95%        .1593606       .2326124      Skewness        3.440809
   99%        .3075759       .3075759      Kurtosis        16.95135
```

Some 5% of our sample has an **xdist** measure in excess of 0.15. Let's force them to reveal their identities:

```
. list foreign make weight mpg if xdist>.15
         foreign  make                  weight     mpg
 24. Domestic  Ford Fiesta              1,800       28
 26. Domestic  Linc. Continental        4,840       12
 27. Domestic  Linc. Mark V             4,720       12
 43. Domestic  Plym. Champ              1,800       34
```

In order to understand why these cars are on this list, you must remember that the explanatory variables in our model are **weight** and **foreign** and that **xdist** measures distance in this metric. The Ford Fiesta and the Plymouth Champ are the two lightest domestic cars in our data. The Lincolns are the two heaviest domestic cars.

◁

## Prediction with weighted data

**predict** can be used after frequency-weighted (**fweight**) estimation just as it is used after unweighted estimation. The technical note below concerns use of **predict** after analytically weighted (**aweight**) estimation.

## ❑ Technical Note

After analytically weighted estimation, **predict** is only willing to calculate the prediction (no options), residual (**residual** option), standard error of the prediction (**stdp** option), and the diagonal elements of the projection matrix (**hat** option). Moreover, the results produced by **hat** need to be adjusted, as will be described. For analytically weighted estimation, the standard error of the forecast and residuals, the standardized and studentized residuals, and Cook's $D$ are not statistically well-defined concepts.

To obtain the correct values of the diagonal elements of the hat matrix, you use `predict` with the `hat` option to make a first, partially adjusted calculation, and then follow that by completing the adjustment. Assume you estimated a linear regression model weighting the data with the variable `w` (`[aweight=w]`). Begin by creating a new variable `w0`:

```
. predict resid if e(sample), resid
. summarize w if resid~=. & e(sample)
. gen w0=w/r(mean)
```

Some caution is necessary at this step—the `summarize w` must be performed on the same sample as you used to estimate the model, which means you must include `if e(sample)` to restrict the prediction to the estimation sample. We created the residual and then included the modifier 'if resid~=.' so that if the dependent variable or any of the independent variables is missing, the corresponding observations will be excluded from the calculation of the average value of the original weight.

To correct `predict`'s `hat` calculation, you multiply the result by `w0`:

```
. predict myhat, hat
. replace myhat = w0 * myhat
```

❑

# Acknowledgments

The robust estimate of variance was first implemented in Stata by Mead Over, Dean Jolliffe, and Andrew Foster (1996).

# Saved Results

`regress` saves in `e()`:

Scalars

| | | | |
|---|---|---|---|
| e(N) | number of observations | e(F) | $F$ statistic |
| e(mss) | model sum of squares | e(rmse) | root mean square error |
| e(df_m) | model degrees of freedom | e(ll_r) | log likelihood |
| e(rss) | residual sum of squares | e(ll_r0) | log likelihood, constant-only model |
| e(df_r) | residual degrees of freedom | e(N_clust) | number of clusters |
| e(r2) | $R$-squared | | |

Macros

| | | | |
|---|---|---|---|
| e(cmd) | regress | e(wexp) | weight expression |
| e(depvar) | name of dependent variable | e(clustvar) | name of cluster variable |
| e(model) | ols or iv | e(vcetype) | covariance estimation method |
| e(wtype) | weight type | e(predict) | program used to implement predict |

Matrices

| | | | |
|---|---|---|---|
| e(b) | coefficient vector | e(V) | variance–covariance matrix of the estimators |

Functions

| | |
|---|---|
| e(sample) | marks estimation sample |

## Methods and Formulas

Variables printed in lowercase and not boldfaced (e.g., $x$) are scalars. Variables printed in lowercase and boldfaced (e.g., $\mathbf{x}$) are column vectors. Variables printed in uppercase and boldfaced (e.g., $\mathbf{X}$) are matrices.

Let $\mathbf{v}$ be a column vector of weights specified by the user. If no weights are specified, then $\mathbf{v} = \mathbf{1}$. Let $\mathbf{w}$ be a column vector of normalized weights. If no weights are specified or if the user specified `fweight`s or `iweight`s, $\mathbf{w} = \mathbf{v}$. Otherwise, $\mathbf{w} = \{\mathbf{v}/(\mathbf{1}'\mathbf{v})\}(\mathbf{1}'\mathbf{1})$.

The *number of observations*, $n$, is defined as $\mathbf{1}'\mathbf{w}$. In the case of `iweight`s, this is truncated to an integer. The *sum of the weights* is $\mathbf{1}'\mathbf{v}$. Define $c = 1$ if there is a constant in the regression and zero otherwise. Define $k$ as the number of right-hand-side (rhs) variables (including the constant).

Let $\mathbf{X}$ denote the matrix of observations on the rhs variables, $\mathbf{y}$ the vector of observations on the left-hand-side (lhs) variable, and $\mathbf{Z}$ the matrix of observations on the instruments. If the user specifies no instruments, then $\mathbf{Z} = \mathbf{X}$. In the following formulas, if the user specifies weights, then $\mathbf{X}'\mathbf{X}$, $\mathbf{X}'\mathbf{y}$, $\mathbf{y}'\mathbf{y}$, $\mathbf{Z}'\mathbf{Z}$, $\mathbf{Z}'\mathbf{X}$, and $\mathbf{Z}'\mathbf{y}$ are replaced by $\mathbf{X}'\mathbf{DX}$, $\mathbf{X}'\mathbf{Dy}$, $\mathbf{y}'\mathbf{Dy}$, $\mathbf{Z}'\mathbf{DZ}$, $\mathbf{Z}'\mathbf{DX}$, and $\mathbf{Z}'\mathbf{Dy}$, respectively, where $\mathbf{D}$ is a diagonal matrix whose diagonal elements are the elements of $\mathbf{w}$. We suppress the $\mathbf{D}$ below to simplify the notation.

If no instruments are specified, define $\mathbf{A}$ as $\mathbf{X}'\mathbf{X}$ and $\mathbf{a}$ as $\mathbf{X}'\mathbf{y}$. Otherwise, define $\mathbf{A}$ as $\mathbf{X}'\mathbf{Z}(\mathbf{Z}'\mathbf{Z})^{-1}(\mathbf{X}'\mathbf{Z})'$ and $\mathbf{a}$ as $\mathbf{X}'\mathbf{Z}(\mathbf{Z}'\mathbf{Z})^{-1}\mathbf{Z}'\mathbf{y}$.

The coefficient vector $\mathbf{b}$ is defined as $\mathbf{A}^{-1}\mathbf{a}$. Although not shown in the notation, unless `hascons` is specified, $\mathbf{A}$ and $\mathbf{a}$ are accumulated in deviation form and the constant calculated separately. This comment applies to all statistics listed below.

The *total sum of squares*, TSS, equals $\mathbf{y}'\mathbf{y}$ if there is no intercept and $\mathbf{y}'\mathbf{y} - \{(\mathbf{1}'\mathbf{y})^2/n\}$ otherwise. The *degrees of freedom* are $n - c$.

The *error sum of squares*, ESS, is defined as $\mathbf{y}'\mathbf{y} - 2\mathbf{b}\mathbf{X}'\mathbf{y} + \mathbf{b}'\mathbf{X}'\mathbf{Xb}$ if there are instruments and as $\mathbf{y}'\mathbf{y} - \mathbf{b}'\mathbf{X}'\mathbf{y}$ otherwise. The *degrees of freedom* are $n - k$.

The *model sum of squares*, MSS, equals TSS − ESS. The *degrees of freedom* are $k - c$.

The *mean square error*, $s^2$, is defined as ESS$/(n - k)$. The *root mean square error* is $s$, its square root.

The $F$ statistic with $k - c$ and $n - k$ degrees of freedom is defined as

$$F = \frac{\text{MSS}}{(k - c)s^2}$$

if no instruments are specified. If instruments are specified and $c = 1$, then $F$ is defined as

$$F = \frac{(\mathbf{b} - \mathbf{c})'\mathbf{A}(\mathbf{b} - \mathbf{c})}{(k - 1)s^2}$$

where $\mathbf{c}$ is a vector of $k - 1$ zeros and $k$th element $\mathbf{1}'\mathbf{y}/n$. Otherwise, $F$ is defined as *missing*. (In this case, you may use the `test` command to construct any $F$ test you wish.)

The *R-squared*, $R^2$, is defined as $R^2 = 1 - \text{ESS}/\text{TSS}$.

The *adjusted R-squared*, $R_a^2$, is $1 - (1 - R^2)(n - c)/(n - k)$.

If `robust` is not specified, the conventional estimate of variance is $s^2\mathbf{A}^{-1}$. The handling of `robust` is described below.

## A general notation for the robust variance calculation

Put aside all context of linear regression and the notation that goes with it—we will return to it. First, we are going to establish a notation for describing robust variance calculations.

The calculation formula for the robust variance calculation is

$$\widehat{\mathcal{V}} = q_c \widehat{\mathbf{V}} \left( \sum_{k=1}^{M} \mathbf{u}_k^{(G)\prime} \mathbf{u}_k^{(G)} \right) \widehat{\mathbf{V}}$$

where

$$\mathbf{u}_k^{(G)} = \sum_{j \in G_k} w_j \mathbf{u}_j$$

$G_1$, $G_2$, ..., $G_M$ are the clusters specified by `cluster()` and $w_j$ are the user-specified weights, normalized if `fweight`s are specified, and equal to 1 if no weights are specified. (In the case of `fweight`s, the formula for $\widehat{\mathcal{V}}$ is modified to produce the same results as if the dataset were expanded and the calculation made on unweighted data, meaning $w_k^{(G)} = \sum_{j \in G_k} w_j$ is introduced into the denominator.)

If `cluster()` is not specified, $M = N$ and each cluster contains one observation. The inputs into this calculation are

1. $\widehat{\mathbf{V}}$, which is typically a conventionally calculated variance matrix;

2. $\mathbf{u}_j$, $j = 1, \ldots, N$, a row vector of scores; and

3. $q_c$, a constant finite-sample adjustment.

Thus, we can now describe how estimators apply the robust calculation formula by defining $\widehat{\mathbf{V}}$, $\mathbf{u}_j$, and $q_c$.

Two definitions are popular enough for $q_c$ to deserve a name. The regression-like formula for $q_c$ (Fuller et al. 1986) is

$$q_c = \frac{N-1}{N-k} \frac{M}{M-1}$$

where $M$ is the number of clusters and $N$ the number of observations. In the case of weights, $N$ refers to the sum of the weights if frequency weights and the number of observations in the dataset (ignoring weights) in all other cases. Also note that, weighted or not, $M = N$ when `cluster()` is not specified and, in that case, $q_c = N/(N-k)$.

The asymptotic-like formula for $q_c$ is

$$q_c = \frac{M}{M-1}$$

where $M = N$ if `cluster()` is not specified.

See [U] **23.11 Obtaining robust variance estimates** and [P] **_robust** for a discussion of the robust variance estimator and a development of these formulas.

## Robust calculation for regress

In the case of `regress`, $\widehat{\mathbf{V}} = \mathbf{A}^{-1}$ (*sic*). The other terms are

No instruments, `robust`, but not `hc2` or `hc3`:

$$\mathbf{u}_j = (y_j - \mathbf{x}_j \mathbf{b}) \mathbf{x}_j$$

and $q_c$ is given by its regression-like definition.

No instruments, `hc2`:

$$\mathbf{u}_j = \frac{1}{\sqrt{1 - h_{jj}}} (y_j - \mathbf{x}_j \mathbf{b}) \mathbf{x}_j$$

where $q_c = 1$ and $h_{jj} = \mathbf{x}_j (\mathbf{X}'\mathbf{X})^{-1} \mathbf{x}_j'$.

No instruments, `hc3`:

$$\mathbf{u}_j = \frac{1}{1 - h_{jj}} (y_j - \mathbf{x}_j \mathbf{b}) \mathbf{x}_j$$

where $q_c = 1$ and $h_{jj} = \mathbf{x}_j (\mathbf{X}'\mathbf{X})^{-1} \mathbf{x}_j'$.

Instrumental variables:

$$\mathbf{u}_j = (y_j - \mathbf{x}_j \mathbf{b}) \widehat{\mathbf{x}}_j$$

where $q_c$ is given by its regression-like definition, and

$$\widehat{\mathbf{x}}_j' = \mathbf{P} \mathbf{z}_j'$$

where $\mathbf{P} = (\mathbf{X}'\mathbf{Z})(\mathbf{Z}'\mathbf{Z})^{-1}$.

## Methods and formulas for predict

We begin by assuming that we have already estimated the regression model, or in the case of commands referred here, a latent or underlying regression model

$$\mathbf{y} = \mathbf{X}\mathbf{b} + \mathbf{e}$$

where $\mathbf{X}$ is $n \times k$.

Denote the previously estimated coefficient vector by $\mathbf{b}$ and its estimated variance matrix by $\mathbf{V}$. `predict` works by recalling various aspects of the model, such as $\mathbf{b}$, and combining that information with the data currently in memory. Let us write $\mathbf{x}_j$ for the $j$th observation currently in memory and let $s^2$ be the mean square error of the regression.

Let us further write $\mathbf{V} = s^2 (\mathbf{X}'\mathbf{X})^{-1}$. Let $k$ be the number of independent variables including the intercept, if any, and let $y_j$ be the observed value of the dependent variable.

The *predicted value* (**xb** option) is defined $\widehat{y}_j = \mathbf{x}_j \mathbf{b}$.

Let $\ell_j$ represent a lower bound for an observation $j$ and $u_j$ represent an upper bound. The probability that $y_j|\mathbf{x}_j$ would be observed in the interval $(\ell_j, u_j)$ —option $\mathtt{pr}(\ell, u)$ —is

$$P(\ell_j, u_j) = \Pr(\ell_j < \mathbf{x}_j\mathbf{b} + e_j < u_j) = \Phi\left(\frac{u_j - \widehat{y}_j}{s}\right) - \Phi\left(\frac{\ell_j - \widehat{y}_j}{s}\right)$$

where for the options $\mathtt{pr}(\ell, u)$, $\mathtt{e}(\ell, u)$, and $\mathtt{ystar}(\ell, u)$, $\ell_j$ and $u_j$ can be anywhere in the range $(-\infty, +\infty)$.

The option $\mathtt{e}(\ell, u)$ computes the expected value of $y_j|\mathbf{x}_j$ conditional on $y_j|\mathbf{x}_j$ being in the interval $(\ell_j, u_j)$, i.e., when, $y_j|\mathbf{x}_j$ is censored. It can be expressed

$$E(\ell_j, u_j) = E(\mathbf{x}_j\mathbf{b} + e_j \mid \ell_j < \mathbf{x}_j\mathbf{b} + e_j < u_j) = \widehat{y}_j - s\frac{\phi\left(\frac{u_j - \widehat{y}_j}{s}\right) - \phi\left(\frac{\ell_j - \widehat{y}_j}{s}\right)}{\Phi\left(\frac{u_j - \widehat{y}_j}{s}\right) - \Phi\left(\frac{\ell_j - \widehat{y}_j}{s}\right)}$$

where $\phi$ is the normal density and $\Phi$ is the cumulative normal.

We can also compute $\mathtt{ystar}(\ell, u)$ —the expected value of $y_j|\mathbf{x}_j$ where $y_j$ is assumed truncated at $\ell_j$ and $u_j$:

$$y_j^* = \begin{cases} \ell_j & \text{if } \mathbf{x}_j\mathbf{b} + e_j \leq \ell_j \\ \mathbf{x}_j\mathbf{b} + u & \text{if } \ell_j < \mathbf{x}_j\mathbf{b} + e_j < u_j \\ u_j & \text{if } \mathbf{x}_j\mathbf{b} + e_j \geq u_j \end{cases}$$

This computation can be expressed in several ways, but the most intuitive formulation involves a combination of the two statistics just defined:

$$y_j^* = P(-\infty, \ell_j)\ell_j + P(\ell_j, u_j)E(\ell_j, u_j) + P(u_j, +\infty)u_j$$

A diagonal element of the projection matrix (**hat**) or (**leverage**) is given by

$$h_j = \mathbf{x}_j(\mathbf{X}'\mathbf{X})^{-1}\mathbf{x}_j'$$

The *standard error of the prediction* (**stdp**) is defined $s_{p_j} = \sqrt{\mathbf{x}_j\mathbf{V}\mathbf{x}_j'}$

and can also be written $s_{p_j} = s\sqrt{h_j}$.

The *standard error of the forecast* (**stdf**) is defined as $s_{f_j} = s\sqrt{1 + h_j}$.

The *standard error of the residual* (**stdr**) is defined as $s_{r_j} = s\sqrt{1 - h_j}$.

The *residuals* (**residuals**) are defined as $\widehat{e}_j = y_j - \widehat{y}_j$.

The *standardized residuals* (**rstandard**) are defined as $\widehat{e}_{s_j} = \widehat{e}_j/s_{r_j}$.

The *studentized residuals* (**rstudent**) are defined as

$$r_j = \frac{\widehat{e}_j}{s_{(j)}\sqrt{1 - h_j}}$$

where $s_{(j)}$ represents the root mean square error with the $j$th observation removed, which is given by

$$s_{(j)}^2 = \frac{s^2(T - k)}{T - k - 1} - \frac{\widehat{e}_j^2}{(T - k - 1)(1 - h_j)}$$

Cook's $D$ (cooksd) is given by

$$D_j = \frac{\widehat{e}_{s_j}^2 (s_{p_j}/s_{r_j})^2}{k} = \frac{h_j \widehat{e}_j^2}{ks^2(1-h_j)^2}$$

DFITS (dfits) is given by

$$\text{DFITS}_j = r_j \sqrt{\frac{h_j}{1-h_j}}$$

Welsch distance (welsch) is given by

$$W_j = \frac{r_j \sqrt{h_j(n-1)}}{1-h_j}$$

COVRATIO (covratio) is given by

$$\text{COVRATIO}_j = \frac{1}{1-h_j}\left(\frac{n-k-\widehat{e}_j^2}{n-k-1}\right)^k$$

The DFBETAs (dfbeta) for a particular regressor $x_i$ are given by

$$\text{DFBETA}_j = \frac{r_j u_j}{\sqrt{U^2(1-h_j)}}$$

where $u_j$ are the residuals obtained from a regression of $x_j$ on the remaining $x$'s and $U^2 = \sum_j u_j^2$.

# References

Alexandersson, A. 1998. gr32: Confidence ellipses. *Stata Technical Bulletin* 46: 10–13. Reprinted in *Stata Technical Bulletin Reprints*, vol. 8, pp. 54–57.

Belsley, D. A., E. Kuh, and R. E. Welsch. 1980. *Regression Diagnostics*. New York: John Wiley & Sons.

Chatterjee, S., A. S. Hadi, and B. Price. 2000. *Regression Analysis by Example*. 3d ed. New York: John Wiley & Sons.

Cook, R. D. 1977. Detection of influential observations in linear regression. *Technometrics* 19: 15–18.

Davidson, R. and J. G. MacKinnon. 1993. *Estimation and Inference in Econometrics*. New York: Oxford University Press.

Draper, N. and H. Smith. 1998. *Applied Regression Analysis*. 3d ed. New York: John Wiley & Sons.

Fuller, W. A., W. Kennedy, D. Schnell, G. Sullivan, H. J. Park. 1986. *PC Carp*. Ames, IA: Statistical Laboratory, Iowa State University.

Hamilton, L. C. 1992. *Regression with Graphics*. Pacific Grove, CA: Brooks/Cole Publishing Company.

Johnston, J. and J. DiNardo. 1997. *Econometric Methods*. 4th ed. New York: McGraw–Hill.

Kmenta, J. 1997. *Elements of Econometrics*. 2d ed. Ann Arbor: University of Michigan Press.

Long, J. S. and J. Freese. 2000. sg152: Listing and interpreting transformed coefficients from certain regression models. *Stata Technical Bulletin* 57: 27–34.

MacKinnon, J. G. and H. White. 1985. Some heteroskedasticity consistent covariance matrix estimators with improved finite sample properties. *Journal of Econometrics* 29: 305–325.

Mosteller, F. and J. W. Tukey. 1977. *Data Analysis and Regression*. Reading, MA: Addison–Wesley Publishing Company.

Over, M., D. Jolliffe, and A. Foster. 1996. sg46: Huber correction for two-stage least squares estimates. *Stata Technical Bulletin* 29: 24–25. Reprinted in *Stata Technical Bulletin Reprints*, vol. 5, pp. 140–142.

Plackett, R. L. 1972. The discovery of the method of least squares. *Biometrika* 59: 239–251.

Ramsey, F. and D. W. Schafer. 1996. *The Statistical Sleuth: A Course in Methods of Data Analysis*. Belmont, CA: Duxbury Press.

Rawlings, J. O. 1988. *Applied Regression Analysis: A Research Tool*. Pacific Grove, CA: Wadsworth & Brooks/Cole Advanced Books and Software.

Rogers, W. H. 1991. smv2: Analyzing repeated measurements—some practical alternatives. *Stata Technical Bulletin* 4: 10–16. Reprinted in *Stata Technical Bulletin Reprints*, vol. 1, pp. 123–131.

Royston, P. and G. Ambler. 1998. sg79: Generalized additive models. *Stata Technical Bulletin* 42: 38–43. Reprinted in *Stata Technical Bulletin Reprints*, vol. 7, pp. 217–224.

Tyler, J. H. 1997. sg73: Table making program. *Stata Technical Bulletin* 40: 18–23. Reprinted in *Stata Technical Bulletin Reprints*, vol. 7, pp. 186–192.

Weesie, J. 1998. sg77: Regression analysis with multiplicative heteroskedasticity. *Stata Technical Bulletin* 42: 28–32. Reprinted in *Stata Technical Bulletin Reprints*, vol. 7, pp. 204–210.

Weisberg, S. 1985. *Applied Linear Regression*. 2d ed. New York: John Wiley & Sons.

Welsch, R. E. 1982. Influence functions and regression diagnostics. In *Modern Data Analysis*, ed. R. L. Launer and A. F. Siegel, 149–169. New York: Academic Press.

Welsch, R. E. and E. Kuh. 1977. *Technical Report 923-77: Linear Regression Diagnostics*. Cambridge, MA: Sloan School of Management, Massachusetts Institute of Technology.

White, H. 1980. A heteroskedasticity-consistent covariance matrix estimator and a direct test for heteroskedasticity. *Econometrica* 48: 817–838.

Wooldridge, J. M. 2000. *Introductory Econometrics: A Modern Approach*. Cincinnati, OH: South-Western College Publishing.

Zimmerman, F. 1998. sg93: Switching regressions. *Stata Technical Bulletin* 45: 30–33. Reprinted in *Stata Technical Bulletin Reprints*, vol. 8, pp. 183–186.

# Also See

| | |
|---|---|
| **Complementary:** | [R] **adjust**, [R] **lincom**, [R] **linktest**, [R] **lrtest**, [R] **mfx**, [R] **predict**, [R] **sw**, [R] **test**, [R] **testnl**, [R] **vce**, [R] **xi** |
| **Related:** | [R] **anova**, [R] **areg**, [R] **cnsreg**, [R] **heckman**, [R] **ivreg**, [R] **mvreg**, [R] **qreg**, [R] **reg3**, [R] **rreg**, [R] **sureg**, [R] **svy estimators**, [R] **tobit**, [R] **truncreg**, [R] **xtgee**, [R] **xtgls**, [R] **xtintreg**, [R] **xtpcse**, [R] **xtreg**, [R] **xtregar**, [P] **_robust** |
| **Background:** | [U] **16.5 Accessing coefficients and standard errors**, [U] **23 Estimation and post-estimation commands**, [U] **23.11 Obtaining robust variance estimates**, [U] **23.13 Weighted estimation** |

# Title

> **regression diagnostics** — Regression diagnostics

# Syntax

avplot *indepvar* [ , *graph_options* ]

avplots [ , *graph_options* ]

cprplot *indepvar* [ , *graph_options* <u>bw</u>idth(#) ]

acprplot *indepvar* [ , *graph_options* <u>bw</u>idth(#) ]

lvr2plot [ , *graph_options* ]

rvfplot [ , *graph_options* ]

rvpplot *indepvar* [ , *graph_options* ]

ovtest [ , <u>rhs</u> ]

hettest [ *varlist* ]

dwstat

dfbeta [ *indepvar* [ *indepvar* ... ] ]

vif

dwstat is for use with time-series data. You must tsset your data before using dwstat; see [R] **tsset**.

*(Continued on next page)*

## Syntax for predict after regress

predict [*type*] *newvarname* [if *exp*] [in *range*] [, *statistic* ]

where *statistic* is

| | |
|---|---|
| xb | $\mathbf{x}_j\mathbf{b}$, fitted values (the default) |
| pr(*a*,*b*) | $\Pr(y_j \mid a < y_j < b)$ |
| e(*a*,*b*) | $E(y_j \mid a < y_j < b)$ |
| ystar(*a*,*b*) | $E(y_j^*)$, $y_j^* = \max\{a, \min(y_j, b)\}$ |
| cooksd | Cook's distance |
| leverage \| hat | leverage (diagonal elements of hat matrix) |
| residuals | residuals |
| rstandard | standardized residuals |
| rstudent | studentized (jackknifed) residuals |
| stdp | standard error of the prediction |
| stdf | standard error of the forecast |
| stdr | standard error of the residual |
| * covratio | COVRATIO |
| * dfbeta(*varname*) | DFBETA for *varname* |
| * dfits | DFITS |
| * welsch | Welsch distance |

and *a* and *b* may be numbers or variables; *a* equal to '.' means $-\infty$; *b* equal to '.' means $+\infty$.

Unstarred statistics are available both in and out of sample; type predict ... if e(sample) ... if wanted only for the estimation sample. Starred statistics are calculated only for the estimation sample even when if e(sample) is not specified.

See [R] **regress** for more information on the options for predict.

## Description

These commands, collectively, provide tools for diagnosing sensitivity to individual observations, analyzing residuals, and assessing specification.

avplot graphs an added-variable plot (a.k.a. partial-regression leverage plot, a.k.a. partial regression plot, a.k.a. adjusted partial residual plot) after **regress**. *indepvar* may be an independent variable (a.k.a. predictor, a.k.a. carrier, a.k.a. covariate) that is currently in the model or not.

avplots graphs all the added-variable plots in a single image.

cprplot graphs a component-plus-residual plot (a.k.a. partial residual plot) after **regress**. *indepvar* must be an independent variable that is currently in the model.

acprplot graphs an augmented component-plus-residual plot (a.k.a. augmented partial residual plot) as described by Mallows (1986). This seems to work better than the component-plus-residual plot for identifying nonlinearities in the data.

lvr2plot graphs a leverage-versus-squared-residual plot (a.k.a. L-R plot).

rvfplot graphs a residual-versus-fitted plot, a graph of the residuals against the fitted values.

rvpplot graphs a residual-versus-predictor plot (a.k.a. independent variable plot, a.k.a. carrier plot), a graph of the residuals against the specified predictor.

ovtest performs two flavors of the Ramsey (1969) regression specification error test (RESET) for omitted variables. This test amounts to estimating $y = \mathbf{xb} + \mathbf{zt} + u$ and then testing $\mathbf{t} = \mathbf{0}$. If option rhs is not specified, powers of the fitted values are used for $\mathbf{z}$. If rhs is specified, powers of the individual elements of $\mathbf{x}$ are used.

hettest performs two flavors of the Cook and Weisberg (1983) test for heteroskedasticity. This test amounts to testing $\mathbf{t} = \mathbf{0}$ in $\text{Var}(e) = \sigma^2 \exp(\mathbf{zt})$. If *varlist* is not specified, the fitted values are used for $\mathbf{z}$. If *varlist* is specified, the variables specified are used for $\mathbf{z}$.

dwstat computes the Durbin–Watson $d$ statistic (Durbin and Watson 1950) to test for first-order serial correlation in the disturbances. For an example using dwstat, see [R] **prais**.

dfbeta will calculate one, more than one, or all the DFBETAs after regress. Although predict will also calculate DFBETAs, predict can do this for only one variable at a time. dfbeta is a convenience tool for those who want to calculate DFBETAs for multiple variables. The names for the new variables created are chosen automatically and begin with the letters DF.

vif calculates the variance inflation factors (VIFs) for the independent variables specified in a linear regression model.

predict will calculate various statistics in addition to fitted values after regress. See table above.

## Options

bwidth(#) specifies the bandwidth for the lowess curve through the points; see [R] **ksm**. cprplot and acprplot allow, in addition to graph's standard point-connect options, connect(k), which places a lowess curve through the points. The default bandwidth is 0.8, although we typically recommend reducing the number. In general, we do *not* recommend specifying connect(k) because it (1) is slow and (2) does not appear to work well at identifying nonlinearities in the points. (This is due more to shortcomings of the component-plus-residual plots rather than of lowess.) When a line is needed to guide the eye, we recommend connect(m) or, if smoother curves appeal to you, connect(s) with the appropriate bands() option; see [G] **graph options**.

rhs, used with ovtest, specifies that powers of the right-hand-side (explanatory) variables are to be used in the test rather than powers of the fitted values.

*graph_options* are any of the options allowed with graph, twoway; see [G] **graph options**.

## Options for predict

For more information on the options for predict, see [R] **regress**.

*(Continued on next page)*

# Remarks

Remarks are presented under the headings

> *Residual-versus-fitted plots*
> *Formal tests for violations of assumptions*
> *L-R plots*
> *Added-variable plots*
> *Component-plus-residual plots*
> *Residual versus predictor plots*
> *Influence statistics from predict*
> *Fitted values and residuals*
> *Leverage or the diagonal elements of the hat matrix*
> *Standard error of the residual, prediction, and forecast*
> *Standardized and studentized residuals*
> *DFITS, Cook's Distance, and Welsch Distance*
> *COVRATIO*
> *DFBETAs*
> *Calculate variance inflation factors with vif*

These commands concern identifying influential data in linear regression. This is, unfortunately, a field that is dominated by jargon, codified and sometimes begun by Belsley, Kuh and Welsch (1980). In the words of Chatterjee and Hadi (1986, 416), "Belsley, Kuh, and Welsch's book, *Regression Diagnostics*, was a very valuable contribution to the statistical literature, but it unleashed on an unsuspecting statistical community a computer speak (à la Orwell) the likes of which we have never seen". Things have only gotten worse since then. Chatterjee and Hadi's (1986, 1988) own attempt to clean up the jargon did not improve matters (see Hoaglin and Kempthorne 1986, Velleman 1986, and Welsch 1986). We apologize for the jargon and, for our contribution to the jargon in the form of inelegant command names, we apologize most of all.

Model *sensitivity* refers to how estimates are affected by subsets of our data. Imagine data on $y$ and $x$ and assume the data are to be fit by the regression $y_i = \alpha + \beta x_i + \epsilon_i$. Our regression will be $y_i = a + bx_i + e_i$, so $a$ and $b$ are our estimates of $\alpha$ and $\beta$. Now imagine you were told that the $a$ and $b$ you estimate would be very different if you deleted a small portion of your dataset. In fact, let's assume that they would change dramatically if you deleted just a single point. This should bother you. As a data analyst, you would like to think that you are summarizing tendencies that apply to all the data, but you have just been told that the model you estimated is unduly influenced by a single point and that, as a matter of fact, there is another model that applies to the rest of the data—a model you have ignored.

The search for subsets of the data which, if deleted, would change your results markedly is the main topic of this entry.

There are three key issues in identifying model sensitivity to individual observations, which go by the names *residuals*, *leverage*, and *influence*. In our $y_i = a + bx_i + e_i$ regression, the residuals are, of course, $e_i$—they reveal how much our fitted value $\widehat{y}_i = a + bx_i$ differs from the observed $y_i$. A point $(x_i, y_i)$ with a corresponding large residual is called an outlier. We are interested in outliers because we somehow feel that such points will exert undue influence on our estimates. Our feelings are generally right, but there are exceptions. It is possible that a point could have a huge residual and yet not affect our estimated $b$ at all. Nevertheless, studying observations with large residuals almost always pays off.

$(x_i, y_i)$ can be an outlier in another way—just as $y_i$ can be far from $\widehat{y}_i$, $x_i$ can be far from the center of mass of the other $x$'s. Such an "outlier" should interest you just as much as the more traditional outliers. Picture a scatterplot of $y$ against $x$ with thousands of points in some sort of mass at the lower left of the graph and a single point at the upper right of the graph. Now run a regression line through the points—your regression line will come very close to the point at the upper right of the graph and may, in fact, go through it. That is, this isolated point will not appear as an outlier as measured by residuals because its residual will be small. Yet this point might have a dramatic effect on our resulting estimates in the sense that, were we to delete the point, the estimates would change markedly. Such a point is said to have high leverage. Just as with traditional outliers, a high leverage point does not necessarily have an undue effect on regression estimates, but if it does not, it is more the exception than the rule.

Now all of this is a most unsatisfactory state of affairs. Points with large residuals may, but need not, have a large effect on our results, and points with small residuals may still have a large effect. Points with high leverage may, but need not, have a large effect on our results, and points with low leverage may still have a large effect. Can't we identify the influential points and simply have the computer list them for us? We can, but we will have to define what we mean by influential.

"Influential" is defined with respect to some statistic. For instance, we might ask which points in our data have a large effect on our estimated $a$, or which points have a large effect on our estimated $b$, or which points have a large effect on our estimated standard error of $b$, and so on, but we should not be surprised when the answers to these questions are different. In any case, obtaining such measures is not difficult—all we have to do is estimate the regression excluding each observation one at a time and record the statistic of interest which, in the day of the modern computer, is not too onerous. Moreover, we can save considerable computer time by doing algebra ahead of time and working out formulas that will calculate the same answers as if we ran each of the regressions. (We will ignore the question of pairs of observations that, together, exert undue influence, and triples, and so on, which remains largely unsolved and for which the brute force estimate-every-possible-regression procedure is not a viable alternative.)

We have, however, begged the question. We have not given you a list of the "influential" observations, but many lists, each calculated with respect to a specific statistic, along with an explanation of why the original question was not meaningful. These lists can themselves be useful, but you are left to extract the information from them on your own.

## Residual-versus-fitted plots

▷ Example

Using the automobile dataset described in [U] **9 Stata's on-line tutorials and sample datasets**, we will use `regress` to estimate a model of `price` on `weight`, `mpg`, `foreign`, and the interaction of `foreign` with `mpg`.

```
. gen forXmpg=foreign*mpg
. regress price weight mpg forXmpg foreign
```

| Source | SS | df | MS | | |
|---|---|---|---|---|---|
| Model | 350319665 | 4 | 87579916.3 | | |
| Residual | 284745731 | 69 | 4126749.72 | | |
| Total | 635065396 | 73 | 8699525.97 | | |

Number of obs = 74
F( 4, 69) = 21.22
Prob > F = 0.0000
R-squared = 0.5516
Adj R-squared = 0.5256
Root MSE = 2031.4

| price | Coef. | Std. Err. | t | P>\|t\| | [95% Conf. Interval] | |
|---|---|---|---|---|---|---|
| weight | 4.613589 | .7254961 | 6.36 | 0.000 | 3.166264 | 6.060914 |
| mpg | 263.1875 | 110.7961 | 2.38 | 0.020 | 42.15527 | 484.2197 |
| forXmpg | -307.2166 | 108.5307 | -2.83 | 0.006 | -523.7294 | -90.70369 |
| foreign | 11240.33 | 2751.681 | 4.08 | 0.000 | 5750.878 | 16729.78 |
| _cons | -14449.58 | 4425.72 | -3.26 | 0.002 | -23278.65 | -5620.51 |

Once you have estimated a model, you may use any of the **regression diagnostics** commands. **rvfplot** (read residual-versus-fitted plot) graphs the residuals against the fitted values:

```
. rvfplot, border yline(0)
```

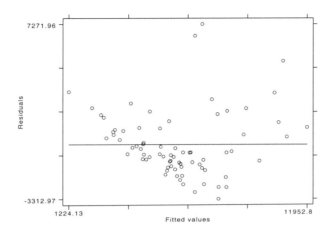

All the diagnostic plot commands allow the options of **graph, twoway**; we specified **border** to draw a border around the graph and **yline(0)** to draw a line across the graph at $y = 0$; see [G] **graph options**.

In a well-fitted model, there should be no pattern to the residuals plotted against the fitted values—something not true of our model. Ignoring the two outliers at the top center of the graph, we see curvature in the pattern of the residuals, suggesting a violation of the assumption that **price** is linear in our independent variables. Alternatively, we might have seen increasing or decreasing variation in the residuals—heteroskedasticity. Any pattern whatsoever indicates a violation of the least-squares assumptions.

We will ignore these problems and plow ahead.

◁

## Formal tests for violations of assumptions

▷ Example

Before plowing ahead, two of the regression diagnostic commands are designed to test for certain violations that **rvfplot** less formally attempts to detect. **hettest** tests for heteroskedasticity—the increasing or decreasing variation in the residuals with fitted values—and **ovtest** tests for omitted variables—a pattern in the residuals. Here is the result of running these two commands on our model:

*(Continued on next page)*

```
. ovtest

Ramsey RESET test using powers of the fitted values of price
        Ho:  model has no omitted variables
                    F(3, 66) =      7.77
                    Prob > F =      0.0002

. hettest

Cook-Weisberg test for heteroskedasticity using fitted values of price
      Ho: Constant variance
           chi2(1)    =      6.50
           Prob > chi2 =      0.0108
```

We find evidence of both problems.

So why bother with the graph when the tests seem so much easier to interpret? In part, it is a matter of taste: both are designed to uncover the same problem and both are, in fact, going about it in similar ways. One is based on a formal calculation while the other is based on your judgment in evaluating a graph. On the other hand, the tests are seeking evidence of quite specific problems while your judgment is more general. The careful analyst will use both.

Note that we performed the omitted-variable test first. Omitted variables are a more serious problem than heteroskedasticity. Were this not a manual, having found evidence of omitted variables, we would never have run the `hettest` command, at least not until we solved the omitted-variable problem.

◁

## ❏ Technical Note

`ovtest` and `hettest` both perform two flavors of their respective tests. By default, `ovtest` looks for evidence of omitted variables by estimating the original model augmented by $\hat{y}^2$, $\hat{y}^3$, and $\hat{y}^4$, the fitted values from the original model. Under the assumption of no misspecification, the coefficients on the powers of the fitted values will be zero. With the `rhs` option, `ovtest` instead augments the original model with powers (second through fourth) of the explanatory variables (omitting, of course, 0/1 explanatory variables).

`hettest`, by default, looks for heteroskedasticity by modeling the variance as a function of the fitted values. If, however, you specify a variable or variables, the variance will be modeled as a function of the variable(s) specified. This amounts to using a finer tool. A priori, perhaps there is some reason to suspect heteroskedasticity and to suspect that the heteroskedasticity is a function of a car's weight. Then using a test that focuses on weight will be more powerful than a general test. In the example above, we had no such a priori expectations.

❏

# L-R plots

## ▷ Example

One of the most useful diagnostic graphs is provided by `lvr2plot` (read leverage-versus-residual-squared plot), a graph of leverage against the (normalized) residuals squared. Using our price model:

. lvr2plot, border

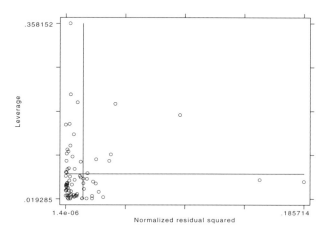

The lines on the chart show the average values of leverage and the (normalized) residuals squared. Points above the horizontal line have higher-than-average leverage; points to the right of the vertical line have larger-than-average residuals.

One point immediately catches our eye and three to five more make us pause. The point at the top of the graph is high leverage and a smaller-than-average residual. The other points that bother us all have higher-than-average leverage, three with smaller-than average residuals and two with larger-than-average residuals.

Since lvr2plot allows any of the options of graph, a less pretty but more useful version of the above graph specifies make be used as the symbol (see [G] **graph options**):

. lvr2plot, s([make]) trim(12) border

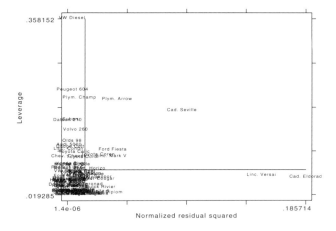

The VW Diesel, Plymouth Champ, Plymouth Arrow, and Peugeot 604 are the points that cause us the most concern. When we further examine our data, we discover that the VW Diesel is the only diesel in our data and that the data for the Plymouth Arrow were entered incorrectly into the computer. No such simple explanations were found for the Plymouth Champ and Peugeot 604.

Your data may not have such handy labels as our automobile data. If we had typed lvr2plot, s([_n]) border, however, we would have obtained a graph with the observation numbers used as the plotting symbols, which would have served our identification purposes as well.

◁

# Added-variable plots

▷ Example

We will continue with our price model including the four suspicious cars. A third, useful diagnostic graph is provided by avplot (read added-variable plot, also known as the partial-regression leverage plot).

One of the wonderful features of one-regressor regressions (regressions of $y$ on a single $x$) is that you can graph the data and the regression line. There is no easier way to understand the regression than to examine such a graph. Unfortunately, you cannot do this when you have more than one regressor. With two regressors, it is still theoretically possible—the graph must be drawn in three dimensions, but with three regressors, the graphs would be four-dimensional; with four, five-dimensional; and so on.

The added-variable plot is an attempt to project multidimensional data back to the two-dimensional world for each of the original regressors. This is, of course, impossible without making some concessions. Call the coordinates on an added-variable plot $y$ and $x$. The added-variable plot has the following properties:

1. There is a one-to-one correspondence between $(x_i, y_i)$ and the $i$th observation used in the original regression.

2. A regression of $y$ on $x$ has the same coefficient and standard error (up to a degree-of-freedom adjustment) as the estimated coefficient and standard error for the regressor in the original regression.

3. The "outlierness" of each observation in determining the slope is in some sense preserved.

It is equally important to note the properties that are not listed. The $y$ and $x$ coordinates of the added-variable plot cannot be used to identify functional form, or at least, not well (see Mallows 1986). In the construction of the added-variable plot, the relationship between $y$ and $x$ is forced to be linear.

Let us examine the added-variable plot for mpg in our price regression:

(*Graph on next page*)

. avplot mpg, border

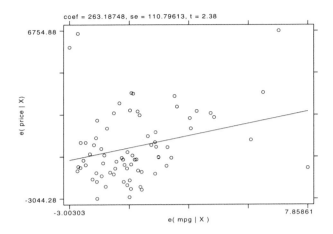

This graph suggests a problem in the determination of the coefficient on mpg. Were this a one-regressor regression, the two points at the top-left corner and the one at the top right would cause us concern, and so it does in our more complicated multiple-regressor case. To identify the problem points, we retyped our command, modifying it to read avplot mpg, border s([make]), and discovered the two cars at the top left are the Cadillac Eldorado and the Lincoln Versailles; the point at the top right is the Cadillac Seville. These three cars account for 100% of the luxury cars in our data, suggesting our model is misspecified. By the way, the point at the lower right of the graph, also cause for concern, is the Plymouth Arrow, our data-entry error.

◁

## ❏ Technical Note

Stata's avplot command can be used with regressors already in the model, as we just did, or with potential regressors not yet in the model. In either case, avplot will produce the correct graph. The name "added-variable plot" is unfortunate in the case when the variable is already among the list of regressors, but is, we feel, still preferable to the name "partial-regression leverage plot" assigned by Belsley, Kuh and Welsch (1980, 30) and more in the spirit of the original use of such plots by Mosteller and Tukey (1977, 271–279). Welsch (1986, 403), however, disagrees: "I am sorry to see that Chatterjee and Hadi [1986] endorse the term 'added-variable plot' when $X_j$ is part of the original model" and goes on to suggest the name "adjusted partial residual plot".

❏

## ▷ Example

Added-variable plots are so useful that you should be sure to look at them for every regressor in your data. avplots makes this easy:

*(Graph on next page)*

```
. avplots, border
```

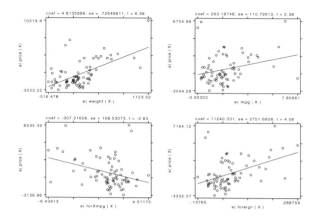

In order to make the legends (barely) readable, we typed `set textsize` 140 before drawing the graph and then reset the default by typing `set textsize` 100 afterwards; see [G] **graph textsize**.

Also see Hamilton (1992, 128–129, 142) for an interesting suggestion on graphing the added-variable plot with symbol size proportional to the DFBETAs. Instructions for drawing such graphs in Stata are included.

◁

## Component-plus-residual plots

▷ Example

Added-variable plots are quite successful at identifying outliers but they cannot be used to identify functional form. The component-plus-residual plot (Ezekiel 1924; Larsen and McCleary 1972) is another attempt at projecting multidimensional data into a two-dimensional form but with different properties. While the added-variable plot can identify outliers, the component-plus-residual plot cannot. It can, however, be used to examine the functional-form assumptions of the model. Both plots have the property that a regression line through the coordinates has a slope equal to the estimated coefficient in the regression model.

To illustrate this, we are going to begin with a different model:

```
. regress price mpg weight
```

| Source   | SS        | df | MS         |
|----------|-----------|----|------------|
| Model    | 187716578 | 2  | 93858289.0 |
| Residual | 447348818 | 71 | 6300687.58 |
| Total    | 635065396 | 73 | 8699525.97 |

```
Number of obs =      74
F(  2,    71) =   14.90
Prob > F      =  0.0000
R-squared     =  0.2956
Adj R-squared =  0.2757
Root MSE      =  2510.1
```

| price  | Coef.    | Std. Err. | t     | P>\|t\| | [95% Conf. Interval] |          |
|--------|----------|-----------|-------|---------|----------------------|----------|
| mpg    | -55.9393 | 75.24136  | -0.74 | 0.460   | -205.9663            | 94.08771 |
| weight | 1.710992 | .5861682  | 2.92  | 0.005   | .5422063             | 2.879779 |
| _cons  | 2197.9   | 3190.768  | 0.69  | 0.493   | -4164.31             | 8560.11  |

Now, we will tell you that the effects of mpg in this model are nonlinear—if you added mpg squared to the model, its coefficient would have a $t$ statistic of 2.38, the $t$ statistic on mpg would become $-2.48$, and weight's effect would become about one-third of its current value and become statistically insignificant. Pretend you do not know this.

The component-plus-residual plot for mpg is

. cprplot mpg, border c(s) bands(13)

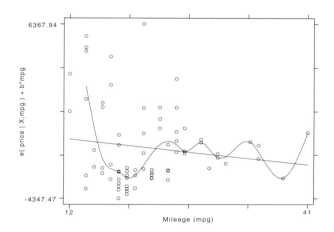

You are supposed to examine the above graph for nonlinearities or, equivalently, ask yourself if the regression line, which has slope equal to the estimated effect of mpg in the original model, fits the data adequately. To assist your eye and ours, we added a cubic spline. Perhaps you see some nonlinearity, but we assert that, if we had not previously told you what you are now pretending we did not and if we had not added the cubic spline, you would not be overly bothered by the graph.

Mallows (1986) proposed an augmented component-plus-residual plot that would be more sensitive to detecting nonlinearity:

. acprplot mpg, border c(s) bands(13)

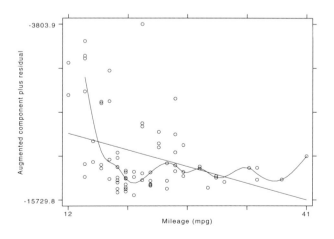

It does do somewhat better.

◁

❑ Technical Note

Rather than specifying `c(s)` —shorthand for `connect(s)` —we could have specified `connect(k)` with either of these plots and obtained a lowess curve through the data. See `bwidth()` under *Options* above for our comment on the value of this.

❑

## Residual versus predictor plots

▷ Example

The residual versus predictor plot is a simple way to look for violations of the regression assumptions. If the assumptions are correct, there should be no pattern in the graph. Using our `price` on `mpg` and `weight` model:

        . rvpplot mpg, border yline(0)

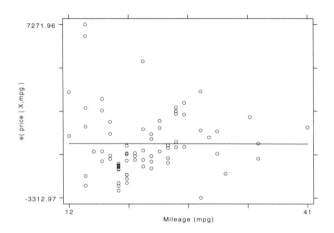

Remember, any pattern counts as a problem, and in this graph we see that the variation in the residuals decreases as `mpg` increases.

◁

## Influence statistics from predict

After estimating a model with `regress`, various statistics may be obtained with `predict`. Many of the statistics can only be computed over the estimation sample. To be assured that we are restricting a statistic to the observations in the estimation sample, we add `if e(sample)` to our `predict` command.

# Fitted values and residuals

▷ Example

Typing `predict` *newvar* with no options creates *newvar* containing the fitted values. Typing `predict` *newvar*, `resid` creates *newvar* containing the residuals. Thus, restricting the predictions to the estimation sample, the graph of residuals versus fitted created by `rvfplot` could also be drawn by typing

```
. predict fitted if e(sample)
(option xb assumed; fitted values)
. predict e if e(sample), resid
. graph e fitted
```

More usefully, returning to our `price` on `weight`, `mpg`, `forXmpg`, and `foreign` model, the five cars whose prices we most underpredict are

```
. predict e if e(sample)
(option xb assumed; fitted values)
. sort e
. list make price e in 1/5
```

| | make | price | e |
|---|---|---|---|
| 1. | Ford Fiesta | 4,389 | 1224.128 |
| 2. | Plym. Horizon | 4,482 | 2280.001 |
| 3. | Buick Opel | 4,453 | 2681.596 |
| 4. | Plym. Champ | 4,425 | 2803.253 |
| 5. | Chev. Chevette | 3,299 | 2917.528 |

and the five we most overpredict are

```
. list make price e in -5/1
```

| | make | price | e |
|---|---|---|---|
| 70. | Linc. Mark V | 13,594 | 10484.81 |
| 71. | Volvo 260 | 11,995 | 10667.33 |
| 72. | Cad. Seville | 15,906 | 10869.65 |
| 73. | Linc. Continental | 11,497 | 11038.44 |
| 74. | Peugeot 604 | 12,990 | 11952.82 |

◁

# Leverage or the diagonal elements of the hat matrix

▷ Example

`predict` *newvar*, `hat` and `predict` *newvar*, `leverage` mean the same thing—both create *newvar* containing the diagonal elements of the hat matrix. Thus, a graph of leverage versus the residuals squared, similar to that created by `lvr2plot`, could be created by typing

```
. predict lev if e(sample), leverage
. predict e if e(sample), resid
. gen esq=e*e
. graph lev esq
```

More usefully, the five cars with the highest leverage in our `price` on `weight`, `mpg`, `forXmpg`, and `foreign` model are

```
. predict lev if e(sample), leverage
. sort lev
. list make price lev e in -5/l
          make             price       lev        e
70. Cad. Seville          15,906   .1814299   5036.348
71. Plym. Arrow            4,647   .2030623  -3312.968
72. Plym. Champ            4,425   .2059959   1621.747
73. Peugeot 604           12,990   .2212826   1037.184
74. VW Diesel              5,397   .3581521   999.7209
```

◁

# Standard error of the residual, prediction, and forecast

See [R] **regress**.

# Standardized and studentized residuals

The terms "standardized" and "studentized" residuals have meant different things to different authors, so excuse us for a second while we get technical. `predict` defines the standardized residual as $\widehat{e}_i = e_i/(s\sqrt{1-h_i})$ and the studentized residual as $r_i = e_i/(s_{(i)}\sqrt{1-h_i})$, which is the same as defined in, for instance, Bollen and Jackman (1990, 264), or what Chatterjee and Hadi (1988, 74) call the "externally studentized" residual. Our "standardized" residual is the same as what Chatterjee and Hadi (1988, 74) call the "internally studentized" residual.

Standardized and studentized residuals are attempts to adjust residuals for their standard errors. Although the $\epsilon_i$ theoretical residuals are homoskedastic by assumption (i.e., they all have the same variance), the calculated $e_i$ are not. In fact,

$$\text{Var}(e_i) = \sigma^2(1 - h_i)$$

where $h_i$ are the leverage measures obtained from the diagonal elements of hat matrix. Thus, observations with the greatest leverage have corresponding residuals with the smallest variance.

Standardized residuals use the root mean square error of the regression for $\sigma$. Studentized residuals use the root mean square error of a regression omitting the observation in question for $\sigma$. In general, studentized residuals are preferable to standardized residuals for purposes of outlier identification. Studentized residuals can be interpreted as the $t$ statistic for testing the significance of a dummy variable equal to 1 in the observation in question and 0 elsewhere (Belsley, Kuh, and Welsch 1980). Such a dummy variable would effectively absorb the observation and so remove its influence in determining the other coefficients in the model. Caution must be exercised here, however, because of the simultaneous testing problem. One cannot simply list the residuals that would be individually significant at the 5% level—their joint significance would be far less (their joint significance *level* would be far greater).

▷ Example

In the opening comments for this entry, we distinguished residuals from leverage and speculated on the impact of an observation with a small residual but large leverage. If we had adjusted the residuals for their standard errors, however, the adjusted residual would have been (relatively) larger and perhaps large enough so that we could simply examine the adjusted residuals. Taking our `price` on `weight`, `mpg`, `forXmpg`, and `foreign` model, we can obtain the in-sample standardized and studentized residuals by typing

```
. predict esta if e(sample), rstandard
. predict estu if e(sample), rstudent
```

Under the subheading *L-R plots*, we discovered that the VW Diesel had the highest leverage in our data but a corresponding small residual. The standardized and studentized residuals for the VW Diesel are

```
. list make price esta estu if make=="VW Diesel"
        make              price      esta       estu
74. VW Diesel             5,397   .6142691   .6114758
```

The studentized residual of 0.611 can be interpreted as the $t$ statistic for including a dummy variable for VW Diesel in our regression. Such a variable would not be significant. Studentized residuals are no substitute for examining the leverage versus residual-squared plot.

◁

## DFITS, Cook's Distance, and Welsch Distance

DFITS (Welsch and Kuh 1977), Cook's Distance (Cook 1977), and Welsch Distance (Welsch 1982) are three attempts to summarize the information in the leverage versus residual-squared plot into a single statistic. That is, the goal is to create an index that is affected by the size of the residuals—outliers—and the size of $h_i$—leverage. Viewed mechanically, one way to write DFITS (Bollen and Jackman 1990, 265) is

$$\text{DFITS}_i = r_i \sqrt{\frac{h_i}{1 - h_i}}$$

where $r_i$ are the studentized residuals. Thus, large residuals increase the value of DFITS as do large values of $h_i$. Viewed more traditionally, DFITS is a scaled difference between predicted values for the $i$th case when the regression is estimated with and without the $i$th observation and hence the name.

The mechanical relationship between DFITS and Cook's Distance $D_i$ (Bollen and Jackman 1990, 266) is

$$D_i = \frac{1}{k} \frac{s_{(i)}^2}{s^2} \text{DFITS}_i^2$$

where $k$ is the number of variables (including the constant) in the regression, $s$ is the root mean square error of the regression, and $s_{(i)}$ is the root mean square error when the $i$th observation is omitted. Viewed more traditionally, $D_i$ is a scaled measure of the distance between the coefficient vectors when the $i$th observation is omitted.

The mechanical relationship between DFITS and Welsch's Distance $W_i$ (Chatterjee and Hadi 1988, 123) is

$$W_i = \text{DFITS}_i \sqrt{\frac{n-1}{1 - h_i}}$$

The more traditional interpretation of $W_i$ is difficult as it is based on the empirical influence curve. Note that whereas DFITS and Cook's distance are quite similar, the Welsch distance measure includes another normalization by leverage.

Belsley, Kuh, and Welsch (1980, 28) suggest that DFITS values greater than $2\sqrt{k/n}$ deserve further investigation and so values of Cook's distance greater than $4/n$ should also be examined (Bollen and Jackman 1990, 265–266). Following similar logic, the cutoff for Welsch distance is approximately $3\sqrt{k}$ (Chatterjee and Hadi 1988, 124).

▷ Example

Using our `price` on `weight`, `mpg`, `forXmpg`, and `foreign` model, we can obtain the DFITS influence measure by typing

    . predict dfits, dfits

Note that we did not specify `if e(sample)` in computing the DFITS statistic. DFITS is only available over the estimation sample, so specifying `if e(sample)` would have been redundant. It would have done no harm, but it would not have changed the results.

Our model has $k = 5$ independent variables ($k$ includes the constant) and $n = 74$ observations; following the $2\sqrt{k/n}$ cutoff advice:

    . list make price e dfits if dfits>2*sqrt(5/74)

|     | make            | price  | e        | dfits    |
|-----|-----------------|--------|----------|----------|
| 40. | Cad. Eldorado   | 14,500 | 7271.96  | .9564455 |
| 43. | Linc. Versailles| 13,466 | 6560.912 | .8760136 |
| 59. | Linc. Mark V    | 13,594 | 3109.193 | .5200413 |
| 62. | Ford Fiesta     | 4,389  | 3164.872 | .5724172 |
| 70. | Cad. Seville    | 15,906 | 5036.348 | 1.356619 |

Calculating Cook's distance and listing the observations greater than the suggested $4/n$ cutoff,

    . predict cooksd if e(sample), cooksd
    . list make price e cooksd if cooksd>4/74

|     | make            | price  | e         | cooksd   |
|-----|-----------------|--------|-----------|----------|
| 40. | Cad. Eldorado   | 14,500 | 7271.96   | .1492676 |
| 43. | Linc. Versailles| 13,466 | 6560.912  | .1308004 |
| 62. | Ford Fiesta     | 4,389  | 3164.872  | .0638815 |
| 70. | Cad. Seville    | 15,906 | 5036.348  | .3328515 |
| 71. | Plym. Arrow     | 4,647  | -3312.968 | .1700736 |

It is worth comparing this list with the preceding one.

Finally, using Welsch distance and the suggested $3\sqrt{k}$ cutoff,

    . predict wd, welsch
    . list make price e wd if wd>3*sqrt(5)

|     | make            | price  | e        | wd       |
|-----|-----------------|--------|----------|----------|
| 40. | Cad. Eldorado   | 14,500 | 7271.96  | 8.394372 |
| 43. | Linc. Versailles| 13,466 | 6560.912 | 7.703005 |
| 70. | Cad. Seville    | 15,906 | 5036.348 | 12.81125 |

Note that here we did not need to specify `if e(sample)` since `welsch` automatically restricts the prediction to the estimation sample.

◁

## COVRATIO

COVRATIO (Belsley, Kuh, and Welsch 1980) measures the influence of the $i$th observation by considering the effect on the variance–covariance matrix of the estimates. The measure is the ratio of the determinants of the covariances matrix, with and without the $i$th observation. The resulting formula is

$$\text{COVRATIO}_i = \frac{1}{1 - h_i} \left( \frac{n - k - \widehat{e}_i^2}{n - k - 1} \right)^k$$

where $\widehat{e}_i$ is the standardized residual.

For noninfluential observations, the value of COVRATIO is approximately 1. Large values of the residuals or large values of leverage will cause deviations from 1, although if both are large, COVRATIO may tend back toward 1 and therefore not identify such observations (Chatterjee and Hadi 1988, 139).

Belsley, Kuh, and Welsch (1980) suggest that observations for which

$$|\text{COVRATIO}_i - 1| \geq \frac{3k}{n}$$

are worthy of further examination.

▷ Example

Using our **price** on **weight**, **mpg**, **forXmpg**, and **foreign** model, we can obtain the COVRATIO measure and list the observations outside the suggested cutoff by typing

```
. predict covr, covratio
. list make price e covr if abs(covr-1)>=3*5/74

          make            price        e         covr
40. Cad. Eldorado        14,500   7271.9604    0.381424
43. Linc. Versailles     13,466   6560.9116    0.476170
65. Audi 5000             9,690    591.2883    1.206842
67. Volvo 260            11,995   1327.6681    1.211888
68. Datsun 210            4,589     19.8183    1.284801
69. Subaru               3,798   -909.5894    1.264677
70. Cad. Seville         15,906   5036.3481    0.738697
72. Plym. Champ           4,425   1621.7467    1.277820
73. Peugeot 604          12,990   1037.1838    1.348219
74. VW Diesel             5,397    999.7209    1.630653
```

The **covratio** option automatically restricts the prediction to the estimation sample.

◁

## DFBETAs

DFBETAs are perhaps the most direct influence measure of interest to model builders. DFBETAs focus on one coefficient and measure the difference between the regression coefficient when the $i$th observation is included and excluded, the difference being scaled by the estimated standard error of the coefficient. Belsley, Kuh, and Welsch (1980, 28) suggest observations with $|\text{DFBETA}_i| > 2/\sqrt{n}$ as deserving special attention, but it is also common practice to use 1 (Bollen and Jackman 1990, 267), meaning that the observation shifted the estimate at least one standard error.

▷ Example

Using our **price** on **weight**, **mpg**, **forXmpg**, and **foreign** model, let us first ask which observations have the greatest impact on the determination of the coefficient on **foreign**. We will use the suggested $2/\sqrt{n}$ cutoff:

```
. predict dfor, dfbeta(foreign)
. list make price foreign dfor if abs(dfor)>2/sqrt(74)

          make            price   foreign        dfor
12. Cad. Eldorado        14,500  Domestic   -.5290519
13. Cad. Seville         15,906  Domestic    .8243419
28. Linc. Versailles     13,466  Domestic   -.5283729
42. Plym. Arrow           4,647  Domestic   -.6622424
43. Plym. Champ           4,425  Domestic    .2371104
64. Peugeot 604          12,990   Foreign    .2552032
69. Toyota Corona         5,719   Foreign   -.256431
```

Note that the Cadillac Seville shifted the `foreign` coefficient .82 standard deviations!

Now let us ask which observations have the greatest effect on the `mpg` coefficient:

```
. predict dmpg, dfbeta(mpg)
. list make price mpg dmpg if abs(dmpg)>2/sqrt(74)
        make              price       mpg       dmpg
12. Cad. Eldorado        14,500        14   -.5970351
13. Cad. Seville         15,906        21    1.134269
28. Linc. Versailles     13,466        14   -.6069287
42. Plym. Arrow           4,647        28   -.8925859
43. Plym. Champ           4,425        34    .3186909
```

Once again we see the Cadillac Seville heading the list, suggesting that our regression results may be dominated by this one car.

◁

▷ Example

You can use `predict, dfbeta()` or the `dfbeta` command to generate the DFBETAs. `dfbeta` makes up names for the new variables automatically and, without arguments, generates the DFBETAs for all the variables in the regression:

```
. dfbeta
            DFweight:  DFbeta(weight)
              DFmpg:  DFbeta(mpg)
          DFforXmpg:  DFbeta(forXmpg)
          DFforeign:  DFbeta(foreign)
```

`dfbeta` created four new variables in our dataset: DFweight, containing the DFBETAs for `weight`; DFmpg, containing the DFBETAs for `mpg`; and so on. Alternatively, had we only wanted the DFBETAs for `mpg` and `weight`, we might have typed

```
. dfbeta mpg weight
              DFmpg:  DFbeta(mpg)
            DFweight:  DFbeta(weight)
```

In the above example, we typed `dfbeta mpg weight` instead of `dfbeta`—had we typed `dfbeta` followed by `dfbeta mpg weight`, here is what would have happened:

```
. dfbeta
            DFweight:  DFbeta(weight)
              DFmpg:  DFbeta(mpg)
          DFforXmpg:  DFbeta(forXmpg)
          DFforeign:  DFbeta(foreign)
. dfbeta mpg weight
                DF1:  DFbeta(mpg)
                DF2:  DFbeta(weight)
```

`dfbeta` would have made up different names for the new variables. `dfbeta` never replaces existing variables—it instead makes up a different name, so you need to pay attention to `dfbeta`'s output.

◁

# Calculate variance inflation factors with vif

Problems arise in regression when the predictors are highly correlated. In this situation, there may be a significant change in the regression coefficients if one adds or deletes an independent variable. The estimated standard errors of the fitted coefficients are inflated, or the estimated coefficients may not be statistically significant even though a statistical relation exists between the dependent and independent variables.

Data analysts rely on these facts to check informally for the presence of multicollinearity. vif, another command for use after **regress**, calculates the variance inflation factors and tolerances for each of the independent variables.

The output shows the variance inflation factors together with their reciprocals. Some analysts compare the reciprocals with a predetermined tolerance. In the comparison, if the reciprocal of the VIF is smaller than the tolerance, the associated predictor variable is removed from the regression model. However, most analysts rely on informal rules of thumb applied to the VIF; see Chatterjee, Hadi, and Price (2000). According to these rules, there is evidence of multicollinearity if

1. The largest VIF is greater than 10 (some choose a more conservative threshold value of 30).

2. The mean of all the VIFs is considerably larger than 1.

▷ Example

We examine a regression model fit using the ubiquitous automobile dataset:

```
. regress price mpg rep78 trunk headroom length turn displ gear_ratio
```

| Source | SS | df | MS | | | Number of obs = | 69 |
|---|---|---|---|---|---|---|---|
| Model | 264102049 | 8 | 33012756.2 | | | F( 8, 60) = | 6.33 |
| Residual | 312694909 | 60 | 5211581.82 | | | Prob > F     = | 0.0000 |
| | | | | | | R-squared    = | 0.4579 |
| | | | | | | Adj R-squared = | 0.3856 |
| Total | 576796959 | 68 | 8482308.22 | | | Root MSE     = | 2282.9 |

| price | Coef. | Std. Err. | t | P>\|t\| | [95% Conf. Interval] | |
|---|---|---|---|---|---|---|
| mpg | -144.84 | 82.12751 | -1.76 | 0.083 | -309.1195 | 19.43948 |
| rep78 | 727.5783 | 337.6107 | 2.16 | 0.035 | 52.25638 | 1402.9 |
| trunk | 44.02061 | 108.141 | 0.41 | 0.685 | -172.2935 | 260.3347 |
| headroom | -807.0996 | 435.5802 | -1.85 | 0.069 | -1678.39 | 64.19061 |
| length | -8.688914 | 34.89848 | -0.25 | 0.804 | -78.49626 | 61.11843 |
| turn | -177.9064 | 137.3455 | -1.30 | 0.200 | -452.6383 | 96.82551 |
| displacement | 30.73146 | 7.576952 | 4.06 | 0.000 | 15.5753 | 45.88762 |
| gear_ratio | 1500.119 | 1110.959 | 1.35 | 0.182 | -722.1303 | 3722.368 |
| _cons | 6691.976 | 7457.906 | 0.90 | 0.373 | -8226.057 | 21610.01 |

```
. vif
```

| Variable | VIF | 1/VIF |
|---|---|---|
| length | 8.22 | 0.121614 |
| displacement | 6.50 | 0.153860 |
| turn | 4.85 | 0.205997 |
| gear_ratio | 3.45 | 0.290068 |
| mpg | 3.03 | 0.330171 |
| trunk | 2.88 | 0.347444 |
| headroom | 1.80 | 0.554917 |
| rep78 | 1.46 | 0.686147 |
| Mean VIF | 4.02 | |

The results are mixed. Although we do not have any VIFs greater than 10, the mean VIF is greater than 1, though not considerably so. One could continue the investigation of collinearity, but given that other authors advise that collinearity is only a problem when VIFs exist that are greater than 30 (contradicting our rule above), we will not do so here.

◁

▷ Example

This example comes from a dataset described in Neter, Wasserman, and Kutner (1989) which examines body fat as modeled by caliper measurements on the triceps, midarm, and thigh.

```
. use bodyfat
(Body Fat)
. regress bodyfat tricep thigh midarm
```

| Source | SS | df | MS |
|---|---|---|---|
| Model | 396.984607 | 3 | 132.328202 |
| Residual | 98.4049068 | 16 | 6.15030667 |
| Total | 495.389513 | 19 | 26.0731323 |

Number of obs = 20
F( 3, 16) = 21.52
Prob > F = 0.0000
R-squared = 0.8014
Adj R-squared = 0.7641
Root MSE = 2.48

| bodyfat | Coef. | Std. Err. | t | P>|t| | [95% Conf. Interval] | |
|---|---|---|---|---|---|---|
| triceps | 4.334085 | 3.015511 | 1.44 | 0.170 | -2.058512 | 10.72668 |
| thigh | -2.856842 | 2.582015 | -1.11 | 0.285 | -8.330468 | 2.616785 |
| midarm | -2.186056 | 1.595499 | -1.37 | 0.190 | -5.568362 | 1.19625 |
| _cons | 117.0844 | 99.78238 | 1.17 | 0.258 | -94.44474 | 328.6136 |

```
. vif
```

| Variable | VIF | 1/VIF |
|---|---|---|
| triceps | 708.84 | 0.001411 |
| thigh | 564.34 | 0.001772 |
| midarm | 104.61 | 0.009560 |
| Mean VIF | 459.26 | |

In this example, we see very strong evidence of multicollinearity in our model. Further investigation reveals that the measurements on the thigh and the triceps are highly correlated:

```
. corr triceps thigh midarm
(obs=20)
```

| | triceps | thigh | midarm |
|---|---|---|---|
| triceps | 1.0000 | | |
| thigh | 0.9238 | 1.0000 | |
| midarm | 0.4578 | 0.0847 | 1.0000 |

If we remove the predictor `tricep` from the model (since it had the highest VIF), we get

```
. regress bodyfat thigh midarm
```

| Source | SS | df | MS |
|---|---|---|---|
| Model | 384.279748 | 2 | 192.139874 |
| Residual | 111.109765 | 17 | 6.53586854 |
| Total | 495.389513 | 19 | 26.0731323 |

Number of obs = 20
F( 2, 17) = 29.40
Prob > F = 0.0000
R-squared = 0.7757
Adj R-squared = 0.7493
Root MSE = 2.5565

| bodyfat | Coef. | Std. Err. | t | P>\|t\| | [95% Conf. Interval] | |
|---|---|---|---|---|---|---|
| thigh | .8508818 | .1124482 | 7.57 | 0.000 | .6136367 | 1.088127 |
| midarm | .0960295 | .1613927 | 0.60 | 0.560 | -.2444792 | .4365383 |
| _cons | -25.99696 | 6.99732 | -3.72 | 0.002 | -40.76001 | -11.2339 |

. vif

| Variable | VIF | 1/VIF |
|---|---|---|
| midarm | 1.01 | 0.992831 |
| thigh | 1.01 | 0.992831 |
| Mean VIF | 1.01 | |

Note how the coefficients change and how the estimated standard errors for each of the regression coefficients become much smaller. The calculated value of $R^2$ for the overall regression for the subset model does not appreciably decline when we remove the correlated predictor. Removing an independent variable from the model is one way to deal with multicollinearity. Other methods include ridge regression, weighted least squares, and restricting the use of the fitted model to data that follow the same pattern of multicollinearity. In economic studies, it is sometimes possible to estimate the regression coefficients from different subsets of the data using cross-section and time series.

◁

# Saved Results

ovtest saves in r():

Scalars

| | | | |
|---|---|---|---|
| r(p) | two-sided $p$-value | r(df) | degrees of freedom |
| r(F) | $F$ statistic | r(df_r) | residual degrees of freedom |

hettest saves in r():

Scalars

| | | | |
|---|---|---|---|
| r(df) | degrees of freedom | r(chi2) | $\chi^2$ |

# Acknowledgment

ovtest and hettest are based on programs originally written by Richard Goldstein (1991, 1992).

# Methods and Formulas

All regression fit and diagnostic commands are implemented as ado-files.

The formulas for all the statistics produced by predict after regress can be found under the [R] regress entry.

For all the regression diagnostics, we assume that a regression model has already been estimated as

$$\mathbf{y} = \mathbf{Xb} + \mathbf{e}$$

where $\mathbf{X}$ is $n \times k$. Formulas for obtaining those estimates are given in [R] **regress**. Let $s^2$ be the mean square error of the regression.

The omitted-variable test (Ramsey 1969) reported by **ovtest** estimates the regression $y_i = \mathbf{x}_i\mathbf{b} + \mathbf{z}_i\mathbf{t} + u_i$ and then performs a standard $F$ test of $\mathbf{t} = \mathbf{0}$. The default test uses $\mathbf{z}_i = (\widehat{y}_i^2, \widehat{y}_i^3, \widehat{y}_i^4)$. If **rhs** is specified, $\mathbf{z}_i = (x_{1i}^2, x_{1i}^3, x_{1i}^4, x_{2i}^2, \ldots, x_{mi}^4)$. In either case, the variables are normalized to have minimum 0 and maximum 1 before powers are calculated.

The heteroskedasticity test (Cook and Weisberg 1983) models $\mathrm{Var}(e_i) = \sigma^2 \exp(\mathbf{z}\mathbf{t})$ where $\mathbf{z}$ is either a variable list specified by the user or equal to the fitted values $\mathbf{x}\widehat{\beta}$. The test is of $\mathbf{t} = \mathbf{0}$. Mechanically, **hettest** estimates the model $\widehat{e}_i^2 = a + \mathbf{z}_i\mathbf{t} + v_i$ and then forms the score test $S$ equal to the model sum of squares divided by 2. Under the null hypothesis, $S$ has the $\chi^2$ distribution with $m$ degrees of freedom, where $m$ is the number of columns of $\mathbf{z}$.

The Durbin–Watson $d$ statistic reported by **dwstat** is

$$
d = \frac{\sum\limits_{j=1}^{n-1} (\widehat{e}_{i+1} - \widehat{e}_i)^2}{\sum\limits_{j=1}^{n} \widehat{e}_i^2}
$$

where $\widehat{e}_i$ represents the residual of the $i$th observation.

The variance inflation factor (VIF) (Chatterjee, Hadi, and Price 2000, 240–242) for $x_j$ is given by

$$
\mathrm{VIF}(x_j) = \frac{1}{1 - R_j^2}
$$

where $R_j^2$ is the square of the multiple correlation coefficient that results when $x_j$ is regressed against all the other explanatory variables.

# References

Baum, C. F. and V. Wiggins. 2000a. sg135: Test for autoregressive conditional heteroskedasticity in regression error distribution. *Stata Technical Bulletin* 55: 13–14.

———. 2000b. sg136: Tests for serial correlation in regression error distribution. *Stata Technical Bulletin* 55: 14–15.

Baum, C. F., N. J. Cox, and V. Wiggins. 2000. sg137: Tests for heteroskedasticity in regression error distribution. *Stata Technical Bulletin* 55: 15–17.

Belsley, D. A., E. Kuh, and R. E. Welsch. 1980. *Regression Diagnostics*. New York: John Wiley & Sons.

Bollen, K. A. and R. W. Jackman. 1990. Regression diagnostics: an expository treatment of outliers and influential cases. In *Modern Methods of Data Analysis*, ed. J. Fox and J. S. Long, 257–291. Newbury Park, CA: Sage Publications.

Chatterjee, S. and A. S. Hadi. 1986. Influential observations, high leverage points, and outliers in linear regression. *Statistical Science* 1: 379–416.

———. 1988. *Sensitivity Analysis in Linear Regression*. New York: John Wiley & Sons.

Chatterjee, S., A. S. Hadi, and B. Price. 2000. *Regression Analysis by Example*. 3d ed. New York: John Wiley & Sons.

Cook, R. D. 1977. Detection of influential observations in linear regression. *Technometrics* 19: 15–18.

Cook, R. D. and S. Weisberg. 1982. *Residuals and Influence in Regression*. New York: Chapman & Hall.

———. 1983. Diagnostics for heteroscedasticity in regression. *Biometrika* 70: 1–10.

Durbin, J. and G. S. Watson. 1950. Testing for serial correlation in least-squares regression. *Biometrika* 37: 409–428.

——. 1951. Testing for serial correlation in least-squares regression. *Biometrika* 38: 159–178.

Ezekiel, M. 1924. A method of handling curvilinear correlation for any number of variables. *Journal of the American Statistical Association* 19: 431–453.

Goldstein, R. 1991. srd5: Ramsey test for heteroskedasticity and omitted variables. *Stata Technical Bulletin* 2: 27. Reprinted in *Stata Technical Bulletin Reprints*, vol. 1, p. 177.

——. 1992. srd14: Cook–Weisberg test of heteroskedasticity. *Stata Technical Bulletin* 10: 27–28. Reprinted in *Stata Technical Bulletin Reprints*, vol. 2, pp. 183–184.

Hamilton, L. C. 1992. *Regression with Graphics*. Pacific Grove, CA: Brooks/Cole Publishing Company.

Hardin, J. W. 1995. sg32: Variance inflation factors and variance-decomposition proportions. *Stata Technical Bulletin* 24: 17–22. Reprinted in *Stata Technical Bulletin Reprints*, vol. 4, pp. 154–160.

Hoaglin, D. C. and P. J. Kempthorne. 1986. Comment [on Chatterjee and Hadi 1986]. *Statistical Science* 1: 408–412.

Hoaglin, D. C. and R. E. Welsch. 1978. The hat matrix in regression and ANOVA. *The American Statistician* 32: 17–22.

Larsen, W. A. and S. J. McCleary. 1972. The use of partial residual plots in regression analysis. *Technometrics* 14: 781–790.

Long, J. S. and J. Freese. 2000. sg145: Scalar measures of fit for regression models. *Stata Technical Bulletin* 56: 34–40.

Mallows, C. L. 1986. Augmented partial residuals. *Technometrics* 28: 313–319.

Mosteller, F. and J. W. Tukey. 1977. *Data Analysis and Regression*. Reading, MA: Addison–Wesley Publishing Company.

Neter, J., W. Wasserman, and M. H. Kutner. 1989. *Applied Linear Regression Models*. Homewood, IL: Irwin.

Ramsey, J. B. 1969. Tests for specification errors in classical linear least squares regression analysis. *Journal of the Royal Statistical Society*, Series B 31: 350–371.

Ramsey, J. B. and P. Schmidt. 1976. Some further results on the use of OLS and BLUS residuals in specification error tests. *Journal of the American Statistical Association* 71: 389–390.

Rousseeuw, P. J. and A. M. Leroy. 1987. *Robust Regression and Outlier Detection*. New York: John Wiley & Sons.

Ryan, T. P. 1997. *Modern Regression Methods*. New York: John Wiley & Sons.

Velleman, P. F. 1986. Comment [on Chatterjee and Hadi 1986]. *Statistical Science* 1: 412–413.

Velleman, P. F. and R. E. Welsch. 1981. Efficient computing of regression diagnostics. *The American Statistician* 35: 234–242.

Weisberg, S. 1985. *Applied Linear Regression*. 2d ed. New York: John Wiley & Sons.

Welsch, R. E. 1982. Influence functions and regression diagnostics. In *Modern Data Analysis*, ed. R. L. Launer and A. F. Siegel, 149–169. New York: Academic Press.

——. 1986. Comment [on Chatterjee and Hadi 1986]. *Statistical Science* 1: 403–405.

Welsch, R. E. and E. Kuh. 1977. *Technical Report 923-77: Linear Regression Diagnostics*. Cambridge, MA: Sloan School of Management, Massachusetts Institute of Technology.

## Also See

| | |
|---|---|
| **Complementary:** | [R] **predict**, [R] **regress** |
| **Background:** | [U] **23 Estimation and post-estimation commands**, *Stata Graphics Manual* |

# Title

---
**rename** — Rename variable
---

# Syntax

rename *old_varname new_varname*

renpfix *old_stub* [*new_stub*]

# Description

rename changes the name of an existing variable; the contents of the variable are unchanged.

renpfix renames all variables that start with *old_stub* to start with *new_stub*. If *new_stub* is not specified, the *old_stub* prefix is removed.

# Remarks

▷ Example

It is easy to make poor choices when naming variables. With rename, you can change the names of variables freely. For instance, say you have data on employees. The data contain the variables empno, sex, and inc. You decide to rename the inc variable:

    . rename inc income

Your data now contain the three variables empno, sex, and income.

◁

▷ Example

You have a number of variables which start with the prefix year (the variables are year86, year87, and so on). You wish to rename them to begin with the prefix yr:

    . renpfix year yr

The variables are now named yr86, yr87, and so on.

◁

# Methods and Formulas

renpfix is implemented as an ado-file.

# Also See

**Complementary:**     [R] **generate**

116

# Title

> **reshape** — Convert data from wide to long and vice versa

# Syntax

*Basic syntax*

reshape wide *varlist*, i(*varlist*) [j(*varname* [*values*]) string atwl(*chars*)]

reshape long *varlist*, i(*varlist*) [j(*varname* [*values*]) string atwl(*chars*)]

reshape wide

reshape long

reshape error

*Advanced syntax*

reshape i *varlist*

reshape j *varname* [*values*] [, string]

reshape xij *fvarlist* [, atwl(*chars*)]

reshape xi [*varlist*]

reshape [query]

reshape clear

where *values* is $\quad \#[-\#]\ [\#[-\#]\ \ldots]$

and *fvarlist* is a list of variable names, some of which may have an @ character denoting where the j suffix appears.

# Description

reshape converts data from *wide* to *long* form and vice versa.

# Options

i(*varlist*) specifies the variable(s) whose unique values denote a logical observation.

j(*varname* [ *values* ]) specifies the variable whose unique values denote a subobservation. *values* list the unique values to be used from *varname*, which typically are not explicitly stated since reshape will determine them automatically from the data.

string specifies that the j() may contain string values.

atwl(*chars*) specifies that *chars* should be substituted for the @ character when converting the data to the long form.

117

# Remarks

Remarks are presented under the headings

> *Description of basic syntax*
> *Mistakes*
> *Other mistakes*
> *reshape long and reshape wide without arguments*
> *Missing variables*
> *Advanced issues with basic syntax: i()*
> *Advanced issues with basic syntax: j()*
> *Advanced issues with basic syntax: xij*
> *Advanced issues with basic syntax: the atwl() option*
> *Advanced issues with basic syntax: string identifiers for j()*
> *Advanced issues with basic syntax: second-level nesting*
> *Description of advanced syntax*

## Description of basic syntax

Think of the data as a collection of observations $X_{ij}$. One such collection might be

| i | | $\ldots\ldots X_{ij} \ldots\ldots$ | | | | i | j | | $X_{ij}$ |
|---|---|---|---|---|---|---|---|---|---|
| id | sex | inc80 | inc81 | inc82 | | id | year | sex | inc |
| 1 | 0 | 5000 | 5500 | 6000 | | 1 | 80 | 0 | 5000 |
| 2 | 1 | 2000 | 2200 | 3300 | | 1 | 81 | 0 | 5500 |
| 3 | 0 | 3000 | 2000 | 1000 | | 1 | 82 | 0 | 6000 |
| | | | | | | 2 | 80 | 1 | 2000 |
| | | | | | | 2 | 81 | 1 | 2200 |
| | | | | | | 2 | 82 | 1 | 3300 |
| | | | | | | 3 | 80 | 0 | 3000 |
| | | | | | | 3 | 81 | 0 | 2000 |
| | | | | | | 3 | 82 | 0 | 1000 |

reshape converts from one form to the other:

```
. reshape long inc, i(id) j(year)        /* goes from left form to right */
. reshape wide inc, i(id) j(year)        /* goes from right form to left */
```

In this example, one observation is, at least logically speaking,

| i | | $\ldots\ldots X_{ij} \ldots\ldots$ | | | | i | j | | $X_{ij}$ |
|---|---|---|---|---|---|---|---|---|---|
| id | sex | inc80 | inc81 | inc82 | | id | year | sex | inc |
| 1 | 0 | 5000 | 5500 | 6000 | or | 1 | 80 | 0 | 5000 |
| | | | | | | 1 | 81 | 0 | 5500 |
| | | | | | | 1 | 82 | 0 | 6000 |

and you should think of this single observation as $X_{ij}$.

The i variable denotes the logical observation and is often called the group identifier. i is the variable id in our data.

j denotes the subobservation and is often called the subgroup or within-group identifier. The variable year (when the data are in long form) corresponds to j. There is no j variable in the wide form. Instead, the inc variable is suffixed with the values of j, forming inc80, inc81, and inc82.

That leaves only the variable sex, which we did not specify when we typed

```
. reshape long inc, i(id) j(year)
```

or

```
. reshape wide inc, i(id) j(year)
```

Since **sex** is not specified, it is assumed to be constant within **i**. **reshape** verifies this assumption before converting the data.

▷ Example

Here is an example with two $X_{ij}$ variables with the data in wide form:

```
. list, nodisplay
        id   sex   inc80   inc81   inc82   ue80   ue81   ue82
  1.     1     0    5000    5500    6000      0      1      0
  2.     2     1    2000    2200    3300      1      0      0
  3.     3     0    3000    2000    1000      0      0      1
```

To convert this into the long form, we type

```
. reshape long inc ue, i(id) j(year)
(note: j = 80 81 82)
Data                                    wide    ->    long
─────────────────────────────────────────────────────────────
Number of obs.                             3    ->       9
Number of variables                        8    ->       5
j variable (3 values)                           ->    year
xij variables:
                        inc80 inc81 inc82      ->    inc
                          ue80 ue81 ue82       ->    ue
─────────────────────────────────────────────────────────────
```

Note that there is no variable named **year** in our original, wide dataset. **year** will be a new variable in our long dataset. After this conversion we have

```
. list
        id   year   sex    inc    ue
  1.     1     80     0   5000     0
  2.     1     81     0   5500     1
  3.     1     82     0   6000     0
  4.     2     80     1   2000     1
  5.     2     81     1   2200     0
  6.     2     82     1   3300     0
  7.     3     80     0   3000     0
  8.     3     81     0   2000     0
  9.     3     82     0   1000     1
```

We can return to our original dataset using **reshape wide**.

```
. reshape wide inc ue, i(id) j(year)
(note:  j = 80 81 82)
Data                                    long    ->    wide
─────────────────────────────────────────────────────────────
Number of obs.                             9    ->       3
Number of variables                        5    ->       8
j variable (3 values)                   year    ->    (dropped)
xij variables:
                                         inc    ->    inc80 inc81 inc82
                                          ue    ->    ue80 ue81 ue82
─────────────────────────────────────────────────────────────
```

```
. list, nodisplay
       id   inc80   ue80   inc81   ue81   inc82   ue82   sex
  1.    1    5000      0    5500      1    6000      0     0
  2.    2    2000      1    2200      0    3300      0     1
  3.    3    3000      0    2000      0    1000      1     0
```

Converting from wide to long creates the j (year) variable. Converting from long to wide drops the j (year) variable.

◁

## ❏ Technical Note

When starting with data in wide form, if you do not have a group identifier variable (the i (*varlist*) required option), you can easily create one by using generate; see [R] **generate**. For instance, in the last example, if we did not have the id variable in our dataset, we could have created it by typing

```
. generate id = _n
```

❏

## Mistakes

In many cases, reshape detects when the data do not conform to the assumptions implicit in reshaping; an error is issued and the data remain unchanged.

## ▷ Example

The following wide data contain a mistake.

```
. list
         id      sex     inc80     inc81     inc82
  1.      1        0      5000      5500      6000
  2.      2        1      2000      2200      3300
  3.      3        0      3000      2000      1000
  4.      2        0      2400      2500      2400
. reshape long inc, i(id) j(year)
(note:   j = 80 81 82)
i=id does not uniquely identify the observations;
there are multiple observations with the same value of id.
Type "reshape error" for a listing of the problem observations.
r(9);
```

The i variable must be unique when the data are in the wide form; we said i(id), yet we have two observations for which id is 2. (Is person 2 a male or female?)

◁

## ▷ Example

It is not a mistake when the i variable is repeated when the data are in the long form, but the following data have a similar mistake.

```
. list
         id     year      sex       inc
  1.      1       80        0      5000
  2.      1       81        0      5500
  3.      1       82        0      6000
  4.      1       81        0      5400
. reshape wide inc, i(id) j(year)
(note:   j = 80 81 82)
year not unique within id;
there are multiple observations at the same year within id.
Type "reshape error" for a listing of the problem observations.
r(9);
```

In the long form, i(id) does not have to be unique, but j(year) must be unique within i; otherwise, what is the value of inc in 1981 for which id==1?

reshape told us to type reshape error to view the problem observations.

```
. reshape error
(note:  j = 80 81 82)

i (id) indicates the top-level grouping such as subject id.
j (year) indicates the subgrouping such as time.
The data are in the long form;  j should be unique within i.

There are multiple observations on the same year within id.

The following 2 out of 4 observations have repeated year values:
              id       year
     2.        1         81
     3.        1         81

(data now sorted by id year)
```

◁

## ▷ Example

Finally, consider some (long form) data which have no mistakes. We list the first four observations.

```
. list in 1/4
            id      year     sex      inc      ue
     1.      1       80       0      5000       0
     2.      1       81       0      5500       1
     3.      1       82       0      6000       0
     4.      2       80       1      2000       1
```

Say what we type to convert it to wide form, however, is mistaken in that we forget to mention the ue variable (which varies within person).

```
. reshape wide inc, i(id) j(year)
(note:  j = 80 81 82)
ue not constant within id
Type "reshape error" for a listing of the problem observations.
r(9);
```

In this case, reshape observed that ue was not constant within i and so could not restructure the data so that there were single observations on i. We should have typed

```
. reshape wide inc ue, i(id) j(year)
```

◁

In summary, there are three cases in which reshape will refuse to convert the data:

1. The data are in the wide form and i is not unique;

2. The data are in the long form and j is not unique within i;

3. The data are in the long form and an unmentioned variable is not constant within i.

## Other mistakes

There are obviously other mistakes one might make, but in such situations reshape will probably convert the data and produce a surprising result.

▷ Example

Suppose that we forget to mention that variable `ue` varies within `id` in the following wide data.

```
. list, nodisplay
        id   sex   inc80   inc81   inc82   ue80   ue81   ue82
 1.      1     0    5000    5500    6000      0      1      0
 2.      2     1    2000    2200    3300      1      0      0
 3.      3     0    3000    2000    1000      0      0      1
. reshape long inc, i(id) j(year)
(note: j = 80 81 82)
Data                                wide   ->   long

Number of obs.                         3   ->      9
Number of variables                    8   ->      7
j variable (3 values)                      ->   year
xij variables:
                    inc80 inc81 inc82   ->   inc

. list, nodisplay
        id    year   sex    inc   ue80   ue81   ue82
 1.      1      80     0   5000      0      1      0
 2.      1      81     0   5500      0      1      0
 3.      1      82     0   6000      0      1      0
 4.      2      80     1   2000      1      0      0
 5.      2      81     1   2200      1      0      0
 6.      2      82     1   3300      1      0      0
 7.      3      80     0   3000      0      0      1
 8.      3      81     0   2000      0      0      1
 9.      3      82     0   1000      0      0      1
```

We did not state that `ue` varied within `i`, so the variables `ue80`, `ue81`, and `ue82` were left as is. `reshape` did not complain. There is no real problem here because no information has been lost. In fact, this may actually be the result we wanted. Probably, however, we simply forgot to include `ue` among the $X_{ij}$ variables.

If you obtain an unanticipated result, here is how to undo it:

1. If you typed `reshape long` ... to produce the result, type `reshape wide` (without arguments) to undo it.

2. If you typed `reshape wide` ... to produce the result, type `reshape long` (without arguments) to undo it.

So we can type

```
. reshape wide
```

to get back to our original data and then type the `reshape long` command that we intended:

```
. reshape long inc ue, i(id) j(year)
```

◁

## reshape long and reshape wide without arguments

Whenever you type a `reshape long` or `reshape wide` command with arguments, `reshape` remembers it. Thus, you might

```
. reshape long inc ue, i(id) j(year)
```

and work with the data like that. You could then type

> . reshape wide

to convert the data back to the wide form. Then later you could type

> . reshape long

to convert them back to the long form. If you save the data, you can even continue using reshape wide and reshape long without arguments during a future Stata session.

Be careful. If you create new $X_{ij}$ variables, you must tell reshape about them by typing out the full reshape command, although no real damage will be done if you forget. If you are converting from long to wide form, reshape itself will catch your error and refuse. If you are converting from wide to long, reshape will convert the data, but the result will be surprising: remember what happened when we forgot to mention variable ue and ended up with ue80, ue81, and ue82 in our long data; see the example in the section above titled *Other mistakes*. You can reshape long to undo the unwanted change and then try again.

## Missing variables

When converting data from wide form to long form, reshape does not demand that all the variables exist. Missing variables are treated like variables with missing observations.

▷ Example

Let's drop ue81 from the wide form of the data.

```
. list, nodisplay

        id    sex    inc80    inc81    inc82    ue80    ue82
  1.     1      0     5000     5500     6000       0       0
  2.     2      1     2000     2200     3300       1       0
  3.     3      0     3000     2000     1000       0       1

. reshape long inc ue, i(id) j(year)
(note:   j = 80 81 82)
(note: ue81 not found)

Data                                    wide   ->   long

Number of obs.                             3   ->      9
Number of variables                        7   ->      5
j variable (3 values)                          ->   year
xij variables:
                          inc80 inc81 inc82   ->   inc
                          ue80 ue81 ue82      ->   ue

. list

        id    year    sex     inc     ue
  1.     1      80      0    5000      0
  2.     1      81      0    5500      .
  3.     1      82      0    6000      0
  4.     2      80      1    2000      1
  5.     2      81      1    2200      .
  6.     2      82      1    3300      0
  7.     3      80      0    3000      0
  8.     3      81      0    2000      .
  9.     3      82      0    1000      1
```

Notice that `reshape` placed missing values where ue81 values were unavailable. If we reshaped these data back to the wide form by typing

    . reshape wide inc ue, i(id) j(year)

the variable ue81 would be created and it would contain all missing values.

◁

## Advanced issues with basic syntax: i()

The i() option can indicate one i variable (as our past examples have illustrated) or multiple variables. An example of multiple i variables would be hospital id and patient id within each hospital.

    . reshape ... , i(hid pid)

Unique pairs of values for hid and pid in the data define the grouping variable for `reshape`.

## Advanced issues with basic syntax: j()

The j() option takes a variable name (as our past examples have illustrated) or a variable name and a list of values. When the values are not provided, `reshape` deduces them from the data. Specifying the values with the j() option is rarely needed.

`reshape` never makes a mistake when the data are in long form—when you type `reshape wide`. The values are easily obtained by tabulating the j variable.

`reshape` can make a mistake when the data are in wide form—when you type `reshape long` if your variables are poorly named. Pretend you have the variables inc80, inc81, and inc82, recording income in each of the indicated years, and you have a variable named inc2, which is not income but when the area was reincorporated. You type

    . reshape long inc, i(id) j(year)

`reshape` sees the variables inc2, inc80, inc81, and inc82 and decides that there are four groups j = 2, 80, 81, and 82.

The easiest way to solve the problem is to rename the inc2 variable to something other than 'inc' followed by a number; see [R] **rename**.

Alternatively, you can keep the name and specify the j values. To perform the reshape you would type

    . reshape long inc, i(id) j(year 80-82)

or

    . reshape long inc, i(id) j(year 80 81 82)

The dash notation for value ranges can be mixed with individual numbers. `reshape` would understand 80 82-87 89 91-95 as a valid values specification.

At the other extreme, you can omit the j() option altogether with `reshape long`. If you do, the j variable will be named _j.

## Advanced issues with basic syntax: xij

When specifying variable names, you may include @ characters to indicate where the numbers go.

▷ Example

Let's reshape the following data from wide to long:

```
. list, nodisplay
           id    sex   inc80r   inc81r   inc82r      ue80     ue81     ue82
  1.        1      0     5000     5500     6000         0        1        0
  2.        2      1     2000     2200     3300         1        0        0
  3.        3      0     3000     2000     1000         0        0        1
. reshape long inc@r ue, i(id) j(year)
(note:  j = 80 81 82)
Data                                      wide   ->   long

Number of obs.                               3   ->      9
Number of variables                          8   ->      5
j variable (3 values)                            ->   year
xij variables:
                   inc80r inc81r inc82r       ->   incr
                        ue80 ue81 ue82        ->   ue

. list
           id    year    sex    incr     ue
  1.        1      80      0    5000      0
  2.        1      81      0    5500      1
  3.        1      82      0    6000      0
  4.        2      80      1    2000      1
  5.        2      81      1    2200      0
  6.        2      82      1    3300      0
  7.        3      80      0    3000      0
  8.        3      81      0    2000      0
  9.        3      82      0    1000      1
```

At most one @ character may appear in each name. If no @ character appears, results are as if the @ character appeared at the end of the name. So the equivalent reshape command to the one above is

```
. reshape long inc@r ue@, i(id) j(year)
```

inc@r specifies variables named inc#r in the wide form and incr in the long form. The @ notation may similarly be used for converting data from long to wide:

```
. reshape wide inc@r ue, i(id) j(year)
```

◁

## Advanced issues with basic syntax: the atwl() option

Option atwl() is for use when @ characters are also specified. atwl stands for at-when-long. When you specify a name such as inc@r or ue@, in the long form the name becomes incr and ue, and the @ character is changed into nothing. atwl() allows you to change it into something.

If you specify atwl(X), the long form names become incXr and ueX. If you specify atwl(yr), the long form names become incyrr and ueyr.

## Advanced issues with basic syntax: string identifiers for j()

The string option allows j to take on string values.

▷ Example

Consider the following wide data on husbands and wives. In these data, incm is the income of the man and incf the income of the woman.

```
. list
           id      kids      incm      incf
  1.        1         0      5000      5500
  2.        2         1      2000      2200
  3.        3         2      3000      2000
```

These data can be reshaped into separate observations for males and females by typing

```
. reshape long inc, i(id) j(sex) string
(note:  j = f m)
```

| Data | wide | -> | long |
|------|------|-----|------|
| Number of obs. | 3 | -> | 6 |
| Number of variables | 4 | -> | 4 |
| j variable (2 values) | | -> | sex |
| xij variables: | | | |
| | incf incm | -> | inc |

The string option specifies that j will take on nonnumeric values. The result is

```
. list
           id      sex      kids       inc
  1.        1        f         0      5500
  2.        1        m         0      5000
  3.        2        f         1      2200
  4.        2        m         1      2000
  5.        3        f         2      2000
  6.        3        m         2      3000
```

sex will be a string variable. Similarly, these data can be converted from long to wide by typing

```
. reshape wide inc, i(id) j(sex) string
```

◁

Strings are not limited to being single characters or even of the same length. The location of the string identifier in the variable name may be specified using the @ notation.

▷ Example

Suppose our variables are named id, kids, incmale, and incfem.

```
. list
           id      kids    incmale    incfem
  1.        1         0      5000      5500
  2.        2         1      2000      2200
  3.        3         2      3000      2000
```

```
. reshape long inc, i(id) j(sex) string
(note:  j = fem male)
```

| Data | | wide | -> | long |
|---|---|---|---|---|
| Number of obs. | | 3 | -> | 6 |
| Number of variables | | 4 | -> | 4 |
| j variable (2 values) | | | -> | sex |
| xij variables: | | | | |
| | incfem incmale | | -> | inc |

```
. list
```

| | id | sex | kids | inc |
|---|---|---|---|---|
| 1. | 1 | fem | 0 | 5500 |
| 2. | 1 | male | 0 | 5000 |
| 3. | 2 | fem | 1 | 2200 |
| 4. | 2 | male | 1 | 2000 |
| 5. | 3 | fem | 2 | 2000 |
| 6. | 3 | male | 2 | 3000 |

If the wide data had variables named minc and finc, then the appropriate reshape command would have been

```
. reshape long @inc, i(id) j(sex) string
```

The resulting variable in the long format will be named inc.

As with numbers, strings may be placed in the middle of the variable names. If the variables were named incMome and incFome, the reshape command would be

```
. reshape long inc@ome, i(id) j(sex) string
```

Be careful with string identifiers because it is easy to be surprised by the result. Consider a person with wide data having variables named incm, incf, uem, uef, agem, and agef. To make the data long, the person types

```
. reshape long inc ue age, i(id) j(sex) string
```

Along with these variables, the person innocently has the variable agenda. reshape will decide the sexes are m, f, and nda. This would not happen without the string option if the variables were named inc0, inc1, ue0, ue1, age0, and age1, even with variable agenda present in the data.

◁

## Advanced issues with basic syntax: second-level nesting

Sometimes the data may have more than one possible j variable for reshaping; suppose your data have both a year variable and a sex variable. One logical observation in the data might be represented in any of the following four forms:

```
. list in 1/4    /* The long-long form */
```

| | hid | sex | year | inc |
|---|---|---|---|---|
| 1. | 1 | f | 90 | 3200 |
| 2. | 1 | f | 91 | 4700 |
| 3. | 1 | m | 90 | 4500 |
| 4. | 1 | m | 91 | 4600 |

```
. list in 1/2    /* The long-year wide-sex form */
```

| | hid | year | minc | finc |
|---|---|---|---|---|
| 1. | 1 | 90 | 4500 | 3200 |
| 2. | 1 | 91 | 4600 | 4700 |

```
. list in 1/2      /* The wide-year long-sex form */
            hid          sex          inc90            inc91
    1.        1            f          3200             4700
    2.        1            m          4500             4600

. list in 1        /* The wide-wide form */
            hid        minc90         minc91          finc90         finc91
    1.        1          4500           4600            3200           4700
```

**reshape** can convert any of these forms to any other. Converting all the way from the long–long form to the wide–wide form (or the wide–wide to the long–long, or the long–wide to the wide–long, or the wide–long to the long–wide) takes two **reshape** commands. Here is how we would do it:

| From | | To | | Command |
|------|-----|------|------|---------|
| year | sex | year | sex | |
| long | long | long | wide | reshape wide @inc, i(hid year) j(sex) string |
| long | wide | long | long | reshape long @inc, i(hid year) j(sex) string |
| long | long | wide | long | reshape wide inc, i(hid sex) j(year) |
| wide | long | long | long | reshape long inc, i(hid sex) j(year) |
| long | wide | wide | wide | reshape wide minc finc, i(hid) j(year) |
| wide | wide | long | wide | reshape long minc finc, i(hid) j(year) |
| wide | long | wide | wide | reshape wide @inc90 @inc91, i(hid) j(sex) string |
| wide | wide | wide | long | reshape long @inc90 @inc91, i(hid) j(sex) string |

## Description of advanced syntax

The advanced syntax is simply a different way of specifying the **reshape** command and it has one seldom-used feature that provides extra control. Rather than typing a single **reshape** command to describe the data and perform the conversion, such as

```
. reshape long inc, i(id) j(year)
```

you type a sequence of **reshape** commands. The initial commands describe the data and the last command performs the conversion:

```
. reshape i id
. reshape j year
. reshape xij inc
. reshape long
```

**reshape i** corresponds to i() in the basic syntax.

**reshape j** corresponds to j() in the basic syntax.

**reshape xij** corresponds to the variables specified in the basic syntax.

In addition, there is one more specification which has no counterpart in the basic syntax:

```
. reshape xi varlist
```

In the basic syntax, all unspecified variables are assumed to be constant within i. The advanced syntax works the same way unless you specify the **reshape xi** command. **reshape xi** names the constant-within-i variables. If you specify **reshape xi**, any variables that are not explicitly specified are dropped from the data during the conversion.

As a practical matter, it would probably be better if you explicitly dropped the unwanted variables before conversion. For instance, suppose the data have variables inc80, inc81, inc82, sex, age, and age2 and that you no longer want the age2 variable. You could specify

```
. reshape xi sex age
```

or

```
. drop age2
```

and leave `reshape xi` unspecified.

`reshape xi` does have one minor advantage. It saves `reshape` from going to the work of determining which variables are unspecified. This saves a relatively small amount of computer time.

Another advanced-syntax feature is `reshape query`. This is equivalent to typing `reshape` by itself. `reshape query` presents a report on what `reshape` parameters have been defined. `reshape i`, `reshape j`, `reshape xij`, and `reshape xi` specifications may be given in any order and may be repeated to change or correct what has been specified.

Finally, `reshape clear` clears the definitions. Recall that `reshape` definitions are stored with the dataset when you save it. `reshape clear` provides a way to erase the definitions if you want.

The basic syntax of `reshape` is implemented in terms of the advanced syntax. This means that you can mix basic and advanced syntaxes.

## Acknowledgment

This version of `reshape` was based, in part, on the work of Jeroen Weesie from Utrecht University, Netherlands (Weesie 1997).

## Saved Results

`reshape` stores the following characteristics with the data (see [P] **char**):

| | |
|---|---|
| _dta[ReS_i] | i variable name(s) |
| _dta[ReS_j] | j variable name |
| _dta[ReS_jv] | j values if specified |
| _dta[ReS_Xij] | $X_{ij}$ variable name(s) |
| _dta[ReS_Xi] | $X_i$ variable name(s) if specified |
| _dta[ReS_atwl] | atwl() value if specified |
| _dta[ReS_str] | 1 if option string specified; otherwise 0 |

## Methods and Formulas

`reshape` is implemented as an ado-file.

## References

Gould, W. W. 1997. stata48: Updated reshape. *Stata Technical Bulletin* 39: 4–16. Reprinted in *Stata Technical Bulletin Reprints*, vol. 7, pp. 5–20.

Weesie, J. 1997. dm48: An enhancement of reshape. *Stata Technical Bulletin* 38: 2–4. Reprinted in *Stata Technical Bulletin Reprints*, vol. 7, pp. 40–43.

## Also See

| | |
|---|---|
| **Complementary:** | [R] **save**, |
| | [P] **char** |
| **Related:** | [R] **stack**, [R] **xpose** |

# Title

**#review** — Review previous commands

# Syntax

#review [ $\#_1$ [ $\#_2$ ] ]

# Description

The **#review** command displays the last few lines typed at the terminal.

# Remarks

**#review** (pronounced *pound-review*) is a Stata preprocessor command. *#commands* do not generate a return code, nor do they generate ordinary Stata errors. The only error message associated with *#commands* is "unrecognized #command".

The **#review** command displays the last few lines typed at the terminal. If no arguments follow **#review**, the last 5 lines typed at the terminal are displayed. The first argument specifies the number of lines to be reviewed, so **#review** 10 displays the last 10 lines typed. The second argument specifies the number of lines to be displayed, so **#review** 10 5 displays 5 lines, starting at the 10th previous line.

Stata reserves a buffer for **#review** lines and stores as many previous lines in the buffer as will fit, rolling out the oldest line to make room for the newest. Requests to **#review** lines no longer stored will be ignored. Only lines typed at the terminal are placed in the **#review** buffer. See [U] **13.5 Editing previous lines**.

▷ Example

Typing **#review** by itself will show the last five lines you typed at the terminal:

```
. #review
5 use mydata
4 * comments go into the #review buffer, too
3 describe
2 tabulate marriage educ [freq=number]
1 tabulate marriage educ [freq=number], chi2
. _
```

Typing **#review** 15 2 shows the 15th and 14th previous lines:

```
. #review 15 2
15 replace x=. if x<200
14 summarize x
. _
```

◁

# Also See

**Background:**     [U] **13.5 Editing previous lines**,
                    [U] **19.1.3 Long lines in do-files**

130

# Title

**roc** — Receiver Operating Characteristic (ROC) analysis

# Syntax

**roctab** *refvar classvar* [*weight*] [if *exp*] [in *range*] [, <u>bam</u>ber <u>han</u>ley <u>d</u>etail

<u>lor</u>enz <u>t</u>able <u>bino</u>mial <u>l</u>evel(*#*) <u>noref</u>line <u>gr</u>aph <u>summ</u>ary *graph_options* ]

**rocfit** *refvar classvar* [*weight*] [if *exp*] [in *range*] [, <u>cont</u>inuous(*#*)

<u>g</u>enerate(*newvar*) <u>l</u>evel(*#*) nolog *maximize_options* ]

**rocplot** [, <u>conf</u>band <u>l</u>evel(*#*) <u>noref</u>line *graph_options* ]

**roccomp** *refvar classvar* [*classvars*] [*weight*] [if *exp*] [in *range*] [, by(*varname*)

<u>binormal</u> <u>l</u>evel(*#*) test(*matname*) <u>noref</u>line <u>separate</u> graph <u>summ</u>ary

*graph_options* ]

**rocgold** *refvar goldvar classvar* [*classvars*] [*weight*] [if *exp*] [in *range*] [, <u>g</u>raph

<u>summ</u>ary <u>sid</u>ak *roccomp_options* ]

fweights are allowed; see [U] **14.1.6 weight**.

# Description

The above commands are used to perform Receiver Operating Characteristic (ROC) analyses with rating and discrete classification data.

The two variables *refvar* and *classvar* must be numeric. The reference variable indicates the true state of the observation such as diseased and nondiseased or normal and abnormal, and must be coded as 0 and 1. The rating or outcome of the diagnostic test or test modality is recorded in *classvar*, which must be at least ordinal, with higher values indicating higher risk.

**roctab** is used to perform nonparametric ROC analyses. By default, **roctab** calculates the area under the ROC curve. Optionally, **roctab** can plot the ROC curve, display the data in tabular form, and produce Lorenz-like plots.

**rocfit** estimates maximum-likelihood ROC models assuming a binormal distribution of the latent variable.

**rocplot** may be used after **rocfit** to plot the fitted ROC curve and simultaneous confidence bands.

**roccomp** tests the equality of two or more ROC areas obtained from applying two or more test modalities to the same sample or to independent samples. **roccomp** expects the data to be in wide form when comparing areas estimated from the same sample, and in long form for areas estimated from independent samples.

rocgold independently tests the equality of the ROC area of each of several test modalities, specified by *classvar*, against a "gold" standard ROC curve, *goldvar*. For each comparison, rocgold reports the raw and the Bonferroni adjusted significance probability. Optionally, Šidák's adjustment for multiple comparisons can be obtained.

# Options

## Options unique to roctab

bamber specifies that the standard error for the area under the ROC curve be calculated using the method suggested by Bamber (1975). Otherwise, standard errors are obtained as suggested by DeLong, DeLong, and Clarke-Pearson (1988).

hanley specifies that the standard error for the area under the ROC curve be calculated using the method suggested by Hanley and McNeil (1982). Otherwise, standard errors are obtained as suggested by DeLong, DeLong, and Clarke-Pearson (1988).

detail outputs a table displaying the sensitivity, specificity, percent of subjects correctly classified, and two likelihood ratios for each possible cut-point of *classvar*.

lorenz specifies that Gini and Pietra indices be reported. Optionally, graph will plot the Lorenz-like curve.

table outputs a $2 \times k$ contingency table displaying the raw data.

binomial specifies that exact binomial confidence intervals be calculated.

## Options unique to rocfit

continuous(#) specifies that the continuous *classvar* should be divided into # groups of approximately equal length. This option is required when *classvar* takes on more than 20 distinct values.

continuous(.) may be specified to indicate that *classvar* is to be used as it is, even though it could have more than 20 distinct values.

generate(*newvar*) specifies the new variable that is to contain the values indicating the groups produced by continuous(#). generate() may only be specified with continuous().

nolog prevents rocfit from showing the iteration log.

*maximize_options* control the maximization process; see [R] **maximize**. You should never have to specify any of these options.

## Option unique to rocplot

confband specifies that simultaneous confidence bands be plotted around the ROC curve.

## Options unique to roccomp and rocgold

by(*varname*) is required when comparing independent ROC areas. The by() variable identifies the groups to be compared.

binormal specifies that the areas under the ROC curves to be compared should be estimated using the binormal distribution assumption. By default, areas to be compared are computed using the trapezoidal rule.

test(*matname*) specifies the contrast matrix to be used when comparing ROC areas. By default, the null hypothesis that all areas are equal is tested.

separate is meaningful only with roccomp; it says that each ROC curve should be placed on its own graph rather than one curve on top of the other.

sidak (rocgold only) requests that the significance probability be adjusted for the effect of multiple comparisons using Šidák's method. Bonferroni's adjustment is reported by default.

## Options common to several commands

level(*#*) specifies the confidence level, in percent, for the confidence intervals. For rocplot, it specifies the confidence level for the confidence bands. The default is level(95) or as set by set level; see [R] **level**.

graph produces graphical output of the ROC curve. For roctab, if lorenz is specified, graphical output of a Lorenz-like curve will be produced.

summary reports the area under the ROC curve, its standard error, and its confidence interval. If lorenz is specified with roctab, Lorenz indices are reported. This option is only needed when also specifying graph.

norefline suppresses the plotting of the 45-degree reference line from the graphical output of the ROC curve.

*graph_options* are any of the options allowed with graph, twoway; see [G] **graph options**.

## Remarks

Receiver Operating Characteristic (ROC) analysis is used to quantify the accuracy of diagnostic tests or other evaluation modality used to discriminate between two states or conditions. For ease of presentation, we will refer to these two states as normal and abnormal, and to the discriminatory test as a diagnostic test. The discriminatory accuracy of a diagnostic test is measured by its ability to correctly classify known normal and abnormal subjects. The analysis uses the ROC curve, a graph of the sensitivity versus 1 − specificity of the diagnostic test. The sensitivity is the fraction of positive cases that are correctly classified by the diagnostic test, while the specificity is the fraction of negative cases that are correctly classified. Thus, the sensitivity is the true-positive rate, and the specificity the true-negative rate.

The global performance of a diagnostic test is commonly summarized by the area under the ROC curve. This area can be interpreted as the probability that the result of a diagnostic test of a randomly selected abnormal subject will be greater than the result of the same diagnostic test from a randomly selected normal subject. The greater the area under the ROC curve, the better the global performance of the diagnostic test.

Both nonparametric methods and parametric (semi-parametric) methods have been suggested for generating the ROC curve and for calculating its area. In the following sections we present these approaches, and in the last section we present tests for comparing areas under ROC curves.

Remarks are presented under the headings

> *Nonparametric* ROC *curves*
> *Parametric* ROC *curves*
> *Lorenz-like curves*
> *Comparing areas under the* ROC *curve*

## Nonparametric ROC curves

The points on the nonparametric ROC curve are generated by using each possible outcome of the diagnostic test as a classification cut-point and computing the corresponding sensitivity and 1 − specificity. These points are then connected by straight lines, and the area under the resulting ROC curve is computed using the trapezoidal rule.

▷ Example

Hanley and McNeil (1982) presented data from a study in which a reviewer was asked to classify, using a nine point scale, a random sample of 109 tomographic images from patients with neurological problems. The rating scale was as follows: 1–definitely normal, 2–probably normal, 3–questionable, 4–probably abnormal, and 5–definitely abnormal. The true disease status was normal for 58 of the patients and abnormal for the remaining 51 patients.

Here we list 9 of the 109 observations.

```
. list disease rating in 1/9
          disease      rating
    1.        1           5
    2.        0           1
    3.        1           5
    4.        0           4
    5.        0           1
    6.        0           3
    7.        1           5
    8.        0           5
    9.        0           1
```

For each observation, `disease` identifies the true disease status of the subject (0 = normal, 1 = abnormal), and `rating` contains the classification value assigned by the reviewer.

We can use `roctab` to calculate and plot the nonparametric ROC curve by specifying both the `summary` and `graph` options. By also specifying the `table` option, we obtain a contingency table summarizing our dataset.

```
. roctab disease rating, table graph summary
```

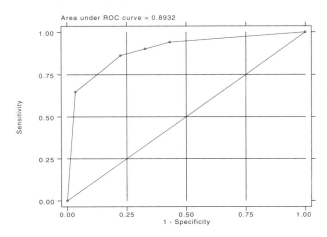

```
                                    rating
     disease |      1         2         3         4         5  |   Total
 ------------+-------------------------------------------------+--------
           0 |     33         6         6        11         2  |      58
           1 |      3         2         2        11        33  |      51
 ------------+-------------------------------------------------+--------
       Total |     36         8         8        22        35  |     109
```

```
                    ROC                      -Asymptotic Normal-
           Obs      Area     Std. Err.      [95% Conf. Interval]
         ----------------------------------------------------------
           109     0.8932      0.0307        0.83295     0.95339
```

By default, `roctab` reports the area under the curve, its standard error and its confidence interval. The `graph` option can be used to plot the ROC curve.

The ROC curve is plotted by computing the sensitivity and specificity using each value of the rating variable as a possible cut-point. A point is plotted on the graph for each of the cut-points. These plotted points are joined by straight lines to form the ROC curve, and the area under the ROC curve is computed using the trapezoidal rule.

We can tabulate the computed sensitivities and specificities for each of the possible cut-points by specifying `detail`.

```
. roctab disease rating, detail
Detailed report of Sensitivity and Specificity

                                        Correctly
  Cut point   Sensitivity   Specificity  Classified      LR+          LR-
------------------------------------------------------------------------------
 ( >= 1 )       100.00%        0.00%       46.79%       1.0000
 ( >= 2 )        94.12%       56.90%       74.31%       2.1835        0.1034
 ( >= 3 )        90.20%       67.24%       77.98%       2.7534        0.1458
 ( >= 4 )        86.27%       77.59%       81.65%       3.8492        0.1769
 ( >= 5 )        64.71%       96.55%       81.65%      18.7647        0.3655
 ( >  5 )         0.00%      100.00%       53.21%                     1.0000
------------------------------------------------------------------------------
```

```
                    ROC                      -Asymptotic Normal-
           Obs      Area     Std. Err.      [95% Conf. Interval]
         ----------------------------------------------------------
           109     0.8932      0.0307        0.83295     0.95339
```

Each cut-point in the table indicates the ratings used to classify tomographs as being from an abnormal subject. For example, the first cut-point, $(>= 1)$, indicates that all tomographs rated as 1 or greater are classified as coming from abnormal subjects. Because all tomographs have a rating of 1 or greater, all are considered abnormal. Consequently, all abnormal cases are correctly classified (sensitivity $= 100\%$), but none of the normal patients are classified correctly (specificity $= 0\%$). For the second cut-point $(>= 2)$, tomographs with ratings of 1 are classified as normal and those with ratings of 2 or greater are classified as abnormal. The resulting sensitivity and specificity are 94.12% and 56.90%, respectively. Using this cut-point, we correctly classified 74.31% of the 109 tomographs. Similar interpretations can be used on the remaining cut-points. As mentioned, each cut-point corresponds to a point on the nonparametric ROC curve. The first cut-point, $(>= 1)$, corresponds to the point at (1,1) and the last cut-point, $(> 5)$, to the point at (0,0).

`detail` also reports two likelihood ratios suggested by Choi (1998): the likelihood ratio for a positive test result (LR+) and the likelihood ratio for a negative test result (LR–). The likelihood ratio for a positive test result is the ratio of the probability of a positive test among the truly positive subjects to the probability of a positive test among the truly negative subjects. The likelihood ratio for a negative test result (LR–) is the ratio of the probability of a negative test among the truly positive subjects to the probability of a negative test among the truly negative subjects. Choi points out that LR+ corresponds to the slope of the line from the origin to the point on the ROC curve determined by the cut-point. Similarly, LR– corresponds to the slope from the point (1,1) to the point on the ROC curve determined by the cut-point.

By default, `roctab` calculates the standard error for the area under the curve using an algorithm suggested by DeLong, DeLong, and Clarke-Pearson (1988) and asymptotic normal confidence intervals. Optionally, standard errors based on methods suggested by Bamber (1975) or Hanley and McNeil (1982) can be computed by specifying `bamber` or `hanley` respectively, and an exact binomial confidence interval can be obtained by specifying `binomial`.

```
. roctab disease rating, bamber
                      ROC        Bamber      —Asymptotic Normal—
           Obs        Area       Std. Err.   [95% Conf. Interval]

           109       0.8932      0.0306        0.83317      0.95317
. roctab disease rating, hanley binomial
                      ROC        Hanley      — Binomial Exact —
           Obs        Area       Std. Err.   [95% Conf. Interval]

           109       0.8932      0.0320        0.81559      0.94180
```
◁

## Parametric ROC curves

Dorfman and Alf (1969) developed a generalized approach for obtaining maximum likelihood estimates of the parameters for a smooth fitting ROC curve. The most commonly used method, and the one implemented here, is based upon the binormal model.

The model assumes the existence of an unobserved continuous latent variable that is normally distributed (perhaps after a monotonic transformation) in both the normal and abnormal populations with means $\mu_n$ and $\mu_a$, and variances $\sigma_n^2$ and $\sigma_a^2$, respectively. The model further assumes that the $K$ categories of the rating variable result from partitioning the unobserved latent variable by $K - 1$ fixed boundaries. The method fits a straight line to the empirical ROC points plotted using normal probability scales on both axes. Maximum likelihood estimates of the line's slope and intercept and the $K - 1$ boundaries are obtained simultaneously. See *Methods and Formulas* for details.

The intercept from the fitted line is a measurement of $(\mu_a - \mu_n)/\sigma_a$, and the slope measures $\sigma_n/\sigma_a$.

Thus, the intercept is the standardized difference between the two latent population means, and the slope is the ratio of the two standard deviations. The null hypothesis of no difference between the two population means is evaluated by testing if the intercept = 0, and the null hypothesis that the variances in the two populations are equal is evaluated by testing if the slope = 1.

▷ Example

We use Hanley and McNeil's (1982) dataset, described in the previous example, to fit a smooth ROC curve assuming a binormal model.

```
. rocfit disease rating

Fitting binormal model:
Iteration 0:    log likelihood = -123.68069
Iteration 1:    log likelihood = -123.64867
Iteration 2:    log likelihood = -123.64855
Iteration 3:    log likelihood = -123.64855
```

```
Binormal model of disease on rating                Number of obs    =         109
Goodness-of-fit chi2(2) =          0.21
Prob > chi2             =          0.9006
Log likelihood          =       -123.64855
```

|  | Coef. | Std. Err. | z | P>\|z\| | [95% Conf. Interval] | |
|---|---|---|---|---|---|---|
| intercept | 1.656782 | 0.310456 | 5.34 | 0.000 | 1.048300 | 2.265265 |
| slope (*) | 0.713002 | 0.215882 | -1.33 | 0.092 | 0.289881 | 1.136123 |
| _cut1 | 0.169768 | 0.165307 | 1.03 | 0.152 | -0.154227 | 0.493764 |
| _cut2 | 0.463215 | 0.167235 | 2.77 | 0.003 | 0.135441 | 0.790990 |
| _cut3 | 0.766860 | 0.174808 | 4.39 | 0.000 | 0.424243 | 1.109477 |
| _cut4 | 1.797938 | 0.299581 | 6.00 | 0.000 | 1.210770 | 2.385106 |

| Index | Indices from binormal fit | | | |
|---|---|---|---|---|
|  | Estimate | Std. Err. | [95% Conf. Interval] | |
| ROC area | 0.911331 | 0.029506 | 0.853501 | 0.969161 |
| delta(m) | 2.323671 | 0.502370 | 1.339044 | 3.308298 |
| d(e) | 1.934361 | 0.257187 | 1.430284 | 2.438438 |
| d(a) | 1.907771 | 0.259822 | 1.398530 | 2.417012 |

(*) z test for slope==1

rocfit outputs the MLE for the intercept and slope of the fitted regression line along with, in this case, 4 boundaries (because there are 5 ratings) labeled _cut1 through _cut4. In addition, rocfit also computes and reports 4 indices based on the fitted ROC curve: the area under the curve (labeled ROC area), $\delta(m)$ (labeled delta(m)), $d_e$ (labeled d(e)), and $d_a$ (labeled d(a)). More information about these indices can be found in the *Methods and Formulas* section and in Erdreich and Lee (1981).

Note that in the output table we are testing whether or not the variances of the two latent populations are equal by testing if the slope $= 1$.

We plot the fitted ROC curve.

   . rocplot

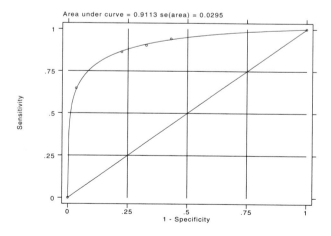

◁

## Lorenz-like curves

For applications where it is known that the risk status increases or decreases monotonically with increasing values of the diagnostic test, the ROC curve and associated indices are useful in assessing the overall performance of a diagnostic test. When the risk status does not vary monotonically with increasing values of the diagnostic test, however, the resulting ROC curve can be nonconvex and its indices unreliable. For these situations, Lee (1999) proposed an alternative to the ROC analysis based on Lorenz-like curves and the associated Pietra and Gini indices.

Lee (1999) mentions at least three specific situations where results from Lorenz curves are superior to those obtained from ROC curves: (1) a diagnostic test with similar means but very different standard deviations in the abnormal and normal populations, (2) a diagnostic test with bimodal distributions in either the normal or abnormal population, and (3) a diagnostic test distributed symmetrically in the normal population and skewed in the abnormal.

When the risk status increases or decreases monotonically with increasing values of the diagnostic test, the ROC and Lorenz curves yield interchangeable results.

▷ Example

To illustrate the use of the `lorenz` option we constructed a fictitious dataset that yields results similar to those presented in Table III of Lee (1999). The data assume that a 12 point rating scale was used to classify 442 diseased and 442 healthy subjects. We list a few of the observations.

```
. list in 1/7, noobs

    disease        class         pop
          0            5          66
          1           11          17
          0            6          85
          0            3          19
          0           10          19
          0            2           7
          1            4          16
```

The data consist of 24 observations, 12 observations from diseased individuals and 12 from nondiseased individuals. Each observation corresponds to one of the 12 classification values of the rating scale variable, `class`. The number of subjects represented by each observation is given by the `pop` variable, making this a frequency-weighted dataset. The data were generated assuming a binormal distribution of the latent variable with similar means for the normal and abnormal populations, but with the standard deviation for the abnormal population 5 times greater than that of the normal population.

*(Continued on next page)*

```
. roctab disease class [fweight=pop], graph summary
```

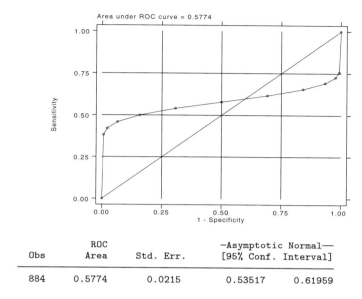

| Obs | ROC Area | Std. Err. | —Asymptotic Normal— [95% Conf. Interval] | |
|-----|----------|-----------|-----------------|-----------------|
| 884 | 0.5774 | 0.0215 | 0.53517 | 0.61959 |

The resulting ROC curve is nonconvex or, as termed by Lee, "wiggly". Lee argues that for this and similar situations, the Lorenz curve and indices are preferred.

```
. roctab disease class [fweight=pop], lorenz summary
```

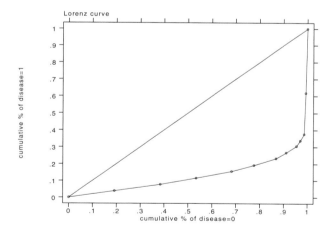

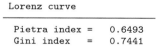

Lorenz curve

| | |
|---|---|
| Pietra index = | 0.6493 |
| Gini index = | 0.7441 |

Like ROC curves, a more bowed Lorenz curve suggests a better diagnostic test. This "bowedness" is quantified by the Pietra index, which is geometrically equivalent to twice the largest triangle that can be inscribed in the area between the curve and the diagonal line, and the Gini index, which is equivalent to twice the area between the Lorenz curve and the diagonal. Lee (1999) provides several additional interpretations for the Pietra and Gini indices. If interested, consult the reference for more information.

◁

## Comparing areas under the ROC curve

The area under multiple ROC curves can be compared using `roccomp`. The command syntax is slightly different if the ROC curves are correlated (i.e., different diagnostic tests applied to the same sample) or independent (i.e., diagnostic tests applied to different samples).

## Correlated data

▷ Example

Hanley and McNeil (1983) presented data from an evaluation of two computer algorithms designed to reconstruct CT images from phantoms. We will call these two algorithms' modalities 1 and 2. A sample of 112 phantoms was selected; 58 phantoms were considered normal and the remaining 54 were abnormal. Each of the two modalities was applied to each phantom and the resulting images rated by a reviewer using a six point scale: 1–definitely normal, 2–probably normal, 3–possibly normal, 4–possibly abnormal, 5–probably abnormal, and 6–definitely abnormal. Because each modality was applied to the same sample of phantoms, the two sets of outcomes are correlated.

We list the first seven observations:

```
. list in 1/7

          mod1       mod2      status
1.          2          1          0
2.          5          5          1
3.          2          1          0
4.          2          3          0
5.          5          6          1
6.          2          2          0
7.          3          2          0
```

Note that the data are in wide form. This is required when dealing with correlated data. Each observation corresponds to one phantom. The variable `mod1` identifies the rating assigned for the first modality, and `mod2` identifies the rating assigned for the second modality. The true status of the phantoms is given by `status=0` if normal and `status=1` if abnormal. The observations with at least one missing rating were dropped from the analysis.

We plot the two ROC curves and compare their areas.

*(Continued on next page)*

. roccomp status mod1 mod2, graph summary symbol(oT)

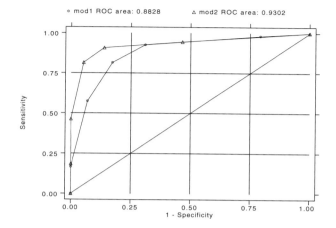

| | Obs | ROC Area | Std. Err. | —Asymptotic Normal—[95% Conf. Interval] | |
|---|---|---|---|---|---|
| mod1 | 112 | 0.8828 | 0.0317 | 0.82067 | 0.94498 |
| mod2 | 112 | 0.9302 | 0.0256 | 0.88005 | 0.98042 |

Ho: area(mod1) = area(mod2)
    chi2(1) =    2.31     Prob>chi2 =   0.1282

By default, `roccomp`, with the **graph** option specified, plots the ROC curves on the same graph. Optionally, the curves can be plotted side by side, each on its own graph, by also specifying **separate**.

For each curve, `roccomp` reports summary statistics and provides a test for the equality of the area under the curves using an algorithm suggested by DeLong, DeLong, and Clarke-Pearson (1988).

Although the area under the ROC curve for modality 2 is larger than that of modality 1, the chi-squared test yielded a significance probability of 0.1282, suggesting that there is no significant difference between these two areas.

The `roccomp` command can also be used to compare more than two ROC areas. To illustrate this, we modified the previous dataset by including a fictitious third modality.

*(Graph on next page)*

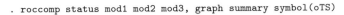

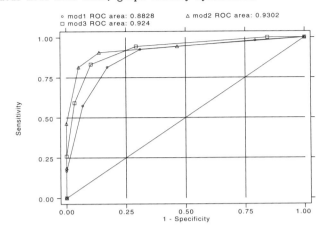

| | Obs | ROC Area | Std. Err. | —Asymptotic Normal—<br>[95% Conf. Interval] | |
|---|---|---|---|---|---|
| mod1 | 112 | 0.8828 | 0.0317 | 0.82067 | 0.94498 |
| mod2 | 112 | 0.9302 | 0.0256 | 0.88005 | 0.98042 |
| mod3 | 112 | 0.9240 | 0.0241 | 0.87670 | 0.97132 |

```
Ho: area(mod1) = area(mod2) = area(mod3)
    chi2(2) =    6.54    Prob>chi2 =   0.0381
```

By default, `roccomp` tests whether the areas under the ROC curves are all equal. Other comparisons can be tested by creating a contrast matrix and specifying `test(matname)`, where *matname* is the name of the contrast matrix.

For example, assume that we are interested in testing whether the area under the ROC for `mod1` is equal to that of `mod3`. To do this, we can first create an appropriate contrast matrix and then specify its name with the `test()` option.

Of course, this is a trivial example because we could have just specified

```
. roccomp status mod1 mod3
```

without including `mod2` to obtain the same test results. However, for illustration we will continue with this example.

The contrast matrix must have its number of columns equal to the number of *classvars* (i.e., the total number of ROC curves), a number of rows less than or equal to the number of *classvars*, and the elements of each row must add to zero.

```
. matrix C=(1,0,-1)
. roccomp status mod1 mod2 mod3, test(C)
```

| | Obs | ROC Area | Std. Err. | —Asymptotic Normal—<br>[95% Conf. Interval] | |
|---|---|---|---|---|---|
| mod1 | 112 | 0.8828 | 0.0317 | 0.82067 | 0.94498 |
| mod2 | 112 | 0.9302 | 0.0256 | 0.88005 | 0.98042 |
| mod3 | 112 | 0.9240 | 0.0241 | 0.87670 | 0.97132 |

```
Ho: Comparison as defined by contrast matrix: C
    chi2(1) =    5.25    .  Prob>chi2 =   0.0220
```

Note that although all three areas are reported, the comparison is made using the specified contrast matrix.

Perhaps more interesting would be a comparison of the area from mod1 and the average area of mod2 and mod3.

```
. matrix C=(1,-.5,-.5)
. roccomp status mod1 mod2 mod3, test(C)
```

| | Obs | ROC Area | Std. Err. | —Asymptotic Normal— [95% Conf. Interval] | |
|---|---|---|---|---|---|
| mod1 | 112 | 0.8828 | 0.0317 | 0.82067 | 0.94498 |
| mod2 | 112 | 0.9302 | 0.0256 | 0.88005 | 0.98042 |
| mod3 | 112 | 0.9240 | 0.0241 | 0.87670 | 0.97132 |

```
Ho: Comparison as defined by contrast matrix: C
      chi2(1) =       3.43        Prob>chi2 =    0.0642
```

Other contrasts could be made. For example, we could test if mod3 is different from at least one of the other two by first creating the following contrast matrix:

```
. matrix C=(-1, 0, 1 \ 0, -1, 1)
. mat list C
C[2,3]
     c1  c2  c3
r1   -1   0   1
r2    0  -1   1
```

◁

## Independent data

▷ Example

In the previous example, we noted that because each test modality was applied to the same sample of phantoms, the classification outcomes were correlated. Now assume that we have collected the same data as presented by Hanley and McNeil (1983), except that we applied the first test modality to one sample of phantoms and the second test modality to a different sample of phantoms. The resulting measurements are now considered independent.

Here are a few of the observations.

```
. list in 1/7
         pop    status    rating       mod
  1.      12        0         1         1
  2.      31        0         1         2
  3.       1        1         1         1
  4.       3        1         1         2
  5.      28        0         2         1
  6.      19        0         2         2
  7.       3        1         2         1
```

Note that the data are in long form. This is required when dealing with independent data. The data consist of 24 observations, 6 observations corresponding to abnormal phantoms and 6 to normal phantoms evaluated using the first modality, and similarly 6 observations corresponding to abnormal phantoms and 6 to normal phantoms evaluated using the second modality. The number of phantoms corresponding to each observation is given by the pop variable. Once again we have frequency-weighted data. The variable mod identifies the modality and rating is the assigned classification.

We can better view our data by using the `table` command.

```
. table status rating [fw=pop], by(mod) row col
```

| mod and status | rating 1 | 2 | 3 | 4 | 5 | 6 | Total |
|---|---|---|---|---|---|---|---|
| **1** | | | | | | | |
| 0 | 12 | 28 | 8 | 6 | 4 | | 58 |
| 1 | 1 | 3 | 6 | 13 | 22 | 9 | 54 |
| Total | 13 | 31 | 14 | 19 | 26 | 9 | 112 |
| **2** | | | | | | | |
| 0 | 31 | 19 | 5 | 3 | | | 58 |
| 1 | 3 | 2 | 5 | 19 | 15 | 10 | 54 |
| Total | 34 | 21 | 10 | 22 | 15 | 10 | 112 |

The `status` variable indicates the true status of the phantoms, `status=0` if normal and `status=1` if abnormal.

We now compare the areas under the two ROC curves.

```
. roccomp status rating [fw=pop], by(mod) graph summary symbol(oT)
```

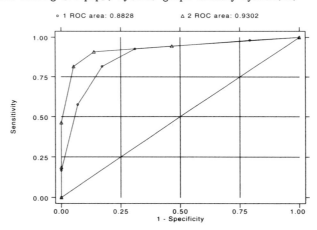

| mod | Obs | ROC Area | Std. Err. | -Asymptotic Normal— [95% Conf. Interval] | |
|---|---|---|---|---|---|
| 1 | 112 | 0.8828 | 0.0317 | 0.82067 | 0.94498 |
| 2 | 112 | 0.9302 | 0.0256 | 0.88005 | 0.98042 |

```
Ho: area(1) = area(2)
    chi2(1) =    1.35      Prob>chi2 =   0.2447
```

◁

## Comparing areas to a gold standard

The area under multiple ROC curves can be compared to a gold standard using `rocgold`. The command syntax is similar to that of `roccomp`. The tests are corrected for the effect of multiple comparisons.

▷ Example

We will use the same data (presented by Hanley and McNeil (1983)) as in the `roccomp` examples. Let's assume the first modality is considered to be the standard to which both the second and third modalities are compared.

We want to plot and compare both the areas of the ROC curves of `mod2` and `mod3` to `mod1`. Since `mod1` is what we are considering to be the gold standard, it is listed first after the reference variable in the `rocgold` command line.

```
. rocgold status mod1 mod2 mod3, graph summary symbol(oTS)
```

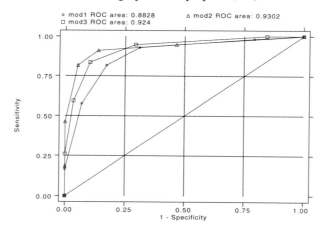

| | ROC Area | Std. Err. | chi2 | df | Pr>chi2 | Bonferroni Pr>chi2 |
|---|---|---|---|---|---|---|
| mod1 (standard) | 0.8828 | 0.0317 | | | | |
| mod2 | 0.9302 | 0.0256 | 2.3146 | 1 | 0.1282 | 0.2563 |
| mod3 | 0.9240 | 0.0241 | 5.2480 | 1 | 0.0220 | 0.0439 |

Equivalently, we could have done this in two steps by using the `roccomp` command.

```
. roccomp status mod1 mod2, graph summary symbol(oT)
```

```
. roccomp status mod1 mod3, graph summary symbol(oT)
```

◁

*(Continued on next page)*

# Saved Results

roctab saves in r():

Scalars

| | | | | |
|---|---|---|---|---|
| r(N) | number of observations | | r(area) | area under the ROC curve |
| r(se) | standard error for the area under the ROC curve | | r(pietra) | Pietra index |
| r(lb) | lower bound of CI for the area under the ROC curve | | r(gini) | Gini index |
| r(ub) | upper bound of CI for the area under the ROC curve | | | |

rocfit saves in e():

Scalars

| | | | | |
|---|---|---|---|---|
| e(N) | number of observations | | e(df_gf) | goodness-of-fit degrees of freedom |
| e(k) | number of parameters | | e(p_gf) | $\chi^2$ goodness-of-fit significance probability |
| e(k_eq) | number of equations | | e(area) | area under the ROC curve |
| e(k_dv) | number of dependent variables | | e(se_area) | standard error for the area under the ROC curve |
| e(df_m) | model degrees of freedom | | | |
| e(ll) | log likelihood | | e(deltam) | $\delta(m)$ |
| e(rc) | return code | | e(se_delm) | standard area for $\delta(m)$ |
| e(ic) | number of iterations | | e(de) | $d_e$ index |
| e(rank) | rank of e(V) | | e(se_de) | standard error for $d_e$ index |
| e(chi2_gf) | goodness-of-fit $\chi^2$ | | e(da) | $d_a$ index |
| | | | e(se_da) | standard error for $d_a$ index |

Macros

| | | | | |
|---|---|---|---|---|
| e(cmd) | rocfit | | e(wexp) | weight expression |
| e(depvar) | names of dependent variables | | e(user) | name of likelihood-evaluator program |
| e(title) | title in estimation output | | e(opt) | type of optimization |
| e(wtype) | weight type | | e(chi2type) | GOF; type of model $\chi^2$ test |

Matrices

| | | | | |
|---|---|---|---|---|
| e(b) | coefficient vector | | e(V) | variance–covariance matrix of the estimators |
| e(ilog) | iteration log (up to 20 iterations) | | | |

Functions

| | |
|---|---|
| e(sample) | marks estimation sample |

roccomp saves in r():

Scalars

| | | | | |
|---|---|---|---|---|
| r(N_g) | number of groups | | r(df) | $\chi^2$ degrees of freedom |
| r(p) | significance probability | | r(chi2) | $\chi^2$ |

Matrices

| | |
|---|---|
| r(V) | variance–covariance matrix |

rocgold saves in r():

Scalars

| | |
|---|---|
| r(N_g) | number of groups |

Matrices

| | | | | |
|---|---|---|---|---|
| r(V) | variance–covariance matrix | | r(p) | significance probability vector |
| r(chi2) | $\chi^2$ vector | | r(p_adj) | adjusted significance probability vector |
| r(df) | $\chi^2$ degrees-of-freedom vector | | | |

# Methods and Formulas

`roctab`, `rocfit`, `rocplot`, `roccomp`, and `rocgold` are implemented as ado-files.

Assume that we applied a diagnostic test to each of $N_n$ normal and $N_a$ abnormal subjects. Further assume that the higher the outcome value of the diagnostic test, the higher the risk of the subject being abnormal. Let $\widehat{\theta}$ be the estimated area under the curve, and let $X_i, i = 1, 2, \ldots, N_a$ and $Y_j, j = 1, 2, \ldots, N_n$ be the values of the diagnostic test for the abnormal and normal subjects, respectively.

## Nonparametric ROC

The points on the nonparametric ROC curve are generated by using each possible outcome of the diagnostic test as a classification cut-point and computing the corresponding sensitivity and $1 -$ specificity. These points are then connected by straight lines, and the area under the resulting ROC curve is computed using the trapezoidal rule.

The default standard error for the area under the ROC curve is computed using the algorithm described by DeLong, DeLong, and Clarke-Pearson (1988). For each abnormal subject, $i$, define

$$V_{10}(X_i) = \frac{1}{N_n} \sum_{j=1}^{N_n} \psi(X_i, Y_j)$$

and for each normal subject, $j$, define

$$V_{01}(Y_j) = \frac{1}{N_a} \sum_{i=1}^{N_a} \psi(X_i, Y_j)$$

where

$$\psi(X, Y) = \begin{cases} 1 & Y < X \\ \frac{1}{2} & Y = X \\ 0 & Y > X \end{cases}$$

Define

$$S_{10} = \frac{1}{N_a - 1} \sum_{i=1}^{N_a} \{V_{10}(X_i) - \widehat{\theta}\}^2$$

and

$$S_{01} = \frac{1}{N_n - 1} \sum_{j=1}^{N_n} \{V_{01}(Y_j) - \widehat{\theta}\}^2$$

The variance of the estimated area under the ROC curve is given by

$$\text{var}(\widehat{\theta}) = \frac{1}{N_a} S_{10} + \frac{1}{N_n} S_{01}$$

The `hanley` standard error for the area under the ROC curve is computed using the algorithm described by Hanley and McNeil (1982). It requires the calculation of two quantities, $Q_1$ and $Q_2$, where $Q_1$ is Pr(two randomly selected abnormal subjects will both have a higher score than a randomly selected normal subject), and $Q_2$ is Pr(one randomly selected abnormal subject will have a higher score than any two randomly selected normal subjects). The Hanley and McNeil variance of the estimated area under the ROC curve is

$$\mathrm{var}(\widehat{\theta}) = \frac{\widehat{\theta}(1 - \widehat{\theta}) + (N_a - 1)(Q_1 - \widehat{\theta^2}) + (N_n - 1)(Q_2 - \widehat{\theta^2})}{N_a N_n}$$

The **bamber** standard error for the area under the ROC curve is computed using the algorithm described by Bamber (1975). For any two $Y$ values, $Y_j$ and $Y_k$, and any $X_i$ value, define

$$b_{yyx} = p(Y_j, Y_k < X_i) + p(X_i < Y_j, Y_k) - 2p(Y_j < X_i < Y_k)$$

and similarly, for any two $X$ values, $X_i$ and $X_l$, and any $Y_j$ value, define

$$b_{xxy} = p(X_i, X_l < Y_j) + p(Y_j < X_i, X_l) - 2p(X_i < Y_j < X_l)$$

Then Bamber's unbiased estimate of the variance for the area under the ROC curve is

$$\mathrm{var}(\widehat{\theta}) = \frac{1}{4}(N_a - 1)(N_n - 1)\{p(X \neq Y) + (N_a - 1)b_{xxy} + (N_n - 1)b_{yyx} - 4(N_a + N_n - 1)(\widehat{\theta} - 0.5)^2\}$$

Asymptotic confidence intervals are constructed and reported by default, assuming a normal distribution for the area under the ROC curve.

Exact binomial confidence intervals are calculated as described in [R] **ci**, with $p$ equal to the area under the ROC curve.

## Parametric ROC curves

Dorfman and Alf (1969) developed a general procedure for obtaining maximum likelihood estimates of the parameters of a smooth fitting ROC curve. The most common method, and the one implemented in Stata, is based upon the binormal model.

The model assumes that there is an unobserved continuous latent variable that is normally distributed in both the normal and abnormal populations. The idea is better explained with the following illustration:

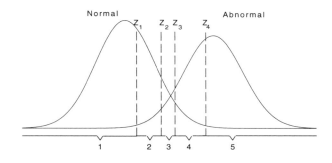

It is assumed that the latent variable is normally distributed for both the normal and abnormal subjects, perhaps after a monotonic transformation, with means $\mu_n$ and $\mu_a$, and variances $\sigma_n^2$ and $\sigma_a^2$, respectively.

This latent variable is assumed to be partitioned into the $k$ categories of the rating variable by $k-1$ fixed boundaries. In the above figure, the $k = 5$ categories of the rating variable identified on the bottom result from the partition of the four boundaries $Z_1$ through $Z_4$.

Let $R_j$ for $j = 1, 2, \ldots, k$ indicate the categories of the rating variable, let $i = 1$ if the subject belongs to the normal group, and let $i = 2$ if the subject belongs to the abnormal group.

Then

$$p(R_j | i = 1) = F(Z_j) - F(Z_{j-1})$$

where $Z_k = (x_k - \mu_n)/\sigma_n$, $F$ is the cumulative normal distribution, $F(Z_0) = 0$ and $F(Z_k) = 1$. Also,

$$p(R_j | i = 2) = F(bZ_j - a) - F(bZ_{j-1} - a)$$

where $b = \sigma_n/\sigma_a$ and $a = (\mu_a - \mu_n)/\sigma_a$.

The parameters $a$, $b$ and the $k-1$ fixed boundaries $Z_j$ are simultaneously estimated by maximizing the log likelihood function

$$\log L = \sum_{i=1}^{2} \sum_{j=1}^{k} r_{ij} \log\{p(R_j | i)\}$$

where $r_{ij}$ is the number of $R_j$'s in group $i$.

The area under the fitted ROC curve is computed as

$$\Phi\left(\frac{a}{\sqrt{1 + b^2}}\right)$$

where $\Phi$ is the standard normal cumulative distribution function.

Point estimates for the ROC curve indices are as follows:

$$\delta(m) = \frac{a}{b} \qquad d_e = \frac{2a}{b+1} \qquad d_a = \frac{a\sqrt{2}}{\sqrt{1 + b^2}}$$

Variances for these indices are computed using the delta method.

The $\delta(m)$ estimates $(\mu_a - \mu_n)/\sigma_n$, $d_e$ estimates $2(\mu_a - \mu_n)/(\sigma_a - \sigma_n)$, and $d_a$ estimates $\sqrt{2}(\mu_a - \mu_n)/(\sigma_a^2 - \sigma_n^2)^2$.

Simultaneous confidence bands for the entire curve are obtained as suggested by Ma and Hall (1993) by first obtaining Working–Hotelling (1929) confidence bands for the fitted straight line in normal probability coordinates, and then transforming them back to ROC coordinates.

## Comparing areas under the ROC curve

Areas under ROC curves are compared using an algorithm suggested by DeLong, DeLong, and Clarke-Pearson (1988). Let $\widehat{\theta} = (\widehat{\theta^1}, \widehat{\theta^2}, \ldots, \widehat{\theta^k})$ be a vector representing the areas under $k$ ROC curves. For the $r$th area, define

$$V_{10}^r(X_i) = \frac{1}{N_n} \sum_{j=1}^{N_n} \psi(X_i^r, Y_j^r)$$

and for each normal subject, $j$, define

$$V_{01}^r(Y_j) = \frac{1}{N_a} \sum_{i=1}^{N_a} \psi(X_i^r, Y_j^r)$$

where

$$\psi(X^r, Y^r) = \begin{cases} 1 & Y^r < X^r \\ \frac{1}{2} & Y^r = X^r \\ 0 & Y^r > X^r \end{cases}$$

Define the $k \times k$ matrix $\mathbf{S_{10}}$ such that the $(r, s)$th element is

$$S_{10}^{r,s} = \frac{1}{N_a - 1} \sum_{i=1}^{N_a} \{V_{10}^r(X_i) - \widehat{\theta^r}\}\{V_{10}^s(X_i) - \widehat{\theta^s}\}$$

and $\mathbf{S_{01}}$ such that the $(r, s)$th element is

$$S_{01}^{r,s} = \frac{1}{N_n - 1} \sum_{j=1}^{N_n} \{V_{01}^r(Y_i) - \widehat{\theta^r}\}\{V_{01}^s(Y_i) - \widehat{\theta^s}\}$$

Then the covariance matrix is

$$S = \frac{1}{N_a} S_{10} + \frac{1}{N_n} S_{01}$$

Let $\mathbf{L}$ be a contrast matrix defining the comparison, so that

$$(\widehat{\theta} - \theta)' \mathbf{L}' (\mathbf{LSL}')^{-1} \mathbf{L}(\widehat{\theta} - \theta)$$

has a chi-squared distribution with degrees of freedom equal to the rank of $\mathbf{LSL}'$.

# References

Bamber, D. 1975. The area above the ordinal dominance graph and the area below the receiver operating characteristic graph. *Journal of Mathematical Psychology* 12: 387–415.

Choi, B. C. K. 1998. Slopes of a receiver operating characteristic curve and likelihood ratios for a diagnostic test. *American Journal of Epidemiology* 148: 1127–1132.

Cleves, M. 1999. sg120: Receiver Operating Characteristic (ROC) analysis. *Stata Technical Bulletin* 52: 19–33. Reprinted in *Stata Technical Bulletin Reprints*, vol. 9, pp. 212–229.

——. 2000a. sg120.1: Two new options added to rocfit command. *Stata Technical Bulletin* 53: 18–19. Reprinted in *Stata Technical Bulletin Reprints*, vol. 9, pp. 230–231.

——. 2000b. sg120.2: Correction to roccomp command. *Stata Technical Bulletin* 54: 26. Reprinted in *Stata Technical Bulletin Reprints*, vol. 9, p. 231.

DeLong, E. R., D. M. DeLong, and D. L. Clarke-Pearson. 1988. Comparing the areas under two or more correlated receiver operating curves: A nonparametric approach. *Biometrics* 44: 837–845.

Dorfman, D. D. and E. Alf. 1969. Maximum likelihood estimation of parameters of signal detection theory and determination of confidence intervals-rating method data. *Journal of Mathematical Psychology* 6: 487–496.

Erdreich, L. S. and E. T. Lee. 1981. Use of relative operating characteristic analysis in epidemiology: a method for dealing with subjective judgment. *American Journal of Epidemiology* 114: 649–662.

Hanley, J. A. and B. J. McNeil. 1982. The meaning and use of the area under a receiver operating characteristic (ROC) curve. *Radiology* 143: 26–36.

——. 1983. A method of comparing the areas under receiver operating characteristic curves derived from the same cases. *Radiology* 148: 839–843.

Lee, W. C. 1999. Probabilistic analysis of global performances of diagnostic test: Interpreting the Lorenz curve-based summary measures. *Statistics in Medicine* 18: 455–471.

Ma, G. and W. J. Hall. 1993. Confidence bands for the receiver operating characteristic curves. *Medical Decision Making* 13: 191–197.

Tobias, A. 2000. sbe36: Summary statistics report for diagnostic tests. *Stata Technical Bulletin* 56: 16–18.

Working, H. and H. Hotelling. 1929. Application of the theory of error to the interpretation of trends. *Journal of the American Statistical Association* 24: 73–85.

## Also See

**Related:**        [R] **logistic**

# Title

rreg — Robust regression

# Syntax

rreg *depvar* [*varlist*] [if *exp*] [in *range*] [, level(#) nolog graph

   tolerance(#) tune(#) genwt(*newvar*) iterate(#) ]

by ... : may be used with rreg; see [R] by.

rreg shares the features of all estimation commands; see [U] 23 Estimation and post-estimation commands.

# Syntax for predict

predict [*type*] *newvarname* [if *exp*] [in *range*] [, xb | stdp | hat | residuals ]

These statistics are available both in and out of sample; type predict ... if e(sample) ... if wanted only for the estimation sample.

# Description

rreg performs one version of robust regression of *depvar* on *varlist*.

Also see *Robust standard errors* in [R] **regress** for standard regression with robust variance estimates and [R] **qreg** for quantile (including median or least-absolute-residual) regression.

# Options

level(#) specifies the confidence level, in percent, for confidence intervals. The default is level(95) or as set by set level; see [U] **23.5 Specifying the width of confidence intervals**.

nolog suppresses display of the iteration log.

graph allows you to graphically watch the convergence of the iterative technique. The weights obtained from the most recent round of estimation are graphed against the weights obtained from the previous round.

tolerance(#) specifies the convergence criteria and defaults to 0.01 if not specified.

tune(#) is the biweight tuning constant. The default is 7, meaning 7 times the median absolute deviation from the median residual (MAD); see *Methods and Formulas*. Lower tuning constants downweight outliers rapidly, but may lead to unstable estimates (below 6 is not recommended). Higher tuning constants produce milder downweighting.

genwt(*newvar*) creates the new variable *newvar* containing the weights assigned to each observation.

iterate(#) limits the number of iterations to #. This allows you to stop the iterations and view results (with a warning that the procedure has not converged). The default is 1,000 (effectively infinite).

152

## Options for predict

xb, the default, calculates the linear prediction.

stdp calculates the standard error of the linear prediction.

hat calculates the diagonal elements of the hat matrix. Note that you must have run the rreg command with the genwt() option.

residuals calculates the residuals.

# Remarks

rreg first performs an initial screening based on Cook's distance > 1 to eliminate gross outliers prior to calculating starting values and then performs, as suggested by Li (1985), Huber iterations followed by biweight iterations.

▷ Example

You wish to examine the relationship between mileage rating, weight, and location of manufacture for the 74 cars in our automobile data. As a point of comparison, you begin by estimating an ordinary regression:

```
. regress mpg weight foreign
```

| Source | SS | df | MS |
|---|---|---|---|
| Model | 1619.2877 | 2 | 809.643849 |
| Residual | 824.171761 | 71 | 11.608053 |
| Total | 2443.45946 | 73 | 33.4720474 |

```
Number of obs =      74
F(  2,    71) =   69.75
Prob > F      =  0.0000
R-squared     =  0.6627
Adj R-squared =  0.6532
Root MSE      =  3.4071
```

| mpg | Coef. | Std. Err. | t | P>|t| | [95% Conf. Interval] |
|---|---|---|---|---|---|
| weight | -.0065879 | .0006371 | -10.34 | 0.000 | -.0078583   -.0053175 |
| foreign | -1.650029 | 1.075994 | -1.53 | 0.130 | -3.7955   .4954422 |
| _cons | 41.6797 | 2.165547 | 19.25 | 0.000 | 37.36172   45.99768 |

You now compare this with the results from rreg:

```
. rreg mpg weight foreign
   Huber iteration 1:  maximum difference in weights = .80280176
   Huber iteration 2:  maximum difference in weights = .2915438
   Huber iteration 3:  maximum difference in weights = .08911171
   Huber iteration 4:  maximum difference in weights = .02697328
Biweight iteration 5:  maximum difference in weights = .29186818
Biweight iteration 6:  maximum difference in weights = .11988101
Biweight iteration 7:  maximum difference in weights = .03315872
Biweight iteration 8:  maximum difference in weights = .00721325
Robust regression estimates
                                        Number of obs =      74
                                        F(  2,    71) =  168.32
                                        Prob > F      =  0.0000
```

| mpg | Coef. | Std. Err. | t | P>|t| | [95% Conf. Interval] |
|---|---|---|---|---|---|
| weight | -.0063976 | .0003718 | -17.21 | 0.000 | -.007139   -.0056562 |
| foreign | -3.182639 | .627964 | -5.07 | 0.000 | -4.434763   -1.930514 |
| _cons | 40.64022 | 1.263841 | 32.16 | 0.000 | 38.1202   43.16025 |

Note the large change in the foreign coefficient.

◁

## ❑ Technical Note

It would have been better had we estimated the previous robust regression by typing `rreg mpg weight foreign, genwt(w)`. The new variable `w` would then contain the estimated weights. Let's pretend that we did do this:

```
. summarize w, detail
                   Robust Regression Weight

              Percentiles      Smallest
   1%               0                0
   5%         .0442957                0
  10%         .4674935                0       Obs                 74
  25%         .8894815         .0442957       Sum of Wgt.         74

  50%         .9690193                         Mean          .8509966
                               Largest         Std. Dev.     .2746451
  75%         .9949395         .9996715
  90%         .9989245         .9996953        Variance      .0754299
  95%         .9996715         .9997343        Skewness     -2.287952
  99%         .9998585         .9998585        Kurtosis      6.874605
```

We discover that three observations in our data were dropped altogether (they have weight 0). We could further explore our data:

```
. sort w

. list make mpg weight w if w<.467
          make            mpg     weight          w
   1. VW Diesel            41      2,040          0
   2. Subaru               35      2,050          0
   3. Datsun 210           35      2,020          0
   4. Plym. Arrow          28      3,260    .04429567
   5. Cad. Seville         21      4,290    .08241943
   6. Toyota Corolla       31      2,200    .10443129
   7. Olds 98              21      4,060    .28141296
```

Being familiar with the automobile data, we immediately spotted two things: The VW is the only diesel in our data and the weight recorded for the Plymouth Arrow is incorrect.

❑

## ▷ Example

If you do not specify any explanatory variables, `rreg` produces a robust estimate of the mean:

```
. rreg mpg
     Huber iteration 1:  maximum difference in weights = .64471879
     Huber iteration 2:  maximum difference in weights = .05098336
     Huber iteration 3:  maximum difference in weights = .0099887
  Biweight iteration 4:  maximum difference in weights = .25197391
  Biweight iteration 5:  maximum difference in weights = .00358606

Robust regression estimates                     Number of obs =      74
                                                F(  0,   73) =       .
                                                Prob > F      =       .
```

| mpg   | Coef.    | Std. Err. | t     | P>\|t\| | [95% Conf. Interval] |          |
|-------|----------|-----------|-------|---------|----------------------|----------|
| _cons | 20.68825 | .641813   | 32.23 | 0.000   | 19.40912             | 21.96738 |

The estimate is given by the coefficient on _cons. The mean is 20.69 with an estimated standard error of .6418. The 95% confidence interval is [19.4, 22.0]. By comparison, ci gives us the standard calculation:

```
. ci mpg
    Variable │     Obs        Mean    Std. Err.      [95% Conf. Interval]
─────────────┼───────────────────────────────────────────────────────────
         mpg │      74     21.2973    .6725511        19.9569     22.63769
```

◁

# Saved Results

rreg saves in e():

Scalars
| e(N)    | number of observations      | e(r2)    | R-squared             |
|---------|-----------------------------|----------|-----------------------|
| e(mss)  | model sum of squares        | e(r2_a)  | adjusted R-squared    |
| e(df_m) | model degrees of freedom    | e(F)     | F statistic           |
| e(rss)  | residual sum of squares     | e(rmse)  | root mean square error|
| e(df_r) | residual degrees of freedom |          |                       |

Macros
| e(cmd)    | rreg                         | e(model)   | ols                             |
|-----------|------------------------------|------------|---------------------------------|
| e(depvar) | name of dependent variable   | e(predict) | program used to implement predict|
| e(genwt)  | variable containing the weights |         |                                 |

Matrices
| e(b) | coefficient vector | e(V) | variance–covariance matrix of the estimators |
|------|--------------------|------|---------------------------------------------|

Functions
| e(sample) | marks estimation sample |
|-----------|-------------------------|

# Methods and Formulas

rreg is implemented as an ado-file.

See Berk (1990), Goodall (1983), and Rousseeuw and Leroy (1987) for a general description of the issues and methods. Hamilton (1991, 1992) provides a more detailed description of rreg and some Monte Carlo evaluations.

rreg begins by estimating the regression (see [R] **regress**), calculating Cook's $D$ (see [R] **predict** and [R] **regression diagnostics**), and excluding any observation for which $D > 1$.

Thereafter rreg works iteratively: it performs a regression, calculates case weights based on absolute residuals, and regresses again using those weights. Iterations stop when the maximum change in weights drops below tolerance(). Weights derive from one of two weight functions, Huber weights and biweights. Huber weights (Huber 1964) are used until convergence and then, based on that result, biweights are used until convergence. The biweight was proposed by A. E. Beaton and J. W. Tukey (1974, 151–152) after the Princeton robustness study (Andrews et al. 1972) had compared various estimators. Both weighting functions are used because Huber weights have problems dealing with severe outliers while biweights sometimes fail to converge or have multiple solutions. The initial Huber weighting should improve the behavior of the biweight estimator.

Huber weighting: Cases with small residuals receive weights of 1; cases with larger residuals receive gradually smaller weights. Let $e_i = y_i - \mathbf{X}_i\mathbf{b}$ represent the $i$th-case residual. The $i$th scaled residual $u_i = e_i/s$ is calculated, where $s = M/.6745$ is the residual scale estimate and $M = \mathrm{med}(|e_i - \mathrm{med}(e_i)|)$ is the median absolute deviation from the median residual. Huber estimation obtains case weights:

$$w_i = \begin{cases} 1 & \text{if } |u_i| \leq c_h \\ c_h/|u_i| & \text{otherwise} \end{cases}$$

**rreg** defines $c_h = 1.345$, so downweighting begins with cases whose absolute residual exceed $(1.345/.6745)M \approx 2M$.

Biweight: All cases with nonzero residuals receive some downweighting, according to the smoothly decreasing biweight function

$$w_i = \begin{cases} \{1 - (u_i/c_b)^2\}^2 & \text{if } |u_i| \leq c_b \\ 0 & \text{otherwise} \end{cases}$$

where $c_b = 4.685 \cdot \mathtt{tune()}/7$. Thus, when $\mathtt{tune()} = 7$, cases with absolute residuals of $(4.685/.6745)M \approx 7M$ or more are assigned 0 weight and thus effectively dropped. Goodall (1983, 377) suggests using a value between 6 and 9, inclusive, for $\mathtt{tune()}$ in the biweight case and states that performance is good between 6 and 12, inclusive.

The tuning constants $c_h = 1.345$ and $c_b = 4.685$ (assuming $\mathtt{tune()}$ is set at the default 7) give **rreg** about 95% of the efficiency of OLS when applied to data with normally distributed errors (Hamilton 1991). Lower tuning constants downweight outliers more drastically (but give up Gaussian efficiency); higher tuning constants make the estimator more like OLS.

Standard errors are calculated using the pseudovalues approach described in Street, Carroll, and Ruppert (1988).

## Acknowledgment

The current version of **rreg** is due to Lawrence Hamilton, Department of Sociology, University of New Hampshire.

## References

Andrews, D. F., P. J. Bickel, F. R. Hampel, P. J. Huber, W. H. Rogers, and J. W. Tukey. 1972. *Robust Estimates of Location: Survey and Advances.* Princeton: Princeton University Press.

Beaton, A. E. and J. W. Tukey. 1974. The fitting of power series, meaning polynomials, illustrated on band-spectroscopic data. *Technometrics* 16: 146–185.

Berk, R. A. 1990. A primer on robust regression. In *Modern Methods of Data Analysis*, ed. J. Fox and J. S. Long, 292–324. Newbury Park, CA: Sage Publications.

Goodall, C. 1983. M-estimators of location: an outline of the theory. In *Understanding Robust and Exploratory Data Analysis*, ed. D. C. Hoaglin, F. Mosteller, and J. W. Tukey, 339–431. New York: John Wiley & Sons.

Gould, W. W. and W. H. Rogers. 1994. Quantile regression as an alternative to robust regression. *1994 Proceedings of the Statistical Computing Section*. Alexandria, VA: American Statistical Association.

Hamilton, L. C. 1991. srd1: How robust is robust regression? *Stata Technical Bulletin* 2: 21–26. Reprinted in *Stata Technical Bulletin Reprints*, vol. 1, pp. 169–175.

——. 1992. *Regression with Graphics*. Pacific Grove, CA: Brooks/Cole Publishing Company.

——. 1998. *Statistics with Stata 5*. Pacific Grove, CA: Brooks/Cole Publishing Company.

Huber, P. J. 1964. Robust estimation of a location parameter. *Annals of Mathematical Statistics* 35: 73–101.

Li, G. 1985. Robust regression. In *Exploring Data Tables, Trends, and Shapes*, ed. D. C. Hoaglin, F. Mosteller, and J. W. Tukey, 281–340. New York: John Wiley & Sons.

Mosteller, F. and J. W. Tukey. 1977. *Data Analysis and Regression*. Reading, MA: Addison–Wesley.

Relles, D. A. and W. H. Rogers. 1977. Statisticians are fairly robust estimators of location. *Journal of the American Statistical Association* 72: 107–111.

Rousseeuw, P. J. and A. M. Leroy. 1987. *Robust Regression and Outlier Detection*. New York: John Wiley & Sons.

Street, J. O., R. J. Carroll, and D. Ruppert. 1988. A note on computing robust regression estimates via iteratively reweighted least squares. *The American Statistician* 42: 152–154.

## Also See

| | |
|---|---|
| **Complementary:** | [R] **lincom**, [R] **linktest**, [R] **mfx**, [R] **predict**, [R] **test**, [R] **testnl**, [R] **vce**, [R] **xi** |
| **Related:** | [R] **qreg**, [R] **regress**, [R] **regression diagnostics** |
| **Background:** | [U] **16.5 Accessing coefficients and standard errors**, [U] **23 Estimation and post-estimation commands** |

# Title

**runtest** — Test for random order

# Syntax

runtest *varname* [in *range*] [ , <u>c</u>ontinuity <u>d</u>rop <u>m</u>ean <u>s</u>plit <u>t</u>hreshold(#) ]

# Description

runtest tests whether the observations of *varname* are serially independent—that is, whether they occur in a random order—by counting how many runs there are above and below a threshold. By default, the median is used as the threshold. A small number of runs indicates positive serial correlation; a large number, negative serial correlation.

# Options

**continuity** specifies a continuity correction that may be helpful in small samples. If there are fewer than 10 observations either above or below the threshold, however, the tables in Swed and Eisenhart (1943) provide more reliable critical values. By default, no continuity correction is used.

**drop** directs runtest to ignore any values of *varname* that are equal to the threshold value when counting runs and tabulating observations. By default, runtest counts a value as above the threshold when it is strictly above the threshold and as below the threshold when it is less than or equal to the threshold.

**mean** directs runtest to tabulate runs above and below the mean rather than the median.

**split** directs runtest to randomly split values of *varname* that are equal to the threshold. In other words, when *varname* is equal to threshold, a "coin" is flipped. If it comes up heads, the value is counted as above the threshold. If it comes up tails, the value is counted as below the threshold.

**threshold(#)** specifies an arbitrary threshold to use in counting runs. For example, if *varname* has already been coded as a 0/1 variable, the median generally will not be a meaningful separating value.

# Remarks

runtest performs a nonparametric test of the hypothesis that the observations of *varname* occur in a random order by counting how many runs there are above and below a threshold. If *varname* is positively serially correlated, it will tend to remain above or below its median for several observations in a row, that is, there will be relatively few runs. If, on the other hand, *varname* is negatively serially correlated, observations above the median will tend to be followed by observations below the median and vice versa, that is, there will be relatively many runs.

By default, runtest uses the median for the threshold and this is not necessarily the best choice. If **mean** is specified, the mean is used instead of the median. If **threshold(#)** is specified, # is used. Since runtest divides the data into two states—above and below the threshold—it is appropriate for data which are already binary, for example: win or lose, live or die, rich or poor, etc. Such variables are often coded as 0 for one state and 1 for the other. In this case, specify **threshold(0)** since, by default, runtest separates the observations into those that are greater than the threshold and those that are less than *or equal* to the threshold.

As with most nonparametric procedures, the treatment of ties complicates the test. Observations equal to the threshold value are ties and can be treated in one of three ways. By default, they are treated as if they were below the threshold. If **drop** is specified, they are omitted from the calculation and the total number of observations is adjusted. If **split** is specified, each is randomly assigned to the above- and below-threshold groups. The random assignment is different each time the procedure is run unless you specify the random number seed; see [R] **generate**.

▷ Example

We can use **runtest** to check regression residuals for serial correlation.

```
. regress ...
  (output omitted)
. predict resid, resid
. graph resid year, c(l) yli(0) ylab xlab title(Regression residuals)
```

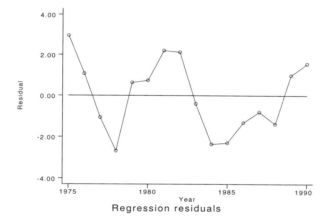

The graph gives the impression that these residuals are positively correlated. Excursions above or below zero—the natural threshold for regression residuals—tend to last for several observations. **runtest** can evaluate the statistical significance of this impression.

```
. runtest resid, thresh(0)
N(resid <= 0) = 8
N(resid >  0) = 8
          obs = 16
      N(runs) = 5
            z  = -2.07
     Prob>|z|  = .04
```

There are 5 runs in these sixteen observations. Using the normal approximation to the true distribution of the number of runs, the 5 runs in this series are fewer than would be expected if the residuals were serially independent. The $p$-value is 0.03, indicating a two-sided significant result at the 5 percent level. If the alternative hypothesis is positive serial correlation, rather than any deviation from randomness, then the one-sided $p$-value is $.03/2 = .015$. With so few observations, however, the normal approximation may be inaccurate. (Tables compiled by Swed and Eisenhart list 5 runs as the 5 percent critical value for a one-sided test.)

**runtest** is a nonparametric test. It ignores the magnitudes of the observations and notes only whether the values are above or below the threshold. We can demonstrate this feature by reducing the information about the regression residuals in this example to a 0/1 variable that indicates only whether a residual is positive or negative.

```
. generate byte sign = resid>0
. runtest sign, thresh(0)
 N(sign <= 0) = 8
 N(sign >  0) = 8
          obs = 16
     N(runs) = 5
          z  = -2.07
   Prob>|z| = .04
```

As expected, **runtest** produces the same answer as before.

◁

## ❏ Technical Note

The run test can also be used to test the null hypothesis that two samples are drawn from the same underlying distribution. The run test is sensitive to differences in the shapes, as well as the locations, of the empirical distributions.

Suppose, for example, that two different additives are added to the oil in ten different cars during an oil change. The cars are run until a viscosity test determines that another oil change is needed, and the number of miles traveled between oil changes is recorded. The data are

```
. list
        additive      miles
  1.        1         4024
  2.        1         4756
  3.        1         7993
  4.        1         5025
  5.        1         4188
  6.        2         3007
  7.        2         1988
  8.        2         1051
  9.        2         4478
 10.        2         4232
```

To test whether the additives generate different distributions of miles between oil changes, sort the data by **miles**, then use **runtest** to see whether the marker for each additive occurs in random order:

```
. sort miles
. runtest additive, thresh(1)
 N(additive <= 1) = 5
 N(additive >  1) = 5
              obs = 10
         N(runs) = 4
              z  = -1.34
       Prob>|z| = .18
```

In this example, the additives do not produce statistically different results.

❏

## ❏ Technical Note

A test that is related to the run test is the runs up-and-down test. In the latter test, the data are classified not by whether they lie above or below a threshold, but by whether they are steadily increasing or decreasing. Thus, an unbroken string of increases in the variable of interest is counted as one run, as is an unbroken string of decreases. According to Madansky (1988), the run test is superior to the runs up-and-down test for detecting trends in the data, but the runs up-and-down test is superior for detecting autocorrelation.

`runtest` can be used to perform a runs up-and-down test. Using the regression residuals from the example above, we can perform a `runtest` on their first differences:

```
. generate resid_D = resid - resid[_n-1]
(1 missing value generated)
. runtest resid_D, thresh(0)
 N(resid_D <= 0) = 7
 N(resid_D >  0) = 8
            obs = 15
        N(runs) = 6
              z = -1.33
       Prob>|z| = .18
```

Edgington (1961) has compiled a table of the small sample distribution of the runs up-and-down statistic, and this table is reprinted in Madansky (1988). For large samples, the $z$ statistic reported by `runtest` is incorrect for the runs up-and-down test. Let $N$ be the number of observations (15 in this example) and let $r$ be the number of runs (6). The expected number of runs in the runs up-and-down test is

$$\mu_r = \frac{2N - 1}{3}$$

the variance is

$$\sigma_r^2 = \frac{16N - 29}{90}$$

and the correct $z$ statistic is

$$\widehat{z} = \frac{r - \mu_r}{\sigma_r}$$

❏

## ❏ Technical Note

`runtest` will tolerate missing values at the beginning or end of a series, as occurred in the technical note above (generating first differences resulted in a missing value for the first observation). `runtest`, however, will issue an error message if there are any missing observations in the interior of the series (in the portion covered by the **in** *range* modifier). If you wish to perform the test anyway, simply **drop** the missing observations before using `runtest`.

❏

## Saved Results

runtest saves in r():

Scalars

| | | | |
|---|---|---|---|
| r(N) | number of observations | r(p) | $p$-value of $z$ |
| r(N_below) | number below the threshold | r(z) | $z$ statistic |
| r(N_above) | number above the threshold | r(n_runs) | number of runs |
| r(mean) | expected number of runs | r(Var) | variance of the number of runs |

## Methods and Formulas

runtest is implemented as an ado-file.

runtest begins by calculating the number of observations below the threshold, $n_0$, the number of observations above the threshold, $n_1$, the total number of observations, $N = n_0 + n_1$, and the number of runs, $r$. These statistics are always reported, so the exact tables of critical values in Swed and Eisenhart (1943) may be consulted if necessary.

The expected number of runs under the null is

$$\mu_r = \frac{2n_0n_1}{N} + 1$$

the variance is

$$\sigma_r^2 = \frac{2n_0n_1\left(2n_0n_1 - N\right)}{N^2\left(N - 1\right)}$$

and the normal approximation test statistic is

$$\widehat{z} = \frac{r - \mu_r}{\sigma_r}$$

## Acknowledgments

runtest was written by Sean Becketti, a past editor of the *Stata Technical Bulletin*.

## References

Edgington, E. S. 1961. Probability table for number of runs of signs of first differences in ordered series. *Journal of the American Statistical Association* 56: 156–159.

Madansky, A. 1988. *Prescriptions for Working Statisticians*. New York: Springer-Verlag.

Swed, F. S. and C. Eisenhart. 1943. Tables for testing randomness of grouping in a sequence of alternatives. *Annals of Mathematical Statistics* 14: 83–86.

## Also See

**Related:**     [R] **ksmirnov**, [R] **kwallis**, [R] **signrank**

# Title

| |
|---|
| **sample** — Draw random sample |

# Syntax

sample # $\left[\text{if } exp\right]$ $\left[\text{in } range\right]$ $\left[\,, \text{ by}(groupvars)\,\right]$

# Description

sample draws a # percent pseudo-random sample of the data in memory, thus discarding $100-\#$ percent of the observations. Observations not meeting the optional if and in criteria are kept (sampled at 100%).

"Sampling" here is defined as drawing observations without replacement; see [R] **bstrap** for sampling with replacement.

If you are serious about drawing random samples, you must first set the random number seed; see [R] **generate**.

# Options

by(*groupvars*) specifies that a # percent sample is to be drawn within each set of values of *groupvars*, thus maintaining the proportion of each group.

# Remarks

▷ Example

You have data on the characteristics of hospital patients and wish to draw a 10% sample of the data in memory. You type

```
. sample 10
(5229 observations deleted)
```

The resulting sample size will be the closest integer to $(10/100)N$, where $N$ is the number of observations prior to sampling. Thus, if your original dataset had 5,854 observations, the resulting dataset will have 585 observations; if your original dataset had 5,856 observations, the resulting dataset will have 586 observations.

◁

▷ Example

Among the variables in your data is race; race==0 denotes whites and race==1 denotes nonwhites. To keep 100% of the nonwhite patients but only 10% of the white patients, type

```
. sample 10 if race==0
(4183 observations deleted)
```

◁

▷ Example

If you instead wish to keep 10% of the white patients and 10% of the nonwhite patients, you type

```
. sample 10, by(race)
(5228 observations deleted)
```

This differs from typing simply **sample 10** in that, with **by()**, **sample** holds constant the ratio of white to nonwhite patients.

◁

❑ Technical Note

You have a large dataset on disk containing 125,235 observations. You wish to draw a 10% sample of this dataset without loading the entire dataset (perhaps because the dataset will not fit in memory). **sample** will not solve this problem—the dataset must be loaded first—but it is rather easy to solve it yourself. Pretend **bigdata.dct** contains the dictionary for this dataset; see [R] **infile**. One solution is

```
. infile using bigdata if uniform()<=.1
dictionary {
     etc.
}
(12,580 observations read)
```

The **if** modifier on the end of **infile** drew uniformly distributed random numbers over the interval 0 and 1 and kept each observation if the random number was less than or equal to 0.1. This, however, did not draw an exact 10% sample—the sample was only expected to contain 10% of the observations and in this case we obtained just more than 10%. This is probably a good enough solution.

If the sample must contain precisely 12,524 observations, however, after getting too many observations we could

```
. gen u=uniform()
. sort u
. keep in 1/12524
(56 observations deleted)
```

That is, we put the resulting sample in random order and keep the first 12,524 observations. Now our only problem is making sure that, at the first step, we have more than 12,524 observations. In this case, we were lucky, but half the time we will not be so lucky—after typing **infile ... if uniform()<=.1**, we will have less than a 10% sample. The solution, of course, is to draw more than a 10% sample initially and then cut it back to 10%.

How much bigger than 10% do we need? That depends on the number of records in the original dataset, which in our example is 125,235.

A little experimentation with **bitesti** (see [R] **bitest**) provides the answer:

```
. bitesti 125235 12524 .102
          N    Observed k    Expected k    Assumed p    Observed p
     125235         12524       12773.97      0.10200       0.10000
  Pr(k >= 12524)              = 0.990466   (one-sided test)
  Pr(k <= 12524)              = 0.009777   (one-sided test)
  Pr(k <= 12524 or k >= 13025) = 0.019584  (two-sided test)
```

To wit: initially drawing a 10.2% sample will yield a sample larger than 10% 99 times out of 100. If we draw a 10.4% sample, we are virtually assured of having enough observations (type `bitesti 125235 12524 .104` for yourself).

❑

## Methods and Formulas

`sample` is implemented as an ado-file.

## References

Weesie, J. 1997. dm46: Enhancement to the sample command. *Stata Technical Bulletin* 37: 6–7. Reprinted in *Stata Technical Bulletin Reprints*, vol. 7, pp. 37–38.

## Also See

**Related:**      [R] **bstrap**

# Title

**sampsi** — Sample size and power determination

# Syntax

sampsi #$_1$ #$_2$ $\left[ \right.$, <u>alpha</u>(#) <u>power</u>(#) <u>n1</u>(#) n2(#) <u>ratio</u>(#) pre(#) post(#)

   <u>sd1</u>(#) sd2(#) <u>method</u>(post|change|ancova|all) r0(#) r1(#) r01(#)

   <u>onesample</u> <u>onesid</u>ed $\left. \right]$

# Description

    sampsi estimates required sample size or power of tests for studies comparing two groups. sampsi can be used when comparing means or proportions for simple studies where only one measurement of the outcome is planned, and for comparing mean summary statistics for more complex studies where repeated measurements of the outcome on each experimental unit are planned.

    If n1(#) and/or n2(#) is specified, sampsi computes power; otherwise, it computes sample size. For simple studies, if sd1(#) and/or sd2(#) is specified, sampsi assumes a comparison of means; otherwise, it assumes a comparison of proportions. In the case of repeated measurements sampsi, sd1(#) and/or sd2(#) must always be specified. sampsi is an immediate command; all its arguments are numbers.

# Options

    alpha(#) is the significance level of the test. The default is alpha(0.05) unless set level has been used to reset the default significance level for confidence intervals. If a set level #$_{lev}$ command has been issued, the default value is alpha($1 - \#_{lev}/100$). See [R] **level**.

    power(#) $= 1 - \beta$ is the power of the test. The default is power(0.90).

    n1(#) and n2(#) are the sizes of sample 1 and sample 2, respectively. One or both must be specified when computing power. If neither n1(#) nor n2(#) is specified, then sampsi computes sample size. When the onesample option is used, n1(#) is the size of the single sample (note that it can be abbreviated as n(#)). If only one of n1(#) or n2(#) is specified, then the unspecified one is computed using the formula: ratio $=$ n2/n1.

    ratio(#) is the ratio of sample sizes for two-sample tests: ratio $=$ n2/n1. The default is ratio(1).

    pre(#) specifies the number of baseline measurements (pre-randomization) planned in a repeated–measure study. The default is pre(0).

    post(#) specifies the number of follow-up measurements (post-randomization) planned in a repeated–measure study. The default is post(1).

    sd1(#) and sd2(#) are the standard deviations of population 1 and population 2, respectively. One or both must be specified when doing a comparison of means. When the onesample option is used, sd1(#) is the standard deviation of the single sample (note that it can be abbreviated as sd(#)). If only one of sd1(#) or sd2(#) is specified, sampsi assumes that sd1 $=$ sd2. If neither sd1(#) nor sd2(#) is specified, sampsi assumes a test of proportions. In the case of repeated measurements, sd1(#) and/or sd2(#) must be specified.

`method(post|change|ancova|all)` specifies the analysis method to be used with repeated measures. `change` and `ancova` can only be used if baseline measurements are planned. The default is `method(all)`, which means use all three methods. Each method is described in the *Methods and Formulas* section.

`r0(#)` specifies the correlation between baseline measurements in repeated–measurement studies. If `r0(#)` is not specified, `sampsi` assumes that `r0 = r1`.

`r1(#)` specifies the correlation between follow-up measurements in repeated–measurement studies. `r1(#)` must be specified.

`r01(#)` specifies the correlation between baseline and follow-up measurements in repeated–measurement studies. If `r01(#)` is not specified, `sampsi` assumes that `r01 = r1`.

`onesample` indicates a one-sample test. The default is two-sample.

`onesided` indicates a one-sided test. The default is two-sided.

# Remarks

Remarks are presented under the headings

> *Studies with a single measurement of the outcome*
> *Two-sample test of equality of means*
> *One-sample test of mean*
> *Two-sample test of equality of proportions*
> *One-sample test of proportion*
> *Clinical trials with repeated measures*

## Studies with a single measurement of the outcome

For simple studies, where only one measurement of the outcome is planned, `sampsi` computes sample size or power for four types of tests:

1. Two-sample comparison of mean $\mu_1$ of population 1 with mean $\mu_2$ of population 2. The null hypothesis is $\mu_1 = \mu_2$, and normality is assumed. The postulated values of the means are $\mu_1 = \#_1$ and $\mu_2 = \#_2$, and the postulated standard deviations are `sd1(#)` and `sd2(#)`.

2. One-sample comparison of the mean $\mu$ of a population with a hypothesized value $\mu_0$. The null hypothesis is $\mu = \mu_0$, and normality is assumed. The first argument $\#_1$ to `sampsi` is $\mu_0$. The second argument $\#_2$ is the postulated value of $\mu$; i.e., the alternative hypothesis is $\mu = \#_2$. The postulated standard deviation is `sd1(#)`. To get this test, the `onesample` option must be given.

3. Two-sample comparison of proportion $p_1$ with proportion $p_2$. The null hypothesis is $p_1 = p_2$, and the postulated values are $p_1 = \#_1$ and $p_2 = \#_2$.

4. One-sample comparison of a proportion $p$ with a hypothesized value $p_0$. The null hypothesis is $p = p_0$, where $p_0 = \#_1$. The alternative hypothesis is $p = \#_2$. To get this test, the `onesample` option must be given.

Examples of these follow.

# Two-sample test of equality of means

▷ Example

We are doing a study of the relationship of oral contraceptives (OC) and blood pressure (BP) level for women ages 35–39 (Rosner 2000, 307—308). From a pilot study, it was determined that the mean and standard deviation BP of OC users were 132.86 and 15.34 respectively. The mean and standard deviation of OC nonusers in the plot study were found to be 127.44 and 18.23. Since it is easier to find OC nonusers than users, we decide that $n_2$, the size of the sample of OC nonusers, should be twice $n_1$, the size of the sample of OC users; that is, $r = n_2/n_1 = 2$. To compute the sample sizes for $\alpha = 0.05$ (two-sided) and the power of 0.80, we issue the following command:

```
. sampsi 132.86 127.44, p(0.8) r(2) sd1(15.34) sd2(18.23)

Estimated sample size for two-sample comparison of means

Test Ho: m1 = m2, where m1 is the mean in population 1
                    and m2 is the mean in population 2

Assumptions:

              alpha =    0.0500  (two-sided)
              power =    0.8000
                 m1 =    132.86
                 m2 =    127.44
                sd1 =     15.34
                sd2 =     18.23
              n2/n1 =      2.00

Estimated required sample sizes:
                 n1 =       108
                 n2 =       216
```

We now find out that we only have enough money to study 100 subjects from each group. We can compute the power for $n_1 = n_2 = 100$ by typing

```
. sampsi 132.86 127.44, n1(100) sd1(15.34) sd2(18.23)

Estimated power for two-sample comparison of means

Test Ho: m1 = m2, where m1 is the mean in population 1
                    and m2 is the mean in population 2

Assumptions:

              alpha =    0.0500  (two-sided)
                 m1 =    132.86
                 m2 =    127.44
                sd1 =     15.34
                sd2 =     18.23
     sample size n1 =       100
                 n2 =       100
              n2/n1 =      1.00

Estimated power:
              power =    0.6236
```

Note that we did not have to give n2(#) or ratio(#), since ratio(1) is the default.

◁

# One-sample test of mean

▷ Example

Suppose that we wish to test the effects of a low-fat diet on serum cholesterol levels. We will measure the difference in cholesterol level for each subject before and after being on the diet. Since there is only one group of subjects, all on the diet, this is a one-sample test, and we must use the `onesample` option with `sampsi`.

Our null hypothesis is that the mean of individual differences in cholesterol level will be zero; i.e., $\mu = 0\,mg/100\,ml$. If the effect of the diet is as large as a mean difference of $-10\,mg/100\,ml$, then we wish to have power of 0.95 for rejecting the null hypothesis. Since we expect a reduction in levels, we want to use a one-sided test with $\alpha = 0.025$. Based on past studies, we estimate that the standard deviation of the difference in cholesterol levels will be about $20\,mg/100\,ml$. To compute the required sample size, we type

```
. sampsi 0 -10, sd(20) onesam a(0.025) onesided p(0.95)
Estimated sample size for one-sample comparison of mean
  to hypothesized value
Test Ho: m =      0, where m is the mean in the population
Assumptions:
            alpha =   0.0250  (one-sided)
            power =   0.9500
    alternative m =     -10
               sd =      20
Estimated required sample size:
                n =      52
```

We decide to conduct the study with $n = 60$ subjects, and we wonder what the power will be at a one-sided significance level of $\alpha = 0.01$:

```
. sampsi 0 -10, sd(20) onesam a(0.01) onesided n(60)
Estimated power for one-sample comparison of mean
  to hypothesized value
Test Ho: m =      0, where m is the mean in the population
Assumptions:
            alpha =   0.0100  (one-sided)
    alternative m =     -10
               sd =      20
    sample size n =      60
Estimated power:
            power =   0.9390
```

◁

# Two-sample test of equality of proportions

▷ Example

We want to conduct a survey on people's opinions of the President's performance. Specifically, we want to determine whether members of the President's party have a different opinion from people with another party affiliation. Using past surveys as a guide, we estimate that only 25 percent of members of the President's party will say that the President is doing a poor job, whereas 40 percent of members of other parties will rate the President's performance as poor. We compute the required sample sizes for $\alpha = 0.05$ (two-sided) and the power of 0.90 by typing

```
. sampsi 0.25 0.4

Estimated sample size for two-sample comparison of proportions

Test Ho: p1 = p2, where p1 is the proportion in population 1
                  and p2 is the proportion in population 2
Assumptions:

          alpha =   0.0500  (two-sided)
          power =   0.9000
             p1 =   0.2500
             p2 =   0.4000
          n2/n1 =   1.00

Estimated required sample sizes:
             n1 =      216
             n2 =      216
```

To compute the power for a survey with a sample of $n_1 = 300$ members of the President's party and a sample of $n_2 = 150$ members of other parties, type

```
. sampsi 0.25 0.4, n1(300) r(0.5)

Estimated power for two-sample comparison of proportions

Test Ho: p1 = p2, where p1 is the proportion in population 1
                  and p2 is the proportion in population 2
Assumptions:

            alpha =   0.0500  (two-sided)
               p1 =   0.2500
               p2 =   0.4000
   sample size n1 =      300
               n2 =      150
            n2/n1 =     0.50

Estimated power:
            power =   0.8790
```

◁

# One-sample test of proportion

▷ Example

Someone claims that females are more likely than males to study French. Our null hypothesis is that the proportion of female French students is 0.5. We wish to compute the sample size that will give us 80% power to reject the null hypothesis if the true proportion of female French students is 0.75:

```
. sampsi 0.5 0.75, power(0.8) onesample

Estimated sample size for one-sample comparison of proportion
  to hypothesized value

Test Ho: p = 0.5000, where p is the proportion in the population
Assumptions:

          alpha =   0.0500  (two-sided)
          power =   0.8000
  alternative p =   0.7500

Estimated required sample size:
              n =       29
```

What is the power if the true proportion of female French students is only 0.6, and the biggest sample of French students we can survey is $n = 200$?

```
. sampsi 0.5 0.6, n(200) onesam
Estimated power for one-sample comparison of proportion
  to hypothesized value

Test Ho: p = 0.5000, where p is the proportion in the population

Assumptions:

            alpha =   0.0500   (two-sided)
    alternative p =   0.6000
    sample size n =      200

Estimated power:
            power =   0.8123
```

◁

## Clinical trials with repeated measures

In randomized controlled trials (RCTs) comparing a standard treatment with an experimental therapy is not unusual for the study design to allow for repeated measurements of the outcome. Typically one or more measurements are taken at baseline immediately before randomization and additional measurements are taken at regular intervals during follow-up. Depending on the analysis method planned and the correlations between measurements at different time points, there can be a great increase in efficiency (variance reduction) from such designs over a simple study with only one measurement of the outcome.

Frison & Pocock (1992) discuss three methods used in RCTs to compare two treatments using a continuous outcome measured at different times on each patient.

Post-treatment means (POST): Uses the mean of each patient's follow-up measurements as the summary measurement. It compares the two groups using a simple $t$ test. This method ignores any baseline measurements.

Mean changes (CHANGE): Uses each patient's difference between the mean of the follow-up measurements and the mean of baseline measurements as the summary measurement. It compares the two groups using a simple $t$ test.

Analysis of covariance (ANCOVA): The mean baseline measurement for each patient is used as a covariate in a linear model for treatment comparisons of follow-up means.

`method()` is used to specify which of these three analyses is planned to be used. `sampsi` will calculate the decrease in variance of the estimate of treatment effect based on the number of measurements at baseline, the number of measurements during follow-up, and the correlations between measurements at different times and use it to estimate power and/or sample size.

▷ Example

We are designing a clinical trial comparing a new medication for the treatment of angina to a placebo. We are planning on performing an exercise stress test on each patient four times during the study, once at time of treatment randomization and 3 more times at 4, 6 and 8 weeks after randomization. From each test we will measure the time in seconds from the beginning of the test until the patient is unable to continue due to angina pain. From a previous pilot study we estimated the means (sds) for the new drug and the placebo group to be 498 seconds (20.2) and 485 seconds (19.5) respectively, and an overall correlation at follow-up of 0.7. We will analyze these data by comparing each patient's difference between the mean of post-treatment measurements and the mean of baseline measurements, i.e., the change method. To compute the number of subjects needed for allocation to each treatment group for $\alpha = 0.05$ (two-sided) and power of 90%, we issue the command:

```
. sampsi 498 485, sd1(20.2) sd2(19.5) method(change) pre(1) post(3) r1(.7)

Estimated sample size for two samples with repeated measures

Assumptions:
          alpha =   0.0500  (two-sided)
                                            power =    0.9000
                                               m1 =       498
                                               m2 =       485
                                              sd1 =      20.2
                                              sd2 =      19.5
                                            n2/n1 =      1.00
              number of follow-up measurements =         3
   correlation between follow-up measurements =     0.700
             number of baseline measurements =         1
     correlation between baseline & follow-up =     0.700

Method: CHANGE
  relative efficiency =      2.500
     adjustment to sd =      0.632
          adjusted sd1 =    12.776
          adjusted sd2 =    12.333

Estimated required sample sizes:
                 n1 =        20
                 n2 =        20
```

The output from `sampsi` for repeated measurements includes the specified parameters used to estimate the sample sizes or power, the relative efficiency of the design, and the adjustment to the standard deviation. These last two are the inverse and the square root of the calculated improvement in the variance compared to a similar study where only one measurement is planned.

We see that we need to allocate 20 subjects to each treatment group. Assume that we only have funds to enroll 30 patients into our study. If we randomly assigned 15 patients to each treatment group, what would be the expected power of our study assuming all other parameters remain the same?

```
. sampsi 498 485, sd1(20.2) sd2(19.5) meth(change) pre(1) post(3) r1(.7) n1(15) n2(15)

Estimated power for two samples with repeated measures

Assumptions:
                                          alpha =   0.0500  (two-sided)
                                             m1 =       498
                                             m2 =       485
                                            sd1 =      20.2
                                            sd2 =      19.5
                               sample size n1 =        15
                                             n2 =        15
                                          n2/n1 =      1.00
              number of follow-up measurements =         3
   correlation between follow-up measurements =     0.700
             number of baseline measurements =         1
     correlation between baseline & follow-up =     0.700

Method: CHANGE    .
  relative efficiency =      2.500
     adjustment to sd =      0.632
          adjusted sd1 =    12.776
          adjusted sd2 =    12.333

Estimated power:
              power =      0.809
```

If we enroll 30 patients into our study instead of the recommended 40 the power of the study decreases from 90% to approximately 81%.

◁

# Saved Results

sampsi saves in r():

Scalars

| | |
|---|---|
| r(N_1) | sample size $n_1$ |
| r(N_2) | sample size $n_2$ |
| r(power) | power |
| r(adj) | Adjustment to the SE |

# Methods and Formulas

sampsi is implemented as an ado-file.

In the following formulas, $\alpha$ is the one-sided significance level (half of the two-sided significance level), $1 - \beta$ is the power, $z_{1-\alpha}$ is the $(1 - \alpha)$-quantile of the normal distribution, and $r = n_2/n_1$ is the ratio of sample sizes.

1. The required sample sizes for a two-sample test of equality of means (assuming normality) are

$$n_1 = \frac{(\sigma_1^2 + \sigma_2^2/r)(z_{1-\alpha} + z_{1-\beta})^2}{(\mu_1 - \mu_2)^2}$$

and $n_2 = rn_1$ (Rosner 2000, 308).

2. For a one-sample test of a mean where the null hypothesis is $\mu = \mu_0$ and the alternative hypothesis is $\mu = \mu_A$, the required sample size (assuming normality) is

$$n = \left\{ \frac{(z_{1-\alpha} + z_{1-\beta})\sigma}{\mu_A - \mu_0} \right\}^2$$

(Pagano and Gauvreau 2000, 247–248).

3. The required sample sizes for a two-sample test of equality of proportions (using a normal approximation with a continuity correction) are

$$n_1 = \frac{n'}{4} \left\{ 1 + \sqrt{1 + \frac{2(r + 1)}{n'r \,|p_1 - p_2|}} \right\}^2$$

$$n_2 = rn_1$$

where

$$n' = \frac{\left\{ z_{1-\alpha}\sqrt{(r + 1)\overline{pq}} + z_{1-\beta}\sqrt{rp_1q_1 + p_2q_2} \right\}^2}{r(p_1 - p_2)^2}$$

and $\bar{p} = (p_1 + rp_2)/(r + 1)$ and $\bar{q} = 1 - \bar{p}$ (Fleiss 1981, 45).

4. For a one-sample test of proportion where the null hypothesis is $p = p_0$ and the alternative hypothesis is $p = p_A$, the required sample size (using a normal approximation) is

$$n = \left\{ \frac{z_{1-\alpha}\sqrt{p_0(1 - p_0)} + z_{1-\beta}\sqrt{p_A(1 - p_A)}}{p_A - p_0} \right\}^2$$

(Pagano and Gauvreau 2000, 332).

5. For repeated measurements, Frison & Pocock (1992) discuss three methods for use in randomized clinical trials to compare two treatments using a continuous outcome measured at different times on each patient. Each uses the average of baseline measurements $\bar{x}_0$ and follow-up measurements $\bar{x}_1$:

POST outcome is $\bar{x}_1$ where the analysis is by simple $t$ test.

CHANGE outcome is $\bar{x}_1 - \bar{x}_0$ where the analysis is by simple $t$ test.

ANCOVA outcome is $\bar{x}_1 - \beta\bar{x}_0$ where the $\beta$ is estimated by analysis of covariance, correcting for the average at baseline.

ANCOVA will always be the most efficient of the three approaches. $\beta$ is set so that $\beta\bar{x}_0$ accounts for the largest possible variation of $\bar{x}_1$.

For a study with one measurement each at baseline and follow-up, CHANGE will be more efficient than POST provided that the correlation between measurements at baseline and measurements at follow-up is more than 0.5. POST ignores all baseline measurements, which tends to make it unpopular. CHANGE is the method most commonly used. With more than one baseline measurement, CHANGE and ANCOVA tend to produce similar sample sizes and power.

The improvements in variance of the estimate of treatment effect over a study with only one measurement depends on the number of measurements $p$ at baseline, the number of measurements during follow-up, and on the correlations between measurements at baseline $\bar{\rho}_{\mathrm{pre}}$, between measurements at follow-up $\bar{\rho}_{\mathrm{post}}$, and between measurements at baseline and measurements at follow-up $\bar{\rho}_{\mathrm{mix}}$. The improvements in variance for the POST method are given by

$$\frac{1 + (r - 1)\bar{\rho}_{\mathrm{post}}}{r}$$

for the CHANGE method by

$$\frac{1 + (r - 1)\bar{\rho}_{\mathrm{post}}}{r} + \frac{1 + (p - 1)\bar{\rho}_{\mathrm{pre}}}{p} - 2\bar{\rho}_{\mathrm{mix}}$$

and for the ANCOVA method by

$$\frac{1 + (r - 1)\bar{\rho}_{\mathrm{post}}}{r} - \frac{\bar{\rho}_{\mathrm{mix}}^2 p}{1 + (p - 1)\bar{\rho}_{\mathrm{pre}}}$$

Often the three correlations are assumed equal. In data from a number of trials, Frison & Pocock found $\bar{\rho}_{\mathrm{pre}}$ and $\bar{\rho}_{\mathrm{post}}$ typically had values around 0.7, while $\bar{\rho}_{\mathrm{mix}}$ was nearer 0.5. This is consistent with the common finding that measurements closer in time are more strongly correlated.

Power calculations are based on estimates of a single variance at all time points.

## Acknowledgments

sampsi is based on the sampsiz command written by Joseph Hilbe of Arizona State University (Hilbe 1993). Paul Seed of United Medical & Dental Schools of Guy's & St Thomas's Hospitals (Seed 1997, 1998) expanded the command to allow for repeated measurements.

## References

Fleiss, J. L. 1981. *Statistical Methods for Rates and Proportions.* New York: John Wiley & Sons.

Frison, L. and S. Pocock. 1992. Repeated measurements in clinical trials: analysis using mean summary statistics and its implications for design. *Statistics in Medicine* 11: 1685-1704.

Hilbe, J. 1993. sg15: Sample size determination for means and proportions. *Stata Technical Bulletin* 11: 17–20. Reprinted in *Stata Technical Bulletin Reprints,* vol. 2, pp. 145–149.

Pagano, M. and K. Gauvreau. 2000. *Principles of Biostatistics.* 2d ed. Pacific Grove, CA: Brooks/Cole.

Rosner, B. 2000. *Fundamentals of Biostatistics.* 5th ed. Pacific Grove, CA: Duxbury Press.

Seed, P. 1997. sbe18: Sample size calculations for clinical trials with repeated measures data. *Stata Technical Bulletin* 40: 16–18. Reprinted in *Stata Technical Bulletin Reprints,* vol. 7, pp. 121–125.

——. 1998. sbe18.1: Update of sampsi. *Stata Technical Bulletin* 45: 21. Reprinted in *Stata Technical Bulletin Reprints,* vol. 8, p. 84.

## Also See

**Background:** [U] **22 Immediate commands**

# Title

| **save** — Save and use datasets |
|---|

# Syntax

$\underline{\text{sa}}$ve $\left[\textit{filename}\right]$ $\left[, \underline{\text{no}}\text{label old replace all}\right]$

$\underline{\text{u}}$se $\textit{filename}$ $\left[, \text{clear} \underline{\text{no}}\text{label}\right]$

$\underline{\text{u}}$se $\left[\textit{varlist}\right]$ $\left[\text{if } \textit{exp}\right]$ $\left[\text{in } \textit{range}\right]$ using $\textit{filename}$ $\left[, \text{clear} \underline{\text{no}}\text{label}\right]$

# Description

**save** stores the dataset currently in memory on disk under the name *filename*. If *filename* is not specified, the name under which the data was last known to Stata ($S_FN) is used. If *filename* is specified without an extension, '.dta' is used.

**use** loads a Stata-format dataset previously saved by **save** into memory. If *filename* is specified without an extension, '.dta' is assumed.

In the second syntax for **use**, a subset of the data may be read.

# Options

nolabel with **save** omits value labels from the saved dataset. The associations between variables and value label names, however, are saved along with the dataset label and variable labels. With use, nolabel prevents value labels in the saved data from being loaded. In either case, it is unlikely that you will ever want to specify this option.

old writes datasets that are readable by someone with Stata 6.0. If your dataset contains variable names longer than 8 characters or value labels longer than 8 characters, Stata will refuse to save.

replace permits **save** to overwrite an existing dataset. replace may not be abbreviated.

all is for use by programmers. If specified, e(sample) will be saved with the dataset. You could run a regression, save mydata, all, drop _all, use mydata, and predict yhat if e(sample).

clear permits the data to be loaded even if there is a dataset already in memory and even if that dataset has changed since the data were last **saved**.

# Remarks

Stata keeps the data on which you are working in your computer's memory. You get the data there in the first place by using the input, infile, insheet, or infix commands; see [U] **24 Commands to input data**. Thereafter, you can **save** the data on disk so that you can easily **use** it in the future. Stata stores your data on disk in a compressed format that only Stata understands. This does not mean, however, that you are locked into using only Stata. Anytime you wish you can use the outfile or outsheet commands to create an ASCII-format dataset that all software packages understand; see [R] **outfile** and [R] **outsheet**.

176

Stata goes to a lot of trouble to keep you from accidentally losing your data. When you attempt to leave Stata by typing `exit`, Stata checks that your data have been safely stored on disk. If not, Stata refuses to let you leave. (You can tell Stata that you want to leave anyway by typing `exit, clear`.) Similarly, when you `save` your data in a disk file, Stata checks to make sure that the disk file does not already exist. If it does exist, Stata refuses. You can use the `replace` option to tell Stata that it is okay to overwrite an existing file.

▷ Example

Somehow you have entered data into Stata for the first time. You have the following data:

```
. describe
Contains data
  obs:          39
  vars:          5
  size:        936 (99.6% of memory free)
```

| variable name | storage type | display format | value label | variable label |
|---|---|---|---|---|
| acc_rate | float | %9.0g | | Accident rate |
| spdlimit | float | %9.0g | | Speed limit |
| acc_pts | float | %9.0g | | Access points per mile |
| rate | float | %9.0g | rcat | Accident rate per million vehicle miles |
| spdcat | float | %9.0g | scat | Speed limit category |

```
Sorted by:
     Note:  dataset has changed since last saved
```

You have a dataset containing 39 observations on 5 variables, and evidently you have gone to much trouble to prepare this dataset. You have used the `label data` command to label the data Minnesota Highway Data, the `label variable` command to label all the variables, and the `label define` and `label values` commands to attach value labels to the last two variables. (See [U] **15.6.3 Value labels** for how you did this.)

Notice that at the end of the `describe`, Stata notes: "dataset has changed since last saved". This is Stata's way of gently reminding you that these data have not been put away safely. Let's `save` your data:

```
. save hiway
file hiway.dta saved
```

We type `save hiway` and Stata stores the data in a file named `hiway.dta`. (The `.dta` suffix was automatically added by Stata.) Now when we `describe` our data, we no longer get the warning that our dataset has not been saved; instead we are told where the data are saved:

*(Continued on next page)*

```
. describe
Contains data from hiway.dta
  obs:            39                          Minnesota Highway Data, 1973
  vars:            5                          21 Jul 2000 11:42
  size:          936 (99.7% of memory free)
```

| variable name | storage type | display format | value label | variable label |
|---|---|---|---|---|
| acc_rate | float | %9.0g | | Accident rate |
| spdlimit | float | %9.0g | | Speed limit |
| acc_pts | float | %9.0g | | Access points per mile |
| rate | float | %9.0g | rcat | Accident rate per million vehicle miles |
| spdcat | float | %9.0g | scat | Speed limit category |

```
Sorted by:
```

Just to prove to you that the data have really been saved, let's eliminate the copy of the data in memory by typing drop _all:

```
. drop _all
. describe
Contains data
  obs:             0
  vars:            0
  size:            0 (100.0% of memory free)
Sorted by:
```

We now have no data in memory. Since we stored our data, we can retrieve it by typing use hiway:

```
. use hiway
(Minnesota Highway Data, 1973)
. describe
Contains data from hiway.dta
  obs:            39                          Minnesota Highway Data, 1973
  vars:            5                          21 Jul 2000 11:42
  size:          936 (99.7% of memory free)
```

| variable name | storage type | display format | value label | variable label |
|---|---|---|---|---|
| acc_rate | float | %9.0g | | Accident rate |
| spdlimit | float | %9.0g | | Speed limit |
| acc_pts | float | %9.0g | | Access points per mile |
| rate | float | %9.0g | rcat | Accident rate per million vehicle miles |
| spdcat | float | %9.0g | scat | Speed limit category |

```
Sorted by:
```

◁

▷ Example

Continuing with our previous example, we have saved our data in the file hiway.dta. We continue to work with our data and discover an error; we made a mistake when we typed one of the values for the variable spdlimit:

```
. list in 1/3

      acc_rate    spdlimit    acc_pts      rate     spdcat
  1.      1.61          50        2.2    Below 4   Above 60
  2.      1.81          60        6.8    Below 4   55 to 60
  3.      1.84          55         14    Below 4   55 to 60
```

Notice that in the first observation, the variable `spdlimit` is 50 whereas the `spdcat` variable indicates that the speed limit is over 60 miles per hour. We check our original copy of the data and discover that the `spdlimit` variable ought to be 70. We fix it using the `replace` command:

```
. replace spdlimit=70 in 1
(1 real change made)
```

If we were to `describe` our data now, Stata would warn us that our data have now changed since the data were last saved:

```
. describe
Contains data from hiway.dta
  obs:            39                          Minnesota Highway Data, 1973
  vars:            5                          21 Jul 2000 11:42
  size:          936 (99.7% of memory free)
```

| variable name | storage type | display format | value label | variable label |
| --- | --- | --- | --- | --- |
| acc_rate | float | %9.0g | | Accident rate |
| spdlimit | float | %9.0g | | Speed limit |
| acc_pts | float | %9.0g | | Access points per mile |
| rate | float | %9.0g | rcat | Accident rate per million vehicle miles |
| spdcat | float | %9.0g | scat | Speed limit category |

```
Sorted by:
    Note:  dataset has changed since last saved
```

We take our cue and attempt to `save` the data again:

```
. save hiway
file hiway.dta already exists
r(602);
```

Stata refused to honor our request, telling us instead, "file hiway.dta already exists". Stata will not let you accidentally overwrite an existing dataset. To `replace` the data, you have to tell Stata explicitly by typing `save hiway, replace`. If you want to save the file under the same name as it was last known to Stata, you can omit the filename:

```
. save, replace
file hiway.dta saved
```

Now our data are saved.

◁

## ❑ Technical Note

If you are working with really large datasets, you may one day `use` your data and have the following occur:

```
. use employee
insufficient memory
r(950);
```

If this occurs, you need to increase the amount of memory allocated to Stata; see [U] **7 Setting the size of memory**.

❏

## Also See

**Complementary:**    [R] **compress**

**Related:**    [R] **outfile**, [R] **outsheet**

**Background:**    [U] **7 Setting the size of memory**,
                [U] **14.6 File-naming conventions**,
                [U] **24 Commands to input data**

# Title

**saved results** — Saved results

# Syntax

<u>ret</u>urn <u>list</u>

<u>est</u>imates <u>list</u>

<u>sret</u>urn <u>list</u>

# Description

Results of calculations are saved by many Stata commands so that they can be easily accessed and substituted into subsequent commands.

return list lists results stored in r().

estimates list lists results stored in e().

sreturn list lists results stored in s().

This entry discusses using saved results. Programmers wishing to save results should see [P] **return**.

# Remarks

Stata commands are classified as being

| | |
|---|---|
| r class | general commands that save results in r() |
| e class | estimation commands that save results in e() |
| s class | parsing commands that save results in s() |
| n class | commands that do not save in r(), e(), or s() |

You can look at the *Saved Results* section of the manual entry of a command to determine whether it is r, e, s, or n class, but it is easy enough to guess.

Commands producing statistical results are either r class or e class. They are e class if they present estimation results and r class otherwise. No commands are s class—that is a class used by programmers. n class commands explicitly state where the result is to go. For instance, generate and replace are n class because their syntax is generate *varname* = ... and replace *varname* = ....

After executing a command, you can type return list, estimates list, or sreturn list to see what has been saved:

```
. summarize mpg
```

| Variable | Obs | Mean | Std. Dev. | Min | Max |
|---|---|---|---|---|---|
| mpg | 74 | 21.2973 | 5.785503 | 12 | 41 |

```
. return list

scalars:
                  r(N) =  74
              r(sum_w) =  74
               r(mean) =  21.2972972972973
                r(Var) =  33.47204738985561
                 r(sd) =  5.785503209735141
                r(min) =  12
                r(max) =  41
                r(sum) =  1576
```

Following summarize, we can use r(N), r(mean), r(Var), etc., in expressions:

```
. gen double mpgstd = (mpg-r(mean))/sqrt(r(Var))

. summarize mpgstd
    Variable │      Obs        Mean    Std. Dev.       Min         Max
─────────────┼─────────────────────────────────────────────────────────
      mpgstd │       74    -1.64e-16           1   -1.606999     3.40553
```

We must be careful to use results stored in r() soon because they will be replaced the next time we execute another r-class command. For instance, although r(mean) was 21.3 (approximately) after summarize mpg, it is $-1\mathrm{e}{-16}$ now because we just ran summarize again.

e class is really no different from r class except for where results are stored and that, when an estimation command stores results, it tends to store a lot of them:

```
. regress mpg weight displ
(output omitted )

. estimates list

scalars:
                  e(N) =  74
               e(df_m) =  2
               e(df_r) =  71
                  e(F) =  66.78504752026517
                 e(r2) =  .6529306984682528
               e(rmse) =  3.45606176570828
                e(mss) =  1595.409691543724
                e(rss) =  848.0497679157352
               e(r2_a) =  .643154098425105
                 e(ll) =  -195.2397979466294
               e(ll_0) =  -234.3943376482347

macros:
             e(depvar) : "mpg"
                e(cmd) : "regress"
            e(predict) : "regres_p"
              e(model) : "ols"

matrices:
                  e(b) :  1 x 3
                  e(V) :  3 x 3

functions:
             e(sample)
```

These e-class results will stick around until we run another estimation command. Typing return list and estimates list is the easy way to find out what a command stores.

Both r- and e-class results come in four flavors: scalars, macros, matrices, and functions. (s-class results come in only one flavor—macros—and as we said earlier, s class is used solely by programmers, so let's ignore it.)

Scalars are just that—numbers by any other name. We can subsequently refer to r(mean) or e(rmse) in numeric expressions and obtain the result to full precision.

Macros are strings. For instance, e(depvar) contains "mpg". We can refer to it, too, in subsequent expressions, but really that would be of most use to programmers and they will refer to it using constructs like "`e(depvar)'". In any case, macros are macros and you obtain their contents just as you would a local macro, by enclosing their name in single quotes. The name in this case is the full name, so `e(depvar)' is mpg.

Matrices are matrices and all estimation commands store e(b) and e(V) containing the coefficient vector and variance–covariance matrix of the estimates (VCE).

Functions are saved by e-class commands only and the only function existing is e(sample). e(sample) evaluates to 1 (meaning true) if the observation was used in the previous estimation and to 0 (meaning false) otherwise.

## ❑ Technical Note

Pretend that some command set r(scalar) and r(macro), the first being stored as a scalar and the second as a macro. In theory, in subsequent use you are supposed to refer to r(scalar) and `r(macro)'. In fact, however, you can refer to either one with or without quotes, so you could refer to `r(scalar)' and r(macro). Programmers sometimes do this.

In the case of r(scalar), when you refer to r(scalar), you are referring to the full double-precision saved result. Think of r(scalar) without quotes as a function returning the value of the saved result scalar. When you refer to r(scalar) in quotes, Stata understands `r(scalar)' to mean "substitute the printed result of evaluating r(scalar)". Pretend that r(scalar) equals the number 23. Then, `r(scalar)' is 23, the character 2 followed by 3.

Referring to r(scalar) in quotes is sometimes useful. For instance, say you want to use the immediate command ci with r(scalar). The immediate command ci requires its arguments to be numbers—numeric literals in programmer's jargon—and it will not take an expression. Thus, you could not type 'ci r(scalar) ...'. You could, however, type 'ci `r(scalar)' ...' because `r(scalar)' is just a numeric literal.

In the case of r(macro), you are supposed to refer to it in quotes: `r(macro)'. If, however, you omit the quotes in an expression context, Stata evaluates the macro and then pretends it is the result of function-returning-string. There are side effects of this, the most important being that the result is trimmed to 80 characters.

Referring to r(macro) without quotes is never a good idea; the feature was included merely for completeness.

You can even refer to r(matrix) in quotes (assume r(matrix) is a matrix). `r(matrix)' does not result in the matrix being substituted; it returns the word matrix. Programmers sometimes find that useful.

❑

# Also See

**Related:**       [P] **return**

**Background:**   [U] **21.8 Accessing results calculated by other programs**,
                  [U] **21.9 Accessing results calculated by estimation commands**

# Title

scobit — Maximum-likelihood skewed logit estimation

# Syntax

scobit *depvar* [*indepvars*] [*weight*] [if *exp*] [in *range*] [, level(*#*) asis

    or noconstant robust cluster(*varname*) score(*newvar₁* [*newvar₂*])

    offset(*varname*) constraints(*numlist*) nolog *maximize_options* ]

by ... : may be used with scobit; see [R] **by**.

fweights, iweights, and pweights are allowed; see [U] **14.1.6 weight**.

This command shares the features of all estimation commands; see [U] **23 Estimation and post-estimation commands**.

# Syntax for predict

predict [*type*] *newvarname* [if *exp*] [in *range*] [, { p | xb | stdp } nooffset ]

These statistics are available both in and out of sample; type predict ... if e(sample) ... if wanted only for the estimation sample.

# Description

scobit estimates a maximum-likelihood skewed logit model.

See [R] **logistic** for a list of related estimation commands.

# Options

level(*#*) specifies the confidence level, in percent, for confidence intervals. The default is level(95) or as set by set level; see [U] **23.5 Specifying the width of confidence intervals**.

asis forces retention of perfect predictor variables and their associated perfectly predicted observations and may produce instabilities in maximization; see [R] **probit**.

or reports the estimated coefficients transformed to odds ratios, i.e., $e^b$ rather than $b$. Standard errors and confidence intervals are similarly transformed. This option affects how results are displayed, not how they are estimated. or may be specified at estimation or when replaying previously estimated results.

noconstant suppresses the constant term (intercept) in the model.

robust specifies that the Huber/White/sandwich estimator of variance is to be used in place of the traditional calculation; see [U] **23.11 Obtaining robust variance estimates**. robust combined with cluster() allows observations which are not independent within cluster (although they must be independent between clusters).

If you specify pweights, robust is implied; see [U] **23.13 Weighted estimation**.

cluster(*varname*) specifies that the observations are independent across groups (clusters) but not necessarily within groups. *varname* specifies to which group each observation belongs; e.g., cluster(personid) in data with repeated observations on individuals. cluster() affects the estimated standard errors and variance–covariance matrix of the estimators (VCE), but not the estimated coefficients; see [U] **23.11 Obtaining robust variance estimates**. cluster() can be used with pweights to produce estimates for unstratified cluster-sampled data.

cluster() implies robust; specifying robust cluster() is equivalent to typing cluster() by itself.

score(*newvar₁* [*newvar₂*]) creates *newvar₁* containing $u_{ij} = \partial \ln L_j / \partial (\mathbf{x}_j \mathbf{b})$ for each observation $j$ in the sample. The score vector is $\sum \partial \ln L_j / \partial \mathbf{b} = \sum u_{ij} \mathbf{x}_j$; i.e., the product of *newvar* with each covariate summed over observations. The second new variable *newvar₂* contains $u_{ij} = \partial \ln L_j / \partial (\ln \alpha)$. See [U] **23.12 Obtaining scores**.

offset(*varname*) specifies that *varname* is to be included in the model with coefficient constrained to be 1.

constraints(*numlist*) specifies by number the linear constraints to be applied during estimation. The default is to perform unconstrained estimation. Constraints are specified using the constraint command; see [R] **constraint**. See [R] **reg3** for the use of constraints in multiple-equation contexts.

nolog suppresses the iteration log.

*maximize_options* control the maximization process; see [R] **maximize**. You should never have to specify them.

## Options for predict

p, the default, calculates the probability of a positive outcome.

xb calculates the linear prediction.

stdp calculates the standard error of the linear prediction.

nooffset is relevant only if you specified offset(*varname*) for scobit. It modifies the calculations made by predict so that they ignore the offset variable; the linear prediction is treated as $\mathbf{x}_j \mathbf{b}$ rather than $\mathbf{x}_j \mathbf{b} + \text{offset}_j$.

# Remarks

scobit performs maximum likelihood estimation of models with dichotomous dependent variables coded as 0/1 (or, more precisely, coded as 0 and not 0).

▷ Example

You have data on the make, weight, and mileage rating of 22 foreign and 52 domestic automobiles. You wish to estimate a model explaining whether a car is foreign based on its mileage. Here is an overview of your data:

```
. describe

Contains data from auto.dta
    obs:            74                         1978 Automobile Data
   vars:             4                         7 Jul 2000 13:51
   size:         1,998 (99.7% of memory free)

              storage  display   value
variable name   type   format    label       variable label

make           str18   %-18s                  Make and Model
mpg            int     %8.0g                  Mileage (mpg)
weight         int     %8.0gc                 Weight (lbs.)
foreign        byte    %8.0g     origin       Car type

Sorted by:  foreign
     Note:  dataset has changed since last saved


. inspect foreign

  foreign:  Car type                           Number of Observations
                                                             Non-
                                              Total  Integers  Integers

    |  #                          Negative       -        -        -
    |  #                          Zero          52       52        -
    |  #                          Positive      22       22        -
    |  #
    |  #    #                     Total         74       74        -
    |  #    #                     Missing        -
    +---------------------------              -----
   0                      1                      74
       (2 unique values)
```

foreign is labeled and all values are documented in the label.

The variable `foreign` takes on two unique values, 0 and 1. The value 0 denotes a domestic car and 1 denotes a foreign car.

The model you wish to estimate is

$$\Pr(\texttt{foreign} = 1) = F(\beta_0 + \beta_1\texttt{mpg})$$

where $F(z) = 1 - 1/\{1 + \exp(z)\}^\alpha$.

To estimate this model, you type

```
. scobit foreign mpg

Fitting comparison logit model:

Iteration 0:   log likelihood =  -45.03321
Iteration 1:   log likelihood = -39.380959
Iteration 2:   log likelihood = -39.288802
Iteration 3:   log likelihood =  -39.28864

Fitting full model:

Iteration 0:   log likelihood =  -39.28864
Iteration 1:   log likelihood = -39.286393
Iteration 2:   log likelihood = -39.284415
Iteration 3:   log likelihood = -39.284234
Iteration 4:   log likelihood = -39.284197
Iteration 5:   log likelihood = -39.284196

Skewed logit regression                        Number of obs    =        74
```

```
                                         Zero outcomes      =          52
       Log likelihood =  -39.2842        Nonzero outcomes   =          22
```

| foreign | Coef. | Std. Err. | z | P>\|z\| | [95% Conf. Interval] | |
|---|---|---|---|---|---|---|
| mpg | .1813879 | .2407362 | 0.75 | 0.451 | -.2904463 | .6532222 |
| _cons | -4.274883 | 1.399305 | -3.06 | 0.002 | -7.017471 | -1.532295 |
| /lnalpha | -.4450405 | 3.879885 | -0.11 | 0.909 | -8.049476 | 7.159395 |
| alpha | .6407983 | 2.486224 | | | .0003193 | 1286.133 |

```
Likelihood ratio test of alpha=1:    chi2(1) =      0.01    Prob > chi2 = 0.9249
note: Likelihood ratio tests are recommended for inference with scobit models.
```

You find that cars yielding better gas mileage are less likely to be foreign. The likelihood-ratio test at the bottom of the output indicates that the model is not significantly different from a logit model. Therefore, we should use the more parsimonious model.

See [R] **maximize** for an explanation of the output.

◁

❏ Technical Note

Stata interprets a value of 0 as a negative outcome (failure) and treats all other values (except missing) as positive outcomes (successes). Thus, if your dependent variable takes on the values 0 and 1, 0 is interpreted as failure and 1 as success. If your dependent variable takes on the values 0, 1, and 2, 0 is still interpreted as failure, but both 1 and 2 are treated as successes.

If you prefer a more formal statement, when you type scobit $y$ $x$, Stata estimates the model

$$\Pr(y_j \neq 0 \mid \mathbf{x}_j) = 1 - 1 \Big/ \Big\{ 1 + \exp(\mathbf{x}_j \boldsymbol{\beta}) \Big\}^\alpha$$

❏

# Robust standard errors

If you specify the robust option, scobit reports robust standard errors as described in [U] **23.11 Obtaining robust variance estimates**. In the case of the model of foreign on mpg, the robust calculation increases the standard error of the coefficient on mpg by around 25 percent:

```
. scobit foreign mpg, robust nolog
Skewed logit regression                  Number of obs      =          74
                                         Zero outcomes      =          52
       Log likelihood =  -39.2842        Nonzero outcomes   =          22
```

| foreign | Coef. | Robust Std. Err. | z | P>\|z\| | [95% Conf. Interval] | |
|---|---|---|---|---|---|---|
| mpg | .1813879 | .3028487 | 0.60 | 0.549 | -.4121847 | .7749606 |
| _cons | -4.274883 | 1.335521 | -3.20 | 0.001 | -6.892455 | -1.657311 |
| /lnalpha | -.4450405 | 4.71561 | -0.09 | 0.925 | -9.687466 | 8.797385 |
| alpha | .6407983 | 3.021755 | | | .0000621 | 6616.919 |

Without `robust`, the standard error for the coefficient on `mpg` was reported to be .241 with resulting confidence interval of $[-.29, .65]$.

Specifying the `cluster()` option has the ability to relax the independence assumption required by the skewed logit estimator to being just independence between clusters. To demonstrate this, we will switch to a different dataset.

You are studying the unionization of women in the United States and have a dataset with 26,200 observations on 4,434 women between 1970 and 1988. For our purposes, we will use the variables `age` (the women were 14–26 in 1968 and your data thus span the age range of 16–46), `grade` (years of schooling completed, ranging from 0 to 18), `not_smsa` (28% of the person-time was spent living outside an SMSA—standard metropolitan statistical area), `south` (41% of the person-time was in the South), and `southXt` (`south` interacted with year, treating 1970 as year 0). You also have variable `union`. Overall, 22% of the person-time is marked as time under union membership and 44% of these women have belonged to a union.

You estimate the following model, ignoring that women are observed an average of 5.9 times each in these data:

```
. scobit union age grade not_smsa south southXt, nolog
Skewed logit regression                    Number of obs   =      26200
                                           Zero outcomes   =      20389
Log likelihood =  -13544.2                 Nonzero outcomes =      5811
```

| union | Coef. | Std. Err. | z | P>|z| | [95% Conf. Interval] | |
|---|---|---|---|---|---|---|
| age | .0085889 | .0023036 | 3.73 | 0.000 | .004074 | .0131039 |
| grade | .0447166 | .0057073 | 7.83 | 0.000 | .0335304 | .0559027 |
| not_smsa | -.1906374 | .0317694 | -6.00 | 0.000 | -.2529042 | -.1283707 |
| south | -.6446248 | .0557704 | -11.56 | 0.000 | -.7539328 | -.5353169 |
| southXt | .0068271 | .0047299 | 1.44 | 0.149 | -.0024433 | .0160976 |
| _cons | -10.82928 | 63.79145 | -0.17 | 0.865 | -135.8582 | 114.1997 |
| /lnalpha | 8.862483 | 63.79069 | 0.14 | 0.890 | -116.165 | 133.8899 |
| alpha | 7061.995 | 450489.5 | | | 3.55e-51 | 1.40e+58 |

```
Likelihood ratio test of alpha=1:   chi2(1) =     3.07    Prob > chi2 = 0.0799
note: Likelihood ratio tests are recommended for inference with scobit models.
```

The reported standard errors in this model are probably meaningless. Women are observed repeatedly and so the observations are not independent. Looking at the coefficients, you find a large southern effect against unionization and little time trend. The `robust` and `cluster()` options provide a way to estimate this model and obtain correct standard errors:

*(Continued on next page)*

```
. scobit union age grade not_smsa south southXt, robust cluster(id) nolog
```

Skewed logit regression                    Number of obs    =     26200
                                           Zero outcomes    =     20389
Log likelihood =  -13544.2                 Nonzero outcomes =      5811

                    (standard errors adjusted for clustering on idcode)

| union | Coef. | Robust Std. Err. | z | P>|z| | [95% Conf. Interval] | |
|---|---|---|---|---|---|---|
| age | .0085889 | .0033835 | 2.54 | 0.011 | .0019575 | .0152204 |
| grade | .0447166 | .0125938 | 3.55 | 0.000 | .0200332 | .0693999 |
| not_smsa | -.1906374 | .0641961 | -2.97 | 0.003 | -.3164594 | -.0648155 |
| south | -.6446248 | .0833872 | -7.73 | 0.000 | -.8080608 | -.4811889 |
| southXt | .0068271 | .0063044 | 1.08 | 0.279 | -.0055292 | .0191834 |
| _cons | -10.82928 | .9164861 | -11.82 | 0.000 | -12.62556 | -9.033003 |
| /lnalpha | 8.862483 | .7782417 | 11.39 | 0.000 | 7.337157 | 10.38781 |
| alpha | 7061.995 | 5495.939 | | | 1536.338 | 32461.45 |

What is important to understand is that `scobit, robust cluster()` is robust to assumptions about within-cluster correlation. That is, it inefficiently sums within cluster for the standard error calculation rather than attempting to exploit what might be assumed about the within-cluster correlation (as do the `xtgee` population-averaged models; see [R] **xtgee**).

❑ Technical Note

The scobit model can be very difficult to fit because of the functional form. It is not uncommon for it to require many iterations or for the optimizer to print out warning and informative messages during the optimization. See [R] **maximize** for details about the optimizer.

❑

## Obtaining predicted values

Once you have estimated a model, you can obtain the predicted probabilities using the `predict` command for both the estimation sample and other samples; see [U] **23 Estimation and post-estimation commands** and [R] **predict**. Here we will make only a few additional comments.

`predict` without arguments calculates the predicted probability of a positive outcome. With the **xb** option, it calculates the linear combination $x_j b$, where $x_j$ are the independent variables in the $j$th observation and $b$ is the estimated parameter vector.

With the `stdp` option, `predict` calculates the standard error of the prediction, which is *not* adjusted for replicated covariate patterns in the data.

▷ Example

Previously, we estimated the model `scobit foreign mpg`. To obtain predicted probabilities:

```
. predict p
(option p assumed; Pr(foreign))
```

```
. summarize foreign p
    Variable │     Obs        Mean    Std. Dev.         Min         Max
─────────────┼───────────────────────────────────────────────────────
     foreign │      74    .2972973    .4601885           0           1
           p │      74    .2974049     .182352    .0714664     .871624
```

◁

## Saved Results

scobit saves in e():

Scalars

| | | | |
|---|---|---|---|
| e(N) | number of observations | e(ll_c) | log likelihood, comparison model |
| e(k) | number of variables | e(N_clust) | number of clusters |
| e(k_eq) | number of equations | e(rc) | return code |
| e(k_dv) | number of dependent variables | e(chi2) | $\chi^2$ |
| e(df_m) | model degrees of freedom | e(chi2_c) | $\chi^2$ for comparison test |
| e(ll) | log likelihood | e(p) | significance |
| e(ll_0) | log likelihood, constant-only model | e(ic) | number of iterations |
| e(N_f) | number of failure (zero) outcomes | e(N_s) | number of success (nonzero) outcomes |

Macros

| | | | |
|---|---|---|---|
| e(cmd) | scobit | e(user) | name of likelihood-evaluator program |
| e(depvar) | name of dependent variable | e(opt) | type of optimization |
| e(title) | title in estimation output | e(chi2type) | Wald or LR; type of model $\chi^2$ test |
| e(wtype) | weight type | e(chi2_ct) | Wald or LR; type of model $\chi^2$ test |
| e(wexp) | weight expression | | corresponding to e(chi2_c) |
| e(clustvar) | name of cluster variable | e(offset) | offset |
| e(vcetype) | covariance estimation method | e(predict) | program used to implement predict |
| | | e(cnslist) | constraint numbers |

Matrices

| | | | |
|---|---|---|---|
| e(b) | coefficient vector | e(V) | variance–covariance matrix of the estimators |

Functions

| | |
|---|---|
| e(sample) | marks estimation sample |

## Methods and Formulas

scobit is implemented as an ado-file.

Skewed logit analysis is an alternative to logit which relaxes the assumption that individuals with initial probability of .5 are most sensitive to changes in independent variables.

The log-likelihood function for skewed logit is

$$\ln L = \sum_{j \in S} w_j \ln F(\mathbf{x}_j \mathbf{b}) + \sum_{j \notin S} w_j \ln \left\{ 1 - F(\mathbf{x}_j \mathbf{b}) \right\}$$

where $S$ is the set of all observations $j$ such that $y_j \neq 0$, $F(z) = 1 - 1/\left\{ 1 + \exp(z) \right\}^\alpha$, and $w_j$ denotes the optional weights. $\ln L$ is maximized as described in [R] **maximize**.

If robust standard errors are requested, the calculation described in *Methods and Formulas* of [R] **regress** is carried forward with

$$\mathbf{u}_j^1 = \mathbf{x}_j \frac{\alpha \exp(\mathbf{x}_j \mathbf{b})}{\left\{1 + \exp(\mathbf{x}_j \mathbf{b})\right\}[\{1 + \exp(\mathbf{x}_j \mathbf{b})\}^\alpha - 1]}$$

$$\mathbf{u}_j^2 = \frac{\alpha \ln\left\{1 + \exp(\mathbf{x}_j \mathbf{b})\right\}}{\left\{1 + \exp(\mathbf{x}_j \mathbf{b})\right\}[\{1 + \exp(\mathbf{x}_j \mathbf{b})\}^\alpha - 1]}$$

for the positive outcomes and

$$\mathbf{u}_j^1 = -\mathbf{x}_j \frac{\alpha \exp(\mathbf{x}_j \mathbf{b})}{1 + \exp(\mathbf{x}_j \mathbf{b})}$$

$$\mathbf{u}_j^2 = \alpha \ln\left\{1 + \exp(\mathbf{x}_j \mathbf{b})\right\}$$

for the negative outcomes.

# References

Nagler, J. 1994. Scobit: An alternative estimator to logit and probit. *American Journal of Political Science* 38: 230–255.

# Also See

| | |
|---|---|
| **Complementary:** | [R] **adjust**, [R] **constraint**, [R] **lincom**, [R] **linktest**, [R] **lrtest**, [R] **mfx**, [R] **predict**, [R] **test**, [R] **testnl**, [R] **vce**, [R] **xi** |
| **Related:** | [R] **biprobit**, [R] **cloglog**, [R] **cusum**, [R] **glm**, [R] **glogit**, [R] **logistic**, [R] **logit**, [R] **probit** |
| **Background:** | [U] **16.5 Accessing coefficients and standard errors**, [U] **23 Estimation and post-estimation commands**, [U] **23.11 Obtaining robust variance estimates**, [U] **23.12 Obtaining scores**, [R] **maximize** |

# Title

---

**sdtest** — Variance comparison tests

---

# Syntax

$$\texttt{sdtest } varname = \# \;\left[\texttt{if } exp\right]\;\left[\texttt{in } range\right]\;\left[\texttt{, }\underline{\texttt{level}}(\#)\right]$$

$$\texttt{sdtest } varname_1 = varname_2 \;\left[\texttt{if } exp\right]\;\left[\texttt{in } range\right]\;\left[\texttt{, }\underline{\texttt{level}}(\#)\right]$$

$$\texttt{sdtest } varname \;\left[\texttt{if } exp\right]\;\left[\texttt{in } range\right]\texttt{, by}(groupvar)\;\left[\underline{\texttt{level}}(\#)\right]$$

$$\texttt{sdtesti } \#_{\text{obs}}\;\left\{\#_{\text{mean}}\mid . \right\}\;\#_{\text{sd}}\;\#_{\text{val}}\;\left[\texttt{, }\underline{\texttt{level}}(\#)\right]$$

$$\texttt{sdtesti } \#_{\text{obs},1}\;\left\{\#_{\text{mean},1}\mid . \right\}\;\#_{\text{sd},1}\;\#_{\text{obs},2}\;\left\{\#_{\text{mean},2}\mid . \right\}\;\#_{\text{sd},2}\;\left[\texttt{, }\underline{\texttt{level}}(\#)\right]$$

$$\texttt{robvar } varname \;\left[\texttt{if } exp\right]\;\left[\texttt{in } range\right]\texttt{, by}(groupvar)$$

by ... : may be used with `sdtest` (but not with `sdtesti`) and `robvar`; see [R] **by**.

# Description

**sdtest** performs tests on the equality of standard deviations (variances). In the first form, **sdtest** tests that the standard deviation of *varname* is #. In the second form, **sdtest** tests that *varname*$_1$ and *varname*$_2$ have the same standard deviation. In the third form, **sdtest** performs the same test, using the standard deviations of the two groups defined by *groupvar*.

**sdtesti** is the immediate form of **sdtest**; see [U] **22 Immediate commands**.

Both the traditional $F$ test for the homogeneity of variances and Bartlett's generalization of this test to $K$ samples are very sensitive to the assumption that the data are drawn from an underlying Gaussian distribution. Levene (1960) proposed a test statistic for equality of variance that was found to be robust under nonnormality. Subsequently, Brown and Forsythe (1974) proposed alternative formulations of Levene's test statistic that use more robust estimators of central tendency in place of the mean. These reformulations were demonstrated to be more robust than Levene's test when dealing with skewed populations.

**robvar** reports Levene's robust test statistic ($W_0$) for the equality of variances between the two groups defined by *groupvar* and the two statistics proposed by Brown and Forsythe that replace the mean in Levene's formula with alternative location estimators. The first alternative ($W_{50}$) replaces the mean with the median. The second alternative replaces the mean with the 10 percent trimmed mean ($W_{10}$).

# Options

**level(#)** specifies the confidence level, in percent, for confidence intervals of the means. The default is level(95) or as set by **set level**; see [U] **23.5 Specifying the width of confidence intervals**.

**by(*groupvar*)** specifies the *groupvar* that defines the two groups to be compared. Do not confuse the by() option with the by ... : prefix; both may be specified.

## Remarks

sdtest performs two different statistical tests: one testing equality of variances and the other testing that the standard deviation is equal to a known constant. Which test it performs is determined by whether you type a variable name or a number to the right of the equal sign.

▷ Example

You have a sample of 74 automobiles. For each automobile, you know the mileage rating. You wish to test whether the overall standard deviation is 5:

```
. sdtest mpg = 5
One-sample test of variance
```

| Variable | Obs | Mean | Std. Err. | Std. Dev. | [95% Conf. Interval] | |
|---|---|---|---|---|---|---|
| mpg | 74 | 21.2973 | .6725511 | 5.785503 | 19.9569 | 22.63769 |

```
                          Ho: sd(mpg) = 5
                          chi2(73) = 97.738
      Ha: sd(mpg) < 5       Ha: sd(mpg) ~= 5          Ha: sd(mpg) > 5
      P < chi2 = 0.9717   2*(P > chi2) = 0.0565     P > chi2 = 0.0283
```

◁

▷ Example

You are testing the effectiveness of a new fuel additive. You run an experiment on 12 cars, running each without and with the additive. The data can be found in [R] **ttest**. The results for each car are stored in the variables **mpg1** and **mpg2**:

```
. sdtest mpg1=mpg2
Variance ratio test
```

| Variable | Obs | Mean | Std. Err. | Std. Dev. | [95% Conf. Interval] | |
|---|---|---|---|---|---|---|
| mpg1 | 12 | 21 | .7881701 | 2.730301 | 19.26525 | 22.73475 |
| mpg2 | 12 | 22.75 | .9384465 | 3.250874 | 20.68449 | 24.81551 |
| combined | 24 | 21.875 | .6264476 | 3.068954 | 20.57909 | 23.17091 |

```
                      Ho: sd(mpg1) = sd(mpg2)
            F(11,11) observed  = F_obs      =    0.705
            F(11,11) lower tail = F_L   = F_obs   =    0.705
            F(11,11) upper tail = F_U   = 1/F_obs =    1.418
   Ha: sd(mpg1) < sd(mpg2)   Ha: sd(mpg1) ~= sd(mpg2)   Ha: sd(mpg1) > sd(mpg2)
      P < F_obs = 0.2862     P < F_L + P > F_U = 0.5725    P > F_obs = 0.7138
```

You cannot reject the hypothesis that the standard deviations are the same.

In [R] **ttest**, we draw an important distinction between paired and unpaired data which, in this example, means whether there are 12 cars in a before-and-after experiment or 24 different cars. For sdtest, on the other hand, there is no distinction. Had the data been unpaired and stored as described in [R] **ttest**, we could have typed sdtest mpg, by(treated), and the results would have been the same.

◁

# Immediate form

▷ Example

Immediate commands are used not with data but with reported summary statistics. For instance, to test whether a variable on which we have 75 observations and a reported standard deviation of 6.5 comes from a population with underlying standard deviation 6:

```
. sdtesti 75 . 6.5 6
```
One-sample test of variance

|   | Obs | Mean | Std. Err. | Std. Dev. | [95% Conf. Interval] |
|---|---|---|---|---|---|
| x | 75 | . | .7505553 | 6.5 | . . |

Ho: sd(x) = 6
chi2(74) = 86.847

| Ha: sd(x) < 6 | Ha: sd(x) ~= 6 | Ha: sd(x) > 6 |
|---|---|---|
| P < chi2 = 0.8542 | 2*(P > chi2) = 0.2916 | P > chi2 = 0.1458 |

The mean plays no role in the calculation and so may be omitted.

To test whether the variable comes from a population with the same standard deviation as another for which we have a calculated standard deviation of 7.5 over 65 observations:

```
. sdtesti 75 . 6.5  65 . 7.5
```
Variance ratio test

|   | Obs | Mean | Std. Err. | Std. Dev. | [95% Conf. Interval] |
|---|---|---|---|---|---|
| x | 75 | . | .7505553 | 6.5 | . . |
| y | 65 | . | .9302605 | 7.5 | . . |
| combined | 140 | . | . | . | . . |

Ho: sd(x) = sd(y)

$F(74,64)$ observed   = F_obs        =   0.751
$F(74,64)$ lower tail = F_L   = F_obs    =   0.751
$F(74,64)$ upper tail = F_U   = 1/F_obs =   1.331

| Ha: sd(x) < sd(y) | Ha: sd(x) ~= sd(y) | Ha: sd(x) > sd(y) |
|---|---|---|
| P < F_obs = 0.1172 | P < F_L + P > F_U = 0.2383 | P > F_obs = 0.8828 |

◁

# Robust test

▷ Example

We wish to test whether the standard deviation of the length of stay for patients hospitalized for a given medical procedure differs by gender. Our data consist of observations on the length of hospital stay for 1778 patients; 884 males and 894 females. Length of stay, lengthstay, is highly skewed (Skewness coefficient = 4.912591), and thus violates Bartlett's normality assumption. Therefore, we use robvar to compare the variances.

```
. robvar lengthstay, by(sex)
```

|            | Summary of Length of stay in days |           |       |
| sex        | Mean      | Std. Dev. |       Freq. |
| --- | --- | --- | --- |
| male       | 9.0874434 | 9.7884747 |         884 |
| female     | 8.800671  | 9.1081478 |         894 |
| Total      | 8.9432508 | 9.4509466 |        1778 |

W0  = .55505315   df(1, 1776)   Pr > F = .45635888
W50 = .42714734   df(1, 1776)   Pr > F = .51347664
W10 = .44577674   df(1, 1776)   Pr > F = .50443411

For these data, we cannot reject the null hypothesis that the variances are equal. However, Bartlett's test yields a significance probability of 0.0319 due to the pronounced skewness of the data.

◁

## ❑ Technical Note

robvar implements both the conventional Levene's test centered at the mean and a median centered test. In a simulation study, Conover, Johnson, and Johnson (1981) compare the properties of the two tests and recommend using the median test for asymmetric data, although for small sample sizes the test is somewhat conservative. See Carroll and Schneider (1985) for an explanation of why both mean- and median-centered tests have approximately the same level for symmetric distributions, but for asymmetric distributions the median test is closer to the correct level.

❑

# Saved Results

sdtest and sdtesti save in r():

Scalars

| r(N)   | number of observations  | r(sd)   | standard deviation                        |
| --- | --- | --- | --- |
| r(p_1) | lower one-sided $p$-value | r(sd_1) | standard deviation for first variable     |
| r(p_u) | upper one-sided $p$-value | r(sd_2) | standard deviation for second variable    |
| r(p)   | two-sided $p$-value       | r(df_1) | numerator degrees of freedom              |
| r(F)   | $F$ statistic             | r(df_2) | denominator degrees of freedom            |

robvar saves in r():

Scalars

| r(N)      | number of observations                | r(w10)   | Brown and Forsythe's $F$ statistic (trimmed mean) |
| --- | --- | --- | --- |
| r(w50)    | Brown and Forsythe's $F$ statistic (median) | | |
| r(p_w50)  | Brown and Forsythe's $p$-value        | r(p_w10) | Brown and Forsythe's $p$-value (trimmed mean) |
| r(w0)     | Levene's $F$ statistic                | | |
| r(p_w0)   | Levene's $p$-value                    | r(df_1)  | numerator degrees of freedom              |
|           |                                       | r(df_2)  | denominator degrees of freedom            |

## Methods and Formulas

`sdtest` and `sdtesti` are implemented as ado-files.

See Hoel (1984, 279–284, 298–300) or Pagano and Gauvreau (2000, chapter 11) for an introduction and explanation of the calculation of these tests.

The test for $\sigma = \sigma_0$ is given by

$$\chi^2 = \frac{(n-1)s^2}{\sigma_0^2}$$

which is distributed as $\chi^2$ with $n - 1$ degrees of freedom.

The test for $\sigma_x^2 = \sigma_y^2$ is given by

$$F = \frac{s_x^2}{s_y^2}$$

which is distributed as $F$ with $n_x - 1$ and $n_y - 1$ degrees of freedom.

`robvar` is also implemented as an ado-file.

Let $X_{ij}$ be the $j$th observation of $X$ for the $i$th group. Let $Z_{ij} = |X_{ij} - \overline{X}_i|$ where $\overline{X}_i$ is the mean of $X$ in the $i$th group. Levene's test statistic is

$$W_0 = \frac{\sum_i n_i (\overline{Z}_i - \overline{Z})^2 / (g - 1)}{\sum_i \sum_j (Z_{ij} - \overline{Z}_i)^2 / \sum_i (n_i - 1)}$$

where $n_i$ is the number of observations in group $i$ and $g$ is the number of groups. $W_{50}$ is obtained by replacing $\overline{X}_i$ with the $i$th group median of $X_{ij}$, while $W_{10}$ is obtained by replacing $\overline{X}_i$ with the 10 percent trimmed mean for group $i$.

## References

Brown, M. B. and A. B. Forsythe. 1974. Robust test for the equality of variances. *Journal of the American Statistical Association* 69: 364–367.

Carroll, R. J. and H. Schneider. 1985. A note on Levene's test for equality of variances. *Statistics & Probability Letters* 3(4): 191–194.

Cleves, M. 1995. sg35: Robust tests for the equality of variances. *Stata Technical Bulletin* 25: 13–15. Reprinted in *Stata Technical Bulletin Reprints*, vol. 5, pp. 91–93.

——. 2000. sg35.2: Robust tests for the equality of variances update to Stata 6. *Stata Technical Bulletin* 53: 17–18. Reprinted in *Stata Technical Bulletin Reprints*, vol. 9, pp. 158–159.

Conover, W. J., M. E. Johnson, and M. M. Johnson. 1981. A comparative study of tests for homogeneity of variances, with applications to the outer continental shelf bidding data. *Technometrics* 23: 351–361.

Hoel, P. G. 1984. *Introduction to Mathematical Statistics*. 5th ed. New York: John Wiley & Sons.

Levene, H. 1960. Robust tests for equality of variances. *Contributions to Probability and Statistics*. ed. I. Olkin, 278–292. California: Stanford University Press.

Pagano, M. and K. Gauvreau. 2000. *Principles of Biostatistics*, 2d ed. Pacific Grove, CA: Brooks/Cole.

Seed, P. 2000. sbe33: Comparing several methods of measuring the same quantity. *Stata Technical Bulletin* 55: 2–9.

Tobias, A. 1998. gr28: A graphical procedure to test equality of variances. *Stata Technical Bulletin* 42: 4–6. Reprinted in *Stata Technical Bulletin Reprints*, vol. 7, pp. 68–70.

## Also See

**Related:**         [R] **ttest**

**Background:**      [U] **22 Immediate commands**

# Title

**search** — Search Stata documentation

# Syntax

search *word* [*word* ...] [, <u>a</u>uthor <u>en</u>try <u>ex</u>act faq <u>h</u>istorical or <u>man</u>ual stb]

# Description

search searches a keyword database. It is available in all versions of Stata. In addition, all users except Stata for Unix (console) users can also access some of search's features by pulling down **Help**.

Capitalization of the words following search is irrelevant, as is the inclusion or exclusion of special characters such as commas, hyphens, and the like.

# Options

author specifies that the search is to be performed on the basis of author's name rather than keywords.

entry specifies that the search is to be performed on the basis of entry ids rather than keywords.

exact prevents matching on abbreviations.

faq limits the search to the FAQs posted on the Stata web site: http://www.stata.com.

historical adds to the search entries that are of historical interest only. By default, such entries are not listed. Past entries are classified as historical if they discuss a feature that later became an official part of Stata. Updates to historical entries will always be found, even if historical is not specified.

or specifies that an entry should be listed if any of the words typed after search are associated with the entry. The default is to list the entry only if all the words specified are associated with the entry.

manual limits the search to entries in the *Stata Documentation*; that is, the search is limited to the *Stata User's Guide*, the *Stata Reference Manuals*, the *Stata Graphics Manual*, and the *Stata Programming Manual*.

stb limits the search to entries in the *Stata Technical Bulletin*.

# Remarks

See [U] **8 Stata's on-line help and search facilities** for a tutorial introduction to search. search is one of Stata's most useful commands. To understand the advanced features of search, you need to know how it works.

search has a database—files—containing the titles, etc., of every entry in the *Stata User's Guide*, the *Stata Reference Manuals*, the *Stata Graphics Manual*, the *Stata Programming Manual*, the inserts in the *Stata Technical Bulletin*, and the FAQs posted on the Stata web site. In these files is a list of words, called keywords, associated with each entry.

198

When you type `search` *xyz*, `search` reads the database and compares the list of keywords with *xyz*. If it finds *xyz* in the list or a keyword that allows an abbreviation of *xyz*, it displays the entry.

When you type `search` *xyz abc*, `search` does the same thing, but displays an entry only if it contains both keywords. The order does not matter, so you can `search linear regression` or `search regression linear`.

Obviously, how many entries `search` finds depends on how the search database was constructed. We have included a plethora of keywords under the theory that, for a given request, it is better to list too much rather than risk listing nothing at all. Still, you are in the position of guessing the keywords. Do you look up normality test, normality tests, or tests of normality? Answer: normality test would be best, but all would work. In general, use the singular and strike the unnecessary words. We provide guidelines for specifying keywords in [U] **8.5 More on search**.

## Author searches

`search` ordinarily compares the words following `search` with the keywords for the entry. If you specify the `author` option, however, it compares the words with the author's name. In the search database, we have filled in author names for all STB inserts.

For instance, in [R] **kdensity** in this manual you will discover that Isaías H. Salgado-Ugarte wrote the first version of Stata's `kdensity` command and published it in the STB. Assume you read his original and found the discussion useful. You might now wonder what else he has written in the STB. To find out, you type

```
. search Salgado-Ugarte, author
  (output omitted)
```

Names like Salgado-Ugarte are confusing to many people. `search` does not require you to specify the entire name; what you type is compared with each "word" of the name and, if any part matches, the entry is listed. The dash is a special character and you can omit it. Thus, you can obtain the same list by looking up Salgado, Ugarte, or Salgado Ugarte without the dash.

Actually, to find all entries written by Salgado-Ugarte, you need to type

```
. search Salgado-Ugarte, author historical
  (output omitted)
```

Prior inserts in the STB that provide a feature that later was superseded by a built-in feature of Stata are marked as historical in the search database and, by default, not listed. The `historical` option ensures that all entries are listed.

## Entry id searches

If you specify the `entry` option, `search` compares what you have typed with the entry id. The entry id is not the title—it is the reference listed to the left of the title that tells you where to look. For instance, in

```
[R]    regress . . . . . . . . . . . . . . . . . . . Linear regression
       (help regress)
```

[R] **regress** is the entry id. This is a reference, of course, to this manual. In

```
FAQ       . . . . . . . . . . Analysis of multiple failure-time survival data
          . . . . . . . . . . . . . . . . . . . . . . . . . . . . M. Cleves
          11/99   How do I analyze multiple failure-time data using Stata?
                  http://www.stata.com/support/faqs/stat/stmfail.html
```

"FAQ" is the entry id. In

"STB-40 dm51" is the entry id.

search with the entry option searches these entry ids.

Thus, one could generate a table of contents for the *User's Guide* by typing

```
. search [U], entry
  (output omitted)
```

You could generate a table of contents for the 26th issue of the STB by typing

```
. search STB-26, entry historical
  (output omitted)
```

The historical option in this case is possibly important. STB-26 was published in July 1995 and perhaps some of its inserts have already been marked historical.

You could obtain a complete list of all inserts associated with sg53 by typing

```
. search sg53, entry historical
  (output omitted)
```

Again, we include the historical option in case any of the relevant inserts have been marked historical.

## Return codes

In addition to indexing the entries in the *User's Guide*, the *Reference Manuals*, the *Graphics Manual*, and the *Programming Manual*, search also can be used to search return codes.

To see information on return code 131, type

```
. search rc 131
  [R]    . . . . . . . . . . . . . . . . . . . . . . . . . . Return code 131
         not possible with test;
         You requested a test of a hypothesis that is nonlinear in the
         variables.  test tests only linear hypotheses.  Use testnl.
```

If you want a list of all Stata return codes, type

```
. search error, entry
  (output omitted)
```

## Also See

**Complementary:**    [R] **help**, [R] **net search**

**Background:**    [U] **8 Stata's on-line help and search facilities**

# Title

**separate** — Create separate variables

# Syntax

**separate** *varname* [**if** *exp*] [**in** *range*] , **by**(*byvar* | *exp*) [ **generate**(*stubname*)

**sequential** **missing** ]

# Description

**separate** creates new variables containing values from *varname*.

# Options

**by**(*byvar* | *exp*) is not optional. It specifies a single variable defining the categories or a logical expression, which is used to categorize the observations into two groups.

If **by**(*byvar*) is specified, *byvar* may be a numeric or string variable taking on any values.

If **by**(*exp*) is specified, the expression must evaluate to true (1), false (0), or missing.

**generate**(*stubname*) specifies how the new variables are to be named. If not specified, **separate** uses the name of the original variable, shortening it if necessary. If **generate()** is specified, *separate* uses *stubname*. If any of the resulting names is too long when the values are suffixed, it is not shortened and an error message is issued.

**sequential** specifies that categories are to be numbered sequentially from 1. By default, **separate** uses the actual values recorded in the original variable if possible and sequential numbers otherwise. **separate** considers it possible to use the original values if they are all nonnegative integers less than 10,000.

**missing** additionally creates a variable for the category missing if missing occurs (*byvar* takes on the value missing or *exp* evaluates to missing). The resulting variable is named in the usual manner but with an appended underscore; e.g., **bp_**. By default, **separate** creates no such variable. Note that the contents of the other variables are unaffected by whether **missing** is specified.

# Remarks

▷ Example

You have data on the miles per gallon (mpg) and country of manufacture of 74 automobiles. You want to compare the distributions of mpg for domestic and foreign automobiles by plotting the quantiles of the two distributions (see [R] **diagplots**).

```
. separate mpg, by(foreign)
```

| variable name | storage type | display format | value label | variable label |
|---|---|---|---|---|
| mpg0 | byte | %8.0g | | mpg, foreign == Domestic |
| mpg1 | byte | %8.0g | | mpg, foreign == Foreign |

```
. list mpg* foreign
              mpg       mpg0       mpg1    foreign
     1.        14          .         14    Foreign
     2.        17          .         17    Foreign
     3.        17          .         17    Foreign
   (output omitted)
    22.        41          .         41    Foreign
    23.        14         14          .    Domestic
    24.        16         16          .    Domestic
   (output omitted)
    73.        19         19          .    Domestic
    74.        18         18          .    Domestic

. qqplot mpg0 mpg1, border ylabel xlabel
```

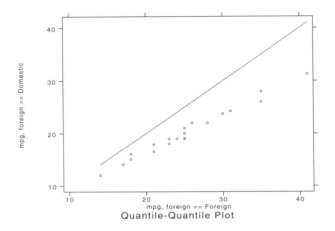

In our auto dataset, the foreign cars have better gas mileage.

◁

## Saved Results

separate saves in r():

Macros
    r(varlist)   names of the newly created variables

## Methods and Formulas

separate is implemented as an ado-file.

## Acknowledgment

separate was originally written by Nicholas J. Cox of the University of Durham.

## Also See

**Related:**    [R] **tabulate**

# Title

---
**serrbar** — Graph standard error bar chart

---

# Syntax

serrbar *mvar svar xvar* [if *exp*] [in *range*] [, s̲cale(*#*) *graph_options* ]

# Description

serrbar graphs *mvar* ± scale × *svar* against *xvar*. Usually, but not necessarily, *mvar* and *svar* will contain means and standard errors or standard deviations of some variable, so that a standard error bar chart is produced.

# Options

scale(*#*) controls the length of the bars. The upper and lower limits of the bars will be *mvar* + scale × *svar* and *mvar* − scale × *svar*. The default is scale(1).

*graph_options* are any of the options allowed with graph, twoway; see [G] **graph options**. The defaults are connect(.II) and symbol(Oii). If changing the defaults, remember that Stata is graphing three variables on the *y* axis: *mvar*, *mvar* + scale × *svar*, and *mvar* − scale × *svar*. However, connect(l), for example, is legal, as serrbar automatically extends the option to connect(lII).

# Remarks

▷ Example

In quality-control applications, the three most commonly used variables with this command are the process mean, process standard deviation, and time. For instance, you have data on the average weights and standard deviations from an assembly line in San Francisco for the period January 8 to January 16. Your data are

```
. list
          date       mean        std
1.         108     192.22       3.94
2.         109     192.64       2.83
3.         110     192.37       4.58
4.         113     194.76       3.25
5.         114     192.69       2.89
6.         115     195.02       1.73
7.         116     193.40       2.62
```

You type serrbar mean std date, scale(2) but, after seeing the result, decide to make it fancier:

204

. serrbar mean std date, sca(2) yline(195) ylab xlab border rlab(195) yscale(180,210)
        title(Observed Weight Variation) t1(San Francisco plant, 1/8 to 1/16)

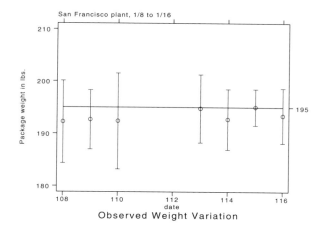

## Methods and Formulas

serrbar is implemented as an ado-file.

## Acknowledgment

serrbar was written by Nicholas J. Cox of the University of Durham.

## Also See

| | |
|---|---|
| **Related:** | [R] **qc** |
| **Complementary:** | *Stata Graphics Manual* |

# Title

> **set** — Quick reference for system parameters

# Description

This entry provides a quick reference to Stata's **set** commands.

# Remarks

| Command | Description | Default | See |
|---------|-------------|---------|-----|
| set adosize | sets the maximum amount of memory that automatically loaded do-files may consume | 128<br>32 for Small Stata | [P] **sysdir** |
| set checksum | determines whether files should be prevented from being downloaded from Internet if checksums do not match | on | [R] **checksum** |
| set dp | determines whether period or comma is to be used as the decimal point | period | [R] **format** |
| set graphics | determines whether graphs are displayed on your monitor | on | [G] **graph** |
| set level | default significance level for confidence intervals for all commands that report confidence intervals | 95 | [R] **level** |
| set linesize | sets the line width for both the screen and the log file | 1 less than full width of the screen | [R] **log** |
| set logtype | sets default log filetype | smcl | [R] **log** |
| set matsize | maximum number of variables that can be included in any model-estimation command | 40 | [R] **matsize** |
| set memory | memory allocated to Stata's data areas, in kilobytes | 1000<br>(400 for Small Stata; cannot be changed) | [R] **memory** |
| set more | pause when —more— is displayed before continuing when the user presses a key | on | [R] **more** |

*(Table continued on next page)*

206

| Command | Description | Default | See |
|---|---|---|---|
| set obs | number of observations in the current dataset | current number of observations | [R] **obs** |
| set output | specifies output to be displayed<br>set output proc displays all output;<br>set output inform suppresses command output;<br>set output error suppresses all output except error messages | proc | [P] **quietly** |
| set rmsg | indicates whether return message indicating execution time is to be displayed at the completion of each command | off | [P] **rmsg** |
| set pagesize | sets number of lines between —more— messages | 2 less than physical number of lines on the screen | [R] **more** |
| set seed | specifies initial value of the random number seed used by the uniform() function | 123456789 | [R] **generate** |
| set trace | indicates whether to trace the execution of programs for debugging | off | [P] **program** |
| set type | specifies the default type assigned to new variables | float | [R] **generate** |
| set virtual | indicates whether Stata should work to arrange its memory to keep objects close together | off | [R] **memory** |

## Also See

**Complementary:**    [R] **limits**, [R] **query**

# Title

shell — Temporarily invoke operating system

# Syntax

$\{ \underline{\text{sh}}\text{ell} \mid ! \}$ [operating_system_command]

winexec program_name [program_args]

$\{ \underline{\text{xsh}}\text{ell} \mid !! \}$ [operating_system_command]

Command availability:

| command | Stata for ... Windows | Macintosh | Unix GUI | Unix console |
|---------|----------|-----------|----------|--------------|
| shell | X | – | X | X |
| winexec | X | – | X | – |
| xshell | – | – | X | – |

As the table reveals, these commands are not available with Stata for Macintosh.

# Description

shell (synonym: '!') allows you to send commands to your operating system or to enter your operating system for interactive use.

winexec allows you to start other programs (such as browsers) from within Stata and without Stata waiting for the program to complete before continuing.

xshell (Stata for Unix GUI only) brings up an xterm in which the command is to be executed.

# Remarks

Remarks are presented under the headings

> *Stata for Windows*
> *Stata for Unix GUI*
> *Stata for Unix console*

# Stata for Windows

shell, without arguments, preserves your session and then invokes your operating system. The Command window will disappear and a DOS window will appear, indicating that you may not do anything in Stata until you exit the DOS shell. To reenter Stata, type exit to your operating system's prompt. Your Stata session is reestablished just as if you had never left.

For instance, you are using Stata for Windows and suddenly realize that there are two things you have to do. You need to enter your operating system for a few minutes. Rather than exiting Stata, doing what you have to do, and then restarting Stata, you type shell in the Command window. A DOS window appears:

```
Microsoft(R) Windows 98
    (C)Copyright Microsoft Corp 1981-1998.
D:\arr\gph> _
```

208

You can now do whatever you need to do in DOS, and Stata will wait until you exit the DOS window before continuing.

Experienced Stata users seldom type out the word `shell`. They type '`!`'. In addition, you do not have to enter your operating system, issue a command, and then exit back to Stata. If you want to execute a single command, you can type the command right after the word `shell` or the exclamation point:

> . !rename try15.dta final.dta

If you do this, the DOS window will flash into and out of existence as the command is executed. You may, however, find that the DOS window does not flash out of existence as it should. If so, see the technical note at the close of this subsection.

Stata for Windows users can also use the `winexec` command. `winexec` allows you to launch any Windows application from within Stata. You can think of it as a shortcut for clicking on the Windows **Start** button, choosing **Run...**, and typing a command.

For instance, assume that you are working in Stata and decide that you want to run a text editor application while Stata runs:

> . winexec notepad
>
> ( *The Windows application Notepad will start and run at the same time as Stata* )

You could even pass a filename to your text editor:

> . winexec notepad c:\docs\myfile.txt

You may need to specify a complete path to the executable that you wish to launch:

> . winexec c:\windows\notepad c:\docs\myfile.txt

The important difference between `winexec` and `shell` is that Stata does not wait for whatever program `winexec` launches to complete before continuing. Stata will wait for whatever program `shell` launches to complete before it will perform any further commands.

## ❑ Technical Note

If, when you use the `shell` to issue a command, the DOS window does not flash out of existence, that is because Windows has the preference set that prevents the window from closing after executing a command. For example, if you typed `!dir`, a DOS window would appear, a directory listing would appear in that window, but the window would not go away and return you to Stata until you closed the window by hand.

You may view this as desirable behavior, but if you do not, you can change it. Under Windows, navigate to C:\Windows. You can do this by double-clicking on the **My Computer** icon on your desktop, then double-clicking on the **C:** drive in the **My Computer** window, and then double-clicking on the **Windows** folder in the **C:** drive window.

In the **Windows** folder, you will find an icon named `command.com`. Click once on this icon with your right mouse button and a menu will appear. Choose **Properties** from that menu, and a tabbed dialog box will appear. Click on the **Program** tab, and you will see a *Close on exit* check box near the bottom of the dialog box. Check this box if you want your DOS shells to close automatically after they complete whatever commands you issue when shelling from Stata for Windows.

❑

❑ Technical Note

Although we do not recommend it, Stata for Windows users can change the shell that Stata calls. By default, Stata for Windows calls the program `command.com` for a DOS shell when running under Windows ME, 98, or 95, and calls `cmd.exe` when running under Windows 2000 or NT.

If you wish to change the shell which Stata calls, set the global macro $S_SHELL to contain the name of the executable program Stata is to use for the shell.

❑

## Stata for Unix GUI

`shell`, without arguments, preserves your session and then invokes your operating system. The Command window will disappear and an `xterm` window will appear, indicating that you may not do anything in Stata until you exit the `xterm` window. To reenter Stata, type `exit` to the Unix prompt. Your Stata session is reestablished just as if you had never left.

For instance, you are using Stata for Windows and suddenly realize that there are two things you have to do. You need to enter your operating system for a few minutes. Rather than exiting Stata, doing what you have to do, and then restarting Stata, you type `shell` in the Command window. An `xterm` window will appear:

```
mycomputer$ _
```

You can now do whatever you need to do, and Stata will wait until you exit the window before continuing.

Experienced Stata users seldom type out the word `shell`. They type '!'. In addition, you do not have to enter your operating system, issue a command, and then exit back to Stata. If you want to execute a single command, you can type the command right after the word `shell` or the exclamation point:

```
. !mv try15.dta final.dta
```

Be careful, because in some cases you will want to type

```
. !!vi myfile.do
```

and, in other cases,

```
. winexec xedit myfile.do
```

!! is a synonym for `xshell`—a command different from, but related to, `shell`—and `winexec` is a different and related command, too.

Before we get into this, understand that if all you want is a shell from which you can issue Unix commands, type `shell` or !:

```
. !

mycomputer$ _
```

When you are through, type `exit` to the Unix prompt and you will return to Stata:

```
mycomputer$ exit

. _
```

If, on the other hand, you want to specify to Stata the Unix command that you want executed, then you have to think because you need to decide whether you want to use shell, xshell, or winexec. The answer depends on whether whatever it is you want to execute needs a terminal window or is an X application:

| | |
|---|---|
| ... does not need a terminal window: | use shell ... (synonym: ! ... ) |
| ... needs a terminal window: | use xshell ... (synonym: !! ... ) |
| ... is an X application: | use winexec ... (no synonym) |

When you type shell mv try15.dta final.dta, Stata invokes your shell (/bin/sh, /bin/csh, etc.) and executes the specified command (mv in this case), routing the standard output and standard error back to Stata. Typing '!mv try15.dta final.dta' is the same as typing 'shell mv try15.dta final.dta'.

When you type xshell vi myfile.do, Stata invokes an xterm window (which in turn invokes a shell), and executes the command there. Typing '!!vi myfile.do' is equivalent to typing xshell vi myfile.do'.

When you type winexec xedit myfile.do, Stata directly invokes the command specified (xedit in this case). No xterm window is brought up nor a shell invoked because, in this case, xterm does not need it. xterm is an X application that will create its own window in which to run. Actually, you could have typed !!xedit myfile.do. That would have brought up an unnecessary xterm window from which xedit would have been executed and that would not matter. You could even have typed !xedit myfile.do. That would have invoked an unnecessary shell from which xedit would have been executed and that would not matter, either. The important difference, however, is that shell and xshell wait until the process completes before allowing Stata to continue and winexec does not.

❏ Technical Note

You can set Stata global macros to control the behavior of shell and xshell. The macros are

| | |
|---|---|
| $S_SHELL | defines the shell to be used by shell when you type a command following shell. Default is something like "/bin/sh -c", although this can vary depending on how your Unix environment variables are set. |
| $S_XSHELL | defines shell to be used by shell and xshell when they are typed without arguments. Default is "xterm". |
| $S_XSHELL2 | defines shell to be used by xshell when it is typed with arguments. Default is "xterm -e". |

For instance, if you type in Stata

    . global S_XSHELL2 "/usr/X11R6/bin/xterm -e"

then later were you to type

    . !!vi myfile.do

Stata would issue the command '/usr/X11R6/bin/xterm -e vi myfile.do' to Unix.

If you do make changes, we recommend that you record the changes in your profile.do file.

❏

## Stata for Unix console

shell, without arguments, preserves your session and then invokes your operating system. Your Stata session will be suspended until you exit the shell, at which point your Stata session is reestablished just as if you had never left.

For instance, you are using Stata and suddenly realize that there are two things you have to do. You need to enter your operating system for a few minutes. Rather than exiting Stata, doing what you have to do, and then restarting Stata, you type shell. A Unix prompt appears:

```
. shell
(Type exit to return to Stata)
$ _
```

You can now do whatever you need to do and type exit when you finish. You will return to Stata just as if you never left.

Experienced Stata users seldom type out the word shell. They type '!'. In addition, you do not have to enter your operating system, issue a command, and then exit back to Stata. If you want to execute a single command, you can type the command right after the word shell or the exclamation point. If you want to edit the file myfile.do and if vi is the name of your favorite editor, you could type

```
. !vi myfile.do
```
          *Stata puts you inside your editor.*
          *When you exit your editor:*

```
. _
```

## Also See

**Complementary:**     [R] **query**

**Related:**     [R] **cd**, [R] **copy**, [R] **dir**, [R] **erase**, [R] **mkdir**, [R] **type**

# Title

> **signrank** — Sign, rank, and median tests

# Syntax

**signrank** *varname* =*exp* [**if** *exp*] [**in** *range*]

**signtest** *varname* =*exp* [**if** *exp*] [**in** *range*]

**ranksum** *varname* [**if** *exp*] [**in** *range*], **by**(*groupvar*)

**median** *varname* [**if** *exp*] [**in** *range*], **by**(*groupvar*) [ **exact**

    **medianties**(**drop** | **above** | **below** | **split**) ]

by ... : may be used with **signrank**, **signtest**, **ranksum**, and **median**; see [R] **by**.

# Description

    **signrank** tests the equality of *matched* pairs of observations using the Wilcoxon matched-pairs signed-ranks test (Wilcoxon 1945). The null hypothesis is that both distributions are the same.

    **signtest** also tests the equality of *matched* pairs of observations (Arbuthnott 1710, but better explained by Snedecor and Cochran 1989) by calculating the differences between *varname* and the *expression*. The null hypothesis is that the median of the differences is zero; no further assumptions are made about the distributions. This, in turn, is equivalent to the hypothesis that the true proportion of positive (negative) signs is one-half.

    **ranksum** tests the hypothesis that two independent samples (i.e., *unmatched* data) are from populations with the same distribution using the Wilcoxon rank-sum test, which is also known as the Mann–Whitney two-sample statistic (Wilcoxon 1945; Mann and Whitney 1947).

    **median** performs a nonparametric $k$-sample test on the equality of medians. It tests the null hypothesis that the $k$ samples were drawn from populations with the same median. In the case of two samples, the test chi-squared statistic is computed both with and without a continuity correction.

# Options

    **by**(*groupvar*) is not optional. It specifies the name of the grouping variable.

    **exact** is only valid for the **median** test. It displays the significance calculated by Fisher's exact test. In the case of two samples, both one- and two-sided probabilities are displayed.

    **medianties**(**drop** | **above** | **below** | **split**) is only valid for the **median** test. It specifies how values equal to the overall median are to be handled. The median test computes the median for *varname* using all observations and then divides the observations into those falling above the median and those falling below the median. When the value for an observation is equal to the sample median, they can be dropped from the analysis by specifying **medianties**(**drop**); added to the group above or below the median by specifying **medianties**(**above**) or **medianties**(**below**), respectively; or if there is more than one observation with values equal to the median, they can be equally divided into the two groups by specifying **medianties**(**split**). If this option is not specified, **medianties**(**below**) is assumed.

213

# Remarks

▷ Example

You are testing the effectiveness of a new fuel additive. You run an experiment with 12 cars. You first run each car without the fuel treatment and measure the mileage. You then add the fuel treatment and repeat the experiment. The results of the experiment are

| Without Treatment | With Treatment | Without Treatment | With Treatment |
|---|---|---|---|
| 20 | 24 | 18 | 17 |
| 23 | 25 | 24 | 28 |
| 21 | 21 | 20 | 24 |
| 25 | 22 | 24 | 27 |
| 18 | 23 | 23 | 21 |
| 17 | 18 | 19 | 23 |

We create two variables called mpg1 and mpg2 representing mileage without and with the treatment, respectively. We can test the null hypothesis that the treatment had no effect by typing

```
. signrank mpg1=mpg2
Wilcoxon signed-rank test
```

| sign | obs | sum ranks | expected |
|---|---|---|---|
| positive | 3 | 13.5 | 38.5 |
| negative | 8 | 63.5 | 38.5 |
| zero | 1 | 1 | 1 |
| all | 12 | 78 | 78 |

```
unadjusted variance       162.50
adjustment for ties        -1.62
adjustment for zeros       -0.25
                          ------
adjusted variance         160.62

Ho: mpg1 = mpg2
            z =   -1.973
  Prob > |z| =    0.0485
```

The output indicates that we can reject the null hypothesis at any level above 4.85%.

◁

▷ Example

signtest tests that the median of the differences is zero, making no further assumptions, whereas signrank assumed that the distributions are equal as well. Using the data above,

*(Continued on next page)*

```
. signtest mpg1=mpg2
```

Sign test

| sign | observed | expected |
|---|---|---|
| positive | 3 | 5.5 |
| negative | 8 | 5.5 |
| zero | 1 | 1 |
| all | 12 | 12 |

One-sided tests:
  Ho: median of mpg1 - mpg2 = 0 vs.
  Ha: median of mpg1 - mpg2 > 0
    Pr(#positive >= 3) =
      Binomial(n = 11, x >= 3, p = 0.5) =  0.9673

  Ho: median of mpg1 - mpg2 = 0 vs.
  Ha: median of mpg1 - mpg2 < 0
    Pr(#negative >= 8) =
      Binomial(n = 11, x >= 8, p = 0.5) =  0.1133

Two-sided test:
  Ho: median of mpg1 - mpg2 = 0 vs.
  Ha: median of mpg1 - mpg2 ~= 0
    Pr(#positive >= 8 or #negative >= 8) =
      min(1, 2*Binomial(n = 11, x >= 8, p = 0.5)) =  0.2266

The summary table indicates that there were 3 comparisons for which mpg1 exceeded mpg2, 8 comparisons for which mpg2 exceeded mpg1, and one comparison for which they were the same.

The output below the summary table is based on the binomial distribution. The significance of the one-sided test, where the alternative hypothesis is that the median of mpg2 − mpg1 is greater than zero, is 0.1133. The significance of the two-sided test, where the alternative hypothesis is simply that the median of the differences is different from zero, is $0.2266 = 2 \times 0.1133$.

◁

▷ Example

ranksum and median are for use with *unmatched* data. This time we assume that you ran the experiment with 24 cars; 12 cars with the fuel treatment and 12 cars without. You input these data by creating a dataset with 24 observations. mpg records the mileage rating, and treat records a 0 if the mileage corresponds to untreated fuel and a 1 if it corresponds to treated fuel.

```
. ranksum mpg, by(treat)
```

Two-sample Wilcoxon rank-sum (Mann-Whitney) test

| treat | obs | rank sum | expected |
|---|---|---|---|
| 0 | 12 | 128 | 150 |
| 1 | 12 | 172 | 150 |
| combined | 24 | 300 | 300 |

| | |
|---|---|
| unadjusted variance | 300.00 |
| adjustment for ties | -4.04 |
| adjusted variance | 295.96 |

Ho: mpg(treat==0) = mpg(treat==1)
        z =  -1.279
  Prob > |z| =  0.2010

These results indicate that the medians are not statistically different at any level smaller than 20.1%. Similarly, the median test

```
. median mpg, by(treat) exact
Median test

    Greater
   than the                 treat
    median           0            1  |   Total
  ----------+----------------------------+---------
        No           7            5  |      12
       yes           5            7  |      12
  ----------+----------------------------+---------
     Total  |        12           12  |      24

          Pearson chi2(1) =   0.6667   Pr = 0.414
        Fisher's exact =                    0.684
 1-sided Fisher's exact =                   0.342

   Continuity corrected:
          Pearson chi2(1) =   0.1667   Pr = 0.683
```

fails to reject the null hypothesis that there is no difference between the two fuel additives.

It is worthwhile to compare the results from these two tests with those obtained from the signrank and signtest where we found significant differences. A experiment run on 24 different cars is not as powerful as a before-and-after comparison using the same 12 cars.

◁

# Saved Results

signrank saves in r():

Scalars

| | | | |
|---|---|---|---|
| r(N_neg) | number of negative comparisons | r(sum_neg) | sum of the negative ranks |
| r(N_pos) | number of positive comparisons | r(z) | $z$ statistic |
| r(N_tie) | number of tied comparisons | r(Var_a) | adjusted variance |
| r(sum_pos) | sum of the positive ranks | | |

signtest saves in r():

Scalars

| | | | |
|---|---|---|---|
| r(N_neg) | number of negative comparisons | r(p_2) | two-sided probability |
| r(N_pos) | number of positive comparisons | r(p_neg) | one-sided probability of negative comparison |
| r(N_tie) | number of tied comparisons | r(p_pos) | one-sided probability of positive comparison |

ranksum saves in r():

Scalars

| | | | |
|---|---|---|---|
| r(N_1) | sample size $n_1$ | r(group1) | value of variable for first group |
| r(N_2) | sample size $n_2$ | r(sum_obs) | actual sum of ranks for first group |
| r(z) | $z$ statistic | r(sum_exp) | expected sum of ranks for first group |
| r(Var_a) | adjusted variance | | |

median saves in r():

Scalars

| | | | |
|---|---|---|---|
| r(N) | sample size | r(group) | number of groups compared |
| r(chi2) | Pearson's $\chi^2$ | r(chi2_cc) | continuity corrected Pearson's $\chi^2$ |
| r(p) | significance of Pearson's $\chi^2$ | r(p_cc) | continuity corrected significance |
| r(p_exact) | Fisher's exact $p$ | r(p1_exact) | one-sided Fisher's exact $p$ |

# Methods and Formulas

signrank, signtest, ranksum, and median are implemented as ado-files.

For a practical introduction to these techniques with an emphasis on examples rather than theory, see Bland (2000) or Sprent (1993). For a summary of all these tests, see Snedecor and Cochran (1989).

## signrank

Both the sign test and Wilcoxon signed-rank tests test the null hypothesis that the distribution of a random variable $D = varname - exp$ has median zero. The sign test makes no additional assumptions, but the Wilcoxon signed-rank test makes the additional assumption that the distribution of $D$ is symmetric. If $D = X_1 - X_2$, where $X_1$ and $X_2$ have the same distribution, then it follows that the distribution of $D$ is symmetric about zero. Thus, the Wilcoxon signed-rank test is often described as a test of the hypothesis that two distributions are the same; i.e., $X_1 \sim X_2$.

Let $d_j$ denote the difference for any matched pair of observations:

$$d_j = x_{1j} - x_{2j} = varname - exp$$

for $j = 1, 2, \ldots, n$.

Rank the absolute values of the differences $|d_j|$ and assign any tied values the average rank. Consider the signs of $d_j$ and let

$$r_j = \text{sign}(d_j) \, \text{rank}(|d_j|)$$

be the signed-ranks. Our test statistic is

$$T_{\text{obs}} = \sum_{j=1}^{n} r_j = (\text{sum of ranks for } + \text{ signs}) - (\text{sum of ranks for } - \text{ signs})$$

The null hypothesis is that the distribution of $d_j$ is symmetric about 0. Hence, the likelihood is unchanged if we flip signs on the $d_j$, and thus the randomization datasets are the $2^n$ possible sign changes for the $d_j$. Thus, the randomization distribution of our test statistic $T$ can be computed by considering all the $2^n$ possible values of

$$T = \sum_{j=1}^{n} S_j r_j$$

where the $r_j$ are the observed signed-ranks (considered fixed) and $S_j$ is either $+1$ or $-1$.

With this distribution, the mean and variance of $T$ are given by

$$E(T) = 0 \quad \text{and} \quad \text{Var}_{\text{adj}}(T) = \sum_{j=1}^{n} r_j^2$$

Note that the test statistic for the Wilcoxon signed-rank test is often expressed (equivalently) as the sum of the positive signed-ranks, $T_+$, where

$$E(T_+) = \frac{n(n+1)}{4} \quad \text{and} \quad \text{Var}_{\text{adj}}(T_+) = \frac{1}{4}\sum_{j=1}^{n} r_j^2$$

Zeros and ties do not affect the theory above and the exact variance is still given by the above formula for $\text{Var}_{\text{adj}}(T_+)$. When we observe $d_j = 0$, $d_j$ will always be zero in each of the randomization datasets (using $\text{sign}(0) = 0$). When we have ties, we can assign averaged ranks for each group of ties and then treat them the same as the other ranks.

The "unadjusted variance" reported by `signrank` is the variance that the randomization distribution would have had if there had been no ties or zeros:

$$\text{Var}_{\text{unadj}}(T_+) = \frac{1}{4}\sum_{j=1}^{n} j^2 = \frac{n(n+1)(2n+1)}{24}$$

The adjustment for zeros is the change in the variance when the ranks for the zeros are signed to make $r_j = 0$:

$$\Delta\text{Var}_{\text{zero adj}}(T_+) = -\frac{1}{4}\sum_{j=1}^{n_0} j^2 = -\frac{n_0(n_0+1)(2n_0+1)}{24}$$

where $n_0$ is the number of zeros. The adjustment for ties is the change in the variance when the ranks (for nonzero observations) are replaced by averaged ranks:

$$\Delta\text{Var}_{\text{ties adj}}(T_+) = \text{Var}_{\text{adj}}(T_+) - \text{Var}_{\text{unadj}}(T_+) - \Delta\text{Var}_{\text{zero adj}}(T_+)$$

Using a normal approximation, we calculate

$$z = \frac{T_+ - E(T_+)}{\sqrt{\text{Var}_{\text{adj}}(T_+)}}$$

## signtest

The test statistic for the sign test is the number $n_+$ of differences

$$d_j = x_{1j} - x_{2j} = varname - exp$$

greater than zero. Assuming that the probability of a difference being equal to zero is exactly zero, then, under the null hypothesis, $n_+ \sim \text{Binomial}(n, p = \frac{1}{2})$, where $n$ is the total number of observations.

But what if some differences are zero? This question has a ready answer if we view the test from the perspective of Fisher's Principle of Randomization (Fisher 1935). Fisher's idea (stated in a modern way) was to look at a family of transformations of the observed data such that the a priori likelihood (under the null hypothesis) of the transformed data is the same as the likelihood of the observed data. The distribution of the test statistic is then produced by calculating its value for each of the transformed "randomization" datasets, assuming that each dataset is equally likely.

For the sign test, the "data" are simply the set of signs of the differences. Under the null hypothesis of the sign test, the probability that $d_j$ is less than zero is equal to the probability that $d_j$ is greater than zero. Thus, we can transform the observed signs by flipping any number of them, and the set of signs will have the same likelihood. The $2^n$ possible sign changes form the family of randomization datasets. If we have no zeros, this procedure again leads to $n_+ \sim \text{Binomial}(n, p = \frac{1}{2})$.

If we do have zeros, changing their signs leaves them as zeros. So, if we observe $n_0$ zeros, each of the $2^n$ sign-change datasets will also have $n_0$ zeros. Hence, the values of $n_+$ calculated over the sign-change datasets range from 0 to $n - n_0$, and the "randomization" distribution of $n_+$ is $\text{Binomial}(n - n_0, p = \frac{1}{2})$.

## ranksum

For the Wilcoxon rank-sum test, we have two independent random variables $X_1$ and $X_2$, and we test the null hypothesis that $X_1 \sim X_2$. We have a sample of size $n_1$ from $X_1$ and another of size $n_2$ from $X_2$.

The data are then ranked without regard to the sample to which they belong. If the data are tied, averaged ranks are used. Wilcoxon's test statistic (Wilcoxon 1945) is the sum of the ranks for the observations in the first sample:

$$T = \sum_{i=1}^{n_1} R_{1i}$$

Mann and Whitney's $U$ statistic (Mann and Whitney 1947) is the number of pairs $(X_{1i}, X_{2j})$ such that $X_{1i} > X_{2j}$. These statistics differ only by a constant:

$$U = T - \frac{n_1(n_1 + 1)}{2}$$

Again Fisher's Principle of Randomization provides a method for calculating the distribution of the test statistic, ties or not. The randomization distribution consists of the $\binom{n}{n_1}$ ways to choose $n_1$ ranks from the set of all $n = n_1 + n_2$ ranks and assign them to the first sample.

It is a straightforward exercise to verify that

$$E(T) = \frac{n_1(n + 1)}{2} \qquad \text{and} \qquad \text{Var}(T) = \frac{n_1 n_2 s^2}{n}$$

where $s$ is the standard deviation of the combined ranks $r_i$ for both groups:

$$s^2 = \frac{1}{n - 1} \sum_{i=1}^{n} (r_i - \bar{r})^2$$

This formula for the variance is exact and holds both when there are no ties and when there are ties and we use averaged ranks. (Indeed, the variance formula holds for the randomization distribution of choosing $n_1$ numbers from any set of $n$ numbers.)

Using a normal approximation, we calculate

$$z = \frac{T - E(T)}{\sqrt{\mathrm{Var}(T)}}$$

## median

The median test examines whether it is likely that two or more samples came from populations with the same median. The null hypothesis is that the samples were drawn from populations with the same median. The alternative hypothesis is that at least one sample was drawn from a population with a different median. The test should be used only with ordinal or interval data.

Assume that we have score values for $k$ independent samples to be compared. The median test is performed by first computing the median score for all observations combined, regardless of the sample group. Each score is compared to this computed grand median and is classified as being above the grand median, below the grand median, or equal to the grand median. Observations with scores equal to the grand median can be dropped, added to the "above" group, added to the "below" group, or split between the two groups.

Once all observations are classified, the data are cast into a $2 \times k$ contingency table and a Pearson's chi-squared test or Fisher's exact test is performed.

## References

Arbuthnott, J. 1710. An argument for divine providence, taken from the constant regularity observ'd in the births of both sexes. *Philosophical Transactions* 27: 186–190.

Bland, M. 2000. *An Introduction to Medical Statistics*. 3d ed. Oxford: Oxford University Press.

Fisher, R. A. 1935. *Design of Experiments*. Edinburgh: Oliver and Boyd.

Goldstein, R. 1997. sg69: Immediate Mann–Whitney and binomial effect-size display. *Stata Technical Bulletin* 36: 29–31. Reprinted in *Stata Technical Bulletin Reprints*, vol. 6, pp. 187–189.

Mann, H. B. and D. R. Whitney. 1947. On a test of whether one of two random variables is stochastically larger than the other. *Annals of Mathematical Statistics* 18: 50–60.

Newson, R. 2000a. snp15: somersd–Confidence intervals for nonparametric statistics and their differences. *Stata Technical Bulletin* 55: 47–55.

———. 2000b. snp15.1: Update to somersd. *Stata Technical Bulletin* 57: 35.

Perkins, A. M. 1998. snp14: A two-sample multivariate nonparametric test. *Stata Technical Bulletin* 42: 47–49. Reprinted in *Stata Technical Bulletin Reprints*, vol. 7, pp. 243–245.

Snedecor, G. W. and W. G. Cochran. 1989. *Statistical Methods*. 8th ed. Ames, IA: Iowa State University Press.

Sprent, P. 1993. *Applied Nonparametric Statistical Methods*. 2d ed. London: Chapman & Hall.

Sribney, W. M. 1995. crc40: Correcting for ties and zeros in sign and rank tests. *Stata Technical Bulletin* 26: 2–4. Reprinted in *Stata Technical Bulletin Reprints*, vol. 5, pp. 5–8.

Wilcoxon, F. 1945. Individual comparisons by ranking methods. *Biometrics* 1: 80–83.

## Also See

**Related:**    [R] **kwallis**, [R] **nptrend**, [R] **runtest**, [R] **ttest**

# Title

| simul — Monte Carlo simulations |
| --- |

# Syntax

simul *progname*, <u>r</u>eps(#) [ <u>a</u>rgs(*whatever*) <u>d</u>ots <u>double</u> <u>sa</u>ving(*filename*)

<u>e</u>very(#) replace <u>noi</u>sily ]

# Description

simul eases the programming task of performing Monte Carlo type simulations. *progname* is the name of a program that performs a single simulation. Typing simul *progname*, reps(#) iterates *progname* # replications and collects the results.

simul calls *progname* in two ways. At the outset, simul issues "*progname* ?" and expects *progname* to set the global macro S_1 to contain the list of variable names under which results are to be stored. Thereafter, simul issues "*progname postname*" calls and expects it to perform a single simulation and to store the results using post *postname*. Details of post can be found in [P] **postfile**, but enough information is provided below to use post successfully.

# Options

reps(#) is not optional—it specifies the number of replications to be performed.

args(*whatever*) specifies any arguments to be passed to *progname* on invocation. The query call is then of the form "*progname* ? *whatever*" and subsequent calls of the form "*progname postname whatever*".

dots requests that a dot be placed on the screen at the beginning of every call to *progname*, thus providing entertainment during long simulations.

double specifies that the simulation results are to be stored as doubles, meaning 8-byte reals. By default, they are stored as floats, meaning 4-byte reals.

saving(*filename*) creates a Stata data file (.dta file) containing the simulation results.

every(#) specifies that results are to be written to disk every #th repetition. every() should only be specified in conjunction with saving() when performing simulations that take a long time. This will allow recovery of partial results should your computer crash. See [P] **postfile**.

replace indicates that the file specified by saving() may already exist and, if it does, it should be overwritten.

noisily requests that any output from the user-defined program be displayed.

# Remarks

For an introduction to Monte Carlo methods, see Johnston and DiNardo (1997, 348–358).

*progname* must have the following outline:

```
program define progname
        if "`1´" == "?" {
                global S_1 "variable names"
                exit
        }
        perform single simulation
        post `1´ (result1) (result2) ...
end
```

There must be the same number of results following the `post `1´` command as there are variable names following the `global S_1` command.

## ▷ Example

Make a dataset containing means and variances of 100-observation samples from a lognormal distribution (as a first step in evaluating, say, the coverage of a 95%, *t*-based confidence interval). Perform the experiment 10,000 times.

```
program define lnsim
        version 7.0
        if "`1´" == "?" {
                global S_1 "mean var"
                exit
        }
        drop _all
        set obs 100
        gen z = exp(invnorm(uniform()))
        summarize z
        post `1´ (r(mean)) (r(Var))
end
```

The last line of our program, `post `1´ ...`, saves the calculated results. `summarize` saves the mean in `r(mean)` and the variance in `r(Var)`. Had we wanted to save the mean divided by the standard deviation and the standard deviation, the last line could have read

```
post `1´ (r(mean)/sqrt(r(Var))) (sqrt(r(Var)))
```

In our version, we save the mean and variance. `lnsim` can be executed 10,000 times by typing

```
. simul lnsim, reps(10000)
. describe
Contains data
  obs:         10,000
  vars:             2                           16 Sep 2000 10:39
  size:       120,000 (94.1% of memory free)
```

| variable name | storage type | display format | value label | variable label |
|---|---|---|---|---|
| mean | float | %9.0g | | |
| var | float | %9.0g | | |

```
Sorted by:
. summarize
```

| Variable | Obs | Mean | Std. Dev. | Min | Max |
|---|---|---|---|---|---|
| mean | 10000 | 1.649879 | .216586 | 1.069133 | 2.896868 |
| var | 10000 | 4.689451 | 4.458131 | .7389911 | 106.0029 |

◁

❑ Technical Note

(Debugging a simulation.) Before executing our `lnsim` simulator, we can verify that it works by executing it interactively. We can first check that, when called with a question mark, `lnsim` sets the global macro $S_1 correctly:

```
. lnsim ?
. display "$S_1"
```

We can then try executing `lnsim` to perform a single simulation:

```
. postfile debug mean var using myfile
. lnsim debug
. postclose debug
. use myfile, clear
. erase myfile.dta
```

When we execute `lnsim`, we will see the output it produces (which, in our case, is the result of the `summarize`). When we execute `lnsim` through `simul`, this output is suppressed.

Here are the details of the testing: The `postfile` command opens a file for posted results; see [P] **postfile**. `simul` normally handles this for us, but the command shown will work in all cases. (The post commands also require we choose a name for tracking the results. We chose `debug`, but you can choose any name that appeals to you.) Once the post file is started, invoking `lnsim debug` will perform a single simulation. We then close the file and examine it.

If things go wrong—if the program `lnsim` ends with an error—we must still type `postclose debug` and remember to `erase myfile.dta`. If we do not, a small amount of Stata's memory will remain allocated to our test simulation for the rest of the session. If things do go wrong, it would be useful to trace the execution of our program. Here is what we would do, from the top:

```
. postfile debug mean var using myfile      /* our first test */
. lnsim debug
   ( big problems; nonzero return code )
. postclose debug                           /* clear this simulation */
. erase myfile.dta

. postfile debug using myfile               /* start again */
. set trace on                              /* trace execution of our program */
. lnsim debug
   ( trace output appears )
   ( things still go wrong, of course )
. set trace off                             /* stop tracing */
. postclose debug                           /* clear simulation */
. erase myfile.dta
```

❑

▷ Example

(Passing arguments to the simulation.) Consider a more complicated problem. Let's experiment with estimating $y_j = a + bx_j + u_j$ when the true model has $a = 1$, $b = 1$, and $u_j = z_j + cx_j$ and $z_j$ is $N(0, 1)$. We will keep the parameter estimates and standard errors and experiment with varying $c$. $x_j$ will be fixed across experiments but will originally be generated as $N(0, 1)$. We begin by interactively making the true data:

```
. drop _all
. set obs 100
. gen x = invnorm(uniform())
. gen true_y = 1+2*x
. save truth
```

Our program is

```
program define hetero
        version 7.0
        if "`1'" == "?" {
                global S_1 "a se_a b se_b"
                exit
        }
        use truth, clear
        gen y = true_y + (invnorm(uniform()) + `2'*x)
        regress y x
        post `1' (_b[_cons]) (_se[_cons]) (_b[x]) (_se[x])
end
```

Note the use of `2' in our statement for generating y. `2' refers to the second argument received by hetero. (`1', the first argument, is the name we must place after the post command.) We can run 10,000 simulations, setting our argument to 3, by typing

```
. simul hetero, args(3) reps(10000)
```

Our program hetero could, however, be more efficient because it rereads the file truth once every replication. It would be better if we could read the data just once and, in fact, we can because we can use the query call to initialize ourselves. A faster version reads

```
program define hetero
        version 7.0
        if "`1'" == "?" {
                use truth, clear              (load the data just once)
                global S_1 "a se_a b se_b"
                exit
        }
        gen y = true_y + 2*(invnorm(uniform()) + `2'*x)
        regress y x
        post `1' (_b[_cons]) (_se[_cons]) (_b[x]) (_se[x])
        drop y
end
```

◁

## ❏ Technical Note

Lest you worry, in complicated situations posts can be nested, i.e., you can do simulations of simulations and simulations of bootstraps. Stata's bstrap command (see [R] bstrap) works much like simul except that it feeds the user-written program a bootstrap sample. Say we want to evaluate the bootstrap estimator of the standard error of the median when applied to lognormally distributed data. We want to perform a simulation, the result being a dataset of medians and bootstrap estimated standard errors.

As background, summarize calculates summary statistics, leaving the mean in r(mean) and the variance in r(Var). summarize with the detail option also calculates summary statistics, but more of them, and leaves the median in r(p50).

Thus, our plan is to perform simulations by randomly drawing a dataset: we calculate the median of our random sample; we use `bstrap` to obtain a dataset of medians calculated from bootstrap samples of our random sample; the standard deviation of those medians is our estimate of the standard error; and we save the median and standard error.

Our programs are

```
program define bsse /* to be called by simul */
        version 7.0
        if "`1'" == "?" {
                global S_1 "med bs_se"
                exit
        }
        drop _all                       (make a sample)
        set obs 100
        gen x = invnorm(uniform())
        bstrap seofmed, rep(100) leave    (obtain bootstrap results)
        summarize midp                    (obtain standard error)
        post `1' (r(mean)) (sqrt(r(Var)))
end

program define seofmed /* to be called by bstrap */
        version 7.0
        if "`1'" == "?" {
                global S_1 "midp"
                exit
        }
        summarize x, detail
        post `1' (r(p50))
end
```

We can obtain final results, running our simulation 1,000 times, by typing

```
. simul bsse, reps(1000)

. summarize
```

| Variable | Obs | Mean | Std. Dev. | Min | Max |
|---|---|---|---|---|---|
| med | 1000 | .002578 | .121661 | -.4340888 | .3749412 |
| bs_se | 1000 | .1268964 | .028928 | .0513692 | .2481588 |

# References

Gould, W. 1994. ssi6.1: Simplified Monte Carlo simulations. *Stata Technical Bulletin* 20: 22–24. Reprinted in *Stata Technical Bulletin Reprints*, vol. 4, pp. 207–210.

Hamilton, L. C. 1998. *Statistics with Stata 5*. Pacific Grove, CA: Brooks/Cole Publishing Company.

Johnston, J. and J. DiNardo. 1997. *Econometric Methods*. 4th ed. New York: McGraw–Hill.

Weesie, J. 1998. ip25: Parameterized Monte Carlo simulations: an enhancement to the simulation command. *Stata Technical Bulletin* 43: 13–15. Reprinted in *Stata Technical Bulletin Reprints*, vol. 8, pp. 75–77.

# Also See

| Complementary: | [R] **bstrap**, |
|---|---|
| | [P] **postfile** |

# Title

sktest — Skewness and kurtosis test for normality

# Syntax

sktest *varlist* [*weight*] [if *exp*] [in *range*] [, noadjust ]

aweights and fweights are allowed.

# Description

For each variable in *varlist*, sktest presents a test for normality based on skewness and another based on kurtosis and then combines the two tests into an overall test statistic. sktest requires a minimum of 8 observations to make its calculations.

# Options

noadjust suppresses the empirical adjustment made by Royston (1991c) to the overall $\chi^2$ and its significance level and presents the unaltered test as described by D'Agostino, Balanger, and D'Agostino, Jr. (1990).

# Remarks

Also see [R] **swilk** for the Shapiro–Wilk and Shapiro–Francia tests for normality. Those tests are, in general, preferred for nonaggregated data (Gould and Rogers 1991, Gould 1992, Royston 1991c).

▷ Example

Using our automobile dataset, we will test whether the variables mpg and trunk are normally distributed:

```
. sktest mpg trunk
```

Skewness/Kurtosis tests for Normality

| Variable | Pr(Skewness) | Pr(Kurtosis) | adj chi2(2) | joint Prob>chi2 |
|---|---|---|---|---|
| mpg | 0.002 | 0.080 | 10.95 | 0.0042 |
| trunk | 0.912 | 0.044 | 4.19 | 0.1228 |

We can reject the hypothesis that mpg is normally distributed but cannot reject the hypothesis that trunk is normally distributed, at least at the 12% level. In the case of trunk, the problem is that the tails are too thick (too much kurtosis). Based on skewness alone, one could not reject the hypothesis that trunk is normally distributed.

◁

❏ Technical Note

sktest implements the test as described by D'Agostino et al. (1990) but with the adjustment made by Royston (1991c). In the above example, had we specified the noadjust option, the $\chi^2$ values would have been 13.13 for mpg and 4.05 for trunk. With the adjustment, it is also possible that the $\chi^2$ value will show as '.'. This should be interpreted as an absurdly large number; the data are most certainly not normal.

❏

## Saved Results

sktest saves in r():

Scalars

| | |
|---|---|
| r(chi2) | $\chi^2$ |
| r(P_skew) | Pr(skewness) |
| r(P_kurt) | Pr(kurtosis) |
| r(P_chi2) | Pr($\chi^2$) |

## Methods and Formulas

sktest is implemented as an ado-file.

sktest implements the test described by D'Agostino, Balanger, and D'Agostino, Jr. (1990) with the empirical correction developed by Royston (1991c).

The relative merits of the skewness and kurtosis test versus the Shapiro–Wilk and Shapiro–Francia tests have been a subject of debate. The interested reader is directed to the articles in the *Stata Technical Bulletin*. Our recommendation is to use Shapiro–Francia whenever possible; that is, whenever dealing with nonaggregated or ungrouped data (Gould and Rogers 1991, Gould 1992); see [R] **swilk**. If normality is rejected, use sktest to determine the source of the problem.

## Acknowledgment

sktest has benefited greatly by the comments and work of Patrick Royston of the MRC Clinical Trials Unit, London; at this point, the program should be viewed as due as much to Royston as to us except, of course, for any errors.

## References

D'Agostino, R. B., A. Balanger and R. B. D'Agostino, Jr. 1990. A suggestion for using powerful and informative tests of normality. *The American Statistician* 44(4): 316–321.

——. 1991. sg3.3: Comment on tests of normality. *Stata Technical Bulletin* 3: 20. Reprinted in *Stata Technical Bulletin Reprints*, vol. 1, pp. 105–106.

Gould, W. W. 1991. sg3: Skewness and kurtosis tests of normality. *Stata Technical Bulletin* 1: 20–21. Reprinted in *Stata Technical Bulletin Reprints*, vol. 1, pp. 99–101.

——. 1992. sg3.7: Final summary of tests of normality. *Stata Technical Bulletin* 5: 10–11. Reprinted in *Stata Technical Bulletin Reprints*, vol. 1, pp. 114–115.

Gould, W. W. and W. H. Rogers. 1991. sg3.4: Summary of tests of normality. *Stata Technical Bulletin* 3: 20–23. Reprinted in *Stata Technical Bulletin Reprints*, vol. 1, pp. 106–110.

Royston, P. 1991a. sg3.1: Tests for departure from normality. *Stata Technical Bulletin* 2: 16–17. Reprinted in *Stata Technical Bulletin Reprints*, vol. 1, pp. 101–104.

——. 1991b. sg3.2: Shapiro–Wilk and Shapiro–Francia tests. *Stata Technical Bulletin* 3: 19. Reprinted in *Stata Technical Bulletin Reprints*, vol. 1, p. 105.

——. 1991c. sg3.5: Comment on sg3.4 and an improved D'Agostino test. *Stata Technical Bulletin* 3: 23–24. Reprinted in *Stata Technical Bulletin Reprints*, vol. 1, pp. 110–112.

——. 1991d. sg3.6: A response to sg3.3: comment on tests of normality. *Stata Technical Bulletin* 4: 8–9. Reprinted in *Stata Technical Bulletin Reprints*, vol. 1, pp. 112–114.

# Also See

**Related:**   [R] **ladder**, [R] **lv**, [R] **swilk**

# Title

> **smooth** — Robust nonlinear smoother

# Syntax

smooth *smoother*[,<u>twice</u>] *varname* [if *exp*] [in *range*], <u>generate</u>(*newvar*)

where *smoother* is specified as $Sm[Sm[\ldots]]$ and $Sm$ is one of

$$\{\,1\,|\,2\,|\,3\,|\,4\,|\,5\,|\,6\,|\,7\,|\,8\,|\,9\,\}\,[\text{R}]$$
$$3[\text{R}]\text{S}[\text{S}\,|\,\text{R}]\,[\text{S}\,|\,\text{R}]\ldots$$
$$\text{E}$$
$$\text{H}$$

Letters may be specified in lowercase if preferred. Examples of *smoother*[,<u>twice</u>] include

| | | | | |
|---|---|---|---|---|
| 3RSSH | 3RSSH,twice | 4253H | 4253H,twice | 43RSR2H,twice |
| 3rssh | 3rssh,twice | 4253h | 4253h,twice | 43rsr2h,twice |

# Description

smooth applies the specified resistant, nonlinear smoother to *varname* and stores the smoothed series in *newvar*.

# Options

generate(*newvar*) is not optional; it specifies the name of the new variable that will contain the smoothed values.

# Remarks

Smoothing is an exploratory data analysis technique for making the general shape of a series apparent. In this approach (Tukey 1977), the observed data series is assumed to be the sum of an underlying process that evolves smoothly (the smooth) and of an unsystematic noise component (the rough); that is,

$$\text{data} = \text{smooth} + \text{rough}$$

Smoothed values $z_t$ are obtained by taking medians (or some other location estimate) of each point in the original data $y_t$ and a few of the points around it. The number of points used is called the span of the smoother. Thus, a span-3 smoother produces $z_t$ by taking the median of $y_{t-1}$, $y_t$, and $y_{t+1}$. smooth provides running median smoothers of spans one to nine—indicated by the digit that specifies their span. Median smoothers are resistant to isolated outliers and so provide robustness to spikes in the data. Since the median is also a nonlinear operator, such smoothers are known as robust (or resistant) nonlinear smoothers.

229

smooth also provides the Hanning linear, nonrobust smoother, indicated by the letter H. Hanning is a span 3 smoother with binomial weights. Repeated applications of H—for example, HH, HHH, etc.— provide binomial smoothers of span 5, 7, etc. See Cox (1997) for a graphical application of this fact.

Since a single smoother usually cannot adequately separate the smooth from the rough, compound smoothers—multiple smoothers applied in sequence—are used. The smoother 35H, for instance, smooths the data with a span-3 median smoother, then smooths the result with a span-5 median smoother, and finally smooths that result with the Hanning smoother. smooth allows you to specify any number of smoothers in any sequence.

Three refinements can be combined with the running median and Hanning smoothers. First, the end points of a smooth can be given special treatment. This is specified by the E operator. Second, smoothing by 3, the span-3 running median, tends to produce flat-topped hills and valleys. The splitting operator, S, "splits" these repeated values, applies the end-point operator to them, and then "rejoins" the series. Finally, it is sometimes useful to repeat an odd-span median smoother or the splitting operator until the smooth no longer changes. Following a digit or an S with an R specifies this type of repetition.

Even the best smoother may fail to separate the smooth from the rough adequately. To guard against losing any of the systematic component of the data series, after smoothing, the smoother can be reapplied to the resulting rough and any recovered signal can be added back to the original smooth. The twice operator specifies this procedure. More generally, an arbitrary smoother can be applied to the rough (using a second smooth command) and the recovered signal can be added back to the *smooth*. This more general procedure is called reroughing (Tukey 1977).

The details of each of the smoothers and operators are explained in the *Methods and Formulas* below.

## ▷ Example

smooth is designed to recover the general features of a series that has been contaminated with noise. To demonstrate this, we construct a series, add noise to it, and then smooth the noisy version to recover an estimate of the original data. First we construct and display the data:

```
. drop _all
. set obs 10
. generate time = _n
. generate x = _n^3 - 10*_n^2 + 5*_n
. label variable x "Signal"
. generate z = x + 50*invnorm(uniform())
. label variable z "Observed series"
. graph x z time, c(l.) s(.o) title(Underlying signal and observed series)
```

*(Graph on next page)*

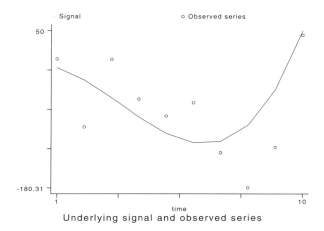

Underlying signal and observed series

Now we smooth the noisy series, z, assumed to be the only data we would observe:

```
. smooth 4253eh,twice z, gen(sz)
. label variable sz "Smoothed series"
. graph x z sz time, c(l.l) s(.op)
                    title(Underlying signal, observed series, and smoothed series)
```

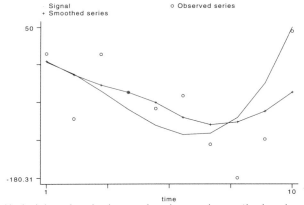

Underlying signal, observed series, and smoothed series

◁

▷ Example

Salgado-Ugarte and Curts-Garcia (1993) provide data on the frequencies of observed fish lengths. In this example, the series to be smoothed—the frequencies—is ordered by fish length rather than by time.

```
. use fish, clear
. smooth 4253eh,twice freq, gen(sfreq)
. lab var sfreq "4253EH,twice of frequencies"
```

. graph sfreq freq length, c(l.) s(po) title(Smoothed frequencies of fish lengths)

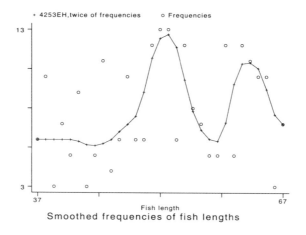

Smoothed frequencies of fish lengths

◁

❑ Technical Note

smooth allows missing values at the beginning and end of the series, but missing values in the middle are not allowed. Leading and trailing missing values are ignored. If you wish to ignore missing values in the middle of the series, you must drop the missing observations before using smooth. Doing so, of course, would violate an assumption of smooth. smooth assumes that observations are equally spaced; each observation represents a year, a quarter, or a month (or a one-year birth-rate category). In practice, smooth produces good results as long as the spaces between adjacent observations are not too variable.

Smoothing is usually applied to time series, but any variable with a natural order can be smoothed. For example, a smoother might be applied to the birth rate recorded by the age of the mothers (birth rate for 17-year olds, birth rate for 18-year olds, and so on).

❑

## Methods and Formulas

smooth is implemented as an ado-file.

## Running median smoothers of odd span

The smoother 3 defines
$$z_t = \text{median}(y_{t-1}, y_t, y_{t+1})$$
The smoother 5 defines
$$z_t = \text{median}(y_{t-2}, y_{t-1}, y_t, y_{t+1}, y_{t+2})$$
and so on. The smoother 1 defines $z_t = \text{median}(y_t)$ and so does nothing.

End points are handled by using smoothers of shorter, odd span. Thus, in the case of 3,

$$z_1 = y_1$$
$$z_2 = \text{median}(y_1, y_2, y_3)$$
$$\vdots$$
$$z_{N-1} = \text{median}(y_{N-2}, y_{N-1}, y_N)$$
$$Z_N = y_N$$

In the case of 5,

$$z_1 = y_1$$
$$z_2 = \text{median}(y_1, y_2, y_3)$$
$$z_3 = \text{median}(y_1, y_2, y_3, y_4, y_5)$$
$$z_4 = \text{median}(y_2, y_3, y_4, y_5, y_6)$$
$$\vdots$$
$$z_{N-2} = \text{median}(y_{N-4}, y_{N-3}, y_{N-2}, y_{N-1}, y_N)$$
$$z_{N-1} = \text{median}(y_{N-2}, y_{N-1}, y_N)$$
$$Z_N = y_N$$

and so on.

## Running median smoothers of even span

Define the median() function as returning the linearly interpolated value when given an even number of arguments. Thus, the smoother 2 defines

$$z_{t+.5} = (y_t + y_{t+1})/2$$

The smoother 4 defines $z_{t+.5}$ as the linearly interpolated median of $(y_{t-1}, y_t, y_{t+1}, y_{t+2})$, and so on. In all cases, end points are handled by using smoothers of shorter, even span. Thus, in the case of 4,

$$z_{.5} = y_1$$
$$z_{1.5} = \text{median}(y_1, y_2) = (y_1 + y_2)/2$$
$$z_{2.5} = \text{median}(y_1, y_2, y_3, y_4)$$
$$\vdots$$
$$z_{N-2.5} = \text{median}(y_{N-4}, y_{N-3}, y_{N-2}, y_N)$$
$$z_{N-1.5} = \text{median}(y_{N-2}, y_{N-1})$$
$$z_{N-.5} = \text{median}(y_{N-1}, y_N)$$
$$z_{N+.5} = y_N$$

As defined above, an even-span smoother increases the length of the series by one observation. However, the series can be recentered on the original observation numbers and the "extra" observation can be eliminated by smoothing the series again with another even-span smoother. For instance, the smooth of 4 illustrated above could be followed by a smooth of 2 to obtain

$$z_1^* = (z_{.5} + z_{1.5})/2$$
$$z_2^* = (z_{1.5} + z_{2.5})/2$$
$$z_3^* = (z_{2.5} + z_{3.5})/2$$

$$\vdots$$

$$z_{N-2}^* = (z_{N-2.5} + z_{N-1.5})/2$$
$$z_{N-1}^* = (z_{N-1.5} + z_{N-.5})/2$$
$$z_N^* = (z_{N-.5} + z_{N+.5})/2$$

smooth keeps track of the number of even smoothers applied to the data and expands and shrinks the length of the series accordingly. To ensure that the final smooth has the same number of observations as *varname*, smooth requires you to specify an even number of even-span smoothers. However, the pairs of even-span smoothers need not be contiguous; for instance, 4253 and 4523 are both allowed.

## Repeat operator

R indicates that a smoother is to be repeated until convergence, that is, until repeated applications of the smoother produce the same series. Thus, 3 applies the smoother of running medians of span 3. 33 applies the smoother twice. 3R produces the result of repeating 3 an infinite number of times. R should only be used with odd-span smoothers, since even-span smoothers are not guaranteed to converge.

The smoother 453R2 applies a span-4 smoother, followed by a span-5 smoother, followed by repeated applications of a span-3 smoother, followed by a span-2 smoother.

## End-point rule

The end-point rule E modifies the values $z_1$ and $z_N$ according to the following formulas:

$$z_1 = \text{median}(3z_2 - 2z_3, z_1, z_2)$$
$$z_N = \text{median}(3z_{N-2} - 2z_{N-1}, z_N, z_{N-1})$$

When the end-point rule is not applied, end points are typically "copied-in"; that is, $z_1 = y_1$ and $z_N = y_N$.

## Splitting operator

The smoothers 3 and 3R can produce flat-topped hills and valleys. The split operator attempts to eliminate such hills and valleys by splitting the sequence, applying the end-point rule E, rejoining the series, and then resmoothing by 3R.

The S operator may be applied only after 3, 3R, or S.

It is recommended that the S operator be repeated once (SS) or until no further changes take place (SR).

## Hanning smoother

H is the Hanning linear smoother:

$$z_t = (y_{t-1} + 2y_t + y_{t+1})/4$$

End points are copied in: $z_1 = y_1$ and $z_N = y_N$. H should be applied only after all nonlinear smoothers.

## Twicing

A smoother divides the data into a smooth and a rough:

$$\text{data} = \text{smooth} + \text{rough}$$

If the smoothing is successful, the rough should exhibit no pattern. Twicing refers to applying the smoother to the observed, calculating the rough, and then applying the smoother to the rough. The resulting "smoothed rough" is then added back to the smooth from the first step.

## Acknowledgments

smooth was originally written by William Gould (1992)—at which time it was named nlsm—and was inspired by Salgado-Ugarte and Curts-Garcia (1992). Salgado-Ugarte and Curts-Garcia (1993) subsequently reported anomalies in nlsm's treatment of even-span median smoothers. smooth corrects these problems and incorporates other improvements, but otherwise is essentially the same as originally published.

## References

Cox, N. J. 1997. gr22: Binomial smoothing plot. *Stata Technical Bulletin* 35: 7–9. Reprinted in *Stata Technical Bulletin Reprints*, vol. 6, pp. 36–38.

Gould, W. 1992. sed7.1: Resistant nonlinear smoothing using Stata. *Stata Technical Bulletin* 8: 9–12. Reprinted in *Stata Technical Bulletin Reprints*, vol. 2, pp. 104–107.

Salgado-Ugarte, I. and J. Curts-Garcia. 1992. sed7: Resistant smoothing using Stata. *Stata Technical Bulletin* 7: 8–11. Reprinted in *Stata Technical Bulletin Reprints*, vol. 2, pp. 99–103.

——. 1993. sed7.2: Twice reroughing procedure for resistant nonlinear smoothing. *Stata Technical Bulletin* 11: 14–16. Reprinted in *Stata Technical Bulletin Reprints*, vol. 2, pp. 108–111.

Sasieni, P. 1998. gr27: An adaptive variable span running line smoother. *Stata Technical Bulletin* 41: 4–7. Reprinted in *Stata Technical Bulletin Reprints*, vol. 7, pp. 63–68.

Tukey, J. W. 1977. *Exploratory Data Analysis*. Reading, MA: Addison–Wesley Publishing Company.

Velleman, P. F. 1977. Robust nonlinear data smoothers: Definitions and recommendations. *Proceedings of the National Academy of Sciences USA* 74(2): 434–436.

——. 1980. Definition and comparison of robust nonlinear data smoothing algorithms. *Journal of the American Statistical Association* 75(371): 609–615.

Velleman, P. F. and D. C. Hoaglin. 1981. *Applications, Basics, and Computing of Exploratory Data Analysis*. Boston: Duxbury Press.

## Also See

**Related:**     [R] **ksm**

# Title

> **snapspan** — Convert snapshot data to time-span data

# Syntax

snapspan *idvar* *timevar* *varlist* $\left[\,,\ \underline{\text{g}}\text{enerate}(newt0var)\ \text{replace}\,\right]$

# Description

**snapspan** converts snapshot data to time-span data. See *Remarks* below for a description of snapshot and time-span data. Time-span data are required for use with survival-analysis commands such as **cox**, **stcox**, **streg**, and **stset**.

*idvar* records the subject id; it may be string or numeric.

*timevar* records the time of the snapshot; it must be numeric and may be recorded on any scale: date, hour, minute, second, etc.

*varlist* are the "event" variables: the variables that occur at the instant of *timevar*. *varlist* is also to include retrospective variables: variables that are to apply to the time span ending at the time of the current snapshot. The other variables are assumed to be measured at the time of the snapshot and thus apply from the time of the snapshot forward. See *Specifying varlist* below.

# Options

**generate**(*newt0var*) adds *newt0var* to the dataset containing the entry time for each converted time-span record. We recommend creating this variable if you plan to use **cox**, **weibull**, etc. If you instead intend to use the st system and first **stset** your data, you may safely skip this option because **stset** can determine the beginning of the time span for itself, although specifying **generate**() now and then specifying **stset** ..., **time0**(*newt0var*) ..., would not hurt.

**replace** specifies that it is okay to change the data in memory even though the dataset has not been saved on disk in its current form.

# Remarks

## Snapshot and time-span datasets

**snapspan** converts a snapshot dataset to a time-span dataset. A snapshot dataset records a subject *id*, a *time*, and then other variables measured at the *time*:

Snapshot datasets:

| idvar | timevar | x1 | x2 | ... |
|-------|---------|----|----|-----|
| 47 | 12 | 5 | 27 | ... |
| 47 | 42 | 5 | 18 | ... |
| 47 | 55 | 5 | 19 | ... |

236

| idvar | datevar | x1 | x2 | ... |
|---|---|---|---|---|
| 122 | 14jul1998 | 5 | 27 | ... |
| 122 | 12aug1998 | 5 | 18 | ... |
| 122 | 08sep1998 | 5 | 19 | ... |

| idvar | year | x1 | x2 | ... |
|---|---|---|---|---|
| 122 | 1994 | 5 | 27 | ... |
| 122 | 1995 | 5 | 18 | ... |
| 122 | 1997 | 5 | 19 | ... |

A time-span dataset records a span of time (*time0*, *time1*):

```
                                          some variables assumed
                                           to occur at time1
          |<— other variables assumed constant over span —>|
          |_____|—> time
          time0                                           time1
```

It is time-span data that are required, for instance, by survival-analysis commands such as cox, weibull, etc. and by stset and the st system. The variables assumed to occur at time1 are the failure or event variables. All the other variables are assumed to be constant over the span.

Time-span datasets:

| idvar | time0 | time1 | x1 | x2 | ... | event |
|---|---|---|---|---|---|---|
| 47 | 0 | 12 | 5 | 13 | ... | 0 |
| 47 | 12 | 42 | 5 | 27 | ... | 0 |
| 47 | 42 | 55 | 5 | 18 | ... | 1 |

| idvar | time0 | time1 | x1 | x2 | ... | event |
|---|---|---|---|---|---|---|
| 122 | 01jan1998 | 14jul1998 | 5 | 13 | ... | 0 |
| 122 | 14jul1998 | 12aug1998 | 5 | 27 | ... | 0 |
| 122 | 12aug1998 | 08sep1998 | 5 | 18 | ... | 1 |

| idvar | time0 | time1 | x1 | x2 | ... | event |
|---|---|---|---|---|---|---|
| 122 | 1993 | 1994 | 5 | 13 | ... | 0 |
| 122 | 1994 | 1995 | 5 | 27 | ... | 0 |
| 122 | 1995 | 1997 | 5 | 18 | ... | 1 |

To convert snapshot data to time-span data, you need to distinguish between event and nonevent variables. Event variables happen at an instant.

Say one has a snapshot dataset containing variable e recording an event (e = 1 might record surgery, or death, or becoming unemployed, etc.) and the rest of the variables—call them x1, x2, etc.—recording characteristics (such as sex, birth date, blood pressure, weekly wage, etc.). The same data, in snapshot and time-span form, would be

In snapshot form:

| id | time | x1 | x2 | e |
|---|---|---|---|---|
| 1 | 5 | a1 | b1 | e1 |
| 1 | 7 | a2 | b2 | e2 |
| 1 | 9 | a3 | b3 | e3 |
| 1 | 11 | a4 | b4 | e4 |

In time-span form:

| id | time0 | time | x1 | x2 | e |
|---|---|---|---|---|---|
| 1 | . | 5 | . | . | e1 |
| 1 | 5 | 7 | a1 | b1 | e2 |
| 1 | 7 | 9 | a2 | b2 | e3 |
| 1 | 9 | 11 | a3 | b3 | e4 |

snapspan converts data from the form on the left to the form on the right:

```
. snapspan id time e
```

The form on the right is suitable for use by cox and stset and the other survival-analysis commands.

## Specifying varlist

The *varlist*—the third variable on—specifies the "event" variables.

In fact, the *varlist* specifies the variables that are to apply to the time span ending at the time of the current snapshot. The other variables are assumed to be measured at the time of the snapshot and thus apply from the time of the snapshot forward.

Thus, *varlist* should include retrospective variables.

For instance, say the snapshot recorded bp, blood pressure; smokes, the answer to the question whether the patient smoked in the last two weeks; and event, a variable recording examination, surgery, etc. Then *varlist* should include smokes and event. The remaining variables, bp and the rest, would be assumed to apply from the time of snapshot forward.

Suppose the snapshot recorded ecs, employment change status (hired, fired, promoted, etc.); wage, the current hourly wage; and ms, current marital status. Then varlist should include esc and ms (assuming snapshot records are not generated for reason of ms change). The remaining variables, wage and the rest, would be assumed to apply from the time of the snapshot forward.

## Methods and Formulas

snapspan is implemented as an ado-file.

## Also See

| | |
|---|---|
| **Complementary:** | [R] st stset |
| **Background:** | [R] st |

# Title

**sort** — Sort data

# Syntax

<u>so</u>rt *varlist* [in *range*]

# Description

sort arranges the observations of the current data into ascending order of the values of the variables in the *varlist*. There is no limit to the number of variables in the *varlist*. Missing numeric values are interpreted to be larger than any other number, so are placed last. When sorting on a string variable, null strings are placed first. The dataset is marked as being sorted by *varlist* unless **in** *range* is specified. If **in** *range* is specified, only those observations are rearranged. The unspecified observations remain in the same place.

# Remarks

Sorting data is one of the more common tasks involved in the processing of data. Sometimes, before Stata can perform some task, the data must be in a specific order. For example, the use of the **by** *varlist*: prefix requires that the data be sorted in order of *varlist*. Match merging two datasets with the **merge** command places similar requirements on both datasets. You use the **sort** command to fulfill these requirements.

▷ Example

Sorting data can also be informative. Suppose that you have data on automobiles, and each car's make and mileage rating (called **make** and **mpg**) are included among the variables in the data. You want to list the five cars with the lowest mileage rating in your data:

```
. sort mpg
. list make mpg in 1/5
        make              mpg
    1. Linc. Continental   12
    2. Linc. Mark V        12
    3. Linc. Versailles    14
    4. Merc. XR-7          14
    5. Cad. Deville        14
```

◁

▷ Example

Stata keeps track of the order of your data. For instance, we just sorted the above data on **mpg**. When we ask Stata to **describe** the data in memory, it tells us how the dataset is sorted:

```
. describe
Contains data from auto.dta
   obs:            74                          1978 Automobile Data
  vars:             3                          7 Jul 2000 13:51
  size:         1,924 (99.7% of memory free)

               storage   display    value
variable name    type    format     label      variable label

make             str18   %-18s                 Make and Model
mpg              int     %8.0g                 Mileage (mpg)
weight           int     %8.0gc                Weight (lbs.)

Sorted by:  mpg
     Note:  dataset has changed since last saved
```

Stata keeps track of changes in sort order. If we were to make a change to the mpg variable, Stata would know that the data are no longer sorted. Remember that the first observation in our data has mpg equal to 12, as does the second. Let's change the value of the first observation:

```
. replace mpg=13 in 1
(1 real change made)
. describe
Contains data from auto.dta
   obs:            74                          1978 Automobile Data
  vars:             3                          7 Jul 2000 13:51
  size:         1,924 (99.7% of memory free)

               storage   display    value
variable name    type    format     label      variable label

make             str18   %-18s                 Make and Model
mpg              int     %8.0g                 Mileage (mpg)
weight           int     %8.0gc                Weight (lbs.)

Sorted by:
     Note:  dataset has changed since last saved
```

After making the change, Stata indicates that our dataset is "Sorted by:" nothing. Let's put the dataset back as it was:

```
. replace mpg=12 in 1
(1 real change made)
. sort mpg
```

◁

## ❑ Technical Note

Stata is not very bright about tracking changes in the sort order and will sometimes decide that a dataset is not sorted when in fact it is. For instance, if we were to change the first observation of our auto dataset from 12 miles per gallon to 10, Stata would decide that the dataset is "Sorted by:" nothing, just as it did in the example above when we changed mpg from 12 to 13. Our change in the previous example did change the order of the data, so Stata was correct. Changing mpg from 12 to 10, however, does not really affect the sort order.

As far as Stata is concerned, any change to the variables on which the data are sorted means that the data are no longer sorted, even if the change actually leaves the order unchanged. Stata may be dumb, but it is also fast. It sorts already-sorted datasets instantly, so Stata's ignorance costs us little. ❑

## ▷ Example

Data can be sorted by more than one variable, and in such cases the sort order is lexicographic. If we `sort` the data by two variables, for instance, the data are placed in ascending order of the first variable, and then observations that share the same value of the first variable are placed in ascending order of the second variable. Let's order our automobile data by `mpg` and within `mpg` by `weight`:

```
. sort mpg weight
. list in 1/8
        make             mpg    weight
  1. Linc. Mark V         12     4,720
  2. Linc. Continental    12     4,840
  3. Peugeot 604          14     3,420
  4. Linc. Versailles     14     3,830
  5. Cad. Eldorado        14     3,900
  6. Merc. Cougar         14     4,060
  7. Merc. XR-7           14     4,130
  8. Cad. Deville         14     4,330
```

The data are in ascending order of `mpg` and, within each `mpg` category, the data are in ascending order of `weight`. The lightest car that achieves 14 miles per gallon in our data is the Peugeot 604.

◁

## ❏ Technical Note

The sorting technique used by Stata is fast. A side-effect is that the order of variables not included in the *varlist* is not maintained. If you wish to maintain the order of additional variables, include them at the end of the *varlist*. There is no limit to the number of variables by which you may `sort`.

❏

## ▷ Example

It is sometimes desirable to order a dataset by descending sequence of something. Perhaps we wish to obtain a list of the five cars achieving the best mileage rating. The `sort` command will order the data only into ascending sequences. Another command, `gsort`, will order the data in ascending or descending sequences; see [R] **gsort**. Alternatively, you can create the negative of a variable and achieve the desired result:

```
. gen negmpg = -mpg
. sort negmpg
. list in 1/5
        make            mpg    weight    negmpg
  1. VW Diesel          41     2,040      -41
  2. Subaru             35     2,050      -35
  3. Datsun 210         35     2,020      -35
  4. Plym. Champ        34     1,800      -34
  5. Toyota Corolla     31     2,200      -31
```

We find that the VW Diesel tops our list.

◁

▷ Example

sort may also be used on string variables. The data are sorted alphabetically:

```
. sort make
. list in 1/5
        make           mpg    weight    negmpg
  1. AMC Concord         22     2,930      -22
  2. AMC Pacer           17     3,350      -17
  3. AMC Spirit          22     2,640      -22
  4. Audi 5000           17     2,830      -17
  5. Audi Fox            23     2,070      -23
```

◁

❑ Technical Note

Bear in mind that Stata takes "alphabetically" to mean that all uppercase letters come before lowercase letters. As far as Stata is concerned, the following list is sorted:

```
. list
        myvar
  1.    ALPHA
  2.    Alpha
  3.     BETA
  4.     Beta
  5.    alpha
  6.     beta
```

❑

# Also See

| | |
|---|---|
| **Complementary:** | [R] **describe** |
| **Related:** | [R] **gsort** |
| **Background:** | [U] **14 Language syntax** |

# Title

**spearman** — Spearman's and Kendall's correlations

# Syntax

spearman *varname*$_1$ *varname*$_2$ [if *exp*] [in *range*]

ktau *varname*$_1$ *varname*$_2$ [if *exp*] [in *range*]

by ... : may be used with spearman and ktau; see [R] **by**.

# Description

spearman displays Spearman's rank correlation coefficient $\rho$ and calculates the significance for a test of the hypothesis that *varname*$_1$ and *varname*$_2$ are independent.

ktau displays Kendall's rank correlation coefficients $\tau_a$ and $\tau_b$ along with Kendall's score and a test of the hypothesis that *varname*$_1$ and *varname*$_2$ are independent. ktau is intended for use on small and moderate-sized datasets; it requires considerable computation time for very large datasets.

# Remarks

▷ Example

We wish to calculate the correlation between marriage rate (mrgrate) and median age (medage) in state data. We can calculate the standard Pearson correlation coefficient and significance by typing

```
. pwcorr mrgrate medage, sig
              mrgrate   medage

    mrgrate    1.0000

     medage    0.0011   1.0000
               0.9941
```

We can calculate the Spearman rank correlation coefficient by typing

```
. spearman mrgrate medage
 Number of obs =        50
 Spearman's rho =     -0.4869

 Test of Ho: mrgrate and medage are independent
     Prob > |t| =       0.0003
```

The large difference in the results is caused by a single observation. Nevada's marriage rate is almost 10 times higher than the state with the next highest marriage rate. An important feature of the Spearman rank correlation coefficient is its lesser sensitivity to extreme values.

We can calculate Kendall's rank correlations by typing

```
. ktau mrgrate medage
  Number of obs =        50
Kendall's tau-a =    -0.3486
Kendall's tau-b =    -0.3544
Kendall's score =    -427
     SE of score =   119.343   (corrected for ties)

Test of Ho: mrgrate and medage are independent
        Prob > |z| =      0.0004   (continuity corrected)
```

◁

## ❏ Technical Note

According to Conover (1999, 323), "Spearman's $\rho$ tends to be larger than Kendall's $\tau$ in absolute value. However, as a test of significance, there is no strong reason to prefer one over the other because both will produce nearly identical results in most cases".

❏

## Saved Results

**spearman** saves in **r()**:

Scalars

| | | | |
|---|---|---|---|
| r(N) | number of observations | r(p) | two-sided $p$-value |
| r(rho) | $\rho$ | | |

**ktau** saves in **r()**:

Scalars

| | | | |
|---|---|---|---|
| r(N) | number of observations | r(tau_b) | $\tau_b$ |
| r(p) | two-sided $p$-value | r(score) | Kendall's score |
| r(tau_a) | $\tau_a$ | r(se_score) | standard error of score |

## Methods and Formulas

**spearman** and **ktau** are implemented as ado-files.

Spearman's (1904) rank correlation is calculated as Pearson's correlation computed on the ranks and average ranks (Conover 1999, 314–315). Ranks are as calculated by **egen**; see [R] **egen**. The significance is calculated using the approximation $p = 2 * \text{ttail}(n - 2, \widehat{\rho}\sqrt{n-2}/\sqrt{1-\widehat{\rho}^2})$.

Kendall's (1938; also see Kendall and Gibbons 1990) score $S$ is defined as $C - D$, where $C$ $(D)$ is the number of concordant (discordant) pairs. If we let $N = n(n-1)/2$ be the total number of pairs, then $\tau_a$ is given by $\tau_a = S/N$ and $\tau_b$ is given by

$$\tau_b = \frac{S}{\sqrt{N-U}\sqrt{N-V}}$$

where $U = \sum u_i(u_i - 1)/2$ with $u_i$ the multiplicities of the values of *varname*$_1$ ($V$ and $v_i$ defined similarly for *varname*$_2$). Under the null hypothesis of independence between *varname*$_1$ and *varname*$_2$, the variance of $S$ is exactly (Kendall and Gibbons 1990, 66)

$$\mathrm{Var}(S) = \frac{1}{18}\left\{ n(n-1)(2n+5) - \sum u_i(u_i-1)(2u_i+5) - \sum v_i(v_i-1)(2v_i+5) \right\}$$
$$+ \frac{1}{9n(n-1)(n-2)}\left\{ \sum u_i(u_i-1)(u_i-2) \right\}\left\{ \sum v_i(v_i-1)(v_i-2) \right\}$$
$$+ \frac{1}{2n(n-1)}\left\{ \sum u_i(u_i-1) \right\}\left\{ \sum v_i(v_i-1) \right\}$$

Using a normal approximation with a continuity correction, we calculate

$$z = \frac{|S| - 1}{\sqrt{\mathrm{Var}(S)}}$$

Note that for the hypothesis of independence the statistics $S$, $\tau_a$, and $\tau_b$ produce equivalent tests and give the same significance.

## Acknowledgment

The original version of `ktau` was written by Sean Becketti, a past editor of the *Stata Technical Bulletin*.

## References

Conover, W. J. 1999. *Practical Nonparametric Statistics*. 3d ed. New York: John Wiley & Sons.

Jeffreys, H. 1961. *Theory of Probability*. Oxford: Oxford University Press.

Kendall, M. G. 1938. A new measure of rank correlation. *Biometrika* 30: 81–93.

Kendall, M. G. and J. D. Gibbons. 1990. *Rank Correlation Methods*. 5th ed. New York: Oxford University Press.

Newson, R. 2000a. snp15: somersd–Confidence intervals for nonparametric statistics and their differences. *Stata Technical Bulletin* 55: 47–55.

——. 2000b. snp15.1: Update to somersd. *Stata Technical Bulletin* 57: 35.

Spearman, C. 1904. The proof and measurement of association between two things. *American Journal of Psychology* 15: 72–101.

Wolfe, F. 1997. sg64: pwcorrs: An enhanced correlation display. *Stata Technical Bulletin* 35: 22–25. Reprinted in *Stata Technical Bulletin Reprints*, vol. 6, pp. 163–167.

——. 1999. sg64.1: Update to pwcorrs. *Stata Technical Bulletin* 49: 17. Reprinted in *Stata Technical Bulletin Reprints*, vol. 9, p. 159.

## Also See

**Related:**      [R] **correlate**, [R] **nptrend**

# Title

spikeplot — Spike plots and rootograms

# Syntax

spikeplot *varname* [if *exp*] [in *range*] [*weight*] [, round(#) frac root zero(#)

graph_options ]

fweights, aweights, and iweights are allowed; see [U] **14.1.6 weight**.

# Description

spikeplot produces a frequency plot for a variable in which the frequencies are depicted as vertical lines from zero. The frequency may be a count, a fraction, or the square root of the count (Tukey's rootogram, *circa* 1965). The vertical lines may also originate from a different baseline than zero at the user's option.

# Options

round(#) rounds the values of *varname* to the nearest multiple of #. This effectively specifies the bin width.

frac specifies that the vertical scale should be the proportion of total values (percentage) rather than the count.

root specifies that the vertical scale is to show square roots. This option may not be specified if frac is specified.

zero(#) specifies a constant to use as the baseline. The vertical bars are drawn from the baseline to the bin height.

*graph_options* are the usual graph options for **graph, twoway**. By default, the l2title() graph option is set to "Frequency", "Fraction" if frac is specified, or "Root of frequency" if root is specified. The b2title() option is set to the variable label of *varname* by default, c() is set to c(||) so that a vertical line is used to draw the bins, and s() is set to s(ii) so that point markers are not included in the output.

# Remarks

A weakness of the **graph, histogram** command is that it is limited to a maximum of 50 bins. The spikeplot command has no such limit and can be used for either categorical or continuous variables (possibly using the **round** option).

▷ Example

Cox and Brady (1997a) present an illustrative example using the age structure of the population of Ghana from the 1960 census (rounded to the nearest 1000). The dataset has ages from 0 (less than one year) to 90. To view the distribution of ages, we would like to use each integer from 0 to 90 as the bins for the dataset.

. spikeplot age [fw=pop], l2("Population in 1000s") ylab xlab(0(10)90) xtick(5(10)85)

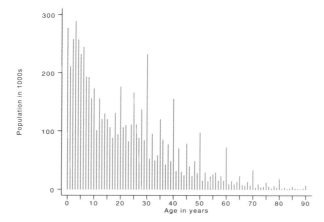

The resulting graph shows a "heaping" of ages at the multiples of 5. In addition, ages ending in even numbers are more frequent than ages ending in odd numbers (except for 5). This preference for reporting ages is well-known in demography and other social sciences.

Note also that we used the l2() option to override the default title of "Frequency" and that we used the xlab() and xtick() options with *numlists* to further customize the resulting graph. See [U] **14.1.8 numlist** for details on specifying *numlists*.

◁

▷ Example

The rootogram is a plot of the square-root transformation of the frequency counts. Note that the square root of a normal distribution is a multiple of another normal distribution:

```
. set seed 1234567
. set obs 5000
obs was 0, now 5000
. gen normal = invnorm(uniform())
. label var normal "Gaussian(0,1) random numbers"
```

*(Graph on next page)*

```
. spikeplot normal, round(.10) xlab(-4(1)4) ylab
```

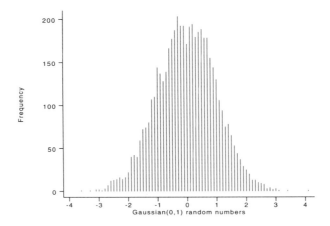

```
. spikeplot normal, round(.10) xlab(-4(1)4) ylab root
```

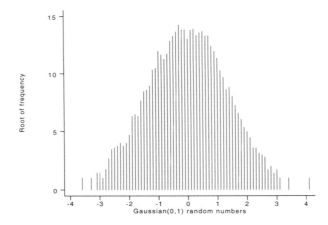

As such, the same experience one has for interpreting a histogram in terms of normality applies to interpreting the rootogram for normality.

This example also shows how the **round()** option is used to bin the values for a spike plot of a continuous variable.

◁

## ▷ Example

spikeplot can also be used to produce time-series plots. *varname* should be the time variable, and weights should be specified as the values for those times. To get a plot of daily rainfalls, we type

```
. spikeplot day [w=rain] if rain, l2("Daily rainfall in mm") gap(5) xlab ylab
```

The **zero** option may be used to set a different baseline, as when it is desired to show variations relative to an average or some other measure of level.

◁

# Acknowledgments

The original version of spikeplot was written by Nicholas J. Cox of the University of Durham and Anthony R. Brady of the Imperial College School of Medicine (1997).

# References

Cox, N. J. and A. R. Brady. 1997a. gr25: Spike plots for histograms, rootograms, and time-series plots. *Stata Technical Bulletin* 36: 8–11. Reprinted in *Stata Technical Bulletin Reprints*, vol. 6, pp. 50–54.

——. 1997b. gr25.1: Spike plots for histograms, rootograms, and time series plots: update. *Stata Technical Bulletin* 40: 12. Reprinted in *Stata Technical Bulletin Reprints*, vol. 7, p. 58.

Tukey, J. W. 1965. The future of processes of data analysis. Reprinted in *The Collected Works of John W. Tukey, Volume IV: Philosophy and Principles of Data Analysis: 1965–1986*, ed. L. V. Jones, 517–547 (1986). Monterey, CA: Wadsworth & Brooks/Cole.

# Also See

| | |
|---|---|
| **Related:** | [R] **hist** |
| **Background:** | *Stata Graphics Manual* |

# Title

st — Survival-time data

# Description

The term st refers to survival-time data and the commands—all of which begin with the letters st—for analyzing these data. If you have data on individual subjects with observations recording that this subject came under observation at time $t_0$, and then, later, at $t_1$, a failure or censoring was observed, you have what we call survival-time data.

If you have subject-specific data, with observations recording not a span of time, but measurements taken on the subject at that point in time, then you have what we call a snapshot dataset, see [R] **snapspan**.

If you have data on populations, with observations recording the number of units under test at time $t$ (subjects alive) and the number of subjects that failed or were lost due to censoring, you have what we call count-time data; see [R] **ct**.

The st commands are

| stset | [R] **st stset** | Declare data to be survival-time data |
|---|---|---|
| stdes | [R] **st stdes** | Describe survival-time data |
| stsum | [R] **st stsum** | Summarize survival-time data |
| stvary | [R] **st stvary** | Report which variables vary over time |
| stfill | [R] **st stfill** | Fill in by carrying forward values of covariates |
| stgen | [R] **st stgen** | Generate variables reflecting entire histories |
| stsplit | [R] **st stsplit** | Split time-span records |
| stjoin | [R] **st stsplit** | Join time-span records |
| stbase | [R] **st stbase** | Form baseline dataset |
| sts | [R] **st sts** | Generate, graph, list, and test the survivor and cumulative hazard functions |
| stir | [R] **st stir** | Report incidence-rate comparison |
| stci | [R] **st stci** | Confidence intervals for means and percentiles of survival time |
| strate | [R] **st strate** | Tabulate failure rate |
| stptime | [R] **st stptime** | Calculate person-time |
| stmh | [R] **st strate** | Calculates rate ratios using Mantel–Haenszel method |
| stmc | [R] **st strate** | Calculates rate ratios using Mantel–Cox method |
| stcox | [R] **st stcox** | Estimate Cox proportional hazards model |
| stphtest | [R] **st stcox** | Test of Cox proportional hazards assumption |
| stphplot | [R] **st stphplot** | Graphical assessment of the Cox proportional hazards assumption |
| stcoxkm | [R] **st stphplot** | Graphical assessment of the Cox proportional hazards assumption |
| streg | [R] **st streg** | Estimate parametric survival models |
| stcurve | [R] **st streg** | Plot fitted survival functions |
| sttocc | [R] **st sttocc** | Convert survival-time data to case–control data |
| sttoct | [R] **st sttoct** | Convert survival-time data to count-time data |
| cttost | [R] **ct cttost** | Convert count-time data to survival-time data |
| snapspan | [R] **snapspan** | Convert snapshot data to time-span data |
| st_* | [P] **st st_is** | Survival analysis subroutines for programmers |

250

The st commands are used for analyzing time-to-absorbing-event (single failure) data and for analyzing time-to-repeated-event (multiple failure) data.

You begin an analysis by stsetting your data, which tells Stata the key survival-time variables. This is described in [R] **st stset**. Once you have stset your data, you can use the other st commands. If you save your data after stsetting it, you will not have to re-stset it in the future; Stata will remember.

The subsequent st entries are printed in this manual in alphabetical order. You can skip around, but if you want to be an expert on all of Stata's survival analysis capabilities, we suggest the above reading order.

# References

Cleves, M. 1999. ssa13: Analysis of multiple failure-time data with Stata. *Stata Technical Bulletin* 49: 30–39. Reprinted in *Stata Technical Bulletin Reprints*, vol. 9, pp. 338–349.

# Also See

**Complementary:**    [R] **st stset**; [R] **ct**, [R] **snapspan**

# Title

> **st stbase** — Form baseline dataset

# Syntax

stbase [if *exp*] [in *range*] [, at(*#*) gap(*newvar*) replace nopreserve noshow]

stbase is for use with survival-time data; see [R] **st**. You must stset your data before using this command.

# Description

stbase without the at() option converts multiple-record st data to st data with every variable set to its value at baseline, defined as the earliest time at which each subject was observed. stbase without at() does nothing to single-record st data.

stbase, at() converts single- or multiple-record st data to a cross-sectional dataset (not st data) recording the number of failures at the specified time. All variables are given their values at baseline—the earliest time at which each subject was observed. In this form, single-failure data could be analyzed by logistic regression and multiple-failure data by Poisson regression, for instance.

stbase is appropriate for use with single- or multiple-record, single- or multiple-failure, st data.

# Options

at(*#*) changes what stbase does. Without the at() option, stbase produces another, related st dataset. With the at() option, stbase produces a related cross-sectional dataset.

gap(*newvar*) is allowed only with at(); it specifies the name of a new variable to be added to the data containing time on gap. If gap() is not specified, the new variable will be named gap or gaptime depending on which name does not already exist in the data.

replace specifies that it is okay to change the data in memory even though the dataset has not been saved to disk in its current form.

nopreserve is for use by programmers using stbase as a subroutine. It says not to preserve the original dataset so that it can be restored should an error be detected or should the user press *Break*. Programmers would specify this option if, in their program, they had already preserved the original data.

noshow prevents stbase from showing the key st variables. This option is rarely used since most people type stset, show or stset, noshow to reset once and for all whether they want to see these variables mentioned at the top of the output of every st command; see [R] **st stset**.

# Remarks

Remarks are presented under the headings

*stbase without the at() option*
*stbase with the at() option*
*Single-failure st data where all subjects enter at 0*
*Single-failure st data where all subjects enter after time 0*
*Single-failure st data with gaps and perhaps delayed entry*
*Multiple-failure st data*

252

## stbase without the at() option

Once you type stbase, you may not streset your data even though the data are st. streset will refuse to run to protect you: the data are changed and if the original rules were reapplied, they might produce different, incorrect results. The st commands use four key variables:

| | |
|---|---|
| _t0 | the time at which the record came under observation |
| _t | the time at which the record left observation |
| _d | 1 if the record left under failure, 0 otherwise |
| _st | whether the observation is to be used (contains 1 or 0) |

These variables are adjusted by stbase. The variables _t0 and _t, in particular, were derived from your variables according to options you specified at the time you stset the data, which might include an origin() rule, an entry() rule, and the like. Once intervening observations are eliminated, those rules will not necessarily produce the same results as they did previously.

To illustrate how stbase works, consider multiple-record, time-varying st data, on which you have performed some analysis. You now wish to compare your results with a simpler, non-time-varying analysis. For instance, suppose the variable bp measures blood pressure, and that readings were taken on bp at various times. Perhaps you estimated the model

    . stcox drug bp sex

using these data. You now wish to estimate that same model, but this time using the value of bp at baseline. You do this by typing

    . stbase

    . stcox drug bp sex

Another way you could perform the analysis is

    . gen bp0 = bp

    . stfill bp0, baseline

    . stcox drug bp0 sex

See [R] **st stfill**. Which you use makes no difference but, if there were a lot of explanatory variables, stbase would be easier.

stbase changes the data to record the same events, but changes the values of all other variables to their values at the earliest time the subject was observed.

In addition, stbase simplifies the st data where possible. For instance, say one of your subjects has three records in the original data and ends in a failure:

After running stbase, this subject would have a single record in the data:

Here are some other examples of how stbase would process records with gaps and multiple failure events:

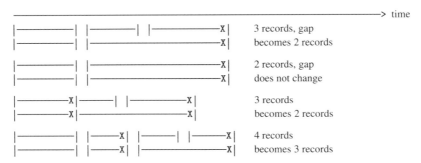

In each of the examples above, the second and subsequent records that stbase creates have the values of the other variables recorded in the first record.

The simplification of the records makes no difference to the st commands; whether a person has

or

makes no difference if all the covariates are the same. The simplification does, however, make it easier for human beings to read the data.

## stbase with the at() option

stbase, at() produces a dataset that is not st. The st dataset is converted to a cross-sectional dataset recording the status of each subject at the specified time. Four "new" variables are created:

> the first entry time for the subject,
> the time on gap,
> the time at risk, and
> the number of failures during the time at risk.

The names given to those variables are related to how your data are stset. Pretend your stset command was

        . stset var1, failure(var2) time0(var3) ...

Then

|  |  |  |
|---|---|---|
| the first entry time | will be named | *var3* or time0 or _t0 |
| the time on gap | will be named | gap() or gap or gaptime |
| the time at risk | will be named | *var1* |
| the number of (or whether) failures | will be named | *var2* or failure or _d |

The ors are mentioned because, for instance, if you did not specify a *var2* variable when you stset your data, stbase, at() looks around for a name.

You need not memorize this; the names are obvious from the output produced by stbase, at().

Let us consider the actions of stbase, at(), with some particular st datasets. Pretend the command given is

        . stbase, at(5)

thus producing a cross-section at analysis time 5.

Note that the value of time specified with the at() option must correspond to time in the analysis scale, i.e., *t*. See [R] **st stset** for a definition of analysis time.

## Single-failure st data where all subjects enter at 0

The result of stbase, at(5) would be one record per subject. Any subject who was censored before time 5 would not appear in the data; the rest would. Those that failed after time 5 will be recorded as having been censored at time 5 (*failvar* = 0): those that failed at time 5 or earlier will have *failvar* = 1.

*timevar* will contain

| | |
|---|---|
| for the failures: | |
| time of failure | if failed on or before time 5, or |
| 5 | because the subject has not failed yet |
| for the censored: | |
| 5 | because the subject has not failed yet |

Among the analyses appropriate to perform with the data would be

1. logistic regression of *failvar* on any of the characteristics; and

2. incidence rate analysis, summing the failures (perhaps within strata) and the time-at-risk *timevar*.

With these data, you could examine 5-year survival probabilities.

## Single-failure st data, some subjects enter after time 0

The data produced by stbase, at(5) would be similar to that above except

1. persons who enter on or after time 5 would not be included in the data (because they have not entered yet), and

2. the time-at-risk *timevar* would properly account for when each patient entered.

*timevar* (the time at risk) will contain

| | |
|---|---|
| for the failures: | |
| time of failure or less | if failed on or before time 5 (or less because the subject may not have entered at 0); or |
| 5 or less | because the subject has not failed yet (or less because subject may not have entered at time 0) |
| for the censored: | |
| 5 or less | because the subject has not failed yet (or less because the subject may not have entered at time 0) |

Depending on the analysis you are performing, you may have to discard those that enter late. That is easy to do because t0 contains the first time of entry.

Among the things appropriate to do with these data would be

1. logistic regression of *failvar* on any of the characteristics, but only if one restricted the sample to if t0 == 0 because those who entered after time 0 have a lesser risk of failing over the fixed interval.

2. incidence rate analysis, summing the failures (perhaps within stratum) and the time-at-risk *timevar*. In this case, you would have to do nothing differently from what one did in the previous example. The time-at-risk variable already includes the time of entry for each patient.

## Single-failure st data with gaps and perhaps delayed entry

These data will be similar to the delayed-entry, no-gap data, but gap will no longer contain 0 in all the observations. It will be 0 for those who have no gap.

If analyzing these data, you could perform

1. logistic regression, but the sample must be restricted to if t0 == 0 & gap == 0; or

2. incidence rate analysis, and nothing would need to be done differently; the time-at-risk *timevar* accounts for late entry and gaps.

## Multiple-failure st data

The multiple-failure case parallels the single-failure case except that fail will not solely contain 0 and 1; it will contain 0, 1, 2, ..., depending on the number of failures observed. Regardless of late entry, gaps, etc., the following would be appropriate:

1. Poisson regression of fail, the number of events, but remember to specify exposure(*timevar*); and

2. incidence rate analysis.

## Methods and Formulas

stbase is implemented as an ado-file.

## Also See

| | |
|---|---|
| **Complementary:** | [R] **st stfill**, [R] **st stgen**, [R] **st stset**, [R] **st sttocc** |
| **Background:** | [R] **st** |

# Title

> **st stci** — Confidence intervals for means and percentiles of survival time

# Syntax

$$\texttt{stci} \begin{bmatrix} \texttt{if } exp \end{bmatrix} \begin{bmatrix} \texttt{in } range \end{bmatrix} \begin{bmatrix} \texttt{, by}(varlist) \underline{\texttt{m}}\texttt{edian} \underline{\texttt{e}}\texttt{mean} \underline{\texttt{r}}\texttt{mean} \underline{\texttt{cc}}\texttt{orr} \texttt{p}(\#) \end{bmatrix}$$

$$\underline{\texttt{nosh}}\texttt{ow} \underline{\texttt{level}}(\#) \texttt{graph} \underline{\texttt{t}}\texttt{max}(\#) \texttt{dd}(\#) \Big]$$

stci is for use with survival-time data; see [R] **st**. You must stset your data before using this command.
by ... : may be used with stci; see [R] **by**.

# Description

stci computes means and percentiles of survival time, standard errors, and confidence intervals. In the case of multiple-event data, survival time is the time until a failure.

stci is appropriate for use with single- or multiple-record, single- or multiple-failure, st data.

# Options

by(*varlist*) requests separate summaries for each group along with an overall total. Observations are in the same group if they have equal values of the variables in *varlist*. *varlist* may contain any number of variables, each of which may be string or numeric.

median specifies median survival times. This is the default.

emean and rmean specify mean survival times. If the longest follow-up time is censored, emean (extended mean) computes the mean survival by exponentially extending the survival curve to zero, and rmean (restricted mean) computes the mean survival time restricted to the longest follow-up time. Note that if the longest follow-up time is a failure, the restricted mean survival time and the extended mean survival time are equal.

ccorr specifies that the standard error for the restricted mean survival time be computed using a continuity correction. ccor is only valid with option rmean.

p(#) specifies the percentile of survival time to be computed. For example, p(25) will compute the 25th percentile of survival times, and p(75) will compute the 75th percentile of survival times. Note that specifying p(50) is the same as specifying the median option.

noshow prevents stci from showing the key st variables. This option is rarely used since most people type stset, show or stset, noshow to reset once and for all whether they want to see these variables mentioned at the top of the output of every st command; see [R] **st stset**.

level(#) specifies the confidence level, in percent, for confidence intervals. The default is level(95) or as set by set level; see [U] **23.5 Specifying the width of confidence intervals**.

graph specifies that the exponentially extended survivor function be plotted. This option is only valid when option emean is also specified, and is not valid in conjunction with the by() option.

tmax(#) is for use with the graph option. It specifies the maximum analysis time to be plotted.

dd(#) specifies the maximum number of decimal digits to be reported for standard errors and confidence intervals. This option affects only how values are reported and not how they are calculated.

# Remarks

## Single-failure data

Here is an example of stci with single-record survival data:

```
. stci
```

|  | no. of subjects | 50% | Std. Err. | [95% Conf. Interval] | |
|---|---|---|---|---|---|
| total | 40 | 232 | 2.562933 | 213 | 239 |

```
. stci, by(group)
```

| group | no. of subjects | 50% | Std. Err. | [95% Conf. Interval] | |
|---|---|---|---|---|---|
| 1 | 19 | 216 | 5.171042 | 190 | 234 |
| 2 | 21 | 233 | 2.179595 | 232 | 280 |
| total | 40 | 232 | 2.562933 | 213 | 239 |

In the above, we obtained the median survival time, by default.

To obtain the 25th or any other percentile of survival time, specify the p(#) option.

```
. stci, p(25)
```

|  | no. of subjects | 25% | Std. Err. | [95% Conf. Interval] | |
|---|---|---|---|---|---|
| total | 40 | 205 | 11.13927 | 164 | 220 |

```
. stci, p(25) by(group)
```

| group | no. of subjects | 25% | Std. Err. | [95% Conf. Interval] | |
|---|---|---|---|---|---|
| 1 | 19 | 190 | 8.411659 | 143 | 213 |
| 2 | 21 | 232 | 14.88531 | 142 | 233 |
| total | 40 | 205 | 11.13927 | 164 | 220 |

Note that the $p$-percentile of survival time is the analysis time at which $p\%$ of subjects have failed and $1 - p\%$ have not. In the above table, 25% of subjects in group 1 failed by time 190, while 25% of subjects in group 2 failed by time 230, indicating a better survival experience for this group.

We can verify the quantities reported by stci by plotting and examining the Kaplan–Meier survival curves.

. sts graph, by(group)

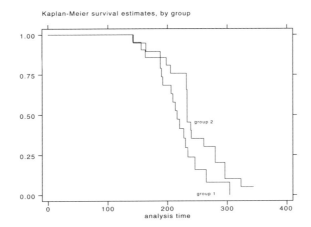

Kaplan-Meier survival estimates, by group

The mean survival time reported by **rmean** is calculated as the area under the Kaplan–Meier survivor function. If the observation with the largest analysis time is censored, then the survivor function does not go to zero. Consequently, the area under the curve underestimates the mean survival time.

In the above graph, notice that the survival probability for **group** = 1 goes to 0 at analysis time 344, but the survivor function for **group** = 2 never goes to 0. For these data, the mean survival time for **group** = 1 will be properly estimated, but it will be underestimated for **group** = 2. When we specify the **rmean** option, Stata will inform us if any of the mean survival times are underestimated.

. stci, rmean by(group)

| group | no. of subjects | restricted mean | Std. Err. | [95% Conf. Interval] | |
|---|---|---|---|---|---|
| 1 | 19 | 218.7566 | 9.122424 | 200.877 | 236.636 |
| 2 | 21 | 241.8571(*) | 11.34728 | 219.617 | 264.097 |
| total | 40 | 231.3522(*) | 7.700819 | 216.259 | 246.446 |

(*) largest observed analysis time is censored, mean is underestimated.

We note that Stata flagged the mean for **group** = 2 and the overall mean as being underestimated.

If the largest observed analysis time is censored, **stci**'s **emean** option will extend the survivor function from the last observed time to zero using an exponential function and will compute the area under the entire curve.

. stci, emean

| | no. of subjects | extended mean |
|---|---|---|
| total | 40 | 234.2557 |

The resulting area needs to be evaluated with care because it is an ad hoc approximation that can at times be misleading. It is recommended that the extended survivor function be plotted and examined. This is facilitated by the use of **stci**'s **graph** option.

```
. stci, emean graph
```

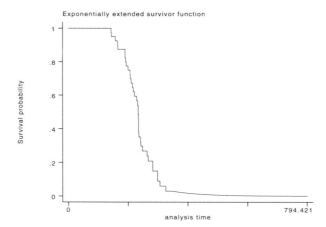

Exponentially extended survivor function

stci also works with multiple-record survival data. Here is a summary of the multiple-record Stanford heart-transplant data introduced in [R] **st stset**:

```
. stci
        failure _d:  died
  analysis time _t:  t1
               id:   id
```

|  | no. of subjects | 50% | Std. Err. | [95% Conf. Interval] |
|---|---|---|---|---|
| total | 103 | 100 | 38.64425 | 69 | 219 |

stci with the by() option may produce results with multiple-record data that, at first, you might think are in error:

```
. stci, by(posttran) noshow
```

| posttran | no. of subjects | 50% | Std. Err. | [95% Conf. Interval] |
|---|---|---|---|---|
| 0 | 103 | 149 | 22.16591 | 69 | 340 |
| 1 | 69 | 96 | 38.01968 | 45 | 285 |
| total | 103 | 100 | 38.64425 | 69 | 219 |

Note that, for the number of subjects, $103 + 69 \neq 103$. Variable **posttran** is not constant for the subjects in this dataset:

```
. stvary posttran
```

subjects for whom the variable is

| variable | constant | varying | never missing | always missing | sometimes missing |
|---|---|---|---|---|---|
| posttran | 34 | 69 | 103 | 0 | 0 |

In this dataset, subjects have one or two records. All subjects were eligible for heart transplantation. They have one record if they die or are lost due to censoring before transplantation, and they have two records if the operation was performed. In that case, the first record records their survival up to transplantation, and the second records their subsequent survival. `posttran` is 0 in the first record and 1 in the second.

Thus, all 103 subjects have records with `posttran = 0` and, when `stci` reported results for this group, it summarized the pretransplantation survival. The median survival time was 149 days.

The `posttran = 1` line of `stci`'s output summarizes the post-transplantation survival: 69 patients underwent transplantation and the median survival time was 96 days. For these data, this is not 96 more days, but 96 days in total. That is, the clock was not reset on transplantation. Thus, without attributing cause, we can describe the differences between the groups as an increased hazard of death at early times followed by a decreased hazard later.

## Multiple-failure data

If you simply type `stci` with multiple-failure data, be aware that the reported survival time is the survival time to the first failure under the assumption that the hazard function is not indexed by number of failures.

Here we have some multiple-failure data:

```
. st
-> stset t, id(id) failure(d) time0(t0) exit(time .) noshow
                id:  id
     failure event:  d ~= 0 & d ~= .
 obs. time interval:  (t0, t]
  exit on or before:  time .
. stci
```

| | no. of subjects | 50% | Std. Err. | [95% Conf. Interval] | |
|---|---|---|---|---|---|
| total | 926 | 420 | 13.42537 | 394 | 451 |

To understand this output, let's also obtain output for each failure separately:

```
. stgen nf = nfailures()
. stci, by(nf)
```

| nf | no. of subjects | 50% | Std. Err. | [95% Conf. Interval] | |
|---|---|---|---|---|---|
| 0 | 926 | 399 | 11.50173 | 381 | 430 |
| 1 | 529 | 503 | 13.68105 | 425 | 543 |
| 2 | 221 | 687 | 16.83127 | 549 | 817 |
| 3 | 58 | . | . | . | . |
| total | 926 | 420 | 13.42537 | 394 | 451 |

The `stgen` command added, for each subject, a variable containing the number of previous failures. For a subject, up to and including the first failure, `nf` is 0. Then `nf` is 1 up to and including the second failure, and then it is 2, and so on; see [R] **st stgen**.

You should have no difficulty interpreting `stci`'s output. The first line, corresponding to `nf = 0`, states that among those who had experienced no failures yet, the median time to first failure is 399.

Similarly, the second line, corresponding to `nf = 1`, is for those who have already experienced one failure. The median time of second failures is 503.

When we simply typed `stci`, we obtained the same information shown as the total line of the more detailed output. The total survival time distribution is an estimate of the distribution of the time to first failure, under the assumption that the hazard function $h(t)$ is the same across failures—that the second failure is no different from the first failure. This is an odd definition of "same" because the clock $t$ is not reset in $h(t)$ upon failure. What is the hazard of a failure—any failure—at time $t$? Answer: $h(t)$.

Another definition of same would have it that the hazard of a failure is given by $h(\tau)$, where $\tau$ is the time since last failure—that the process resets itself. These definitions are different unless $h()$ is a constant function of $t$.

Let's examine this multiple-failure data under the process-replication idea. The key variables in this st data are `id`, `t0`, `t`, and `d`:

```
. st
-> stset t, id(id) failure(d) time0(t0) exit(time .) noshow
               id:  id
    failure event:  d ~= 0 & d ~= .
obs. time interval:  (t0, t]
 exit on or before:  time .
```

Our goal is, for each subject, to reset `t0` and `t` to 0 after every failure event. We are going to have to trick Stata, or at least trick `stset`. `stset` will not let us set data where the same subject has multiple records summarizing the overlapping periods. The trick is create a new id variable that is different for every `id–nf` combination (remember, `nf` is the variable we previously created that records the number of prior failures). Then each of the "new" subjects can have their clock start at time 0:

```
. egen newid = group(id nf)

. sort newid t

. by newid: replace t = t - t0[1]

. by newid: gen newt0 = t0 - t0[1]

. stset t, failure(d) id(newid) time0(newt0)
               id:  newid
    failure event:  d ~= 0 & d ~= .
obs. time interval:  (newt0, t]
 exit on or before:  failure

    1734   total obs.
       0   exclusions

    1734   obs. remaining, representing
    1734   subjects
     808   failures in single failure-per-subject data
  435444   total analysis time at risk, at risk from t =          0
                            earliest observed entry t =          0
                              last observed exit t =          797
```

Note that `stset` no longer thinks we have multiple-failure data. Whereas, with `id`, subjects had multiple failures, `newid` gives a unique identity to each `id–nf` combination. Each "new" subject has at most one failure.

```
. stci, by(nf)

        failure _d:  d
  analysis time _t:  t
                id:  newid

                  no. of
nf               subjects      50%      Std. Err.     [95% Conf. Interval]

         0             926      399      11.22457          381          430
         1             529      384       9.16775          359          431
         2             221      444      7.406977          325          515
         3              58        .             .            .            .

     total            1734      404      10.29992          386          430
```

Compare this table with the one we previously obtained. The number of subjects is the same, but the survival times differ because now we measure the times from one failure to the next, and previously we measured the time from a fixed point. The time between events in these data appears to be independent of event number.

Similarly, we can obtain the mean survival time for these data restricted to the longest follow-up time:

```
. stci, rmean by(nf)

        failure _d:  d
  analysis time _t:  t
                id:  newid

                  no. of  restricted
nf               subjects       mean    Std. Err.     [95% Conf. Interval]

         0             926   399.1802    8.872794       381.79      416.571
         1             529   397.0077(*)  13.36058      370.821      423.194
         2             221   397.8051(*)  25.78559      347.266      448.344
         3              58       471(*)          0          471          471

     total            1734   404.7006    7.021657      390.938      418.463
```
(*) largest observed analysis time is censored, mean is underestimated.

# Saved Results

stci saves in r():

Scalars

| | | | |
|---|---|---|---|
| r(N_sub) | number of subjects | r(se) | standard error |
| r(p#) | #th percentile | r(lb) | lower bound of CI |
| r(rmean) | restricted mean | r(ub) | upper bound of CI |
| r(emean) | extended mean | | |

# Methods and Formulas

stci is implemented as an ado-file.

The percentiles of survival times are obtained from $S(t)$, the Kaplan–Meier product-limit estimate of the survivor function. The 25th percentile, for instance, is obtained as the maximum value of $t$ such that $S(t) \leq .75$. The restricted mean is obtained as the area under the Kaplan–Meier product-limit survivor curve. The extended mean is obtained by extending the Kaplan–Meier product-limit survivor curve to zero using an exponentially fitted curve and then computing the area under the entire curve. Note that if the longest follow-up time ends in failure, the Kaplan–Meier product-limit survivor curve goes to zero and the restricted mean and extended mean are identical.

The large sample standard error for the $p$th percentile of the distribution is given by Klein and Moeschberger (1997, 114) as

$$\frac{p\sqrt{\widehat{g}}}{\sqrt{\widehat{S}(t_p)\widehat{f}(t_p)}}$$

where $\widehat{g}$ is the Greenwood pointwise standard error estimate for $\widehat{S}(t_p)$, and $\widehat{f}(t_p)$ is the estimated density function at the $p$th percentile.

Confidence intervals, however, are not calculated based on this standard error. For a given confidence level, the upper confidence limit for the $p$th percentile is defined as the first time at which the upper confidence limit for $S(t)$ (based on a $\ln\{-\ln S(t)\}$ transformation) is less than or equal to $p$, and similarly, the lower confidence limit is defined as the first time at which the lower confidence limit of $S(t)$ is less than or equal to $p$.

The restricted mean is obtained as the area under the Kaplan–Meier product-limit survivor curve. The extended mean is obtained by extending the Kaplan–Meier product-limit survivor curve to zero by using an exponentially fitted curve and then computing the area under the entire curve. Note that if the longest follow-up time ends in failure, the Kaplan–Meier product-limit survivor curve goes to zero, and the restricted mean and the extended mean are identical.

The standard error for the estimated restricted mean is computed as given by Klein and Moeschberger (1997, 110) and Collett (1994, 295):

$$\widehat{SE} = \sum_{i=1}^{D} \widehat{A}_i \sqrt{\frac{d_i}{R_i(R_i - d_i)}}$$

where the sum is over all distinct failure times, $\widehat{A}_i$ is the estimated area under the curve from time $i$ to the maximum follow-up time, $R_i$ is the number of subjects at risk at time $i$, and $d_i$ is the number of failures at time $i$.

The $100(1 - \alpha)\%$ confidence interval for the estimated restricted mean is computed as

$$\widehat{A}_i \pm Z_{1-\alpha/2}\widehat{SE}$$

# References

Collett, D. 1994. *Modeling Survival Data in Medical Research.* London: Chapman & Hall.

Klein, J. P. and M. L. Moeschberger. 1997. *Survival Analysis: Techniques for Censored and Truncated data.* New York: Springer-Verlag.

# Also See

**Complementary:**     [R] st **stdes**, [R] st **stgen**, [R] st **stir**, [R] st **sts**, [R] st **stset**, [R] st **stvary**

**Background:**     [R] **st**

# Title

---
**st stcox** — Estimate Cox proportional hazards model

---

# Syntax

stcox $[varlist]$ $[if\ exp]$ $[in\ range]$ $[,$ nohr strata(*varnames*) robust

cluster(*varname*) noadjust tvc(*varlist*) texp(*exp*) mgale(*newvar*)

esr(*newvar(s)*) schoenfeld(*newvar(s)*) scaledsch(*newvar(s)*) basehc(*newvar*)

basechazard(*newvar*) basesurv(*newvar*) { breslow | efron | exactm | exactp }

cmd estimate noshow offset(*varname*) level(#) *maximize_options* $]$

stphtest $[,$ km log rank time(*varname*) plot(*varname*) detail *graph_options*

*ksm_options* $]$

stcox is for use with survival-time data; see [R] **st**. You must stset your data before using this command.

by ... : may be used with stcox; see [R] **by**.

stphtest may be used after stcox.

stcox shares the features of all estimation commands; see [U] **23 Estimation and post-estimation commands**.

# Syntax for predict

predict $[type]$ *newvarname* $[if\ exp]$ $[in\ range]$ $[,$ *statistic* nooffset $]$

where *statistic* is

|  |  |  |
|---|---|---|
| hr | hazard ratio (relative hazard), predicted $\exp(\mathbf{x}_j\mathbf{b})$ (the default) |
| xb | linear prediction $\mathbf{x}_j\mathbf{b}$ |
| stdp | standard error of the linear prediction; $\mathrm{SE}(\mathbf{x}_j\mathbf{b})$ |
| * csnell | (partial) Cox–Snell residuals |
| * deviance | deviance residuals |
| * ccsnell | cumulative Cox–Snell residuals |
| * cmgale | cumulative martingale residuals |

Unstarred statistics are available both in and out of sample; type predict ... if e(sample) ... if wanted for only the estimation sample. Starred statistics are calculated for only the estimation sample even when e(sample) is not specified. Note that the (partial) martingale residuals, the efficient score residuals, the Schoenfeld residuals, and the scaled Schoenfeld residuals are available by options specified to the stcox command itself.

# Description

stcox estimates maximum-likelihood proportional hazards models on st data. stcox is appropriate for use with single- or multiple-record, single- or multiple-failure, st data.

stcox is implemented in terms of cox—another Stata command. That does not matter but, in case you were wondering, cox and stcox produce the same results, and there is nothing one command can do that the other command cannot. stcox is the preferred command because it is easier to use, allows the use of stphtest, and allows a richer set of statistics from predict.

stphtest can be used after stcox to test the proportional hazard assumption based on Schoenfeld residuals. Use of this command requires that you previously specified stcox's schoenfeld() option (if the global test is desired) and/or stcox's scaledsch() option (if the detailed test is desired). For graphical assessment of the proportional hazard assumptions, see [R] **st stphplot**.

# Options

## Options for stcox

nohr specifies that coefficients rather than exponentiated coefficients are to be displayed or, said differently, coefficients rather than hazard ratios. This option affects only how results are displayed and not how they are estimated. nohr may be specified at estimation time or when redisplaying previously estimated results (which you do by typing stcox).

strata(*varnames*) specifies up to 5 strata variables. Observations with equal values of the strata variables are assumed to be in the same stratum. Stratified estimates (equal coefficients across strata but baseline hazard unique to each stratum) are then estimated.

robust specifies that the robust method of calculating the variance–covariance matrix (Lin and Wei 1989) is to be used instead of the conventional inverse-matrix-of-negative-second-derivatives method. If you specify robust, and if you have previously stset an id() variable, the robust calculation will be clustered on the id() variable.

cluster(*varname*) implies robust and specifies a variable on which clustering is to be based. This overrides the default clustering, if any. You seldom need to specify this option, since specifying robust implies cluster() if an id() variable is stset.

noadjust is for use with robust, cluster(), or pweights. noadjust prevents the estimated variance matrix from being multiplied by $N/(N-1)$ or $g/(g-1)$, where $g$ is the number of clusters. The default adjustment is somewhat arbitrary because it is not always clear how to count observations or clusters. In such cases, however, the adjustment is likely to be biased toward 1, so we would still recommend making it.

tvc(*varlist*) is used to specify those variables that vary continuously with respect to time, i.e., time-varying covariates. This is a convenience option used to speed up calculations and to avoid the need to have to stsplit the data over many failure times.

texp(*exp*) is used in conjunction with tvc(*varlist*) to specify which function of analysis time should be multiplied by the time-varying covariates. For example, specifying texp(ln(_t)) would cause the time-varying covariates to be multiplied by the logarithm of analysis time. If tvc(*varlist*) is used without texp(*exp*), it is understood that you mean texp(_t), and thus the time-varying covariates are multiplied by the analysis time.

Both tvc(*varlist*) and texp(*exp*) are further explained in the section on *Cox regression with continuously time-varying covariates* below.

mgale(*newvar*) adds *newvar* containing the partial martingale residuals, which are fully described in *Methods and Formulas* below. If each observation in your data represents a different subject (single record per subject data), then the partial martingale residuals are the martingale residuals.

If you have multiple records per subject data, the value that `mgale()` stores in each observation is the observation's contribution to the martingale residual, and these partial residuals can be summed within `id()` to obtain the subject's martingale residual. Say you specify `mgale(pmr)` and that you have previously `stset, id(patid)`. Then, `egen mr = sum(pmr), by(patid)` would create the martingale residuals.

`esr(`*newvar(s)*`)` adds *newvar(s)* containing the partial efficient score residuals, which are fully described in *Methods and Formulas* below. If each observation in your data represents a different subject (single record per subject data), then the partial efficient score residuals are the efficient score residuals.

If you have multiple records per subject data, then the values `esr()` stores are each observation's contribution to the score residuals, and these partial residuals can be summed within `id()` to form the subject's efficient score residuals. This could be accomplished as noted under `mgale()` above.

One efficient score residual variable is created for each regressor in the model; the first new variable corresponds to the first regressor, the second to the second, and so on.

`schoenfeld(`*newvar(s)*`)` adds *newvar(s)* containing the Schoenfeld residuals, which are fully described under *Methods and Formulas*. This option is not available in conjunction with the `exactm` and `exactp` options. Schoenfeld residuals are calculated and are reported only at failure times.

One Schoenfeld residual variable is created for each regressor in the model; the first new variable corresponds to the first regressor, the second to the second, and so on.

`scaledsch(`*newvar(s)*`)` adds *newvar(s)* containing the scaled Schoenfeld residuals, which are fully described under *Methods and Formulas*. This option is not available if `exactm` or `exactp` have been specified. Scaled Schoenfeld residuals are calculated and reported only at failure times.

One scaled Schoenfeld residual variable is created for each regressor in the model; the first new variable corresponds to the first regressor, the second to the second, and so on.

**NOTE:** The easiest way to specify the preceding three options is `esr(`*stub*`*)`, where *stub* is a short name of your choosing. Stata then creates variables *stub*1, *stub*2, etc. Alternatively, you may specify each variable explicitly, in which case there must be as many (and no more) variables specified in `esr()` as regressors in the model.

One caution is necessary for the preceding three options: `stcox` will drop variables from the model due to collinearity. This is a desirable feature. A side-effect is that the score residual variable, the Schoenfeld residual variable, and the scaled Schoenfeld residual variable may not align with the regressors in the way you expect. Say you estimate a model by typing

    . stcox x1 x2 x3, esr(r1 r2 r3)

Usually, `r1` will contain the residual associated with `x1`, `r2` the residual associated with `x2`, etc.

Now assume that `x2` is dropped due to collinearity. In that case, `r1` will correspond to `x1`, `r2` to `x3`, and `r3` will contain 0. This happens because, after omitting the collinear variables, there are only two variables in the model: `x1` and `x3`.

`basehc(`*newvar*`)` adds *newvar* to the data containing the estimated baseline hazard contributions as described by Kalbfleisch & Prentice (1980, 85). These are used to construct the product-limit type estimator for the baseline survival function generated by `basesurv()`. If `strata()` is also specified, baseline estimates for each stratum are provided.

`basechazard(`*newvar*`)` adds *newvar* to the data containing the estimated cumulative baseline hazard. If `strata()` is also specified, cumulative baseline estimates for each stratum are provided.

basesurv(*newvar*) adds *newvar* to the data containing the estimated baseline survival function. Note that, in the null model, this is equivalent to the Kaplan–Meier product-limit estimate. If strata() is also specified, baseline estimates for each stratum are provided.

breslow, efron, exactm, and exactp specify the method for handling tied failures in the calculation of the model (and residuals). breslow is the default. Each method is described in the *Methods and Formulas* section below. Note that efron and the exact methods require substantially more computer time than the default breslow option. exactm and exactp may not be specified with robust or cluster(), or with tvc().

cmd displays the underlying cox command that stcox would execute, but does not execute the command; i.e., it does not estimate the model.

estimate forces estimation of the null model. All Stata estimation commands redisplay results when the command name is typed without arguments. So does stcox. What if you wish to estimate a Cox model on $x_j b$, where $x_j b$ is defined as 0? Logic says you would type stcox. There are no explanatory variables, so there is nothing to type following the command. Unfortunately, stcox looks the same as stcox typed without arguments, which is a request to redisplay results.

To estimate the null model, type stcox, estimate.

noshow prevents stcox from showing the key st variables. This option is rarely used since most people type stset, show or stset, noshow to reset once and for all whether they want to see these variables mentioned at the top of the output of every st command; see [R] **st stset**.

offset(*varname*) specifies a variable that is to be entered directly into the link function with coefficient 1.

level(*#*) specifies the confidence level, in percent, for confidence intervals. The default is level(95) or as set by set level; see [U] **23.5 Specifying the width of confidence intervals**.

*maximize_options* control the maximization process; see [R] **maximize**. You should never have to specify them.

## Options for stphtest

km, log, rank, and time() are used to specify the time scaling function.

By default, stphtest performs the tests using the identity function, i.e., analysis time itself.

km specifies that 1 minus the Kaplan–Meier product limit estimate be used.

log specifies that the natural log of analysis time be used.

rank specifies that the rank of analysis time be used.

time(*varname*) specifies a variable containing an arbitrary monotonic transformation of analysis time. It is your responsibility to ensure that *varname* is a monotonic transform.

plot(*varname*) is used to request that a smoothed plot of scaled Schoenfeld residuals versus time be produced for the covariate specified by *varname*. By default, the smoothing is performed using the running mean method implemented in ksm, but other smoothers can be specified. See [R] **ksm** for more details and options.

detail specifies that a separate test of the proportional hazard assumption be produced for each covariate in the Cox model. By default, stphtest produces only the global test.

*graph_options* are any of the options allowed with graph, twoway; see [G] **graph options**.

*ksm_options* are any of the options allowed with ksm; see [R] **ksm**.

## Options for predict

hr, the default, calculates the relative hazard (hazard ratio); that is, the exponentiated linear prediction, $\exp(\mathbf{xb})$.

xb calculates the linear prediction from the estimated model. That is, the model can be thought of as estimating a set of parameters $b_1, b_2, \ldots, b_k$, and the linear prediction is $\widehat{y}_j = b_1 x_{1j} + b_2 x_{2j} + \cdots + b_k x_{kj}$, often written in matrix notation as $\widehat{y}_j = \mathbf{x}_j \mathbf{b}$.

It is important to understand that the $x_{1j}$, $x_{2j}$, $\ldots$, $x_{kj}$ used in the calculation are obtained from the data currently in memory and do not have to correspond to the data on the independent variables used in estimating the model (obtaining the $b_1$, $b_2$, $\ldots$, $b_k$).

stdp calculates the standard error of the prediction; that is, the standard error of $\widehat{y}_j$.

csnell calculates the (partial) Cox–Snell generalized residuals. If you have a single observation per subject, csnell calculates the usual Cox–Snell residual. Otherwise, csnell calculates the additive contribution of this observation to the subject's overall Cox–Snell residual. In such cases, see option ccsnell below.

In order to specify option csnell, you must have specified 'stcox ..., mgale(*newvar*) ...' when you estimated the model. The name specified for the new variable does not matter, but you must have specified the mgale() option or predict will return an error.

deviance calculates the deviance residual. In the case of multiple-record data, only one value per subject is calculated, and it is placed on the last record for the subject.

In order to specify option deviance, you must have specified 'stcox ..., mgale(*newvar*) ...' when you estimated the model. See the comment for option csnell above.

ccsnell calculates the cumulative Cox–Snell residual in multiple-record data. This is based on calculating the partial Cox–Snell residuals (see option csnell above) and then summing them. Only one value per subject is recorded—the overall sum—and it is placed on the last record for the subject. ccsnell is the same as csnell in single-record survival data.

In order to specify option ccsnell, you must have specified 'stcox ..., mgale(*newvar*) ...' when you estimated the model. See the comment for option csnell above.

cmgale calculates the cumulative martingale residual in multiple-record data. This is based on summing the partial martingale residuals available from stcox. Only one value per subject is recorded—the overall sum—and it is placed on the last record for the subject. cmgale is the same as mgale in single-record survival data.

In order to specify option cmgale, you must have specified 'stcox ..., mgale(*newvar*) ...' when you estimated the model. See the comment for option csnell above.

nooffset is relevant only if you specified offset(*varname*) for stcox. It modifies the calculations made by predict so that they ignore the offset variable; the linear prediction is treated as $\mathbf{x}_j \mathbf{b}$ rather than $\mathbf{x}_j \mathbf{b} + \text{offset}_j$.

(*Continued on next page*)

# Remarks

Remarks are presented under the headings

Cox regression with uncensored data
Cox regression with censored data
Treatment of tied failure times
Cox regression with discrete time-varying covariates
Cox regression with continuous time-varying covariates
Robust estimate of variance
Cox regression with multiple failure data
Stratified estimation
Obtaining the baseline hazard and survivor function estimates
Cox regression residuals
Checking and testing the proportional hazard assumption

In the Cox proportional hazards model, the hazard is assumed to be

$$h(t) = h_0(t)e^{\beta_1 x_1 + \cdots + \beta_k x_k}$$

The Cox model provides estimates of $\beta_1, \ldots, \beta_k$, but provides no direct estimate of $h_0(t)$, called the baseline hazard. Formally, the function $h_0(t)$ is not estimated, but it is possible to recover an estimate of the cumulative hazard $H_0(t)$ and, from that, an estimate of the baseline survivor function $S_0(t)$.

stcox estimates the Cox proportional hazards model, which is to say, it provides estimates of $\beta$ and its variance–covariance matrix.

stcox, basehc(*newvar*) estimates the Cox proportional hazards model and calculates the set of baseline hazard contributions used to estimate the baseline survival function $S_0(t)$.

stcox, basechazard(*newvar*) estimates the Cox proportional hazards model and estimates the cumulative baseline hazard function $H_0(t)$.

stcox, basesurv(*newvar*) estimates the Cox model and estimates the baseline survival function $S_0(t)$.

The three baseline options may also be used in combination to concurrently produce estimates of their respective functions. In addition, stcox with the strata() option will produce stratified Cox regression estimates. In the stratified estimator, the hazard at time $t$ for a subject in group $i$ is assumed to be

$$h_i(t) = h_{0i}(t)e^{\beta_1 x_1 + \cdots + \beta_k x_k}$$

That is, the coefficients are assumed to be the same regardless of group, but the baseline hazard is allowed to be group-specific. If you specify the strata() option, the baseline options produce the group-specific estimates of the baseline functions.

Finally, whether or not you specify strata(), stcox can produce either of two variance estimators for $\beta$. The default is the conventional, inverse-matrix-of-negative-second-derivatives calculation. The theoretical justification for this estimator is based on likelihood theory.

The robust option instead switches to the robust measure developed by Lin and Wei (1989). This variance estimator is a variant of the estimator discussed in [U] **23.11 Obtaining robust variance estimates**.

❏ Technical Note

   stcox is, in fact, nothing more than the cox command ([R] **cox**) in disguise. Putting aside convenience, the only difference between the two commands is that cox, by default, reports coefficients ($\beta_1$, $\beta_2$, ...) but will, with the **hr** option, report exponentiated coefficients ($e^{\beta_1}$, $e^{\beta_2}$, ...), whereas stcox, by default, reports exponentiated coefficients but will, with the **nohr** option, report coefficients. Exponentiated coefficients have the interpretation of hazard ratios for a one-unit change in $x$.

   Although the commands are the same, we recommend the use of stcox over cox because stcox specifies various options of the cox command for you, such as the entry-time variable or the censor/dead variable, and thus reduces the chance of error.

❏

   We give examples below with uncensored, censored, time-varying, and recurring failure data, but it does not matter in terms of what you type. Once you have stset your data, to estimate a model you type stcox followed by the names of the explanatory variables. You do this whether your dataset is single- or multiple-record, whether your dataset includes censored observations or delayed entry, and even whether you are analyzing single- or multiple-failure data. In other words, you use stset to describe the properties of the data and then that information is available to stcox—and all the other st commands—so that you do not have to specify it again.

## Cox regression with uncensored data

   You wish to analyze an experiment testing the ability of emergency generators with a new-style bearing to withstand overloads. For this experiment, the overload protection circuit was disabled and then the generators were run overloaded until they burned up. Here are your data:

```
. list
          failtime      load    bearings
    1.         100        15           0
    2.         140        15           1
    3.          97        20           0
    4.         122        20           1
    5.          84        25           0
    6.         100        25           1
    7.          54        30           0
    8.          52        30           1
    9.          40        35           0
   10.          55        35           1
   11.          22        40           0
   12.          30        40           1
```

Twelve generators, half with the new-style bearings and half with the old, were allocated to this destructive test. The first observation reflects an old-style generator (bearings = 0) under a 15 kVA overload. It stopped functioning after 100 hours. The second generator had new-style bearings (bearings = 1) and under the same overload condition lasted 140 hours. Paired experiments were also performed under 20, 25, 30, 35, and 40 kVA overloads.

   You wish to estimate a Cox proportional hazards model in which the failure rate depends on the amount of overload and the style of the bearings. That is, you assume that bearings and load do not affect the shape of the overall hazard function, but they do affect the relative risk of failure. To estimate this model, you type

```
. stcox load bearings
          failure _d:  1 (meaning all fail)
    analysis time _t:  failtime
Iteration 0:   log likelihood = -20.274897
Iteration 1:   log likelihood = -10.515114
Iteration 2:   log likelihood = -8.8700259
Iteration 3:   log likelihood = -8.5915211
Iteration 4:   log likelihood = -8.5778991
Iteration 5:   log likelihood =  -8.577853
Refining estimates:
Iteration 0:   log likelihood =  -8.577853

Cox regression -- Breslow method for ties
No. of subjects =          12                   Number of obs   =         12
No. of failures =          12
Time at risk    =         896
                                                LR chi2(2)      =      23.39
Log likelihood  =    -8.577853                  Prob > chi2     =     0.0000
```

| _t _d | Haz. Ratio | Std. Err. | z | P>|z| | [95% Conf. Interval] | |
|---|---|---|---|---|---|---|
| load | 1.52647 | .2188172 | 2.95 | 0.003 | 1.152576 | 2.021653 |
| bearings | .0636433 | .0746609 | -2.35 | 0.019 | .0063855 | .6343223 |

You find that after controlling for overload, the new-style bearings result in a lower hazard and therefore a longer survival time.

Once an stcox model has been estimated, typing stcox without arguments redisplays the previous results. Options that affect the display, such as nohr—which requests that coefficients rather than hazard ratios be displayed—can be specified when the model is estimated or when it is redisplayed:

```
. stcox, nohr
Cox regression -- Breslow method for ties
No. of subjects =          12                   Number of obs   =         12
No. of failures =          12
Time at risk    =         896
                                                LR chi2(2)      =      23.39
Log likelihood  =    -8.577853                  Prob > chi2     =     0.0000
```

| _t _d | Coef. | Std. Err. | z | P>|z| | [95% Conf. Interval] | |
|---|---|---|---|---|---|---|
| load | .4229578 | .1433485 | 2.95 | 0.003 | .1419998 | .7039157 |
| bearings | -2.754461 | 1.173115 | -2.35 | 0.019 | -5.053723 | -.4551981 |

❑ Technical Note

stcox's iteration log looks like a standard Stata iteration log right up to the point where it says "Refining estimates". The Cox proportional hazards likelihood function is indeed a difficult function, both conceptually and numerically. Up until Stata says "Refining estimates", it maximizes the Cox likelihood in the standard way using double-precision arithmetic. Then, just to be sure that the answers are accurate, Stata switches to quad-precision routines (which is to say, double double precision) and completes the maximization procedure from its current location on the likelihood.

❑

## Cox regression with censored data

You have data on 48 participants in a cancer drug trial. Of these 48, 28 receive the experimental treatment (drug = 1) and 20 receive a placebo (drug = 0). The participants range in age from 47 to 67 years. You wish to analyze time until death, measured in months. Your data include one observation for each patient. The variable studytime records either the month of their death or the last month that they were known to be alive. Some of the patients still live, so together with studytime is died, indicating their health status. Persons known to have died—"noncensored" in the jargon—have died = 1, whereas the patients who are still alive—"censored" in the jargon—have died = 0.

Here is an overview of your data:

```
. st
-> stset studytime, failure(died)

    failure event:  died ~= 0 & died ~= .
obs. time interval:  (0, studytime]
 exit on or before:  failure

. summarize
```

| Variable | Obs | Mean | Std. Dev. | Min | Max |
|---|---|---|---|---|---|
| studytime | 48 | 15.5 | 10.25629 | 1 | 39 |
| died | 48 | .6458333 | .4833211 | 0 | 1 |
| drug | 48 | .5833333 | .4982238 | 0 | 1 |
| age | 48 | 55.875 | 5.659205 | 47 | 67 |
| _st | 48 | 1 | 0 | 1 | 1 |
| _d | 48 | .6458333 | .4833211 | 0 | 1 |
| _t | 48 | 15.5 | 10.25629 | 1 | 39 |
| _t0 | 48 | 0 | 0 | 0 | 0 |

You typed stset studytime, failure(died) previously; that is how st knew about this dataset. To estimate the Cox model, you type

```
. stcox drug age

Iteration 0:   log likelihood = -99.911448
Iteration 1:   log likelihood = -83.551879
Iteration 2:   log likelihood = -83.324009
Iteration 3:   log likelihood = -83.323546
Refining estimates:
Iteration 0:   log likelihood = -83.323546

Cox regression -- Breslow method for ties

No. of subjects =          48                Number of obs   =         48
No. of failures =          31
Time at risk    =         744
                                             LR chi2(2)      =      33.18
Log likelihood  =   -83.323546               Prob > chi2     =     0.0000
```

| _t _d | Haz. Ratio | Std. Err. | z | P>\|z\| | [95% Conf. Interval] |
|---|---|---|---|---|---|
| drug | .1048772 | .0477017 | -4.96 | 0.000 | .0430057    .2557622 |
| age | 1.120325 | .0417711 | 3.05 | 0.002 | 1.041375    1.20526 |

You find that the drug results in a lower hazard and therefore a longer survival time controlling for age. Older patients are more likely to die. The model as a whole is statistically significant.

The hazard ratios reported correspond to a one-unit change in the corresponding variable. It is more typical to report relative risk for 5-year changes in age. To obtain such a hazard ratio, you create a new age variable such that a one-unit change means a 5-year change:

```
. replace age = age/5
age was int now float
(48 real changes made)

. stcox drug age, nolog

Cox regression -- Breslow method for ties

No. of subjects =          48                    Number of obs   =          48
No. of failures =          31
Time at risk    =         744
                                                 LR chi2(2)      =       33.18
Log likelihood  =   -83.323544                   Prob > chi2     =      0.0000
```

| _t _d | Haz. Ratio | Std. Err. | z | P>\|z\| | [95% Conf. Interval] | |
|---|---|---|---|---|---|---|
| drug | .1048772 | .0477017 | -4.96 | 0.000 | .0430057 | .2557622 |
| age | 1.764898 | .3290196 | 3.05 | 0.002 | 1.224715 | 2.543338 |

## Treatment of tied failure times

The proportional hazards model assumes that the hazard function is continuous and thus that there are no tied survival times. Due to the way that time is recorded, however, tied events do occur in survival data. In such cases, the partial likelihood needs to be modified. See the *Methods and Formulas* section for further details on the methods described below.

Stata provides four methods for handling tied failures in the calculation of the Cox model through the options breslow, efron, exactm, and exactp. If there are no ties in the data, the results are identical regardless of the method selected.

When there are tied failure times, we must decide how to handle the calculation of the risk pools for these tied observations. Assume that there are two observations that fail in succession. In the calculation involving the second observation, the first observation is not in the risk pool since failure has already occurred. If the two observations have the same failure time, then how to calculate the risk pool for the second observation and in which order to calculate the two observations are at issue.

There are two views of time. In the first, time is continuous, so ties should not occur. If they have occurred, the likelihood reflects the marginal probability that the tied failure events occurred before the nonfailure events in the risk pool (the order that they occurred is not important). This is called the exact marginal likelihood (option exactm).

In the second view, time is discrete, so ties are expected. The likelihood is changed to reflect this discreteness and calculates the conditional probability that the observed failures are the ones that fail in the risk pool given the observed number of failures. This is called the exact partial likelihood (option exactp).

Let's assume that there are 5 subjects, $e_1, e_2, e_3, e_4, e_5$, in the risk pool and that subjects $e_1$ and $e_2$ fail. It could be that had we been able to observe the events at a better resolution, $e_1$ failed from risk pool $e_1 + e_2 + e_3 + e_4 + e_5$ and then $e_2$ failed from risk pool $e_2 + e_3 + e_4 + e_5$. Alternatively, it could be that $e_2$ failed first from risk pool $e_1 + e_2 + e_3 + e_4 + e_5$ and then $e_1$ failed from risk pool $e_1 + e_3 + e_4 + e_5$.

The Breslow method (option `breslow`) for handling tied values simply says that since we do not know the order, we will use the largest risk pool for each of the tied failure events. In other words, it assumes that $e_1$ failed and $e_2$ failed, both from risk pool $e_1 + e_2 + e_3 + e_4 + e_5$. This approximation is very fast and is the default method for handling ties. If there are many ties in the dataset, this approximation will not be very good as the risk pools include too many observations. The Breslow method is an approximation of the exact marginal likelihood.

The Efron method (option `efron`) for handling tied values says that the first risk pool must be $e_1 + e_2 + e_3 + e_4 + e_5$ and then that the second risk pool is either $e_2 + e_3 + e_4 + e_5$ or $e_1 + e_3 + e_4 + e_5$. From this, Efron noted that the $e_1$ and $e_2$ terms were in the second risk pool with probability 1/2, and so used for the second risk pool $.5(e_1 + e_2) + e_3 + e_4 + e_5$. Efron's approximation is a more accurate approximation of the exact marginal likelihood than Breslow's, but takes longer to calculate.

The exact marginal method (option `exactm`) is a misnomer in the sense that the calculation performed is also an *approximation* of the exact marginal likelihood. It is an approximation because the evaluation of the likelihood (and derivatives) is accomplished using 15-point Gauss–Laguerre quadrature. For small to moderate samples, this is slower than the Efron approximation, but the difference in execution time diminishes when samples become larger. You may want to consider the quadrature when deciding to use this method. If the number of tied deaths is large (on average), the quadrature approximation of the function is not well-behaved. A small amount of empirical checking suggests that if the number of tied deaths is larger (on average) than 30, the quadrature does not approximate the function well.

Viewing time as discrete, the exact partial method (option `exactp`) is the final method available. This approach is equivalent to computing conditional logistic regression where the groups are defined by the risk sets and the outcome is given by the death variable. This is the slowest method to use and can take a significant amount of time if the risk sets and the number of tied failures are large.

## Cox regression with discrete time-varying covariates

In [R] **st stset** we introduce the Stanford heart transplant data—data for which there are one or two records per patient depending on whether they received a new heart.

This dataset (Crowley and Hu 1977) consists of 103 patients admitted to the Stanford Heart Transplantation Program. Patients were admitted into the program after review by a committee and then waited for an available donor heart. While waiting, some died or were transferred out of the program, but 67% received a transplant. The dataset includes the year the patient was accepted into the program along with the patient's age, whether the patient had other heart surgery previously, and whether the patient received a transplant.

In the data, `posttran` becomes 1 when a patient receives a new heart and so is a time-varying covariate. That does not matter in terms of what we type to estimate the model:

```
. stset t1, failure(died) id(id)
  (output omitted )

. stcox age posttran surg year
        failure _d:  died
  analysis time _t:  t1
               id:  id
Iteration 0:   log likelihood = -298.31514
Iteration 1:   log likelihood =  -289.7344
Iteration 2:   log likelihood = -289.53498
Iteration 3:   log likelihood = -289.53378
Iteration 4:   log likelihood = -289.53378
Refining estimates:
Iteration 0:   log likelihood = -289.53378
```

```
Cox regression -- Breslow method for ties

No. of subjects =          103                  Number of obs   =        172
No. of failures =           75
Time at risk    =      31938.1
                                                LR chi2(4)      =      17.56
Log likelihood  =    -289.53378                 Prob > chi2     =     0.0015
```

| _t _d | Haz. Ratio | Std. Err. | z | P>\|z\| | [95% Conf. Interval] |
|---|---|---|---|---|---|
| age | 1.030224 | .0143201 | 2.14 | 0.032 | 1.002536 1.058677 |
| posttran | .9787243 | .3032597 | -0.07 | 0.945 | .5332291 1.796416 |
| surgery | .3738278 | .163204 | -2.25 | 0.024 | .1588759 .8796 |
| year | .8873107 | .059808 | -1.77 | 0.076 | .7775022 1.012628 |

We find that older patients have higher hazards, that patients tend to do better over time, and that patients with prior surgery do better. Whether a patient ultimately receives a transplant does not seem to make much difference.

## Cox regression with continuous time-varying covariates

The basic proportional hazards regression assumes the relationship

$$h(t) = h_0(t) \exp(\beta_1 x_1 + \cdots + \beta_k x_k)$$

where $h_0(t)$ is the baseline hazard function. For most purposes this model is sufficient, but sometimes we may wish to introduce variables of the form $z_i(t) = z_i g(t)$, which vary continuously with time so that

$$h(t) = h_0(t) \exp\{\beta_1 x_1 + \cdots + \beta_k x_k + g(t)(\gamma_1 z_1 + \cdots + \gamma_m z_m)\}$$

where $(z_1, \ldots, z_m)$ are the time-varying covariates and where estimation has the net effect of estimating, say, a regression coefficient $\gamma_i$ for a covariate $g(t)z_i$, which is a function of the current time.

The time-varying covariates $(z_1, \ldots, z_m)$ are specified using the tvc(*varlist*) option, and $g(t)$ is specified using the texp(*exp*) option, where $t$ in $g(t)$ is analysis time. For example, if we want $g(t) = \ln(t)$, we would use texp(ln(_t)) since _t stores the analysis time once the data are stset.

Since the calculations in Cox regression only concern themselves with the times at which failures occur, the above could also be achieved by stsplitting the data at the observed failure times and manually generating the time-varying covariates. In cases where this is feasible, the above merely represents a more convenient way to accomplish this. However, for large datasets with many distinct failure times, using stsplit may produce datasets that are too large to fit in memory, and even if this were not so, the estimation would take far longer to complete. It is for these reasons that the options described above were introduced.

▷ Example

Consider a dataset consisting of 45 observations on recovery time from walking pneumonia. Recovery time (in days) is recorded in the variable time, and there exist measurements on the covariates age, drug1, and drug2, where drug1 and drug2 interact a choice of treatment with initial dosage level. The study was terminated after 30 days, and thus those who had not recovered by that time were censored (cured = 0).

```
. list in 1/12

          age      drug1      drug2       time       cured
  1.       36          0         50       20.6           1
  2.       14          0         50        6.8           1
  3.       43          0        125        8.6           1
  4.       25        100          0         10           1
  5.       50        100          0         30           0
  6.       26          0        100       13.6           1
  7.       21        150          0        5.4           1
  8.       25          0        100       15.4           1
  9.       32        125          0        8.6           1
 10.       28        150          0        8.5           1
 11.       34          0        100         30           0
 12.       40          0         50         30           0
```

Patient 1 took 50 mg of drug number 2 and was cured after 20.6 days, while Patient 5 took 100 mg of drug number 1 and had yet to recover when the study ended, and thus was censored at 30 days.

We run a standard Cox regression after stsetting the data.

```
. stset time, failure(cured)

       failure event:  cured ~= 0 & cured ~= .
obs. time interval:  (0, time]
 exit on or before:  failure

       45  total obs.
        0  exclusions

       45  obs. remaining, representing
       36  failures in single record/single failure data
    677.9  total analysis time at risk, at risk from t =          0
                             earliest observed entry t =          0
                               last observed exit t =           30

. stcox age drug1 drug2

        failure _d:  cured
  analysis time _t:  time

Iteration 0:   log likelihood = -116.54385
Iteration 1:   log likelihood = -102.77311
Iteration 2:   log likelihood = -101.92794
Iteration 3:   log likelihood = -101.92504
Iteration 4:   log likelihood = -101.92504
Refining estimates:
Iteration 0:   log likelihood = -101.92504

Cox regression -- Breslow method for ties

No. of subjects =          45                  Number of obs   =         45
No. of failures =          36
Time at risk    =  677.9000034
                                               LR chi2(3)      =      29.24
Log likelihood  =   -101.92504                 Prob > chi2     =     0.0000
```

| _t _d | Haz. Ratio | Std. Err. | z | P>|z| | [95% Conf. Interval] |
|---|---|---|---|---|---|
| age | .8759449 | .0253259 | -4.58 | 0.000 | .8276873 .9270162 |
| drug1 | 1.008482 | .0043249 | 1.97 | 0.049 | 1.000041 1.016994 |
| drug2 | 1.00189 | .0047971 | 0.39 | 0.693 | .9925323 1.011337 |

The output includes $p$-values for the tests of the null hypotheses that each regression coefficient is zero or, equivalently, that each hazard ratio is one. That all hazard ratios are apparently close to one is a matter of scale; however, we can see that drug number 1 significantly increases the risk of being cured and so is an effective drug, while drug number 2 is ineffective.

Suppose now that we wish to fit a model in which we account for the effect that as time goes by, the actual level of the drug remaining in the body diminishes, say, at an exponential rate. If it is known that the half-life of both drugs is close to 2 days, then we can say that the actual concentration level of the drug in the patient's blood is proportional to the initial dosage times $\exp(-0.35t)$, where $t$ is analysis time. We now fit a model that reflects this change.

```
. stcox age, tvc(drug1 drug2) texp(exp(-0.35*_t)) nolog
         failure _d:  cured
   analysis time _t:  time
Cox regression -- Breslow method for ties
No. of subjects =          45             Number of obs   =         45
No. of failures =          36
Time at risk    =  677.9000034
                                          LR chi2(3)      =      36.98
Log likelihood  =   -98.052763            Prob > chi2     =     0.0000
```

| _t _d | Haz. Ratio | Std. Err. | z | P>\|z\| | [95% Conf. Interval] | |
|---|---|---|---|---|---|---|
| rh | | | | | | |
| age | .8614636 | .028558 | -4.50 | 0.000 | .8072706 | .9192948 |
| t | | | | | | |
| drug1 | 1.304744 | .1135967 | 3.06 | 0.002 | 1.100059 | 1.547514 |
| drug2 | 1.200613 | .1113218 | 1.97 | 0.049 | 1.001103 | 1.439882 |

```
note: second equation contains variables that continuously vary with respect to
      time; variables are interacted with current values of exp(-0.35*_t).
```

The first equation, rh, reports the results (hazard ratios) for the covariates that do not vary over time; the second equation, t, reports the results for the time-varying covariates.

As the level of drug in the blood system decreases, the drug's effectiveness will diminish. Accounting for this serves to unmask the effects of both drugs in that we now see increased effects on both. In fact, the effect on recovery time of drug number 2 now becomes significant.

❏ Technical Note

The interpretation of hazard ratios requires careful consideration here. For the first model, the hazard ratio for, say, drug1 is interpreted as the proportional change in hazard when the dosage level of drug1 is increased by one unit. For the second model, the hazard ratio for drug1 is the proportional change in hazard when the blood concentration level, i.e., drug1*$\exp(-0.35t)$, increases by one.

❏

Since the number of observations in our data is relatively small, for illustrative purposes we can stsplit the data at each recovery time, manually generate the blood concentration levels, and re-estimate the second model.

```
. gen id=_n
. streset, id(id)
  (output omitted )
. stsplit, at(failures)
  (31 failure times)
  (812 observations (episodes) created)
. gen drug1emt = drug1*exp(-0.35*_t)
. gen drug2emt = drug2*exp(-0.35*_t)
```

```
. stcox age drug1emt drug2emt

          failure _d:  cured
    analysis time _t:  time
                  id:  id

Iteration 0:   log likelihood = -116.54385
Iteration 1:   log likelihood = -99.321912
Iteration 2:   log likelihood =  -98.07369
Iteration 3:   log likelihood =  -98.05277
Iteration 4:   log likelihood = -98.052763
Refining estimates:
Iteration 0:   log likelihood = -98.052763

Cox regression -- Breslow method for ties

No. of subjects =           45          Number of obs    =        857
No. of failures =           36
Time at risk    = 677.9000034
                                        LR chi2(3)       =      36.98
Log likelihood  =   -98.052763          Prob > chi2      =     0.0000
```

| _t _d | Haz. Ratio | Std. Err. | z | P>\|z\| | [95% Conf. Interval] | |
|---|---|---|---|---|---|---|
| age | .8614636 | .028558 | -4.50 | 0.000 | .8072706 | .9192948 |
| drug1emt | 1.304744 | .1135967 | 3.06 | 0.002 | 1.100059 | 1.547514 |
| drug2emt | 1.200613 | .1113218 | 1.97 | 0.049 | 1.001103 | 1.439882 |

Note that we get the same answer. However, this required more work for both Stata and for the user.

◁

The full functionality of stcox is available with time-varying covariates, including the generation of residuals and baseline functions. The only exception to this rule is when the exactm or exactp options are specified for handling ties, in which case the tvc(*varlist*) option is currently not supported. In those cases, you must use the stsplit approach outlined above.

▷ Example

For a final demonstration, we will use the cancer data illustrated earlier in this entry and generate some baseline survival probabilities. We then compare these to the baseline survival probabilities generated after the data are stsplit.

```
. use cancer,clear
(Patient Survival in Drug Trial)
. stset studytime, failure(died)
(output omitted)
. quietly stcox age, tvc(drug) texp(ln(_t)) bases(s1)
. summ s1
```

| Variable | Obs | Mean | Std. Dev. | Min | Max |
|---|---|---|---|---|---|
| s1 | 48 | .9262653 | .1253034 | .5820062 | .9999141 |

```
. gen id=_n
. streset, id(id)
(output omitted)
. stsplit, at(failures)
(21 failure times)
(534 observations (episodes) created)
. gen druglnt = drug*ln(_t)
```

```
. quietly stcox age druglnt, bases(s2)
. sort id _t
. by id: gen tosum=1 if _n==_N
(534 missing values generated)
. summ s2 if tosum==1
    Variable |       Obs        Mean    Std. Dev.         Min          Max
-------------+---------------------------------------------------------------
          s2 |        48    .9262653    .1253034    .5820062    .9999141
```

◁

## ❑ Technical Note

Finally, it should be noted that the specification of $g(t)$ via the texp(*exp*) option is intended for functions of analysis time, _t only, with the default being texp(_t) if left unspecified. However, specifying any other valid Stata expression will not produce a syntax error, yet in most cases will not yield the anticipated output. For example, specifying texp(*varname*) will not generate interaction terms. This mainly has to do with how the calculations are carried out—by careful summations over risk pools at each failure time.

❑

## Robust estimate of variance

By default, stcox produces the conventional estimate for the variance–covariance matrix of the coefficients (and hence, the reported standard errors). If, however, you specify the robust option, stcox switches to the robust variance estimator (Lin and Wei 1989).

The key to the robust calculation is using the efficient score residuals for each of the subjects in the data for the variance calculation. Even in simple single-record, single-failure survival data, the same subjects appear repeatedly in the risk pools, and the robust calculation tries to account for that.

▷ Example

Reestimating the Stanford Heart transplant data model with robust standard errors, we obtain

```
. stcox age posttran surg year, robust

         failure _d:  died
   analysis time _t:  t1
                 id:  id
Iteration 0:   log likelihood = -298.31514
Iteration 1:   log likelihood =  -289.7344
Iteration 2:   log likelihood = -289.53498
Iteration 3:   log likelihood = -289.53378
Iteration 4:   log likelihood = -289.53378
Refining estimates:
Iteration 0:   log likelihood = -289.53378

Cox regression -- Breslow method for ties

No. of subjects =          103              Number of obs   =        172
No. of failures =           75
Time at risk    =      31938.1
                                            Wald chi2(4)    =      19.68
Log likelihood  =    -289.53378             Prob > chi2     =     0.0006

                   (standard errors adjusted for clustering on id)
```

| _t<br>_d | Haz. Ratio | Robust<br>Std. Err. | z | P>\|z\| | [95% Conf. Interval] | |
|---|---|---|---|---|---|---|
| age | 1.030224 | .0148771 | 2.06 | 0.039 | 1.001474 | 1.059799 |
| posttran | .9787243 | .2961736 | -0.07 | 0.943 | .5408498 | 1.771104 |
| surgery | .3738278 | .1304912 | -2.82 | 0.005 | .1886013 | .7409665 |
| year | .8873107 | .0613176 | -1.73 | 0.084 | .7749139 | 1.01601 |

Note the word `Robust` above `Std. Err.` in the table and the phrase "standard errors adjusted for clustering on id" above the table.

The hazard ratio estimates are the same as before, but the standard errors are slightly different.

◁

## ❑ Technical Note

If you were to reproduce these results using `cox` rather than `stcox`, you would have to specify two options: `robust` and `cluster(id)`. `stcox` knew to specify `cluster(id)` for you when you specified `robust`.

To see the importance of this option, consider simple single-record, single-failure survival data, a piece of which is

```
t0        t        died        x
0        5         1          1
0        9         0          1
0        8         0          0
```

and then consider the absolutely equivalent multiple-record survival data:

```
id        t0        t        died        x
1         0        3         0          1
1         3        5         1          1
2         0        6         0          1
2         6        9         0          1
3         0        3         0          0
3         3        8         0          0
```

Both of these datasets record the same underlying data, so both should produce the same numerical results. This should be true whether or not `robust` is specified.

In the second dataset, were one to ignore `id`, it would appear that there are six observations on six subjects. The key ingredients in the robust calculation are the efficient score residuals, and viewing the data as six observations on six subjects produces different score residuals. Let us call the six score residuals $s_1$, $s_2$, ..., $s_6$ and the three score residuals that would be generated by the first dataset $S_1$, $S_2$, and $S_3$. It turns out that $S_1 = s_1 + s_2$, $S_2 = s_3 + s_4$, and $S_3 = s_5 + s_6$.

That residuals sum is the key to understanding the `cluster()` option. When you specify `cluster(id)`, Stata makes the robust calculation based not on the overly detailed $s_1$, $s_2$, ..., $s_6$, but on $s_1 + s_2$, $s_3 + s_4$, and $s_5 + s_6$. That is, Stata sums residuals within clusters before entering them into subsequent calculations (where they are squared) and that is why results estimated from the second dataset are equal to those estimated from the first. In more complicated datasets with time-varying regressors, delayed entry, and gaps, it is this action of summing within cluster that, in effect, treats the cluster (which is typically a subject) as a unified whole.

Because we had `stset` an `id()` variable, `stcox` knew to specify `cluster(id)` for us when we specified `robust`.

For those of you who are distrustful, specifying the `cmd` option displays the `cox` command that `stcox` would normally execute on your behalf:

```
. stcox age posttran surg year, robust cmd
          failure _d:  died
    analysis time _t:  t1
                 id:   id
-> cox _t age posttran surg year   , robust cluster(id) t0(_t0)  dead(_d)
```

The odd spacing arises because of how `stcox` assembles the command; the spacing does not matter.

□

## Cox regression with multiple failure data

In [R] **st stsum**, we introduce a multiple-failure dataset:

```
. st
-> stset t, id(id) failure(d) exit(time .) noshow
              id:  id
    failure event:  d ~= 0 & d ~= .
  obs. time interval:  (t[_n-1], t]
   exit on or before:  time .

. stdes
```

| Category | total | mean | per subject min | median | max |
|---|---|---|---|---|---|
| no. of subjects | 926 | | | | |
| no. of records | 1734 | 1.87257 | 1 | 2 | 4 |
| (first) entry time | | 0 | 0 | 0 | 0 |
| (final) exit time | | 470.6857 | 1 | 477 | 960 |
| subjects with gap | 0 | | | | |
| time on gap if gap | 0 | . | . | . | . |
| time at risk | 435855 | 470.6857 | 1 | 477 | 960 |
| failures | 808 | .8725702 | 0 | 1 | 3 |

Assume that this dataset contains two variables—x1 and x2—which we believe affect the hazard of failure.

If our interest is simply in analyzing these multiple-failure data as if the baseline hazard remains unchanged as events occur (that is, the hazard may change with time, but time is measured from 0 and is independent of when the last failure occurred), we can type

```
. stcox x1 x2, robust
Iteration 0:   log likelihood = -5034.9569
  (output omitted)
Iteration 3:   log likelihood = -4978.1914
Refining estimates:
Iteration 0:   log likelihood = -4978.1914

Cox regression -- Breslow method for ties

No. of subjects =         926              Number of obs   =       1734
No. of failures =         808
Time at risk    =      435855
                                           Wald chi2(2)    =     152.13
Log likelihood  =   -4978.1914             Prob > chi2     =     0.0000

                (standard errors adjusted for clustering on id)
```

| _t<br>_d | Haz. Ratio | Robust<br>Std. Err. | z | P>\|z\| | [95% Conf. Interval] | |
|---|---|---|---|---|---|---|
| x1 | 2.273456 | .1868211 | 9.99 | 0.000 | 1.935259 | 2.670755 |
| x2 | .329011 | .0523425 | -6.99 | 0.000 | .2408754 | .4493951 |

We chose to estimate this model with robust standard errors—we specified robust—but you could estimate with conventional standard errors if you wished.

In [R] **st stsum**, we discuss analyzing this dataset as time since last failure. We wished to assume that the hazard function remained unchanged with failure except that one restarted the same hazard function. To that end, we made the following changes to our data:

```
. stgen nf = nfailures()

. egen newid = group(id nf)

. sort newid t

. by newid: replace t = t - t0[1]
(808 real changes made)

. by newid: gen newt0 = t0 - t0[1]

. stset t, id(newid) failure(d) time0(newt0) noshow
                id:  newid
     failure event:  d ~= 0 & d ~= .
obs. time interval:  (newt0, t]
 exit on or before:  failure


      1734  total obs.
         0  exclusions

      1734  obs. remaining, representing
      1734  subjects
       808  failures in single failure-per-subject data
    435444  total analysis time at risk, at risk from t =         0
                              earliest observed entry t =         0
                                last observed exit t =         797
```

That is, we took each subject and made numerous newid subjects out of each, with each subject entering at time 0 (now meaning the time of the last failure). id still identifies real subject, but Stata thinks the identifier variable is newid because we stset, id(newid). If we were to estimate a model using robust, we would get

```
. stcox x1 x2, robust nolog

Cox regression -- Breslow method for ties

No. of subjects =        1734              Number of obs   =       1734
No. of failures =         808
Time at risk    =      435444
                                           Wald chi2(2)    =      88.51
Log likelihood  =   -5062.5815             Prob > chi2     =     0.0000
              (standard errors adjusted for clustering on newid)
```

| _t<br>_d | Haz. Ratio | Robust<br>Std. Err. | z | P>\|z\| | [95% Conf. Interval] | |
|---|---|---|---|---|---|---|
| x1 | 2.002547 | .1936906 | 7.18 | 0.000 | 1.656733 | 2.420542 |
| x2 | .2946263 | .0569167 | -6.33 | 0.000 | .2017595 | .4302382 |

Note carefully the message concerning the clustering: standard errors have been adjusted for clustering on `newid`. We, however, want the standard errors adjusted for clustering on `id`, so we must specify the `cluster()` option:

```
. stcox x1 x2, robust cluster(id) nolog
Cox regression -- Breslow method for ties
No. of subjects =        1734                   Number of obs   =        1734
No. of failures =         808
Time at risk    =      435444
                                                Wald chi2(2)    =       93.66
Log likelihood  =    -5062.5815                 Prob > chi2     =      0.0000
                         (standard errors adjusted for clustering on id)
```

| _t _d | Haz. Ratio | Robust Std. Err. | z | P>\|z\| | [95% Conf. Interval] | |
|---|---|---|---|---|---|---|
| x1 | 2.002547 | .1920151 | 7.24 | 0.000 | 1.659452 | 2.416576 |
| x2 | .2946263 | .0544625 | -6.61 | 0.000 | .2050806 | .4232709 |

That is, if you are using **robust**, you must remember to specify **cluster()** for yourself when

1. you are analyzing multiple-failure data, and

2. you have played a trick on Stata to reset time to time-since-last-failure, so what Stata considers the subjects are really subsubjects.

## Stratified estimation

When you type

```
. stcox xvars, strata(svars)
```

you are allowing the baseline hazard functions to differ for the groups identified by *svars*. Said differently, this is equivalent to estimating separate Cox proportional hazards models under the constraint that the coefficients, but not the baseline hazard functions, are equal.

▷ **Example**

Pretend that in the Stanford heart experiment data there was a change in treatment for all patients, pre- and post-transplant, in 1970 and then again in 1973. Further assume that the proportional hazards assumption is not reasonable for these changes in treatment—perhaps the changes result in short-run but little expected long-run benefit. Your interest in the data is not in the effect of these treatment changes but in the effect of transplantation, for which you still find the proportional hazards assumption reasonable. One way you might estimate your model to account for these fictional changes is

```
. gen pgroup = year
. recode pgroup min/69=1 70/72=2 73/max=3
(172 changes made)
```

```
. stcox age posttran surg year, strata(pgroup) nolog

         failure _d:  died
   analysis time _t:  t1
               id:  id

Stratified Cox regr.  -- Breslow method for ties

No. of subjects =          103            Number of obs   =        172
No. of failures =           75
Time at risk    =      31938.1
                                          LR chi2(4)      =      20.67
Log likelihood  =    -213.35033           Prob > chi2     =     0.0004
```

| _t _d | Haz. Ratio | Std. Err. | z | P>\|z\| | [95% Conf. Interval] |
|---|---|---|---|---|---|
| age | 1.027406 | .0150188 | 1.85 | 0.064 | .9983874 1.057268 |
| posttran | 1.075476 | .3354669 | 0.23 | 0.816 | .583567 1.982034 |
| surgery | .2222415 | .1218386 | -2.74 | 0.006 | .0758882 .6508429 |
| year | .5523966 | .1132688 | -2.89 | 0.004 | .3695832 .825638 |

```
                                             Stratified by pgroup
```

Of course, you could obtain the robust estimate of variance by also including the `robust` option.

◁

## Obtaining baseline function estimates

When you specify options `basechazard(`*newvar₁*`)` and `basesurv(`*newvar₂*`)`—which you may do together or separately—you obtain estimates of the baseline cumulative hazard and survival functions. When you specify the option `basehc(`*newvar₃*`)`, you obtain estimates of the baseline hazard contribution at each failure time, which are factors used to develop the product-limit estimator for the survival function generated by `basesurv(`*newvar₂*`)`.

Although in theory $S_0(t) = \exp\{-H_0(t)\}$, where $S_0(t)$ is the baseline survival function and $H_0(t)$ is the baseline cumulative hazard, the estimates produced by `basechazard()` and `basesurv()` do not exactly correspond in this manner, although they closely do. The reason is that `stcox` uses different estimation schemes for each; the exact formulas are given in the *Methods and Formulas* section.

When the model is estimated with the `strata()` option, you obtain estimates of the baseline functions for each stratum.

Let us first understand how `stcox` stores the results.

Mathematically, the baseline hazard contribution $h_i = (1 - \alpha_i)$ (see Kalbfleisch and Prentice 1980, 85) is defined at every analytic time $t_i$ at which a failure occurs and is undefined (or, if you prefer, 0) at other times. Stata stores $h_i$ in observations where a failure occurred and missing values in the other observations. For instance, here are some data on which we have estimated a proportional hazards model and specified the option `basehc(h)`:

```
. list id t0 t1 d h in 1/10
```

|   | id | _t0 | t1 | died | h |
|---|---|---|---|---|---|
| 1. | 1 | 0 | 50 | 1 | .01503465 |
| 2. | 2 | 0 | 6 | 1 | .02035303 |
| 3. | 3 | 0 | 1 | 0 | . |
| 4. | 3 | 1 | 16 | 1 | .03339642 |
| 5. | 4 | 0 | 36 | 0 | . |

|      |   |    |     |   |          |
|------|---|----|-----|---|----------|
| 6.   | 4 | 36 | 39  | 1 | .01365406 |
| 7.   | 5 | 0  | 18  | 1 | .01167142 |
| 8.   | 6 | 0  | 3   | 1 | .02875689 |
| 9.   | 7 | 0  | 51  | 0 | .        |
| 10.  | 7 | 51 | 675 | 1 | .06215003 |

Here is the interpretation: At time $t1 = 50$, the hazard contribution $h_1$ is .0150. At time $t1 = 6$, the hazard contribution $h_2$ is .0204.

In observation 3, no hazard contribution is stored. Observation 3 contains a missing because observation 3 did not fail at time 1.

All of which is to say that values of the hazard contributions are stored only in observations that are marked as failing.

The baseline survivor function $S_0(t)$ is defined at all values of $t$: it changes its value when failures occur and, at times when no failures occur, $S_0(t)$ is equal to its value at the time of the last failure.

Here are some data in which we specified both `basehc(h)` and `basesurv(s)`:

```
. list id t0 t1 d h s in 1/10
```

|      | id | t0 | t1  | died | h        | s        |
|------|----|----|-----|------|----------|----------|
| 1.   | 1  | 0  | 50  | 1    | .01503465 | .68100303 |
| 2.   | 2  | 0  | 6   | 1    | .02035303 | .89846438 |
| 3.   | 3  | 0  | 1   | 0    | .        | .99089681 |
| 4.   | 3  | 1  | 16  | 1    | .03339642 | .84087361 |
| 5.   | 4  | 0  | 36  | 0    | .        | .7527663 |
| 6.   | 4  | 36 | 39  | 1    | .01365406 | .73259264 |
| 7.   | 5  | 0  | 18  | 1    | .01167142 | .82144038 |
| 8.   | 6  | 0  | 3   | 1    | .02875689 | .93568733 |
| 9.   | 7  | 0  | 51  | 0    | .        | .6705895 |
| 10.  | 7  | 51 | 675 | 1    | .06215003 | .26115633 |

At time $t1 = 50$, the baseline survivor function is .6810 or, more precisely, $S_0(50 + 0) = .6810$. What we mean by $S(t)$ is $S(t+0)$, the probability of surviving just beyond time $t$. This is done to clarify that the probability does not include failure at precisely time $t$.

Understanding what is stored is easier if we sort by $t1$:

```
. sort t1
. list id t0 t1 d h s in 1/18
```

|      | id | t0 | t1 | died | h        | s        |
|------|----|----|----|------|----------|----------|
| 1.   | 15 | 0  | 1  | 1    | .00910319 | .99089681 |
| 2.   | 20 | 0  | 1  | 0    | .        | .99089681 |
| 3.   | 3  | 0  | 1  | 0    | .        | .99089681 |
| 4.   | 45 | 0  | 1  | 0    | .        | .99089681 |
| 5.   | 61 | 0  | 2  | 1    | .02775802 | .96339147 |
| 6.   | 75 | 0  | 2  | 1    | .02775802 | .96339147 |
| 7.   | 43 | 0  | 2  | 1    | .02775802 | .96339147 |
| 8.   | 46 | 0  | 2  | 0    | .        | .96339147 |
| 9.   | 95 | 0  | 2  | 0    | .        | .96339147 |
| 10.  | 39 | 0  | 2  | 0    | .        | .96339147 |
| 11.  | 42 | 0  | 3  | 1    | .02875689 | .93568733 |
| 12.  | 6  | 0  | 3  | 1    | .02875689 | .93568733 |
| 13.  | 54 | 0  | 3  | 1    | .02875689 | .93568733 |
| 14.  | 68 | 0  | 3  | 0    | .        | .93568733 |
| 15.  | 23 | 0  | 3  | 0    | .        | .93568733 |
| 16.  | 60 | 0  | 3  | 0    | .        | .93568733 |
| 17.  | 72 | 0  | 4  | 0    | .        | .93568733 |
| 18.  | 94 | 0  | 4  | 0    | .        | .93568733 |

Note that the baseline hazard contribution is stored on every failure record—and if multiple failures occur at a time, the value of the hazard contribution is repeated—and the baseline survival is stored on every record. (More correctly, baseline values are stored on records that meet the criterion and which were used in estimation. If some observations are explicitly or implicitly excluded from the estimation, their baseline values will be set to missing no matter what.)

With this listing, we get a better indication as to how the hazard contributions are used to calculate the survival function. Since the patient with $id = 15$ died at time $t_1 = 1$, his hazard contribution is $h_{15} = .00910319$. Since that was the only death at $t_1 = 1$, the estimated survival function at this time is $S_0(1) = 1 - h_{15} = 1 - .00910319 = .99089681$. The next death occurs at time $t_1 = 2$, and the hazard contribution at this time for patient 61 is $h_{61} = .02775802$. Multiplying the previous survival function value by $1 - h_{61}$ gives the new survival function at $t_1 = 2$ as $S_0(2) = .96339147$. The other survival function values are then calculated in succession, using this method at each failure time. At times when no failures occur, the survival function remains unchanged.

If we had estimated a stratified model—if we had specified the **strata()** option—the recorded baseline hazard contribution and survival on each record would be for the stratum of the record.

## ❑ Technical Note

If you want the baseline hazard contribution stored on every record for which it is defined and not just the failure records, you would do the following:

```
. sort _t _d
. by _t: replace h = h[_N]
```

The above assumes that you specified **basehc(h)** when estimating the Cox model. If you also specified the **strata()** option, say **strata(group)**, the instructions would be

```
. sort group _t _d
. by group _t: replace h = h[_N]
```

In both of these examples, all we did was place the data in time order: we put the failures at the end of each time group, and then copied the last value of **h** within each time to all the observations for that time.

It is a useful test of your understanding to consider obtaining the estimate $S_0(t)$ from the $h_i$'s for yourself. One way you could do that is

```
. sort _t _d
. by _t: keep if _d & _n==_N
. gen s = 1-h
. replace s = s[_n-1]*s if _n>1
```

If you had obtained stratified estimates, the equivalent code would be

```
. sort group _t _d
. by group _t: keep if _d & _n==_N
. gen s = 1-h
. by group: replace s = s[_n-1]*s if _n>1
```

❑

## ▷ Example

One thing to do with the baseline functions is to graph them. Remember, baseline functions refer to the values of the functions when all covariates are set to 0. Let's graph the survival curve for the heart transplant model we have been estimating and, to make the baseline curve reasonable, let us do that at **age** = 40 and **year** = 70. (The following technical note provides important information on why baseline values should be chosen to be reasonable, which is to say, in the range of the data.)

Thus, we will begin by creating variables that, when 0, correspond to the baseline values we desire, and then re-estimate our model, specifying the basesurv() option:

```
. gen age40 = age - 40

. gen year70 = year - 70

. stcox age40 posttran surg year70, bases(s) nolog
Cox regression -- Breslow method for ties
No. of subjects =          103        Number of obs   =        172
No. of failures =           75
Time at risk    =       31938.1
                                       LR chi2(4)      =      17.56
Log likelihood  =     -289.53378       Prob > chi2     =     0.0015
```

| _t _d | Haz. Ratio | Std. Err. | z | P>\|z\| | [95% Conf. Interval] |  |
|---|---|---|---|---|---|---|
| age40 | 1.030224 | .0143201 | 2.14 | 0.032 | 1.002536 | 1.058677 |
| posttran | .9787243 | .3032597 | -0.07 | 0.945 | .5332291 | 1.796416 |
| surgery | .3738278 | .163204 | -2.25 | 0.024 | .1588759 | .8796 |
| year70 | .8873107 | .059808 | -1.77 | 0.076 | .7775022 | 1.012628 |

```
. summarize s
```

| Variable | Obs | Mean | Std. Dev. | Min | Max |
|---|---|---|---|---|---|
| s | 172 | .629187 | .2530009 | .130666 | .9908968 |

Note first that our adjustments to the variables did not affect the model estimated. Also, for your information, the s variable we have just generated is the s variable we listed above.

Here is a graph of the baseline survival curve:

```
. graph s _t, c(J) s(i) sort
```

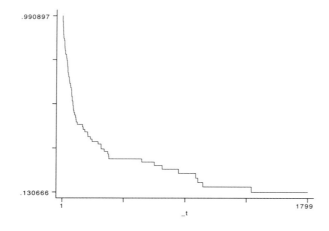

❏ Technical Note

If you specify the `basechazard()` or `basesurv()` options, for numerical accuracy reasons it is important that the baseline functions correspond to something reasonable in your data. Remember, the baseline functions correspond to all covariates equal to 0 in your Cox model.

Consider, for instance, a Cox model that included the variable calendar year among the covariates. Say `year` varied between 1980 and 1996. Then the baseline functions would correspond to year 0, almost 2,000 years in the past. Say the estimated coefficient on `year` was $-.2$ (meaning the hazard ratio for one year to the next is a reasonable 0.82).

Think carefully about the contribution to the predicted log cumulative hazard: it would be approximately $-.2 \times 2,000 = -400$. Now $e^{-400} \approx 10^{-173}$ which, on a digital computer, is 1. There is simply no hope that $H_0(t)e^{-400}$ will produce an accurate estimate of $H(t)$.

Even with less extreme numbers, problems arise even in the calculation of the baseline survivor function. Baseline hazard contributions very near 1 produce baseline survivor functions with the steps differing by tens of orders of magnitudes, because the calculation of the survivor function is cumulative. Producing a meaningful graph of such a survivor function is hopeless, and adjusting the survivor function (as opposed to the hazard contribution) to other values of the covariates is too much work.

For these reasons, it is important that covariate values of 0 be meaningful if you are going to specify the `basechazard()` or `basesurv()` options. As the baseline values move to absurdity, the first problem you will encounter is a baseline survivor function that is too hard to interpret, even though the baseline hazard contributions are estimated accurately. Further out, the procedure Stata uses to estimate the baseline hazard contributions will break down—it will produce results that are exactly 1.

This, in fact, occurs with the Stanford heart transplant data:

```
. stcox age posttran surg year, basec(ch) bases(s)
(output omitted )
. summarize ch s
```

| Variable | Obs | Mean | Std. Dev. | Min | Max |
|---|---|---|---|---|---|
| ch | 172 | 745.1134 | 682.8671 | 11.88239 | 2573.637 |
| s | 172 | 1.45e-07 | 9.43e-07 | 0 | 6.24e-06 |

The hint that there are problems is that the values of `ch` are huge and the values of `s` are close to zero. In this dataset, it is `age` (which ranges from 8 to 64 with a mean value of 40) and `year` (which ranges from 67 to 74) that are the problems. The baseline functions correspond to a newborn at the turn of the century on the waiting list for a heart transplant!

To obtain accurate estimates of the baseline functions, you should type

```
. gen age40 = age-40
. gen year70 = year-70
. stcox age40 posttran surg year70, basec(ch) bases(s)
(output omitted )
. summarize ch s
```

| Variable | Obs | Mean | Std. Dev. | Min | Max |
|---|---|---|---|---|---|
| ch | 172 | .5685743 | .521076 | .0090671 | 1.963868 |
| s | 172 | .629187 | .2530009 | .130666 | .9908968 |

Adjusting the variables makes no difference in terms of the coefficient (and hence hazard ratio) estimates, but it changes the values at which the baseline functions are estimated to be within the range of the data.

❏

## Cox regression residuals

Stata can calculate score residuals, efficient score residuals (esr), martingale residuals, Schoenfeld residuals, and scaled Schoenfeld residuals with options specified to the `stcox` command. Cox–Snell and deviance residuals can be calculated with options to `predict` and, in the case of time-varying covariates and multiple observations per subject, cumulative martingale and cumulative Cox–Snell residuals can also be calculated using `predict`.

Although the uses of residuals vary and depend on the data and user preferences, traditional and suggested uses are the following: Cox–Snell residuals are useful in assessing overall model fit; martingale residuals are useful in determining the functional form of covariates to be included in the model and are occasionally useful in assessing lack of fit; Schoenfeld and score residuals are useful for checking and testing the proportional hazard assumption, examining leverage points, and identifying outliers; and deviance residuals are useful in examining model accuracy and identifying outliers.

▷ Example

Let us first examine the use of Cox–Snell residuals. Using the cancer data, we first perform a Cox regression requesting that martingale residuals be calculated. Martingale residuals must be requested because these are used by `predict` to calculate the Cox–Snell residuals. If we forget, `predict` will issue an error message reminding us of this.

```
. use cancer
(Patient Survival in Drug Trial)
. stset studytime, failure(died)
  (output omitted )
. stcox age drug, mgale(mg)
  (output omitted )
. predict cs, csnell
```

The first command performs the Cox regression, calculates the martingale residuals, and saves them in the variable `mg`. In the second command, the `csnell` option tells `predict` to output to a new variable, `cs`, the Cox–Snell residuals. If the Cox regression model fits the data, then these residuals should have a standard censored exponential distribution with hazard ratio 1. We can verify the model's fit by calculating, based for example on the Kaplan–Meier survival estimates or the Aalen–Nelson estimator, an empirical estimate of the cumulative hazard function, using the Cox–Snell residuals as the time variable and the data's original censoring variable. If the model fits the data, then the plot of the cumulative hazard versus `cs` should be a straight line with slope 1.

To do this, we first `stset` the data, specifying `cs` as our new failure time variable and `died` as the failure/censoring indicator. We then use the `sts generate` command to generate the variable `km` containing the Kaplan–Meier survival estimates. Lastly, we generate the cumulative hazard `H` using the relationship $H = -\ln s$ and plot it against `cs`.

```
. stset cs, failure(died)
      failure event:  died ~= 0 & died ~= .
obs. time interval:  (0, cs]
 exit on or before:  failure
 exit on or before:  failure
```

```
       48  total obs.
        0  exclusions
```

```
       48  obs. remaining, representing
       31  failures in single record/single failure data
       31  total analysis time at risk, at risk from t =          0
                            earliest observed entry t =          0
                                last observed exit t =   3.343572
```

```
. sts generate km=s

. gen double H=-ln(km)
(1 missing value generated)
. graph H cs cs, c(ll) s(..) xlab ylab
```

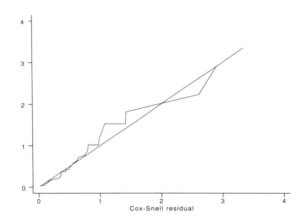

We specified cs twice in the graph command so that a reference 45° line is plotted. Comparing the jagged line with the reference line, we observe that the Cox model does not fit these data too badly.

❏ Technical Note

The statement "if the Cox regression model fits the data, then the Cox–Snell residuals have a standard censored exponential distribution with hazard ratio 1" only holds if the true parameters $\beta$ and the true cumulative baseline hazard function, $H_0(t)$, are used in the calculation of the residuals. Since we use estimates $\widehat{\beta}$ and $\widehat{H}_0(t)$, deviations from the 45° line in the above plots could be partially due to uncertainty about these estimates. This is particularly important for small sample sizes and in the right-hand tail of the distribution where the baseline hazard is more variable due to the reduced effective sample caused by prior failures and censoring.

❏

Let us now examine the martingale residuals. Remember that these have already been calculated and are stored in the variable mg. In the following graph, we use the ksm command to plot these residuals against `studytime`, against rank of `studytime`, and against each of the two covariates—age and `drug`.

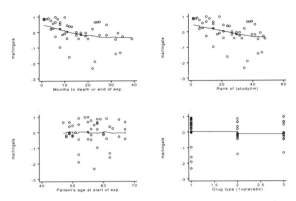

Martingale residuals with an overimposed running mean smoother

We used the `ksm` command to obtain a plot of the running mean smoother to ease interpretation. Alternatively, a lowess smoother or other smoother could be used; see [R] **ksm**. Martingale residuals can be interpreted as the difference over time of the observed number of failures minus that predicted by the model. If the model fits, we expect to see the smooth curve roughly equal to zero everywhere in plots of martingale residuals versus survival time or ranked survival time. In our top two plots, the smooth curve is slightly above zero for patients with short survival times, and slightly below zero for patients with longer survival times, suggesting a slight lack of fit.

Plots of martingale residuals versus individual covariates are useful in assessing whether an adequate functional form of the covariate has been used in the model. If the smooth curve is close to being linear, then the functional form of the covariate is adequate and no transformation is necessary. If the fitted smooth curve is far from linear, however, a transformed covariate may provided a better fit. In our example, the fitted curves are fairly linear for both covariates, so no transformation is necessary. Note that a linear smooth curve does not necessarily imply that the best functional form of the covariate is being used, only that the form selected is adequate.    ◁

Plots of martingale residuals are sometimes difficult to interpret because these residuals are skewed, taking values in $(-\infty, 1)$. For this reason, deviance residuals are preferred for examining model accuracy and outlier identification.

▷ Example

Using the cancer data, we can calculate the deviance residual using `predict`. It is necessary that martingale residuals be calculated and saved when fitting the Cox model since `predict` requires that. Deviance residuals are a rescaling of the martingale residuals so that they are symmetric about zero and thus more like residuals obtained from linear regression. Plots of these residuals against survival time, rank order of survival, or observation number can be useful in identifying aberrant observations and assessing model fit.

```
. stcox age drug, mgale(mg)
  (output omitted )
. quietly predict double dev, deviance
```

. ksm dev studytime, xlab ylab

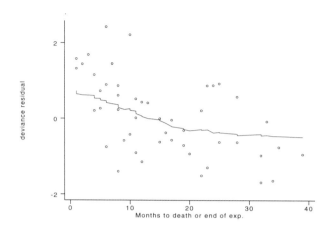

. egen rtime = rank(studytime)

. ksm dev rtime, xlab ylab

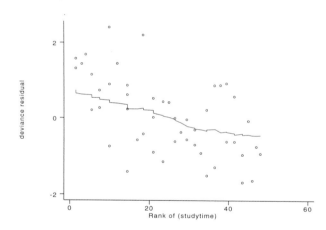

We used the `ksm` command to obtain a plot of the running mean smoother to ease interpretation. We can see from these plots that the deviance residuals are slightly larger for short survival times and then decrease. This pattern suggests that the Cox model will slightly underestimate the probability of failure for patients with short study times and will slightly overestimate the probability of failure for patients with longer times.

Deviance residuals are also useful in identifying possible outliers. Examination of the graph above reveals two observations as possible outliers. Both have deviance residuals greater than 2. The first patient, a 55 year old on drug 3, with a deviance residual of 2.42 and a predicted hazard ratio of 4.25, died at 6 months. The second patient, a 54 year old on drug 3, with a deviance residual of 2.21 and a predicted hazard ratio of 3.81, died at 10 months. Given these patients' covariate structure and predicted hazard ratio, they should have lived longer. Note that predicted hazard ratio can be obtained using `predict`'s `hr` option.

◁

In evaluating the adequacy of the fitted model, it is important to determine if any one or any group of observations has a disproportionate influence on the estimated parameters. This is known as influence or leverage analysis. The preferred method of performing influence or leverage analysis is to compare the estimated parameter, $\widehat{\beta}$, obtained from the full data, with estimated parameters $\widehat{\beta}_{(i)}$, obtained by fitting the model to the $n-1$ observations remaining after the $i$th observation is removed. If $\widehat{\beta} - \widehat{\beta}_{(i)}$ is close to zero, then the $i$th observation has little influence on the estimate. The process is repeated for all observations included in the original model. To compute these differences for a dataset with $n$ observations, we would have to execute `stcox` $n$ additional times, which could be impractical for large datasets. In such cases, an approximation to $\widehat{\beta} - \widehat{\beta}_{(i)}$ based on the efficient score residuals can be calculated as

$$\boldsymbol{\Delta}' \mathbf{V}(\widehat{\beta})$$

where $\mathbf{V}(\widehat{\beta})$ is the variance–covariance matrix and $\boldsymbol{\Delta}'$ is the matrix of efficient score residuals. The difference $\widehat{\beta} - \widehat{\beta}_{(i)}$ is commonly referred to as `dfbeta` in the literature; see [R] **regression diagnostics**.

## ▷ Example

We now perform an influence analysis using the cancer data. To do this, we first obtain the efficient score residuals by typing `stcox age drug, esr(esr*)`. This command generates two new variables, `esr1` and `esr2`, corresponding to the two covariates in the model. The first variable, `esr1`, contains the efficient score residuals corresponding to the first covariate listed in the model (`age`), and the second variable, `esr2`, contains the efficient score residuals corresponding to the second covariate listed in the model (`drug`). We then use the `mkmat` command to create a matrix of the efficient score residuals, we obtain the variance–covariance matrix, and then we multiply the two matrices.

```
. stcox age drug, esr(esr*)
(output omitted )
. mkmat esr1 esr2, matrix(esr)
. mat V = e(V)
. mat Inf = esr*V
. svmat Inf, names(s)
```

The last command saves the estimates of `dfbeta` $= \widehat{\beta} - \widehat{\beta}_{(i)}$ in the variables `s1` and `s2`. We can now label these new variables and plot them versus time or observation number to identify observations with disproportionate influence.

```
. label var s1 "dfbeta - Age"
. label var s2 "dfbeta - Drug"
. graph s1 studytime, xlab ylab yline(0)
```

*(Graphs on next page)*

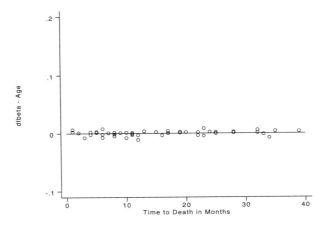

```
. graph s2 studytime, xlab ylab yline(0)
```

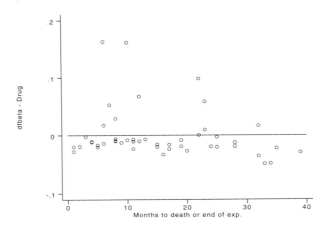

◁

## Checking and testing the proportional hazard assumption

The most important assumption of the Cox proportional hazards model is that the hazard ratio is proportional over time. Using an example from Garrett (1997), suppose a group of cancer patients on an experimental treatment are followed for 10 years. If the hazard of dying for the nontreated group is twice the rate as that for the treated group (HR = 2.0), the proportional hazards assumption implies that this ratio is the same at one year, two years, or at any point on the time scale. Because the Cox model is constrained to follow this assumption, it is important to evaluate its validity. If the assumption fails, alternative modeling choices would be more appropriate (e.g., a stratified Cox model).

We provide three programs, stphtest, stphplot and stcoxkm, which can be used to evaluate the proportional hazards assumption. Both stphplot and stcoxkm are graphical methods documented separately. See [R] **st stphplot** for complete description of these tests.

The test of proportional hazards implemented in `stphtest` is based on the generalization by Grambsch and Therneau (1994). They showed that many of the popular tests for proportional hazards are in fact tests of nonzero slope in a generalized linear regression of the scaled Schoenfeld residuals on functions of time. The `stphtest` command tests, for individual covariates and globally, the null hypothesis of zero slope in the appropriate regression. The test of zero slope is equivalent to testing that the log hazard ratio function is constant over time; thus, rejection of the null hypothesis of a zero slope indicates deviation from the proportional hazards assumption. The choice of time function depends on the problem at hand. The `stphtest` command allows three common choices as options, `log`, `rank` and `km`, and allows the use of any user-defined function of time through the `time()` option. Additionally, when no option is specified the tests are performed using analysis time without further transformation.

▷ Example

This example uses data from a leukemia remission study (Garrett 1997). The data consist of 42 patients who are followed over time to examine how long (`weeks`) before they go out of remission (`relapse`: 1 = yes, 0 = no). Half the patients received a new experimental drug, and the other half received a standard drug (`treatment1`: 1 = drug A, 0 = standard). White blood cell count, a strong indicator of the presence of leukemia, is divided into three categories (`wbc3cat`: 1 = normal, 2 = moderate, 3 = high).

```
. describe
Contains data from leukemia.dta
  obs:           42                        Leukemia Remission Study
  vars:           8                        4 Aug 2000 10:45
  size:         504 (90.1% of memory free)
```

|                | storage | display | value |                        |
|----------------|---------|---------|-------|------------------------|
| variable name  | type    | format  | label | variable label         |
| weeks          | byte    | %8.0g   |       | Weeks in Remission     |
| relapse        | byte    | %8.0g   | yesno | Relapse                |
| treatment1     | byte    | %8.0g   | trt1lbl | Treatment I          |
| treatment2     | byte    | %8.0g   | trt2lbl | Treatment II         |
| wbc3cat        | byte    | %9.0g   | wbclbl | White Blood Cell Count |
| wbc1           | byte    | %8.0g   |       | wbc3cat==Normal        |
| wbc2           | byte    | %8.0g   |       | wbc3cat==Moderate      |
| wbc3           | byte    | %8.0g   |       | wbc3cat==High          |

```
Sorted by:  weeks
```

In this example, we examine whether the proportional hazards assumption holds for a model with covariates `wbc2`, `wbc1`, and `treatment1`. After `stset`ting the data, we first run `stcox`, saving both the scaled and the nonscaled Schoenfeld residuals, and then use `stphtest`. `stphtest` requires that we request scaled Schoenfeld residuals if we want a separate test for each covariate and that we request the unscaled residuals if we want the global test. If we forget when we estimate the Cox model, `stphtest` will remind us.

```
. stset weeks, failure(relapse)

     failure event:  relapse ~= 0 & relapse ~= .
obs. time interval:  (0, weeks]
 exit on or before:  failure
```

```
    42  total obs.
     0  exclusions
```

```
    42  obs. remaining, representing
    30  failures in single record/single failure data
   541  total analysis time at risk, at risk from t =          0
                         earliest observed entry t =          0
                            last observed exit t =         35
```

```
. stcox treatment1 wbc2 wbc3, scaledsch(sca*) schoenfeld(sch*) nolog

        failure _d:  relapse
   analysis time _t:  weeks

Cox regression -- Breslow method for ties
```

| | | | |
|---|---|---|---|
| No. of subjects = | 42 | Number of obs   = | 42 |
| No. of failures = | 30 | | |
| Time at risk     = | 541 | | |
| | | LR chi2(3)    = | 33.02 |
| Log likelihood  =   -77.476905 | | Prob > chi2   = | 0.0000 |

| _t _d | Haz. Ratio | Std. Err. | z | P>\|z\| | [95% Conf. Interval] | |
|---|---|---|---|---|---|---|
| treatment1 | .2834551 | .1229874 | -2.91 | 0.004 | .1211042 | .6634517 |
| wbc2 | 3.637825 | 2.201306 | 2.13 | 0.033 | 1.111134 | 11.91015 |
| wbc3 | 10.92214 | 7.088783 | 3.68 | 0.000 | 3.06093 | 38.97284 |

```
. stphtest, rank detail

    Test of proportional hazards assumption

    Time:  Rank(t)
```

| | rho | chi2 | df | Prob>chi2 |
|---|---|---|---|---|
| treatment1 | -0.02802 | 0.02 | 1 | 0.8755 |
| wbc2 | -0.10665 | 0.32 | 1 | 0.5735 |
| wbc3 | -0.02238 | 0.02 | 1 | 0.8987 |
| global test | | 0.51 | 3 | 0.9159 |

Because we saved both the Schoenfeld residuals and the scaled Schoenfeld residuals by specifying the detail option on the stphtest command, both covariate-specific and global tests were produced. We can see that there is no evidence that the proportional hazards assumption has been violated. When we saved the residuals using stcox, it does not matter what we named them, it just matters that we did save them.

Another variable on this dataset measures a different drug (treatment2: 1 = drug B, 0 = standard). We now wish to examine the proportional hazards assumption for the previous model by substituting treatment2 for treatment1.

After dropping the previous Schoenfeld and scaled Schoenfeld residuals, we fit a new Cox model and perform the test for proportional hazards.

```
. stcox treatment2 wbc2 wbc3, scaledsch(sca*) schoenfeld(sch*) nolog

         failure _d:  relapse
   analysis time _t:  weeks

Cox regression -- Breslow method for ties

No. of subjects =            42                    Number of obs   =          42
No. of failures =            30
Time at risk    =           541
                                                   LR chi2(3)      =       23.93
Log likelihood  =    -82.019053                    Prob > chi2     =      0.0000
```

| _t _d | Haz. Ratio | Std. Err. | z | P>\|z\| | [95% Conf. Interval] | |
|---|---|---|---|---|---|---|
| treatment2 | .8483777 | .3469054 | -0.40 | 0.688 | .3806529 | 1.890816 |
| wbc2 | 3.409628 | 2.050784 | 2.04 | 0.041 | 1.048905 | 11.08353 |
| wbc3 | 14.0562 | 8.873693 | 4.19 | 0.000 | 4.078529 | 48.44314 |

```
. stphtest, rank detail

     Test of proportional hazards assumption

     Time:  Rank(t)
```

| | rho | chi2 | df | Prob>chi2 |
|---|---|---|---|---|
| treatment2 | -0.63673 | 15.47 | 1 | 0.0001 |
| wbc2 | -0.17380 | 0.90 | 1 | 0.3426 |
| wbc3 | -0.08294 | 0.21 | 1 | 0.6481 |
| global test | | 15.76 | 3 | 0.0013 |

treatment2 clearly violates the proportional hazards assumption. A single hazard ratio describing the effect of this drug is inappropriate.

◁

## ❏ Technical Note

The test of the proportional hazards assumption is based on the principle that the assumption restricts $\beta_j(t) = \beta$ for all $t$, which implies that a plot of $\beta_j(t)$ versus time will have a slope of zero. Grambsch and Therneau (1994) showed that $E(s_j^*) + \widehat{\beta} \approx \beta(t_j)$, where $s_j^*$ is the scaled Schoenfeld residual and $\widehat{\beta}$ is the estimated coefficient from the Cox model. Thus, a plot of $s_j^* + \beta$ versus some function of time provides a graphical assessment of the assumption.

❏

## ❏ Technical Note

The tests of the proportional hazards assumption assume homogeneity of variance across risk sets. This allows the use of the estimated overall (pooled) variance–covariance matrix in the equations. Although these tests have been shown by Grambsch and Therneau (1994) to be fairly robust to departures from this assumption, care must be exercised where this assumption may not hold, particularly when performing a stratified Cox model. In such cases, we recommend that the proportional hazards assumption be checked separately for each stratum.

❏

# Acknowledgments

We thank Peter Sasieni of the Imperial Cancer Research Fund for his statistical advice and guidance in implementing the robust variance estimator for this command. We would also like to thank Joanne M. Garrett of the University of North Carolina at Chapel Hill for her contributions to the `stphtest` command.

# Saved Results

`stcox` saves in `e()`:

Scalars

| | | | |
|---|---|---|---|
| e(N) | number of observations | e(ll) | log likelihood |
| e(N_sub) | number of subjects | e(ll_0) | log likelihood, constant-only model |
| e(risk) | total time at risk | e(N_clust) | number of clusters |
| e(df_m) | model degrees of freedom | e(chi2) | $\chi^2$ |
| e(r2_p) | pseudo $R$-squared | | |

Macros

| | | | |
|---|---|---|---|
| e(cmd) | cox | e(chi2type) | Wald or LR; type of model $\chi^2$ test |
| e(cmd2) | stcox | e(offset) | offset |
| e(depvar) | _t | e(mgale) | var. containing partial martingale residuals |
| e(clustvar) | name of cluster variable | e(vl_esr) | variables containing partial efficient score residuals |
| e(N_fail) | number of failures | | |
| e(t0) | _t0 | e(vl_sch) | variables containing Schoenfeld residuals |
| e(method) | requested estimation method | e(vl_ssc) | variables containing scaled Schoenfeld residuals |
| e(ties) | method used for handling ties | | |
| e(texp) | function used for time-varying covariates | e(bases) | variable containing baseline survival function |
| e(vcetype) | covariance estimation method | e(basec) | variable containing baseline cumulative haz. function |
| e(predict) | program used to implement **predict** | e(basehc) | variable containing baseline hazard contributions |

Matrices

| | | | |
|---|---|---|---|
| e(b) | coefficient vector | e(V) | variance–covariance matrix of the estimators |

Functions

| | |
|---|---|
| e(sample) | marks estimation sample |

`stphtest` saves in `r()`:

Scalars

| | | | |
|---|---|---|---|
| r(df) | global test degrees of freedom | r(chi2) | global test $\chi^2$ |

# Methods and Formulas

stcox and stphtest are implemented as ado-files.

The proportional hazards model with time-dependent explanatory variables was first suggested by Cox (1972). For an introductory explanation, see, for example, Hosmer and Lemeshow (1999, Chapters 3, 4, and 7), Kahn and Sempos (1989, 193–198), and Selvin (1996, 391–422). For a comprehensive review of the methods in this entry, see Klein and Moeschberger (1997). For a detailed development, see Kalbfleisch and Prentice (1980).

stcox executes cox to obtain results, and the methods and formulas presented below are applicable to both cox and stcox.

Let $\mathbf{x}_i$ be the row vector of covariates for the time interval $(t_{0i}, t_i]$ for the $i$th observation in the dataset $(i = 1, \ldots, N)$. cox, and thus stcox, obtain parameter estimates $\widehat{\boldsymbol{\beta}}$ by maximizing the partial log-likelihood function

$$\ln L = \sum_{j=1}^{D} \left[ \sum_{k \in D_j} \mathbf{x}_k \boldsymbol{\beta} - d_j \ln \left\{ \sum_{i \in R_j} \exp(\mathbf{x}_i \boldsymbol{\beta}) \right\} \right]$$

where $j$ indexes the ordered failure times $t_{(j)}$ $(j = 1, \ldots, D)$, $D_j$ is the set of $d_j$ observations that fail at $t_{(j)}$, $d_j$ is the number of failures at $t_{(j)}$, and $R_j$ is the set of observations $k$ that are at risk at time $t_{(j)}$ (i.e., all $k$ such that $t_{0i} < t_{(j)} \le t_i$). See Kalbfleisch and Prentice (1980, equation (4.8), 74). This formula for $\ln L$ handles ties using the Peto–Breslow approximation (Peto 1972; Breslow 1974).

The variance of $\widehat{\boldsymbol{\beta}}$ is estimated by the conventional inverse matrix of (negative) second derivatives of $\ln L$ unless robust is specified, in which case the method of Lin and Wei (1989) is used. If cluster() is specified, the efficient score residuals are summed within cluster before application of the sandwich (robust) estimator.

See [R] **maximize** for a description of the maximization algorithm and for the translation of estimated results to hazard ratios when hr is specified.

mgale() stores in each observation the observation's contribution to the martingale residual, which we call the "partial" martingale residual—partial is our terminology. The derivative of $\ln L$ can be written as

$$\frac{\partial \ln L}{\partial \boldsymbol{\beta}} = \sum_{j=1}^{D} \sum_{i=1}^{N} \mathbf{x}_i \, dM_i(t_{(j)})$$

where

$$dM_i(t_{(j)}) = \delta_{ij} - I(t_{0i} < t_{(j)} \le t_i) \frac{d_j \exp(\mathbf{x}_i \boldsymbol{\beta})}{\sum_{\ell \in R_j} \exp(\mathbf{x}_\ell \boldsymbol{\beta})}$$

with $\delta_{ij} = 1$ if observation $i$ fails at $t_{(j)}$ and 0 otherwise. $I(\cdot)$ is the indicator function. $dM_i(t_{(j)})$ is the increment of the martingale residual for the $i$th observation due to the failures at time $t_{(j)}$. The mgale() option saves the partial martingale residuals $\Delta M_i$, which are the sum of the $dM_i(t_{(j)})$ over all failure times $t_{(j)}$ such that $t_{0i} < t_{(j)} \le t_i$. For single-record data, the partial martingale residual is the martingale residual. For multiple-record data, the martingale residual for an individual can be obtained by summing the partial martingale residuals over all observations belonging to the individual.

For a discussion of martingale residuals, see, for instance, Fleming and Harrington (1991, 163–197).

The increments of the efficient score residuals are

$$dF_{ij} = x_{ij}^* \, dM_i(t_{(j)})$$

where

$$x_{ij}^* = x_i - \frac{\sum_{\ell \in R_j} x_\ell \exp(x_\ell \beta)}{\sum_{\ell \in R_j} \exp(x_\ell \beta)}$$

When the esr() option is specified, cox and stcox create $p = \dim(x)$ new variables containing $\Delta F_i$, which are the sum of $dF_{ij}$ over all failure times $t_{(j)}$ such that $t_{0i} < t_{(j)} \le t_i$. The efficient score residuals for an individual can be obtained by summing $\Delta F_i$ over all observations $i$ belonging to the individual.

The baseline hazard contribution, if requested, is obtained as $h_j = 1 - \widehat{\alpha}_j$, where $\widehat{\alpha}_j$ is the solution of

$$\sum_{k \in D_j} \frac{\exp(x_k \beta)}{1 - \widehat{\alpha}_j^{\exp(x_k \beta)}} = \sum_{l \in R_j} \exp(x_l \beta)$$

(Kalbfleisch and Prentice 1980, equation (4.23), 85).

The baseline survivor function, if requested, is obtained as

$$S_0(t_{(j)}) = \prod_{h=0}^{j-1} \widehat{\alpha}_h$$

where $\widehat{\alpha}_0 = 1$.

The baseline cumulative hazard function, if requested, is related to the baseline survivor function calculation, yet the values of $\widehat{\alpha}_j$ are set at their starting values and are not iterated. Equivalently,

$$H_0(t_{(j)}) = \sum_{h=0}^{j-1} \frac{d_j}{\sum_{l \in R_j} \exp(x_l \beta)}$$

Tied values are handled using one of four approaches. The log likelihoods corresponding to the four approaches are given with weights (exactp does not allow weights) and offsets by

(*Continued on next page*)

$$L_{\mathrm{breslow}} = \sum_{j=1}^{D} \sum_{i \in D_j} \left[ w_i(x_i\boldsymbol{\beta} + \mathrm{offset}_i) - w_i \ln \left\{ \sum_{\ell \in R_j} w_\ell \exp(x_\ell\boldsymbol{\beta} + \mathrm{offset}_\ell) \right\} \right]$$

$$L_{\mathrm{efron}} = \sum_{j=1}^{D} \sum_{k=1}^{d_j} \left\{ \frac{1}{d_j} \sum_{i \in D_j} w_i(x_i\boldsymbol{\beta} + \mathrm{offset}_i) - \right.$$
$$\left. \left( \frac{1}{d_j} \sum_{i \in D_j} w_i \right) \ln \sum_{\ell \in R_j} w_\ell f_{kj\ell} \exp(x_\ell\boldsymbol{\beta} + \mathrm{offset}_\ell) \right\}$$

$$f_{kj\ell} = \begin{cases} \dfrac{d_j - k + 1}{d_j} & \text{if } \delta_{\ell j} = 1 \\ 1 & \text{otherwise} \end{cases}$$

$$L_{\mathrm{exactm}} = \sum_{j=1}^{D} \ln \int_0^{\infty} \prod_{\ell \in D_j} \left\{ 1 - \exp\left( -\frac{e_\ell}{s}t \right) \right\}^{w_\ell} \exp(-t)dt$$

$$e_\ell = \exp(x_\ell\boldsymbol{\beta} + \mathrm{offset}_\ell)$$

$$s = \sum_{\substack{k \in R_j \\ k \notin D_j}} w_k \exp(x_k\boldsymbol{\beta} + \mathrm{offset}_k) = \text{sum of weighted nondeath risk scores}$$

$$L_{\mathrm{exactp}} = \sum_{j=1}^{D} \left\{ \sum_{i \in R_j} \delta_{ij}(x_i\boldsymbol{\beta} + \mathrm{offset}_i) - \ln f(r_j, d_j) \right\}$$

$$f(r, d) = f(r - 1, d) + f(r - 1, d - 1) \exp(x_k\boldsymbol{\beta} + \mathrm{offset}_k)$$

$$k = r^{\mathrm{th}} \text{ observation in the set } R_j$$

$$f(r, d) = \begin{cases} 0 & \text{if } r < d \\ 1 & \text{if } d = 0 \end{cases}$$

Calculations for the exact marginal log-likelihood (and associated derivatives) are obtained with 15-point Gauss–Laguerre quadrature. The `breslow` and `efron` options both provide approximations of the exact marginal log-likelihood. The `efron` approximation is a better (closer) approximation, but the `breslow` is a much faster approximation. The choice of which approximation to use in a given situation should generally be driven by the proportion of ties in the data.

Note that weights are not allowed with the `exactp` method.

Cox–Snell residuals are calculated using

$$r_{C_i} = \delta_i. - r_{M_i}$$

where $r_{M_i}$ are the martingale residuals and $\delta_i.$ is a censoring indicator equal to 1 if the $i$ observation is a failure and 0 otherwise. The martingale residuals are nonnegative values following an exponential distribution with mean 1. Modified Cox–Snell residuals are defined similarly, except that the residual is augmented by some positive constant if the observation is censored. The most common modifications are to add either 1 or the Crowley–Hu adjustment of $\ln 2 \approx .693$ (which is the median of an exponential distribution with parameter 1).

Martingale residuals are calculated using

$$r_{M_i} = \delta_{i.} - \sum_{j=1}^{D} I(t_{0i} < t_{(j)} \le t_i) \frac{d_j \exp(x_i\boldsymbol{\beta} + \text{offset}_i)}{\sum\limits_{\ell \in R_j} \exp(x_\ell\boldsymbol{\beta} + \text{offset}_\ell)}$$

These residuals are in $(-\infty, 1)$.

Using the Breslow–Peto approach, we have

$$r_{M_i} = 1 - \exp(x_i\boldsymbol{\beta} + \text{offset}_i) \sum_{k:t_k \le t_i} \frac{w_k \delta_{k.}}{\sum_{\ell \in R_i} w_\ell \exp(x_\ell\boldsymbol{\beta} + \text{offset}_\ell)}$$

Using the Efron approach, we have

$$r_{M_i} = \left\{ w_i - \frac{1}{d_i} \left( \sum_{j=1}^{d_i} w_i \right) \frac{\exp(x_i\boldsymbol{\beta} + \text{offset}_i)}{\sum_{\ell \in R_i} w_\ell f_{ij\ell} \exp(x_\ell\boldsymbol{\beta} + \text{offset}_\ell)} \right\} \Big/ w_i$$

Deviance residuals are calculated using

$$r_{D_i} = \text{sign}(r_{M_i}) \left[ -2 \left\{ r_{M_i} + \delta_{i.} \log(\delta_{i.} - r_{M_i}) \right\} \right]^{1/2}$$

These are expected to be symmetric about zero, but do not necessarily sum to zero.

Schoenfeld residuals are calculated using the Breslow–Peto approach as

$$r_{uS_i} = \sum_{j=1}^{D} \delta_{ij} \left\{ x_{ui} - \frac{\sum\limits_{\ell \in R_j} x_{u\ell} \exp(x_\ell\boldsymbol{\beta} + \text{offset}_\ell)}{\sum\limits_{\ell \in R_j} \exp(x_\ell\boldsymbol{\beta} + \text{offset}_\ell)} \right\}$$

Using the Efron approach, we have

$$r_{uS_i} = \sum_{j=1}^{D} \delta_{ij} \left\{ x_{ui} - \frac{\sum\limits_{\ell \in R_j} x_{u\ell} f_{ij\ell} \exp(x_\ell\boldsymbol{\beta} + \text{offset}_\ell)}{\sum\limits_{\ell \in R_j} f_{ij\ell} \exp(x_\ell\boldsymbol{\beta} + \text{offset}_\ell)} \right\}$$

Note that these are for each of the covariates, $u = 1, \ldots, p$.

Grambsch and Therneau (1994) presented a scaled adjustment for the Schoenfeld residuals which permits the interpretation of the smoothed residuals as a nonparametric estimate of the log hazard ratio function. These are defined at each death event as

$$r_{uS_i^*} = \widehat{\beta}_u + D(S\widehat{V}^{-1})_{ui}$$

where $D$ is the total number of deaths, $S$ is the matrix of Schoenfeld residuals, and $\widehat{V}$ is the variance matrix estimate. These residuals are centered at $\widehat{\beta}_u$ for each of the covariates and should have slope zero when plotted against functions of time. The `stphtest` command uses these residuals, tests the null hypothesis that the slope is equal to zero for each covariate in the model, and performs the global test proposed by Grambsch and Therneau (1994). The test of zero slope is equivalent to testing that the log hazard ratio function is constant over time.

For a specified function of time, $g(t)$, the statistic for testing individual covariates is

$$\frac{\sum_{i=1}^{d_i}\left\{g_i(t) - \overline{g}(t)\right\}r_{uS_i^*}}{\sqrt{d\widehat{V_{uu}}\sum_{i=1}^{d_i}\left\{g_i(t) - \overline{g}(t)\right\}^2}}$$

which is asymptotically distributed as a $\chi^2$ random variate with 1 degree of freedom.

The statistic for the global tests is calculated as

$$\left[\sum_{i=1}^{d_i}\left\{g_i(t) - \overline{g}(t)\right\}r_{uS_i^*}\right]'\left[\frac{d\widehat{V}}{\sum_{i=1}^{d_i}\left\{g_i(t) - \overline{g}(t)\right\}^2}\right]\left[\sum_{i=1}^{d_i}\left\{g_i(t) - \overline{g}(t)\right\}r_{uS_i^*}\right]$$

which is asymptotically distributed as a $\chi^2$ random variate with $p$ degrees of freedom.

The equations for the scaled Schoenfeld residuals and the two test statistics just described assume homogeneity of variance across risk sets. Although these tests are fairly robust to deviations from this assumption, care must be exercised, particularly when dealing with a stratified Cox model.

# References

Breslow, N. E. 1974. Covariance analysis of censored survival data. *Biometrics* 30: 89–99.

Cleves, M. 1999. ssa13: Analysis of multiple failure-time data with Stata. *Stata Technical Bulletin* 49: 30–39. Reprinted in *Stata Technical Bulletin Reprints*, vol. 9, pp. 338–349.

Cox, D. R. 1972. Regression models and life-tables (with discussion). *Journal of the Royal Statistical Society*, Series B 34: 187–220.

——. 1975. Partial likelihood. *Biometrika* 62: 269–276.

Cox, D. R. and D. Oakes. 1984. *Analysis of Survival Data*. London: Chapman & Hall.

Cox, D. R. and E. J. Snell. 1968. A general definition of residuals (with discussion). *Journal of the Royal Statistical Society B* 30: 248–275.

Crowley, J. and M. Hu. 1977. Covariance analysis of heart transplant survival data. *Journal of the American Statistical Association* 72: 27–36.

Fleming, T. R. and D. P. Harrington. 1991. *Counting Processes and Survival Analysis*. New York: John Wiley & Sons.

Garrett, J. M. 1997. gr23: Graphical assessment of the Cox model proportional hazards assumption. *Stata Technical Bulletin* 35: 9–14. Reprinted in *Stata Technical Bulletin Reprints*, vol. 6, pp. 38–44.

Grambsch, P. M. and T. M. Therneau. 1994. Proportional hazards tests and diagnostics based on weighted residuals. *Biometrika* 81: 515–526.

Hosmer, D. W., Jr., and S. Lemeshow. 1999. *Applied Survival Analysis*. New York: John Wiley & Sons.

Jenkins, S. P. 1997. sbe17: Discrete time proportional hazards regression. *Stata Technical Bulletin* 39: 22–32. Reprinted in *Stata Technical Bulletin Reprints*, vol. 7, pp. 109–121.

Kahn, H. A. and C. T. Sempos. 1989. *Statistical Methods in Epidemiology*. New York: Oxford University Press.

Kalbfleisch, J. D. and R. L. Prentice. 1980. *The Statistical Analysis of Failure Time Data.* New York: John Wiley & Sons.

Klein, J. P. and M. L. Moeschberger. 1997. *Survival Analysis: Techniques for Censored and Truncated data.* New York: Springer-Verlag.

Lin, D. Y. and L. J. Wei. 1989. The robust inference for the Cox proportional hazards model. *Journal of the American Statistical Association* 84: 1074–1078.

Peto, R. 1972. Contribution to the discussion of paper by D. R. Cox. *Journal of the Royal Statistical Society*, Series B 34: 205–207.

Rogers, W. H. 1994. ssa4: *Ex post* tests and diagnostics for a proportional hazards model. *Stata Technical Bulletin* 19: 23–27. Reprinted in *Stata Technical Bulletin Reprints*, vol. 4, pp. 186–191.

Schoenfeld, D. 1982. Partial residuals for the proportional hazards regression model. *Biometrika* 69: 239–241.

Selvin, S. 1996. *Statistical Analysis of Epidemiologic Data.* 2d ed. New York: Oxford University Press.

## Also See

| | |
|---|---|
| **Complementary:** | [R] **adjust**, [R] **lincom**, [R] **linktest**, [R] **lrtest**, [R] **mfx**, [R] **predict**, [R] **st stphplot**, [R] **st sts**, [R] **st stset**, [R] **test**, [R] **testnl**, [R] **vce** |
| **Related:** | [R] **st streg** |
| **Background:** | [U] **16.5 Accessing coefficients and standard errors**, [U] **23 Estimation and post-estimation commands**, [U] **23.11 Obtaining robust variance estimates**, [R] **maximize**, [R] **st** |

# Title

> **st stdes** — Describe survival-time data

# Syntax

stdes [if *exp*] [in *range*] [, weight noshow]

stdes is for use with survival-time data; see [R] **st**. You must stset your data before using this command. by ... : may be used with stdes; see [R] **by**.

# Description

stdes presents a brief description of the st data in a computer or data-based sense rather than in an analytical or statistical sense.

stdes is appropriate for use with single- or multiple-record, single- or multiple-failure, st data.

# Options

weight specifies that you wish the description to use weighted rather than unweighted statistics. weight does nothing unless you specified a weight when you stset the data. The weight option, and ignoring the weights, is unique to stdes. The purpose of stdes is to describe the data in a computer sense—the number of records, etc.—and for that purpose, the weights are best ignored.

noshow prevents stdes from showing the key st variables. This option is rarely used since most people type stset, show or stset, noshow to reset once and for all whether they want to see these variables mentioned at the top of the output of every st command; see [R] **st stset**.

# Remarks

Here is an example of stdes with single-record survival data:

```
. stdes

        failure _d:  dead
   analysis time _t:  time
```

|                       |       | \|————— per subject —————\| | | | |
|-----------------------|-------|------|------|--------|------|
| Category              | total | mean | min  | median | max  |
| no. of subjects       | 40    |      |      |        |      |
| no. of records        | 40    | 1    | 1    | 1      | 1    |
| (first) entry time    |       | 0    | 0    | 0      | 0    |
| (final) exit time     |       | 227.95 | 142 | 231   | 344  |
| subjects with gap     | 0     |      |      |        |      |
| time on gap if gap    | 0     |      |      |        |      |
| time at risk          | 9118  | 227.95 | 142 | 231   | 344  |
| failures              | 36    | .9   | 0    | 1      | 1    |

307

In this dataset, there is one record per subject. The purpose of this summary is not analysis—it is to describe how the data are arranged. Looking at this, one can quickly see that there is one record per subject (the number of subjects equals the number of records but, if there is any doubt, we can also see that the minimum and maximum number of records per subject is 1), that all the subjects entered at time 0, that the subjects exited between times 142 and 344 (median 231), that there are no gaps (as there could not be if there is only one record per subject), that the total time at risk is 9,118 (distributed reasonably evenly across the subjects), and that the total number of failures is 36 (with a maximum of 1 failure per subject).

Here is a description of the multiple-record Stanford heart transplant data that we introduced in [R] **st stset**:

```
. stdes

        failure _d:  died
  analysis time _t:  t1
               id:  id
```

| Category | total | mean | per subject min | median | max |
|---|---|---|---|---|---|
| no. of subjects | 103 | | | | |
| no. of records | 172 | 1.669903 | 1 | 2 | 2 |
| (first) entry time | | 0 | 0 | 0 | 0 |
| (final) exit time | | 310.0786 | 1 | 90 | 1799 |
| subjects with gap | 0 | | | | |
| time on gap if gap | 0 | . | . | . | . |
| time at risk | 31938.1 | 310.0786 | 1 | 90 | 1799 |
| failures | 75 | .7281553 | 0 | 1 | 1 |

In this dataset, patients have one or two records. Although not revealed by the output, a patient has one record if the patient never received a heart transplant and two if the patient did receive a transplant; the first reflecting the patient's survival up to the time of transplantation and the second their subsequent survival:

```
. stset, noshow          /* to not show the st marker variables */

. stdes if ~transplant
```

| Category | total | mean | per subject min | median | max |
|---|---|---|---|---|---|
| no. of subjects | 34 | | | | |
| no. of records | 34 | 1 | 1 | 1 | 1 |
| (first) entry time | | 0 | 0 | 0 | 0 |
| (final) exit time | | 96.61765 | 1 | 21 | 1400 |
| subjects with gap | 0 | | | | |
| time on gap if gap | 0 | . | . | . | . |
| time at risk | 3285 | 96.61765 | 1 | 21 | 1400 |
| failures | 30 | .8823529 | 0 | 1 | 1 |

(*Continued on next page*)

. stdes if transplant

| Category | total | per subject | | | |
|---|---|---|---|---|---|
| | | mean | min | median | max |
| no. of subjects | 69 | | | | |
| no. of records | 138 | 2 | 2 | 2 | 2 |
| (first) entry time | | 0 | 0 | 0 | 0 |
| (final) exit time | | 415.2623 | 5.1 | 207 | 1799 |
| subjects with gap | 0 | | | | |
| time on gap if gap | 0 | . | . | . | . |
| time at risk | 28653.1 | 415.2623 | 5.1 | 207 | 1799 |
| failures | 45 | .6521739 | 0 | 1 | 1 |

Finally, here is the stdes from multiple-failure data:

. stdes

| Category | total | per subject | | | |
|---|---|---|---|---|---|
| | | mean | min | median | max |
| no. of subjects | 926 | | | | |
| no. of records | 1734 | 1.87257 | 1 | 2 | 4 |
| (first) entry time | | 0 | 0 | 0 | 0 |
| (final) exit time | | 470.6857 | 1 | 477 | 960 |
| subjects with gap | 6 | | | | |
| time on gap if gap | 411 | 68.5 | 16 | 57.5 | 133 |
| time at risk | 435444 | 470.2419 | 1 | 477 | 960 |
| failures | 808 | .8725702 | 0 | 1 | 3 |

Note that the maximum number of failures per subject observed is 3, although 50% had just one failure, and that 6 of the subjects have a gap in their histories.

## Saved Results

stdes saves in r():

Scalars

| | | | |
|---|---|---|---|
| r(N_sub) | number of subjects | r(gap) | total gap, if gap |
| r(N_total) | number of records | r(gap_min) | minimum gap, if gap |
| r(N_min) | minimum number of records | r(gap_mean) | mean gap, if gap |
| r(N_mean) | mean number of records | r(gap_med) | median gap, if gap |
| r(N_med) | median number of records | r(gap_max) | maximum gap, if gap |
| r(N_max) | maximum number of records | r(tr) | total time at risk |
| r(t0_min) | minimum first entry time | r(tr_min) | minimum time at risk |
| r(t0_mean) | mean first entry time | r(tr_mean) | mean time at risk |
| r(t0_med) | median first entry time | r(tr_med) | median time at risk |
| r(t0_max) | maximum first entry time | r(tr_max) | maximum time at risk |
| r(t1_min) | minimum final exit time | r(N_fail) | number of failures |
| r(t1_mean) | mean final exit time | r(f_min) | minimum number of failures |
| r(t1_med) | median final exit time | r(f_mean) | mean number of failures |
| r(t1_max) | maximum final exit time | r(f_med) | median number of failures |
| r(N_gap) | number of subjects with gap | r(f_max) | maximum number of failures |

## Methods and Formulas

stdes is implemented as an ado-file.

## Also See

| | |
|---|---|
| **Complementary:** | [R] **st stset**, [R] **st stsum**, [R] **st stvary** |
| **Background:** | [R] **st** |

# Title

> **st stfill** — Fill in by carrying forward values of covariates

# Syntax

$$\texttt{stfill } varlist \; [\texttt{if } exp] \; [\texttt{in } range] \;, \; \{ \underline{\texttt{b}}\texttt{aseline} \,|\, \underline{\texttt{f}}\texttt{orward} \} \; [\underline{\texttt{nosh}}\texttt{ow}]$$

stfill is for use with survival-time data; see [R] **st**. You must stset your data before using this command.

# Description

stfill is intended for use with multiple-record st data; data for which id() has been stset. stfill may be used with single-record data, but it literally does nothing. That is, stfill is appropriate for use with multiple-record, single- or multiple-failure, st data.

stfill, baseline changes variables to contain the value at the earliest time each subject was observed, making the variable constant over time. stfill, baseline changes all subsequent values of the specified variables to equal the first value whether they originally contained missing or not.

stfill, forward fills in missing values of each variable with that of the most recent time at which the variable was last observed. stfill, forward changes only missing values.

You must specify either the baseline or the forward option.

if *exp* and in *range* operate slightly differently from their usual definitions to work as you would expect. if and in restrict where changes can be made to the data but, no matter what, all stset observations are used to provide the values to be carried forward.

# Options

baseline specifies that values are to be replaced with the values at baseline, the earliest time at which the subject was observed. All values of the specified variables are replaced, missing and nonmissing.

forward specifies that values are to be carried forward, and that previously observed, nonmissing values are to be used to fill in later values that are missing in the specified variables.

noshow prevents stsum from showing the key st variables. This option is rarely used since most people type stset, show or stset, noshow to reset once and for all whether they want to see these variables mentioned at the top of the output of every st command; see [R] **st stset**.

# Remarks

stfill serves two purposes:

1. to assist in fixing data errors, and

2. to make baseline analyses easier.

Let us begin with repairing broken data.

You have a multiple-record st dataset which, due to how it was constructed, has a problem with the gender variable:

```
. stvary sex
        failure _d:  myopic
  analysis time _t:  t
               id:  id

          subjects for whom the variable is
                                          never     always   sometimes
    variable |  constant     varying      missing   missing    missing
    ---------+----------------------------------------------------------
         sex |      131           1            22         0        110
```

Note that for 110 subjects, sex is sometimes missing and, for one more subject, the value of sex changes over time! The sex change is an error, but the missing values occurred because sometimes the subject's sex was not filled in on the revisit forms. We will assume you have checked the changing-sex subject and determined that the baseline record is correct in that case, too.

```
. stfill sex, baseline
        failure _d:  myopic
  analysis time _t:  t
               id:  id

replace all values with value at earliest observed:
        sex:  221 real changes made
. stvary sex
        failure _d:  myopic
  analysis time _t:  t
               id:  id

          subjects for whom the variable is
                                          never     always   sometimes
    variable |  constant     varying      missing   missing    missing
    ---------+----------------------------------------------------------
         sex |      132           0           132         0          0
```

The sex variable is now completely filled in.

In this same dataset, there is another variable—bp, blood pressure—that is not always filled in because readings were not always taken.

```
. stvary bp
        failure _d:  myopic
  analysis time _t:  t
               id:  id

          subjects for whom the variable is
                                          never     always   sometimes
    variable |  constant     varying      missing   missing    missing
    ---------+----------------------------------------------------------
          bp |       18         114             9         0        123
```

(bp is constant for 18 patients because it was only taken once—at baseline.) Anyway, you decide it will be good enough, when bp is missing, to use the previous value of bp:

```
. stfill bp, forward noshow
replace missing values with previously observed values:
            bp:   263 real changes made
. stvary bp, noshow
```

|          |          |         | subjects for whom the variable is |                  |                  |                     |
|---------:|:--------:|:-------:|:-----:|:----------------:|:----------------:|:-------------------:|
| variable | constant | varying |       | never missing | always missing | sometimes missing |
| bp       | 18       | 114     |       | 132              | 0                | 0                   |

So much for data repair and fabrication.

Much later, deep in analysis, you are concerned about the bp variable and decide to compare results with a model that simply includes blood pressure at baseline. You are undecided on the issue and want to have both variables in your data:

```
. gen bp0 = bp
. stfill bp0, baseline
replace all values with value at earliest observed:
            bp0:   406 real changes made
. stvary bp bp0
```

|          |          |         | subjects for whom the variable is |                  |                  |                     |
|---------:|:--------:|:-------:|:-----:|:----------------:|:----------------:|:-------------------:|
| variable | constant | varying |       | never missing | always missing | sometimes missing |
| bp       | 18       | 114     |       | 132              | 0                | 0                   |
| bp0      | 132      | 0       |       | 132              | 0                | 0                   |

## Methods and Formulas

stfill is implemented as an ado-file.

## Also See

**Complementary:**  [R] **st stbase**, [R] **st stgen**, [R] **st stset**, [R] **st stvary**

**Background:**  [R] **st**

# Title

**st stgen** — Generate variables reflecting entire histories

# Syntax

stgen [*type*] *newvar* = *function*

where *function* is

> ever(*exp*)
> never(*exp*)
> always(*exp*)
> min(*exp*)
> max(*exp*)
> when(*exp*)
> when0(*exp*)
> count(*exp*)
> count0(*exp*)
> minage(*exp*)
> maxage(*exp*)
> avgage(*exp*)
> nfailures()
> ngaps()
> gaplen()
> hasgap()

stgen is for use with survival-time data; see [R] **st**. You must stset your data before using this command.

# Description

stgen provides a convenient way to generate new variables reflecting entire histories—variables you could create for yourself using generate (and especially, generate with the **by** *varlist*: prefix), but that would require too much thought and there would be too much chance of making a mistake.

These functions are intended for use with multiple-record survival data but may be used with single-record data. With single-record data, each function reduces to a single generate, and generate would be a more natural way to approach the problem.

stgen is appropriate for use with multiple-record, single- or multiple-failure, st data.

If your interest is in generating calculated values such as the survivor function, etc., see [R] **st sts**.

# Functions

In the description of the functions below, note that when we say time units, we mean the same units as *timevar* from stset *timevar*, .... For instance, if *timevar* is the number of days since 01 January 1960 (a Stata date), then time units are days. If *timevar* is in years—years since 1960 or years since diagnosis or whatever—then time units are years.

When we say variable X records a "time" we mean a variable recording when something occurred recorded in the same units and with the same base as *timevar*. If *timevar* is a Stata date, then "time" is correspondingly a Stata date.

When we say $t$ units, or analysis time units, we mean a variable in the units *timevar*/scale() from stset *timevar*, scale(...) .... If you did not specify a scale(), then $t$ units are the same as time units. Alternatively, say *timevar* is recorded as a Stata date and you specified scale(365.25). Then $t$ units are years. Caution: if you specified a nonconstant scale—scale(myvar) where myvar varies from subject to subject—then $t$ units are different for every subject.

When we say "an analysis time", we mean when something occurred recorded in the units (*timevar*-origin())/scale(). We only speak about analysis time in terms of the beginning and end of each time-span record.

Although in the *Description* we said stgen creates variables reflecting entire histories, it is important to understand that stgen restricts itself to the stset observations, and entire history thus means the entire history as it is currently stset. If you really want to use entire histories as recorded in the data, type streset, past or streset, past future before using stgen and then type streset to reset to the original analysis sample.

The functions are

ever(*exp*) creates *newvar* containing 1 (true) if the expression is ever true (nonzero) and 0 otherwise. For instance,

. stgen everlow = ever(bp<100)

would create everlow containing, for each subject, uniformly 1 or 0. Every record for a subject would contain everlow = 1 if, on any stset record for the subject, bp < 100, and otherwise everlow would be 0.

never(*exp*) is the reverse of ever(); it creates *newvar* containing 1 (true) if the expression is always false (0) and 0 otherwise. For instance,

. stgen neverlow = never(bp<100)

would create neverlow containing, for each subject, uniformly 1 or 0. Every record for a subject would contain neverlow = 1 if, on every stset record for the subject, bp < 100 is false.

always(*exp*) creates *newvar* containing 1 (true) if the expression is always true (nonzero) and 0 otherwise. For instance,

. stgen lowlow = always(bp<100)

would create lowlow containing, for each subject, uniformly 1 or 0. Every record for a subject would contain lowlow = 1 if, on every stset record for a subject, bp < 100.

min(*exp*) and max(*exp*) create newvar containing the minimum or maximum nonmissing value of *exp* within id(). min() and max() are often used with variables recording "a time" (see definition above), such as min(visitdat).

when(*exp*) and when0(*exp*) create newvar containing the "time" when *exp* first became true within the previously stset id(). Note that the result is in time, not $t$ units; see definition above.

when() and when0() differ about when the *exp* became true. Records record time spans (*time0*, *time1*]. when() assumes the expression became true at the end of the time span, *time1*. when0() assumes the expression became true at the beginning of the time span, *time0*.

For example, assume you previously 'stset myt, failure(*eventvar*=...) ...'. when() would be appropriate for use with *eventvar*, and presumably when0() would be appropriate for use with the remaining variables.

count(*exp*) and count0(*exp*) create *newvar* containing the number of occurrences when *exp* is true within id().

count() and count0() differ in when they assume *exp* occurs. count() assumes *exp* corresponds to the end of the time-span record. Thus, even if *exp* is true in this record, the count would remain unchanged until the next record.

count0() assumes *exp* corresponds to the beginning of the time-span record. Thus, if *exp* is true in this record, the count is immediately updated.

For example, assume you previously 'stset myt, failure(*eventvar*=...) ...'. count() would be appropriate for use with *eventvar*, and presumably count0() would be appropriate for use with the remaining variables.

minage(*exp*), maxage(*exp*), and avgage(*exp*) return the elapsed time, in time units, since *exp* at the beginning, end, or middle of the record, respectively. *exp* is expected to evaluate to a time in time units. minage(), maxage(), and avgage() would be appropriate for use with the result of when(), when0(), min(), and max(), for instance.

Also see [R] **st stsplit**; stsplit will divide the time-span records into new time-span records that record specified intervals of ages.

nfailures() creates *newvar* containing the cumulative number of failures for each subject as of the entry time for the observation. nfailures() is intended for use with multiple-failure data; with single-failure data, nfailures() is always 0. In multiple-failure data,

    . stgen nfail = nfailures()

might create, for a particular subject, the following:

| id | time0 | time1 | fail | x | nfail |
|----|-------|-------|------|---|-------|
| 93 | 0 | 20 | 0 | 1 | 0 |
| 93 | 20 | 30 | 1 | 1 | 0 |
| 93 | 30 | 40 | 1 | 2 | 1 |
| 93 | 40 | 60 | 0 | 1 | 2 |
| 93 | 60 | 70 | 0 | 2 | 2 |
| 93 | 70 | 80 | 1 | 1 | 2 |

Note that the total number of failures for this subject is 3 and yet the maximum of the new variable nfail is 2. At time 70, the beginning of the last record, there had been 2 failures previously, and there were 2 failures up to but not including time 80.

ngaps() creates *newvar* containing the cumulative number of gaps for each subject as of the entry time for the record. Delayed entry (an opening gap) is not considered a gap. For example,

    . stgen ngap = ngaps()

might create, for a particular subject, the following:

| id | time0 | time1 | fail | x | ngap |
|----|-------|-------|------|---|------|
| 94 | 10 | 30 | 0 | 1 | 0 |
| 94 | 30 | 40 | 0 | 2 | 0 |
| 94 | 50 | 60 | 0 | 1 | 1 |
| 94 | 60 | 70 | 0 | 2 | 1 |
| 94 | 82 | 90 | 1 | 1 | 2 |

gaplen() creates *newvar* containing the time on gap, measured in analysis time units, for each subject as of the entry time for the observation. Delayed entry (an opening gap) is not considered a gap. Continuing with the previous example,

```
. stgen gl = gaplen()
```

would produce

| id | time0 | time1 | fail | x | ngap | gl |
|----|-------|-------|------|---|------|-----|
| 94 | 10 | 30 | 0 | 1 | 0 | 0 |
| 94 | 30 | 40 | 0 | 2 | 0 | 0 |
| 94 | 50 | 60 | 0 | 1 | 1 | 10 |
| 94 | 60 | 70 | 0 | 2 | 1 | 0 |
| 94 | 82 | 90 | 1 | 1 | 2 | 12 |

hasgap() creates *newvar* containing uniformly 1 if the subject ever has a gap, and 0 otherwise. Delayed entry (an opening gap) is not considered a gap.

# Remarks

stgen does nothing you cannot do in other ways, but it is convenient.

It is worth considering how you would obtain results like those created by stgen should you need something that stgen will not create for you. Pretend you have an st dataset for which you have previously

```
. stset t, failure(d) id(id)
```

Assume this is some of the data:

| id | t | d | bp |
|----|----|---|-----|
| 27 | 30 | 0 | 90 |
| 27 | 50 | 0 | 110 |
| 27 | 60 | 1 | 85 |
| 28 | 11 | 0 | 120 |
| 28 | 40 | 1 | 130 |

If we were to type

```
. stgen everlow = ever(bp<100)
```

then the new variable everlow would contain for these two subjects

| id | t | d | bp | everlow |
|----|----|---|-----|---------|
| 27 | 30 | 0 | 90 | 1 |
| 27 | 50 | 0 | 110 | 1 |
| 27 | 60 | 1 | 85 | 1 |
| 28 | 11 | 0 | 120 | 0 |
| 28 | 40 | 1 | 130 | 0 |

Variable everlow is 1 for subject 27 because in two of the three observations, bp $< 100$, and everlow is 0 for subject 28 because everlow is never less than 100 in either of the two observations.

Here is one way we could have created everlow for ourselves:

```
. gen islow = bp<100
. sort id
. by id: gen sumislow = sum(islow)
. by id: gen everlow = sumislow[_N]>0
. drop islow sumislow
```

The generic term for code like the above is explicit subscripting, and if you want to know more, see [U] **16.7 Explicit subscripting**.

Anyway, that is what stgen did for us although, internally, stgen used denser code which was equivalent to

```
. by id, sort: gen everlow=sum(bp<100)
. by id: replace everlow = everlow[_N]>0
```

Obtaining things like the time on gap is no more difficult. When we `stset` the data, `stset` created variable `_t0` to record the entry time. Then `stgen`'s `gaplen` function is equivalent to

```
. sort id _t
. by id: gen gaplen = _t0-_t[_n-1]
```

Seeing this, you should realize that if all you wanted was the cumulative length of the gap before the current record, you could type

```
. sort id _t
. by id: gen curgap = sum(_t0-_t[_n-1])
```

and if, instead, you wanted a variable that was 1 if there were a gap just before this record and 0 otherwise, you could type

```
. sort id _t
. by id: gen iscurgap = (_t0-_t[_n-1])>0
```

All of this is to convince you that, despite the usefulness of `stgen`, understanding [U] **16.7 Explicit subscripting** really is worth your while.

▷ Example

Let us use the `stgen` commands to real effect. We have a multiple-record, multiple-failure dataset.

```
. st
-> stset t, id(id) failure(d) time0(t0) exit(time .) noshow
                id:  id
     failure event:  d ~= 0 & d ~= .
obs. time interval:  (t0, t]
 exit on or before:  time .
. stdes
```

| Category | total | |———— per subject ————| | | |
|---|---|---|---|---|---|
| | | mean | min | median | max |
| no. of subjects | 926 | | | | |
| no. of records | 1734 | 1.87257 | 1 | 2 | 4 |
| (first) entry time | | 0 | 0 | 0 | 0 |
| (final) exit time | | 470.6857 | 1 | 477 | 960 |
| subjects with gap | 6 | | | | |
| time on gap if gap | 411 | 68.5 | 16 | 57.5 | 133 |
| time at risk | 435444 | 470.2419 | 1 | 477 | 960 |
| failures | 808 | .8725702 | 0 | 1 | 3 |

Also in this dataset are two covariates, `x1` and `x2`. We wish to estimate a Cox model on these data but wish to assume that the baseline hazard for first failures is different from that for second and subsequent failures.

Note that our data contain 6 subjects with gaps. Since it is possible that failures might have occurred during the gap, we begin by dropping those 6 subjects:

```
. stgen hg = hasgap()
. drop if hg
(14 observations deleted)
```

The 6 subjects had 14 records among them. That done, we can create variable `nf` containing the number of failures and, from that, variable `group` which will be 0 when subjects have experienced no previous failures and 1 thereafter:

```
. stgen nf = nfailures()
. gen byte group = nf>0
```

We can now estimate our stratified model:

```
. stcox x1 x2, strata(group) robust
Iteration 0:  log likelihood = -4499.9966
Iteration 1:  log likelihood = -4444.7797
Iteration 2:  log likelihood = -4444.4596
Iteration 3:  log likelihood = -4444.4596
Refining estimates:
Iteration 0:  log likelihood = -4444.4596

Stratified Cox regr. -- Breslow method for ties

No. of subjects =        920              Number of obs   =       1720
No. of failures =        800
Time at risk    =     432153
                                          Wald chi2(2)    =     102.78
Log likelihood  =   -4444.4596            Prob > chi2     =     0.0000
                    (standard errors adjusted for clustering on id)
```

| _t _d | Haz. Ratio | Robust Std. Err. | z | P>\|z\| | [95% Conf. Interval] | |
|---|---|---|---|---|---|---|
| x1 | 2.087903 | .1961725 | 7.84 | 0.000 | 1.736738 | 2.510074 |
| x2 | .2765613 | .052277 | -6.80 | 0.000 | .1909383 | .4005806 |

Stratified by group

## Methods and Formulas

`stgen` is implemented as an ado-file.

## Also See

Complementary:     [R] **st stci**, [R] **st sts**, [R] **st stset**, [R] **st stvary**

Background:        [U] **16.7 Explicit subscripting**,
                   [R] **st**

# Title

> **st stir** — Report incidence-rate comparison

# Syntax

> stir *exposedvar* [if *exp*] [in *range*] [, <u>strata</u>(*varname*) <u>nosh</u>ow *ir_options* ]

stir is for use with survival-time data; see [R] **st**. You must stset your data before using this command.

by ... : may be used with stir; see [R] **by**.

# Description

stir reports point estimates and confidence intervals for the incidence rate ratio and difference. stir is an interface to the ir command; see [R] **epitab**.

By the logic of ir, *exposedvar* should be a 0/1 variable, 0 meaning unexposed and 1 meaning exposed. stir, however, will allow any two-valued coding and even allow *exposedvar* to be a string variable.

stir may not be used with pweighted data.

stir is appropriate for use with single- or multiple-record, single- or multiple-failure, st data.

# Options

<u>strata</u>(*varname*) specifies that the calculation is to be stratified on *varname*, which may be a numeric or a string variable. Within-stratum statistics are shown and then combined with Mantel–Haenszel weights.

noshow prevents stir from showing the key st variables. This option is rarely used since most people type stset, show or stset, noshow to reset once and for all whether they want to see these variables mentioned at the top of the output of every st command; see [R] **st stset**.

*ir_options* refers to the options of ir including, most importantly, level(#), estandard, istandard, and standard(*varname*) —see [R] **epitab**—but you can specify any of the options ir allows except by() (which is stir's strata() option).

(*Continued on next page*)

# Remarks

stir examines the incidence rate and time at risk.

```
. stir group
note:  Exposed <-> group==2 and Unexposed <-> group==1
```

|  | group<br>Exposed | Unexposed | Total |
|---|---|---|---|
| Failure | 19 | 17 | 36 |
| Time | 5023 | 4095 | 9118 |
| Incidence Rate | .0037826 | .0041514 | .0039482 |

|  | Point estimate | [95% Conf. Interval] | |  |
|---|---|---|---|---|
| Inc. rate diff. | -.0003688 | -.002974 | .0022364 | |
| Inc. rate ratio | .9111616 | .448426 | 1.866097 | (exact) |
| Prev. frac. ex. | .0888384 | -.8660967 | .551574 | (exact) |
| Prev. frac. pop | .04894 | | | |

|  | | |
|---|---|---|
| (midp)   Pr(k<=19) = | 0.3900 | (exact) |
| (midp) 2*Pr(k<=19) = | 0.7799 | (exact) |

# Saved Results

stir saves in r():

Scalars

| | | | |
|---|---|---|---|
| r(p) | one-sided $p$-value | r(ub_irr) | upper bound of CI for irr |
| r(ird) | incidence rate difference | r(afe) | attributable (prev.) fraction among exposed |
| r(lb_ird) | lower bound of CI for ird | r(lb_afe) | lower bound of CI for afe |
| r(ub_ird) | upper bound of CI for ird | r(ub_afe) | upper bound of CI for afe |
| r(irr) | incidence rate ratio | r(afp) | attributable fraction for the population |
| r(lb_irr) | lower bound of CI for irr | | |

# Methods and Formulas

stir is implemented as an ado-file.

stir simply accumulates numbers of failures and time at risk by exposed and unexposed (by strata, if necessary) and passes the calculation to ir; see [R] **epitab**.

# Also See

**Complementary:**    [R] **st stset**, [R] **st stsum**

**Background:**    [R] **st**; [R] **epitab**

# Title

> **st stphplot** — Graphical assessment of the Cox proportional hazards assumption

# Syntax

stphplot $\left[\text{if } exp\right]$, $\left\{\text{ by}(varname) \mid \underline{\text{stra}}\text{ta}(varname) \right\}$

$\left[\underline{\text{adj}}\text{ust}(varlist) \underline{\text{noln}}\text{time} \underline{\text{noneg}}\text{ative} \underline{\text{zero}} \underline{\text{nosh}}\text{ow} \textit{ graph\_options}\right]$

stcoxkm $\left[\text{if } exp\right]$, by(varname) $\left[\underline{\text{sep}}\text{arate}\right.$

$\underline{\text{ties}}(\left\{\underline{\text{bres}}\text{low} \mid \underline{\text{efr}}\text{on} \mid \text{exactp} \mid \text{exactm}\right\}) \underline{\text{nosh}}\text{ow} \textit{ graph\_options}\left.\right]$

stphplot and stcoxkm are for use with survival-time data; see [R] **st**. You must stset your data before using these commands.

# Description

stphplot plots $-\ln\left(-\ln(\text{survival})\right)$ curves for each category of a nominal or ordinal covariate versus $\ln(\text{analysis time})$. These are often referred to as "log-log" plots. Optionally, these estimates can be adjusted for covariates. The proportional hazards assumption is not violated when the curves are parallel.

stcoxkm plots Kaplan–Meier observed survival curves and compares them with the Cox predicted curves for the same variable. The closer the observed values are to the predicted, the less likely it is that the proportional hazards assumption has been violated. Do not run stcox before this command; stcoxkm will execute stcox itself to estimate the model and obtain predicted values.

# Options

by(*varname*) specifies the nominal or ordinal covariate. You must specify by() with stcoxkm and you must specify either by() or strata() with stphplot.

strata(*varname*) is an alternative to by() for stphplot. Rather than separate Cox models being estimated for each value of *varname*, a single, stratified Cox model is estimated. You must also specify adjust(*varlist*) with the strata(*varname*) option; see [R] **st sts graph**.

adjust(*varlist*) adjusts the estimates to that for *average* values of the *varlist* specified. Alternatively the estimates can be adjusted to *zero* values of *varlist* by specifying the zero option. adjust(*varlist*) can be specified with by(); it is required with strata(*varname*).

nolntime specifies that curves be plotted against analysis time instead of against $\ln(\text{analysis time})$.

nonegative specifies that $\ln\left\{-\ln(\text{survival})\right\}$ curves be plotted instead of $-\ln\left\{-\ln(\text{survival})\right\}$.

zero is used with adjust() to specify that the estimates be adjusted to the 0 values of the *varlist* rather than average values.

noshow prevents stphplot and stcoxkm from showing the key st variables. This option is rarely used since most people type stset, show or stset, noshow to reset once and for all whether they want to see these variables mentioned at the top of the output of every st command; see [R] **st stset**.

separate is used with stcoxkm to produce separate plots of predicted and observed for each value of the variable specified with by().

ties(breslow | efron | exactm | exactp) is used to specify one of the methods available to stcox for handling tied failures. If not specified, ties(breslow) is assumed; see [R] **st stcox**.

*graph_options* are most of the options allowed with graph, twoway; see [G] **graph options**. If ylabel() is selected, values for the $y$-axis must be included.

# Remarks

What follows is paraphrased from Garrett (1997). Any errors are ours.

The most important assumption of the Cox proportional hazards model is that the hazard ratio is proportional over time. For example, suppose a group of cancer patients on an experimental treatment are followed for 10 years. If the hazard of dying for the nontreated group is twice the rate as that of the treated group (HR = 2.0), the proportional hazards assumption implies that this ratio is the same at one year, at two years, or at any point on the time scale. Because the Cox model, by definition, is constrained to follow this assumption, it is important to evaluate its validity before modeling. If the assumption fails, alternative modeling choices would be more appropriate (e.g., a stratified Cox model).

We provide three programs, stphplot, stcoxkm, and stphtest, which can be used to evaluate the proportional hazards assumption. Both stphplot and stcoxkm are graphical methods, whereas stphtest performs statistical tests based on the distribution of Schoenfeld residuals and is described in [R] **st stcox**.

The two commands stphplot and stcoxkm provide graphical methods for assessing violations of the proportional hazards assumption. Although using graphs to assess the validity of the assumption is subjective, it can be a helpful tool.

stphplot plots $-\ln\left(-\ln(\text{survival})\right)$ curves for each category of a nominal or ordinal covariate versus ln(analysis time). These are often referred to as "log–log" plots. Optionally, these estimates can be adjusted for covariates. If the plotted lines are reasonably parallel, the proportional hazards assumption has not been violated, and it would be appropriate to base the estimate for that variable on a single baseline survivor function.

Another graphical method of evaluating the proportional hazards assumption, though less common, is to plot the Kaplan–Meier observed survival curves and compare them with the Cox predicted curves for the same variable. This plot is produced with stcoxkm. When the predicted and observed curves are close together, the proportional hazards assumption has not been violated.

▷ Example

These examples use data from a leukemia remission study (Garrett 1997). The data consist of 42 patients who are followed over time to see how long (weeks) it takes them to go out of remission (relapse: 1 = yes, 0 = no). Half the patients receive a new experimental drug and the other half receive a standard drug (treatment1: 1 = drug A, 0 = standard). White blood cell count, a strong indicator of the presence of leukemia, is divided into three categories (wbc3cat: 1 = normal, 2 = moderate, 3 = high).

```
. describe
Contains data from leukemia.dta
  obs:           42                           Leukemia Remission Study
  vars:           8                           4 Aug 2000 10:45
  size:         504 (99.8% of memory free)
```

```
              storage  display   value
variable name  type    format    label    variable label

weeks          byte    %8.0g              Weeks in Remission
relapse        byte    %8.0g     yesno    Relapse
treatment1     byte    %8.0g     trt1lbl  Treatment I
treatment2     byte    %8.0g     trt2lbl  Treatment II
wbc3cat        byte    %9.0g     wbclbl   White Blood Cell Count
wbc1           byte    %8.0g              wbc3cat==Normal
wbc2           byte    %8.0g              wbc3cat==Moderate
wbc3           byte    %8.0g              wbc3cat==High
```

```
Sorted by:  weeks

. stset weeks, failure(relapse)

     failure event:  relapse ~= 0 & relapse ~= .
obs. time interval:  (0, weeks]
 exit on or before:  failure
```

```
   42  total obs.
    0  exclusions

   42  obs. remaining, representing
   30  failures in single record/single failure data
  541  total analysis time at risk, at risk from t =          0
                           earliest observed entry t =          0
                               last observed exit t =         35
```

In this example, we examine whether the proportional hazards assumption holds for drug A versus the standard drug (treatment1). First, we will use stphplot, followed by stcoxkm.

```
. stphplot, by(treatment1) c(ll) xlabel ylabel
```

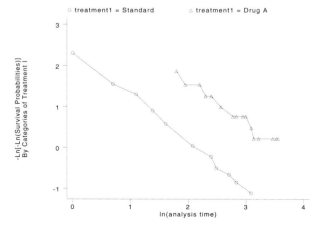

Figure 1.

```
. stcoxkm, by(treatment1) c(llll) s(OOST) xlabel
```

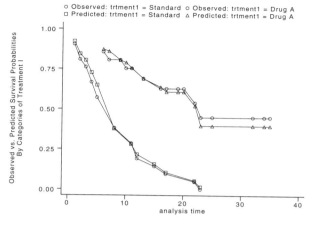

Figure 2.

Figure 1 (`stphplot`) displays lines that are parallel, implying the proportional hazards assumption for `treatment1` has not been violated. This is confirmed in Figure 2 (`stcoxkm`) where the observed values and predicted values are close together.

The graph in Figure 3 is the same as Figure 1, adjusted for white blood cell count (using two dummy variables). The adjustment variables were centered temporarily by `stphplot` before the adjustment was made.

```
. stphplot, strata(treatment1) c(ll) xlabel ylabel adj(wbc2 wbc3)
```

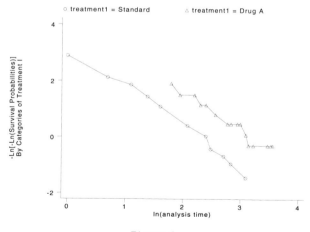

Figure 3.

Note that the lines in Figure 3 are still parallel, although somewhat closer together. Examining the proportional hazards assumption on a variable without adjustment for covariates is usually adequate as a diagnostic tool before using the Cox model. However, if it is known that adjustment for covariates in a final model is necessary, one may wish to re-examine whether the proportional hazards assumption still holds.

There is another variable in this dataset which measures a different drug (`treatment2`: 1 = drug B, 0 = standard). We wish to examine the proportional hazards assumption for this variable.

```
. stphplot, by(treatment2) c(ll) xlabel ylabel
```

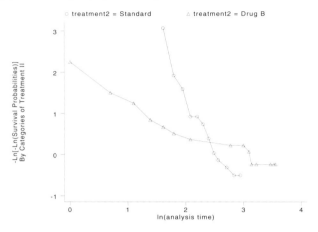

Figure 4.

```
. stcoxkm, by(treatment2) c(llll) s(....) xlabel separate
```

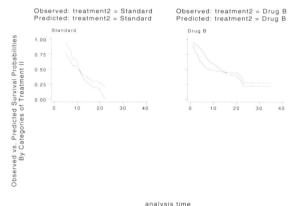

Figure 5.

Clearly this variable violates the proportion hazards assumption. In figure 4, we see that not only are the lines nonparallel, they cross in the data region. And in figure 5, we see that there are considerable differences between the observed and predicted values. We have overestimated the positive effect of drug B for the first half of the study and have underestimated it in the later weeks. A single hazard ratio describing the effect of this drug would be inappropriate. We definitely would want to stratify this variable in our Cox model.

◁

# Methods and Formulas

stphplot and stcoxkm are implemented as ado-files.

For a single covariate, $x$, the Cox proportional hazard model reduces to

$$h(t; x) = h_0(t) \exp(\mathbf{x}\boldsymbol{\beta})$$

where $h_0(t)$ is the baseline hazard function from the Cox model. Let $S_0(t)$ and $H_0(t)$ be the corresponding Cox baseline survivor and baseline cumulative hazard functions respectively.

The proportional hazards assumption implies that

$$H(t) = H_0(t) \exp(\mathbf{x}\boldsymbol{\beta})$$

or

$$\ln H(t) = \ln H_0(t) + \mathbf{x}\boldsymbol{\beta}$$

where $H(t)$ is the cumulative hazard function. Thus, under the proportional hazards assumption, the logs of the cumulative hazard functions at each level of the covariate have equal slope. This is the basis for the method implemented in stphplot.

The proportional hazards assumption also implies that

$$S(t) = S_0(t)^{\exp(\mathbf{x}\boldsymbol{\beta})}$$

Let $\widehat{S}(t)$ be the estimated survivor function based on the Cox model. This function is a step function like the Kaplan–Meier estimate and, in fact, reduces to the Kaplan–Meier estimate when $\mathbf{x} = \mathbf{0}$. Thus, for each level of the covariate of interest, we can assess violations of the proportional hazards assumption by comparing these survival estimates with estimates calculated independently of the model. See, for example, Kalbfleisch and Prentice (1980) or Hess (1995).

stcoxkm plots Kaplan–Meier estimated curves for each level of the covariate together with the Cox model predicted baseline survival curve. The closer the observed values are to the predicted, the less likely it is that the proportional hazards assumption has been violated.

# Acknowledgment

The original versions of stphplot and stcoxkm were written by Joanne M. Garrett, University of North Carolina at Chapel Hill.

# References

Garrett, J. M. 1997. gr23: Graphical assessment of the Cox model proportional hazards assumption. *Stata Technical Bulletin* 35: 9–14. Reprinted in *Stata Technical Bulletin Reprints*, vol. 6, pp. 38–44.

——. 1998. ssa12: Predicted survival curves for the Cox proportional hazards model. *Stata Technical Bulletin* 44: 37–41. Reprinted in *Stata Technical Bulletin Reprints*, vol. 8, pp. 285–290.

Hess, K. R. 1995. Graphical methods for assessing violations of the proportional hazards assumption in Cox regression. *Statistics in Medicine* 14: 1707–1723.

Kalbfleisch, J. D. and R. L. Prentice. 1980. *The Statistical Analysis of Failure Time Data*. New York: John Wiley & Sons.

## Also See

**Related:** [R] **st stcox**, [R] **st stset**

**Background:** [R] **st**

# Title

> **st stptime** — Calculate person-time, incidence rates, and SMR

# Syntax

stptime $[$if $exp]$ $[$, at(*numlist*) by(*varname*) trim per(*#*) dd(*#*) level(*#*)

    noshow jackknife smr(*groupvar ratevar*) using(*filename*) title(*string*)

    output(*filename*$[$,replace$]$) $]$

stptime is for use with survival-time data; see [R] **st**. You must stset your data before using this command.
by ... : may be used with stptime; see [R] **by**.

# Description

stptime calculates person-time and incidence rates. stptime also implements computation of standardized mortality/morbidity ratios (SMR), after merging the data with a suitable file of standard rates specified with the using() option.

# Options

at(*numlist*) specifies time intervals at which person-time are to be computed. The intervals are specified in analysis-time $t$ units. If at() is not specified, overall person-time and incidence rates are computed.

If, for example, we specify at(5(5)20) and the trim option is not specified, person-time is reported for the intervals $t = (0 - 5]$, $t = (5 - 10]$, $t = (10 - 15]$, and $t = (15 - 20]$.

by(*varlist*) specifies a categorical variable by which incidence rates or SMR are to be computed.

trim specifies that observations less than or equal to the minimum or greater than the maximum value listed in at() are to be excluded from the computations.

per(*#*) defines the units used to report the rates. For example, if the analysis time is in years, specifying per(1000) results in rates per 1,000 person-years.

dd(*#*) specifies the maximum number of decimal digits to be reported for rates, ratios, and confidence intervals. This option affects only how values are displayed and not how they are calculated.

level(*#*) specifies the confidence level, in percent, for confidence intervals. The default is level(95) or as set by set level; see [U] **23.5 Specifying the width of confidence intervals**.

noshow prevents stptime from showing the key st variables. This option is rarely used since most people type stset, show or stset, noshow to reset once and for all whether they want to see these variables mentioned at the top of the output of every st command; see [R] **st stset**.

jackknife specifies that jackknife confidence intervals be produced. This is the default if pweights or iweights were specified when the dataset was stset.

smr(*groupvar ratevar*) specifies two variables in the using() dataset. The *groupvar* identifies the age-group or calendar-period variable used to match the data in memory and the using() dataset. The *ratevar* variable contains the appropriate reference rates. stptime then calculates SMRs rather than incidence rates.

using(*filename*) specifies the filename that contains a file of standard rates that is to be merged with the data so that SMR can be calculated.

title(*string*) replaces the default "person-time" label on the output table with the string specified with this option.

output(*filename*[,replace]) saves a summary dataset in *filename*. The file contains counts of failures and person-time, incidence rates (or SMRs), confidence limits, and categorical variables identifying the time intervals. This could be used for further calculations, or simply as input to the table command.

# Remarks

stptime computes and tabulates the person-time and incidence rate, formed from the number of failures divided by the person-time, by different levels of one or more categorical explanatory variables specified by *varlist*. Confidence intervals for the rate are also given. By default, the confidence intervals are calculated using the quadratic approximation to the Poisson log-likelihood for the log rate parameter. However, whenever the Poisson assumption is questionable, jackknife confidence intervals can also be calculated.

stptime can also calculate and report SMRs if the data have been merged with a suitable file of reference rates.

If pweights or iweights were specified when the dataset was stset, stptime calculates jackknife confidence intervals by default.

The summary dataset can be saved to a file specified with the output() option, thus enabling further analysis or a more elaborate graphical display.

▷ Example

We begin with a simple fictitious example from Clayton and Hills' (1997, 42) book. Thirteen subjects were followed until the development of a particular disease. Here are the data for the first six subjects:

```
. list if _n < 6
            id       year      fail
    1.       1       19.6         1
    2.       2       10.8         1
    3.       3       14.1         1
    4.       4        3.5         1
    5.       5        4.8         1
```

The id variable identifies the subject, year records the time to failure in years, and fail is the failure indicator, which is one for all 30 subjects in the data. To use stptime, we must first stset the data.

```
. stset year, fail(fail) id(id)
                id:  id
     failure event:  fail ~= 0 & fail ~= .
obs. time interval:  (year[_n-1], year]
exit on or before:   failure

       30  total obs.
        0  exclusions

       30  obs. remaining, representing
       30  subjects
       30  failures in single failure-per-subject data
    261.9  total analysis time at risk, at risk from t =          0
                             earliest observed entry t =          0
                               last observed exit t =         36.5
```

We can use **stptime** to obtain overall person-time of observation and disease incidence rate.

```
. stptime, title(person-years)
         failure _d:  fail
    analysis time _t:  year
                id:  id

Cohort     | person-years  failures      rate    [95% Conf. Interval]
-----------+-----------------------------------------------------------
     total |       261.9        30  .11454754     .08009     .1638299
```

Note that the total 261.9 person-years reported by **stptime** matches what **stset** reported as total analysis time at risk. **stptime** computed an incidence rate of .11454754 per person-years. In epidemiology, incidence rates are often presented per 1000 person-years. We can do this by specifying **per(1000)**.

```
. stptime, title(person-years) per(1000)
         failure _d:  fail
    analysis time _t:  year
                id:  id

Cohort     | person-years  failures      rate    [95% Conf. Interval]
-----------+-----------------------------------------------------------
     total |       261.9        30  114.54754   80.09001    163.8299
```

More interesting would be to compare incidence rates at 10 year intervals. We will specify **dd(4)** to display rates to 4 decimal places.

```
. stptime, per(1000) at(0(10)40) dd(4)
         failure _d:  fail
    analysis time _t:  year
                id:  id

Cohort     | person-time  failures      rate    [95% Conf. Interval]
-----------+-----------------------------------------------------------
  (0 - 10] |    188.8000        18   95.3390    60.0676    151.3215
 (10 - 20] |     55.1000        10  181.4882    97.6506    337.3044
 (20 - 30] |     11.5000         1   86.9565    12.2490    617.3106
      > 30 |      6.5000         1  153.8462    21.6713   1092.1648
-----------+-----------------------------------------------------------
     total |    261.9000        30  114.5475    80.0900    163.8299
```

▷ Example

Using the diet data (Clayton and Hills 1997) described in Example 1 of [R] st stsplit, we will use stptime to tabulate age-specific person-years and CHD incidence rates. Recall that in this dataset, coronary heart disease (CHD) has been coded as fail = 1, 3, or 13.

We first stset the data: failure codes for CHD are specified; origin is set to date of birth, making age analysis time; and the scale is set to 365.25, so analysis time is measured in years.

```
. use diet, clear
(Diet data with dates)
. stset dox, origin(time dob) enter(time doe) id(id) scale(365.25) fail(fail==1 3 13)

                 id:  id
      failure event:  fail == 1 3 13
 obs. time interval:  (dox[_n-1], dox]
  enter on or after:  time doe
  exit on or before:  failure
    t for analysis:   (time-origin)/365.25
             origin:  time dob

       337  total obs.
         0  exclusions

       337  obs. remaining, representing
       337  subjects
        46  failures in single failure-per-subject data
  4603.669  total analysis time at risk, at risk from t =          0
                              earliest observed entry t =   30.07529
                                last observed exit t =   69.99863
```

The incidence of CHD per 1,000 person-years can be tabulated in 10-year intervals.

```
. stptime , at(40(10)70) per(1000) trim

           failure _d:  fail == 1 3 13
     analysis time _t:  (dox-origin)/365.25
               origin:  time dob
    enter on or after:  time doe
                   id:  id
                 note:  _group<=40 trimmed
```

| Cohort | person-time | failures | rate | [95% Conf. Interval] | |
|---|---|---|---|---|---|
| (40 - 50] | 907.00616 | 6 | 6.6151701 | 2.971936 | 14.72457 |
| (50 - 60] | 2107.0335 | 18 | 8.5428161 | 5.382338 | 13.55911 |
| (60 - 70] | 1493.3005 | 22 | 14.732467 | 9.700602 | 22.37444 |
| total | 4507.3402 | 46 | 10.205575 | 7.644246 | 13.62512 |

◁

The SMR for a cohort is the ratio of the total number of observed deaths to the number expected from age-specific reference rates. This expected number can be found by multiplying the person time in each cohort by the reference rate for that cohort. Using the smr option to define the cohort variable and reference rate variable in the using() dataset, stptime calculates SMRs and confidence intervals. Note that the per() option must still be specified. For example, if the reference rates are per 100,000, then specify per(100000).

▷ Example

In `smrchd.dta`, we have age-specific CHD rates per 1000 person-years for a reference population. We can merge these data with our current data and use `stptime` to obtain SMRs and confidence intervals.

```
. stptime , smr(ageband rate) using(smrchd) at(40(10)70) per(1000) trim
        failure _d:  fail == 1 3 13
   analysis time _t:  (dox-origin)/365.25
           origin:  time dob
   enter on or after:  time doe
              id:  id
            note:  _group<=40 trimmed
```

| Cohort | person-time | observed failures | expected failures | SMR | [95% Conf. Interval] | |
|---|---|---|---|---|---|---|
| (40 - 50] | 907.00616 | 6 | 5.62344 | 1.067 | .4793445 | 2.374931 |
| (50 - 60] | 2107.0335 | 18 | 18.7526 | .95987 | .6047571 | 1.523496 |
| (60 - 70] | 1493.3005 | 22 | 22.8475 | .96291 | .6340263 | 1.462382 |
| total | 4507.3402 | 46 | 47.2235 | .97409 | .7296197 | 1.300475 |

The `stptime` command can also be used to calculate person-time and incidence rates or SMRs by categories of the explanatory variable. In our diet data, the variable `hienergy` is coded 1 if the total energy consumption is more than 2.75 Mcals, and 0 otherwise. We want to compute the person-years and incidence rates for these two levels of `hienergy`.

```
. stptime , by(hienergy) per(1000)
        failure _d:  fail == 1 3 13
   analysis time _t:  (dox-origin)/365.25
           origin:  time dob
   enter on or after:  time doe
              id:  id
```

| hienergy | person-time | failures | rate | [95% Conf. Interval] | |
|---|---|---|---|---|---|
| 0 | 2059.4305 | 28 | 13.595992 | 9.387478 | 19.69123 |
| 1 | 2544.2382 | 18 | 7.0748093 | 4.457431 | 11.2291 |
| total | 4603.6687 | 46 | 9.9920309 | 7.484296 | 13.34002 |

We can also compute the incidence rate for the two levels of `hienergy` and the three previously defined age cohorts:

*(Continued on next page)*

```
. stptime, by(hienergy) at(40(10)70) per(1000) trim
          failure _d:  fail == 1 3 13
    analysis time _t:  (dox-origin)/365.25
              origin:  time dob
    enter on or after:  time doe
                  id:  id
```

| hienergy | person-time | failures | rate | [95% Conf. Interval] | |
|---|---|---|---|---|---|
| 0 | | | | | |
| (40 - 50] | 346.87474 | 2 | 5.76577 | 1.442006 | 23.05407 |
| (50 - 60] | 979.33744 | 12 | 12.253182 | 6.958701 | 21.57593 |
| > 60 | 699.14031 | 14 | 20.024593 | 11.85961 | 33.81091 |
| | | | | | |
| 1 | | | | | |
| (40 - 50] | 560.13142 | 4 | 7.1411813 | 2.680213 | 19.02702 |
| (50 - 60] | 1127.6961 | 6 | 5.3205824 | 2.390329 | 11.84297 |
| > 60 | 794.16016 | 8 | 10.073535 | 5.037751 | 20.14314 |
| | | | | | |
| total | 4507.3402 | 46 | 10.205575 | 7.644246 | 13.62512 |

or compute the corresponding SMR.

```
. stptime, smr(ageband rate) using(smrchd) by(hienergy) at(40(10)70) per(1000) trim
          failure _d:  fail == 1 3 13
    analysis time _t:  (dox-origin)/365.25
              origin:  time dob
    enter on or after:  time doe
                  id:  id
```

| hienergy | person-time | observed failures | expected failures | SMR | [95% Conf. Interval] | |
|---|---|---|---|---|---|---|
| 0 | | | | | | |
| (40 - 50] | 346.87474 | 2 | 2.15062 | .9299629 | .2325815 | 3.718399 |
| (50 - 60] | 979.33744 | 12 | 8.7161 | 1.376762 | .7818765 | 2.424262 |
| > 60 | 699.14031 | 14 | 10.6968 | 1.308797 | .7751381 | 2.209863 |
| | | | | | | |
| 1 | | | | | | |
| (40 - 50] | 560.13142 | 4 | 3.47281 | 1.151803 | .4322924 | 3.068875 |
| (50 - 60] | 1127.6961 | 6 | 10.0365 | .5978183 | .2685763 | 1.330671 |
| > 60 | 794.16016 | 8 | 12.1507 | .658401 | .3292648 | 1.316545 |
| | | | | | | |
| total | 4507.3402 | 46 | 47.2235 | .9740906 | .7296197 | 1.300475 |

◁

# Methods and Formulas

stptime is implemented as an ado-file.

# References

Clayton, D. G. and M. Hills. 1993. *Statistical Models in Epidemiology*. Oxford: Oxford University Press.

# Also See

| **Complementary:** | [R] **st strate**; [R] **st stci**, [R] **st stir**, [R] **st stset**, [R] **st stsplit** |
|---|---|
| **Related:** | [R] **epitab** |
| **Background:** | [R] **st** |

# Title

st strate — Tabulate failure rates and rate ratios

# Syntax

strate [*varlist*] [if *exp*] [in *range*] [, per(#) jackknife cluster(*varname*)

  miss smr(*varname*) output(*filename*[,replace]) nolist level(#)

  graph nowhisker *graph_options*]

stmh *varname* [*varlist*] [if *exp*] [in *range*] [, by(*varlist*) compare(*codes1*,*codes2*)

  miss level(#)]

stmc *varname* [*varlist*] [if *exp*] [in *range*] [, by(*varlist*) compare(*codes1*,*codes2*)

  miss level(#)]

strate, stmh, and stmc are for use with survival-time data; see [R] st. You must stset your data before using these commands.

by ... : may be used with stmh and stmc; see [R] by.

# Description

strate tabulates rates by one or more categorical variables declared in *varlist*. An optional summary dataset which includes event counts and rate denominators can be saved for further analysis or display. The combination of the commands stsplit and strate implements most if not all the functions of the special purpose "person-years" programs in widespread use in epidemiology. See, for example, Clayton and Hills (1993) and see [R] st stsplit. If your interest is solely in the calculation of person-years, see [R] st stptime.

stmh calculates stratified rate ratios and significance tests using a Mantel–Haenszel-type method.

stmc calculates rate ratios stratified finely by time, using the Mantel–Cox method. The corresponding significance test (the log-rank test) is also calculated.

Both stmh and stmc can be used to estimate the failure rate ratio for two categories of the explanatory variable specified by the first argument of *varlist*. Categories to be compared may be defined by specifying them with the compare() option. The remaining variables in *varlist* before the comma are categorical variables which are to be "controlled for" using stratification. Strata are defined by cross-classification of these variables.

Alternatively, stmh and stmc may be used to carry out trend tests for a metric explanatory variable. In this case, a one-step Newton approximation to the log-linear Poisson regression coefficient is computed.

# Options

## Options for strate

per(#) defines the units used to report the rates. For example, if the analysis time is in years, specifying per(1000) results in rates per 1,000 person-years.

jackknife specifies that jackknife confidence intervals be produced. This is the default if weights were specified when the dataset was stset.

cluster(*varname*) defines a categorical variable which indicates clusters of data to be used by the jackknife. If the jackknife option is selected and this option is not specified, the cluster variable is taken as the id variable defined in the st data. Specifying cluster() implies jackknife.

miss specifies that missing values of the explanatory variables are to be treated as extra categories. The default is to exclude such observations.

smr(*varname*) specifies a reference rate variable. strate then calculates SMRs rather than rates. This option will usually follow using stsplit to split the follow-up records by age bands and possibly calendar periods.

output(*filename*[,replace]) saves a summary dataset in *filename*. The file contains counts of failures and person-time, rates (or SMRs), confidence limits, and all the categorical variables in the *varlist*. This could be used for further calculations, or simply as input to the table command.

nolist suppresses the output. This is used only when saving results to a file specified by output().

level(#) specifies the confidence level, in percent, for confidence intervals. The default is level(95) or as set by set level; see [U] **23.5 Specifying the width of confidence intervals**.

graph produces a graph of the rate against the numerical code used for the categories of *varname*.

nowhisker omits the confidence intervals from the graph.

*graph_options* are any of the options allowed with graph, twoway; see [G] **graph options**.

## Options unique to stmh and stmc

by(*varlist*) specifies categorical variables by which the rate ratio is to be tabulated.

A separate rate ratio is produced for each category or combination of categories of *varlist*, and a test for unequal rate ratios (effect modification) is displayed.

In an analysis for log-linear trend the test is an approximation since the estimates are themselves based on a quadratic approximation of the log likelihood.

compare(*codes1*,*codes2*) specifies the categories of the exposure variable to be compared. The first code defines the numerator categories, and the second the denominator categories.

When compare is absent and there are only two categories, the larger is compared with the smaller; when there are more than two categories an analysis for log-linear trend is carried out.

# Remarks

Remarks are presented under the headings

>*Tabulation of rates using strate*
>*Stratified rate ratios using stmh*
>*Log-linear trend test for metric explanatory variables using stmh*
>*Controlling for age with fine strata using stmc*

## Tabulation of rates using strate

strate tabulates the rate, formed from the number of failures divided by the person-time, by different levels of one or more categorical explanatory variables specified by *varlist*. Confidence intervals for the rate are also given. By default, the confidence intervals are calculated using the quadratic approximation to the Poisson log-likelihood for the log rate parameter. However, whenever the Poisson assumption is questionable, jackknife confidence intervals can also be calculated. The jackknife option also allows for the case where there are multiple records for the same cluster (usually subject).

strate can also calculate and report SMRs if the data have been merged with a suitable file of reference rates.

The summary dataset can be saved to a file specified with the output() option, thus enabling further analysis or more elaborate graphical display.

If weights were specified when the dataset was stset, strate calculates jackknife confidence intervals by default.

▷ Example

Using the diet data (Clayton and Hills 1997) described in Example 1 of [R] **st stsplit**, we will use strate to tabulate age-specific CHD. Recall that in this dataset, coronary heart disease (CHD) has been coded as fail = 1, 3, or 13.

We first stset the data: failure codes for CHD are specified; origin is set to date of birth, making age analysis time; and the scale is set to 365.25, so analysis time is measured in years.

```
. use diet, clear
(Diet data with dates)
. stset dox, origin(time doe) id(id) scale(365.25) fail(fail==1 3 13)
                id:  id
     failure event:  fail == 1 3 13
obs. time interval:  (dox[_n-1], dox]
 exit on or before:  failure
     t for analysis:  (time-origin)/365.25
            origin:  time doe

       337  total obs.
         0  exclusions

       337  obs. remaining, representing
       337  subjects
        46  failures in single failure-per-subject data
  4603.669  total analysis time at risk, at risk from t =         0
                              earliest observed entry t =         0
                                 last observed exit t =  20.04107
```

Now we stsplit the data into 10-year age bands.

```
. stsplit ageband=dob, at(40(10)70) trim
(26 + 0 obs. trimmed due to lower and upper bounds)
(418 observations=episodes created)
```

stsplit added 418 observations to the dataset in memory and generated a new variable, ageband, which identifies each observation's age group.

The CHD rate per 1,000 person-years can now be tabulated against ageband:

```
. strate ageband, per(1000) graph xlab ylab
            failure _d:  fail == 1 3 13
    analysis time _t:  (dox-origin)/365.25
             origin:  time doe
                 id:  id
               note:  ageband<=40 trimmed
```

Estimated rates (per 1000) and lower/upper bounds of 95% confidence intervals
(729 records included in the analysis)

| ageband | _D | _Y | _Rate | _Lower | _Upper |
|---|---|---|---|---|---|
| 40 | 6 | 0.9070 | 6.6152 | 2.9719 | 14.7246 |
| 50 | 18 | 2.1070 | 8.5428 | 5.3823 | 13.5591 |
| 60 | 22 | 1.4933 | 14.7325 | 9.7006 | 22.3744 |

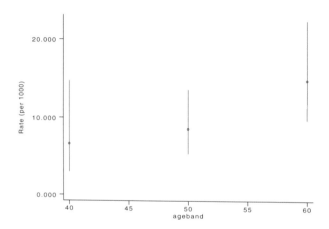

Since we specified the graph option, a plot of the estimated rate and confidence intervals was also generated.

◁

The SMR for a cohort is the ratio of the total number of observed deaths to the number expected from age-specific reference rates. This expected number can be found by first expanding on age, using stsplit, and then multiplying the person years in each age band by the reference rate for that band. merge (see [R] merge) can be used to add the reference rates to the dataset. Using the smr option to define the variable containing the reference rates, strate calculates SMRs and confidence intervals. Note that the per() option must still be specified. For example, if the reference rates are per 100,000, then specify per(100000). When reference rates are available by age and calendar period, stsplit must be called twice to expand on both time scales before merging the data with the reference rate file.

▷ Example

In smrchd.dta we have age-specific CHD rates per 1000 person-years for a reference population. We can merge these data with our current data and use strate to obtain SMRs and confidence intervals.

```
. merge ageband using smrchd
```

```
. strate ageband, per(1000) smr(rate)
           failure _d:  fail == 1 3 13
     analysis time _t:  (dox-origin)/365.25
               origin:  time doe
                   id:  id
                 note:  ageband<=40 trimmed
Estimated SMRs and lower/upper bounds of 95% confidence intervals
(729 records included in the analysis)
  ageband     _D         _E       _SMR     _Lower      _Upper
       40      6       5.44     1.1025     0.4953      2.4541
       50     18      16.86     1.0679     0.6728      1.6949
       60     22      22.40     0.9822     0.6467      1.4916
```

◁

# Stratified rate ratios using stmh

The stmh command is used for estimating rate ratios, controlled for confounding, using stratification. It can be used to estimate the ratio of the rates of failure for two categories of the explanatory variable. Categories to be compared may be defined by specifying the codes of the levels using compare().

The first variable listed on the command line after stmh is the explanatory variable used in comparing rates, and the remaining, if any, are categorical variables which are to be controlled for using stratification.

▷ Example

To illustrate this command, let us return to the diet data. Recall that the variable hienergy is coded 1 if the total energy consumption is more than 2.75 Mcals and 0 otherwise. We want to compare the rate for hienergy, level 1 with the rate for level 0, controlled for ageband.

To do this, we first stset and stsplit the data into age bands as before, and then we use stmh:

```
. use diet
(Diet data with dates)
. stset dox, origin(time dob) enter(time doe) id(id) scale(365.25) fail(fail==1 3 13)
  (output omitted )
. stsplit ageband=dob, at(40(10)70) trim
(26 + 0 obs. trimmed due to lower and upper bounds)
(418 observations=episodes created)
. stmh hienergy, c(1,0) by(ageband)
           failure _d:  fail == 1 3 13
     analysis time _t:  (dox-origin)/365.25
               origin:  time dob
       enter on or after:  time doe
                   id:  id
                 note:  ageband<=40 trimmed
Maximum likelihood estimate of the rate ratio
  comparing hienergy==1 vs. hienergy==0
  by ageband

RR estimate, and lower and upper 95% confidence limits
  ageband     RR    Lower   Upper
       40    1.24    0.23    6.76
       50    0.43    0.16    1.16
       60    0.50    0.21    1.20
```

```
Overall estimate controlling for ageband
```

| RR | chi2 | P>chi2 | [95% Conf. Interval] | |
|---|---|---|---|---|
| 0.534 | 4.36 | 0.0369 | 0.293 | 0.972 |

```
Approx test for unequal RRs (effect modification): chi2(2) =     1.19
                                                    Pr>chi2 =   0.5514
```

Note that since the RR estimates are approximate, the test for unequal rate ratios is also approximate.

We can also compare the effect of `hienergy` between jobs, controlling for `ageband`.

```
. stmh hienergy ageband, c(1,0) by(job)
            failure _d:  fail == 1 3 13
      analysis time _t:  (dox-origin)/365.25
                origin:  time dob
      enter on or after:  time doe
                    id:  id
                  note:  ageband<=40 trimmed
Mantel-Haenszel estimate of the rate ratio
  comparing hienergy==1 vs. hienergy==0
  controlling for ageband
  by job
RR estimate, and lower and upper 95% confidence limits
     job     RR   Lower   Upper
       0   0.42    0.13    1.33
       1   0.64    0.22    1.87
       2   0.51    0.21    1.26
Overall estimate controlling for ageband job
```

| RR | chi2 | P>chi2 | [95% Conf. Interval] | |
|---|---|---|---|---|
| 0.521 | 4.88 | 0.0271 | 0.289 | 0.939 |

```
Approx test for unequal RRs (effect modification): chi2(2) =     0.28
                                                    Pr>chi2 =   0.8695
```

◁

## Log-linear trend test for metric explanatory variables using stmh

`stmh` may also be used to carry out trend tests for a metric explanatory variable. In addition, a one-step Newton approximation to the log-linear Poisson regression coefficient is computed.

The diet dataset contains the height for each patient recorded in the variable `height`. We can test for a trend of heart disease rates with height controlling for age band by typing

```
. stmh height ageband
            failure _d:  fail == 1 3 13
      analysis time _t:  (dox-origin)/365.25
                origin:  time dob
      enter on or after:  time doe
                    id:  id
                  note:  ageband<=40 trimmed
Score test for trend of rates with height
  with an approximate estimate of the
  rate ratio for a one unit increase in height
  controlling for ageband
```

RR estimate, and lower and upper 95% confidence limits

| RR | chi2 | P>chi2 | [95% Conf. Interval] | |
|---|---|---|---|---|
| 0.906 | 18.60 | 0.0000 | 0.866 | 0.948 |

stmh tested for trend of heart disease rates with height within age bands, and provided a rough estimate of the rate ratio for a 1 cm increase in height—this estimate is a one-step Newton approximation to the maximum likelihood estimate. It is not consistent, but it does provide a useful indication of the size of the effect.

We see that the rate ratio is significantly less than 1, so there is clear evidence for a decreasing rate with increasing height (about 9% decrease in rate per cm increase in height).

## Controlling for age with fine strata using stmc

The stmc (Mantel–Cox) command is used to control for variation of rates on a time scale by breaking up time into very short intervals, or *clicks*.

Usually this approach is used only to calculate significance tests, but the rate ratio estimated remains just as useful as in the coarsely stratified analysis from stmh. The method may be viewed as an approximate form of Cox regression.

The rate ratio produced by stmc is controlled for analysis time, separately for each level of the variables specified with by(), and then combined to give a rate ratio controlled for both time and the by() variables.

▷ Example

For example, to obtain the effect of high energy controlled for age by stratifying very finely, we must first stset the data specifying the date of birth, dob, as the origin (so analysis time is age), and then we use stmc:

```
. stset dox, origin(time dob) enter(time doe) id(id) scale(365.25) fail(fail==1 3 13)
(output omitted )
. stmc hienergy
          failure _d:  fail == 1 3 13
    analysis time _t:  (dox-origin)/365.25
              origin:  time dob
   enter on or after:  time doe
                  id:  id
Mantel-Cox comparisons
Mantel-Haenszel estimates of the rate ratio
    comparing hienergy==1 vs. hienergy==0
    controlling for time (by clicks)
Overall Mantel-Haenszel estimate, controlling for time from dob
```

| RR | chi2 | P>chi2 | [95% Conf. Interval] | |
|---|---|---|---|---|
| 0.537 | 4.20 | 0.0403 | 0.293 | 0.982 |

The rate ratio of 0.537 is quite close to that obtained with stmh when controlling for age using 10-year age bands.

◁

## Saved Results

stmh and stmc save in r():

Scalars
  r(RR)          overall rate ratio

## Methods and Formulas

strate, stmh, and stmc are implemented as ado-files.

## Acknowledgments

The original versions of strate, stmh, and stmc were written by David Clayton, MRC Biostatistical Research Unit, Cambridge, and Michael Hills, London School of Hygiene and Tropical Medicine (retired).

## References

Clayton, D. G. and M. Hills. 1993. *Statistical Models in Epidemiology*. Oxford: Oxford University Press.

——. 1995. ssa7: Analysis of follow-up studies. *Stata Technical Bulletin* 27: 19–26. Reprinted in *Stata Technical Bulletin Reprints*, vol. 5, pp. 219–227.

——. 1997. ssa10: Analysis of follow-up studies with Stata 5.0. *Stata Technical Bulletin* 40: 27–39. Reprinted in *Stata Technical Bulletin Reprints*, vol. 7, pp. 253–268.

## Also See

| | |
|---|---|
| **Complementary:** | [R] **st stci**, [R] **st stir**, [R] **st stptime**, [R] **st stset**, [R] **st stsplit** |
| **Related:** | [R] **epitab** |
| **Background:** | [R] **st** |

# Title

st **streg** — Estimate parametric survival models

# Syntax

streg [*varlist*] [if *exp*] [in *range*] [, dist(*distname*) nohr time tr level(*#*)

    robust cluster(*varname*) score(*newvar(s)*) ancillary(*varname*) anc2(*varname*)

    strata(*varname*) frailty(gamma | invgaussian) noshow constraints(*numlist*)

    cmd nolog *maximize_options*]

stcurve [, cumhaz survival hazard range(*# #*) at(*varname=#* [*varname=#*...])

    [at1(*varname=#* [*varname=#*...]) [at2(*varname=#* [*varname=#*...]) [...]]]

    outfile(*filename*,[replace]) *graph_options*]

where *distname* is one of { exponential | weibull | gompertz | lognormal | lnormal | loglogistic | llogistic | gamma }

lognormal and lnormal are synonyms; loglogistic and llogistic are synonyms.

streg is for use with survival-time data; see [R] st. You must stset your data before using streg.

by ... : may be used with streg; see [R] by.

stcurve may be used after streg.

streg shares the features of all estimation commands; see [U] **23 Estimation and post-estimation commands**.

# Syntax for predict

predict [*type*] *newvarname* [if *exp*] [in *range*] [, *statistic* ]

where *statistic* is

| | |
|---|---|
| median time | predicted median survival time (the default) |
| median lntime | predicted median ln(survival time) |
| mean time | predicted mean survival time |
| mean lntime | predicted mean ln(survival time) |
| hazard | predicted hazard |
| hr | predicted hazard ratio |
| xb | linear prediction $\mathbf{x}_j\mathbf{b}$ |
| stdp | standard error of the linear prediction; $\mathrm{SE}(\mathbf{x}_j\mathbf{b})$ |
| surv | predicted $S(depvar)$ or $S(depvar|t_0)$ |
| csnell | (partial) Cox–Snell residuals |
| mgale | (partial) martingale-like residuals |
| deviance | deviance residuals |
| csurv | predicted $S(depvar|$ earliest $t_0$ for subject) |
| ccsnell | cumulative Cox–Snell residuals |
| cmgale | cumulative martingale-like residuals |

All statistics are available both in and out of sample; type `predict ... if e(sample) ...` if wanted only for the estimation sample.

When no option is specified, the predicted median survival time is calculated for all models. The predicted hazard ratio option `hr` is only available for the exponential, Weibull, and Gompertz models. The `mean time` and `mean lntime` options are not available for the Gompertz model, and the `mean time` option is not available for the generalized log-gamma model. The `mean time` and `mean lntime` options are not available if `frailty(distname)` is specified.

## Description

`streg` performs maximum likelihood estimation of parametric regression survival-time models. These commands are appropriate for use with single- or multiple-record, single- or multiple-failure, st data. Survival models currently supported are exponential, Weibull, Gompertz, lognormal, log-logistic, and generalized gamma.

Also see [R] **st stcox** for estimation of proportional hazards models.

`stcurve` is used after `streg` to plot the cumulative hazard, survival, and hazard functions at the mean value of the covariates or at values specified by the `at()` options.

`predict` is used after `streg` to generate a variable containing the specified predicted values or residuals.

## Options

### Options for streg

`dist(distname)` specifies the survival model to be estimated. If `dist(distname)` is not specified, `streg` will use the same distribution as the previous time `streg` was used or, if there is no previous time, it will issue an error message.

For instance, typing `streg x1 x2, dist(weibull)` will estimate a Weibull model. Subsequently, you do not need to specify `dist(weibull)` to estimate other Weibull regression models.

If `frailty(distname)` is specified, then `dist(distname)` and `frailty(distname)` will carry over to each subsequent estimation if neither is specified then. However, if in a subsequent estimation `dist(distname)` is specified without `frailty(distname)`, then a model without frailty is estimated.

The currently supported distributions are listed in the syntax diagram, but new ones may have been added. Type `help streg` for an up-to-date list.

All Stata estimation commands, including `streg`, redisplay results when the command name is typed without arguments. If you wish to estimate a model without any explanatory variables, type `streg, dist(distname)`.

`nohr`, which can be specified when the model is estimated or when redisplaying results, specifies that coefficients rather than exponentiated coefficients are to be displayed or, said differently, coefficients rather than hazard ratios are displayed. This option affects only how results are displayed and not how they are estimated.

This option is valid only for models with a proportional hazard ratio parameterization: exponential, Weibull, and Gompertz. These three models, by default, report hazard ratios (exponentiated coefficients).

time specifies that the model is to be estimated in the accelerated failure-time metric rather than in the log relative-hazard metric. This option is only valid for the exponential and Weibull models since they have both a hazard ratio and an accelerated failure-time parameterization. For these two models, in the log relative-hazard metric, estimates of $(\beta, \sigma)$ are produced, and in the accelerated failure-time metric, estimates of $(-\sigma\beta, \sigma)$ are produced. Regardless of metric, the likelihood function is the same and models are equally appropriate viewed in either metric; it is just a matter of changing interpretation.

time must be specified when the model is estimated.

tr is appropriate only for the log-logistic, lognormal, and gamma models, or for the exponential and Weibull models when estimated in log expected time. tr specifies that exponentiated coefficients are to be displayed, which have the interpretation of time ratios.

tr may be specified when the model is estimated or when results are redisplayed.

level(#) specifies the confidence level, in percent, for confidence intervals. The default is level(95) or as set by set level; see [U] **23.5 Specifying the width of confidence intervals**.

robust specifies that the robust method of calculating the variance–covariance matrix is to be used instead of the conventional inverse-matrix-of-negative-second-derivatives method. If you specify robust, and if you have previously stset an id() variable, the robust calculation will be clustered on the id() variable.

We especially recommend that you specify robust if you have stset an id() variable because the assumption that justifies the conventional variance estimate—the independence of the observations—is presumably false.

cluster(*varname*) implies robust and specifies a variable on which clustering is to be based. This overrides the default clustering, if any. See the discussion under *Robust estimates of variance* in [R] **st stcox**; what is said there is appropriate here as well. Unless you are analyzing repeated failure data and have created pseudo-ids to allow time to measure time since last failure, you should not have to specify this option.

score(*newvar(s)*) requests that *newvar(s)* be created containing the score function(s). One new variable is specified in the case of an exponential model, two variables are specified for Weibull, lognormal, Gompertz, and log-logistic models, and three new variables are specified in the case of gamma.

The first new variable will contain $\partial(\ln L_j)/\partial(\mathbf{x}_j\boldsymbol{\beta})$.

The second and third new variables, if they exist, will contain $\partial(\ln L_j)$ with respect to the second and third ancillary parameters. See Table 1 for a list of ancillary parameters.

ancillary(*varlist*) specifies that the ancillary parameter for the Weibull, lognormal, Gompertz, and log-logistic distributions and the first ancillary parameter (sigma) of the generalized log-gamma distribution are to be estimated as a linear combination of *varlist*. This option is not available if frailty(*distname*) is specified.

anc2(*varlist*) specifies that the second ancillary parameter (kappa) for the generalized log-gamma distribution is to be estimated as a linear combination of *varlist*. This option is not available if frailty(*distname*) is specified.

strata(*varname*) specifies a stratification variable. Observations with equal values of the variable are assumed to be in the same stratum. Stratified estimates (equal coefficients across strata but intercepts and ancillary parameters unique to each stratum) are then estimated. This option is not available if frailty(*distname*) is specified.

frailty(gamma | invgaussian) specifies the assumed distribution of the observation level frailty or heterogeneity. The estimated model will, in addition to the standard parameter estimates, produce an estimate of the variance of the frailties and a likelihood-ratio test of the null hypothesis that this variance is zero. When this null hypothesis is true, the model reduces to the model with frailty(*distname*) not specified.

noshow prevents streg from showing the key st variables. This option is rarely used since most people type stset, show or stset, noshow to reset once and for all whether they want to see these variables mentioned at the top of the output of every st command; see [R] **st stset**.

constraints(*numlist*) specifies by number the linear constraints to be applied during estimation. The default is to perform unconstrained estimation. Constraints are specified using the constraint command; see [R] **constraint**. See [R] **reg3** for the use of constraints in multiple-equation contexts.

cmd displays the underlying command that streg would execute but does not estimate the model.

nolog prevents streg from showing the iteration log.

*maximize_options* control the maximization process; see [R] **maximize**. You should never have to specify them, with the exception of frailty models, in which case specifying difficult may aid convergence.

## Options for stcurve

cumhaz requests that the cumulative hazard function be plotted.

survival requests that the survival function be plotted.

hazard requests that the hazard function be plotted.

range(*# #*) specifies the range of the time axis to be plotted. If this option is not specified, stcurve will plot the desired curve on an interval expanding from the earliest to the latest time in the data.

at(*varname=#...*) requests that the covariates specified by *varname* be set to *#*. By default, stcurve evaluates the function by setting each covariate to its mean value. This option causes the function to be evaluated at the value of the covariates listed in at() and at the mean of all unlisted covariates.

at1(*varname=#...*), at2(*varname=#...*), ..., at10(*varname=#...*) specify that multiple curves (up to 10) are to be plotted on the same graph. at1(), at2(), ..., at10() work like the at() option. They request that the function be evaluated at the value of the covariates specified and at the mean of all unlisted covariates. at1() specifies the values of the covariates for the first curve, and at2() specifies the values of the covariates for the second curve, and so on.

outfile(*filename* [,replace]) saves in *filename*.dta the values used to plot the curve(s).

*graph_options* are most of the options allowed with graph, twoway; see [G] **graph options**.

## Options for predict

median time calculates the predicted median survival time in analysis time units. Note that this is the prediction from time 0 conditional on constant covariates. When no options are specified with predict, the predicted median survival time is calculated for all models.

median lntime calculates the natural logarithm of what median time produces.

mean time calculates the predicted mean survival time in analysis time units. Note that this is the prediction from time 0 conditional on constant covariates. This option is neither available for the Gompertz and gamma regressions, nor when frailty(*distname*) is used.

**mean lntime** calculates the mean of the natural logarithm of **time**. This option is neither available for Gompertz regression, nor when **frailty**(*distname*) is used.

**hazard** calculates the predicted hazard.

**hr** calculates the hazard ratio. This option is valid only for models having a proportional hazard parameterization.

**xb** calculates the linear prediction from the estimated model. That is, all models can be thought of as estimating a set of parameters $b_1$, $b_2$, ..., $b_k$, and the linear prediction is $\widehat{y}_j = b_0 + b_1 x_{1j} + b_2 x_{2j} + \cdots + b_k x_{kj}$, often written in matrix notation as $\widehat{y}_j = \mathbf{x}_j \mathbf{b}$.

It is important to understand that the $x_{1j}$, $x_{2j}$, ..., $x_{kj}$ used in the calculation are obtained from the data currently in memory, and do not have to correspond to the data on the independent variables used in estimating the model (obtaining the $b_1$, $b_2$, ..., $b_k$).

**stdp** calculates the standard error of the prediction; that is, the standard error of $\widehat{y}_j$.

**surv** calculates each observation's predicted survivor probability $S(t|t_0)$, where $t_0$ is _t0, the analysis time at which each record became at risk. For multiple-record data, also see the **csurv** option below.

**csnell** calculates the (partial) Cox–Snell residual. If you have a single observation per subject, then **csnell** calculates the usual Cox–Snell residual. Otherwise, **csnell** calculates the additive contribution of this observation to the subject's overall Cox–Snell residual.

**mgale** calculates the (partial) martingale-like residual. The issues are the same as with **csnell** above.

**deviance** calculates the deviance residual. In the case of multiple-record data, only one value per subject is calculated and it is placed on the last record for the subject.

**csurv** calculates the predicted $S(t|\text{earliest } t_0)$ for each subject in multiple-record data. This is based on calculating the conditional survivor values $S(t|t_0)$ (see option **csurv** above) and then multiplying them together.

**ccsnell** calculates the (cumulative) Cox–Snell residual in multiple-record data. This is based on calculating the partial Cox–Snell residuals (see option **csnell** above) and then summing them. Only one value per subject is recorded—the overall sum—and it is placed on the last record for the subject.

**cmgale** calculates the (cumulative) martingale-like residual in multiple-record data. This is based on calculating the partial martingale-like residuals (see option **mgale** above) and then summing them. Only one value per subject is recorded—the overall sum—and it is placed on the last record for the subject.

# Remarks

Remarks are presented under the headings

> *Introduction*
> *Distributions*
> > *Weibull and exponential models*
> > *Gompertz model*
> > *Lognormal and log-logistic models*
> > *Generalized gamma model*
> *Examples*
> *Frailty models*
> *Parameterization of ancillary parameters*
> *Stratified estimation*
> *Fitted curves*
> *predict*

## Introduction

Two frequently used models for adjusting survival functions for the effects of covariates are the accelerated failure-time (AFT) model and the multiplicative or proportional hazard rate (PH) model. In the accelerated failure-time model, the natural logarithm of the survival time $\ln t$ is expressed as a linear function of the covariates, yielding the linear model

$$\ln t_j = \mathbf{x}_j \boldsymbol{\beta} + z_j$$

where $\mathbf{x}_j$ is a vector of covariates, $\boldsymbol{\beta}$ is a vector of regression coefficients, and $z_j$ is the error with density $f()$. The distributional form of the error term determines the regression model. If we let $f()$ be the normal density, the lognormal regression model is obtained. Similarly, by letting $f()$ be the logistic density, the log-logistic regression is obtained. Setting $f()$ equal to the extreme-value density yields the exponential and the Weibull regression models, and when $f()$ follows a three-parameter gamma density, the generalized log-gamma regression or simply the generalized gamma regression is obtained.

The effect of the accelerated failure-time (AFT) model is to change the time scale by a factor of $\exp(-\mathbf{x}_j \boldsymbol{\beta})$. Depending on whether this factor is greater than or less than 1, time is either accelerated or decelerated (degraded). Thus, accelerated failure time does not necessarily imply a positive acceleration of time.

In the proportional hazard (PH) rate model, the concomitant covariates have a multiplicative effect on the hazard function

$$h(t_j) = h_0(t)g(\mathbf{x}_j)$$

where $h_0(t)$ is the baseline hazard function and $g(\mathbf{x}_j)$ is a nonnegative function of the covariates. A popular choice, and the one adopted here, is to let $g(\mathbf{x}_j)$ equal the relative risk: $g(\mathbf{x}_j) = e^{\mathbf{x}_j \boldsymbol{\beta}}$. The function $h_0(t)$ may either be left unspecified, yielding the Cox proportional hazard model (see [R] **st stcox**), or take a specific parametric form. For the **streg** command, $h_0(t)$ is assumed to be parametric. Three regression models are currently implemented as proportional hazard (PH) models: the exponential, Weibull, and Gompertz models. Note that the exponential and Weibull models are implemented as both AFT and PH models, and that Gompertz is only implemented as a PH model.

More specific information regarding the parameterization of accelerated failure-time and proportional hazard models is presented in the next section. For more detailed information about these distributions, please consult the references.

(*Continued on next page*)

## Distributions

Six parametric survival distributions are currently supported by `streg`. The parameterization and ancillary parameters for each distribution are summarized in Table 1:

Table 1. Parametric survival distributions supported by `streg`

| Distribution | Metric | Survival function | Parameterization | Ancillary parameters |
|---|---|---|---|---|
| Exponential | PH | $e^{-\lambda_j t_j}$ | $\lambda = e^{\mathbf{x}_j \boldsymbol{\beta}}$ | |
| Exponential | AFT | $e^{-\lambda_j t_j}$ | $\lambda = e^{-\mathbf{x}_j \boldsymbol{\beta}}$ | |
| Weibull | PH | $e^{-\lambda_j t_j^p}$ | $\lambda_j = e^{\mathbf{x}_j \boldsymbol{\beta}}$ | $p$ |
| Weibull | AFT | $e^{-\lambda_j t_j^p}$ | $\lambda_j = e^{-\mathbf{x}_j \boldsymbol{\beta} p}$ | $p$ |
| Gompertz | PH | $e^{-\frac{e^{\lambda_j}}{\gamma}(e^{\gamma t_j}-1)}$ | $\lambda_j = \mathbf{x}_j \boldsymbol{\beta}$ | $\gamma$ |
| Lognormal | AFT | $1 - \Phi\left(\frac{\ln(t_j)-\mu_j}{\sigma}\right)$ | $\mu_j = \mathbf{x}_j \boldsymbol{\beta}$ | $\sigma$ |
| Log-logistic | AFT | $\frac{1}{1+(\lambda_j t_j)^{\frac{1}{\gamma}}}$ | $\lambda_j = e^{-\mathbf{x}_j \boldsymbol{\beta}}$ | $\gamma$ |
| Generalized gamma | | | | |
| if $\kappa > 0$ | AFT | $1 - I(\gamma, u)$ | $\lambda_j = \mathbf{x}_j \boldsymbol{\beta}$ | $\sigma, \kappa$ |
| if $\kappa = 0$ | AFT | $1 - \Phi(z)$ | $\lambda_j = \mathbf{x}_j \boldsymbol{\beta}$ | $\sigma, \kappa$ |
| if $\kappa < 0$ | AFT | $I(\gamma, u)$ | $\lambda_j = \mathbf{x}_j \boldsymbol{\beta}$ | $\sigma, \kappa$ |

where PH = proportional hazard, AFT = accelerated failure time, $\Phi(z)$ is the standard normal cumulative distribution, $\gamma = |\kappa|^{-2}$, $u = \gamma \exp(|\kappa| z)$, $I(a, x)$ is the incomplete gamma function, and $z = \text{sign}(\kappa)\{\ln(t_j) - \lambda_j\}/\sigma$

Plotted in Figure 1 are example hazard functions for five of the six distributions. The exponential hazard (not separately plotted) is a special case of the Weibull hazard when the Weibull ancillary parameter $p = 1$. The generalized gamma (not plotted) is extremely flexible, and therefore can take a multitude of shapes.

(*Graphs on next page*)

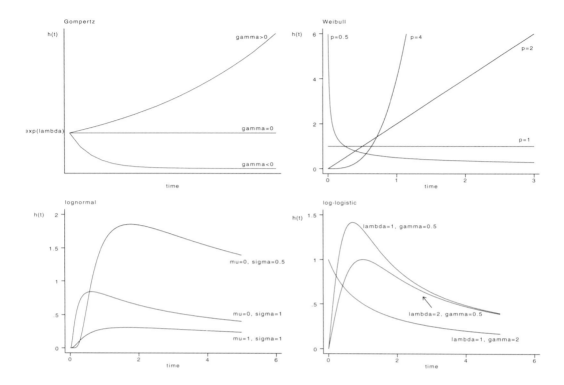

Figure 1. Example plots of hazard functions

## Weibull and exponential models

The Weibull and exponential models are parameterized as both proportional hazard and accelerated failure-time models. The Weibull distribution is suitable for modeling data with monotone hazard rates that either increase or decrease exponentially with time, while the exponential distribution is suitable for modeling data with constant hazard (see Figure 1).

For the proportional hazard model, $h_0(t) = 1$ for exponential regression, and $h_0(t) = p\,t^{p-1}$ for Weibull regression, where $p$ is the shape parameter to be estimated from the data. Some authors refer not to $p$ but to $\sigma = 1/p$.

The accelerated failure-time model equation is written as

$$\ln(t_j) = \mathbf{x}_j \boldsymbol{\beta}^\star + z_j$$

where $z_j$ has an extreme-value distribution scaled by $\sigma$. Let $\boldsymbol{\beta}$ be the vector of regression coefficients derived from the proportional hazard model, so that $\boldsymbol{\beta}^\star = -\sigma\boldsymbol{\beta}$. Note that this relationship only holds if the ancillary parameter $p$ is a constant; it does not hold when the ancillary parameter is parameterized in terms of covariates.

streg uses, by default, for the exponential and Weibull models, the proportional hazard interpretation because (1) it makes it easier to compare results with those produced by stcox, and (2) this parameterization makes it clear that these models are applicable to time-varying covariates, delayed entry, and even multiple failures.

You can, however, specify option time to choose the accelerated failure-time parameterization, and you can do this even with time-varying covariates, delayed entry, or multiple failures. There is no estimation issue, but it should be understood that, in those cases, the predicted value of the accelerated time model is the predicted log time of failure conditional on entry at time 0 with constant covariates. To be clear, consider a subject with the following data:

| t0 | t1 | d | x |
|----|----|---|---|
| 50 | 62 | 1 | 3 |

These data say that the subject was under observation over $(50, 62]$ with $x = 3$, and failed at time 62. The data will be used appropriately to estimate the parameters, whichever parameterization you choose. Say you choose the accelerated time parameterization. The predicted value from the estimated model might be 2.3 for this subject. That merely means that, for a person who enters at time 0 with $x = 3$, the predicted time of first failure would be $e^{2.3} = 9.97$.

The Weibull hazard and survival functions are

$$h(t) = p\lambda t^{p-1}$$

$$S(t) = \exp(-\lambda t^p)$$

where $\lambda$ is parameterized as described in Table 1. If $p = 1$, then these functions reduce to those of the exponential.

## Gompertz model

The Gompertz regression is parameterized only as a proportional hazards model. First described in 1825, this model has been extensively used by medical researchers and biologists modeling mortality data. The Gompertz distribution implemented is the two-parameter function as described in Lee (1992), with the following hazard, survival, and density functions:

$$h(t) = e^{\lambda + \gamma t} = e^\lambda e^{\gamma t}$$

$$S(t) = e^{-\frac{e^\lambda}{\gamma}(e^{\gamma t} - 1)}$$

$$f(t) = e^{(\lambda + \gamma t) - \frac{e^\lambda}{\gamma}(e^{\gamma t} - 1)}$$

The model is implemented by parameterizing $\lambda_j = \mathbf{x}_j \boldsymbol{\beta}$, implying that $h_0(t) = e^{\gamma t}$ where $\gamma$ is an ancillary parameter to be estimated from the data. This parameterization yields the proportional hazard model, specifically

$$h(t_j) = e^{\gamma t_j} e^{\mathbf{x}_j \boldsymbol{\beta}}$$

This distribution is suitable for modeling data with monotone hazard rates that either increase or decrease exponentially with time (see Figure 1).

When $\gamma$ is positive, the hazard function increases with time; when $\gamma$ is negative, the hazard function decreases with time; and when $\gamma$ is zero, the hazard function is equal to exp(a) for all $t$, which is to say, the model reduces to an exponential.

Some recent survival analysis texts, such as Klein and Moeschberger (1997), restrict $\gamma$ to be strictly positive. Note that if $\gamma < 0$, then as $t$ goes to infinity, the survivor function $S(t)$ exponentially decreases to a nonzero constant, implying that there is a nonzero probability of never failing (living forever). That is, there is always a nonzero hazard rate, yet it decreases exponentially. By restricting $\gamma$ to be positive, one is assured that the survivor function always goes to zero as $t$ tends to infinity.

Although the above argument may be desirable from a mathematical perspective, in Stata's implementation, we took the more traditional approach of not restricting $\gamma$. We did this because in survival studies subjects are not followed forever—there is a date when the study ends, and in many investigations, specifically in medical research, an exponentially-decreasing hazard rate is clinically appealing.

## Lognormal and log-logistic models

The lognormal and log-logistic models are implemented in only the accelerated failure-time form. These two distributions are similar and tend to produce comparable results. In the case of the lognormal distribution, the natural logarithm of time follows a normal distribution; whereas for the log-logistic distribution, the natural logarithm of time follows a logistic distribution.

The lognormal hazard, survival, and density functions are

$$h(t) = \frac{\frac{1}{t\sigma\sqrt{2\pi}} \exp\left[\frac{-1}{2\sigma^2}\left\{\ln(t) - \mu\right\}^2\right]}{1 - \Phi\left\{\frac{\ln(t) - \mu}{\sigma}\right\}}$$

$$S(t) = 1 - \Phi\left\{\frac{\ln(t) - \mu}{\sigma}\right\}$$

$$f(t) = \frac{1}{t\sigma\sqrt{2\pi}} \exp\left[\frac{-1}{2\sigma^2}\left\{\ln(t) - \mu\right\}^2\right]$$

where $\Phi(z)$ is the standard normal cumulative distribution function.

The lognormal regression is implemented by setting $\mu_j = \mathbf{x}_j\boldsymbol{\beta}$ and treating the standard deviation $\sigma$ as an ancillary parameter to be estimated from the data.

The log-logistic regression is obtained if $z_j$ has a logistic density. The log-logistic hazard, survival, and density functions are

$$h(t) = \frac{\lambda^{\frac{1}{\gamma}} t^{\frac{1}{\gamma} - 1}}{\gamma\left\{1 + (\lambda t)^{\frac{1}{\gamma}}\right\}}$$

$$S(t) = \frac{1}{1 + (\lambda t)^{\frac{1}{\gamma}}}$$

$$f(t) = \frac{\lambda^{\frac{1}{\gamma}} t^{\frac{1}{\gamma}-1}}{\gamma \{1 + (\lambda t)^{\frac{1}{\gamma}}\}^2}$$

This model is implemented by parameterizing $\lambda_j = e^{-\mathbf{x}_j \boldsymbol{\beta}}$ and treating the scale parameter $\gamma$ as an ancillary parameter to be estimated from the data.

Unlike the exponential, Weibull, and Gompertz distributions, the lognormal and the log-logistic distributions are indicated for data exhibiting nonmonotonic hazard rates, specifically initially increasing and then decreasing rates (Figure 1).

## Generalized gamma model

The generalized gamma model is implemented only in the accelerated failure-time form. The three-parameter generalized gamma survival and density functions are

$$S(t) = \begin{cases} 1 - I(\gamma, u), & \text{if } \kappa > 0 \\ 1 - \Phi(z), & \text{if } \kappa = 0 \\ I(\gamma, u), & \text{if } \kappa < 0 \end{cases}$$

$$f(t) = \begin{cases} \frac{\gamma^{\gamma}}{\sigma t \sqrt{\gamma} \Gamma(\gamma)} \exp(z\sqrt{\gamma} - u), & \text{if } \kappa \neq 0 \\ \frac{1}{\sigma t \sqrt{2\pi}} \exp(-z^2/2), & \text{if } \kappa = 0 \end{cases}$$

where $\gamma = |\kappa|^{-2}$, $z = \text{sign}(\kappa)\{\ln(t) - \mu\}/\sigma$, $u = \gamma \exp(|\kappa|z)$, $\Phi(z)$ is the standard normal cumulative distribution function, and $I(a, x)$ is the incomplete gamma function. See the `gammap(a,x)` entry in [U] **16.3.2 Statistical functions** to see how the incomplete gamma function is implemented in Stata.

This model is implemented by parameterizing $\lambda_j = \mathbf{x}_j \boldsymbol{\beta}$ and treating the parameters $\kappa$ and $\sigma$ as ancillary parameters to be estimated from the data.

The hazard function of the generalized gamma distribution is extremely flexible, allowing for a large number of possible shapes, including as special cases the Weibull distribution when $\kappa = 1$, the exponential when $\kappa = 1$ and $\sigma = 1$, and the lognormal distribution when $\kappa = 0$. The generalized gamma model is, therefore, commonly used for evaluating and selecting an appropriate parametric model for the data. The Wald or likelihood-ratio test can be used to test the hypotheses that $\kappa = 1$ or that $\kappa = 0$.

## Examples

▷ Example

The Weibull distribution provides a good illustration of `streg`, since this distribution is parameterized as both AFT and PH and serves to compare and contrast the two approaches.

You wish to analyze an experiment testing the ability of emergency generators with new-style bearings to withstand overloads. This dataset is described in [R] **st stcox**. This time, you wish to estimate a Weibull model:

```
. streg load bearings, dist(weibull)

        failure _d:  1 (meaning all fail)
   analysis time _t:  failtime

Fitting constant-only model:

Iteration 0:   log likelihood = -13.666193
Iteration 1:   log likelihood = -9.7427276
Iteration 2:   log likelihood = -9.4421169
Iteration 3:   log likelihood = -9.4408287
Iteration 4:   log likelihood = -9.4408286

Fitting full model:

Iteration 0:   log likelihood = -9.4408286
Iteration 1:   log likelihood =  -2.078323
Iteration 2:   log likelihood =  5.2226016
Iteration 3:   log likelihood =  5.6745808
Iteration 4:   log likelihood =  5.6934031
Iteration 5:   log likelihood =  5.6934189
Iteration 6:   log likelihood =  5.6934189

Weibull regression -- log relative-hazard form
```

| | | | | | | |
|---|---|---|---|---|---|---|
| No. of subjects = | | 12 | | Number of obs | = | 12 |
| No. of failures = | | 12 | | | | |
| Time at risk   = | | 896 | | | | |
| | | | | LR chi2(2) | = | 30.27 |
| Log likelihood = | | 5.6934189 | | Prob > chi2 | = | 0.0000 |

| _t | Haz. Ratio | Std. Err. | z | P>|z| | [95% Conf. Interval] | |
|---|---|---|---|---|---|---|
| load | 1.599315 | .1883807 | 3.99 | 0.000 | 1.269616 | 2.014631 |
| bearings | .1887995 | .1312109 | -2.40 | 0.016 | .0483546 | .7371644 |
| /ln_p | 2.051552 | .2317074 | 8.85 | 0.000 | 1.597414 | 2.505691 |
| p | 7.779969 | 1.802677 | | | 4.940241 | 12.25202 |
| 1/p | .1285352 | .0297826 | | | .0816192 | .2024193 |

Since we did not specify otherwise, this model was estimated in the hazard metric, which is the default for dist(weibull). The estimates are directly comparable to those produced by stcox: stcox estimated a hazard ratio of 1.526 for load and .0636 for bearings.

In this case, however, we estimated the baseline hazard function as well, assuming it is Weibull. The estimates are the full maximum-likelihood estimates. The shape parameter is fitted as $\ln p$, but streg then reports $p$ and $1/p = \sigma$ so that you can think about the parameter however you wish.

We find that $p$ is greater than 1, which means that the hazard of failure increases with time and, in this case, increases dramatically. After 100 hours, the bearings are over 1 million times more likely to fail per second than after 10 hours (or, to be precise, $(100/10)^{7.78-1}$). Based on our knowledge of generators, we would expect this; it is the accumulation of heat due to friction that causes bearings to expand and seize.

◁

## ❑ Technical Note

Regression results are often presented in a metric other than the natural regression coefficients, i.e., as hazard ratios, relative risk ratios, odd ratios, etc. When this occurs, the standard errors are calculated using the delta method.

However, the $Z$ test and $p$-values given are calculated from the natural regression coefficients and their standard errors. The reason for this is that, although a test based on say a hazard ratio and its standard error would be asymptotically equivalent to that based on a regression coefficient, in real samples a hazard ratio will tend to have a more skewed distribution since it is an exponentiated regression coefficient. Also, it is more natural to think of these tests as testing whether a regression coefficient is nonzero, rather than testing whether a transformed regression coefficient is unequal to some nonzero value (one in the case of a hazard ratio).

Finally, the confidence intervals given are obtained by transforming the end points of the corresponding confidence interval for the untransformed regression coefficient. This has the advantage of ensuring that, say, strictly positive quantities such as hazard ratios have confidence intervals which do not overlap zero.

❏

## ▷ Example

The previous model was estimated in the log relative-hazard metric and exponentiated coefficients—hazard ratios—were reported. If we wanted to see the unexponentiated coefficients, we could redisplay results and specify the `nohr` option:

```
. streg, nohr

Weibull regression -- log relative-hazard form
No. of subjects =          12                  Number of obs   =          12
No. of failures =          12
Time at risk    =         896
                                               LR chi2(2)      =       30.27
Log likelihood  =     5.6934189                Prob > chi2     =      0.0000
```

| _t | Coef. | Std. Err. | z | P>\|z\| | [95% Conf. Interval] | |
|---|---|---|---|---|---|---|
| load | .4695753 | .1177884 | 3.99 | 0.000 | .2387143 | .7004363 |
| bearings | -1.667069 | .6949745 | -2.40 | 0.016 | -3.029194 | -.3049443 |
| _cons | -45.13191 | 10.60663 | -4.26 | 0.000 | -65.92053 | -24.34329 |
| /ln_p | 2.051552 | .2317074 | 8.85 | 0.000 | 1.597414 | 2.505691 |
| p | 7.779969 | 1.802677 | | | 4.940241 | 12.25202 |
| 1/p | .1285352 | .0297826 | | | .0816192 | .2024193 |

◁

*(Continued on next page)*

▷ Example

We could just as well estimate this model in the accelerated failure-time metric:

```
. streg load bearings, dist(weibull) time nolog
        failure _d:  1 (meaning all fail)
  analysis time _t:  failtime
```

Weibull regression -- accelerated failure-time form

| | | |
|---|---|---|
| No. of subjects = | 12 | Number of obs = | 12 |
| No. of failures = | 12 | | |
| Time at risk = | 896 | | |
| | | LR chi2(2) = | 30.27 |
| Log likelihood = | 5.6934189 | Prob > chi2 = | 0.0000 |

| _t | Coef. | Std. Err. | z | P>\|z\| | [95% Conf. Interval] |
|---|---|---|---|---|---|
| load | -.060357 | .0062214 | -9.70 | 0.000 | -.0725507   -.0481632 |
| bearings | .2142771 | .0746451 | 2.87 | 0.004 | .0679753   .3605789 |
| _cons | 5.80104 | .1752301 | 33.11 | 0.000 | 5.457595   6.144485 |
| /ln_p | 2.051552 | .2317074 | 8.85 | 0.000 | 1.597414   2.505691 |
| p | 7.779969 | 1.802677 | | | 4.940241   12.25202 |
| 1/p | .1285352 | .0297826 | | | .0816192   .2024193 |

This is the same model as previously estimated, but presented in a different metric. Calling the previous coefficients $b$, these coefficients are $-\sigma b = -b/p$. For instance, in the previous example, the coefficient on load was reported as .4695753, and note that $-.4695753/7.779969 = -.06035696$.

◁

▷ Example

The advantage of the log relative-hazard metric is that it allows an easier interpretation of results in complicated datasets. Below we have multiple records per subject on a failure that can occur repeatedly:

```
. stdes
```

| | | per subject | | | |
|---|---|---|---|---|---|
| Category | total | mean | min | median | max |
| no. of subjects | 926 | | | | |
| no. of records | 1734 | 1.87257 | 1 | 2 | 4 |
| (first) entry time | | 0 | 0 | 0 | 0 |
| (final) exit time | | 470.6857 | 1 | 477 | 960 |
| subjects with gap | 6 | | | | |
| time on gap if gap | 411 | 68.5 | 16 | 57.5 | 133 |
| time at risk | 435444 | 470.2419 | 1 | 477 | 960 |
| failures | 808 | .8725702 | 0 | 1 | 3 |

In this dataset, subjects have up to 4 records—most have 2—and have up to 3 failures—most have 1—and, although you cannot tell from the above output, the data have time-varying covariates as well. There are even 6 subjects with gaps in their histories, meaning that, for a while, they went unobserved. Although we could estimate in the accelerated failure-time metric, it is easier to interpret results in the log relative-hazard metric:

```
. streg x1 x2, dist(weibull) robust

Fitting constant-only model:

Iteration 0:   log likelihood = -1398.2504
Iteration 1:   log likelihood = -1382.8224
Iteration 2:   log likelihood = -1382.7457
Iteration 3:   log likelihood = -1382.7457

Fitting full model:

Iteration 0:   log likelihood = -1382.7457
Iteration 1:   log likelihood = -1328.4186
Iteration 2:   log likelihood = -1326.4483
Iteration 3:   log likelihood = -1326.4449
Iteration 4:   log likelihood = -1326.4449

Weibull regression -- log relative-hazard form

No. of subjects =         926          Number of obs    =      1734
No. of failures =         808
Time at risk    =      435444
                                       Wald chi2(2)     =    154.45
Log likelihood  =   -1326.4449         Prob > chi2      =    0.0000

             (standard errors adjusted for clustering on id)
```

| _t | Haz. Ratio | Robust Std. Err. | z | P>\|z\| | [95% Conf. Interval] | |
|---|---|---|---|---|---|---|
| x1 | 2.240069 | .1812848 | 9.97 | 0.000 | 1.911504 | 2.625111 |
| x2 | .3206515 | .0504626 | -7.23 | 0.000 | .2355458 | .436507 |
| /ln_p | .1771265 | .0310111 | 5.71 | 0.000 | .1163458 | .2379071 |
| p | 1.193782 | .0370205 | | | 1.123384 | 1.268591 |
| 1/p | .8376738 | .0259772 | | | .7882759 | .8901674 |

A one-unit change in x1 approximately doubles the hazard of failure, whereas a one-unit change in x2 cuts the hazard to one-third. We also see that these data are close to being exponentially distributed; $p$ is nearly 1.

◁

▷ Example

The multiple-failure data above are close enough to exponentially distributed that we will re-estimate the model using exponential regression:

```
. streg x1 x2, dist(exp) robust

Iteration 0:   log likelihood = -1398.2504
Iteration 1:   log likelihood = -1343.6083
Iteration 2:   log likelihood = -1341.5932
Iteration 3:   log likelihood = -1341.5893
Iteration 4:   log likelihood = -1341.5893

Exponential regression -- log relative-hazard form

No. of subjects =         926          Number of obs    =      1734
No. of failures =         808
Time at risk    =      435444
                                       Wald chi2(2)     =    166.92
Log likelihood  =   -1341.5893         Prob > chi2      =    0.0000

             (standard errors adjusted for clustering on id)
```

| _t | Haz. Ratio | Robust Std. Err. | z | P>\|z\| | [95% Conf. Interval] | |
|---|---|---|---|---|---|---|
| x1 | 2.19065 | .1684399 | 10.20 | 0.000 | 1.884186 | 2.54696 |
| x2 | .3037259 | .0462489 | -7.83 | 0.000 | .2253552 | .4093511 |

◁

▷ Example

A reasonable question to ask is "Given that we have several possible parametric models, how can we select one?" When parametric models are nested, the likelihood-ratio or Wald tests can be used to discriminate between them. This can certainly be done in the case of Weibull versus exponential, or gamma versus Weibull or lognormal. When models are not nested, however, these tests are unsuitable and the task of discriminating between models becomes difficult. A common approach to this problem is to use the Akaike information criterion (AIC). Akaike (1974) proposed penalizing each log likelihood to reflect the number of parameters being estimated in a particular model and then comparing them. In our case, the AIC can be defined as

$$AIC = -2(\log \text{ likelihood}) + 2(c + p + 1)$$

where $c$ is the number of model covariates and $p$ is the number of model-specific ancillary parameters listed in Table 1. Although the best-fitting model is the one with the largest log likelihood, the preferred model is the one with the smallest AIC value.

Using the `cancer.dta` distributed with Stata, let's first fit a generalized gamma model and test the hypothesis that $\kappa = 0$ (test for the appropriateness of the lognormal), and then test the hypothesis that $\kappa = 1$ (test for the appropriateness of the Weibull).

```
. streg drug age, dist(gamma) nolog

        failure _d:  died
   analysis time _t:  studytime

Gamma regression -- accelerated failure-time form

No. of subjects =          48                  Number of obs   =          48
No. of failures =          31
Time at risk    =         744
                                               LR chi2(2)      =       35.74
Log likelihood  =   -42.619647                 Prob > chi2     =      0.0000
```

| _t | Coef. | Std. Err. | z | P>\|z\| | [95% Conf. Interval] | |
|---|---|---|---|---|---|---|
| drug | .7861776 | .1571202 | 5.00 | 0.000 | .4782278 | 1.094128 |
| age | -.0644245 | .0202083 | -3.19 | 0.001 | -.104032 | -.024817 |
| _cons | 5.108207 | 1.104842 | 4.62 | 0.000 | 2.942758 | 7.273657 |
| /ln_sig | -.5174026 | .2086128 | -2.48 | 0.013 | -.9262762 | -.108529 |
| /kappa | .8532808 | .4910887 | 1.74 | 0.082 | -.1092353 | 1.815797 |
| sigma | .5960668 | .1243472 | | | .3960257 | .8971529 |

The Wald test of the hypothesis that $\kappa = 0$ (test for the appropriateness of the lognormal) is performed and reported on the output above, $p = 0.082$, suggesting that lognormal is perhaps not an adequate model for these data.

The Wald test for $\kappa = 1$ is

$$\left( \frac{.8532808 - 1}{.4910887} \right)^2 = .08925925$$

which yields a $\chi^2(1)$ significance of .7651, providing strong support against rejecting the Weibull model.

We now fit the exponential, Weibull, log-logistic, and lognormal models separately. To be able to directly compare coefficients, we will ask Stata to report the exponential and Weibull models in accelerated failure-time form by specifying the `time` option. The output from fitting these models and the results from the generalized gamma model are summarized in Table 2.

Table 2. Summary of results obtained from `streg` using `cancer.dta`

|  | Exponential | Weibull | Lognormal | Log-logistic | Generalized gamma |
|---|---|---|---|---|---|
| Age | −.078479 | −.063094 | −.073804 | −.068521 | −.064425 |
| Drug | 1.014594 | 0.769945 | 0.834785 | 0.827980 | 0.786178 |
| Constant | 6.629056 | 5.101301 | 5.299195 | 5.046001 | 5.108207 |
| Ancillary |  | 1.757749 | 0.763802 | 0.421766 | 0.596067 |
| Kappa |  |  |  |  | 0.853281 |
| Log-likelihood | −48.837598 | −42.662838 | −44.093049 | −43.785510 | −42.619647 |
| AIC | 103.675196 | 93.325676 | 96.186098 | 95.571020 | 95.239294 |

We can see that the largest log likelihood was obtained for the generalized gamma model; however, the Weibull model is preferred by the AIC. In fact, if you are curious enough about this example, you can perform a Gompertz regression and obtain an even smaller AIC value.

◁

# Frailty models

A frailty model is a survival model with unobservable heterogeneity, or *frailty*. At the observation level, frailty is introduced as an unobservable multiplicative effect $\alpha$ on the hazard function such that

$$h(t|\alpha) = \alpha h(t)$$

where $h(t)$ is a non-frailty hazard function, say, the hazard function of any of the six parametric models supported by `streg` described earlier in this entry. The frailty $\alpha$ is a random positive quantity, and for purposes of model identifiability is assumed to have mean one and variance $\theta$.

Exploiting the relationship between the cumulative hazard function and survival function yields the expression for the survival function, given the frailty

$$S(t|\alpha) = \exp\left\{ -\int_0^t h(u|\alpha)du \right\} = \exp\left\{ -\alpha \int_0^t \frac{f(u)}{S(u)}du \right\} = \{S(t)\}^\alpha$$

where $S(t)$ is the survival function that corresponds to $h(t)$. Furthermore, the probability density function, given the frailty, is

$$f(t|\alpha) = -S'(t|\alpha) = \alpha f(t) \{S(t)\}^{\alpha-1}$$

where $f(t)$ is the probability density function that corresponds to $h(t)$ and $S(t)$.

Since $\alpha$ is unobservable, it needs to be integrated out of $f(t|\alpha)$. Let $g(\alpha)$ be the probability density function of $\alpha$, in which case an estimable form of our frailty model is achieved as

$$f_\theta(t) = \int_0^\infty f(t|\alpha) g(\alpha) d\alpha = \int_0^\infty \alpha f(t) \{S(t)\}^{\alpha-1} g(\alpha) d\alpha$$

yielding (in the usual way) the survival function for the frailty model

$$S_\theta(t) = 1 - \int_0^t f_\theta(u) du$$

At this stage, the only missing piece is the choice of frailty distribution $g(\alpha)$. In theory, any continuous distribution supported on the positive numbers that has expectation one and finite variance $\theta$ is allowed here. For purposes of mathematical tractability, however, we limit the choice to one of either the Gamma$(1/\theta, \theta)$ distribution or the Inverse-Gaussian distribution with parameters one and $1/\theta$, denoted as IG$(1, 1/\theta)$. The Gamma$(a, b)$ distribution has probability density function

$$g(x) = \frac{x^{a-1} e^{-x/b}}{\Gamma(a) b^a}$$

and the IG$(a, b)$ distribution has density

$$g(x) = \left( \frac{b}{2\pi x^3} \right)^{1/2} \exp \left\{ -\frac{b}{2a} \left( \frac{x}{a} - 2 + \frac{a}{x} \right) \right\}$$

Therefore, performing the integrations described above will show that specifying `frailty(gamma)` will result in the frailty survival model (in terms of the non-frailty survival function $S(t)$)

$$S_\theta(t) = [1 - \theta \ln \{S(t)\}]^{-1/\theta}$$

and specifying `frailty(invgaussian)` will give

$$S_\theta(t) = \exp \left\{ \frac{1}{\theta} \left( 1 - [1 - 2\theta \ln \{S(t)\}]^{1/2} \right) \right\}$$

Note here that regardless of the choice of frailty distribution, $\lim_{\theta \to 0} S_\theta(t) = S(t)$, and thus the frailty model reduces to $S(t)$ when there is no heterogeneity present.

As a result, using the `frailty(`*distname*`)` option will fit a survival model based on $S_\theta(t)$, where `dist(`*distname*`)` determines the form of $S(t)$ which is used within $S_\theta(t)$, based on the list of available parametric forms given in Table 1. The output of the estimation remains unchanged from the non-frailty version, except for the additional estimation of $\theta$ and a likelihood-ratio test of $H_0 : \theta = 0$. For more information on frailty models, the interested reader is referred to Hougaard (1986) and the references therein.

▷ Example

Consider as an example a survival analysis of data on women with breast cancer. Our hypothetical dataset consists of analysis times on 80 women with covariates `age`, `smoking`, and `dietfat`, which measures the average weekly calories from fat $(\times 10^3)$ in the patient's diet over the course of the study.

```
. list in 1/12

         age    smoking    dietfat         t    dead
  1.      30          1      4.919      14.2       0
  2.      50          0      4.437      8.21       1
  3.      47          0       5.85      5.64       1
  4.      49          1      5.149      4.42       1
  5.      52          1      4.363      2.81       1
  6.      29          0      6.153        35       0
  7.      49          1       3.82      4.57       1
  8.      27          1      5.294        35       0
  9.      47          0      6.102      3.74       1
 10.      59          0      4.446      2.29       1
 11.      35          0      6.203      15.3       0
 12.      26          0      4.515        35       0
```

The data are such that they are well fit by a Weibull model for the distribution of survival time conditional on age, smoking, and dietary fat. By omitting the variable `dietfat` from the model, we hope to introduce unobserved heterogeneity.

```
. stset t, fail(dead)
 (output omitted )
. streg age smoking, dist(weib) frailty(gamma)

      failure _d:  dead
  analysis time _t:  t
Fitting comparison weibull model:

Fitting constant-only model:

Iteration 0:   log likelihood = -137.15363
Iteration 1:   log likelihood =  -136.3927
Iteration 2:   log likelihood = -136.01557
Iteration 3:   log likelihood = -136.01202
Iteration 4:   log likelihood = -136.01201

Fitting full model:

Iteration 0:   log likelihood = -85.933969
Iteration 1:   log likelihood =  -73.61173
Iteration 2:   log likelihood = -68.999447
Iteration 3:   log likelihood = -68.340858
Iteration 4:   log likelihood = -68.136187
Iteration 5:   log likelihood = -68.135804
Iteration 6:   log likelihood = -68.135804

Weibull regression -- log relative-hazard form
                      Gamma frailty

No. of subjects =           80        Number of obs   =         80
No. of failures =           58
Time at risk    =      1257.07
                                      LR chi2(2)      =     135.75
Log likelihood  =    -68.135804       Prob > chi2     =     0.0000
```

| _t | Haz. Ratio | Std. Err. | z | P>|z| | [95% Conf. Interval] | |
|---:|---:|---:|---:|---:|---:|---:|
| age | 1.475948 | .1379987 | 4.16 | 0.000 | 1.228811 | 1.772788 |
| smoking | 2.788548 | 1.457031 | 1.96 | 0.050 | 1.00143 | 7.764894 |
| /ln_p | 1.087761 | .222261 | 4.89 | 0.000 | .6521376 | 1.523385 |
| /ln_the | .3307466 | .5250758 | 0.63 | 0.529 | -.698383 | 1.359876 |
| p | 2.967622 | .6595867 | | | 1.91964 | 4.587727 |
| 1/p | .3369701 | .0748953 | | | .2179729 | .520931 |
| theta | 1.392007 | .7309092 | | | .4973889 | 3.895711 |

Likelihood ratio test of theta=0: chibar2(01) =    22.57 Prob>=chibar2 = 0.000

Alternatively, we could used an Inverse-Gaussian distribution to model the heterogeneity.

```
. streg age smoking, dist(weib) frailty(invgauss) nolog
        failure _d:  dead
   analysis time _t:  t
```

```
Weibull regression -- log relative-hazard form
                      Inverse-Gaussian frailty
```

```
No. of subjects =          80              Number of obs   =        80
No. of failures =          58
Time at risk    =     1257.07
                                           LR chi2(2)      =    125.44
Log likelihood  =    -73.838578            Prob > chi2     =    0.0000
```

| _t | Haz. Ratio | Std. Err. | z | P>|z| | [95% Conf. Interval] | |
|---:|---:|---:|---:|---:|---:|---:|
| age | 1.284133 | .0463256 | 6.93 | 0.000 | 1.196473 | 1.378217 |
| smoking | 2.905409 | 1.252785 | 2.47 | 0.013 | 1.247892 | 6.764528 |
| /ln_p | .7173904 | .1434382 | 5.00 | 0.000 | .4362567 | .9985241 |
| /ln_the | .2374778 | .8568064 | 0.28 | 0.782 | -1.441832 | 1.916788 |
| p | 2.049079 | .2939162 | | | 1.546906 | 2.714273 |
| 1/p | .4880241 | .0700013 | | | .3684228 | .6464518 |
| theta | 1.268047 | 1.086471 | | | .2364941 | 6.799082 |

Likelihood ratio test of theta=0: chibar2(01) =    11.16 Prob>=chibar2 = 0.000

The results are similar with respect to the choice of frailty distribution, with the gamma frailty model producing a slightly higher likelihood. Both models show a statistically significant level of unobservable heterogeneity since the $p$-value for the LR test of $H_0 : \theta = 0$ is virtually zero in both cases.

❑ Technical Note

When significant heterogeneity is present, hazard ratios lose their direct interpretation as a proportional change in hazard for a unit increase in the covariate at question. In this case, hazard ratios are merely exponentiated regression coefficients. However, we retain the title "Haz. Ratio" in the output to ease comparison with output from non-frailty models estimated through `streg`. Also, should the estimated $\theta$ be close to zero, the hazard ratios do regain their proper interpretation.

❑

## ❏ Technical Note

The likelihood-ratio test of $\theta = 0$ is a boundary test, and thus requires careful consideration concerning the calculation of its $p$-value. In particular, the null distribution of the likelihood-ratio test statistic is not the usual $\chi_1^2$, but rather is a 50:50 mixture of a $\chi_0^2$ (point mass at zero) and a $\chi_1^2$, denoted as $\bar{\chi}_{01}^2$. See Gutierrez et al. (2001) for more details.

❏

To verify that the significant heterogeneity is caused by the omission of dietfat, we now refit the Weibull/Inverse-Gaussian frailty model with dietfat included.

```
. streg age smoking dietfat, dist(weib) frailty(invgauss) nolog

      failure _d:  dead
   analysis time _t:  t

Weibull regression -- log relative-hazard form
                     Inverse-Gaussian frailty
No. of subjects =          80            Number of obs   =          80
No. of failures =          58
Time at risk     =     1257.07
                                         LR chi2(3)      =      246.41
Log likelihood  =   -13.352142           Prob > chi2     =      0.0000
```

| _t | Haz. Ratio | Std. Err. | z | P>\|z\| | [95% Conf. Interval] | |
|---|---|---|---|---|---|---|
| age | 1.74928 | .0985246 | 9.93 | 0.000 | 1.566452 | 1.953447 |
| smoking | 5.203553 | 1.704943 | 5.03 | 0.000 | 2.737814 | 9.889993 |
| dietfat | 9.229842 | 2.219332 | 9.24 | 0.000 | 5.761311 | 14.78656 |
| /ln_p | 1.431742 | .0978847 | 14.63 | 0.000 | 1.239892 | 1.623593 |
| /ln_the | -14.29702 | 2687.395 | -0.01 | 0.996 | -5281.494 | 5252.9 |
| p | 4.185987 | .4097441 | | | 3.45524 | 5.071278 |
| 1/p | .2388923 | .0233839 | | | .1971889 | .2894155 |
| theta | 6.18e-07 | .0016604 | | | 0 | . |

```
Likelihood ratio test of theta=0: chibar2(01) =    0.00 Prob>=chibar2 = 1.000
```

Note now that the estimate of the frailty variance component $\theta$ is near zero, and the $p$-value of the test of $H_0 : \theta = 0$ equals one, indicating negligible heterogeneity. A regular Weibull model could be fit to these data (with dietfat included), producing almost identical estimates of the hazard ratios and ancillary parameter $p$, and so such an analysis is omitted here. However, the data analyst would carry out such an estimation, since omitting $\theta$ from the model would decrease the estimated standard errors of the other parameters.

In addition, hazard ratios now regain their original interpretation. Thus, for example, an increase in weekly calories from fat of 1,000 would increase the risk of death by over nine-fold.

◁

## ❏ Technical Note

Finally, it should be noted that the frailty models currently supported by streg are observation-level frailty models, and should not be confused with individual or group-level frailty models often referred to as *shared frailty* models. Shared frailty models are closely related to random effects models where if the data consist of multiple-records for each subject (or group), it is assumed that these multiple observations all share the same individual frailty. The frailty models currently supported by streg use the assumption of observation-level frailties to derive an alternate survival function $S_\theta(t)$. This $S_\theta(t)$ is then treated in the same as any non-frailty survival function for purposes of estimation.

❏

## Parameterization of ancillary parameters

By default, all ancillary parameters are estimated as constant quantities. For example, the ancillary parameter, $p$, of the Weibull distribution is assumed to be a constant not dependent on covariates. streg's ancillary() and anc2() options allow for complete parameterization of parametric survival models. By specifying, for example,

    . streg age drug, dist(weibull) ancillary(drug)

both $\lambda$ and the ancillary parameter, $p$, are parameterized in terms of covariates.

▷ Example

Using the cancer data, we can estimate a fully parameterized log-logistic model by specifying the ancillary() option.

```
. use cancer, clear
(Patient Survival in Drug Trial)
. stset studytime, fail(died)
 (output omitted )
. streg age drug, dist(llogistic) ancillary(age drug) nolog

       failure _d:  died
   analysis time _t:  studytime

Log-logistic regression -- accelerated failure-time form

No. of subjects =           48                 Number of obs   =           48
No. of failures =           31
Time at risk    =          744
                                               LR chi2(2)      =        32.70
Log likelihood  =   -43.279441                 Prob > chi2     =       0.0000
```

| _t | Coef. | Std. Err. | z | P>|z| | [95% Conf. Interval] | |
|---|---|---|---|---|---|---|
| _t | | | | | | |
| age | -.0669416 | .0219207 | -3.05 | 0.002 | -.1099054 | -.0239779 |
| drug | .80442 | .1672889 | 4.81 | 0.000 | .4765397 | 1.1323 |
| _cons | 4.987664 | 1.1597 | 4.30 | 0.000 | 2.714693 | 7.260634 |
| ln_gam | | | | | | |
| age | .0318454 | .0324601 | 0.98 | 0.327 | -.0317752 | .095466 |
| drug | .048045 | .1928167 | 0.25 | 0.803 | -.3298688 | .4259588 |
| _cons | -2.756693 | 1.884842 | -1.46 | 0.144 | -6.450915 | .9375285 |

◁

## Stratified estimation

When we type

    . streg *xvars*, dist( *distname*) strata( *xvar*)

we are asking that a completely stratified model be estimated. By "completely stratified" we mean that both the model's intercept and any ancillary parameters are allowed to vary for each level of the strata variable. That is, we are constraining the coefficients on the covariates to be the same across strata, but allowing the intercept and ancillary parameters to vary.

We demonstrate by fitting a stratified log-normal model to the cancer data.

▷ Example

```
. streg age drug, dist(lnormal) strata(drug) nolog
         failure _d:  died
   analysis time _t:  studytime
note: _Sdrug_3 dropped due to collinearity
Log-normal regression -- accelerated failure-time form
```

| | | | | |
|---|---|---|---|---|
| No. of subjects = | 48 | Number of obs | = | 48 |
| No. of failures = | 31 | | | |
| Time at risk = | 744 | | | |
| | | LR chi2(3) | = | 34.84 |
| Log likelihood = | -41.502368 | Prob > chi2 | = | 0.0000 |

| _t | Coef. | Std. Err. | z | P>\|z\| | [95% Conf. Interval] | |
|---|---|---|---|---|---|---|
| _t | | | | | | |
| age | -.0755916 | .0203052 | -3.72 | 0.000 | -.115389 | -.0357941 |
| drug | .8275575 | .1833025 | 4.51 | 0.000 | .4682913 | 1.186824 |
| _Sdrug_2 | .3291957 | .2680991 | 1.23 | 0.219 | -.1962688 | .8546602 |
| _cons | 5.316234 | 1.171662 | 4.54 | 0.000 | 3.019818 | 7.61265 |
| | | | | | | |
| ln_sig | | | | | | |
| _Sdrug_2 | -.4085853 | .3347414 | -1.22 | 0.222 | -1.064666 | .2474957 |
| _Sdrug_3 | .1691172 | .3429039 | 0.49 | 0.622 | -.502962 | .8411964 |
| _cons | -.275192 | .1641769 | -1.68 | 0.094 | -.5969728 | .0465888 |

◁

Completely stratified models are fit by first generating stratum specific indicator variables (dummy variables), and then adding these as independent variables in the model and as covariates in the ancillary parameter. It is possible to produce a less stratified model by independently generating the indicator variables and using the ancillary() option.

▷ Example

```
. xi i.drug
i.drug          _Idrug_1-3          (naturally coded; _Idrug_1 omitted)
. des _I*
```

| variable name | storage type | display format | value label | variable label |
|---|---|---|---|---|
| _Idrug_2 | byte | %8.0g | | drug==2 |
| _Idrug_3 | byte | %8.0g | | drug==3 |

*(Continued on next page)*

```
. streg age drug, dist(lnormal) ancillary(_Idrug_2 _Idrug_3) nolog

      failure _d:  died
  analysis time _t:  studytime

Log-normal regression -- accelerated failure-time form

No. of subjects =           48             Number of obs   =          48
No. of failures =           31
Time at risk    =          744
                                           LR chi2(2)      =       33.41
Log likelihood  =   -42.220792             Prob > chi2     =      0.0000
```

| _t | Coef. | Std. Err. | z | P>|z| | [95% Conf. Interval] | |
|---|---|---|---|---|---|---|
| _t | | | | | | |
| age | -.0716697 | .0194026 | -3.69 | 0.000 | -.109698 | -.0336413 |
| drug | .9701036 | .2086388 | 4.65 | 0.000 | .561179 | 1.379028 |
| _cons | 5.014549 | 1.103643 | 4.54 | 0.000 | 2.851449 | 7.177649 |
| ln_sig | | | | | | |
| _Idrug_2 | -.4742873 | .3181322 | -1.49 | 0.136 | -1.097815 | .1492403 |
| _Idrug_3 | .3397935 | .3646431 | 0.93 | 0.351 | -.3748939 | 1.054481 |
| _cons | -.2660926 | .1658635 | -1.60 | 0.109 | -.5911791 | .0589939 |

◁

By doing this, we are restricting not only the coefficients on the covariates to be the same across strata, but also the intercept, while allowing the ancillary parameter to differ.

## Fitted curves

stcurve is used after streg to plot the fitted survival, hazard, and cumulative hazard functions. By default, stcurve computes the means of the covariates and evaluates the fitted model at each time in the data, censored or uncensored. The resulting plot is therefore the survival experience of a subject with a covariate pattern equal to the average covariate pattern in the study. It is possible to produce the plot at other values of the covariates using the at() option. You can also specify a time range using the range() option.

▷ Example

Using the cancer data, let's fit a log-logistic regression model and plot its survival curves. After stsetting the data, we can perform a log-logistic regression by issuing the following command:

```
. streg age drug, dist(llog) nolog

      failure _d:  died
  analysis time _t:  studytime

Log-logistic regression -- accelerated failure-time form

No. of subjects =           48             Number of obs   =          48
No. of failures =           31
Time at risk    =          744
                                           LR chi2(2)      =       34.00
Log likelihood  =   -43.78551              Prob > chi2     =      0.0000
```

| _t | Coef. | Std. Err. | z | P>|z| | [95% Conf. Interval] | |
|---|---|---|---|---|---|---|
| age | −.0685208 | .020464 | −3.35 | 0.001 | −.1086295 | −.028412 |
| drug | .8279797 | .1478426 | 5.60 | 0.000 | .5382136 | 1.117746 |
| _cons | 5.046001 | 1.151639 | 4.38 | 0.000 | 2.788829 | 7.303173 |
| /ln_gam | −.8633045 | .1501434 | −5.75 | 0.000 | −1.15758 | −.5690289 |
| gamma | .421766 | .0633254 | | | .3142457 | .5660749 |

Now we wish to plot the survival and the hazard functions:

. stcurve, survival c(l) s(.) xlab ylab

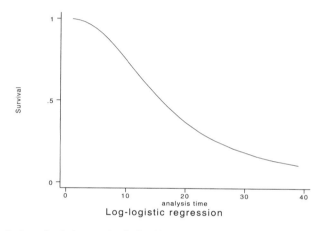

Figure 2. Log-logistic survival distribution at mean value of all covariates

. stcurve, hazard c(l) s(.) xlab ylab

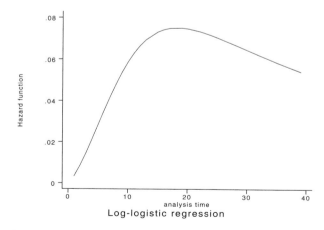

Figure 3. Log-logistic hazard distribution at mean value of all covariates

These plots show the fitted survival and hazard functions evaluated for a cancer patient of average age and receiving the average drug. Of course, the "average drug" has no meaning in this example since `drug` is an indicator variable. It makes more sense to plot the curves at a fixed value (level) of the drug. We can do this using the `at` option. For example, we may want to compare the average-age patient's survival curve under drug 1 and under drug 2.

First, we plot the curve for drug 1 and then for drug 2:

```
. stcurve, surv c(1) s(.) xlab ylab at(drug = 1)
```

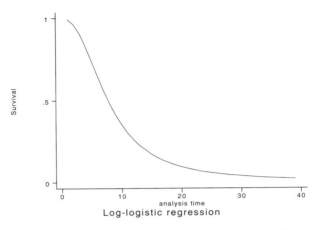

Figure 4. Log-logistic survival distribution at mean age for drug 1

```
. stcurve, surv c(1) s(.) xlab ylab at(drug = 2)
```

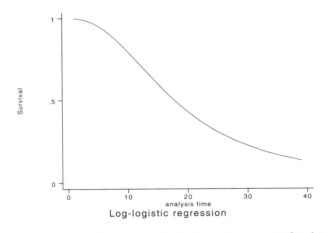

Figure 5. Log-logistic survival distribution at mean age for drug 2

From the plot, we can see that based on the log-logistic model, the survival experience of an average-age patient receiving drug 1 is worse than the survival experience of that same patient receiving drug 2.

◁

## predict

predict after streg is used to generate a variable containing predicted values or residuals.

For a more detailed discussion on residuals, read *Cox regression residuals* in the [R] **st stcox** entry. Many of the concepts and ideas presented there also apply to streg models.

Regardless of the metric used, predict can generate predicted median survival times and median log-survival times for all models, and predicted mean times and mean log-survival times where available. Predicted survival, hazard, and residuals are also available for all models. The predicted hazard ratio—emphasis on ratio—can be calculated only for models with a proportional hazards parameterization; i.e., the Weibull, exponential, and Gompertz models. It is, however, not necessary that these models be estimated in the log-hazard metric. It is possible to perform, for example, a Weibull regression specifying the time option and then to ask that hazard ratios be predicted.

▷ Example

Let's return to the previous example of the emergency generator. Assume that we fit a proportional hazard Weibull model as before:

```
. streg load bearings, dist(weibull) nolog

        failure _d:  1 (meaning all fail)
   analysis time _t:  failtime

Weibull regression -- log relative-hazard form
No. of subjects =          12              Number of obs   =         12
No. of failures =          12
Time at risk    =         896
                                           LR chi2(2)      =      30.27
Log likelihood  =     5.6934189            Prob > chi2     =     0.0000
```

| _t | Haz. Ratio | Std. Err. | z | P>\|z\| | [95% Conf. Interval] | |
|---|---|---|---|---|---|---|
| load | 1.599315 | .1883807 | 3.99 | 0.000 | 1.269616 | 2.014631 |
| bearings | .1887995 | .1312109 | -2.40 | 0.016 | .0483546 | .7371644 |
| /ln_p | 2.051552 | .2317074 | 8.85 | 0.000 | 1.597414 | 2.505691 |
| p | 7.779969 | 1.802677 | | | 4.940241 | 12.25202 |
| 1/p | .1285352 | .0297826 | | | .0816192 | .2024193 |

Now we can predict both the survival time and the log survival time for each observation:

```
. predict time, time

. predict lntime, lntime

. format time lntime %9.4f

. list failtime load bearings time lntime

        failtime    load    bearings       time    lntime
   1.        100      15           0   124.1503    4.8215
   2.        140      15           1   153.8180    5.0358
   3.         97      20           0    91.8088    4.5197
   4.        122      20           1   113.7480    4.7340
   5.         84      25           0    67.8923    4.2179
   6.        100      25           1    84.1163    4.4322
   7.         54      30           0    50.2062    3.9161
   8.         52      30           1    62.2038    4.1304
   9.         40      35           0    37.1273    3.6144
```

| | | | | | |
|---|---|---|---|---|---|
| 10. | 55 | 35 | 1 | 45.9995 | 3.8286 |
| 11. | 22 | 40 | 0 | 27.4556 | 3.3126 |
| 12. | 30 | 40 | 1 | 34.0165 | 3.5268 |

◁

## ▷ Example

Using the cancer data, we can examine the various residuals that Stata produces. For a more detailed discussion on residuals, read *Cox regression residuals* in the [R] **st stcox** entry. Many of the concepts and ideas presented there also apply to **streg** models. For a more technical presentation of these residuals, see *Methods and Formulas*.

We will begin by requesting the generalized Cox–Snell residuals with the command **predict cs, csnell**. The **csnell** option causes **predict** to create a new variable, **cs**, containing the Cox–Snell residuals. If the model fits the data, then these residuals should have a standard exponential distribution with $\lambda = 1$. One way of verifying the fit is to calculate an empirical estimate of the cumulative hazard function, based, for example, on the Kaplan–Meier survival estimates or the Aalen–Nelson estimator, taking the Cox–Snell residuals as the time variable and the censoring variable as before, and plotting it against **cs**. If the model fits the data, then the plot should be a straight line with slope of 1.

To do this after fitting the model, we first **stset** the data, specifying **cs** as our new failure time variable and **died** as the failure indicator. We then use the **sts generate** command to generate the variable **km** containing the Kaplan–Meier survival estimates. Lastly, we generate a new variable **H** and plot it against the **cs**. The commands are

```
.  stset cs, failure(died)
   (output omitted )
.  sts generate km=s
.  generate H=-ln(km)
.  graph H cs cs,c(ll) s(..)
```

We specified **cs** twice in the **graph** command so that a reference 45° line is plotted. We did this separately for each of four distributions. Results are plotted in Figure 6:

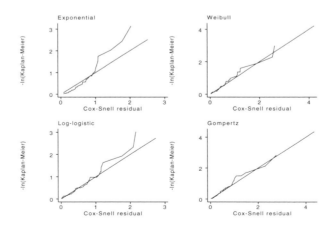

Figure 6. Cox–Snell residuals to evaluate model fit of 4 regression models

The plots indicate that the Weibull and Gompertz models fit the data best, and that the exponential and lognormal fit poorly. These results are consistent with our previous results based on Akaike's information criterion.

◁

▷ Example

Let's now look at the martingale-like and deviance residuals. We use the term "martingale-like" because although these residuals do not arise naturally from martingale theory in the case of parametric survival models as they do for the Cox proportional hazard model, they do share similar form. We can generate these residuals by using predict's mgale option. Martingale residuals take values between $-\infty$ and 1, and therefore are difficult to interpret. The deviance residuals are a rescaling of the martingale-like residuals so that they are symmetric about zero, and thus more like residuals obtained from linear regression. Plots of either set of residuals against survival time, ranked survival time, or observation number can be useful in identifying aberrant observations and in assessing model fit. Using the cancer data, we plotted the deviance residual obtained after fitting a lognormal model:

```
. graph dev studytime, ylab xlab yline(0)
```

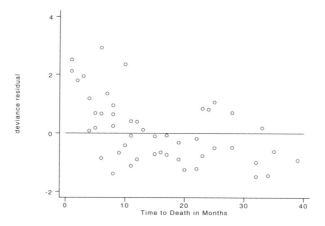

Figure 7. Deviance residuals to evaluate model fit of lognormal model

In this plot, the deviance residual is large for short survival times and then decreases with time. This pattern suggests that the lognormal model will underestimate the probability of failure for patients with short study times, and will overestimate the probability of failure for patients with longer times.

◁

(Continued on next page)

# Saved Results

streg saves in e():

Scalars

| | | | |
|---|---|---|---|
| e(N) | number of observations | e(rc) | return code |
| e(N_sub) | number of subjects | e(chi2) | $\chi^2$ |
| e(k_eq) | number of equations | e(p) | significance |
| e(k_dv) | number of dependent variables | e(ic) | number of iterations |
| e(risk) | total time at risk | e(aux_p) | ancillary parameter (weibull) |
| e(df_m) | model degrees of freedom | e(gamma) | ancillary parameter (gompertz, |
| e(ll) | log likelihood | | loglogistic) |
| e(ll_0) | log likelihood, constant-only model | e(sigma) | ancillary parameter (gamma, lnormal) |
| e(N_clust) | number of clusters | e(kappa) | ancillary parameter (gamma) |
| e(theta) | frailty parameter | e(ll_c) | log likelihood, comparison model |
| e(chi2_c) | $\chi^2$, comparison model | e(p_c) | significance, comparison model |

Macros

| | | | |
|---|---|---|---|
| e(cmd) | model or regression name | e(t0) | _t0 |
| e(cmd2) | streg | e(frm2) | hazard or time |
| e(dead) | _d | e(vcetype) | covariance estimation method |
| e(depvar) | _t | e(user) | name of likelihood-evaluator program |
| e(title) | title in estimation output | e(opt) | type of optimization |
| e(clustvar) | name of cluster variable | e(chi2type) | Wald or LR; type of model $\chi^2$ test |
| e(N_fail) | number of failures | e(predict) | program used to implement predict |
| e(fr_title) | title in output identifying frailty | e(cnslist) | constraint numbers |

Matrices

| | | | |
|---|---|---|---|
| e(b) | coefficient vector | e(V) | variance–covariance matrix of the estimators |

Functions

| | |
|---|---|
| e(sample) | marks estimation sample |

# Methods and Formulas

streg and stcurve are implemented as ado-files.

For an introduction to survival models, see Hosmer and Lemeshow (1999) or Klein and Moeschberger (1997).

Assume that we have selected a specific regression model with known distribution up to a vector parameter $\gamma$, and that we have a sample of time-to-event data with possibly censored observations. A subject known to fail at time $t$ contributes to the likelihood function the value of the density at time $t$ conditional on the entry time $t_0$, $f(t, \gamma|t_0)$, whereas a censored observation, only known to survive up to time $t$, contributes $S(t, \gamma|t_0)$, the probability of surviving beyond time $t$ conditional on the entry time $t_0$. Without loss of generality, assume that the data consist of $N$ subjects, $U$ of whom have uncensored times. streg maximizes the full log-likelihood function

$$\ln L = \sum_{j=1}^{U} \ln\{f(t_j, \gamma|t_{0j})\} + \sum_{j=U+1}^{N} \ln\{S(t_j, \gamma|t_{0j})\}$$

where $f()$ and $S()$ are the appropriate distributions for the desired parametric regression model. `streg` reports maximum likelihood estimates of the parameter vector $\gamma$ and of the covariate coefficients vector $\beta$. The reported log-likelihood value is $L_R = \ln L + T$, where $T = \sum \ln(t_{1j})$ is summed over uncensored observations. This adjustment is to make reported results match those of other statistical software. The intention of the adjustment is to remove the time units from $\ln L$. Whether or not the adjustment is made makes no difference to any test or result, since such tests and results depend on differences in log-likelihood functions and/or their second derivatives.

If the robust estimate of variance is requested, results are transformed as explained in [U] **23.11 Obtaining robust variance estimates** and, in particular, in [P] **_robust**. Note that if observations in the dataset represent repeated observations on the same subjects (that is, there are time-varying covariates), the assumption of independence of the observations is highly questionable, meaning the conventional estimate of variance is not appropriate. We strongly advise the use of the `robust` and `cluster()` options in this case. (`streg` knows to specify `cluster()` if you specify `robust`.)

Assume that we have failure data on $n$ subjects indexed by $j$. Let $\mathbf{Z_j} = (z_{1j}, \ldots, z_{pj})$ be $p$ possibly time-varying covariates for subject $j$. Then, the Cox–Snell (1968) residual $CS_j$ for subject $j$ at time $t_j$ is defined as $\widehat{H}_j(t_j) = -\ln \widehat{S}_j(t_j)$, the estimated cumulative hazard function obtained from the fitted model (Collett 1994, 150). Cox and Snell argued that if the correct model has been fitted to the data, these residuals are $n$ observations from an exponential distribution with unit mean. Thus, a plot of the cumulative hazard rate of the residuals against the residuals themselves should result in a straight line of slope 1. Note that Cox–Snell residuals can never be negative, and therefore are not symmetric about zero. The option `csnell` stores in each observation that observation's contribution to the subject's Cox–Snell residual, which we refer to as a "partial" Cox–Snell residual. The option `ccsnell` stores the subject's overall Cox–Snell residual in the last observation for that subject. If there is only one observation per subject as identified by the `id` option of `stset`, the Cox–Snell residuals stored by `ccsnell` and `csnell` are equal.

Martingale residuals fall out naturally from martingale theory in the case of Cox proportional hazards, but their development does not carry over for parametric survival models. However, martingale-like residuals similar to those obtained in the case of Cox can be derived from the Cox–Snell residuals,

$$M_j(t) = \delta_j - CS_j(t_j)$$

where $CS_j$ are the Cox–Snell residuals as previously described, and $\delta = 1$ if subject $j$ fails at time $t_j$ and 0 otherwise.

Because martingale-like residuals are calculated from the Cox–Snell residuals, they also could be "partial" or not. Partial martingale residuals are generated with the option `mgale`, and overall martingale residuals are generated with the option `cmgale`.

Martingale residuals can be interpreted as a measurement of the difference over time between the number of deaths in the data and the expected number based on the fitted model. These residuals take values between $-\infty$ and 1 and have an expected value of zero, although like the Cox–Snell residuals, they are not symmetric about zero, making them difficult to interpret.

Deviance residuals are a scaling of the martingale-like residuals in an attempt to make them symmetric about zero. They are defined as

$$D_j(t) = \text{sign}\{M_j(t)\} \left( -2 \left[ M_j(t) + \delta_j \ln \left\{ \delta_j - M_j(t) \right\} \right] \right)$$

When the model fits the data, these residuals are symmetric about zero, and thus can be more readily used to examine the data for outliers.

The median survival time is defined as the time, $t$, at which $S(t) = 0.5$ while the mean survival time is defined as

$$\int_0^\infty S(t)dt$$

# References

Akaike, H. 1974. A new look at the statistical model identification. *IEEE Transaction and Automatic Control* AC-19: 716–723.

Cleves, M. 2000. stata54: Multiple curves plotted with stcurv command. *Stata Technical Bulletin* 54: 2–4. Reprinted in *Stata Technical Bulletin Reprints*, vol. 9, pp. 7–10.

Collett, D. 1994. *Modelling Survival Data in Medical Research*. London: Chapman & Hall.

Cox, D. R. and D. Oakes. 1984. *Analysis of Survival Data*. London: Chapman & Hall.

Cox, D. R. and E. J. Snell. 1968. A general definition of residuals (with discussion). *Journal of the Royal Statistical Society B* 30: 248–275.

Crowder, M. J., A. C. Kimber, R. L. Smith, and T. J. Sweeting. 1991. *Statistical Analysis of Reliability Data*. London: Chapman & Hall.

Fisher, R. A. and L. H. C. Tippett. 1928. Limiting forms of the frequency distribution of the largest or smallest member of a sample. *Proceedings of the Cambridge Philosophical Society* 24: 180–190.

Gutierrez, R. G., S. L. Carter, and D. M. Drukker. 2001. On boundary-value likelihood-ratio tests. *Stata Technical Bulletin*, forthcoming.

Hougaard, P. 1986. Survival models for heterogeneous populations derived from stable distributions. *Biometrika* 73: 387–396.

Hosmer, D. W., Jr., and S. Lemeshow. 1999. *Applied Survival Analysis*. New York: John Wiley & Sons.

Kalbfleisch, J. D. and R. L. Prentice. 1980. *The Statistical Analysis of Failure Time Data*. New York: John Wiley & Sons.

Klein, J. P. and M. L. Moeschberger. 1997. *Survival Analysis: Techniques for Censored and Truncated data*. New York: Springer-Verlag.

Lee, E. T. 1992. *Statistical Methods for Survival Data Analysis*. 2d ed. New York: John Wiley & Sons.

Peto, R. and P. Lee. 1973. Weibull distributions for continuous-carcinogenesis experiments. *Biometrics* 29: 457–470.

Pike, M. C. 1966. A method of analysis of a certain class of experiments in carcinogenesis. *Biometrics* 22: 142–161.

Schoenfeld, D. 1982. Partial residuals for the proportional hazards regression model. *Biometrika* 69: 239–241.

Scotto, M. G. and A. Tobias. 1998. sg83: Parameter estimation for the Gumbel distribution. *Stata Technical Bulletin* 43: 32–35. Reprinted in *Stata Technical Bulletin Reprints*, vol. 8, pp. 133–137.

——. 2000. sg146: Parameter estimation for the generalized extreme value distribution. *Stata Technical Bulletin* 56: 40–43.

Weibull, W. 1939. A statistical theory of the strength of materials. *Ingeniörs Vetenskaps Akademien Handlingar*, no. 151. Stockholm: Generalstabens Litografiska Anstalts Förlag.

*(Continued on next page)*

# Also See

| | |
|---|---|
| **Complementary:** | [R] **adjust**, [R] **constraint**, [R] **lincom**, [R] **linktest**, [R] **lrtest**, [R] **mfx**, [R] **predict**, [R] **st sts**, [R] **st stset**, [R] **test**, [R] **testnl**, [R] **vce** |
| **Related:** | [R] **st stcox** |
| **Background:** | [U] **16.5 Accessing coefficients and standard errors**, [U] **23 Estimation and post-estimation commands**, [U] **23.11 Obtaining robust variance estimates**, [R] **maximize**, [R] **st** |

# Title

> **st sts** — Generate, graph, list, and test the survivor and cumulative hazard functions

# Syntax

<u>sts</u> [ <u>graph</u> ] [if *exp*] [in *range*] [, ...]

<u>sts</u> <u>list</u> [if *exp*] [in *range*] [, ...]

<u>sts</u> <u>test</u> *varlist* [if *exp*] [in *range*] [, ...]

<u>sts</u> <u>generate</u> *newvar* = ... [if *exp*] [in *range*] [, ...]

sts is for use with survival-time data; see [R] **st**. You must stset your data before using this command.

See [R] **st sts generate**, [R] **st sts graph**, [R] **st sts list**, and [R] **st sts test** for details of syntax.

# Description

sts reports on and creates variables containing the estimated survivor and related functions such as the Nelson–Aalen cumulative hazard function. In the case of the survivor function, sts tests and produces Kaplan–Meier estimates or, via Cox regression, adjusted estimates.

sts graph graphs the estimated survivor or Nelson–Aalen cumulative hazard function.

sts list lists the estimated survivor and related functions.

sts test tests the equality of the survivor function across groups.

sts generate creates new variables containing the estimated survivor function, the Nelson–Aalen cumulative hazard function, or related functions.

sts is appropriate for use with single- or multiple-record, single- or multiple-failure, st data.

▷ Example

| | |
|---|---|
| Graph the Kaplan–Meier survivor function | . sts graph<br>. sts graph, by(drug) |
| Graph the Nelson–Aalen cumulative hazard function | . sts graph, na<br>. sts graph, na by(drug) |
| List the Kaplan–Meier survivor function | . sts list<br>. sts list, by(drug) compare |
| List the Nelson–Aalen cumulative hazard function | . sts list, na<br>. sts list, na by(drug) compare |
| Generate variable containing Kaplan–Meier survivor function | . sts gen surv = s<br>. sts gen surv = s, by(drug) |
| Generate variable containing Nelson–Aalen cumulative hazard function | . sts gen haz = na<br>. sts gen haz = na, by(drug) |
| Test equality of survivor functions | . sts test drug<br>. sts test drug, strata(agecat) |

◁

# Remarks

Remarks are presented under the headings

*Listing, graphing, and generating variables*
*Comparing survivor or cumulative hazard functions*
*Testing equality of survivor functions*
*Adjusted estimates*
*Counting the number lost due to censoring*

sts concerns the survivor function $S(t)$, the probability of surviving to $t$ or beyond, or the cumulative hazard function, $H(t)$. Its subcommands can list and generate variables containing $\widehat{S}(t)$ and $\widehat{H}(t)$, and test the equality of $S(t)$ over groups. In addition:

1. All subcommands share a common syntax.

2. All subcommands deal with either the Kaplan–Meier product-limit or the Nelson–Aalen estimates unless you request adjusted survival estimates.

3. If you request an adjustment, all subcommands perform the adjustment in the same way, which is described below.

The full details of each subcommand are found in the entries following this one, but each subcommand provides so many options to control exactly how the listing looks, how the graph appears, the form of the test to be performed, or what exactly is to be generated, that the simplicity of sts can be easily overlooked.

So, without getting burdened by the details of syntax, let us demonstrate the sts commands using the Stanford heart transplant data introduced in [R] **st stset**.

# Listing, graphing, and generating variables

You can list the overall survivor function by typing sts list and you can graph it by typing sts graph or sts. sts assumes you mean graph when you do not type a subcommand.

Or, you can list the Nelson–Aalen cumulative hazard function by typing sts list, na and you can graph it by typing sts graph, na.

When you type sts list you are shown all the details:

```
. sts list
```

| Time | Beg. Total | Fail | Net Lost | Survivor Function | Std. Error | [95% Conf. Int.] | |
|---|---|---|---|---|---|---|---|
| 1 | 103 | 1 | 0 | 0.9903 | 0.0097 | 0.9331 | 0.9986 |
| 2 | 102 | 3 | 0 | 0.9612 | 0.0190 | 0.8998 | 0.9852 |
| 3 | 99 | 3 | 0 | 0.9320 | 0.0248 | 0.8627 | 0.9670 |
| 5 | 96 | 1 | 0 | 0.9223 | 0.0264 | 0.8507 | 0.9604 |
| (*output omitted*) | | | | | | | |
| 1586 | 2 | 0 | 1 | 0.1519 | 0.0493 | 0.0713 | 0.2606 |
| 1799 | 1 | 0 | 1 | 0.1519 | 0.0493 | 0.0713 | 0.2606 |

When you type sts graph, or just sts, you are shown a graph of the same result detailed by list:

. sts graph

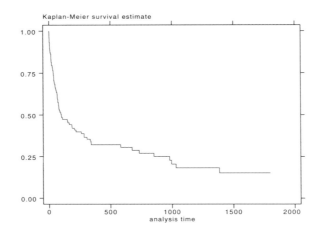

sts generate is a rarely used command. Type sts generate survf = s and you will create a new variable survf containing the same survivor function that list just listed and graph just graphed:

```
. sts gen survf = S
sort t1
. list _t survf in 1/10
             _t      survf
   1.         1    .99029126
   2.         1    .99029126
   3.         1    .99029126
   4.         1    .99029126
   5.         2    .96116505
   6.         2    .96116505
   7.         2    .96116505
   8.         2    .96116505
   9.         2    .96116505
  10.         2    .96116505
```

sts generate is provided in case you want to make a calculation, listing, or graph that sts cannot already do for you.

## Comparing survivor or cumulative hazard functions

sts will allow you to compare survivor or cumulative hazard functions. sts graph and sts graph, na are probably most successful at this. For example, survivor functions can be plotted using

*(Graph on next page)*

. sts graph, by(posttran)

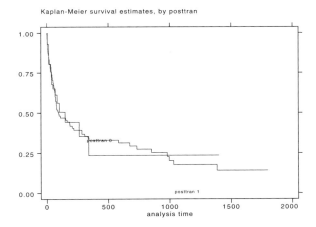

and Nelson–Aalen cumulative hazard functions can be plotted using

. sts graph, na by(posttran)

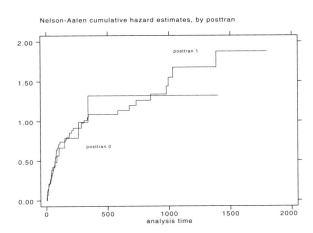

To compare survivor functions, we typed sts graph, just as previously, and then we added by(posttran) to see the survivor functions for the groups designated by posttran. In this case there are two groups, but as far as the sts command is concerned, there could have been more.

To compare cumulative hazard functions, we added na to the previous command.

Just as you can compare survivor functions graphically by typing sts graph, by(posttran) and cumulative hazard functions by typing sts graph, na by(posttran), you can obtain detailed listings by typing sts list, by(posttran) and sts list, na by(posttran) respectively. Below, we list the survivor function and also specify another option—**enter**—which adds a number-who-enter column.

```
. sts list, by(posttran) enter
```

| Time | Beg. Total | Fail | Lost | Enter | Survivor Function | Std. Error | [95% Conf. Int.] | |
|---|---|---|---|---|---|---|---|---|
| posttran=0 | | | | | | | | |
| 0 | 0 | 0 | 0 | 103 | 1.0000 | . | . | . |
| 1 | 103 | 1 | 3 | 0 | 0.9903 | 0.0097 | 0.9331 | 0.9986 |
| 2 | 99 | 3 | 3 | 0 | 0.9603 | 0.0195 | 0.8976 | 0.9849 |
| *(output omitted)* | | | | | | | | |
| 427 | 2 | 0 | 1 | 0 | 0.2359 | 0.1217 | 0.0545 | 0.4882 |
| 1400 | 1 | 0 | 1 | 0 | 0.2359 | 0.1217 | 0.0545 | 0.4882 |
| posttran=1 | | | | | | | | |
| 1 | 0 | 0 | 0 | 3 | 1.0000 | . | . | . |
| 2 | 3 | 0 | 0 | 3 | 1.0000 | . | . | . |
| 3 | 6 | 0 | 0 | 3 | 1.0000 | . | . | . |
| 4 | 9 | 0 | 0 | 2 | 1.0000 | . | . | . |
| 5 | 11 | 0 | 0 | 3 | 1.0000 | . | . | . |
| 5.1 | 14 | 1 | 0 | 0 | 0.9286 | 0.0688 | 0.5908 | 0.9896 |
| 6 | 13 | 0 | 0 | 1 | 0.9286 | 0.0688 | 0.5908 | 0.9896 |
| 8 | 14 | 0 | 0 | 2 | 0.9286 | 0.0688 | 0.5908 | 0.9896 |
| 10 | 16 | 0 | 0 | 2 | 0.9286 | 0.0688 | 0.5908 | 0.9896 |
| *(output omitted)* | | | | | | | | |
| 1586 | 2 | 0 | 1 | 0 | 0.1420 | 0.0546 | 0.0566 | 0.2653 |
| 1799 | 1 | 0 | 1 | 0 | 0.1420 | 0.0546 | 0.0566 | 0.2653 |

It is easier to compare survivor or cumulative hazard functions if they are listed side-by-side and sts list has a compare option to do this:

```
. sts list, by(posttran) compare
```

| posttran | | Survivor Function 0 | 1 |
|---|---|---|---|
| time | 1 | 0.9903 | 1.0000 |
| | 225 | 0.4422 | 0.3934 |
| | 449 | 0.2359 | 0.3304 |
| | 673 | 0.2359 | 0.3139 |
| | 897 | 0.2359 | 0.2535 |
| | 1121 | 0.2359 | 0.1774 |
| | 1345 | 0.2359 | 0.1774 |
| | 1569 | . | 0.1420 |
| | 1793 | . | 0.1420 |
| | 2017 | . | . |

If we include the na option, the cumulative hazard functions will be listed:

```
. sts list, na by(posttran) compare
```

| posttran | | Nelson-Aalen Cum. Haz. 0 | 1 |
|---|---|---|---|
| time | 1 | 0.0097 | 0.0000 |
| | 225 | 0.7896 | 0.9145 |
| | 449 | 1.3229 | 1.0850 |
| | 673 | 1.3229 | 1.1350 |
| | 897 | 1.3229 | 1.3411 |
| | 1121 | 1.3229 | 1.6772 |
| | 1345 | 1.3229 | 1.6772 |
| | 1569 | . | 1.8772 |
| | 1793 | . | 1.8772 |
| | 2017 | . | . |

When you specify `compare`, the same detailed survivor or cumulative hazard function is calculated, but it is then evaluated at ten or so times and those evaluations listed. Above we left it to `sts list` to choose the comparison times, but we can specify them ourselves using the `at()` option:

```
. sts list, by(posttran) compare at(0 100 to 1700)
                  Survivor Function
  posttran             0           1

  time     0       1.0000      1.0000
         100       0.5616      0.4814
         200       0.4422      0.4184
         300       0.3538      0.3680
         400       0.2359      0.3304
         500       0.2359      0.3304
         600       0.2359      0.3139
         700       0.2359      0.2942
         800       0.2359      0.2746
         900       0.2359      0.2535
        1000       0.2359      0.2028
        1100       0.2359      0.1774
        1200       0.2359      0.1774
        1300       0.2359      0.1774
        1400       0.2359      0.1420
        1500            .      0.1420
        1600            .      0.1420
        1700            .      0.1420
```

## Testing equality of survivor functions

`sts test` tests equality of survivor functions:

```
. sts test posttran

Log-rank test for equality of survivor functions
           |   Events        Events
  posttran | observed      expected

  0        |       30         31.20
  1        |       45         43.80

  Total    |       75         75.00
               chi2(1) =      0.13
               Pr>chi2 =    0.7225
```

When you do not specify otherwise, `sts test` performs the log-rank test, but it can also perform the Wilcoxon test:

```
. sts test posttran, wilcoxon

Wilcoxon (Breslow) test for equality of survivor functions
           |   Events        Events       Sum of
  posttran | observed      expected        ranks

  0        |       30         31.20          -85
  1        |       45         43.80           85

  Total    |       75         75.00            0
               chi2(1) =      0.14
               Pr>chi2 =    0.7083
```

`sts test` will also perform stratified tests. This is demonstrated in [R] **st sts test**.

## Adjusted estimates

All the estimates of the survivor function we have seen so far are the Kaplan–Meier product-limit estimates. `sts` can make adjusted estimates of the survivor function. We want to illustrate this and explain how it is done.

The heart transplant dataset is not the best to demonstrate this feature because we are starting with survivor functions that are similar already, so let us switch to data on a fictional drug trial:

```
. stdes
                                     |————————— per subject —————————|
Category                    total        mean       min    median        max

no. of subjects                48
no. of records                 48           1         1         1          1
(first) entry time                          0         0         0          0
(final) exit time                        15.5         1      12.5         39
subjects with gap               0
time on gap if gap              0
time at risk                  744        15.5         1      12.5         39
failures                       31    .6458333         0         1          1
```

This dataset contains 48 subjects, all observed from time 0. The `st` command shows us how the dataset is currently declared:

```
. st
-> stset studytime, failure(died) noshow

       failure event:  died ~= 0 & died ~= .
  obs. time interval:  (0, studytime]
   exit on or before:  failure
```

and the dataset contains variables `age` and `drug`:

```
. summarize age drug
    Variable |       Obs        Mean    Std. Dev.       Min        Max

         age |        48      47.125     9.492718        32         67
        drug |        48    .5833333     .4982238         0          1
```

We are comparing the outcomes of `drug` = 1 with that of the placebo, `drug` = 0. Here are the survivor curves for the two groups:

*(Graph on next page)*

```
. sts graph, by(drug)
```

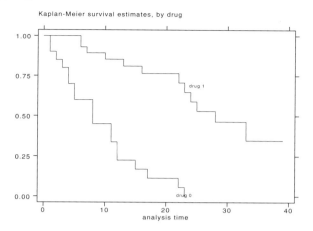

Here are the survivor curves adjusted for age (and scaled to age 50):

```
. gen age50 = age-50
. sts graph, by(drug) adjustfor(age50)
```

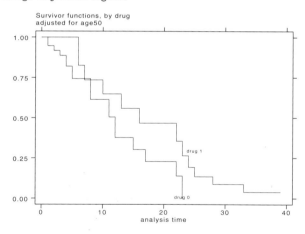

The age difference between the two samples accounts for much of the difference between the survivor functions.

When you type by(*group*) adjustfor(*vars*), sts estimates a separate Cox proportional hazards model on *vars* (estimation via stcox) and retrieves the separately estimated baseline survivor functions. sts graph graphs the baseline survivor functions, sts list lists them, and sts generate saves them.

Thus, sts list can list what sts graph plots:

```
. sts list, by(drug) adjustfor(age50) compare
```

|        |      | Adjusted Survivor Function |        |
|--------|------|--------:|--------:|
| drug   |      | 0       | 1       |
| time   | 1    | 0.9463  | 1.0000  |
|        | 5    | 0.7439  | 1.0000  |
|        | 9    | 0.6135  | 0.7358  |
|        | 13   | 0.3770  | 0.5588  |
|        | 17   | 0.2282  | 0.4668  |
|        | 21   | 0.2282  | 0.4668  |
|        | 25   | .       | 0.1342  |
|        | 29   | .       | 0.0872  |
|        | 33   | .       | 0.0388  |
|        | 37   | .       | 0.0388  |
|        | 41   | .       | .       |

Survivor function adjusted for age50

In both the graph and the listing, it is important that we adjust for variable age50 = age − 50 and not just age. Adjusted survivor functions are adjusted to the adjustfor() variables and scaled to correspond to the adjustfor() variables set to 0. Here is the result of adjusting for age, which is 0 at birth:

```
. sts list, by(drug) adjustfor(age) compare
```

|        |      | Adjusted Survivor Function |        |
|--------|------|--------:|--------:|
| drug   |      | 0       | 1       |
| time   | 1    | 0.9994  | 1.0000  |
|        | 5    | 0.9970  | 1.0000  |
|        | 9    | 0.9951  | 0.9995  |
|        | 13   | 0.9903  | 0.9990  |
|        | 17   | 0.9853  | 0.9987  |
|        | 21   | 0.9853  | 0.9987  |
|        | 25   | .       | 0.9965  |
|        | 29   | .       | 0.9958  |
|        | 33   | .       | 0.9944  |
|        | 37   | .       | 0.9944  |
|        | 41   | .       | .       |

Survivor function adjusted for age

These are equivalent to what we obtained previously but not nearly so informative because of the scaling of the survivor function. Option adjustfor(age) scales the survivor function to correspond to age = 0. age is calendar age and so the survivor function is scaled to correspond to a newborn.

There is another way sts will adjust the survivor function. Rather than specifying by(*group*) adjustfor(*vars*), we specify strata(*group*) adjustfor(*vars*):

*(Continued on next page)*

```
. sts list, strata(drug) adjustfor(age50) compare
             Adjusted Survivor Function
drug                    0              1

time          1    0.9526         1.0000
              5    0.7668         1.0000
              9    0.6417         0.7626
             13    0.4080         0.5995
             17    0.2541         0.5139
             21    0.2541         0.5139
             25         .         0.1800
             29         .         0.1247
             33         .         0.0614
             37         .         0.0614
             41         .              .
```

Survivor function adjusted for age50

When we specify `strata()` instead of `by()`, instead of estimating separate Cox models for each stratum, a single, stratified Cox model is estimated and the stratified baseline survivor function retrieved. That is, `strata()` rather than `by()` constrains the effect of the `adjustfor()` variables to be the same across strata.

## Counting the number lost due to censoring

`sts list`, in the detailed output, shows the number lost in the fourth column:

```
. sts list
              Beg.            Net     Survivor      Std.
    Time      Total   Fail    Lost    Function      Error      [95% Conf. Int.]

       1      48      2       0       0.9583        0.0288     0.8435    0.9894
       2      46      1       0       0.9375        0.0349     0.8186    0.9794
       3      45      1       0       0.9167        0.0399     0.7930    0.9679
    (output omitted)
       8      36      3       1       0.7061        0.0661     0.5546    0.8143
       9      32      0       1       0.7061        0.0661     0.5546    0.8143
      10      31      1       1       0.6833        0.0678     0.5302    0.7957
    (output omitted)
      39       1      0       1       0.1918        0.0791     0.0676    0.3634
```

and `sts graph`, if you specify the `lost` option, will show that number, too:

*(Graph on next page)*

`. sts graph, lost`

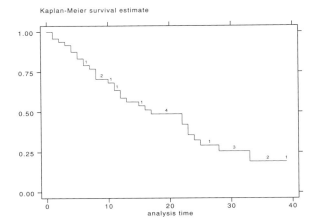

Kaplan-Meier survival estimate

The number on the listing and on the graph is the number net lost, defined as number censored minus number who enter. With simple survival data—data with one observation per subject—net lost corresponds to lost.

With more complicated survival data—meaning delayed entry or multiple records per subject—the number net lost may surprise you. With complicated data, the vague term lost can mean many things. Sometimes subjects are lost but mostly, there are a lot of censorings followed by reentries—a subject is censored at time 5 immediately to reenter the data with different covariates. This is called thrashing.

There are other possibilities: A subject can be lost, but only for a while, and so reenter the data with a gap; a subject can be censored out of one stratum to enter another. There are too many possibilities to dedicate a column in a table or a plotting symbol in a graph to each one. `sts`'s solution is to define lost as net lost, meaning censored-minus-entered, and show that number. How we define lost does not affect the calculation of the survivor function: it merely affects a number that researchers often report.

Censored-minus-entered results in exactly what is desired for simple survival data. Since everybody enters at time 0, censored-minus-entered amounts to calculating censored − 0. The number net lost is the number censored.

In more complicated data, censored-minus-entered results in the number really lost if there are no gaps and no delayed entry. In that case, the subtraction smooths the thrashing. In an interval, 5 might be censored and 3 reenter, so $5 - 3 = 2$ were lost.

In even more complicated data, censored-minus-entered results in something reasonable once you understand how to interpret negative numbers and are cautious in interpreting positive ones. 5 might be censored and 3 might enter (from the five? who can say?), resulting in 2 net lost. Or 3 might be censored and 5 enter, resulting in −2 being lost.

`sts`, by default, reports net lost but will, if you specify the `enter` option, report the pure number censored and the pure number who enter. Sometimes you will want to do that. Earlier in this entry, we used `sts list` to display the survivor functions in the Stanford heart transplant data for subjects pre- and post-transplantation, and we slipped in an `enter` option:

`. sts list, by(posttran) enter`

| Time | Beg. Total | Fail | Lost | Enter | Survivor Function | Std. Error | [95% Conf. Int.] | |
|---|---|---|---|---|---|---|---|---|
| posttran=0 | | | | | | | | |
| 0 | 0 | 0 | 0 | 103 | 1.0000 | . | . | . |
| 1 | 103 | 1 | 3 | 0 | 0.9903 | 0.0097 | 0.9331 | 0.9986 |
| 2 | 99 | 3 | 3 | 0 | 0.9603 | 0.0195 | 0.8976 | 0.9849 |
| 3 | 93 | 3 | 3 | 0 | 0.9293 | 0.0258 | 0.8574 | 0.9657 |
| 4 | 87 | 0 | 2 | 0 | 0.9293 | 0.0258 | 0.8574 | 0.9657 |
| (output omitted) | | | | | | | | |
| 427 | 2 | 0 | 1 | 0 | 0.2359 | 0.1217 | 0.0545 | 0.4882 |
| 1400 | 1 | 0 | 1 | 0 | 0.2359 | 0.1217 | 0.0545 | 0.4882 |
| posttran=1 | | | | | | | | |
| 1 | 0 | 0 | 0 | 3 | 1.0000 | . | . | . |
| 2 | 3 | 0 | 0 | 3 | 1.0000 | . | . | . |
| 3 | 6 | 0 | 0 | 3 | 1.0000 | . | . | . |
| 4 | 9 | 0 | 0 | 2 | 1.0000 | . | . | . |
| 5 | 11 | 0 | 0 | 3 | 1.0000 | . | . | . |
| 5.1 | 14 | 1 | 0 | 0 | 0.9286 | 0.0688 | 0.5908 | 0.9896 |
| 6 | 13 | 0 | 0 | 1 | 0.9286 | 0.0688 | 0.5908 | 0.9896 |
| 8 | 14 | 0 | 0 | 2 | 0.9286 | 0.0688 | 0.5908 | 0.9896 |
| 10 | 16 | 0 | 0 | 2 | 0.9286 | 0.0688 | 0.5908 | 0.9896 |
| (output omitted) | | | | | | | | |
| 1586 | 2 | 0 | 1 | 0 | 0.1420 | 0.0546 | 0.0566 | 0.2653 |
| 1799 | 1 | 0 | 1 | 0 | 0.1420 | 0.0546 | 0.0566 | 0.2653 |

We did that to keep you from being shocked at negative numbers for net lost. In this complicated dataset, the value of posttran changes over time. All patients start with posttran = 0 and later, some change to posttran = 1.

Thus, at time 1 in the posttran = 0 group, 3 are lost, which is to say, lost to the group but not the experiment. Simultaneously, in the posttran = 1 group, we see that 3 enter. Had we not specified the enter option, you would not have seen that 3 enter, and you would have seen that −3 were, in net, lost:

. sts list, by(posttran)

| Time | Beg. Total | Fail | Net Lost | Survivor Function | Std. Error | [95% Conf. Int.] | |
|---|---|---|---|---|---|---|---|
| posttran=0 | | | | | | | |
| 1 | 103 | 1 | 3 | 0.9903 | 0.0097 | 0.9331 | 0.9986 |
| 2 | 99 | 3 | 3 | 0.9603 | 0.0195 | 0.8976 | 0.9849 |
| 3 | 93 | 3 | 3 | 0.9293 | 0.0258 | 0.8574 | 0.9657 |
| 4 | 87 | 0 | 2 | 0.9293 | 0.0258 | 0.8574 | 0.9657 |
| (output omitted) | | | | | | | |
| 427 | 2 | 0 | 1 | 0.2359 | 0.1217 | 0.0545 | 0.4882 |
| 1400 | 1 | 0 | 1 | 0.2359 | 0.1217 | 0.0545 | 0.4882 |
| posttran=1 | | | | | | | |
| 1 | 0 | 0 | −3 | 1.0000 | . | . | . |
| 2 | 3 | 0 | −3 | 1.0000 | . | . | . |
| 3 | 6 | 0 | −3 | 1.0000 | . | . | . |
| 4 | 9 | 0 | −2 | 1.0000 | . | . | . |
| 5 | 11 | 0 | −3 | 1.0000 | . | . | . |
| 5.1 | 14 | 1 | 0 | 0.9286 | 0.0688 | 0.5908 | 0.9896 |
| 6 | 13 | 0 | −1 | 0.9286 | 0.0688 | 0.5908 | 0.9896 |
| 8 | 14 | 0 | −2 | 0.9286 | 0.0688 | 0.5908 | 0.9896 |
| 10 | 16 | 0 | −2 | 0.9286 | 0.0688 | 0.5908 | 0.9896 |
| (output omitted) | | | | | | | |
| 1586 | 2 | 0 | 1 | 0.1420 | 0.0546 | 0.0566 | 0.2653 |
| 1799 | 1 | 0 | 1 | 0.1420 | 0.0546 | 0.0566 | 0.2653 |

In this case, specifying `enter` makes the table easier to explain, but do not jump to the conclusion that specifying `enter` is always a good idea. In this same dataset, let's look at the overall survivor function, first with the `enter` option:

```
. sts list, enter
```

| Time | Beg.<br>Total | Fail | Lost | Enter | Survivor<br>Function | Std.<br>Error | [95% Conf. Int.] | |
|---|---|---|---|---|---|---|---|---|
| 0 | 0 | 0 | 0 | 103 | 1.0000 | . | . | . |
| 1 | 103 | 1 | 3 | 3 | 0.9903 | 0.0097 | 0.9331 | 0.9986 |
| 2 | 102 | 3 | 3 | 3 | 0.9612 | 0.0190 | 0.8998 | 0.9852 |
| 3 | 99 | 3 | 3 | 3 | 0.9320 | 0.0248 | 0.8627 | 0.9670 |
| *(output omitted)* | | | | | | | | |
| 1571 | 3 | 0 | 1 | 0 | 0.1519 | 0.0493 | 0.0713 | 0.2606 |
| 1586 | 2 | 0 | 1 | 0 | 0.1519 | 0.0493 | 0.0713 | 0.2606 |
| 1799 | 1 | 0 | 1 | 0 | 0.1519 | 0.0493 | 0.0713 | 0.2606 |

Note that at time 1, 3 are lost and 3 enter. There is no delayed entry in this dataset and there are no gaps, so it is the same 3 that were lost and reentered and no one was really lost. At time 1571, on the other hand, a patient really was lost. This is all more clearly revealed when we do not specify the `enter` option:

```
. sts list
```

| Time | Beg.<br>Total | Fail | Net<br>Lost | Survivor<br>Function | Std.<br>Error | [95% Conf. Int.] | |
|---|---|---|---|---|---|---|---|
| 1 | 103 | 1 | 0 | 0.9903 | 0.0097 | 0.9331 | 0.9986 |
| 2 | 102 | 3 | 0 | 0.9612 | 0.0190 | 0.8998 | 0.9852 |
| 3 | 99 | 3 | 0 | 0.9320 | 0.0248 | 0.8627 | 0.9670 |
| *(output omitted)* | | | | | | | |
| 1571 | 3 | 0 | 1 | 0.1519 | 0.0493 | 0.0713 | 0.2606 |
| 1586 | 2 | 0 | 1 | 0.1519 | 0.0493 | 0.0713 | 0.2606 |
| 1799 | 1 | 0 | 1 | 0.1519 | 0.0493 | 0.0713 | 0.2606 |

Thus, to summarize:

1. The `sts list` and `graph` commands will show the number lost or censored. `sts list` shows it on the detailed output—you specify no option to see it. `sts graph` shows the number when you specify the `lost` option.

2. By default, the number lost is the net number lost, defined as censored-minus-entered.

3. Both commands allow you to specify the `enter` option and then show the number who actually entered, and the number lost becomes the actual number censored, not censored-minus-entered.

## Saved Results

`sts test` saves in `r()`:

Scalars

| | | | |
|---|---|---|---|
| `r(df)` | degrees of freedom | `r(chi2)` | $\chi^2$ |

# Methods and Formulas

`sts` is implemented as an ado-file.

Unless adjusted estimates are requested, `sts` estimates the survivor function using the Kaplan–Meier product-limit method.

When the `na` option is specified, `sts` estimates the cumulative hazard function using the Nelson–Aalen estimator.

For an introduction to the Kaplan–Meier product-limit method and the log-rank test, see Pagano and Gauvreau (2000, 495–499); for a detailed discussion, see Cox and Oakes (1984), Kalbfleisch and Prentice (1980), or Klein and Moeschberger (1997).

Let $n_t$ be the population alive at time $t$ and $d_t$ the number of failures. Then the nonparametric maximum-likelihood estimate of the survivor function is (Kaplan and Meier 1958)

$$\widehat{S}(t) = \prod_{j|t_j \leq t} \left( \frac{n_j - d_j}{n_j} \right)$$

(Kalbfleisch and Prentice 1980, 12).

The failure function $\widehat{F}(t)$ is defined as $1 - \widehat{S}(t)$.

The standard error reported is given by Greenwood's formula (Greenwood 1926)

$$\widehat{\mathrm{Var}}\{\widehat{S}(t)\} = \widehat{S}^{\,2}(t) \sum_{j|t_j \leq t} \frac{d_j}{n_j(n_j - d_j)}$$

(Kalbfleisch and Prentice 1980, 14). These standard errors, however, are not used for confidence intervals. Instead, the asymptotic variance of $\ln[-\ln \widehat{S}(t)]$

$$\widehat{\sigma}^{\,2}(t) = \frac{\sum \frac{d_j}{n_j(n_j - d_j)}}{\left\{ \sum \ln\left( \frac{n_j - d_j}{d_j} \right) \right\}^2}$$

is used, where sums are calculated over $j|t_j \leq t$ (Kalbfleisch and Prentice 1980, 15). The confidence bounds are then $\widehat{S}(t)^{\exp(\pm z_{\alpha/2}\widehat{\sigma}(t))}$, where $z_{\alpha/2}$ is the $(1 - \alpha/2)$ quantile of the normal distribution. `sts` suppresses reporting the standard error and confidence bounds if the data are `pweighted` since these formulas are no longer appropriate.

When option `adjustfor()` is specified, the survivor function estimate $\widehat{S}(t)$ is the baseline survivor function estimate $\widehat{S}_0(t)$ of `stcox`; see [R] **st stcox**. If `by()` is specified, $\widehat{S}(t)$ is obtained from estimating separate Cox models on `adjustfor()` for each of the `by()` groups. If instead `strata()` is specified, a single Cox model on `adjustfor()`, stratified by `strata()`, is estimated.

The Nelson–Aalen estimator of the cumulative hazard rate function is due to Nelson (1972) and Aalen (1978), and is defined up to the largest observed time as

$$\widehat{H}(t) = \sum_{j|t_j \leq t} \frac{d_j}{n_j}$$

Its variance (Aalen 1978) may be estimated by

$$\widehat{\text{Var}}\{\widehat{H}(t)\} = \sum_{j|t_j \leq t} \frac{d_j}{n_j{}^2}$$

Pointwise confidence intervals are calculated using the asymptotic variance of $\ln \widehat{H}(t)$

$$\widehat{\phi}^2(t) = \frac{\widehat{\text{Var}}\{\widehat{H}(t)\}}{\{\widehat{H}(t)\}^2}$$

The confidence bounds are then $\widehat{H}(t)\exp\{\pm z_{\alpha/2}\widehat{\phi}(t)\}$. If the data are pweighted, these formulas are not appropriate and in that case, confidence intervals are not reported.

## References

Aalen, O. O. 1978. Nonparametric inference for a family of counting processes. *Annals of Statistics* 6: 701–726.

Cleves, M. 1999. stata53: censored option added to sts graph command. *Stata Technical Bulletin* 50: 34–36. Reprinted in *Stata Technical Bulletin Reprints*, vol. 9, pp. 4–7.

Cox, D. R. and D. Oakes. 1984. *Analysis of Survival Data*. London: Chapman & Hall.

Greenwood, M. 1926. The natural duration of cancer. *Reports on Public Health and Medical Subjects* 33: 1–26. London: His Majesty's Stationery Office.

Kalbfleisch, J. D. and R. L. Prentice. 1980. *The Statistical Analysis of Failure Time Data*. New York: John Wiley & Sons.

Kaplan, E. L. and P. Meier. 1958. Nonparametric estimation from incomplete observations. *Journal of the American Statistical Association* 53: 457–481.

Klein, J. P. and M. L. Moeschberger. 1997. *Survival Analysis: Techniques for Censored and Truncated data*. New York: Springer-Verlag.

Nelson, W. 1972. Theory and applications of hazard plotting for censored failure data. *Technometrics* 14: 945–965.

Pagano, M. and K. Gauvreau. 2000. *Principles of Biostatistics*. 2d ed. Pacific Grove, CA: Brooks/Cole.

## Also See

| | |
|---|---|
| **Complementary:** | [R] **st stci**, [R] **st stcox**, [R] **st sts generate**, [R] **st sts graph**, [R] **st sts list**, [R] **st sts test**, [R] **st stset** |
| **Background:** | [R] **st** |

# Title

st sts generate — Create survivor, hazard, and other variables

# Syntax

<u>sts</u> <u>generate</u> *newvar* =

$\big\{$ s $|$ se(s) $|$ h $|$ se(lls) $|$ lb(s) $|$ ub(s) $|$ na $|$ se(na) $|$ lb(na) $|$ ub(na) $|$ n $|$ d $\big\}$

$\big[$ *newvar* = $\{\dots\}$ $\dots\big]$ $\big[$ if *exp* $\big]$ $\big[$ in *range* $\big]$ $\big[$ , by(*varlist*) <u>strata</u>(*varlist*)

<u>ad</u>justfor(*varlist*) <u>level</u>(#) $\big]$

sts generate is for use with survival-time data; see [R] **st**. You must stset your data before using this command.

# Description

sts generate creates new variables containing the estimated survivor (failure) function, the Nelson–Aalen cumulative hazard (integrated hazard) function, and related functions. See [R] **st sts** for an introduction to this command.

sts generate is appropriate for use with single- or multiple-record, single- or multiple-failure, st data.

# Functions

s produces the Kaplan–Meier product-limit estimate of the survivor function $\widehat{S}(t)$ or, if adjustfor() is specified, the baseline survivor function from a Cox regression model on the adjustfor() variables.

se(s) produces the Greenwood, pointwise standard error $\widehat{se}\{\widehat{S}(t)\}$. Option adjustfor() is not allowed in this case.

h produces the estimated hazard component $\Delta H_j = H(t_j) - H(t_{j-1})$, where $t_j$ is the current failure time and $t_{j-1}$ is the previous one. This is mainly a utility function used to calculate the estimated cumulative hazard $H(t_j)$. It is recorded at all the points at which a failure occurs and computed as $d_t/n_t$, where $d_t$ is the number of failures occurring at time $t$ and $n_t$ is the population alive at $t$ before the occurrence of the failures.

se(lls) produces $\widehat{\sigma}(t)$, the standard error of $\ln\{-\ln\widehat{S}(t)\}$.

lb(s) produces the lower bound of the confidence interval for $\widehat{S}(t)$ based on $\ln\{-\ln\widehat{S}(t)\}$; to wit, $\widehat{S}(t)^{\exp(-z_{\alpha/2}\widehat{\sigma}(t))}$, where $z_{\alpha/2}$ is the $(1-\alpha/2)$ quantile of the standard normal distribution.

ub(s) produces the upper bound of the confidence interval for $\widehat{S}(t)$ based on $\ln\{-\ln\widehat{S}(t)\}$; to wit, $\widehat{S}(t)^{\exp(z_{\alpha/2}\widehat{\sigma}(t))}$, where $z_{\alpha/2}$ is the $(1-\alpha/2)$ quantile of the standard normal distribution.

na produces the Nelson–Aalen estimate of the cumulative hazard function. Option adjustfor() is not allowed in this case.

se(na) produces pointwise standard error for the Nelson–Aalen estimate of the cumulative hazard function, $\widehat{H}(t)$. Option adjustfor() is not allowed in this case.

lb(na) produces the lower bound of the confidence interval for $\widehat{H}(t)$ based on the log-transformed cumulative hazard function.

ub(na) produces the corresponding upper bound.

n produces $n_t$, the size of the population at time $t$.

d produces $d_t$, the number failing at time $t$.

## Options

by(*varlist*) produces separate survivor or cumulative hazard functions by making separate calculations for each group identified by equal values of the variables in *varlist*.

strata(*varlist*) is a subtle alternative to by(). First, you may not specify strata() unless you also specify adjustfor(), whereas you may specify by() in either case. Thus, strata() amounts to a modifier of adjustfor() and is discussed below. This option is not available for the Nelson–Aalen function.

adjustfor(*varlist*) adjusts the estimate of the survivor function to that for 0 values of the *varlist* specified. This option is not available with the Nelson–Aalen function. How sts makes the adjustment depends on whether you specify by() or strata(). This is fully discussed in [R] st sts, but here is a quick review:

If you specify strata(), sts performs the adjustment by estimating a stratified-on-group Cox regression model using adjustfor() as the covariates. The stratified, baseline survivor function is then retrieved.

If you specify by(), sts estimates separate Cox regression models for each group. The separately calculated baseline survivor functions are then retrieved.

Be aware that, regardless of method employed, the survivor function is adjusted to 0 values of the covariates.

level(*#*) specifies the confidence level, in percent, for the lb(s), ub(s), lb(na) and ub(na) functions. The default is level(95) or as set by set level; see [U] **23.5 Specifying the width of confidence intervals**.

## Remarks

sts generate is a rarely used command; it gives you access to the calculations listed by sts list and graphed by sts graph.

Use of this command is demonstrated in [R] **st sts**.

## Methods and Formulas

See [R] **st sts**.

## References

See [R] **st sts**.

## Also See

**Complementary:**    [R] **st sts**, [R] **st sts graph**, [R] **st sts list**, [R] **st sts test**, [R] **st stset**

**Background:**    [R] **st**

# Title

> **st sts graph** — Graph the survivor and the cumulative hazard functions

# Syntax

> sts graph [if *exp*] [in *range*] [, by(*varlist*) strata(*varlist*) adjustfor(*varlist*)
>
>     nolabel failure gwood na cna level(#) lost enter separate
>
>     tmin(#) tmax(#) xasis yasis noborder noorigin atrisk noshow
>
>     censored(single | number | multiple) *graph_options* ]

sts graph is for use with survival-time data; see [R] **st**. You must stset your data before using this command.

# Description

sts graph graphs the estimated survivor (failure) function, or optionally the Nelson–Aalen estimated cumulative (integrated) hazard function. See [R] **st sts** for an introduction to this command.

sts graph is appropriate for use with single- or multiple-record, single- or multiple-failure, st data.

# Options

by(*varlist*) produces separate survivor or cumulative hazard functions by making separate calculations for each group identified by equal values of the variables in *varlist*.

If you type sts graph, the single survivor function for all the data—the Kaplan–Meier estimate—is plotted. If you type sts graph, by(sex), the survivor functions for each sex—separate Kaplan–Meier estimates—are graphed (on the same axes).

Similarly, if you type sts graph, na, the Nelson–Aalen cumulative hazard function for all the data is plotted. If you type sts graph, na by(sex), the Nelson–Aalen cumulative hazard function for each sex is graphed (on the same axes).

Typically, you specify a single by() variable, such as by(sex), but up to five are allowed. sts graph often restricts you to one by() variable depending on the other options specified because labeling multiple groups on a graph becomes an impossible problem.

If you have more than one by variable and find yourself in a position of needing only one, use egen to create it; see [R] **egen**. For example, to create a single variable denoting the groups defined by both sex and race, type

> . egen *newvar* = group(sex race)

strata(*varlist*) is a subtle alternative to by(). First, you may not specify strata() unless you also specify adjustfor(), whereas you may specify by() in either case. Thus, strata() amounts to a modifier of adjustfor() and is discussed below. This option is not available with the na option.

394

adjustfor(*varlist*) adjusts the estimate of the survivor function to that for 0 values of the *varlist* specified. This option is not available with the na option.

The two commands

. sts graph, by(group) adjustfor(age)

and

. sts graph, strata(group) adjustfor(age)

graph the survivor functions for each group. The functions graphed would be adjusted for age, meaning an attempt has been made to remove the differences in the functions due to age. How sts does this depends on whether you specify by() or strata(). This is fully discussed in [R] **st sts**, but here is a quick review:

If you specify strata(), sts performs the adjustment by estimating a stratified-on-group Cox regression model using adjustfor() as the covariates. The stratified, baseline survivor function is then retrieved.

If you specify by(), sts estimates separate Cox regression models for each group. The separately calculated baseline survivor functions are then retrieved.

Be aware that, regardless of method employed, the survivor function is adjusted to 0 values of the covariates. Say you are adjusting for age and assume the ages of patients in your sample are 40 to 60. Then

. sts graph, strata(group) adjustfor(age)

will graph results adjusted to age 0. If you want to adjust the function to age 40, you type

. gen age40 = age - 40
. sts graph, strata(group) adjustfor(age40)

nolabel is meaningful only with by() or strata(); it prevents sts graph from labeling the group of the survival, failure or cumulative hazard curves. Sometimes sts graph chooses a poor location for its labels. sts graph does not attempt to label curves when there is more than one by() or strata() variable.

failure specifies that you want $1 - S(t + 0)$, the failure function, graphed.

gwood indicates you want pointwise Greenwood confidence bands drawn around the survivor (failure) function. The default is not to include these bands. gwood is not allowed if you specify the adjustfor() option, nor is it allowed if you have pweighted data.

na specifies that the Nelson–Aalen estimate of the cumulative hazard function be plotted.

cna indicates that you want pointwise confidence bands drawn around the Nelson–Aalen cumulative hazard function. cna is not allowed with pweighted data.

level(#) specifies the confidence level, in percent, for the pointwise confidence interval around the survivor, failure, or cumulative hazard functions; see [U] **23.5 Specifying the width of confidence intervals**.

lost specifies that you wish the numbers lost shown on the plot. These numbers are shown as small numbers over the flat parts of the function.

If enter is not specified, the numbers displayed are the number censored minus the number who enter. If you do specify enter, the numbers displayed are the pure number censored. The logic underlying this is described in [R] **st sts**.

enter specifies that the number who enter are to be shown on the graph as well as the number lost. The number who enter are shown as small numbers beneath the flat parts of the plotted function.

`separate` is meaningful only with `by()` or `strata()`; it requests that each group be placed on its own graph rather than one on top of the other. Sometimes curves have to be placed on separate graphs—such as when you specify `gwood` or `cna`—because otherwise it would be too confusing.

`tmin(#)` specifies that the plotted curve is to be graphed only for $t \geq \#$. This option does not affect the calculation of the function, only the portion that is displayed.

`tmax(#)` specifies that the plotted curve is to be graphed only for $t \leq \#$. This option does not affect the calculation of the function, only the portion that is displayed.

`xasis` and `yasis` prevent `sts graph` from attempting to produce better labels for the axes other than the minimum and maximum.

`yasis` is especially important; by default, `sts graph` scales the vertical (probability) axis to scale from 0 to 1.

Another alternative to `yasis` and `xasis` is to specify `graph`'s `ylabel()` and `xlabel()` options for yourself.

`noborder` is `graph`'s `border` option, but turned around. `sts graph`, by default, draws a border around the graph.

`noorigin` requests that the plot of the survival (failure) curve begin at the first exit time instead of beginning at $t = 0$ (the default). This option is ignored when `na` or `cna` is specified.

`atrisk` specifies that the numbers at risk at the beginning of each time interval be shown on the plot. The numbers at risk are shown as small numbers beneath the flat parts of the plotted function.

`noshow` prevents `sts graph` from showing the key st variables. This option is rarely used since most people type `stset, show` or `stset, noshow` to reset once and for all whether they want to see these variables mentioned at the top of the output of every st command; see [R] **st stset**.

`censored(single | number | multiple)` specifies that tick marks be placed on the graph to indicate censored observations.

`censored(single)` places one tick at each censoring time regardless of the number of censorings at that time.

`censored(number)` places one tick at each censoring time and displays the number of censorings about the tick.

`censored(multiple)` places multiple ticks for multiple censorings at the same time. For instance, if 3 observations are censored at time 5, then 3 ticks are placed at time 5. `censored(multiple)` is intended for use when there are few censored observations; if there are too many, the graph can look bad and in such cases we recommend that `censored(number)` be used.

*graph_options* are most of the options of `graph`, `twoway`, except `by()`, `connect()`, `symbol()`, and `pen()`; see [G] **graph options**.

## Remarks

If you have not read [R] **st sts**, please do so.

What is important to understand about `sts graph` is that only one of its options—`adjustfor()`—modifies the calculation. All the other options merely determine how the results of the calculation are graphed.

If you do not specify `adjustfor()` or `na`, `sts graph` displays the Kaplan–Meier product-limit estimate of the survivor (failure) function. Specify `by()` if you wish to see the results of the calculation performed separately on the different groups.

Specify `adjustfor()` and an adjusted survival curve is calculated. Now if you specify `by()` or `strata()`, this further modifies how the adjustment is made.

Specify `na` or `cna` and `sts graph` displays the Nelson–Aalen estimate of the cumulative hazard function.

We demonstrate many of `sts graph`'s features in [R] **st sts**. This discussion picks up where that entry leaves off.

## Including the number lost on the graph

In [R] **st sts**, we introduced a simple, one-observation-per-subject drug-trial dataset. Here is a graph of the survivor functions, by drug, including the number lost due to censoring:

```
. sts graph, by(drug) lost
```

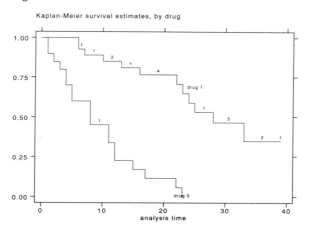

There is no late entry in these data, but pretend there is. Behind the scenes, we just modified the data so that a few subjects entered late. Here is the same graph on the modified data:

```
. sts graph, by(drug) lost
```

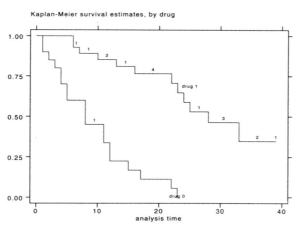

Note the negative numbers. That is because, by default, `lost` means censored-minus-entered. All −1 means is that 1 entered, or 2 entered and 1 was lost, etc. If we specify the `enter` option, we will see the censored and entered separately:

```
. sts graph, by(drug) lost enter
```

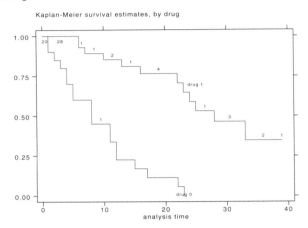

Thus, it might appear that specifying `enter` with `lost` is always a good idea. That is not true.

We have yet another version of the data—the correct data not doctored to have late entry—but in this version we have multiple records per subject. It is the same data, but where there was one record in the first dataset, sometimes there are now two because we have a covariate that is changing over time. Using this dataset, here is the graph with the number lost shown:

```
. sts graph, by(drug) lost
```

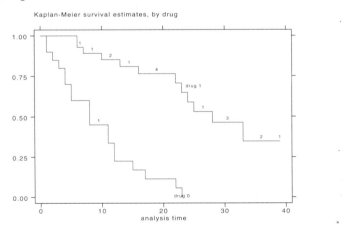

This looks just like the first graph we presented as, indeed, it should. Again we emphasize, the data are logically, if not physically, equivalent. If, however, we graph the number lost and entered, we get a graph showing a lot of activity:

. sts graph, by(drug) lost enter

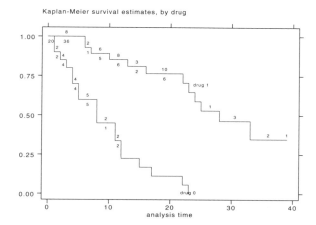

All that activity goes by the name thrashing—subjects are being censored to reenter the data again, but with different covariates. This graph was better when we did not specify **enter** because the censored-minus-entered calculation smoothed out the thrashing.

## Graphing the Nelson–Aalen cumulative hazard function

We can plot the Nelson–Aalen estimate of the cumulative (integrated) hazard function by specifying the **na** option. For example, using the one-observation-per-subject drug-trial dataset, here is a graph of the cumulative hazard functions, by drug:

. sts graph, na by(drug)

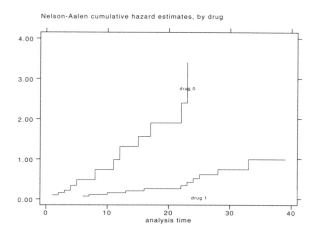

and here is a plot including the number lost due to censoring:

. sts graph, na by(drug) lost

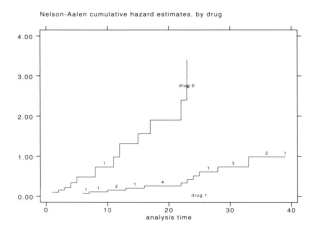

## Methods and Formulas

See [R] **st sts**.

## References

See [R] **st sts**.

## Also See

**Complementary:**    [R] **st sts**, [R] **st sts generate**, [R] **st sts list**, [R] **st sts test**, [R] **st stset**

**Background:**    [R] **st**

# Title

> **st sts list** — List the survivor and the cumulative hazard functions

# Syntax

sts list [if *exp*] [in *range*] [, by(*varlist*) strata(*varlist*) adjustfor(*varlist*) failure

na at(*#* | *numlist*) compare enter level(*#*) noshow ]

sts list is for use with survival-time data; see [R] **st**. You must stset your data before using this command.

# Description

sts list lists the estimated survivor (failure) or the Nelson–Aalen estimated cumulative (integrated) hazard function. See [R] **st sts** for an introduction to this command.

sts list is appropriate for use with single- or multiple-record, single- or multiple-failure, st data.

# Options

by(*varlist*) produces separate survivor or cumulative hazard functions by making separate calculations for each group identified by equal values of the variables in *varlist*.

If you type sts list, the single survivor function for all the data—the Kaplan–Meier estimate—is listed. If you type sts list, by(sex), the survivor function for each sex—separate Kaplan–Meier estimates—are listed.

Similarly, if you type sts list, na, the Nelson–Aalen cumulative hazard function for all the data is listed. If you type sts list, na by(sex), the Nelson–Aalen cumulative hazard function for each sex is listed.

One typically specifies a single by variable, such as by(sex), but up to five are allowed. Thus, you can specify by(sex race).

strata(*varlist*) is a subtle alternative to by(). First, you may not specify strata() unless you also specify adjustfor(), whereas you may specify by() in either case. Thus, strata() amounts to a modifier of adjustfor() and is discussed below. This option is not available with the na option.

adjustfor(*varlist*) adjusts the estimate of the survivor function to that for 0 values of the *varlist* specified. This option is not available with the na option.

The two commands

```
. sts list, by(group) adjustfor(age)
```

and

```
. sts list, strata(group) adjustfor(age)
```

list the survivor functions for each group. The functions listed would be adjusted for age, meaning an attempt has been made to remove the differences in the functions due to age. How sts does this depends on whether you specify by() or strata(). This is fully discussed in [R] **st sts**, but here is a quick review:

401

If you specify `strata()`, `sts` performs the adjustment by estimating a stratified-on-group Cox regression model using `adjustfor()` as the covariates. The stratified, baseline survivor function is then retrieved.

If you specify `by()`, `sts` estimates separate Cox regression models for each group. The separately calculated baseline survivor functions are then retrieved.

Be aware that, regardless of method employed, the survivor function is adjusted to 0 values of the covariates. Say you are adjusting for age and assume that the ages of patients in your sample are 40 to 60. Then

          . sts list, strata(group) adjustfor(age)

will list results adjusted to age 0. If you want to adjust the function to age 40, you type

          . gen age40 = age - 40
          . sts list, strata(group) adjustfor(age40)

`failure` specifies that you want $1 - S(t + 0)$, the failure function, listed.

`na` requests that the Nelson–Aalen estimate of the cumulative hazard function be listed.

`at(#| numlist)` specifies the time values at which the estimated survivor (failure) or cumulative hazard function is to be listed.

The default is to list the function at all the unique time values in the data or, if functions are being compared, at about 10 times chosen over the observed interval. In any case, you can control the points chosen.

`at(5 10 20 30 50 90)` would display the function at the designated times.

`at(10 20 to 100)` would display the function at times 10, 20, 30, 40, ..., 100.

`at(0 5 10 to 100 200)` would display the function at times 0, 5, 10, 15, ..., 100, and 200.

`at(20)` would display the curve at (roughly) 20 equally spaced times over the interval observed in the data. We say roughly because Stata may choose to increase or decrease your number slightly if that would result in rounder values of the chosen times.

`compare` is specified only with `by()` or `strata()`. It states that you wish to compare the survival (failure) or cumulative hazard functions and so want them listed side-by-side rather than first one and then the next.

`enter` specifies that you want the table to contain the number who enter, and, correspondingly, that the number lost is to be displayed as the pure number censored rather than censored-minus-entered. The logic underlying this is explained in [R] **st sts**.

`level(#)` specifies the confidence level, in percent, for the Greenwood pointwise confidence interval of the survivor (failure) or for the pointwise confidence interval of the Nelson–Aalen cumulative hazard function; see [U] **23.5 Specifying the width of confidence intervals**.

`noshow` prevents `sts list` from showing the key st variables. This option is rarely used since most people type `stset, show` or `stset, noshow` to reset once and for all whether they want to see these variables mentioned at the top of the output of every st command; see [R] **st stset**.

# Remarks

What is important to understand about `sts list` is that only one of its options—`adjustfor()`—modifies the calculation. All the other options merely determine how the results of the calculation are displayed.

If you do not specify `adjustfor()` or `na`, `sts list` displays the Kaplan–Meier product-limit estimate of the survivor (failure) function. Specify `by()` if you wish to see the results of the calculation performed separately on the different groups.

Specify `adjustfor()` and an adjusted survival curve is calculated. Now if you specify `by()` or `strata()`, this further modifies how the adjustment is made.

Specify `na` and `sts list` displays the Nelson–Aalen estimate of the cumulative hazard function.

We demonstrate many of `sts list`'s features in [R] **st sts**. This discussion picks up where that entry leaves off.

By default, `sts list` will bury you in output. Using the Stanford heart transplant data introduced in [R] **st stset**, the following produces 154 lines of output.

```
. sts list, by(posttran)
```

| Time | Beg.<br>Total | Fail | Net<br>Lost | Survivor<br>Function | Std.<br>Error | [95% Conf. Int.] | |
|------|------|------|------|------|------|------|------|
| posttran=0 | | | | | | | |
| 1 | 103 | 1 | 3 | 0.9903 | 0.0097 | 0.9331 | 0.9986 |
| 2 | 99 | 3 | 3 | 0.9603 | 0.0195 | 0.8976 | 0.9849 |
| 3 | 93 | 3 | 3 | 0.9293 | 0.0258 | 0.8574 | 0.9657 |
| 4 | 87 | 0 | 2 | 0.9293 | 0.0258 | 0.8574 | 0.9657 |
| (output omitted ) | | | | | | | |
| 1400 | 1 | 0 | 1 | 0.2359 | 0.1217 | 0.0545 | 0.4882 |
| posttran=1 | | | | | | | |
| 1 | 0 | 0 | -3 | 1.0000 | . | . | . |
| 2 | 3 | 0 | -3 | 1.0000 | . | . | . |
| (output omitted ) | | | | | | | |
| 5.1 | 14 | 1 | 0 | 0.9286 | 0.0688 | 0.5908 | 0.9896 |
| 6 | 13 | 0 | -1 | 0.9286 | 0.0688 | 0.5908 | 0.9896 |
| (output omitted ) | | | | | | | |
| 1799 | 1 | 0 | 1 | 0.1420 | 0.0546 | 0.0566 | 0.2653 |

`at()` and `compare()` are the solutions. Here is another detailed, but more useful, view of the heart transplant data:

```
. sts list, at(10 40 to 170) by(posttran)
```

| Time | Beg.<br>Total | Fail | Survivor<br>Function | Std.<br>Error | [95% Conf. Int.] | |
|------|------|------|------|------|------|------|
| posttran=0 | | | | | | |
| 10 | 74 | 12 | 0.8724 | 0.0346 | 0.7858 | 0.9256 |
| 40 | 31 | 11 | 0.6781 | 0.0601 | 0.5446 | 0.7801 |
| 70 | 17 | 2 | 0.6126 | 0.0704 | 0.4603 | 0.7339 |
| 100 | 11 | 1 | 0.5616 | 0.0810 | 0.3900 | 0.7022 |
| 130 | 10 | 1 | 0.5054 | 0.0903 | 0.3199 | 0.6646 |
| 160 | 7 | 1 | 0.4422 | 0.0986 | 0.2480 | 0.6204 |
| posttran=1 | | | | | | |
| 10 | 16 | 1 | 0.9286 | 0.0688 | 0.5908 | 0.9896 |
| 40 | 43 | 6 | 0.7391 | 0.0900 | 0.5140 | 0.8716 |
| 70 | 45 | 9 | 0.6002 | 0.0841 | 0.4172 | 0.7423 |
| 100 | 40 | 9 | 0.4814 | 0.0762 | 0.3271 | 0.6198 |
| 130 | 38 | 1 | 0.4687 | 0.0752 | 0.3174 | 0.6063 |
| 160 | 36 | 1 | 0.4561 | 0.0742 | 0.3076 | 0.5928 |

Note: Survivor function is calculated over full data and evaluated at
      indicated times; it is not calculated from aggregates shown at left.

Notice that we specified `at(10 40 to 170)` when that is not strictly correct; `at(10 40 to 160)` would make sense and so would `at(10 40 to 180)`, but `sts list` is not picky.

Similar output for the Nelson–Aalen estimated cumulative hazard can be produced by specifying the `na` option:

```
. sts list, na at(10 40 to 170) by(posttran)
```

| Time | Beg. Total | Fail | Nelson-Aalen Cum. Haz. | Std. Error | [95% Conf. Int.] | |
|---|---|---|---|---|---|---|
| posttran=0 | | | | | | |
| 10 | 74 | 12 | 0.1349 | 0.0391 | 0.0764 | 0.2382 |
| 40 | 31 | 11 | 0.3824 | 0.0871 | 0.2448 | 0.5976 |
| 70 | 17 | 2 | 0.4813 | 0.1124 | 0.3044 | 0.7608 |
| 100 | 11 | 1 | 0.5646 | 0.1400 | 0.3473 | 0.9178 |
| 130 | 10 | 1 | 0.6646 | 0.1720 | 0.4002 | 1.1037 |
| 160 | 7 | 1 | 0.7896 | 0.2126 | 0.4658 | 1.3385 |
| posttran=1 | | | | | | |
| 10 | 16 | 1 | 0.0714 | 0.0714 | 0.0101 | 0.5071 |
| 40 | 43 | 6 | 0.2929 | 0.1176 | 0.1334 | 0.6433 |
| 70 | 45 | 9 | 0.4981 | 0.1360 | 0.2916 | 0.8507 |
| 100 | 40 | 9 | 0.7155 | 0.1542 | 0.4691 | 1.0915 |
| 130 | 38 | 1 | 0.7418 | 0.1564 | 0.4908 | 1.1214 |
| 160 | 36 | 1 | 0.7689 | 0.1587 | 0.5130 | 1.1523 |

Note:   Nelson-Aalen function is calculated over full data and evaluated at indicated times; it is not calculated from aggregates shown at left.

Here is the result of the survivor functions with the `compare` option:

```
. sts list, at(10 40 to 170) by(posttran) compare
```

| | | Survivor Function | |
|---|---|---|---|
| posttran | | 0 | 1 |
| time | 10 | 0.8724 | 0.9286 |
| | 40 | 0.6781 | 0.7391 |
| | 70 | 0.6126 | 0.6002 |
| | 100 | 0.5616 | 0.4814 |
| | 130 | 0.5054 | 0.4687 |
| | 160 | 0.4422 | 0.4561 |

and of the cumulative hazard functions:

```
. sts list, na at(10 40 to 170) by(posttran) compare
```

| | | Nelson-Aalen Cum. Haz. | |
|---|---|---|---|
| posttran | | 0 | 1 |
| time | 10 | 0.1349 | 0.0714 |
| | 40 | 0.3824 | 0.2929 |
| | 70 | 0.4813 | 0.4981 |
| | 100 | 0.5646 | 0.7155 |
| | 130 | 0.6646 | 0.7418 |
| | 160 | 0.7896 | 0.7689 |

# Methods and Formulas

See [R] **st sts**.

# References

See [R] **st sts**.

# Also See

| | |
|---|---|
| **Complementary:** | [R] **st sts**, [R] **st sts generate**, [R] **st sts graph**, [R] **st sts test**, [R] **st stset** |
| **Background:** | [R] **st**;<br>[U] **14.1.8 numlist** |

# Title

**st sts test** — Test equality of survivor functions

# Syntax

sts test *varlist* [if *exp*] [in *range*] [,

{ <u>log</u>rank | <u>w</u>ilcoxon | <u>tw</u>are | <u>p</u>eto | <u>f</u>h(*p q*)| <u>c</u>ox }

<u>str</u>ata(*varlist*) <u>d</u>etail <u>tr</u>end mat(*matname*$_1$ *matname*$_2$) <u>not</u>itle <u>nosh</u>ow ]

sts test is for use with survival-time data; see [R] **st**. You must stset your data before using this command.

# Description

sts test tests the equality of survivor functions across two or more groups. The log-rank, Wilcoxon, Tarone–Ware, Peto–Peto–Prentice, Fleming–Harrington, and "Cox" tests are provided, in both unstratified and stratified forms.

sts test also provides a test for trend.

See [R] **st sts** for an introduction to this command.

sts test is appropriate for use with single- or multiple-record, single- or multiple-failure, st data.

# Options

logrank, wilcoxon, tware, peto, fh(), and cox specify which test of equality is desired. logrank is the default unless the data are pweighted, in which case, cox is the default and is the only possibility.

wilcoxon specifies the Wilcoxon–Breslow–Gehan test, tware the Tarone–Ware test, peto the Peto–Peto–Prentice test, and fh() the generalized Fleming–Harrington test. When specifying the Fleming–Harrington test, two arguments, $p$ and $q$, are expected. When $p = 0$ and $q = 0$, the Fleming–Harrington test reduces to the log-rank test; and when $p = 1$ and $q = 0$, the test reduces to the Mann–Whitney–Wilcoxon test.

strata(*varlist*) requests that a stratified test be performed.

detail modifies strata(); it requests that, in addition to reporting the overall stratified test, the tests for the individual strata be reported as well. detail is not allowed with cox.

trend specifies that a test for trend of the survivor function across three or more ordered groups be performed.

mat(*matname*$_1$ *matname*$_2$) is not allowed with cox. The other tests are rank tests of the form $\mathbf{u}'\mathbf{V}^{-1}\mathbf{u}$. mat() requests that the vector $\mathbf{u}$ be stored in *matname*$_1$ and that $\mathbf{V}$ be stored in *matname*$_2$.

notitle requests that the title printed above the test be suppressed.

noshow prevents sts test from showing the key st variables. This option is rarely used since most people type stset, show or stset, noshow to reset once and for all whether they want to see these variables mentioned at the top of the output of every st command; see [R] **st stset**.

# Remarks

Remarks are presented under the headings

*The log-rank test*
*The Wilcoxon (Breslow–Gehan) test*
*The Tarone–Ware test*
*The Peto–Peto–Prentice test*
*The generalized Fleming–Harrington tests*
*The "Cox" test*
*The trend test*

`sts test` tests the equality of the survivor function across groups. With the exception of "Cox", these tests are members of a family of statistical tests that are extensions to censored data of traditional nonparametric rank tests for comparing two or more distributions. A technical description of these tests can be found in the *Methods and Formulas* section of this entry. Simply, at each distinct failure time in the data, the contribution to the test statistic is obtained as a weighted standardized sum of the difference between the observed and expected number of deaths in each of the $k$ groups. The expected number of deaths is obtained under the null hypothesis of no differences between the survival experience of the $k$ groups.

The weights or weight function used determine the test statistic. For example, when the weight is 1 at all failure times, the log-rank test is computed, and when the weight is the number of subjects at risk of failure at each distinct failure time, the Wilcoxon–Breslow–Gehan test is computed.

Summarized in the following table are the weights used for each of the statistical tests.

| Test | weight at each distinct failure time $(t_i)$ |
|------|----------------------------------------------|
| Log-rank | 1 |
| Wilcoxon–Breslow–Gehan | $n_i$ |
| Tarone–Ware | $\sqrt{n_i}$ |
| Peto–Peto–Prentice | $\widetilde{S}(t_i)$ |
| Fleming–Harrington | $\widehat{S}(t_{i-1})^p \left[1 - \widehat{S}(t_{i-1})\right]^q$ |

where $\widehat{S}(t_i)$ is the estimated Kaplan–Meier survivor function value for the combined sample at failure time $t_i$, $\widetilde{S}(t_i)$ is a modified estimate of the overall survivor function described in *Methods and Formulas*, and $n_i$ is the number of subjects in the risk pool at failure time $t_i$.

These tests are appropriate for testing the equality of survivor functions across two or more groups. Up to 800 groups are allowed.

The "Cox" test is related to the log-rank test but is performed as a likelihood-ratio (or, alternatively, as a Wald test) on the results from a Cox proportional-hazards regression. The log-rank test should be preferable to what we have labeled the Cox test, but with `pweight`ed data, the log-rank test is not appropriate. In point of fact, whether one performs the log-rank or Cox test makes little substantive difference with most datasets.

`sts test, trend` can be used to test against the alternative hypothesis that the failure rate increases or decreases as the level of the $k$ groups increases or decreases. This test is only appropriate when there is natural ordering of the comparison groups, for example, when each group represents an increasing or decreasing level of a therapeutic agent.

`trend` is not valid when `cox` is specified.

## The log-rank test

sts test, by default, performs the log-rank test which, to be clear, is the exponential scores test (Savage 1956, Mantel and Haenszel 1959, Mantel 1963, Mantel 1966). This test is most appropriate when the hazard functions are thought to be proportional across the groups if they are not equal.

This test statistic is constructed by giving equal weights to the contribution of each failure time to the overall test statistic.

In [R] **st sts**, we demonstrated the use of this command with the heart transplant data, a multiple-record, single-failure st dataset.

```
. sts test posttran

        failure _d:  died
   analysis time _t:  t1
              id:  id

Log-rank test for equality of survivor functions

          |   Events      Events
 posttran |  observed    expected
----------+-----------------------
 0        |      30         31.20
 1        |      45         43.80
----------+-----------------------
 Total    |      75         75.00

           chi2(1) =      0.13
           Pr>chi2 =    0.7225
```

We cannot reject the hypothesis that the survivor functions are the same.

sts test, logrank can also perform the stratified log-rank test. Say it is suggested that calendar year of acceptance also affects survival and that there are three important periods: 1967–69, 1970–72, and 1973–74. Therefore, a stratified test should be performed:

```
. gen group = 1 if year <= 69
(117 missing values generated)
. replace group=2 if year>=70 & year<=72
(78 real changes made)
. replace group=3 if year>=73
(39 real changes made)
. sts test posttran, strata(group)

Stratified log-rank test for equality of survivor functions

          |   Events      Events
 posttran |  observed    expected(*)
----------+-----------------------
 0        |      30         31.51
 1        |      45         43.49
----------+-----------------------
 Total    |      75         75.00
(*) sum over calculations within group
           chi2(1) =      0.20
           Pr>chi2 =    0.6547
```

Still finding nothing, you ask Stata to show the within-strata tests:

```
. sts test posttran, strata(group) detail
```

Stratified log-rank test for equality of survivor functions

-> group = 1

| posttran | Events observed | Events expected |
|---|---|---|
| 0 | 14 | 13.59 |
| 1 | 17 | 17.41 |
| Total | 31 | 31.00 |

```
            chi2(1) =      0.03
            Pr>chi2 =    0.8558
```

-> group = 2

| posttran | Events observed | Events expected |
|---|---|---|
| 0 | 13 | 13.63 |
| 1 | 20 | 19.37 |
| Total | 33 | 33.00 |

```
            chi2(1) =      0.09
            Pr>chi2 =    0.7663
```

-> group = 3

| posttran | Events observed | Events expected |
|---|---|---|
| 0 | 3 | 4.29 |
| 1 | 8 | 6.71 |
| Total | 11 | 11.00 |

```
            chi2(1) =      0.91
            Pr>chi2 =    0.3410
```

-> Total

| posttran | Events observed | Events expected(*) |
|---|---|---|
| 0 | 30 | 31.51 |
| 1 | 45 | 43.49 |
| Total | 75 | 75.00 |

(*) sum over calculations within group

```
            chi2(1) =      0.20
            Pr>chi2 =    0.6547
```

## The Wilcoxon (Breslow–Gehan) test

sts test, wilcoxon performs the generalized Wilcoxon test of Breslow (1970) and Gehan (1965). This test is appropriate when hazard functions are thought to vary in ways other than proportionally and censoring patterns are similar across groups.

The Wilcoxon test statistic is constructed by weighting the contribution of each failure time to the overall test statistic by the number of subjects at risk. Thus, it gives heavier weights to earlier failure times when the number at risk is higher. As a result, this test is susceptible to differences in the censoring pattern of the groups.

sts test, wilcoxon works the same way as sts test, logrank:

. sts test posttran, wilcoxon

Wilcoxon (Breslow) test for equality of survivor functions

| posttran | Events observed | Events expected | Sum of ranks |
|---|---|---|---|
| 0 | 30 | 31.20 | -85 |
| 1 | 45 | 43.80 | 85 |
| Total | 75 | 75.00 | 0 |

chi2(1) =      0.14
Pr>chi2 =    0.7083

and, with the strata() option, sts test, wilcoxon performs the stratified test:

. sts test posttran, wilcoxon strata(group)

Stratified Wilcoxon (Breslow) test for equality of survivor functions

| posttran | Events observed | Events expected(*) | Sum of ranks(*) |
|---|---|---|---|
| 0 | 30 | 31.51 | -40 |
| 1 | 45 | 43.49 | 40 |
| Total | 75 | 75.00 | 0 |

(*) sum over calculations within group

chi2(1) =      0.22
Pr>chi2 =    0.6385

As with sts test, logrank, you can also specify the detail option to see the within-stratum tests.

## The Tarone–Ware test

sts test, tware performs a test suggested by Tarone and Ware (1977, 383), with weights equal to the square root of the number of subjects in the risk pool at time $t_i$.

Like Wilcoxon's test, this test is appropriate when hazard functions are thought to vary in ways other than proportionally and censoring patterns are similar across groups. The test statistic is constructed by weighting the contribution of each failure time to the overall test statistic by the square root of the number of subjects at risk. Thus, like the Wilcoxon test, it gives heavier weights, although not as large, to earlier failure times. Although less susceptible to the failure and censoring pattern in the data than Wilcoxon's test, this could remain a problem if large differences in these patterns exist between groups.

sts test, tware works the same way as sts test, logrank:

```
. sts test posttran, tware
```

Tarone-Ware test for equality of survivor functions

| posttran | Events observed | Events expected | Sum of ranks |
|----------|-----------------|-----------------|--------------|
| 0        | 30              | 31.20           | -9.3375685   |
| 1        | 45              | 43.80           | 9.3375685    |
| Total    | 75              | 75.00           | 0            |

$$\text{chi2}(1) = 0.12$$
$$\text{Pr>chi2} = 0.7293$$

and, with the `strata()` option, `sts test, tware` performs the stratified test:

```
. sts test posttran, tware strata(group)
```

Stratified Tarone-Ware test for equality of survivor functions

| posttran | Events observed | Events expected(*) | Sum of ranks(*) |
|----------|-----------------|--------------------|-----------------|
| 0        | 30              | 31.51              | -7.4679345      |
| 1        | 45              | 43.49              | 7.4679345       |
| Total    | 75              | 75.00              | 0               |

(*) sum over calculations within group

$$\text{chi2}(1) = 0.21$$
$$\text{Pr>chi2} = 0.6464$$

As with `sts test, logrank`, you can also specify the `detail` option to see the within-stratum tests.

## The Peto–Peto–Prentice test

`sts test, peto` performs an alternative to the Wilcoxon test proposed by Peto and Peto (1972) and Prentice (1978). The test uses as the weight function an estimate of the overall survivor function, which is similar to that obtained using the Kaplan–Meier estimator. See *Methods and Formulas* for details.

This test is appropriate when hazard functions are thought to vary in ways other than proportionally but, unlike the Wilcoxon–Breslow–Gehan test, it is not affected by differences in censoring patterns across groups.

`sts test, peto` works the same way as `sts test, logrank`:

```
. sts test posttran, peto
```

Peto-Peto test for equality of survivor functions

| posttran | Events observed | Events expected | Sum of ranks |
|----------|-----------------|-----------------|--------------|
| 0        | 30              | 31.20           | -.86708453   |
| 1        | 45              | 43.80           | .86708453    |
| Total    | 75              | 75.00           | 0            |

$$\text{chi2}(1) = 0.15$$
$$\text{Pr>chi2} = 0.6979$$

and, with the `strata()` option, `sts test, peto` performs the stratified test:

```
. sts test posttran, peto strata(group)
```

Stratified Peto-Peto test for equality of survivor functions

| posttran | Events observed | Events expected(*) | Sum of ranks(*) |
|---|---|---|---|
| 0 | 30 | 31.51 | -.96898006 |
| 1 | 45 | 43.49 | .96898006 |
| Total | 75 | 75.00 | 0 |

(*) sum over calculations within group

```
              chi2(1) =      0.19
              Pr>chi2 =    0.6618
```

As with the previous tests, you can also specify the detail option to see the within-stratum tests.

## The generalized Fleming–Harrington tests

sts test, fh($p\ q$) performs the Fleming and Harrington (1982) class of test statistics. The weight function at each distinct failure time $t$ is the product of the Kaplan–Meier survivor estimate at time $t-1$ raised to the $p$ power and $1-$ the Kaplan–Meier survivor estimate at time $t-1$ raised to the $q$ power. Thus, when specifying the Fleming and Harrington option we must specify two nonnegative arguments, $p$ and $q$.

When $p > q$, the test gives more weights to earlier failures than to later ones. When $p < q$, the opposite is true, and more weight is given to later than to earlier times. When $p$ and $q$ are both zero, the weight is 1 at all failure times and the test reduces to the log-rank test.

sts test, fh($p\ q$) works the same way as sts test, logrank. As we mentioned, if we specify $p = 0$ and $q = 0$ we will get the same results as the log-rank test,

```
. sts test posttran, fh(0 0)
```

Fleming-Harrington test for equality of survivor functions

| posttran | Events observed | Events expected | Sum of ranks |
|---|---|---|---|
| 0 | 30 | 31.20 | -1.1995511 |
| 1 | 45 | 43.80 | 1.1995511 |
| Total | 75 | 75.00 | 0 |

```
              chi2(1) =      0.13
              Pr>chi2 =    0.7225
```

which is what the log-rank test reported.

We could, for example, give more weight to later failures than to earlier ones.

```
. sts test posttran, fh(0 3)
```

Fleming-Harrington test for equality of survivor functions

| posttran | Events observed | Events expected | Sum of ranks |
|---|---|---|---|
| 0 | 30 | 31.20 | -.09364975 |
| 1 | 45 | 43.80 | .09364975 |
| Total | 75 | 75.00 | 0 |

```
              chi2(1) =      0.01
              Pr>chi2 =    0.9139
```

Similar to the previous tests, with the `strata()` option, `sts test, fh()` performs the stratified test:

```
. sts test posttran, fh(0 3) strata(group)
```

Stratified Fleming-Harrington test for equality of survivor functions

| posttran | Events observed | Events expected(*) | Sum of ranks(*) |
|---|---|---|---|
| 0 | 30 | 31.51 | -.1623318 |
| 1 | 45 | 43.49 | .1623318 |
| Total | 75 | 75.00 | 0 |

(*) sum over calculations within group

```
              chi2(1) =      0.05
              Pr>chi2 =    0.8266
```

As with the other tests, you can also specify the `detail` option to see the within-stratum tests.

## The "Cox" test

The term Cox test is our own, and this test is a variation on the log-rank test using Cox regression.

One way of thinking about the log-rank test is as a Cox proportional-hazards model on indicator variables for each of the groups. The log-rank test is a test that the coefficients are zero or, if you prefer, the hazard ratios are one. The log-rank test is, in fact, a score test of that hypothesis performed on a slightly different (partial) likelihood function that handles ties more accurately.

It is generally felt that a (less precise) score test on the precise likelihood function is preferable to a (more precise) likelihood-ratio test on the approximate likelihood function used in Cox regression estimation. In our experience, it makes little difference:

```
. sts test posttran, cox
```

Cox regression-based test for equality of survival curves

| posttran | Events observed | Events expected | Relative hazard |
|---|---|---|---|
| 0 | 30 | 31.20 | 0.9401 |
| 1 | 45 | 43.80 | 1.0450 |
| Total | 75 | 75.00 | 1.0000 |

```
           LR chi2(1) =      0.13
              Pr>chi2 =    0.7222
```

By comparison, `sts test, logrank` also reported $\chi^2 = .13$, although the significance level was 0.7225, meaning the $\chi^2$ values differed in the fourth digit. As mentioned by Kalbfleisch and Prentice (1980, 17), a primary advantage of the log-rank test is the ease with which it can be explained to nonstatisticians, since the test statistic is the difference between the observed and expected number of failures within groups.

Our purpose in offering `sts test, cox` is not to promote its use instead of the log-rank test, but to provide a test for those with sample-weighted data.

If you have sample weights (if you specified `pweights` when you `stset` the data), you cannot run the log-rank or Wilcoxon tests. Perhaps someone has worked out the generalization of these tests to sample-weighted data, but we do not know about it.

The Cox regression model, however, has been generalized to sample-weighted data, and Stata's `stcox` can estimate models with such data. In sample-weighted data, the likelihood-ratio statistic is no longer appropriate, but the Wald test based on the robust estimator of variance is.

Thus, if we treated these data as sample-weighted data, we would obtain

```
. gen one = 1
. stset t1 [pw=one], id(id) time0(_t0) failure(died) noshow
                   id:  id
        failure event:  died ~= 0 & died ~= .
   obs. time interval:  (_t0, t1]
    exit on or before:  failure
               weight:  [pweight=one]

          172  total obs.
            0  exclusions

          172  obs. remaining, representing
          103  subjects
           75  failures in single failure-per-subject data
      31938.1  total analysis time at risk, at risk from t =          0
                             earliest observed entry t =          0
                               last observed exit t =       1799

. sts test posttran, cox
```

Cox regression-based test for equality of survival curves

| posttran | Events observed | Events expected | Relative hazard |
|----------|-----------------|-----------------|-----------------|
| 0        | 30.00           | 31.20           | 0.9401          |
| 1        | 45.00           | 43.80           | 1.0450          |
| Total    | 75.00           | 75.00           | 1.0000          |

```
                Wald chi2(1) =      0.13
                   Pr>chi2 =      0.7181
```

Note that `sts test, cox` now reports the Wald statistic which is, to two digits, 0.13 just like all the others.

## The trend test

When the groups to be compared have a natural order, such as increasing or decreasing age groups, or drug dosage, we may want to test the null hypothesis of no difference in failure rate among the groups versus the alternative hypothesis that the failure rate increases or decreases as we move from one group to the next.

We illustrate this test with a dataset from a carcinogenesis experiment reprinted in Marubini and Grazia (1995, 126). Twenty-nine experimental animals were exposed to three levels (0, 1.5, 2.0) of a carcinogenic agent. The time in days to tumor formation was recorded. Here are a few of the observations:

```
. list in 1/9

         time      event       group       dose
  1.       67          1           2        1.5
  2.      150          1           2        1.5
  3.       47          1           1          2
  4.       75          0           3          0
  5.       58          1           1          2
  6.      136          1           2        1.5
  7.       58          1           1          2
  8.      150          1           2        1.5
  9.       43          0           2        1.5
```

In these data, there are two variables that indicate exposure level. The `group` variable is coded 1, 2, and 3, indicating a one-unit separation between exposures. The `dose` variable records the actual exposure dosage. To test the null hypothesis of no difference among the survival experience of the three groups versus the alternative hypothesis that the survival experience of at least one of the groups is different, it does not matter if we use `group` or `dose`.

```
. stset time, fail(event)

     failure event:  event ~= 0 & event ~= .
obs. time interval:  (0, time]
 exit on or before:  failure
```

```
      29  total obs.
       0  exclusions

      29  obs. remaining, representing
      15  failures in single record/single failure data
    2564  total analysis time at risk, at risk from t =          0
                              earliest observed entry t =         0
                                 last observed exit t =         246
```

```
. sts test group, noshow
```

Log-rank test for equality of survivor functions

| group | Events observed | Events expected |
|-------|-----------------|-----------------|
| 1     | 4               | 6.41            |
| 2     | 6               | 6.80            |
| 3     | 5               | 1.79            |
| Total | 15              | 15.00           |

```
        chi2(2) =     8.05
        Pr>chi2 =   0.0179
```

```
. sts test dose, noshow
```

Log-rank test for equality of survivor functions

| dose | Events observed | Events expected |
|------|-----------------|-----------------|
| 0    | 4               | 6.41            |
| 1.5  | 6               | 6.80            |
| 2    | 5               | 1.79            |
| Total | 15             | 15.00           |

```
              chi2(2) =      8.05
              Pr>chi2 =    0.0179
```

For the trend test, however, the distance between the values is important, so using `group` or `dose` will produce different results.

```
. sts test group, noshow trend
```

Log-rank test for equality of survivor functions

| group | Events observed | Events expected |
|-------|-----------------|-----------------|
| 1     | 4               | 6.41            |
| 2     | 6               | 6.80            |
| 3     | 5               | 1.79            |
| Total | 15              | 15.00           |

```
              chi2(2) =      8.05
              Pr>chi2 =    0.0179
```

Test for trend of survivor functions

```
              chi2(1) =      5.87
              Pr>chi2 =    0.0154
```

```
. sts test dose, noshow trend
```

Log-rank test for equality of survivor functions

| dose | Events observed | Events expected |
|------|-----------------|-----------------|
| 0    | 4               | 6.41            |
| 1.5  | 6               | 6.80            |
| 2    | 5               | 1.79            |
| Total | 15             | 15.00           |

```
              chi2(2) =      8.05
              Pr>chi2 =    0.0179
```

Test for trend of survivor functions

```
              chi2(1) =      3.66
              Pr>chi2 =    0.0557
```

Although the above trend test was constructed using the log-rank test, any of the previously mentioned weight functions can be used. For example, a trend test on the data can be performed using the same weights as the Peto–Peto–Prentice test by specifying the option `peto`.

```
. sts test dose, noshow trend peto
```

Peto-Peto test for equality of survivor functions

| dose | Events observed | Events expected | Sum of ranks |
|------|-----------------|-----------------|--------------|
| 0    | 4               | 6.41            | -1.2792221   |
| 1.5  | 6               | 6.80            | -1.3150418   |
| 2    | 5               | 1.79            | 2.5942639    |
| Total | 15             | 15.00           | 0            |

```
                         chi2(2) =      8.39
                         Pr>chi2 =    0.0150
```

Test for trend of survivor functions

```
                         chi2(1) =      2.85
                         Pr>chi2 =    0.0914
```

## Saved Results

sts test saves in r():

Scalars
r(df)   degrees of freedom          r(chi2)   $\chi^2$

## Methods and Formulas

sts test is implemented as an ado-file.

Let $t_1 < t_2 < \cdots < t_r$ denote the ordered failure times; let $d_j$ be the number of failures at $t_j$ and $n_j$ the population at risk just before $t_j$; and let $d_{ij}$ and $n_{ij}$ denote the same things for group $i$, $i = 1, \ldots, k$.

We are interested in testing the null hypothesis

$$H_o : \lambda_1(t) = \lambda_2(t) = \ldots = \lambda_k(t)$$

where $\lambda(t)$ is the hazard function at time $t$, against the alternative hypothesis that at least one of the $\lambda_i(t)$ is different for some $t_j$.

As described in Klein and Moeschberger (1997, 191–202), Kalbfleisch and Prentice (1980, 17–18), and Collett (1994, 45–46), if the null hypothesis is true, then the expected number of failures in group $i$ at time $t_j$ is $e_{ij} = n_{ij}d_j/n_j$, and the test statistic

$$\mathbf{u}' = \sum_{j=1}^{k} W(t_j)(d_{1j} - e_{1j}, \ldots, d_{rj} - e_{rj})$$

is formed. $W(t_j)$ is a positive weight function defined as zero when $n_{ij}$ is zero. The various test statistics are obtained by selecting different weight functions $W(t_j)$. See the table in the *Remarks* section of this entry for a complete list of these weight functions. The variance matrix $\mathbf{V}$ for $\mathbf{u}$ has elements

$$V_{il} = \sum_{j=1}^{k} \frac{W(t_j)^2 n_{ij} d_j (n_j - d_j)}{n_j(n_j - 1)} \left( \delta_{il} - \frac{n_{ij}}{n_j} \right)$$

where $\delta_{il} = 1$ if $i = l$ and 0 otherwise.

For the unstratified test, statistic $\mathbf{u}'\mathbf{V}^{-1}\mathbf{u}$ is distributed as $\chi^2$ with $k - 1$ degrees of freedom.

For the stratified test, let $\mathbf{u}_s$ and $\mathbf{V}_s$ be the results of performing the above calculation separately within stratum, and define $\mathbf{u} = \sum_s \mathbf{u}_s$ and $\mathbf{V} = \sum_s \mathbf{V}_s$. The $\chi^2$ test is given by $\mathbf{u}'\mathbf{V}^{-1}\mathbf{u}$ redefined in this way.

The "Cox" test is performed by estimating a (possibly stratified) Cox regression using stcox on $k - 1$ indicator variables, one for each of the groups with one of the indicators omitted. The $\chi^2$ test reported is then the likelihood-ratio test (no pweights) or the Wald test (based on the robust estimate of variance); see [R] st stcox.

The reported relative hazards are the exponentiated coefficients from the Cox regression renormalized, and the renormalization plays no role in the calculation of the test statistic. The renormalization is chosen so that the expected-number-of-failures-within-group weighted average of the regression coefficients is 0 (meaning the hazard is 1). Let $b_i$, $i = 1, \ldots, r - 1$ be the estimated coefficients, and define $b_r = 0$. The constant $K$ is then calculated by

$$K = \sum_{i=1}^{r} e_i b_i / d$$

where $e_i = \sum_j e_{ij}$ is the expected number of failures for group $i$, $d$ is the total number of failures across all groups, and $r$ is the number of groups. The reported relative hazards are $\exp(b_i - K)$.

The trend test assumes that there is natural ordering of the $k$ groups, $k > 2$. In this case, we are interested in testing the null hypothesis

$$H_o : \lambda_1(t) = \lambda_2(t) = \ldots = \lambda_k(t)$$

against the alternative hypothesis

$$H_a : \lambda_1(t) \leq \lambda_2(t) \leq \ldots \leq \lambda_k(t)$$

The test uses $\mathbf{u}$ as previously defined with any of the available weight functions. The test statistic is given by

$$\frac{\left(\sum_{i=1}^{k} a_i u_i\right)^2}{\mathbf{a}'\mathbf{V}\mathbf{a}}$$

where $\mathbf{a}$ is a vector of these scores and $a_1 \leq a_2 \leq \ldots \leq a_k$ are scores defining the relationship of interest. A score is assigned to each of the comparison groups.

# References

Breslow, N. E. 1970. A generalized Kruskal–Wallis test for comparing $k$ samples subject to unequal patterns of censorship. *Biometrika* 57: 579–594.

Collett, D. 1994. *Modelling Survival Data in Medical Research.* London: Chapman & Hall.

Gehan, E. A. 1965. A generalized Wilcoxon test for comparing arbitrarily singly censored data. *Biometrika* 52: 203–223.

Harrington, D. P. and T. R. Fleming. 1982. A class of rank test procedures for censored survival data. *Biometrika* 69: 553–566.

Kalbfleisch, J. D. and R. L. Prentice. 1980. *The Statistical Analysis of Failure Time Data.* New York: John Wiley & Sons.

Klein, J. P. and M. L. Moeschberger. 1997. *Survival Analysis: Techniques for Censored and Truncated data.* New York: Springer-Verlag.

Mantel, N. 1963. Chi-squared tests with one degree of freedom: extensions of the Mantel–Haenszel procedure. *Journal of the American Statistical Association* 58: 690–700.

——. 1966. Evaluation of survival data and two new rank-order statistics arising in its consideration. *Cancer Chemotherapy Reports* 50: 163–170.

Mantel, N. and W. Haenszel. 1959. Statistical aspects of the analysis of data from retrospective studies of disease. *Journal of the National Cancer Institute* 22: 719–748. Reprinted in *Evolution of Epidemiologic Ideas*, ed. S. Greenland, 112–141. Newton Lower Falls, MA: Epidemiology Resources.

Marubini, E. and M. Grazia-Valsecchi. 1995. *Analyzing Survival Data from Clinical Trials and Observational Studies.* New York: John Wiley & Sons.

Peto, R. and J. Peto. 1972. Asymptotically efficient rank invariant test procedures (with discussion). *Journal of the Royal Statistical Society* 135: 185–206.

Prentice, R. L. 1978. Linear rank tests with right-censored data. *Biometrika* 65: 167–179.

Savage, I. R. 1956. Contributions to the theory of rank-order statistics—the two-sample case. *Annals of Mathematical Statistics* 27: 590–615.

Tarone, R. E. and J. H. Ware. 1977. On distribution-free tests for equality of survival distributions. *Biometrika* 64: 156–160.

Wilcoxon, F. 1945. Individual comparisons by ranking methods. *Biometrics* 1: 80–83.

# Also See

| | |
|---|---|
| **Complementary:** | [R] **st stcox**, [R] **st sts**, [R] **st sts generate**, [R] **st sts graph**, [R] **st sts list**, [R] **st stset** |
| **Background:** | [R] **st** |

# Title

> **st stset** — Declare data to be survival-time data

# Syntax

**Single-record per subject survival data**

> stset *timevar* $\begin{bmatrix} \text{if} \ exp \end{bmatrix}$ $\begin{bmatrix} weight \end{bmatrix}$ $\begin{bmatrix} , \ \underline{f}\text{ailure}(\textit{failvar}\begin{bmatrix}==\textit{numlist}\end{bmatrix}) \ \text{time0}(\textit{varname}) \end{bmatrix}$
>
> $\underline{o}\text{rigin}(\underline{t}\text{ime} \ exp) \ \underline{sc}\text{ale}(\#) \ \underline{en}\text{ter}(\underline{t}\text{ime} \ exp) \ \underline{ex}\text{it}(\underline{t}\text{ime} \ exp) \ \text{if}(exp) \ \underline{no}\text{show} \ ]$

> streset $\begin{bmatrix} \text{if} \ exp \end{bmatrix}$ $\begin{bmatrix} weight \end{bmatrix}$ $[ , \ \textit{same options as stset} \ ]$

> st $[ , \ \underline{noc}\text{md} \ \underline{not}\text{able} \ ]$

> stset, clear

**Multiple-record per subject survival data**

> stset *timevar* $\begin{bmatrix} \text{if} \ exp \end{bmatrix}$ $\begin{bmatrix} weight \end{bmatrix}$, id(*varname*) $\underline{f}\text{ailure}(\textit{failvar}\begin{bmatrix}==\textit{numlist}\end{bmatrix}) \ [$
>
> $\underline{o}\text{rigin}(\begin{bmatrix}\textit{varname}==\textit{numlist}\end{bmatrix} \ \underline{t}\text{ime} \ exp \ | \ \text{min}) \ \underline{sc}\text{ale}(\#)$
>
> $\underline{en}\text{ter}(\begin{bmatrix}\textit{varname}==\textit{numlist}\end{bmatrix} \ \underline{t}\text{ime} \ exp) \ \underline{ex}\text{it}(\text{failure} \ | \ \begin{bmatrix}\textit{varname}==\textit{numlist}\end{bmatrix} \ \underline{t}\text{ime} \ exp)$
>
> $\text{time0}(\textit{varname}) \ \text{if}(exp) \ \text{ever}(exp) \ \text{never}(exp) \ \text{after}(exp) \ \underline{befo}\text{re}(exp) \ \underline{no}\text{show} \ ]$

> streset $\begin{bmatrix} \text{if} \ exp \end{bmatrix}$ $\begin{bmatrix} weight \end{bmatrix}$ $[ , \ \textit{same options as stset} \ ]$

> streset, { $\underline{\text{past}}$ | $\underline{\text{future}}$ | $\underline{\text{past}}$ $\underline{\text{future}}$ }

> st $[ , \ \underline{noc}\text{md} \ \underline{not}\text{able} \ ]$

> stset, clear

fweights, iweights, and pweights are allowed; see [U] **14.1.6 weight**.

# Examples

| | |
|---|---|
| . stset ftime | (*Time measured from 0, all failed*) |
| . stset ftime, failure(died) | (*Time measured from 0, censoring*) |
| . stset ftime, failure(died) id(id) | (*Time measured from 0, censoring and id*) |
| . stset ftime, failure(died==2,3) | (*Time measured from 0, failure codes*) |
| . stset ftime, failure(died) origin(time dob) | (*Time measured from dob, censoring*) |

**You cannot harm your data using stset, so feel free to experiment.**

# Description

st refers to survival-time data, which are fully described below.

stset declares the data in memory to be survival-time (st) data, informing Stata of key variables and their roles in a survival-time data analysis. When you stset your data, stset runs various data consistency checks to ensure that what you have declared makes sense. Note that if the data are weighted, you specify the weights when you stset the data, not when you issue the individual st commands.

streset changes how the st dataset is declared. In multiple record data, streset can also temporarily set the sample to include records prior to being at risk (called the past) and records after failure (called the future). In that case, typing streset without arguments resets the sample back to the analysis sample.

st displays how the dataset is currently declared.

Whenever you type stset or streset, Stata runs or reruns data consistency checks to ensure that what you are now declaring (or declared in the past) makes sense. Thus, if you have made any changes to your data or simply wish to verify how things are, you can type streset without any options.

stset, clear is for use by programmers. It causes Stata to forget the st markers, making the data no longer st data to Stata. The data remain unchanged. It is not necessary to stset, clear before doing another stset.

## ❑ Technical Note

**Note to Stata version 5.0 users:** stset was changed in Stata 6. Your old Stata 5 st datasets will work with the new st:

1. If you want to use old st datasets with the new st commands, there is nothing special you need to do. You do **not** need to re-stset your data. Just use your dataset and everything will just work.

2. There are syntax changes. If you want to use the old st syntax (perhaps you have old do-files and need to recreate an old analysis), type

       . version 5

   You will then be using the old st system. When you want to use the new st system again, type

       . version 7

3. If you are using version 7 (or version 6), the stset syntax has changed from version 5. Where you previously typed 'stset *timevar failvar*', now type 'stset *timevar*, failure(*failvar*)'.

   In addition, the t0() option is gone. It is literally renamed time0(), and we did that so that you would not use it unthinkingly. Where you used to specify t0(*evar*), you now want to say entry(time *evar*) or time0(*evar*), and you probably want to say the former. The new system draws a distinction among coming at risk (called origin), coming under observation (called entry), and the start date for a record (called time0).

   ❑

# Options for use with stset and streset

id(*idvar*) specifies the subject-id variable; observations with equal, nonmissing values of *idvar* are assumed to be the same subject. *idvar* may be string or numeric. Observations for which *idvar* is missing (. or "") are ignored.

When id() is not specified, each observation is assumed to represent a different subject and thus constitutes a single-record-per-subject survival dataset.

When you specify id(), the data are said to be multiple-record data even if it turns out there is only one record per subject. Perhaps they would better be called potentially multiple-record data.

If you specify id(), stset requires that you specify failure().

Specifying id() never hurts; we recommend it because a few st commands, such as stsplit, require that an id variable have been specified when the dataset was stset.

failure(*failvar*[==*numlist*]) specifies the failure event.

If failure() is not specified, all records are assumed to end in failure. This is allowed with single-record data only.

If failure(*failvar*) is specified, *failvar* is interpreted as an indicator variable; 0 and missing mean censored and all other values are interpreted as representing failure.

If failure(*failvar*==*numlist*) is specified, records with *failvar* taking on any of the values in *numlist* are assumed to end in failures and all other records are assumed to be censored.

origin([*varname*==*numlist*] time *exp* | min) and scale(#) define analysis time or, said differently, origin() defines when a subject becomes at risk. Subjects become at risk when time = origin(). All analyses are performed in terms of time since becoming at risk, called analysis time.

Let us use the terms *time*, for how time is recorded in the data, and *t*, for analysis time. Analysis time *t* is defined

$$t = \frac{time - \texttt{origin()}}{\texttt{scale()}}$$

*t* is time from origin in units of scale.

By default, origin(time 0) and scale(1) are assumed, meaning $t = time$. In that case, it is your responsibility to ensure that *time* in your data is measured as time since becoming at risk. Subjects are exposed at $t = time = 0$ and subsequently fail. Observations with $t = time < 0$ are ignored because information prior to becoming at risk is irrelevant.

origin() plays the substantive role of determining when the clock starts ticking. scale() plays no substantive role, but it can be handy for making *t* units more readable (such as converting days to years).

origin(time *exp*) sets the origin to *exp*. For instance, if *time* were recorded as dates such as 05jun1998 in your data and variable expdate recorded the date when subjects were exposed, you could specify origin(time expdate). If instead all subjects were exposed on 12nov1997, you could specify origin(time mdy(11,12,1997)).

origin(time *exp*) may be used with single- or multiple-record data.

origin(*varname*==*numlist*) is for use with multiple-record data; it specifies the origin indirectly. If *time* were recorded as dates in your data, variable obsdate recorded the (ending) date associated with each record, and subjects came at risk upon, say, having a certain operation—and that operation were indicated by code==217—then you could specify origin(code==217). origin(code==217) would mean, for each subject, the origin time is the earliest time at which code==217 is observed. Records prior to that would be ignored (because $t < 0$). Subjects who never had code==217 would be ignored entirely.

origin(*varname==numlist* time *exp*) sets the origin to be the latter of the two times determined by *varname==numlist* and *exp*.

origin(min) sets origin to the earliest time observed, minus 1. This is a very odd thing to do and is described in *Example 10* under *Remarks* below.

origin() is an important concept; see the entries *Key concepts*, *Two concepts of time*, and *The substantive meaning of analysis time* under *Remarks* below.

scale() makes results more readable. If you have *time* recorded in days (such as Stata dates, which are really days since 01jan1960), specifying scale(365.25) will cause results to be reported in years.

enter([*varname==numlist*] time *exp*) specifies when a subject first comes under observation, meaning that any failures, were they to occur, would be recorded in the data.

Do not confuse enter() and origin(). origin() specifies when a subject first becomes at risk. In many datasets, becoming at risk and coming under observation are coincident. In that case, it is sufficient to specify origin().

enter(time *exp*), enter(*varname==numlist*), and enter(*varname==numlist* time *exp*) follow the same syntax as origin(). In multiple-record data, both *varname==numlist* and time *exp* are interpreted as the earliest time implied and, if both are specified, the later of the two times is used.

exit(failure | [*varname==numlist*] time *exp*) specifies the latest time under which the subject is both under observation and at risk. The emphasis is on latest; obviously subjects also exit the risk pool when their data run out.

exit(failure) is the default. When the first failure event occurs, the subject is removed from the analysis risk pool even if the subject has subsequent records in the data and even if some of those subsequent records document other failure events. Specify exit(time .) if you wish to keep all records for a subject after failure. You want to do this if you have multiple failure data.

exit(*varname==numlist*), exit(time *exp*), and exit(*varname==numlist* time *exp*) follow the same syntax as origin() and entry(). In multiple-record data, both *varname==numlist* and time *exp* are interpreted as the earliest time implied. exit differs from origin() and entry() in that, if both are specified, the earlier of the two times is used.

time0(*varname*) is rarely specified because most datasets do not contain this information. time0() should be used exclusively with multiple-record data, and even then you should consider whether origin() or enter() would be more appropriate.

time0() specifies a mechanical aspect of interpretation about the records in the dataset, namely the beginning of the period spanned by each record. See *Intermediate exit and re-entry times (gaps)* under *Remarks* below.

if(*exp*), ever(*exp*), never(*exp*), after(*exp*), and before(*exp*) select relevant records.

if(*exp*) selects records for which *exp* is true. We strongly recommend specifying this if() option rather than if *exp* following stset or streset. They differ in that if *exp* removes from consideration the data before the calculation of beginning and ending times and other quantities as well. The if() option, on the other hand, sets the restriction after all derived variables are calculated. See *The if() option versus the if exp* under *Remarks* below.

if() may be specified with single- or multiple-record data. The remaining selection options are for use with multiple-record data only.

ever(*exp*) selects only subjects for which *exp* is ever true.

never(*exp*) selects only subjects for which *exp* is never true.

after(*exp*) selects records within subject on or after the first time *exp* is true.

before(*exp*) selects records within subject before the first time *exp* is true.

show and noshow change whether the other st commands are to display the identities of the key st variables at the top of their output.

## Options unique to streset

past expands the stset sample to include the entire recorded past of the relevant subjects, meaning it includes observations before becoming at risk, or excluded due to after(), etc.

future expands the stset sample to include the records on the relevant subjects after the last record that previously was included, if any, which typically means to include all observations after failure or censoring.

past future expands the stset sample to include all records on the relevant subjects.

Typing streset without arguments resets the sample back to the analysis sample. See *Past and future records* under *Remarks* for more information.

## Options for st

nocmd suppresses displaying the last stset command.

notable suppresses displaying the table summarizing what has been stset.

## Remarks

Remarks are presented under the headings

# What is survival-time data?

Survival-time data—what we call st data—documents spans of time ending in an event. For instance,

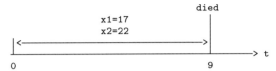

which is to say, x1 = 17 and x2 = 22 over the time span 0 to 9, and then died = 1. More formally, we mean x1 = 17 and x2 = 22 for $0 < t \le 9$, which we often write as $(0, 9]$. However you wish to say it, this information might be recorded by the observation

| id | end | x1 | x2 | died |
|---|---|---|---|---|
| 101 | 9 | 17 | 22 | 1 |

and we call this single-record survival data.

The data can be more complicated. For instance, we might have

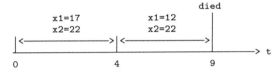

meaning

$$x1 = 17 \text{ and } x2 = 22 \text{ during } (0, 4]$$
$$x1 = 12 \text{ and } x2 = 22 \text{ during } (4, 9], \text{ and then } died = 1.$$

and this would be recorded by the data

| id | begin | end | x1 | x2 | died |
|---|---|---|---|---|---|
| 101 | 0 | 4 | 17 | 22 | 0 |
| 101 | 4 | 9 | 12 | 22 | 1 |

We call this multiple-record survival data.

These two formats allow recording lots of different possibilities. The last observation on a person need not be failure:

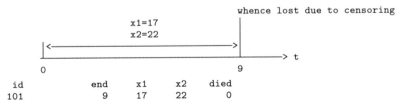

| id | end | x1 | x2 | died |
|---|---|---|---|---|
| 101 | 9 | 17 | 22 | 0 |

or

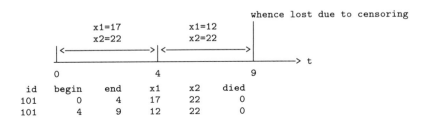

| id | begin | end | x1 | x2 | died |
|---|---|---|---|---|---|
| 101 | 0 | 4 | 17 | 22 | 0 |
| 101 | 4 | 9 | 12 | 22 | 0 |

Multiple-record data might have gaps,

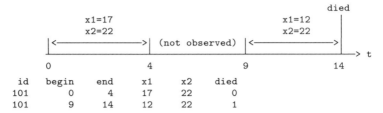

| id  | begin | end | x1 | x2 | died |
|-----|-------|-----|----|----|------|
| 101 | 0     | 4   | 17 | 22 | 0    |
| 101 | 9     | 14  | 12 | 22 | 1    |

or subjects might not be observed from the onset of risk:

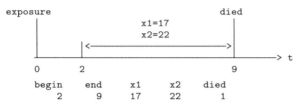

| begin | end | x1 | x2 | died |
|-------|-----|----|----|------|
| 2     | 9   | 17 | 22 | 1    |

and

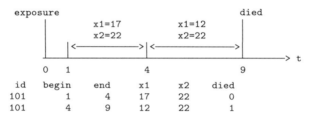

| id  | begin | end | x1 | x2 | died |
|-----|-------|-----|----|----|------|
| 101 | 1     | 4   | 17 | 22 | 0    |
| 101 | 4     | 9   | 12 | 22 | 1    |

The failure event might not be death but instead something that can repeat:

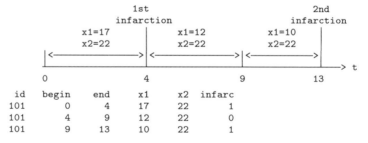

| id  | begin | end | x1 | x2 | infarc |
|-----|-------|-----|----|----|--------|
| 101 | 0     | 4   | 17 | 22 | 1      |
| 101 | 4     | 9   | 12 | 22 | 0      |
| 101 | 9     | 13  | 10 | 22 | 1      |

Our data may be in different time units; rather than $t$ where $t = 0$ corresponds to the onset of risk, we might have time recorded as age,

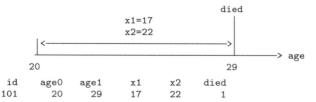

| id  | age0 | age1 | x1 | x2 | died |
|-----|------|------|----|----|------|
| 101 | 20   | 29   | 17 | 22 | 1    |

or time recorded as calendar dates:

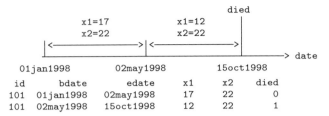

| id  | bdate     | edate     | x1 | x2 | died |
|-----|-----------|-----------|----|----|------|
| 101 | 01jan1998 | 02may1998 | 17 | 22 | 0    |
| 101 | 02may1998 | 15oct1998 | 12 | 22 | 1    |

Finally, you can mix these diagrams however you wish, so we might have time recorded per the calendar, unobserved periods after the onset of risk, subsequent gaps, and multiple failure events.

The st commands analyze data like these and the first step is to tell st about your data using stset. You do not change your data to fit some predefined mold; you describe your data using stset and then the rest of the st commands just do the right thing.

Before we turn to using stset, let us describe one more style of recording time-to-event data because it is common and is inappropriate for use with st. It is inappropriate, but it is easy to convert to the survival-time form. It is called snapshot data. In snapshot data you do not know spans of time, but you have information recorded at various points in time:

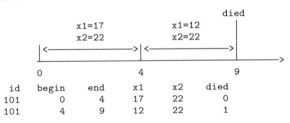

| id  | t | x1 | x2 | died |
|-----|---|----|----|------|
| 101 | 0 | 17 | 22 | 0    |
| 101 | 4 | 12 | 22 | 0    |
| 101 | 9 | .  | .  | 1    |

In this snapshot dataset all we know are the values of x1 and x2 at $t = 0$ and $t = 4$, and we know that the subject died at $t = 9$. Snapshot data can be converted to survival-time data if we are willing to assume that x1 and x2 remained constant between times:

| id  | begin | end | x1 | x2 | died |
|-----|-------|-----|----|----|------|
| 101 | 0     | 4   | 17 | 22 | 0    |
| 101 | 4     | 9   | 12 | 22 | 1    |

The snapspan command makes this conversion. If you have snapshot data, first see [R] **snapspan** to convert it to survival-time data and then use stset to tell st about the converted data, but see *Example 10: Real data* below, first.

## Key concepts

*time*, or better, *time units*, is how time is recorded in your data. It might be numbers such as 0, 1, 2, ..., with *time* = 0 corresponding to some exposure event, or it might be subject's age, or it might be calendar time, or it might be recorded in some other way.

*events* are things that happen at an instant in time, such as being exposed to an environmental hazard, being diagnosed as myopic, becoming employed, being promoted, becoming unemployed, having a heart attack, and dying.

*failure event* is the *event* indicating failure as it is defined for the purpose of analysis. This can be a single or compound event. The *failure* event might be when variable `dead` is 1 or it might be when variable `diag` is any of 115, 121, or 133.

*at risk* means the subject is at risk of the *failure event* occurring. For instance, if the *failure event* is becoming unemployed, a person must be employed. The subject is not *at risk* prior to being employed. Once employed, the subject becomes *at risk* and, once again, the subject is no longer *at risk* once the *failure event* occurs. If subjects become *at risk* upon the occurrence of some *event*, it is called the exposure event. Gaining employment is the exposure event in our example.

*origin* is the *time* when the subject became at risk. If *time* is recorded as numbers such as 0, 1, 2, ..., with *time* = 0 corresponding to the exposure event, then *origin* = 0. Alternatively, *origin* might be the age of the subject when diagnosed or the date when the subject was exposed. Regardless, *origin* is expressed in *time units*.

*scale* is just a fixed number, typically 1, used in mapping *time* to analysis time *t*.

*t*, or *analysis time*, is $(time - origin)/scale$, which is to say, time since onset of being at risk measured in *scale* units.

$t = 0$ corresponds to the onset of risk and *scale* just provides a way to make the units of *t* more readable. You might have *time* recorded in days from 01jan1960 and want *t* recorded in years, in which case *scale* would be 365.25.

*time* is how time is recorded in your data and *t* is how time is reported in the analysis.

*under observation* means that, should the *failure event* occur, it would be observed and recorded in the data. Sometimes subjects are *under observation* only after they are *at risk*. This would be the case, for instance, if subjects enrolled in a study after being diagnosed with cancer and, in order to enroll in the study, subjects were required to be diagnosed with cancer.

Being *under observation* does not mean the subject is necessarily *at risk*. A subject may come *under observation* prior to being *at risk* and, in fact, a subject *under observation* may never come to be *at risk*.

*entry time* and *exit time* mark when a subject is first and last *under observation*. The emphasis here is on the words first and last; *entry time* and *exit time* do not record observational gaps, if any; there is only one *entry time* and one *exit time* per subject.

*entry time* and *exit time* might be expressed as *times* (meaning recorded in *time units*) or they might correspond to the occurrence of some *event* (such as enrolling in the study).

Often the *entry time* corresponds to $t = 0$ or, since $t = (time - origin)/scale$, *time* = *origin*, or, substituting true meanings, the onset of risk.

Often the *exit time* corresponds to when the *failure event* occurs or, failing that, the end of data for the subject.

*delayed entry* means that *entry time* corresponds to $t > 0$; the subject became at risk but it was some time afterwards that the subject was under observation.

*id* refers to a subject identification variable; equal values of *id* indicate that the records are on the same subject. An *id* variable is required for multiple-record data and is optional, but recommended, with single-record data.

*time0* refers to the beginning *time* (meaning recorded in *time units*) of a record. Some datasets have this variable but most do not. If the dataset does not contain the beginning time for each record, then subsequent records are assumed to begin where previous records ended. A *time0* variable may be created for these datasets using the `snapspan` command; see [R] **snapspan**. Do not confuse *time0*—a mechanical aspect of datasets—with *entry time*—a substantive aspect of analysis.

```
patid    addate    curdate    sex    x1    x2    code
  101  18aug1998  23aug1998      1    10    10     177
  101          .  31aug1998      1    20     8     286
  101          .  08sep1998      1    16    11     208
  101          .  11sep1998      1    11    17     401
  102  20aug1998  28aug1998      0    20    19     204
  102          .  07sep1998      0    19     1     401
  103  etc.
```

Rather, what we would have received would have been a snapshot dataset:

```
patid      date    sex    x1    x2    code
  101  18aug1998      1    10    10      22
  101  23aug1998      .    20     8     177
  101  31aug1998      .    16    11     286
  101  08sep1998      .    11    17     208
  101  11sep1998      .     .     .     401
  102  20aug1998      0    20    19      22
  102  28aug1998      .    19     1     204
  102  07sep1998      .     .     .     401
  103  etc.
```

In a snapshot dataset, we have a time (date in this case) and values of the variables as of that instant.

This dataset can be converted to the appropriate form by typing

```
. snapspan patid date code
```

The result would be

```
patid      date    sex    x1    x2    code
  101  18aug1998      .     .     .      22
  101  23aug1998      1    10    10     177
  101  31aug1998      .    20     8     286
  101  08sep1998      .    16    11     208
  101  11sep1998      .    11    17     401
  102  20aug1998      .     .     .      22
  102  28aug1998      0    20    19     204
  102  07sep1998      .    19     1     401
```

This is virtually the same dataset with which we have been working. It differs in two ways:

1. The variable sex is not filled in for all the observations because it was not filled in on the the original form. The hospital wrote down the sex on admission and then never bothered to document it again.

2. We have no admission date (addate) variable. Instead, we have an extra first record for each patient with code = 22 (22 is the code the hospital uses for admissions).

The first problem is easily fixed and the second, it turns out, is not a problem because we can vary what we type when we stset the data.

First, let's fix the problem with variable sex. There are two ways to proceed. One would be simply to fill in the variable ourselves:

```
. by patid (date), sort: replace sex = sex[_n-1] if sex==.
```

Alternatively, we could perform a phony stset that is good enough to set all the data, and then use stfill to fill in the variable for us. Let us begin with the phony stset:

```
. stset date, id(patid) origin(min) fail(code==-1)
                    id:  patid
         failure event:  code == -1
     obs. time interval:  (date[_n-1], date]
      exit on or before:  failure
         t for analysis:  (time-origin)
                 origin:  min

        283  total obs.
          0  exclusions

        283  obs. remaining, representing
         40  subjects
          0  failures in single failure-per-subject data
       2224  total analysis time at risk, at risk from t =          0
                              earliest observed entry t =          0
                                 last observed exit t =          89
```

Typing `stset date, id(patid) origin(min) fail(code == -1)` does not produce anything we would want to use for analysis. This is a trick to get all the data temporarily `stset` so that we can use some st data-management commands on it.

The first part of the trick was to specify `origin(min)`. This defines analysis time as $t = 0$, corresponding to the minimum observed value of time variable, minus 1. The time variable is `date` in this case. Why the minimum minus 1? Because st is bound and determined to ignore observations for which analysis time $t < 0$. `origin(min)` provides a phony definition of $t$ that ensures $t > 0$ for all observations.

The second part of the trick was to specify `fail(code == -1)`, and you might have to vary what you type. We just wanted to choose an event that we know never happens, thus ensuring that no observations are ignored following failure.

Now that we have the dataset `stset`, we can use the other st commands. Do not use the st analysis commands unless you want ridiculous results, but one of the st data-management commands is just what we want:

```
. stfill sex, forward
           failure _d:  code == -1
      analysis time _t:  (date-origin)
               origin:  min
                   id:  patid
replace missing values with previously observed values:
           sex:  203 real changes made
```

Problem one solved.

The second problem concerns the lack of an admission date variable. That is not really a problem because we have a new first observation with `code = 22` recording the date of admission, so every place we previously coded `origin(time addate)`, we substitute `origin(code == 22)`.

Problem two solved.

We also solved the big problem—converting a snapshot dataset into a survival-time dataset; see [R] **snapspan**.

## Two concepts of time

The st system has two concepts of time. The first is *time* in italics, which corresponds to how time is recorded in your data. The second is analysis time, which we write as *t*. Substantively, analysis time is time at risk. stset defines analysis time in terms of *time* via

$$t = \frac{time - \texttt{origin()}}{\texttt{scale()}}$$

*t* and time can be the same thing and, by default they are because, by default, origin() is 0 and scale() is 1.

All the st analysis commands work with analysis time *t*.

By default, if you do not specify the origin() and scale() options, your time variables are expected to be the analysis time variables. This means *time* = 0 corresponds to when subjects became at risk and that means, among other things, that observations for which *time* < 0 are ignored because survival analysis concerns the analysis of persons who are at risk, and no one is at risk prior to *t* = 0.

origin plays the substantive role of determining when the clock starts ticking. If you do not specify origin(), origin(time 0) is assumed, meaning that *t* = *time* and that persons are at risk from *t* = *time* = 0.

In many datasets, *time* and *t* will differ. Time might be calendar time and *t* the length of time since some event, such as being born, being exposed to some risk factor, etc. origin() sets when *t* = 0. scale() merely sets a constant that makes *t* more readable.

The syntax for the origin() option makes it look more complicated than it really is:

origin([*varname* == *numlist*] time *exp* | min)

This says that there are four different ways to specify origin():

origin(time *exp*)
origin(*varname* == *numlist*)
origin(*varname* == *numlist* time *exp*)
origin(min)

The first syntax can be used with single- or multiple-record data. It states that the origin is given by *exp*, which can be a constant for all observations, a variable (and hence varying subject by subject), or even an expression composed of variables and constants. Perhaps origin is a fixed date or a date recorded in the data when the subject was exposed or when the subject turned 18.

The second and third syntaxes are for use with multiple-record data. The second states that origin corresponds to the (earliest) time when the designated event occurred. Perhaps origin is when an operation was performed. The third syntax calculates origin both ways and then selects the later one.

The fourth syntax does something odd; it sets the origin to the minimum time observed, minus 1. This is not useful for analysis but is sometimes useful for playing data-management tricks; see *Example 10: Real data* above.

Let's start with the first syntax. Pretend that you had the data

```
   faildate     x1     x2
   28dec1997    12     22
   12nov1997    15     22
   03feb1998    55     22
```

and that all the observations came at risk on the same date, 01nov1997. You could type

    . stset faildate, origin(time mdy(11,1,1997))

Remember that `stset` secretly adds `_t0` and `_t` to your dataset and that they contain the time span for each record, documented in analysis-time units. After typing `stset`, you can `list` the results:

    . list faildate x1 x2 _t0 _t

          faildate      x1      x2      _t0       _t
       1. 28dec1997      12      22        0       57
       2. 12nov1997      15      22        0       11
       3. 03feb1998      55      22        0       94

Record 1 reflects the period $(0, 57]$ in analysis-time units, which are, in this case, days. `stset` calculated the 57 from $28\text{dec}1997 - 01\text{nov}1997 = 13{,}876 - 13{,}819 = 57$. (Remember that dates such as 28dec1997 are really just integers containing the number of days from 01jan1960, and it is Stata's `%d` display format that makes them display nicely. 28dec1997 is really the number 13,876.)

As another example, we might have data recording exposure and failure dates:

        expdate    faildate      x1      x2
        07may1998  22jun1998      12      22
        02feb1998  11may1998      11      17

The way to `stset` this dataset is

    . stset faildate, origin(time expdate)

and the result, in analysis units, is

    . list expdate faildate x1 x2 _t0 _t

          expdate    faildate      x1      x2      _t0       _t
       1. 07may1998  22jun1998      12      22        0       46
       2. 02feb1998  11may1998      11      17        0       98

There is nothing magic about dates. Our original data could just as well have been

        expdate    faildate      x1      x2
             32          78      12      22
             12         110      11      17

and the final result would still be the same because $78 - 32 = 46$ and $110 - 12 = 98$.

Specifying an expression can sometimes be useful. Suppose that your dataset has the variable `date` recording the date of event and variable `age` recording the subject's age as of `date`. You want to make $t = 0$ correspond to when the subject turned 18. You could type `origin(time date-int((age-18)*365.25))`.

`origin(`*varname*`==`*numlist*`)` is for use with multiple-record data. It states when each subject became at risk indirectly; the subject became at risk at the earliest time that *varname* takes on any of the enumerated values. Pretend you had

        patid        date      x1      x2    event
          101  12nov1997      15      22      127
          101  28dec1997      12      22      155
          101  03feb1998      55      22      133
          101  05mar1998      14      22      127
          101  09apr1998      12      22      133
          101  03jun1998      13      22      101
          102  22nov1997       .       .        .

and assume `event` = 155 represents the onset of exposure. You might `stset` this dataset by typing

    . stset date, id(patid) origin(event==155) ...

If you did that, the information for patient 101 prior to 28dec1997 would be ignored in subsequent analysis. The prior information would not be removed from the dataset; it would just be ignored. Probably something similar would happen for patient 102 or, if patient 102 has no record with event = 155, all the records on the patient would be ignored.

In terms of analysis time, $t = 0$ would correspond to when event 155 occurred. Here are the results in analysis-time units:

```
patid       date     x1    x2    event        _t0          _t
  101   12nov1997    15    22      127          .           .
  101   28dec1997    12    22      155          .           .
  101   03feb1998    55    22      133          0          37
  101   05mar1998    14    22      127         37          67
  101   09apr1998    12    22      133         67         102
  101   03jun1998    13    22      101        102         157
  102   22nov1997     .     .        .          .           .
```

Note that patient 101's second record is excluded from the analysis. That is not a mistake. Records document durations, `date` reflects the end of the time period, and events occur at the end of time periods. Thus, event 155 occurred at the instant `date` = 28dec1997 and the relevant first record for the patient is (28dec1997, 03feb1998] in time units, which is (0, 37] in $t$ units.

## The substantive meaning of analysis time

In specifying `origin()`, you must ask yourself whether two subjects with identical characteristics face the same risk of failure. The answer is that they face the same risk when they have the same value of $t = (time - \mathtt{origin()})/\mathtt{scale()}$ or, equivalently, when the same amount of time has elapsed from `origin()`.

Say we have the following data on smokers who have died:

```
   ddate     x1    x2    reason
11mar1984    23    11      2
15may1994    21     9      1
22nov1993    22    13      2
etc.
```

We wish to analyze death due to `reason==2`. However, typing

```
. stset ddate, fail(reason==2)
```

would probably not be adequate. We would be saying that smokers were at risk of death from 01jan1960. Would it matter? If we planned on doing anything parametric, it would, because parametric hazard functions, except for the exponential, are functions of analysis time and the location of 0 makes a difference.

Even if we were thinking of performing nonparametric analysis, there would probably be difficulties. We would be asserting that two "identical" persons (identical, presumably, in terms of `x1` and `x2`) face the same risk on the same calendar date. Does the risk of death due to smoking really change as the calendar changes?

It would be more reasonable to assume that the risk changes with how long you have been smoking and that our data would likely include that date. We would type

```
. stset ddate, fail(reason==2) origin(time smdate)
```

if `smdate` were the name of the date-started-smoking variable. We would now be saying that the risk is equal when the number of days smoked is the same. We might prefer to see $t$ in years,

```
. stset ddate, fail(reason==2) origin(time smdate) scale(365.25)
```

but that would make no substantive difference.

Consider single-record data on firms which went bankrupt:

```
    incorp    bankrupt    x1    x2  btype
 22jan1983  11mar1984     23    11      2
 17may1992  15may1994     21     9      1
 03nov1991  22nov1993     22    13      2
 etc.
```

Say we wish to examine the risk of a particular kind of bankruptcy, btype == 2, among firms that become bankrupt. Typing

```
. stset bankrupt, fail(btype==2)
```

would be more reasonable than it was in the smoking example. It would not be reasonable if we were thinking of performing any sort of parametric analysis, of course, because then location of $t = 0$ matters, but it might be reasonable for semiparametric analysis. We would be asserting that two "identical" firms (identical with respect to the characteristics we model) have the same risk of bankruptcy when the calendar dates are the same. We would be asserting that the overall state of the economy matters.

Alternatively, it might be reasonable to measure time from the date of incorporation:

```
. stset bankrupt, fail(btype==2) origin(time incorp)
```

Understand that the choice of origin() is a substantive decision.

## Setting the failure event

You set the failure event using the failure() option.

In single-record data, if failure() is not specified, every record is assumed to end in a failure. For instance, with

```
      failtime    load  bearings
 1.        100      15         0
 2.        140      15         1
 etc.
```

you would type stset failtime and the first observation would be assumed to fail at time = 100, the second at time = 140, and so on.

failure(*varname*) specifies that a failure occurs whenever *varname* is not zero and is not missing. For instance, with

```
      failtime    load  bearings  burnout
 1.        100      15         0        1
 2.        140      15         1        0
 3.         97      20         0        1
 4.        122      20         1        0
 5.         84      25         0        1
 6.        100      25         1        1
 etc.
```

you might type stset failtime, failure(burnout). Observations 1, 3, 5, and 6 would be assumed to fail at times 100, 97, 84, and 100, respectively; observations 2 and 4 would be assumed to be censored at times 140 and 122.

Similarly, were the data

|    | failtime | load | bearings | burnout |
|----|----------|------|----------|---------|
| 1. | 100      | 15   | 0        | 1       |
| 2. | 140      | 15   | 1        | 0       |
| 3. | 97       | 20   | 0        | 2       |
| 4. | 122      | 20   | 1        | .       |
| 5. | 84       | 25   | 0        | 2       |
| 6. | 100      | 25   | 1        | 3       |
| *etc.* |       |      |          |         |

the result would be the same. Nonzero, nonmissing values of the failure variable are assumed to represent failures. (Perhaps `burnout` contains a code on how the burn out occurred.)

`failure`(*varname* == *numlist*) specifies that a failure occurs whenever *varname* takes on any of the values of *numlist*. In the above example, specifying

```
. stset failtime, failure(burnout==1 2)
```

would treat observation 6 as censored.

```
. stset failtime, failure(burnout==1 2 .)
```

would also treat observation 4 as a failure.

```
. stset failtime, failure(burnout==1/3 6 .)
```

would treat `burnout==1`, `burnout==2`, `burnout==3`, `burnout==6`, and `burnout==`. as representing failures, and all other values as representing censorings. (Perhaps we want to examine "failure due to meltdown" and these are the codes that represent the various kinds of meltdown.)

`failure()` is treated the same way in both single- and multiple-record data. Consider

|    | patno | t   | x1 | x2 | died |
|----|-------|-----|----|----|------|
| 1. | 1     | 4   | 23 | 11 | 1    |
| 2. | 2     | 5   | 21 | 9  | 0    |
| 3. | 2     | 8   | 22 | 13 | 1    |
| 4. | 3     | 7   | 20 | 5  | 0    |
| 5. | 3     | 9   | 22 | 5  | 0    |
| 6. | 3     | 11  | 21 | 5  | 0    |
| 7. | 4     | ... |    |    |      |

Typing

```
. stset t, id(patno) failure(died)
```

would treat

| | | |
|---|---|---|
| patno==1 | as dying | at t==4 |
| patno==2 | as dying | at t==8 |
| patno==3 | as being censored | at t==11 |

Note that intervening records on the same subject are marked as "censored". Technically, they are not really censored if you think about it carefully; they are simply marked as not failing. Look at the data for subject 3:

| patno | t  | x1 | x2 | died |
|-------|----|----|----|------|
| 3     | 9  | 22 | 5  | 0    |
| 3     | 11 | 21 | 5  | 0    |

The subject is not censored at $t = 9$ because there are more data on the subject; it is merely the case that the subject did not die at that time. At $t = 9$, `x1` changed from 22 to 21. The subject is really censored at $t = 11$ because the subject did not die and there are no more records on the subject.

Typing `stset t, id(patno) failure(died)` would mark the same persons as dying and the same persons as censored as in the previous case. If `died` contained not 0 and 1, but 0 and nonzero, nonmissing codes for the reason for death

|     | patno | t     | x1 | x2 | died |
| --- | ----- | ----- | -- | -- | ---- |
| 1.  | 1     | 4     | 23 | 11 | 103  |
| 2.  | 2     | 5     | 21 | 9  | 0    |
| 3.  | 2     | 8     | 22 | 13 | 207  |
| 4.  | 3     | 7     | 20 | 5  | 0    |
| 5.  | 3     | 9     | 22 | 5  | 0    |
| 6.  | 3     | 11    | 21 | 5  | 0    |
| 7.  | 4     | . . . |    |    |      |

Typing

```
. stset t, id(patno) failure(died)
```

or

```
. stset t, id(patno) failure(died==103 207)
```

would yield the same results; subjects 1 and 2 would be treated as dying and subject 3 as censored.

Typing

```
. stset t, id(patno) failure(died==207)
```

would treat subject 2 as dying and subjects 1 and 3 as censored. Thus, when you specify the values for the code, it is not necessary that the code variable ever contain 0. In

|     | patno | t     | x1 | x2 | died |
| --- | ----- | ----- | -- | -- | ---- |
| 1.  | 1     | 4     | 23 | 11 | 103  |
| 2.  | 2     | 5     | 21 | 9  | 13   |
| 3.  | 2     | 8     | 22 | 13 | 207  |
| 4.  | 3     | 7     | 20 | 5  | 11   |
| 5.  | 3     | 9     | 22 | 5  | 12   |
| 6.  | 3     | 11    | 21 | 5  | 12   |
| 7.  | 4     | . . . |    |    |      |

Typing

```
. stset t, id(patno) failure(died==207)
```

treats patient 2 as dying, and 1 and 3 as censored. Typing

```
. stset t, id(patno) failure(died==103 207)
```

treats patients 1 and 2 as dying and 3 as censored.

## Setting multiple failures

In multiple-record data, records after the first failure event are ignored unless you specify the `exit()` option. Consider the following data:

|     | patno | t     | x1 | x2 | code |
| --- | ----- | ----- | -- | -- | ---- |
| 1.  | 1     | 4     | 21 | 7  | 14   |
| 2.  | 1     | 5     | 21 | 7  | 11   |
| 3.  | 1     | 8     | 22 | 7  | 22   |
| 4.  | 1     | 7     | 20 | 7  | 17   |
| 5.  | 1     | 9     | 22 | 7  | 22   |
| 6.  | 1     | 11    | 21 | 7  | 29   |
| 7.  | 2     | . . . |    |    |      |

Perhaps code 22 represents the event of interest—say the event "visited the doctor". Were you to type `stset t, failure(code == 22)`, the result would be as if the data contained

|     | patno | t | x1 | x2 | code |
|-----|-------|---|----|----|------|
| 1.  | 1     | 4 | 21 | 7  | 14   |
| 2.  | 1     | 5 | 21 | 7  | 11   |
| 3.  | 1     | 8 | 22 | 7  | 22   |

Records after the first occurrence of the failure event are ignored. If you do not want this, you must specify the `exit()` option. Probably you would want to specify `exit(time .)` in this case, meaning subjects are not to exit the risk group until their data run out. Alternatively, perhaps code 142 means "entered the nursing home" and, once that event happens, you no longer want them in the risk group. In that case you would code `exit(code == 142)`; see *Final exit times* below.

## First entry times

Do not confuse `enter()` with `origin()`. `origin()` specifies when a subject first becomes at risk. `enter()` specifies when a subject first comes under observation. In most datasets, becoming at risk and coming under observation are coincident. In that case, it is sufficient to specify `origin()` alone, although you could specify both options.

The issue here has to do with persons who enter the data after they have been at risk of failure. Say we are studying deaths due to exposure to substance X, and we know the date at which a person was first exposed to the substance. We are willing to assume that persons are at risk from the date of exposure forward. A person arrives at our door who was exposed 15 years ago. Can we add this person to our data? The statistical issue is labeled *left-truncation* and the problem is that, had the person died before arriving at our door, we would never have known about her. We can add her to our data, but we must be careful to treat her subsequent survival time as conditional on having already survived 15 years.

Say we are examining visits to the widget repair facility, "failure" being defined as a visit (so failures can be repeated). The risk begins once a person buys a widget. We have a woman who bought a widget three years ago and she has no records on when she has visited the facility in the last three years. Can we add her to our data? Yes, as long as we are careful to treat her subsequent behavior as already being three years after she first became at risk.

The jargon for this is "under observation". All this means is that failures, were they to occur, would be observed. Before being under observation, failures, were they to occur, would not be observed.

If `enter()` is not specified, it is assumed that subjects are under observation at the time they enter the risk group, which is to say, as specified by `origin()`, 0 if `origin()` is not specified, or possibly `time0()`. To be precise, subject $i$ is assumed to first enter the analysis risk pool at

$$time_i = \max\big(\text{earliest } \texttt{time0()} \text{ for } i, \texttt{enter()}, \texttt{origin()}\big)$$

For example, say we have multiple-record data recording "came at risk" (`mycode == 1`), "enrolled in our study" (`mycode == 2`), and "failed due to risk" (`mycode == 3`). We `stset` this dataset by typing

```
. stset time, id(id) origin(mycode==1) enter(mycode==2) failure(mycode==3)
```

The above `stset` correctly handles the came at risk/came under observation problem regardless of the order of events 1, 2, and 3. For instance, if the subject comes under observation before he or she becomes at risk, the subject will be treated as entering the analysis risk pool at the time he or she came at risk.

Say we have the same data in single-record format: variable `riskdate` documents becoming at risk and variable `enr_date` the date of enrollment in our study. We would `stset` this dataset by typing

    . stset time, origin(time riskdate) enter(time enr_date) failure(mycode==3)

As a final example, let's return to the multiple-record way of recording our data and pretend that we started enrolling people in our study on 12jan1998 but that, up until 16feb1998, we do not trust that our records are complete (we had start-up problems). We would `stset` that dataset by typing

    . stset time, origin(mycode==1) enter(mycode==2 time mdy(2,16,1998)) fail(mycode==3)

`enter(`*varname*`==`*numlist* `time` *exp*`)` is interpreted as

$$\max(\text{time of earliest event in } numlist, exp)$$

Thus, persons having `mycode == 2` occurring before 16feb1998 are assumed to be under observation from 16feb1998 and those having `mycode == 2` thereafter are assumed to be under observation from the time of `mycode == 2`.

## Final exit times

`exit()` specifies the latest time under which the subject is both under observation and at risk of the failure event. The emphasis is on latest; obviously subjects also exit the data when their data run out.

When you type

    . stset ..., ... failure(outcome==1/3 5) ...

the result is as if you had typed

    . stset ..., ... failure(outcome==1/3 5) exit(failure) ...

which in turn is the same as

    . stset ..., ... failure(outcome==1/3 5) exit(outcome==1/3 5) ...

When is a person to be removed from the analysis risk pool? When their data end, of course, and in addition, when the event 1, 2, 3, or 5 first occurs. How are they to be removed? According to their status at that time. If the event is 1, 2, 3, or 5 at that instant, then they exit as a failure. If the event is something else, they exit as censored.

Perhaps events 1, 2, 3, and 5 represent death due to heart disease and that is what we are studying. Pretend `outcome == 99` represents death for some other reason. Obviously, once the person dies, they are no longer at risk of dying from heart disease, so we would want to specify

    . stset ..., ... failure(outcome==1/3 5) exit(outcome==1/3 5 99) ...

When we explicitly specify `exit()`, it is our responsibility to list all the reasons a person is to be removed other than simply running out of data. In this case, it would have been a mistake to specify just `exit(99)`, because that would have left persons in the analysis risk pool who died for reasons 1, 2, 3, and 5. We would have treated those people as if they were still at risk of dying.

In fact, it probably would not have mattered had we specified `exit(99)` because, once a person is dead, he or she is unlikely to have any subsequent records anyway. By that logic, we did not even have to specify `exit(99)` because death is death and there should be no records following it.

For other kinds of events, however, `exit()` becomes important. Let us assume the failure event is diagnosed with heart disease. A person may surely have records following diagnosis, but even so,

    . stset ..., ... failure(outcome==22) ...

would be adequate because, by not specifying `exit()`, we are accepting the default that `exit()` is equivalent to `failure()`. Once outcome 22 occurs, subsequent records on the subject will be ignored—they comprise the future history of the subject.

Say, however, that we wish to treat as censored persons diagnosed with kidney disease. We would type

        . stset ..., ... failure(outcome==22) exit(outcome==22 29) ...

assuming `outcome = 29` is "diagnosed with kidney disease". It is now of great importance that we specified `exit(outcome==22 29)` and not just `exit(outcome==29)` because, had we omitted code 22, persons would have remained in the analysis risk pool even after the failure event, i.e., being diagnosed with heart disease.

If, in addition, our data were untrustworthy after 22nov1998 (perhaps not all the data have been entered yet), we would type

        . stset ..., ... failure(outcome==22) exit(outcome==22 29 time mdy(11,22,1998)) ...

If you type `exit(`*varname*`==`*numlist* `time` *exp*`)`, the exit time is taken to be

$$\min(\text{time of earliest event in } numlist, exp)$$

For some analyses, repeated failures are possible. If you have repeated failure data, you specify the `exit()` option and include whatever reasons, if any, that would cause the person to be removed. If there are no such reasons and you wish to retain all observations for the person, you type

        . stset ..., ... exit(time .) ...

`exit(time .)` specifies that the maximum time a person can be in the risk pool is infinite; thus, they will not be removed until their data run out.

## Intermediate exit and re-entry times (gaps)

Gaps arise when a subject is temporarily not under observation. The statistical importance of gaps is that, if failure is death and had the person died, then they would not have been around to be found again. The solution to this is to remove the person from the risk pool during the observational gap.

In order even to know you have gaps, your data must provide starting and ending times for each record. Most datasets provide only ending times and that precludes the possibility of gaps.

`time0()` is how you specifying the beginning times of records. Understand that `time0()` specifies a mechanical aspect of interpretation about the records in the dataset, namely the beginning of the period spanned by each record. Do not confuse `time0()` with `origin()`, which specifies the substantive issue of when a subject became at risk, and do not confuse `time0()` with `enter()`, which specifies when a subject first comes under observation.

`time0()` merely identifies the beginning of the time span covered by each record. Pretend that we had two records on a subject, the first covering the span (40,49] and the second (49,57]:

```
            |<—— record 1 ——>|<- record 2 ->|
  ——————————————————————————————————————————————> time
            40              49             57
```

A `time0()` variable would contain

                            40 in record 1
                            49 in record 2

and not, for instance, 40 and 40. Note that a `time0()` variable varies record-by-record for a subject.

Most datasets merely provide an end-of-record time value, *timevar*, which you specify by typing stset *timevar*, .... When you have multiple records per subject and you do not specify a time0() variable, stset assumes that the records begin where the previous one left off.

## The if() option versus the if exp

Both the if *exp* and if(*exp*) option select records for which *exp* is true. We strongly recommend specifying the if() option in preference to the if *exp*. They differ in that if *exp* removes data from consideration before the calculation of beginning and ending times, and other quantities as well. The if() option, on the other hand, sets the restriction after all derived variables are calculated. To appreciate this difference, consider the following multiple-record data

| patno | t | x1 | x2 | code |
|---|---|---|---|---|
| 3 | 7 | 20 | 5 | 14 |
| 3 | 9 | 22 | 5 | 23 |
| 3 | 11 | 21 | 5 | 29 |

and consider the difference in results between typing

. stset t if x1~=22, failure(code==14)

and

. stset t,  if(x1~=22) failure(code==14)

The first would remove record 2 from consideration at the outset. In constructing beginning and ending times, stset and streset would see

| patno | t | x1 | x2 | code |
|---|---|---|---|---|
| 3 | 7 | 20 | 5 | 14 |
| 3 | 11 | 21 | 5 | 29 |

and so construct the result

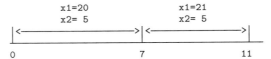

In the second case, the result would be

The latter result is correct and the former incorrect, because $x1 = 21$ is not true in the interval $(7, 9)$.

The only reason to specify if *exp* is to ignore errors in the data—observations that would confuse stset and streset should they see them—without actually dropping the offending observations from the dataset.

You specify the if() option to ignore information in the data that are not themselves errors. Specifying if() yields the same result as specifying if *exp* on the subsequent st commands after the dataset has been stset.

## Past and future records

Consider the hospital-ward data that we have seen before:

```
patid     addate     curdate    sex    x1     x2    code
  101   18aug1998  23aug1998     1     10     10     177
  101           .  31aug1998     1     20      8     286
  101           .  08sep1998     1     16     11     208
  101           .  11sep1998     1     11     17     401
etc.
```

Let us imagine that you `stset` this dataset such that you selected the middle two records. Perhaps you typed

```
. stset curdate, id(patid) origin(time addate) entry(code==286) failure(code==208)
```

The first record for the subject, since it was not selected, is called a *past history record*. If there were more early records that were not selected, they would all be called past history records.

The last record for the subject, since it was not selected, is called a *future history record*. If there were more later records that were not selected, they would all be called future history records.

Were you to type

```
. streset, past
```

the first three records for this subject would be selected.

Were you to type

```
. streset, future
```

the last three records for this subject would be selected.

Were you to type

```
. streset, past future
```

all four records for this subject would be selected.

No matter which, were you then to type

```
. streset
```

the original two records would be selected and things would be back just as they were before.

After typing `streset, past`, or `streset, future`, or `streset, past future`, you would not want to use any analysis commands. `streset` did some strange things, especially with the analysis time variable, in order to include the extra records. It would be the wrong sample, anyway.

You might, however, want to use certain data management commands on the data; especially those for creating new variables.

Typically, it is `streset, past` that is of greater interest. Past records—records prior to being at risk or excluded for other reasons—are not supposed to play a role in survival analysis. `stset` makes sure they do not. But it is sometimes reasonable to ask questions about them such as, was the subject ever on the drug cisplatin? Or has the subject ever been married? Or did the subject ever have a heart attack?

To answer questions like that, you sometimes want to dig into the past. Typing `streset, past` makes that easy and, once the past is set, the data can be used with `stgen` and a few other st commands. You might well type the following:

```
. stset curdate, id(patid) origin(addate) entry(code==286) failure(code==208)
. streset, past
. stgen attack = ever(code==179)
```

```
. streset
. stcox attack ...
```

Do not be concerned about doing something inappropriate while having the past or future set; st will not let you:

```
. stset curdate, id(patid) origin(time addate) entry(code==286) failure(code==208)
(output omitted)
. streset, past
(output omitted)
. stcox x1
you last "streset, past"
you must type "streset" to restore the analysis sample
r(119);
```

## Using streset

streset is a useful tool for gently modifying what you have previously stset. Rather than typing the whole stset command, you can type streset followed by just what has changed.

For instance, you might

```
. stset curdate, id(patid) origin(time addate) entry(code==286) failure(code==208)
```

and then later want to restrict the analysis to subjects who ever have x1>20. You could retype the whole stset command and add ever(x1>20), but it would be easier to type

```
. streset, ever(x1>20)
```

If later you decide you want to remove the restriction, type

```
. streset, ever(.)
```

That is the general rule for resetting options to the default: type '.' as the option's argument.

Be careful using streset because you can make subtle mistakes. In another analysis with another dataset, consider the following:

```
. stset date, fail(code==2) origin(code==1107)
. ...
. streset date, fail(code==9) origin(code==1422) after(code==1423)
. ...
. streset, fail(code==2) origin(code==1107)
```

If, in the last step, the user is trying to get back to the results of the first stset, the user fails. The last streset is equivalent to

```
. stset date, fail(code==9) origin(code==1107) after(code==1423)
```

streset() remembers the previously specified options and uses them if you do not override them. Note that both stset and streset display the current command line. Make sure that you verify that the command is as you intended.

## Performance and multiple-record per subject datasets

stset and streset do not drop data; they simply mark data to be excluded from consideration. Some survival-time datasets can be very large, yet the relevant subsamples small. In such cases you can reduce memory requirements and speed execution by dropping the irrelevant observations.

stset and streset mark the relevant observations by creating a variable named _st (it is always named this). The variable contains 1 and 0; _st = 1 marks the relevant observations and _st = 0 marks the irrelevant ones. If you type

```
. drop if _st==0
```

or equivalently

```
. keep if _st==1
```

or equivalently

```
. keep if _st
```

you will drop the irrelevant observations. All st commands produce the same results whether you do this or not. Be careful, however, if you are planning future stsets or stresets. Observations that are irrelevant right now might be relevant later.

One solution to this conundrum is to keep only those observations that are relevant after setting the entire history:

```
. stset date, fail(code==9) origin(code==1422) after(code==1423)
. streset, past future
. keep if _st
. streset
```

Final note: you may drop the irrelevant observations as marked by _st = 0, but do not drop the _st variable itself. The other st commands expect to find variable _st.

## Sequencing of events within t

Consider the following bit of data:

```
etime    failtime      fail
   0           5           1
   0           5           0
   5           7           1
```

Note all the different events happening at time 5: the first observation fails, the second is censored, and the third enters.

What does it mean for something to happen at time 5? In particular, is it at least potentially possible for the second observation to have failed at time 5, i.e., was it in the risk group when the first observation failed? How about the third observation? Was it in the risk group and could it have potentially failed at time 5?

Stata sequences events within a time as follows:

first,    at time  $t$              the failures occur
then,    at time  $t + 0$          the censorings are removed from the risk group
finally, at time  $t + 0 + 0$   the new entries are added to the risk group

Thus, to answer the questions:

Could the second observation have potentially failed at time 5? Yes.

Could the third observation have potentially failed at time 5? No, because it was not yet in the risk group.

By this logic, the following makes no sense:

```
etime    failtime      fail
   5           5           1
```

because this would mark a subject as failing before being at risk. It would make no difference if fail were 0—the subject would then be marked as being censored too soon. Either way, stset would flag this as an error. If you had a subject who entered and immediately exited, you would code this as

```
etime   failtime      fail
4.99           5         1
```

## Weights

stset allows you to specify fweights, pweights, and iweights.

fweights are Stata's frequency or replication weights. Consider the data

```
failtime      load   bearings       count
     100        15          0           3
     140        15          1           2
      97        20          0           1
```

and the stset command

```
. stset failtime [fw=count]
        failure event:  (assumed to fail at time=failtime)
   obs. time interval:  (0, failtime]
   exit on or before:  failure
               weight:  [fweight=count]

    3   total obs.
    0   exclusions

    3   physical obs. remaining, equal to
    6   weighted obs., representing
    6   failures in single record/single failure data
  677   total analysis time at risk, at risk from t =          0
                              earliest observed entry t =       0
                                  last observed exit t =      140
```

This combination is equivalent to the expanded data

```
failtime      load   bearings
     100        15          0
     100        15          0
     100        15          0
     140        15          1
     140        15          1
      97        20          0
```

and

```
. stset failtime
```

So much for fweights.

pweights are Stata's sampling weights—the inverse of the probability the subject was chosen from the population. pweights are typically integers but they do not have to be. For instance, you might have

```
time0      time       died        sex       reps
    0       300          1          0       1.50
    0       250          0          1       4.50
   30       147          1          0       2.25
```

We now have the desired result and are ready to `stset` our data:

```
. stset t1, failure(died) id(id)
                id:  id
     failure event:  died ~= 0 & died ~= .
obs. time interval:  (t1[_n-1], t1]
 exit on or before:  failure
```

```
         172  total obs.
           2  multiple records at same instant          PROBABLE ERROR
              (t1[_n-1]==t1)
```

```
         170  obs. remaining, representing
         102  subjects
          74  failures in single failure-per-subject data
       31933  total analysis time at risk, at risk from t =        0
                            earliest observed entry t =        0
                             last observed exit t =     1799
```

Well, something went wrong. Two records were excluded. There is a small enough amount of data here that we could just list the dataset and look for the problem, but let's pretend otherwise. We want to find the records which, within patient, are marked as exiting at the same time:

```
. bys id: gen problem = t1==t1[_n-1]
. sort id died
. list id if problem
             id
  60.        38
. list id transplant wait stime died posttran t1 if id==38, nodi
         id  transp~t      wait     stime      died  posttran          t1
  60.     38         1         5         5         0         0           5
  61.     38         1         5         5         1         1           5
```

There is no typographical error in these data—we checked that variables `transplant`, `wait`, and `stime` contain what the original source published. What those variables say is that patient 38 waited 5 days for a heart transplant, received one on the fifth day, and then died on the fifth day, too.

That makes perfect sense, but not to Stata. Remember that Stata orders events within $t$ as failures, followed by censorings, followed by entries. Reading `t1`, Stata went for this literal interpretation: patient 38 was censored at time 5 with `posttran = 0`, then, at time 5, patient 38 died and then, at time 5, patient 38 reentered the data but this time with `posttran = 1`. That made no sense to Stata.

Stata's sequencing of events may surprise you but, trust us, there are good reasons for it and, really, the ordering convention does not matter. To fix this problem, we just have to put a little time between the implied entry at time 5 and the subsequent death:

```
. replace t1 = 5.1 in 61
(1 real change made)
. list id transplant wait stime died posttran t1 if id==38
         id  transp~t      wait     stime      died  posttran          t1
  60.     38         1         5         5         0         0           5
  61.     38         1         5         5         1         1         5.1
```

Now the data make sense both to us and to Stata: Up until time 5, the patient had `posttran = 0`, then at time 5 the value of `posttran` changed to 1, and then at time 5.1, the patient died.

```
. stset t1, id(id) failure(died)
                id:  id
     failure event:  died ~= 0 & died ~= .
obs. time interval:  (t1[_n-1], t1]
exit on or before:  failure
```

```
       172  total obs.
         0  exclusions

       172  obs. remaining, representing
       103  subjects
        75  failures in single failure-per-subject data
   31938.1  total analysis time at risk, at risk from t =          0
                            earliest observed entry t =          0
                                 last observed exit t =       1799
```

This dataset is now ready for use with all the other st commands. Here is an illustration:

```
. stsum, by(posttran)
```

|           |              | incidence | no. of   | ├───── Survival time ─────┤ |     |      |
| posttran  | time at risk | rate      | subjects | 25%                       | 50% | 75%  |
|-----------|--------------|-----------|----------|-----|-----|------|
| 0         | 5936         | .0050539  | 103      | 36  | 149 | 340  |
| 1         | 26002.1      | .0017306  | 69       | 39  | 96  | 979  |
| total     | 31938.1      | .0023483  | 103      | 36  | 100 | 979  |

```
. stcox age posttran surgery year
Iteration 0:   log likelihood = -298.31514
Iteration 1:   log likelihood =  -289.7344
Iteration 2:   log likelihood = -289.53498
Iteration 3:   log likelihood = -289.53378
Iteration 4:   log likelihood = -289.53378
Refining estimates:
Iteration 0:   log likelihood = -289.53378

Cox regression -- Breslow method for ties

No. of subjects =          103          Number of obs   =        172
No. of failures =           75
Time at risk    =      31938.1
                                         LR chi2(4)      =      17.56
Log likelihood  =    -289.53378          Prob > chi2     =     0.0015
```

| _t<br>_d | Haz. Ratio | Std. Err. | z     | P>\|z\| | [95% Conf. Interval] |          |
|----------|------------|-----------|-------|-------|----------|----------|
| age      | 1.030224   | .0143201  | 2.14  | 0.032 | 1.002536 | 1.058677 |
| posttran | .9787243   | .3032597  | -0.07 | 0.945 | .5332291 | 1.796416 |
| surgery  | .3738278   | .163204   | -2.25 | 0.024 | .1588759 | .8796    |
| year     | .8873107   | .059808   | -1.77 | 0.076 | .7775022 | 1.012628 |

# References

Cleves, M. 1999. ssa13: Analysis of multiple failure-time data with Stata. *Stata Technical Bulletin* 49: 30–39. Reprinted in *Stata Technical Bulletin Reprints*, vol. 9, pp. 338–349.

Crowley, J. and M. Hu. 1977. Covariance analysis of heart transplant data. *Journal of the American Statistical Association* 72: 27–36.

Kalbfleisch, J. D. and R. L. Prentice. 1980. *The Statistical Analysis of Failure Time Data*. New York: John Wiley & Sons.

## Also See

| | |
|---|---|
| **Complementary:** | [R] **snapspan**, [R] **st stdes** |
| **Background:** | [R] **st** |

# Title

| st stsplit — Split and join time-span records |
| --- |

# Syntax

### stsplit, syntax one

stsplit *newvarname* $\left[\text{if } exp\right]$ , $\{$ at(*numlist*) | $\underline{\text{e}}$very(*#*) $\}$ $\left[\text{trim } \underline{\text{nopre}}\text{serve}\right]$

### stsplit, syntax two

stsplit *newvarname* $\left[\text{if } exp\right]$ , $\underline{\text{after}}$(*spec*) $\{$ at(*numlist*) | $\underline{\text{e}}$very(*#*) $\}$

$\left[\text{trim } \underline{\text{nopre}}\text{serve}\right]$

where
$$spec = \{\texttt{time}\,|\,\texttt{t}\,|\,\texttt{\_t}\} = \{exp\,|\,\texttt{asis}(exp)\,|\,\texttt{min}(exp)\}$$

### stsplit, syntax three

stsplit $\left[\text{if } exp\right]$ , at($\underline{\text{f}}$ailures) $\left[\underline{\text{st}}\text{rata}(varlist)\ \underline{\text{r}}\text{iskset}(newvar)\ \underline{\text{nopre}}\text{serve}\right]$

### Syntax for stjoin

stjoin $\left[, \underline{\text{c}}\text{ensored}(numlist)\right]$

stsplit and stjoin are for use with survival-time data; see [R] **st**. You must stset your dataset using the id() option before using these commands; see [R] **st stset**.

# Description

stsplit with option at(*numlist*) or every(*#*) splits episodes into two or more episodes at the implied time points since being at risk (syntax one) or after a time point specified via after() (syntax two). Each resulting record contains the follow-up on one subject through one time band. Expansion on multiple time scales may be obtained by repeatedly using stsplit. *newvarname* specifies the name of the variable to be created containing the observation's category. It records the time interval to which each new observation belongs. It is bottom coded.

stsplit, at(failures) (syntax three) performs episode splitting at the failure times (per stratum).

stjoin performs the reverse operation, namely joining episodes back together when that can be done without a loss of information.

# Options

## Options for stsplit, syntax one

at(*numlist*) or every(#) are not optional. They specify the analysis times at which the records are to be split.

at(5(5)20) splits records at $t = 5$, $t = 10$, $t = 15$, and $t = 20$.

If at([...] max) is specified, max is replaced by a suitably large value. For instance, if we wish to split records every five analysis time units from time zero to the largest follow-up time in our data, we could find out what the largest time value is by typing summarize _t and then explicitly typing it into the at() option, or we could just specify at(0(5)max).

every(#) is a shorthand for at(#(#)max), i.e., episodes are split at each positive multiple of #.

trim specifies that observations less than the minimum or greater than the maximum value listed in at() are to be excluded from subsequent analysis. Such observations are not dropped from the data; trim merely sets their value of variable _st to 0 so that they will not be used and yet are still retrievable the next time the dataset is stset.

nopreserve is intended for use by programmers. It speeds the transformation by not saving the original data, which can be restored should things go wrong or if you press *Break*. Programmers often specify this option when they have already preserved the original data. nopreserve changes nothing about the transformation that is made.

## Options for stsplit, syntax two

at(*numlist*) or every(#) are not optional. They specify the analysis times at which the records are to be split.

at(5(5)20) splits the records at $t$, corresponding to 5, 10, 15, and 20 analysis time units after the time expression given by *spec* is evaluated.

If at([...] max) is specified, max is replaced by a suitably large value. For more details on max, see the explanation for at() in the above section.

every(#) is shorthand for at(#(#)max), i.e., episodes are split at each positive multiple of #.

after(*spec*) specifies the reference time for at() or every(). Syntax one above can be thought of as corresponding to after(*time of onset of risk*), although you cannot really type this. You could type, however, after(time= birthdate) or after(time= marrydate).

*spec* has syntax

$$\{\text{time} \mid \text{t} \mid \text{\_t}\} = \{exp \mid \text{asis}(exp) \mid \text{min}(exp)\}$$

where

time specifies that the expression is to be evaluated in the same time units as *timevar* in stset timevar, .... This is the default.

t and _t specify that the expression is to be evaluated in units of "analysis time". t and _t are synonyms; it makes no difference whether you specify one or the other.

*exp* specifies the reference time. In the case of multi-episode data, *exp* should be constant within subject id.

min( *exp* ) specifies that in the case of multi-episode data, the minimum of *exp* is taken within id.

asis(*exp*) specifies that in the case of multi-episode data, *exp* is allowed to vary within id.

trim specifies that observations less than the minimum or greater than the maximum value listed in at() are to be excluded from subsequent analysis. Such observations are not dropped from the data; trim merely sets their value of variable _st to 0 so that they are retrievable the next time the dataset is stset.

nopreserve is intended for use by programmers. See the description under syntax one.

## Options for stsplit, syntax three

strata(*varlist*) specifies up to 5 strata variables. Observations with equal values of the variables are assumed to be in the same stratum. strata() restrict episode splitting to failures that occur within the stratum, and memory requirements are reduced when strata are specified.

riskset(*newvar*) specifies the name for a new variable recording the unique riskset in which an episode occurs, and missing otherwise.

nopreserve is intended for use by programmers. See the description under syntax one.

## Option for stjoin

censored(*numlist*) specifies values of the failure variable, *failvar*, from stset, failure(*failvar*=...), that indicate "no event" (censoring).

If you are using stjoin to rejoin records after stsplit, you do not need to specify censored(). Just do not forget to drop the variable created by stsplit before typing stjoin. See Example 4 below.

Neither do you need to specify censored() if, when you stset your dataset, you specified failure(*failvar*) and not failure(*failvar*=...). In that case, stjoin knows that *failvar* = 0 and *failvar* = . (missing) correspond to no event. Two records can be joined if they are contiguous and record the same data and the first record has *failvar* = 0 or *failvar* = ., meaning no event at that time.

You may need to specify censored(), and you probably do if, when you stset the dataset, you specified failure(*failvar*=...). If stjoin is to join records, it needs to know what events do not count, which is to say, which events can be discarded. If the only such event is *failvar* = ., then you do not need to specify censored().

# Remarks

Remarks are presented under the headings

*What stsplit does and why*
*Using stsplit to split at designated times*
*Time versus analysis time*
*Splitting data on recorded ages*
*Example 1: Splitting on age*
*Example 2: Splitting on age and time-in-study*
*Example 3: Explanatory variables that change with time*
*Using stsplit to split at failure times*
*Example 4: Splitting on failure times to test the proportional hazards assumption*
*Example 5: Cox versus conditional logistic regression*
*Example 6: Joining data split with stsplit*

## What stsplit does and why

stsplit splits records into two or more records based on analysis time or based on a variable that depends on analysis time such as age. The intention is to start with something like

| id | _t0 | _t | x1 | x2 | _d |
|----|-----|----|----|----|----|
| 1  | 0   | 18 | 12 | 11 | 1  |

and produce

| id | _t0 | _t | x1 | x2 | _d | tcat |
|----|-----|----|----|----|----|------|
| 1  | 0   | 5  | 12 | 11 | 0  | 0    |
| 1  | 5   | 10 | 12 | 11 | 0  | 5    |
| 1  | 10  | 18 | 12 | 11 | 1  | 10   |

or

| id | _t0 | _t | x1 | x2 | _d | agecat |
|----|-----|----|----|----|----|--------|
| 1  | 0   | 7  | 12 | 11 | 0  | 30     |
| 1  | 7   | 17 | 12 | 11 | 0  | 40     |
| 1  | 17  | 18 | 12 | 11 | 1  | 50     |

The above alternatives record the same underlying data: subject 1 had x1 $= 12$ and x2 $= 11$ during $0 < t \leq 18$ and, at $t = 18$, the subject failed.

The difference between them is that the first alternative breaks out the analysis time periods 0–5, 5–10, and 10–20 (although subject 1 failed before $t = 20$). The second alternative breaks out age 30–40, 40–50, and 50–60. You cannot tell from what is presented above, but at $t = 0$, subject 1 was 33 years old.

In our example, that the subject started with a single record is not important. The original data on the subject might have been

| id | _t0 | _t | x1 | x2 | _d |
|----|-----|----|----|----|----|
| 1  | 0   | 14 | 12 | 11 | 0  |
| 1  | 14  | 18 | 12 | 9  | 1  |

and then we would have obtained

| id | _t0 | _t | x1 | x2 | _d | tcat |
|----|-----|----|----|----|----|------|
| 1  | 0   | 5  | 12 | 11 | 0  | 0    |
| 1  | 5   | 10 | 12 | 11 | 0  | 5    |
| 1  | 10  | 14 | 12 | 11 | 0  | 10   |
| 1  | 14  | 18 | 12 | 9  | 1  | 10   |

or

| id | _t0 | _t | x1 | x2 | _d | agecat |
|----|-----|----|----|----|----|--------|
| 1  | 0   | 7  | 12 | 11 | 0  | 30     |
| 1  | 7   | 14 | 12 | 11 | 0  | 40     |
| 1  | 14  | 17 | 12 | 9  | 0  | 40     |
| 1  | 17  | 18 | 12 | 9  | 1  | 50     |

In addition, we could just as easily have produced records with analysis time or age recorded in single-year categories. That is, we could start with

| id | _t0 | _t | x1 | x2 | _d |
|----|-----|----|----|----|----|
| 1  | 0   | 14 | 12 | 11 | 0  |
| 1  | 14  | 18 | 12 | 9  | 1  |

and produce

| id | _t0 | _t | x1 | x2 | _d | tcat |
|----|-----|-----|-----|-----|-----|------|
| 1  | 0   | 1   | 12  | 11  | 0   | 0    |
| 1  | 1   | 2   | 12  | 11  | 0   | 1    |
| 1  | 2   | 3   | 12  | 11  | 0   | 2    |

. . .

or

| id | _t0 | _t | x1 | x2 | _d | agecat |
|----|-----|-----|-----|-----|-----|--------|
| 1  | 0   | 1   | 12  | 11  | 0   | 30     |
| 1  | 1   | 2   | 12  | 11  | 0   | 31     |
| 1  | 2   | 3   | 12  | 11  | 0   | 32     |

. . .

Moreover, we can even do this splitting on more than one variable. Let's go back and start with

| id | _t0 | _t | x1 | x2 | _d |
|----|-----|-----|-----|-----|-----|
| 1  | 0   | 18  | 12  | 11  | 1   |

Let's split it into the analysis-time intervals 0–5, 5–10, and 10–20, *and* let's split it into 10-year age intervals 30–40, 40–50, and 50–60. The result would be

| id | _t0 | _t | x1 | x2 | _d | tcat | agecat |
|----|-----|-----|-----|-----|-----|------|--------|
| 1  | 0   | 5   | 12  | 11  | 0   | 0    | 30     |
| 1  | 5   | 7   | 12  | 11  | 0   | 5    | 30     |
| 1  | 7   | 10  | 12  | 11  | 0   | 5    | 40     |
| 1  | 10  | 17  | 12  | 11  | 0   | 10   | 40     |
| 1  | 17  | 18  | 12  | 11  | 1   | 10   | 50     |

Why would we want to do any of this?

We might want to split on a time-dependent variable such as age if we want to estimate a Cox proportional hazards model and include current age among the regressors (although we could instead use stcox's tvc() option), or if we want to make tables by age groups (see, for instance, [R] **st strate**).

## Using stsplit to split at designated times

stsplit's syntax to split at designated times is, ignoring other options,

> stsplit *newvarname* [if *exp*] , at(*numlist*)
>
> stsplit *newvarname* [if *exp*] , at(*numlist*) after(*spec*)

at() specifies the analysis times at which records are to be split. Typing at(5 10 15) splits records at the indicated analysis times, and separates records into the four intervals 0–5, 5–10, 10–15, and 15+.

In the first syntax, the splitting is done on analysis time $t$. In the second syntax, the splitting is done on 5, 10, and 15 analysis time units after the time given by after(*spec*).

In either case, stsplit also creates *newvarname* containing the interval to which each observation belongs. In this case, *newvarname* would contain 0, 5, 10, and 15; 0 if the observation occurred in the interval 0–5, 5 if the observation occurred in the interval 5–10, and so on. To be precise,

```
. stset dox, failure(fail) origin(time dob) enter(time doe) scale(365.25) id(id)
                   id:  id
        failure event:  fail ~= 0 & fail ~= .
   obs. time interval:  (dox[_n-1], dox]
   enter on or after:   time doe
   exit on or before:   failure
       t for analysis:  (time-origin)/365.25
               origin:  time dob
```

```
      337  total obs.
        0  exclusions

      337  obs. remaining, representing
      337  subjects
       80  failures in single failure-per-subject data
 4603.669  total analysis time at risk, at risk from t =          0
                                  earliest observed entry t =  30.07529
                                   last observed exit t =  69.99863
```

Note that the origin is set to date of birth, making time-since-birth analysis time, and the scale is set to 365.25, so that time-since-birth is measured in years.

Let's list a few records and verify that the analysis-time variables _t0 and _t are indeed recorded as we expect:

```
. list id dob doe dox fail _t0 _t if id==1 | id==34, nodisplay
        id        dob        doe        dox  fail        _t0          _t
  1.     1  04Jan2015  16Aug2064  01Dec2076     0   49.615332    61.908282
 34.    34  12Jun1999  16Apr2059  31Dec2066     3   59.843943    67.55373
```

We see that patient 1 was 49.6 years old at time of entry into our study and left at age 61.9. Patient 34 entered the study at age 59.8 and exited the study with CHD at age 67.6.

Now we can split the data by age:

```
. stsplit ageband, at(40(10)70)
(418 observations created)
```

stsplit added 418 observations to the dataset in memory and generated a new variable, ageband, which identifies each observation's age group.

```
. list id _t0 _t ageband fail height if id==1 | id==34, nodisplay
        id        _t0          _t   ageband  fail     height
  1.     1   49.615332          50        40     .    175.387
  2.     1          50          60        50     .    175.387
  3.     1          60   61.908282        60     0    175.387
 61.    34   59.843943          60        50     .      177.8
 62.    34          60    67.55373        60     3      177.8
```

Note that the single record for subject with id = 1 has expanded to three records. The first refers to the age band 40–49, coded 40, and the subject spends _t − _t0 = .384668 years in this band. The second refers to the age band 50–59, coded 50, and the subject spends 10 years in this band, and so on. The follow-up in each of the three bands is censored (fail = .). The single record for the subject with id = 34 is expanded to two age bands; the follow-up for the first band was censored (fail = .) and the follow-up for the second band ended in CHD (fail = 3).

The values for variables which do not change with time, such as height, are simply repeated in the new records. This can lead to much larger datasets after expansion. It may be necessary to drop unneeded variables before using stsplit.

## Example 2: Splitting on age and time-in-study

To use `stsplit` to expand the records on two time scales simultaneously, such as age and time-in-study, we can first expand on the age scale as described in Example 1, and then on the time-in-study scale, with the command

```
. stsplit timeband, at(0(5)25) after(time=doe)
(767 observations created)
. list id _t0 _t ageband timeband fail if id==1 | id==34, nodisplay
```

|      | id | _t0       | _t        | ageband | timeband | fail |
|------|----|-----------|-----------|---------|----------|------|
| 1.   | 1  | 49.615332 | 50        | 40      | 0        | .    |
| 2.   | 1  | 50        | 54.615332 | 50      | 0        | .    |
| 3.   | 1  | 54.615332 | 59.615332 | 50      | 5        | .    |
| 4.   | 1  | 59.615332 | 60        | 50      | 10       | .    |
| 5.   | 1  | 60        | 61.908282 | 60      | 10       | 0    |
| 111. | 34 | 59.843943 | 60        | 50      | 0        | .    |
| 112. | 34 | 60        | 64.843943 | 60      | 0        | .    |
| 113. | 34 | 64.843943 | 67.55373  | 60      | 5        | 3    |

By splitting the data using two time scales, the data are partitioned into time cells corresponding to a *Lexis diagram* as described, for example, in Clayton and Hills (1993). Also see Keiding (1998) for an overview of Lexis diagrams. Each new observation created by splitting the data records the time that the individual spent in a Lexis cell. We can obtain the time spent in the cell by calculating the difference $\_t - \_t0$. For example, the subject with $id = 1$ spent .384668 years $(50 - 49.615332)$ in the cell corresponding to age 40 to 49 and study time 0 to 5, and 4.615332 years $(54.615332 - 50)$ in the cell for age 50 to 59 and study time 0 to 5.

Alternatively, we can do these expansions in reverse order. That is, split first on study time and then on age.

## Example 3: Explanatory variables that change with time

In the previous examples, time, in the form of age or time-in-study, is the explanatory variable which is to be studied or controlled for, but in some studies there are other explanatory variables that vary with time. The `stsplit` command can sometimes be used to expand the records so that in each new record such an explanatory variable is constant over time. For example, in the Stanford heart data (see [R] **st stset**), we would like to split the data and generate the explanatory variable `posttran`, which takes the value 0 before transplantation and 1 thereafter. The follow-up must therefore be divided into time before transplantation and time after.

We first generate for each observation an entry time and an exit time which preserve the correct follow-up time, but in such a way that the time of transplants is the same for all individuals. By summarizing `wait`, the time to transplant, we obtain its maximum value of 310. By selecting a value greater than this maximum, say 320, we now generate two new variables:

```
. gen enter = 320 - wait
. gen exit = 320 + stime
```

Note that we have created a new artificial time scale where all transplants are coded as being performed at time 320. By defining `enter` and `exit` in this manner, we maintain the correct total follow-up time for each patient. We now `stset` and `stsplit` the data:

```
. stset exit, enter(time enter) failure(died) id(id)

                id:  id
     failure event:  died ~= 0 & died ~= .
obs. time interval:  (exit[_n-1], exit]
 enter on or after:  time enter
 exit on or before:  failure

        103  total obs.
          0  exclusions

        103  obs. remaining, representing
        103  subjects
         75  failures in single failure-per-subject data
    34589.1  total analysis time at risk, at risk from t =          0
                               earliest observed entry t =         10
                                  last observed exit t =         2119

. stsplit posttran, at(0,320)
(69 observations=episodes created)

. replace posttran=0 if transplant==0
(34 real changes made)

. replace posttran=1 if posttran==320
(69 real changes made)
```

We replaced `posttran` in the last command so that it is now a 0/1 indicator variable. We can now `generate` our follow-up time `t1` as the difference between our analysis-time variables, `list` the data, and `stset` the dataset.

```
. generate t1 = _t - _t0

. list id enter exit _t0 _t posttran if id==16 | id==44

          id      enter       exit        _t0         _t    posttran
23.       16        300        320        300        320           0
24.       16        300        363        320        363           1
70.       44        320        360        320        360           0

. stset t1, failure(died) id(id)

                id:  id
     failure event:  died ~= 0 & died ~= .
obs. time interval:  (t1[_n-1], t1]
 exit on or before:  failure

        172  total obs.
          0  exclusions

        172  obs. remaining, representing
        103  subjects
         75  failures in single failure-per-subject data
    31938.1  total analysis time at risk, at risk from t =          0
                               earliest observed entry t =          0
                                  last observed exit t =         1799
```

## Using stsplit to split at failure times

`stsplit`'s syntax to split at failure times is, ignoring other options,

$$\text{stsplit } [\text{if } exp], \text{ at(failures)}$$

This form of episode splitting is useful for Cox regression with time-varying covariates. The usefulness of splitting at the failure times is due to a property of the maximum partial likelihood estimator for a Cox regression model: The likelihood is only evaluated at the times at which failures occur in the data, and the computation only depends on the risk pools at those failure times. Changes in covariates between failure times do not affect estimates for a Cox regression model. Thus, to estimate a model with time-varying covariates, all one has to do is define the values of these time-varying covariates at all failure times at which a subject was at risk (e.g., Collett 1994: ch 7). After splitting at failure times, one defines time-varying covariates by referring to the system variable _t (analysis time), or via the *timevar* variable used to stset the data.

After splitting at failure times, all st commands still work fine and will produce the same results as before splitting. Note that to estimate parametric models with time-varying covariates, it does not suffice to specify covariates at failure times. Stata can estimate "piecewise constant" models; the required data manipulation is facilitated by stsplit, {at() | every()}, stegen, and strepl.

## Example 4: Splitting on failure times to test the proportional hazards assumption

Collett (1994, pg 141) presents data on 26 ovarian cancer patients that underwent two different chemotherapy protocols after a surgical intervention. Here are few of the observations:

```
. list in 1/6

        patient       time       cens       treat       age       rdisea
  1.          1        156          1           1        66            2
  2.          2       1040          0           1        38            2
  3.          3         59          1           1        72            2
  4.          4        421          0           2        53            2
  5.          5        329          1           1        43            2
  6.          6        769          0           2        59            2
```

The variable treat indicates the chemotherapy protocol administered, age records the age of the patient at the beginning of the treatment, and rdisea records each patient's residual disease after surgery. After stsetting these data, we fitted a Cox proportional hazard regression model on age and treat to ascertain the effect of treatment, controlling for age.

```
. stset time, failure(cens) id(patient)
                   id:  patient
        failure event:  cens ~= 0 & cens ~= .
  obs. time interval:  (time[_n-1], time]
   exit on or before:  failure
─────────────────────────────────────────────────────────────
     26  total obs.
      0  exclusions
─────────────────────────────────────────────────────────────
     26  obs. remaining, representing
     26  subjects
     12  failures in single failure-per-subject data
  15588  total analysis time at risk, at risk from t =          0
                            earliest observed entry t =          0
                               last observed exit t =       1227
```

Weesie, J. 1998a. ssa11: Survival analysis with time-varying covariates. *Stata Technical Bulletin* 41: 25–43. Reprinted in *Stata Technical Bulletin Reprints*, vol. 7, pp. 268–292.

——. 1998b. dm62: Joining episodes in multi-record survival time data. *Stata Technical Bulletin* 45: 5–6. Reprinted in *Stata Technical Bulletin Reprints*, vol. 8, pp. 27–28.

## Also See

| | |
|---|---|
| **Complementary:** | [R] **st stset** |
| **Background:** | [R] **st** |

# Title

> **st stsum** — Summarize survival-time data

# Syntax

stsum [if *exp*] [in *range*] [, by(*varlist*) <u>nosho</u>w]

stsum is for use with survival-time data; see [R] **st**. You must stset your data before using this command.

by . . . : may be used with stsum; see [R] **by**.

# Description

stsum presents summary statistics: time at risk, incidence rate, number of subjects, and the 25th, 50th, and 75th percentiles of survival time.

stsum is appropriate for use with single- or multiple-record, single- or multiple-failure, st data.

# Options

by(*varlist*) requests separate summaries for each group along with an overall total. Observations are in the same group if they have equal values of the variables in *varlist*. *varlist* may contain any number of variables, each of which may be string or numeric.

noshow prevents stsum from showing the key st variables. This option is rarely used since most people type stset, show or stset, noshow to reset once and for all whether they want to see these variables mentioned at the top of the output of every st command; see [R] **st stset**.

# Remarks

## Single-failure data

Here is an example of stsum with single-record survival data:

```
. stsum
```

|        | time at risk | incidence rate | no. of subjects | Survival time 25% | 50% | 75% |
|--------|-------------|----------------|-----------------|-------|-----|-----|
| total  | 9118        | .0039482       | 40              | 205   | 232 | 261 |

```
. stsum, by(group)
```

| group  | time at risk | incidence rate | no. of subjects | Survival time 25% | 50% | 75% |
|--------|-------------|----------------|-----------------|-------|-----|-----|
| 1      | 4095        | .0041514       | 19              | 190   | 216 | 234 |
| 2      | 5023        | .0037826       | 21              | 232   | 233 | 280 |
| total  | 9118        | .0039482       | 40              | 205   | 232 | 261 |

478

stsum works equally well with multiple-record survival data. Here is a summary of the multiple-record Stanford heart-transplant data introduced in [R] st stset:

```
. stsum

              failure _d:  died
        analysis time _t:  t1
                      id:  id

                 |              incidence      no. of   |------- Survival time -------|
                 | time at risk     rate      subjects     25%       50%        75%
         --------+--------------------------------------------------------------------
           total |    31938.1    .0023483         103       36       100        979
```

stsum with the by() option may produce results with multiple-record data that, at first, you may think in error.

```
. stsum, by(posttran) noshow

                 |              incidence      no. of   |------- Survival time -------|
        posttran | time at risk     rate      subjects     25%       50%        75%
        ---------+--------------------------------------------------------------------
               0 |        5936    .0050539         103       36       149        340
               1 |     26002.1    .0017306          69       39        96        979
        ---------+--------------------------------------------------------------------
           total |     31938.1    .0023483         103       36       100        979
```

Note that, for the time at risk, $5{,}936 + 26{,}002.1 = 31{,}938.1$ but, for the number of subjects, $103 + 69 \neq 103$. Variable posttran is not constant for the subjects in this dataset:

```
. stvary posttran

                      subjects for whom the variable is
                 |                                never    always    sometimes
        variable | constant     varying          missing   missing    missing
        ---------+----------------------------------------------------------------
        posttran |       34          69             103         0          0
```

In this dataset, subjects have one or two records. All subjects were eligible for heart transplantation. They have one record if they die or are lost due to censoring before transplantation, and they have two if the operation was performed. In that case, the first record records their survival up to transplantation and the second records their subsequent survival. posttran is 0 in the first record and 1 in the second.

Thus, all 103 subjects have records with posttran $= 0$ and, when stsum reported results for this group, it summarized the pre-transplantation survival. The incidence of death was .005 and median survival time 149 days.

The posttran $= 1$ line of stsum's output summarizes the post-transplantation survival: 69 patients underwent transplantation, incidence of death was .002, and median survival time 96 days. For these data, this is not 96 more days but 96 days in total. That is, the clock was not reset on transplantation. Thus, without attributing cause, we can describe the differences between the groups as an increased hazard of death at early times followed by a decreased hazard later.

## Multiple-failure data

If you simply type stsum with multiple-failure data, be aware that the reported survival time is the survival time to the first failure under the assumption that the hazard function is not indexed by number of failures.

Here we have some multiple-failure data:

```
. st
-> stset t, id(id) failure(d) time0(t0) exit(time .) noshow
                id:  id
     failure event:  d ~= 0 & d ~= .
 obs. time interval:  (t0, t]
  exit on or before:  time .
. stsum
```

| | time at risk | incidence rate | no. of subjects | Survival time 25% | 50% | 75% |
|---|---|---|---|---|---|---|
| total | 435444 | .0018556 | 926 | 201 | 420 | 703 |

To understand this output, let's also obtain output for each failure separately:

```
. stgen nf = nfailures()
. stsum, by(nf)
```

| nf | time at risk | incidence rate | no. of subjects | Survival time 25% | 50% | 75% |
|---|---|---|---|---|---|---|
| 0 | 263746 | .0020057 | 926 | 196 | 399 | 604 |
| 1 | 121890 | .0018131 | 529 | 252 | 503 | 816 |
| 2 | 38807 | .0014946 | 221 | 415 | 687 | . |
| 3 | 11001 | 0 | 58 | . | . | . |
| total | 435444 | .0018556 | 926 | 201 | 420 | 703 |

The stgen command added, for each subject, a variable containing the number of previous failures. For a subject, up to and including the first failure, nf is 0. Then nf is 1 up to and including the second failure, and then it is 2, and so on; see [R] st stgen.

You should have no difficulty interpreting the detailed output. The first line, corresponding to nf $= 0$, states that among those who had experienced no failures yet, the incidence rate for (first) failure is .0020. The distribution of the time to (first) failure is as shown.

Similarly, the second line, corresponding to nf $= 1$, is for those who have already experienced one failure. The incidence rate for (second) failures is .0018 and the distribution of time of (second) failures is as shown.

When we simply typed stsum, we obtained the same information shown as the total line of the more detailed output. The total incidence rate is easy to interpret, but what is the "total" survival time distribution? Answer: it is an estimate of the distribution of the time to first failure under the assumption that the hazard function $h(t)$ is the same across failures—that the second failure is no different from the first failure. This is an odd definition of same because the clock $t$ is not reset in $h(t)$. What is the hazard of a failure—any failure—at time $t$? Answer: $h(t)$.

Another definition of the same would have it that the hazard of a failure is given by $h(\tau)$, where $\tau$ is the time since last failure—that the process repeats. These definitions are different unless $h()$ is a constant function of $t$ $(\tau)$.

So let's examine these multiple-failure data under the process-replication idea. The key variables in these st data are id, t0, t, and d:

```
. st
-> stset t, id(id) failure(d) time0(t0) exit(time .) noshow
                id:  id
     failure event:  d ~= 0 & d ~= .
 obs. time interval:  (t0, t]
  exit on or before:  time .
```

Our goal is, for each subject, to reset t0 and t to 0 after every failure event. We are going to have to trick Stata, or at least trick stset. stset will not let us set data where the same subject has multiple records summarizing the overlapping periods. So, the trick is create a new id variable that is different for every id−nf combination (remember, nf is the variable we previously created that records the number of prior failures). Then each of the "new" subjects can have their clock start at time 0:

```
. egen newid = group(id nf)
. sort newid t
. by newid: replace t = t - t0[1]
(808 real changes made)
. by newid: gen newt0 = t0 - t0[1]
. stset t, failure(d) id(newid) time0(newt0)
                id:  newid
     failure event:  d ~= 0 & d ~= .
obs. time interval:  (newt0, t]
 exit on or before:  failure

      1734  total obs.
         0  exclusions

      1734  obs. remaining, representing
      1734  subjects
       808  failures in single failure-per-subject data
    435444  total analysis time at risk, at risk from t =          0
                              earliest observed entry t =          0
                               last observed exit t =           797
```

Note that stset no longer thinks we have multiple-failure data. Whereas, with id, subjects had multiple failures, newid gives a unique identity to each id−nf combination. Each "new" subject has at most one failure.

```
. stsum, by(nf)
          failure _d:  d
    analysis time _t:  t
                  id:  newid
```

| nf | time at risk | incidence rate | no. of subjects | Survival time 25% | 50% | 75% |
|---|---|---|---|---|---|---|
| 0 | 263746 | .0020057 | 926 | 196 | 399 | 604 |
| 1 | 121890 | .0018131 | 529 | 194 | 384 | 580 |
| 2 | 38807 | .0014946 | 221 | 210 | 444 | 562 |
| 3 | 11001 | 0 | 58 | . | . | . |
| total | 435444 | .0018556 | 1734 | 201 | 404 | 602 |

Compare this table with the one we previously obtained. The incidence rates are the same but the survival times differ because now we measure the times from one failure to the next and previously we measured the time from a fixed point. The time between events in these data appears to be independent of event number.

❑ Technical Note

The method shown for converting multiple-failure data to replicated-process single-event failure data is completely general. The generic outline of the conversion process is

```
. stgen nf = nfailures()
. egen newid = group(id nf)
. sort newid t
. by newid: replace t = t - t0[1]
. by newid: gen newt0 = t0 - t0[1]
. stset t, failure(d) id(newid) t0(newt0)
```

where *id*, *t*, *t0*, and *d* are the names of your key survival-time variables.

Once you have done this to your data, you need exercise only one caution. If, in estimating models using stcox, stereg, etc., you wish to obtain robust estimates of variance, you should include the option cluster(*id*).

When you specify the **robust** option, stcox, stereg, etc., assume that you mean **robust** cluster(*stset_id_variable*) which, in this case, will be **newid**. The data, however, are really more clustered than that. Two "subjects" with different **newid** values may, in fact, be the same real subject. cluster(*id*) is what is appropriate.

❑

# Saved Results

stsum saves in r():

Scalars

| | | | |
|---|---|---|---|
| r(p25) | 25th percentile | r(risk) | time at risk |
| r(p50) | 50th percentile | r(ir) | incidence rate |
| r(p75) | 75th percentile | r(N_sub) | number of subjects |

# Methods and Formulas

stsum is implemented as an ado-file.

The 25th, 50th, and 75th percentiles of survival times are obtained from $S(t)$, the Kaplan–Meier product-limit estimate of the survivor function. The 25th percentile, for instance, is obtained as the maximum value of $t$ such that $S(t) \le .75$.

# Also See

**Complementary:**     [R] **st stdes**, [R] **st stir**, [R] **st sts**, [R] **st stgen**, [R] **st stset**, [R] **st stvary**

**Background:**     [R] **st**

# Title

> **st sttocc** — Convert survival-time data to case–control data

# Syntax

> sttocc [*varlist*] [, <u>m</u>atch(*matchvarlist*) <u>n</u>umber(*#*) <u>g</u>enerate(*genvarlist*) <u>nodo</u>ts]

sttocc is for use with survival-time data; see [R] **st**. You must stset your data before using this command.

# Description

sttocc (survival time to case–control) generates a nested case–control study dataset from a cohort study dataset by sampling controls from the risk sets. For each case, the controls are chosen randomly from those members of the cohort who are at risk at the failure time of the case. Said differently, the resulting case–control sample is matched with respect to analysis time, the time scale used to compute risk sets. The following variables are added to the dataset:

| | |
|---|---|
| _case | coded 0 for controls, 1 for cases |
| _set | case–control id; matches which cases and controls belong together |
| _time | analysis time of the case's failure |

The names of these three variables can be changed by specifying the generate() option. *varlist* defines variables which, in addition to those used in the creation of the case–control study, will be retained in the final dataset. If *varlist* is not specified, all variables are carried over into the resulting dataset.

When the resulting dataset is analyzed as a matched case–control study, odds ratios will estimate corresponding rate-ratio parameters in the proportional hazards model for the cohort study.

Randomness in the matching is obtained using Stata's uniform() function. To ensure that the sample truly is random, you should set the random-number seed; see [R] **generate**.

# Options

match(*matchvarlist*) specifies additional categorical variables for matching controls to cases. When match() is not specified, cases and controls are matched with respect to time only. If match(*matchvarlist*) is specified, the cases will also be matched by *matchvarlist*.

number(*#*) specifies the number of controls to draw for each case. The default is 1, even though this is not a very sensible choice.

generate(*genvarlist*) specifies variable names for the three new variables _case, _set, and _time.

nodots requests that dots not be placed on the screen at the beginning of each case–control group selection. By default, dots are displayed to provide entertainment.

# Remarks

What follows is paraphrased from Clayton and Hills (1997). Any errors are ours.

Nested case–control studies are an attractive alternative to full Cox regression analysis, particularly when time-varying explanatory variables are involved. They are also attractive when some explanatory variables involve laborious coding. For example, you can create a file with a subset of variables for all subjects in the cohort, generate a nested case–control study, and go on to code the remaining data only for those subjects selected.

In the same way as for Cox regression, the results of the analysis are critically dependent on the choice of analysis time (time scale). The choice of analysis time may be calendar time—so that controls would be chosen from subjects still being followed on the date that the case fails—but other time scales, such as age or time-in-study, may be more appropriate in some studies. Remember that the analysis time set in selecting controls is implicitly included in the model in subsequent analysis.

`match()` requires that controls also be matched to the case with respect to additional categorical variables such as sex. This produces an analysis closely mirroring stratified Cox regression. If we wanted to match on calendar time and 5-year age bands, we could first type 'stsplit ageband ...' to create the age bands and then specify `match(ageband)` on the `sttocc` command. Analyzing the resulting data as a matched case–control study would estimate rate ratios in the underlying cohort which are controlled for calendar time (very finely) and age (less finely). Such analysis could be carried out by Mantel–Haenszel (odds ratio) calculations, for example using `mhodds`, or by conditional logistic regression using `clogit`.

When ties occur between entry times, censoring times, and failure times, the following convention is adopted:

Entry time < Failure time < Censoring time

Thus, censored subjects and subjects entering at the failure time of the case are included in the risk set and are available for selection as controls. Tied failure times are broken at random.

## Example: Creating a nested case–control study

Using the `diet` data introduced in [R] **st stsplit**, we shall illustrate the use of `sttocc` letting age be analysis time. Hence, controls are chosen from subjects still being followed at the age at which the case fails.

```
. use diet, clear
. stset dox, failure(fail) enter(time doe) id(id) origin(time dob) scale(365.25)
                  id:  id
       failure event:  fail ~= 0 & fail ~= .
  obs. time interval:  (dox[_n-1], dox]
   enter on or after:  time doe
   exit on or before:  failure
       t for analysis:  (time-origin)/365.25
               origin:  time dob

        337  total obs.
          0  exclusions

        337  obs. remaining, representing
        337  subjects
         80  failures in single failure-per-subject data
   4603.669  total analysis time at risk, at risk from t =         0
                                   earliest observed entry t =   30.07529
                                      last observed exit t =   69.99863
```

```
. sttocc, match(job) n(5) nodots
              failure _d:  fail
        analysis time _t:  (dox-origin)/365.25
                  origin:  time dob
        enter on or after:  time doe
                      id:  id
             matching for:  job
There were 3 tied times involving failure(s)
 - failures assumed to precede censorings,
 - tied failure times split at random
There are 80 cases
Sampling 5 controls for each case
```

The above two commands create a new dataset in which there are 5 controls per case, matched on job, with the age of the subjects when the case failed recorded in the variable _time. The case indicator is given in _case and the matched set number in _set. Because we did not specify the optional *varlist*, all variables are carried over into the new dataset.

We can verify that the controls were correctly selected:

```
. gen ageentry = (doe-dob)/365.25
. gen ageexit  = (dox-dob)/365.25
. sort _set _case id
. by _set: list id _case _time ageentry ageexit
```

```
-> _set = 1
            id      _case      _time      ageentry      ageexit
  1.        65          0   42.57358      40.11225    56.82409
  2.        66          0   42.57358      40.09309     56.9692
  3.        74          0   42.57358      37.09788    53.39083
  4.        83          0   42.57358      30.07529    46.20123
  5.        86          0   42.57358      38.14921    54.10815
  6.        90          1   42.57358       31.4141    42.57358

-> _set = 2
            id      _case      _time      ageentry      ageexit
  7.       235          0    47.8987      44.58043    51.70431
  8.       250          0    47.8987       43.9562    62.91581
  9.       292          0    47.8987      46.24504    62.28611
 10.       313          0    47.8987      41.50582    57.05133
 11.       334          0    47.8987      47.32923    62.70773
 12.       196          1    47.8987      45.46475     47.8987

-> _set = 3
```
    (*output omitted* )

The controls do indeed belong to the appropriate risk set. Note that the controls in each set enter at an age which is less than that of the case at failure, and exit at an age which is greater than the age of the case at failure. To estimate the effect of high energy, use clogit, just as you would for any matched case–control study:

(*Continued on next page*)

```
. clogit _case hienergy, group(_set) or
Iteration 0:    log likelihood = -143.32699
Iteration 1:    log likelihood = -143.28861
Iteration 2:    log likelihood = -143.28861
Conditional (fixed-effects) logistic regression     Number of obs  =      480
                                                    LR chi2(1)     =     0.10
                                                    Prob > chi2    =   0.7467
Log likelihood = -143.28861                         Pseudo R2      =   0.0004
```

| _case | Odds Ratio | Std. Err. | z | P>\|z\| | [95% Conf. Interval] |
|---|---|---|---|---|---|
| hienergy | .9247363 | .2241581 | -0.32 | 0.747 | .5750225    1.487137 |

## Methods and Formulas

sttocc is implemented as an ado-file.

## Acknowledgments

The original version of sttocc was written by David Clayton, MRC Biostatistical Research Unit, Cambridge, and Michael Hills, London School of Hygiene and Tropical Medicine (retired).

## References

Clayton, D. G. and M. Hills. 1993. *Statistical Models in Epidemiology*. Oxford: Oxford University Press.

——. 1995. ssa7: Analysis of follow-up studies. *Stata Technical Bulletin* 27: 19–26. Reprinted in *Stata Technical Bulletin Reprints*, vol. 5, pp. 219–227.

——. 1997. ssa10: Analysis of follow-up studies with Stata 5.0. *Stata Technical Bulletin* 40: 27–39. Reprinted in *Stata Technical Bulletin Reprints*, vol. 7, pp. 253–268.

Langholz, B. and D. C. Thomas. 1990. Nested case–control and case–cohort methods of sampling from a cohort: a critical comparison. *American Journal of Epidemiology* 131: 169–176.

## Also See

| | |
|---|---|
| **Complementary:** | [R] **st stbase**, [R] **st stdes**, [R] **st stsplit** |
| **Background:** | [R] **st** |

# Title

st sttoct — Convert survival-time data to count-time data

# Syntax

sttoct *newfailvar newcensvar* [*newentvar*] [, by(*varlist*) replace <u>nosh</u>ow ]

sttoct is for use with survival-time data; see [R] **st**. You must stset your data before using this command.

# Description

sttoct converts survival-time (st) data to count-time (ct) data; see [R] **ct**.

There is, currently, absolutely no reason you would want to do this.

# Options

by(*varlist*) specifies that counts are to reflect counts by group where the groups are defined by observations with equal values of *varlist*.

replace specifies that it is okay to proceed with the transformation even though the current dataset has not been saved on disk.

noshow prevents sttoct from showing the key st variables. This option is rarely used since most people type stset, show or stset, noshow to reset once and for all whether they want to see these variables mentioned at the top of every st command; see [R] **st stset**.

# Remarks

sttoct is a never-used command and is included for completeness. The definition of ct data is found in [R] **ct**. In the current version of Stata, all you can do with ct data is convert it to st data (which thus provides access to Stata's survival-analysis capabilities to those with ct data), so there is little point in converting st to ct data.

The converted dataset will contain

| | |
|---|---|
| *varlist* | from by(*varlist*) if specified |
| *t* | the exit time variable previously stset |
| *newfailvar* | number of failures at *t* |
| *newcensvar* | number of censored at *t* (after failures) |
| *newentvar* | if specified, number of entries at *t* (after censorings) |

The resulting dataset will be ctset automatically.

There are two forms of the sttoct command:

1. sttoct *failvar censvar*, ...

2. sttoct *failvar censvar entvar*, ...

That is, it makes a difference whether *entvar* is specified.

## Case 1: entvar not specified

This is possible only if

a. the risk is not recurring;

b. the original st data is single-record data or, if multiple record, all subjects enter at time 0 and have no gaps thereafter; and

c. if by(*varlist*) is specified, subjects do not have changing values of the variables in *varlist* over their histories.

If you do not specify *entvar*, cttost verifies that (a), (b), and (c) are true. If the assumptions are true, cttost converts your data and counts each subject only once. That is, in multiple-record data, all thrashing (censoring followed by immediate reenter with different covariates) is removed.

## Case 2: entvar specified

Any kind of survival-time data can be converted to count-data with an entry variable. You can convert your data in this way whether assumptions (a), (b), and (c) are true or not.

When you specify a third variable, thrashing is not removed even if it could be (even if assumptions (a), (b), and (c) are true).

## Methods and Formulas

sttoct is implemented as an ado-file.

## Also See

| | |
|---|---|
| **Complementary:** | [R] **ct**, [R] **st sttocc**, [P] **st st_is** |
| **Background:** | [R] **st** |

# Title

> **st stvary** — Report which variables vary over time

# Syntax

stvary [*varlist*] [if *exp*] [in *range*] [, noshow]

stvary is for use with survival-time data; see [R] **st**. You must stset your data before using this command.

by ... : may be used with stvary; see [R] **by**.

# Description

stvary is for use with multiple-record datasets—datasets for which id() has been stset. It reports whether values of variables within subject vary over time and on their pattern of missing values. While stvary is intended for use with multiple-record st data, it may be used with single-record data as well, but this produces little useful information.

stvary ignores weights even if you have set them. stvary is intended to provide a summary of the variables in the computer or data-based sense of the word.

# Options

noshow prevents stvary from showing the key st variables. This option is rarely used since most people type stset, show or stset, noshow to reset once and for all whether they want to see these variables mentioned at the top of the output of every st command; see [R] **st stset**.

# Remarks

Consider a multiple-record dataset. A subject's gender, presumably, does not change. His or her age very well might. stvary allows you to verify that values vary in the way that you expect:

```
. stvary
        failure _d:  died
   analysis time _t:  t1
              id:  id

             subjects for whom the variable is
                                           never     always   sometimes
   variable |  constant     varying        missing    missing    missing
   ---------+----------------------------------------------------------------
       year |    103           0             103        0          0
        age |    103           0             103        0          0
      stime |    103           0             103        0          0
    surgery |    103           0             103        0          0
 transplant |    103           0             103        0          0
       wait |    103           0             103        0          0
   posttran |     34          69             103        0          0
```

That 103 values for year are "constant" does not mean year itself is a constant—it means merely that, for each subject, the value of year does not change across the records. Whether the values of year vary across subjects is still an open question.

Now look at the bottom of the table: posttran is constant over time for 34 subjects and varies for the remaining 69.

Below we have another dataset and we will examine just two of the variables:

```
. stvary sex drug
                 subjects for whom the variable is
                                        never     always   sometimes
       variable |  constant   varying  missing    missing   missing
     -----------+--------------------------------------------------
            sex |      119          1      119          3         1
           drug |      121          2      123          0         0
```

Clearly, there are errors in the variable sex; for 119 of the subjects, sex does not change over time, but for one, it does. In addition, we see that we do not know the sex of 3 of the patients but for another, we sometimes know it and sometimes do not. The latter must be a simple data construction error. As for drug, we see that for two of our patients, the drug administered varied over time. Perhaps this is an error or perhaps those two patients were treated differently from all the rest.

## Saved Results

stvary saves in r():

Scalars
    r(cons)     number of subjects for whom variable is constant when not missing
    r(varies)   number of subjects for whom nonmissing values vary
    r(never)    number of subjects for whom variable is never missing
    r(always)   number of subjects for whom variable is always missing
    r(miss)    number of subjects for whom variable is sometimes missing

## Methods and Formulas

stvary is implemented as an ado-file.

## Also See

**Complementary:**    [R] **st stdes**, [R] **st stfill**, [R] **st stset**

**Background:**       [R] **st**

# Title

stack — Stack data

# Syntax

stack *varlist* [if *exp*] [in *range*], { into(*newvars*) | group(*#*) } [ clear wide ]

# Description

stack stacks the variables in *varlist* vertically, resulting in a dataset with variables *newvars* and _N · $(N_v/N_n)$ observations, where $N_v$ is the number of variables in *varlist* and $N_n$ is the number in *newvars*. stack creates the new variable _stack identifying the groups.

# Options

into(*newvars*) identifies the names of the new variables to be created. into() may be specified using variable ranges (e.g., into(v1-v3)). Either into() or group(), but not both, must be specified.

group(*#*) specifies the number of groups of variables in *varlist* to be stacked. The created variables will be named according to the first group in *varlist*. Either into() or group(), but not both, must be specified.

clear indicates your understanding that the dataset in memory will be lost. If you do not specify this option, you will be asked to confirm your intentions.

wide includes any of the original variables in *varlist* that are not specified in *newvars* in the resulting data.

# Remarks

▷ Example

This command is best understood by examples. We begin with artificial but informative examples and end with useful examples:

```
. list

           a          b          c          d
 1.        1          2          3          4
 2.        5          6          7          8
. stack  a b   c d, into(e f) clear
. list
        _stack          e          f
 1.        1          1          2
 2.        1          5          6
 3.        2          3          4
 4.        2          7          8
```

491

That is, the new variable e is formed by stacking a and c while the new variable f is formed by stacking b and d. _stack is automatically created and set equal to 1 for the first (a, b) group and 2 for the second (c, d) group. (Said differently, when _stack==1, the new data e and f contain the values from a and b. When _stack==2, e and f contain values from c and d.)

There are two groups because we specified 4 variables in the *varlist* and 2 variables in the into list and $4/2 = 2$. If there were 6 variables in the *varlist*, there would be $6/2 = 3$ groups. If there were also 3 variables in the into list, there would be $6/3 = 2$ groups. Specifying 6 variables in the *varlist* and 4 variables in the into list would result in an error since $6/4$ is not an integer.

◁

## ▷ Example

Variables may be repeated in the *varlist* and the *varlist* need not contain all the variables:

```
. list

            a           b           c           d
 1.         1           2           3           4
 2.         5           6           7           8
. stack   a b   a c, into(a bc) clear
. list

          _stack          a          bc
 1.          1            1           2
 2.          1            5           6
 3.          2            1           3
 4.          2            5           7
```

a was stacked on a and called a while b was stacked on c and called bc.

If we had wanted the resulting variables to simply be called a and b we could have used

```
. stack   a b   a c, group(2) clear
```

which is equivalent to

```
. stack   a b   a c, into(a b) clear
```

◁

## ▷ Example

Continuing with artificial but informative examples, the **wide** option includes the variables in the original dataset in the output dataset:

```
. list

            a         b         c         d
 1.         1         2         3         4
 2.         5         6         7         8
. stack   a b   c d, into(e f) clear wide
. list, nodisplay
          _stack      e        f        a        b        c        d
 1.         1         1        2        1        2        .        .
 2.         1         5        6        5        6        .        .
 3.         2         3        4        .        .        3        4
 4.         2         7        8        .        .        7        8
```

Note that in addition to the stacked e and f variables, the original a, b, c, and d variables are included. They are set to missing where their values are not appropriate.

◁

## ▷ Example

Finally, the last of the artificial examples. When you specify the `wide` option and repeat the same variable name in both the *varlist* and the `into` list, the variable will contain the stacked values:

```
. list

          a          b          c          d
1.        1          2          3          4
2.        5          6          7          8

. stack a b   a c, into(a bc) clear wide
. list

      _stack          a         bc          b          c
1.        1          1          2          2          .
2.        1          5          6          6          .
3.        2          1          3          .          3
4.        2          5          7          .          7
```

◁

## ▷ Example

(Useful.) You want a single graph of y against x1 and y against x2. You might be tempted to type `graph y x1 x2`, but that would not work. It would graph y against x2 and x1 against x2. One solution is

```
. save mydata
. stack  y x1  y x2, into(yy x12) clear
. gen y1 = yy if _stack==1
. gen y2 = yy if _stack==2
. graph y1 y2 x12
. use mydata, clear
```

The names yy and x12 are supposed to suggest the contents of the variables. yy contains (y,y) and x12 contains (x1,x2). We then make y1 defined at the x1 points but missing at the x2 points—graphing y1 against x12 is the same as graphing y against x1 in the original dataset. Similarly, y2 is defined at the x2 points but missing at x1—graphing y2 against x12 is the same as graphing y against x2 in the original dataset. Therefore, `graph y1 y2 x12` produces the desired graph.

◁

## ▷ Example

You wish to graph y1 against x1 and y2 against x2 on the same graph. The logic is the same as above, but let's go through it. Perhaps you have constructed two cumulative distributions using `cumul` (see [R] **cumul**)

```
. cumul tempjan, gen(cjan)
. cumul tempjuly, gen(cjuly)
```

and want to graph both cumulatives in the same graph. That is, you want to graph `cjan` against `tempjan` and `cjuly` against `tempjuly`. Remember, you could graph the `tempjan` cumulative by typing

```
. graph cjan tempjan, connect(1) symbol(o) sort
```

Graphing the `tempjuly` cumulative is done similarly. To obtain both on the same graph, you must stack the data:

```
. stack  cjuly tempjuly   cjan tempjan, into(c temp) clear
. gen cjan  = c if _stack==1
. gen cjuly = c if _stack==2
. graph cjan cjuly temp, connect(ll) symbol(oo) sort
```

Alternatively, if we specify the `wide` option, we do not have to bother to regenerate `cjan` and `cjuly` since they will automatically be created:

```
. stack  cjuly tempjuly   cjan tempjan, into(c temp) clear wide
. graph cjan cjuly temp, c(ll) s(oo) sort
```

◁

❑ Technical Note

There is a third way, not using the `wide` option, that is exceedingly tricky but sometimes useful:

```
. stack cjuly tempjuly  cjan tempjan, into(c temp) clear
. sort _stack temp
. graph c temp, c(L) s(o)
```

Note the use of `connect`'s capital L rather than lowercase l option. `c(L)` connects points only from left-to-right and, since the data are sorted by `_stack temp`, `temp` increases within the first group (`cjuly` vs. `tempjuly`) and then starts again for the second (`cjan` vs. `tempjan`); see [G] **graph options**.

❑

# Methods and Formulas

`stack` is implemented as an ado-file.

# Also See

**Related:**    [R] **contract**, [R] **reshape**, [R] **xpose**

# Title

**statsby** — Collect statistics for a command across a by list

# Syntax

statsby "*command*" *exp_list* [ , by(*varlist*) <u>t</u>otal <u>s</u>ubsets <u>d</u>ouble clear ]

*exp_list* contains

   *newvarname* = (*exp*)
   (*exp*)
   *eexp*

*eexp* is

   *specname*
   [*eqno*]*specname*

*specname* is

   _b
   _b[]
   _se
   _se[]

*eqno* is

   # #
   *name*

Distinguish between [ ], which are to be typed, and [ ], which indicate optional arguments.

# Description

**statsby** collects statistics for a command across a **by** list. The statistics that can be collected by **statsby** are the saved results, the coefficients, and the standard errors of the coefficients.

*command* is the statistical command to be run. *command* must be bound in double quotes. Compound double quotes (`" and "´) are needed if the command itself contains double quotes.

*exp_list* specifies the statistics to be collected from the execution of the command.

# Options

by(*varlist*) is a list of existing variables that would normally appear in the **by** *varlist*: section of the command if you were to issue the command interactively. If it is not specified, the user-specified command will be run on the entire dataset.

**total** specifies that the user-specified command is to be run on the entire dataset, in addition to the groups specified in the **by** list.

**subsets** specifies that the user-specified command is to be run for each group defined by any combination of the variables in the **by** list.

**double** specifies that the results collected are to be stored as Stata **double**s, meaning 8-byte reals. If **double** is not specified, results are stored as Stata **float**s, meaning 4-byte reals.

clear specifies that it is okay to replace the data in memory with the collection of statistics even though the current data have not been saved to disk.

# Remarks

## Collecting coefficients and standard errors

▷ Example

We begin with an example using the auto.dta dataset. In this example, we want to collect the coefficients from a regression where we model the price of a car on its weight, length, and mpg. We want to run this model for both domestic and foreign cars. This can easily be done by statsby using the extended expression _b.

```
. use auto, clear
(1978 Automobile Data)
. statsby "regress price weight length mpg" _b, by(foreign)

command:        regress price weight length mpg
by:             foreign
statistics:     b_weight=_b[weight]
                b_length=_b[length]
                b_mpg=_b[mpg]
                b_cons=_b[_cons]

. list

          foreign    b_weight    b_length      b_mpg       b_cons
  1.     Domestic    6.767233   -109.9518    142.7663     2359.475
  2.      Foreign    4.784841    13.39052    -18.4072     -6497.49
```

If we were only interested in the coefficient of a particular variable, say mpg, we would specify that particular coefficient; see [U] **16.5 Accessing coefficients and standard errors**.

```
. use auto, clear
(1978 Automobile Data)
. statsby "regress price weight length mpg" mpg=_b[mpg], by(foreign)

command:        regress price weight length mpg
by:             foreign
statistics:     mpg=_b[mpg]

. list

          foreign         mpg
  1.     Domestic    142.7663
  2.      Foreign    -18.4072
```

The extended expression _se is for standard errors.

```
. use auto, clear
(1978 Automobile Data)
. statsby "regress price weight length mpg" _se, by(foreign)

command:        regress price weight length mpg
by:             foreign
statistics:     se_weight=_se[weight]
                se_length=_se[length]
                se_mpg=_se[mpg]
                se_cons=_se[_cons]
```

```
. list

         foreign  se_weight  se_length    se_mpg    se_cons
  1.    Domestic   1.226326   39.48193   134.7221   7770.131
  2.     Foreign   1.670006   50.70229   59.37442   6337.952
```

◁

## ▷ Example

For multiple-equation estimations, we can use [*eqno*] _b ([*eqno*] _se) to get the coefficients (standard errors) of a specific equation, or use _b (_se) to get the coefficients (standard errors) of all the equations. To demonstrate, we run a `heckman` model by `rep78` and collect the coefficients.

```
. use auto, clear
(1978 Automobile Data)
. statsby "heckman price mpg, sel(for=trunk)" _b, by(rep78)
command:      heckman price mpg, sel(for=trunk)
by:           rep78
statistics:   b_mpg=["price"]_b[mpg]
              b_cons=["price"]_b[_cons]
              b_trunk=["foreign"]_b[trunk]
              b_1cons=["foreign"]_b[_cons]
              b_2cons=["athrho"]_b[_cons]
              b_3cons=["lnsigma"]_b[_cons]
. list

Observation 1

        rep78           3       b_mpg    -1114.003      b_cons     35132.14
      b_trunk   -.2692854     b_1cons     1.941074     b_2cons    -16.73255
      b_3cons    8.014194

Observation 2

        rep78           4       b_mpg     -424.909      b_cons     16460.63
      b_trunk   -.1884235     b_1cons     2.510587     b_2cons     .5168093
      b_3cons    7.306929

Observation 3

        rep78           5       b_mpg    -181.0376      b_cons     11508.34
      b_trunk    .3300202     b_1cons    -2.918518     b_2cons    -14.33623
      b_3cons     7.64706
```

To collect the coefficients of the first equation only, we would specify [price] _b instead of _b.

```
. use auto, clear
(1978 Automobile Data)
. statsby "heckman price mpg, sel(for=trunk)" [price]_b, by(rep78)
command:      heckman price mpg, sel(for=trunk)
by:           rep78
statistics:   b_mpg=["price"]_b[mpg]
              b_cons=["price"]_b[_cons]
. list

       rep78       b_mpg      b_cons
  1.       3   -1114.003    35132.14
  2.       4    -424.909    16460.63
  3.       5   -181.0407    11508.62
```

◁

❑ Technical Note

It is possible that the user-specified command would fail on one or more groups. If that happens, statsby will capture the error messages and ignore those groups. This explains why there are only 3 observations in the above example when rep78 has 5 levels. rep78 = 1 and rep78 = 2 do not have enough observations to estimate this particular heckman model.

❑

## Collecting saved results

Results of calculations are saved by many Stata commands; see [U] **16.6 Accessing results from Stata commands**. statsby can collect the saved results and expressions using the saved results. Expressions must be bound in parentheses.

▷ Example

Suppose we want to collect the mean and the median of price, as well as their ratios, and we want to collect them for both domestic and foreign cars.

```
. use auto, clear
(1978 Automobile Data)
. statsby "summarize price, detail" mean=r(mean) median=r(p50) ratio=
> (r(mean)/r(p50)), by(foreign)
command:       summarize price, detail
by:            foreign
statistics:    mean=r(mean)
               median=r(p50)
               ratio=r(mean)/r(p50)
. list
          foreign        mean      median       ratio
     1.   Domestic    6072.423      4782.5    1.269717
     2.    Foreign    6384.682        5759    1.108644
```

◁

❑ Technical Note

In *exp_list*, *newvarname* is not required. If no new variable name is specified, statsby would name the new variables _stat1, _stat2, and so forth.

❑

## A final example

▷ Example

When there are two or more variables in the by(*varlist*), if we want to execute the user-specified command for each group defined by any combination of the variables in the by list, we need to specify the subsets option.

```
. use auto, clear
(1978 Automobile Data)
```

```
. statsby "summarize price, detail" mean=r(mean) median=r(p50),
> by(foreign rep78) subsets
command:      summarize price, detail
by:           foreign rep78
statistics:   mean=r(mean)
              median=r(p50)
. list
           foreign      rep78        mean      median
     1.  Domestic          1      4564.5      4564.5
     2.  Domestic          2    5967.625        4638
     3.  Domestic          3    6607.074        4749
     4.  Domestic          4    5881.556        5705
     5.  Domestic          5      4204.5      4204.5
     6.  Domestic          .    6072.423      4782.5
     7.   Foreign          3    4828.667        4296
     8.   Foreign          4    6261.444        6229
     9.   Foreign          5    6292.667        5719
    10.   Foreign          .    6384.682        5759
    11.          .          1      4564.5      4564.5
    12.          .          2    5967.625        4638
    13.          .          3    6429.233        4741
    14.          .          4      6071.5      5751.5
    15.          .          5        5913        5397
    16.          .          .    6165.257      5006.5
```

In the above dataset, observation 6 is for domestic cars regardless of the repair record; observation 10 is for foreign cars regardless of the repair record; observation 11 is for both foreign cars and domestic cars given that the repair record is 1; and the last observation is for the entire dataset.

◁

# Methods and Formulas

statsby is implemented as an ado-file.

# References

Hardin, J. W. 1996. dm42: Accrue statistics for a command across a by list. *Stata Technical Bulletin* 32: 5–9. Reprinted in *Stata Technical Bulletin Reprints*, vol. 6, pp. 13–18.

Newson, R. 1999. dm65: A program for saving a model fit as a dataset. *Stata Technical Bulletin* 49: 2–5. Reprinted in *Stata Technical Bulletin Reprints*, vol. 9, pp. 19–23.

# Also See

**Related:**      [R] **collapse**, [R] **jknife**

**Background:**   [R] **by**

# Title

**stb** — STB installation instructions

# Description

The *Stata Technical Bulletin* (STB) is a printed and electronic journal with corresponding software. If you want the journal, you must subscribe, but the software is available for free from our web site http://www.stata.com and, for those without Internet access, it is also available on media which can be obtained from Stata Corporation. There is a charge for the media.

The software distributed via the STB includes (1) user-written additions (you may choose which, if any, to install) and (2) official updates.

The STB is published bimonthly—in January, March, May, July, September, and November.

Below are instructions for installing the STB software from our web site; instructions for installing the STB software from media are included with the media.

# Remarks

Each issue of the STB is numbered. STB-1 refers to the first issue (published May 1991), STB-2 to the second (published July 1991), and so on.

An issue of the STB consists of inserts—articles—and these are assigned letter-and-number combinations such as sg84, dm80, sbe26.1, etc. The letters represent a category: sg is the general statistics category and dm the data-management category. The numbers are assigned sequentially, so sg84 is the 84th insert in the general statistics series.

Insert sg84, it turns out, provides a concordance correlation coefficient; it adds a new command called `concord` to Stata. If you installed sg84, you would have that command and its on-line help. Insert sg84 was published in STB-43 (May 1998). Obtaining `concord`, simply requires going to STB-43 and getting sg84.

Sometimes inserts are subsequently updated, either to fix bugs or to add new features. If sg84 were updated, the first update would become sg84.1, the second sg84.2, and so on. As of the date this is being written, sg84 has been updated twice. You could install insert sg84.2, and it would not matter whether you had previously installed sg84. Updates are complete: installing sg84.2 provides all the features of the original insert and more.

For computer naming purposes, insert sg84.2 is referred to as `sg84_2`. When referred to in normal text, however, the insert is still called sg84.2 because that looks nicer.

Inserts are easily available from the Internet. Inserts may be obtained by pointing and clicking or by using command mode. If you do not have Internet access, STB media is available from Stata Corporation, email `stata@stata.com`.

Below we detail how to install an insert. In all cases, we will pretend that you wish to install insert sg84.2 from STB-54. We will also show how to install the official updates.

## Obtaining from Internet by pointing and clicking

1. Pull down **Help** and select **STB and User-written Programs**.

2. Click on *http://www.stata.com*.

3. Click on *stb*.

4. Click on *stb54*

5. Click on *sg84_2*.

6. Click on *(click here to install)*.

Whenever a new STB is released, so are the official updates. These are official additions and fixes to Stata. To obtain and install the official updates,

1. Pull down **Help** and select **Official Updates**

2. Click on *http://www.stata.com*.

3. Scroll down to the heading **Recommendation**. You will be told

    a. *Do nothing; all files up-to-date.* Close help; you are done.

    b. *update ado-files.* You need to update your ado-files.

    c. *update executable.* You need to update your executable.

    d. *update ado-files and executable.* You need to update both.

## Obtaining from Internet via command mode

Type the following:

```
. net from http://www.stata.com
. net cd stb
. net cd stb54
. net describe sg84_2
. net install sg84_2
```

The above could be shortened to

```
. net from http://www.stata.com/stb/stb54
. net describe sg84_2
. net install sg84_2
```

but going about it the long way around is more entertaining, at least the first time.

Whenever a new STB is released, so are the official updates. These are official additions and fixes to Stata. To obtain and install the official updates, type

```
. update from http://www.stata.com
```

At the bottom of the output will appear a **Recommendation**. You will be told

1. *Do nothing; all files are up-to-date.* You are done.

2. *Type* `update ado`. You need to update your ado-files.

3. *Type* `update executable`. You need to update your executable.

4. *Type* `update all`. You need to update both.

## Also See

| | |
|---|---|
| **Complementary:** | [R] **search** |
| **Related:** | [R] **net**, [R] **net search**, [R] **update** |
| **Background:** | [U] **2.4 The Stata Technical Bulletin**, |
| | [U] **32 Using the Internet to keep up to date**, |
| | [GSM] **20 Using the Internet**, |
| | [GSU] **20 Using the Internet**, |
| | [GSW] **20 Using the Internet** |

# Title

> **stem** — Stem-and-leaf displays

# Syntax

>   stem *varname* $\begin{bmatrix} \text{if } exp \end{bmatrix}$ $\begin{bmatrix} \text{in } range \end{bmatrix}$ $\begin{bmatrix} , \underline{\text{d}}\text{igits}(\#) \left\{ \underline{\text{l}}\text{ines}(\#) \mid \underline{\text{w}}\text{idth}(\#) \right\} \end{bmatrix}$
>
>   $\underline{\text{r}}\text{ound}(\#)$ $\underline{\text{p}}\text{rune}$ $\end{bmatrix}$

by ... : may be used with stem; see [R] **by**.

# Description

stem displays stem-and-leaf plots.

# Options

digits(#) sets the number of digits per leaf. The default is 1.

lines(#) sets the number of stems per every data interval of $10^{\text{digits}}$. The value of lines() must divide $10^{\text{digits}}$; that is, if digits(1) is specified, then lines() must divide 10. If digits(2) is specified, then lines() must divide 100, etc. Only one of lines() or width() may be specified. If neither is specified, an appropriate value will be set automatically.

width(#) sets the width of a stem. lines() is equal to $10^{\text{digits}}$/width, and this option is merely an alternative way of setting lines(). The value of width() must divide $10^{\text{digits}}$. Only one of width() or lines() may be specified. If neither is specified, an appropriate value will be set automatically.

round(#) rounds the data to this value and displays the plot in these units. If round() is not specified, noninteger data will be rounded automatically.

prune prevents printing any stems that have no leaves.

Note: If lines() or width() is not specified, digits() may be decreased in some circumstances to make a better-looking plot. If lines() or width() is set, the user-specified value of digits() will not be altered.

# Remarks

▷ Example

Stem-and-leaf displays are a compact way to present considerable information about a batch of data. For instance, using our automobile data (described in [U] **9 Stata's on-line tutorials and sample datasets**):

503

```
. stem mpg
Stem-and-leaf plot for mpg (Mileage (mpg))
   1t | 22
   1f | 44444455
   1s | 66667777
   1. | 88888888899999999
   2* | 00011111
   2t | 22222333
   2f | 444455555
   2s | 666
   2. | 8889
   3* | 001
   3t |
   3f | 455
   3s |
   3. |
   4* | 1
```

The stem-and-leaf display provides a way to list our data. The expression to the left of the vertical bar is called the stem; the digits to the right are called the leaves. All the stems that begin with the same digit and the corresponding leaves, written beside each other, reconstruct an observation of the data. Thus, if we look at the four stems that begin with the digit 1, and their corresponding leaves, we see that we have two cars rated at 12 mpg, 6 cars at 14, 2 at 15, and so on. The car with the highest mileage rating in our data is rated at 41 mpg.

The above plot is a 5-line plot with lines() equal to 5 (5 lines per interval of 10) and width() equal to 2 (2 leaves per stem).

Instead, we could specify lines(2):

```
. stem mpg, lines(2)
Stem-and-leaf plot for mpg (Mileage (mpg))
   1* | 22444444
   1. | 5566667777788888888899999999
   2* | 00011111222223334444
   2. | 555556668889
   3* | 0014
   3. | 55
   4* | 1
```

stem mpg, width(5) would produce the same plot as above.

The stem-and-leaf display provides a crude histogram of our data, one not so pretty as that produced by graph (see [G] **histogram**), but one that is nonetheless quite informative.

◁

▷ Example

Miles per gallon fit easily into a stem-and-leaf display because, in our data, it has two digits. This is not, however, required:

(*Continued on next page*)

```
. stem price, lines(1) digits(3)

Stem-and-leaf plot for price (Price)

    3*** | 291,299,667,748,798,799,829,895,955,984,995
    4*** | 010,060,082,099,172,181,187,195,296,389,424,425,453,482,499, ... (26)
    5*** | 079,104,172,189,222,379,397,705,719,788,798,799,886,899
    6*** | 165,229,295,303,342,486,850
    7*** | 140,827
    8*** | 129,814
    9*** | 690,735
   10*** | 371,372
   11*** | 385,497,995
   12*** | 990
   13*** | 466,594
   14*** | 500
   15*** | 906
```

The (26) at the right of the second stem shows that there were 26 leaves on this stem—too many to display on one line.

We can make a more compact stem-and-leaf plot by rounding. To display stem in units of 100, type

```
. stem price, round(100)

Stem-and-leaf plot for price (Price)

price rounded to nearest multiple of 100
plot in units of 100

    3* | 33778889
    4* | 00001112222344455555667777899
    5* | 11222447788899
    6* | 2233359
    7* | 18
    8* | 18
    9* | 77
   10* | 44
   11* | 45
   12* | 0
   13* | 056
   14* | 5
   15* | 9
```

price, in our data, has four or five digits. stem presented the display in terms of units of 100, so a car that cost $3,291 was treated for display purposes as $3,300.

◁

❑ Technical Note

Stem-and-leaf diagrams have been used in Japanese railway timetables, as shown in Tufte (1990, 46–47).

❑

# Methods and Formulas

stem is implemented as an ado-file.

# References

Emerson, J. D. and D. C. Hoaglin. 1983. Stem-and-leaf displays. In *Understanding Robust and Exploratory Data Analysis*, ed. D. C. Hoaglin, F. Mosteller, and J. W. Tukey, 7–30. New York: John Wiley & Sons.

Tufte, E. R. 1990. *Envisioning Information*. Cheshire, CT: Graphics Press.

Tukey, J. W. 1972. Some graphic and semigraphic displays. In *Statistical Papers in Honor of George W. Snedecor*, ed. T. A. Bancroft and S. A. Brown, 293–316. Ames, IA: Iowa State University Press.

——. 1977. *Exploratory Data Analysis*. Reading, MA: Addison–Wesley Publishing Company.

# Also See

**Related:**     [R] **lv**,
                 [G] **histogram**